Global Problems and the Culture of Capitalism

Richard H. Robbins

State University of New York at Plattsburgh

Allyn and Bacon

Boston • *London* • *Toronto* • *Sydney* • *Tokyo* • *Singapore*

Series Editor: Sarah L. Kelbaugh
Editor-in-Chief, Social Sciences: Karen Hanson
Consulting Editor: Sylvia Shepard
Series Editorial Assistant: Heather Ahlstrom
Sr. Editorial Production Administrator: Susan McIntyre
Editorial Production Service: Ruttle, Shaw & Wetherill, Inc.
Composition Buyer: Linda Cox
Manufacturing Buyer: Megan Cochran
Cover Administrator: Linda Knowles
Electronic Composition: Omegatype Typography, Inc.
Photo Research: Laurie Frankenthaler

Copyright © 1999 by Allyn & Bacon
A Viacom Company
160 Gould Street
Needham Heights, MA 02494

Internet: www.abacon.com

Library of Congress Cataloging-in-Publication Data

Robbins, Richard Howard, 1940–
    Global problems and the culture of capitalism / Richard H. Robbins.
      p.   cm.
    Includes bibliographical references and index.
    ISBN 0-205-19337-4
    1. Economic history—1990–   2. Social problems.   3. Capitalism.
4. Consumption (Economics)   5. Poverty.   I. Title.
HC59.15.R63   1999
330.12'2—dc21   98-23668
                                                                CIP

Printed in the United States of America
10 9 8 7 6 5 4   04 03 02 01 00

Contents

Preface

Over the past 400 to 600 years a culture and society, originating for the most part in Europe and dedicated to the idea of consumption as the ultimate source of well-being, began to expand to all parts of the globe. In many ways it is the most successful culture and society the world has ever seen, its technology, wealth, and power monuments to its success; but accompanying its expansion have been problems—growing social and economic inequality, environmental destruction, mass starvation, and social unrest. Most members of this society and culture perceive these problems as distant from themselves or as challenges for them to meet. However, there is the possibility that these problems, which threaten to negate everything this culture has accomplished, are intrinsic to the culture itself. That is the possibility to be explored in this book.

The outline of this book emerged when, a few years ago, my colleagues at the State University of New York at Plattsburgh, James Armstrong and Mark Cohen, and I began developing a course on global problems. We wanted to create a course that would help students understand the major global issues that they confront in the mass media, problems such as the so-called population explosion, famine and hunger, global environmental destruction, the emergence and spread of new diseases, so-called ethnic conflict and genocides, and terrorism and social protest. We learned quickly that to make the course successful, we had to overcome the often ethnocentric perspectives of the students, perspectives that were often reinforced by media coverage of global affairs. We needed also to compensate for the students' lack of background in anthropology, history and economics, all crucial for understanding the roots of the problems we were to examine. Finally, we needed to illustrate that the problems we examined were relevant to them; that the problems would affect them either directly or indirectly, and that their actions now or in the future would determine the extent to which the origins of these problems could be acknowledged, let alone ever addressed. The form of this book emerged from our efforts at dealing with these pedagogical issues and the classroom interactions that these efforts stimulated.

Many people have contributed to the writing of this book: I have already mentioned my colleagues James Armstrong and Mark Cohen. Others include Alfred Robbins, Yetta Robbins, Michael Robbins, Tom Moran, Philip Devita, Gloria Bobbie, Douglas Skopp, Edward Champagne, Vincent Carey, Larry Soroka, Jennifer Scanlon, Ellen Fitzpatrick, Ann Kimmage, Michael Miranda, John Hess, Jan Rinaldi, Tina Charland, Tim Harnett, Daphne Kutzer, Monica van Beusekom, Peggy Lindsey, Mary Turner, members of the email list H-World, particularly its moderator Patrick Manning, Richard Winkel, moderator of the email list Activ-L (aml@webmap. missouri.edu) and its many contributors, and many of the students who used one or another version of this book in draft form, and who provided invaluable feedback. I would also like to thank the reviewers who have been involved in the process of writing the book: Paul Winther, Eastern Kentucky University; Charles Ellenbaum, College of DuPage; Cynthia Mahmood, University of Maine; Richard Moore, The Ohio State University; and John Aguilar, Arizona State University.

I owe a special debt of gratitude to Sylvia Shephard of Allyn & Bacon for her support of the project, to Sarah Kelbaugh and Susan McIntyre of Allyn & Bacon for guiding the project through to its conclusion, as well as Jane Grochowski and Dan Spinella whose copyediting will make reading the book far easier than it would have been otherwise. And special thanks go to Amy and Rebecca who tolerated with unusual understanding my periods of self-imposed isolation. Needless to say, the final form of the book, for better or worse, is the result of my own decisions.

Few subjects require students and instructors to keep up with current affairs quite as much as the study of global problems and issues. Economic, political, and social events can alter global dynamics without even sophisticated intelligence services being forewarned: an Islamic revolution in Iran, a peasant revolt in Mexico, the collapse of currencies in Asia, or the testing of nuclear devices in India can quickly change global political, social, and economic arrangements. In fact, as this book emphasizes, perpetual growth and change are dominant characteristics of our culture.

To assist students and instructors dealing with global change, we have established a Web site, *The Study of the Global Expansion of Capitalism* (http://www. plattsburgh.edu/legacy/), to provide supplementary material for this book. At the site users will find links to other sites arranged according to the chapters of the book; links to resources on countries, maps, and corporations; and links to news sources, including mainstream media (e.g., *International Herald Tribune, New York Times, Christian Science Monitor*), alternative media sources (e.g., *Newswatch, Green Leaf Weekly, People's Tribune*), and international media sources (e.g., *Africa News Online, South China Morning Post*). There are also links to search engines and general resources relating to global issues and the study of anthropology. The site also contains materials to encourage discussion, along with exercises. In addition, new material is constantly being added to the site to assist instructors and students in the study of global problems.

I welcome from readers any comments, suggestions, or questions. I can be reached on email at robbinrh@splava.cc.plattsburgh.edu or through the Web site devoted to the book at http://www.plattsburgh.edu/legacy/

The Consumer, the Laborer, the Capitalist, and the Nation-State in the Society of Perpetual Growth

[W]hat difference it would make to our understanding if we looked at the world as a whole, a totality, a system, instead of as a sum of self-contained societies and cultures; if we understood better how this totality developed over time; if we took seriously the admonition to think of human aggregates as "inextricably involved with other aggregates, near and far, in weblike, netlike, connections."
—ERIC WOLF, PEOPLE WITHOUT HISTORY

Chapter *1*

Capitalism and the Making of the Consumer

The consumer revolution is a strange chapter in the ethnographic history of the species. For what may have been the first time in its history, a human community willingly harbored a nonreligious agent of social change, and permitted it to transform on a continual and systematic basis virtually every feature of social life.
—GRANT McCRACKEN, CULTURE AND CONSUMPTION

The...metamessage of our time is that the commodity form is natural and inescapable. Our lives can only be well lived (or lived at all) through the purchase of particular commodities. Thus our major existential interest consists of maneuvering for eligibility to buy such commodities in the market. Further, we have been taught that it is right and just—ordained by history, human nature, and God—that the means of life in all its forms be available only as commodities.... Americans live in an overcommodified world, with needs that are generated in the interests of the market and that can be met only through the market.
—STEPHEN FJELLMAN, VINYL LEAVES:
WALT DISNEY WORLD AND AMERICA

On or about December 1910, wrote novelist Virginia Woolf, human character changed.[1] On his repeated visits to the United States, Frenchman André Giegfried noted much the same thing: "A new society has come to life in America," he said.

[1]The quote, which has been widely used (see e.g., Fjellman 1992:5; Lears 1983) appeared in an essay, "Mr. Bennett and Mrs. Brown," which is collected in *The Captain's Death Bed and Other Essays*, but was originally part of a paper Woolf read to the Heretics, Cambridge on May 18, 1924. "On or about December 1910, human character changed.... The change was not sudden and definite.... But a change there was, nevertheless; and since one must be arbitrary, let us date it about the year 1910." Woolf, however, may have been referring as much to changes in literary tastes as she was to broad social changes.

"It was not clear in 1901 or 1904; it was noticeable in 1914, and patent in 1919 and 1925" (cited Leach 1993:266). Samuel Strauss, a journalist and philosopher writing in the 1920s, suggested the term *consumptionism* to characterize this new way of life that, he said, created a person with

> *a philosophy of life that committed human beings to the production of more and more things—"more this year than last year, more next year than this"—and that emphasized the "standard of living" above all other values.*

"From a *moral point of view*," Strauss continued,

> *it is obvious that Americans have come to consider their standard of living as a somewhat sacred acquisition, which they will defend at any price. This means that they would be ready to make many an intellectual or even moral concession in order to maintain that standard. (cited Leach 1993:266)*

There is no question that in America the half century from 1880 to 1930 marked a major transition in the rate and level of commodity consumption—the purchase, use, and waste of what comedian George Carlin called "stuff." Food production grew by almost 40 percent from 1899 to 1905; the production of men's and women's ready-made clothing, along with the production of costume jewelry, doubled between 1890 and 1900; glassware and lamp production went from 84,000 tons in 1890 to 250,563 tons in 1914. In 1890, 32,000 pianos were sold in the United States; by 1904, the number sold increased to 374,000 (Leach 1993:16).

During this period the perfume industry became the country's tenth largest; at one department store, sale of toiletries rose from $84,000 to $522,000 between 1914 and 1926. The manufacture of clocks and watches went from 34 million to 82 million in ten years. By the late 1920s, one of every six Americans owned an automobile. All of this consumption occurred in a society in which 2 percent of the people owned 60 percent of the wealth, while the bottom 50 percent owned only 5 percent.

Of course these figures are dwarfed by what Americans and others around the world consume today. There are as many cars in the United States as there are persons with drivers' licenses, for example. However, although consumption rates were not nearly as high as they are today, the early twentieth century is notable because it marked the early phase of what Ernest Gellner (1983:24) called the *society of perpetual growth*, and the creation of a new type of culture, *consumer capitalism* (see Bodley 1985:67), along with the construction of a new type of person, the *consumer*.

The emergence of the society of perpetual growth and the culture of capitalism marked a new stage in an ongoing global historical process that began (to the extent that it can be said to have a beginning) anytime from the fifteenth to the early nineteenth centuries. The creation of the human type that characterizes this stage, the consumer, followed soon after the emergence of two other historically unique categories of human being: the *capitalist* and the *laborer.* Merchants had existed, of course, for thousands of years, and people had always labored to produce goods

The displays of commodities in shopping malls and department stores, such as Macy's in New York City, helped define the values, attitudes, and aspirations of members of the culture of capitalism.

and, in a fashion, consume what they'd produced. But never before in history has there existed a society founded on categories of people: the capitalist, whose sole purpose is to invest money and accumulate profit; the laborer, whose sole means of support comes from the sale of his or her labor; and the consumer, whose sole purpose is to purchase and consume increasing quantities of goods and services.

By the end of the nineteenth-century, the capitalist and laborer—operating within a set of rules mediated by a new type of political entity, the *nation-state*—had created a revolutionary system for the production of goods that potentially contained the seeds of its own destruction. By the late 1890s, so many goods were being produced that businesspeople and government officials feared overproduction, panic, and the severe economic depression that in fact marked that decade. Out of these fears came what William Leach called "a steady stream of enticements" designed to encourage people to consume and to awaken Americans, as Emily Fogg Mead, the mother of anthropologist Margaret Mead, said, to "the ability to want and choose" (see Leach 1993:16). The consumer was necessary to save industrial capitalism from its own efficiency.

Virtually all Americans, at some point in their lives, play the roles of consumer, laborer, or capitalist; as consumers they buy things; as laborers, they work for wages; and as capitalists they invest money in banks, insurance policies, pension plans, stocks, education, or other enterprises from which they expect to profit. What ties together these roles, and indeed the entire culture, is money. Every culture has its distinct style or elements, rituals or ritual objects, that define for its members what is most important in life. The Dogon of West Africa define their existence through art; the Balinese of Indonesia, through drama and music. The Trobriand Islanders engaged in the accumulation of yams and the ritual exchange of shell necklaces and bracelets; the ancient Aztecs of Mexico in human sacrifice. For the indigenous peoples of the American Plains, the key element of cultural life was the buffalo. For members of the culture of capitalism the key element is money. As Jack Weatherford (1997:11) noted:

> *Money constitutes the focal point of modern world culture. Money defines relationships among people, not just between customer and merchant in the marketplace or employer and laborer in the workplace. Increasingly in modern society, money defines relationships between parent and child, among friends, between politicians and constituents, among neighbors, and between clergy and parishioners. Money forms the central institutions of the modern market and economy, and around it are grouped the ancillary institutions of kinship, religion, and politics. Money is the very language of commerce for the modern world.*

Consumers want to spend as much money as they can, laborers want to earn as much as possible, and capitalists want to invest it so that it can return more. There is the potential for much conflict in these arrangements. Each person, as consumer, wants to pay as little as possible for commodities; while the same person, as laborer, wants to earn as much as possible, thus driving up prices. The capitalist wants to pay each person, as laborer, as little as possible, but wants the person, as consumer, to earn enough to purchase the commodities from which profits accrue. Yet each role also reinforces the other: The capitalist is dependent on the laborer to perform services and produce products and on the consumer to buy them; the laborer is dependent on the capitalist for employment and wages. Furthermore, each role disciplines and drives the other: the consumer in each person, desiring to acquire commodities and the status they may convey, accumulates debt; to pay off the debts accumulated to purchase status-bearing commodities, the consumer must labor to acquire money or must, in the role of capitalist, make investments hoping for greater returns.

We can perhaps best conceptualize the working of the culture of capitalism as sets of relations between capitalists, laborers, and consumers, each depending on the other, yet each placing demands on, and often conflicting with, the others. In this cultural scheme, the nation-state serves as, among its other functions, a mediator, controlling the creation and flow of money and setting and enforcing the rules of interaction. (Figure 1.1 is a highly simplified model, but it serves to underline the key features and unique style of the culture of capitalism.)

Where did the culture of capitalism come from? One of the assumptions of this book is that the emergence of capitalism has been misrepresented by many historians, sociologists, and anthropologists; rather than recognizing it as the emergence of a historically unique culture, they have generally portrayed it as an inevitable historical or evolutionary development. Capitalist culture was equated with "civilization," implying that anything different was "uncivilized." Later it

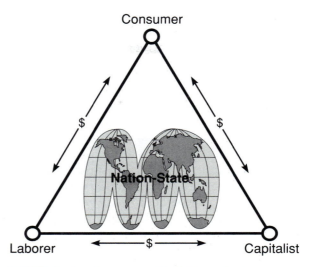

**FIGURE 1.1   Patterns of Relations in the
Culture of Capitalism**

was considered part of a process of "modernization," implying that anything else was "primitive" or "traditional." The emergence of the culture of capitalism, particularly in the so-called third world, was called "economic development," once again implying that anything less was "undeveloped" or "underdeveloped." However, if we look at capitalism as one cultural adaptation out of many, we will be better able to understand and judge the effects it has had on the world's peoples and see its spread not as inevitable development, growth, or modernization, but as the displacement, for better or worse, of one way of life by another. Put another way, there is not much to choosing (as we must if capitalism is equated with progress, modernity, and development) between being modern or primitive, developed or undeveloped, civilized or uncivilized; it is, however, a very different matter in choosing whether to be a member of the culture of capitalism or a Zuni, Guaraní, Mohawk, Chuckchee, Nuer, or Murngin.

The emergence of the culture of capitalism has left little in our lives untouched—it has affected our material, spiritual, and intellectual life; it has reshaped our values; and, as we shall see, it has largely dictated the direction that every institution in our society would take. It has produced wave after wave of consumer goods, revolutionized food production, and prompted previously unimagined developments in technology, communications, and medicine. Most dramatically, at least from the anthropological point of view, "feeding" the consumer has required a level of global integration unmatched in human history. The clothes we wear more often than not are produced in whole or in part by people in Malaysia, Hong Kong, or El Salvador; workers in Brazil probably cut the sugarcane that became the sugar that sweetens our soft drinks; our morning coffee began as coffee beans in the highlands of Colombia; the oranges we eat may have been grown in Spain, packed in cardboard boxes made of Canadian pulpwood, wrapped in plastic produced in New Jersey, and transported on trucks made in France with Italian, Japanese, and American parts. Our radios, televisions, and VCRs are most likely assembled by workers in Mexico, Haiti, or Indonesia; and our automobiles, of course, may have been produced at least in part in Japan, Taiwan, or Korea.

Furthermore, the culture of capitalism is being exported to all parts of the globe. Yet few people are aware of how the culture works and how it affects our lives and those of people all over the world—how American consumption, labor, and investment patterns relate to wages paid to women in Indonesia, the destruction of the rainforests in Paraguay, or the use of water on the American Plains. This is not necessarily the fault of the individual, for, as we shall see, the culture of capitalism purposefully masks from its members the problems that result from its maintenance and spread.

The Focus of This Book

In July 1972, while doing research on bird evolution in New Guinea, biologist Jared Diamond strolled along a tropical beach with a local politician named Yali. Yali, who had helped his people prepare for self-government, questioned Diamond about the origins of the people of New Guinea and about the commodities that Europeans brought to New Guinea, such as steel axes, matches, clothing, and soft drinks—items that people in New Guinea referred to as "cargo." Then he posed for Diamond the key question: "Why is it," he asked, "that you White people developed so much cargo and brought it to New Guinea, but we Black people had so little cargo of our own?" (Diamond 1997:14).

Yali's question goes to the heart of the condition of the modern world: How have such inequalities of wealth evolved? Why do some have so much and others so little? How have a group of societies clustered largely, but not exclusively, in the area of northern Europe, East Asia, and North America come to dominate the societies of the rest of the world politically and economically?

This book tries to answer Yali's question while providing enough background for the reader to begin better to understand other global problems, such as population growth, world hunger, environmental destruction, disease, ethnic conflict, rebellion, and social and religious protest. Although the approach is largely anthropological, we will not hesitate to draw from other disciplines—history, sociology, geography, political science, and economics—when necessary to understand capitalism, and how the culture of capitalism contributes to the global problems that we are discussing.

We can summarize our approach in this book as follows: There has emerged over the past five to six centuries a distinctive culture or way of life dominated by a belief in commodity consumption as the source of well-being. This culture flowered in Western Europe, reached fruition in the United States, and spread to much of the rest of the world, creating what some anthropologists, sociologists, and historians call the *world system.* People disagree on the critical factors in the development of this system and even whether or not it was unique historically, although most agree on certain basic ideas. Among the most important are the assumptions that the driving force behind the spread of the contemporary world system was industrial and corporate capitalism, and that the spread of the world system is related in some way to the resulting division of the world into wealthy nations and poor nations or into wealthy *core,* developed, or industrialized areas and dependent *peripheral,* undeveloped, or nonindustrialized areas.

The spread of the capitalist world system has been accompanied by the creation of distinctive patterns of social relations, ways of viewing the world, methods of food production, distinctive diets, patterns of health and disease, relationships to the environment, and so on. However, the spread of this culture has not gone uncontested; there has been resistance in the form of direct and indirect actions—political, religious, and social protest and revolution. How and why capitalist culture developed and the reasons why some groups resisted and continue to resist its development are among the questions posed in this book.

The book is divided into three parts. Part I (Chapters 1–4) is devoted to an understanding of the social and historical origins of capitalism, specifically the social construction of the consumer, the laborer, the capitalist, and the nation-state. The desire, indeed the necessity, of people to consume more and more is the force that drives the society of perpetual growth, largely defines the relationships between the core and the periphery of the world system, and relates to virtually all of the global problems discussed in later chapters. (The remainder of this chapter is devoted to an examination of the creation of the consumer in the United States.)

Chapter 2 examines the creation and role of the laborer in capitalism and the expansion of capitalism into the peripheral areas of the world. Chapter 3 outlines the evolution of the organization of capital from around A.D. 1400 to the present, the ongoing division of the world into poor nations and wealthy nations, the role of the state in these processes, and the historical interaction of the capitalist, laborer, and consumer. The last chapter in this part, Chapter 4, takes a closer look at the creation of the nation-state and its role in the creation and maintenance of the culture of capitalism.

Part II (Chapters 5–9) examines the relationship between the spread of capitalism and various global problems. Chapter 5 examines the much-discussed problem of population growth. As early as 1798, Thomas Malthus predicted that if the rate of population growth continued as it was then, human population would soon outstrip that population's capacity to feed itself. Malthus predicted disaster; yet today the world produces more than enough food to feed a population of almost six billion and has the capacity to produce even more. *Was Malthus wrong, or are others who are alarmed at the present rate of population growth correct in their assessment that overpopulation is responsible for world poverty, hunger, and environmental degradation?*

World hunger and poverty, and how they relate to the globalization of capitalism are the subjects of Chapter 6. Each year some five million children die of hunger; each day, 600,000 to over one billion people—one in five—go hungry. Overpopulation does not seem to be the only problem—there is more than enough food to feed everyone. *Why, then, do thousands of people starve to death every day?*

Chapter 7 examines environmental problems. Once again, there are dire predictions of environmental disaster, and, once again, overpopulation is often given as a cause. But other forces seem to be at work: The United States, with a relatively low rate of population growth, is by far the world's greatest contributor to environmental pollution. Clearly our consumption patterns are responsible for much environmental devastation. *How and why were these destructive consumption patterns established, and what, if anything, can we do about them?*

Another worldwide threat—disease—is examined in Chapter 8. In the 1960s, the World Health Organization set as its goal the complete eradication of disease. We have certainly eliminated many of them. Smallpox, polio, and plague once took millions of lives but now are nearly forgotten. Yet new diseases keep threatening our lives—AIDS is the best known—and others are constantly appearing. Others seem almost beyond solution; malaria still claims more lives each year worldwide than any other disease. *How does the way we live influence the emergence and spread of disease, and how does the spread of disease relate to the globalization of capitalist culture?*

Chapter 9 examines the fate of indigenous peoples and the origins of ethnic conflict in the world. In general, the development and spread of capitalism has not been conducive to the maintenance of diverse cultures. *Why has its spread resulted in the destruction of indigenous peoples and cultures?* Furthermore, cultural or ethnic diversity is often assumed to be the cause of ethnic strife. Yet diverse cultures have existed side-by-side for centuries without the kind of violence we witness today. *Why in today's world does ethnic diversity frequently seem to lead to violent conflict?*

Part III turns to the sometimes rebellious reactions of peoples who have not fared well in the wake of expanding capitalism. This expansion was rarely uncontested. Chapter 10 examines the reactions and resistance of peasant farmers to the expansion of capitalism and to their increased marginalization in a world of large-scale agriculture. *Why have peasant farmers often been among the first to protest or rebel against capitalist encroachment?*

Chapter 11 focuses on the various forms of social protest that have accompanied the development of capitalist culture: laborers resisting their working conditions, women protesting their places in capitalist cultures, and groups protesting the effects of capitalism on the environment. *How has capitalism created conditions in which people feel compelled to protest and resist?*

The focus of Chapter 12 is on religious protest. Religion has long been a vehicle for expressing resistance to social and cultural change. *How has religion served as a way to resist or protest the development and spread of capitalist culture?*

Finally, Chapter 13 takes a brief look at projections of the future: what will the world be like fifty, one hundred, or two hundred years from now?

The answers to some of these questions are based on specific assumptions. First, a central tenet of anthropology is that personal, social, cultural, and historical factors determine the point of view any person might have regarding a certain phenomenon. No less is true of those participating in the culture of capitalism who have created a view of global events that we share. Consequently these views tend to be, to one extent or another, *ethnocentric;* that is, they describe, evaluate, and judge events solely from a specific cultural perspective. Among the major purposes of anthropology is to teach ways to avoid ethnocentrism and appreciate the importance of understanding the beliefs and behaviors of others from their perspectives rather than from our own, a view anthropologists refer to as *cultural relativism.* To some extent ethnocentrism is unavoidable, and the job of the person who interprets global events—whether a journalist, economist, sociologist, or anthropologist—is to make the event comprehensible to those people for whom that person is writing. Our assumption is that to minimize cultural bias we must recognize that our views of events are partially influenced by our culture and, for that reason, we must make our own culture an object of analysis.

Second, we assume that an understanding of global events requires us to recognize that no contemporary culture or society exists independent of what social scientists refer to as the *world system,* and that each falls within either the core or the periphery of that system. Using this terminology to refer to different parts of the world permits us to avoid the more value-laden distinctions implicit in the use of terms such as *developed* or *undeveloped, modern* or *traditional, first, second,* or *third world.* World system theorists often include a third category, *semiperiphery,* to denote those nation-states or regions that are moving toward the core or have moved out of the core. These distinctions recognize that countries can move from one category to another. For example, the three nation-states that world system theorists consider to have been dominant in the past four centuries—the Netherlands, the United Kingdom, and the United States—all began as semiperipheral to the world system.

Third, we assume that global events and actions cannot be adequately understood without considering the events that preceded them; we must develop a historical perspective. For example, we live in a period of human history largely defined by a sequence of events that began some two to five hundred years ago, loosely termed the *industrial revolution.* Because each of us has lived during only a particular phase of that history, we tend to take it for granted that the world has always been as it is today. Yet the modern industrial world order is, in historical terms, a very recent event. We are deceived by our biology, by our limited life span, into thinking of sixty, seventy, or eighty years as a long time, but in the perspective of human history it is a fleeting moment. Human beings have for most of their existence lived as bands of gatherers and hunters, for a shorter time as agriculturists and farmers, and only recently as industrialists and wage laborers. Yet the industrial revolution has transformed the world and human societies as no other event in history has. We cannot understand the events, issues, and problems of today's world without understanding the how's and why's of this transformation.

It will be clear that the emergence of capitalism represents a culture that is in many ways the most successful that has ever been developed in terms of accommodating large numbers of individuals in relative and absolute comfort and luxury. It has not been as successful, however, in integrating all in equal measure, and its failure here remains one of its major problems. It has solved the problems of feeding large numbers of people (although certainly not all), and it has provided unprecedented advances in health and medicine (but, again, not for all). It has promoted the development of amazingly complex technological instruments and fostered a level of global communication without precedent. It has united people in common pursuits as has no other culture. Yet it remains to be seen when the balance sheet is tallied whether capitalism represents the epitome of "progress" that some claim.

Culture and the Construction of the Consumer

The culture of capitalism is devoted to encouraging the production and sale of commodities. For capitalists, the culture encourages the accumulation of profit; for laborers, it encourages the accumulation of wages; for consumers, it encourages the accumulation of goods. In other words, capitalism defines sets of people who, behaving according to a set of learned rules, act as they must act.

There is nothing natural about this behavior. People are not naturally driven to accumulate wealth. There are societies in which such accumulation is discouraged. Human beings do not have an innate drive to accumulate commodities; again, there are plenty of societies in which such accumulation is discouraged. People are not driven to work; in fact, contrary to popular notions, members of capitalist culture work far more than, say, people who live by gathering and hunting. How does *culture,* as anthropologists use the term, encourage people to behave in some ways and not in others? Specifically, how does the culture of capitalism encourage the accumulation of profit, wages, and commodities? How does it, in effect, encourage perpetual growth and what amounts to perpetual change?

It is not easy to describe the effects of culture on people's lives; anthropologists have noted that culture consists of all learned beliefs and behaviors, the rules by which we order our lives, and the meanings that human beings construct to interpret their universes and their places in them. Yet, using these abstract descriptions, it is difficult to understand how pervasive our culture can be in determining our view of the world. It may help, therefore, to provide a metaphor for culture in the form of a belief and practice of another culture: the sandpaintings of the Navajo of the American Southwest.

Among the Navajo people, there is a healing practice in which a curer draws on the ground a miniature representation of the universe, using colored sand, cornmeal, or other bits of material. Although there are perhaps a thousand versions of these drawings, each contains vital elements of what, for the Navajo, defines the general conditions of existence. Navajo conceptions of space are indicated by symbols of the world's directions; conceptions of social life are indicated by the distribution of Navajo houses (*hogans*) and mythic beings; values are represented in the stories and chants associated with each sandpainting; material items critical to Navajo existence (e.g., horses or ritual items) are also portrayed. Once the work is completed, the patient sits on or in the sandpainting, and a curing ceremony, accompanied by chanting and prayer, proceeds. Illness, the Navajo claim, is the result of persons' losing their proper places in the world; the aim of the ceremony is to restore the patient to that place. When the ceremony is completed and harmony restored, the sandpainter destroys the painting.

Navajo sandpainting contains all the elements of what anthropologists often mean by the term *culture*. Like the sandpainting, a culture serves to define the universe as it is supposed to exist for a people. The sandpainting contains the key elements and symbols that people use to locate themselves in physical and social space. It affirms the place of the person in the created world and the values that govern people's lives. Like the sandpainting, particular cultural representations serve as therapeutic frames that communicate to us who and what we are, and how we figure in the larger order of things. These representations are therapeutic because they help people resolve the contradictions and ambiguities that are inherent in any cultural definition of reality and self.

Furthermore, every society has its sandpainters, those individuals who are given or who take responsibility for representing the universe to others, and who have the power to define those elements that are essential for others in locating and defining their identities. In some societies, as among the Navajo, it is the curer or

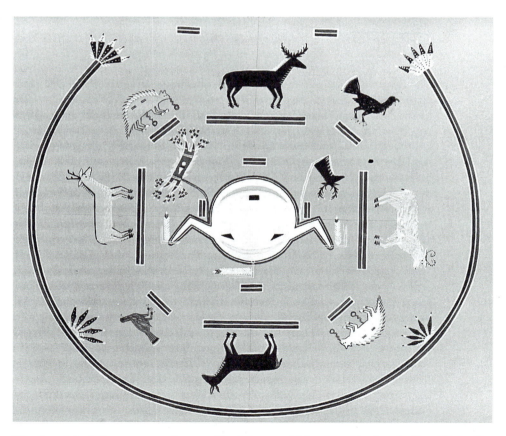

Navajo sandpaintings serve as therapeutic stages on which a person's place in the universe is defined and ritually enacted.

the shaman or the mythmaker or storyteller; in others, it is the priest, poet, writer, artist, singer, or dancer. In capitalism, the sandpainter works in churches, synagogues, or mosques, and in theaters, in front of television sets, at sporting events, or in the shopping malls that reaffirm the vision of abundance central to the consumers' view of the world. Contemporary sandpainters, who include marketing specialists, advertisers, government agents, corporate public relations specialists, entertainers, and journalists, among others, create a vision of the world designed to maximize the production and consumption of goods. They have helped to create a culture in which the prime elements are commodities, and in which the consumer's first duty is to buy (or "Shop till You Drop," as a popular bumper sticker advises). It is a culture in which virtually all our everyday activities—work, leisure, the fulfillment of social responsibilities, and so on—take place in the context of commodities, and in which shopping, like the sandpainting cure, serves as a therapeutic activity. These contemporary sandpainters construct for us a culture in which at one time or another every individual enacts the identity of consumer. The question we need to explore first is, *how was the universe of the consumer and the consumer itself created?*

The Construction of the Consumer

The consumer did not, of course, appear full blown in the United States of the early twentieth century. Even in the eighteenth century, merchants in Great Britain, France, and elsewhere were concerned that more goods were being produced than could be sold and devised means to create demands (see Carrier 1995). But merchants generally paid little attention to how goods were marketed or presented, assuming that when people needed their products, they would buy them. It was this attitude that was to undergo a profound change in the United States of a century ago.

The change did not occur naturally. In fact, the culture of nineteenth-century America emphasized not unlimited consumption but moderation and self-denial. People, workers in particular, were expected to be frugal and save their money; spending, particularly on luxuries, was seen as "wasteful." People purchased only necessities—basic foodstuffs, clothing, household utensils, and appliances—or shared basic items when they could. If we look at a typical inventory of the possessions of an American family of 1870–1880, we will find a pattern very different from that of today. In 1870, 53 percent of the population lived and worked on farms and produced much of what they consumed. One Vermont farm wife recorded making 421 pies, 152 cakes, 2,140 doughnuts, and 1,038 loaves of bread in one year (Sutherland 1989:71). Household items were relatively simple—a dinner table, wooden chairs, beds, perhaps a carpet or rug. There were few appliances to aid housework—cookstoves, eggbeaters, apple-parers, pea-shellers, and coffee mills, but most other housework required muscle; even hand-cranked washing machines were not available until the late 1870s. Although only the poorest or most isolated families did not buy some ready-made clothing, most of the items people wore were made at home and were largely functional. Furthermore, because the vast majority of American families lived on farms, most of the family capital was invested in farming tools and implements. There were, of course, exceptions. The wealthy members of society competed with each other in the ostentatious display of wealth and luxury, as they had for centuries (see Jardine 1996). But they represented a small percentage of the population.

Of course, Americans did not yet have electricity, the automobile had yet to be invented, and the money supply was far more limited than it is today. Nevertheless, to transform buying habits, luxuries had to be transformed into necessities. In America, this was accomplished largely in three ways. First, there was a major transformation of the meaning of goods and how they were presented and displayed. For most of the eighteenth and nineteenth centuries, retailers paid little attention to how goods were displayed. The first department store—Bon Marché—opened in Paris in 1852, allowing people to wander through the store with no expectations that they make a purchase. Enterprises such as Bon Marché were devoted to "the arousal of free-floating desire," as Rosalind Williams put it (cited McCracken 1988:25). The displays of commodities helped define bourgeois culture, converting the culture, values, attitudes, and aspirations of the bourgeoisie into goods, thus shaping and transforming them (Miller 1994).

But Bon Marché was an exception. In stores in the United States, most products were displayed in bulk, and little care was taken to arrange them in any special way. Prepackaged items with company labels did not even exist until the 1870s, when Ivory Soap and Quaker Oats appeared (Carrier 1995:102). Shop windows, if they existed, were simply filled with items that had been languishing in back rooms or warehouses for years. Even the few large department stores of the mid-nineteenth-century, such as that of Alexander Turney Stewart, the Marble Palace in New York, paid little attention to display. It was not until the 1890s and the emergence of the department store in the United States as a major retail establishment that retailers began to pay attention to how products were presented to the public.

The department store evolved into a place to display goods as objects in themselves. When Marshall Field's opened in Chicago in 1902, six string orchestras filled the various floors with music and American Beauty roses along with other cut flowers and potted palms bedecked all the counters. Nothing was permitted to be sold on the first day, and merchants in the district closed so that their employees could visit Field's. Later elaborate theatrical productions were put on in the stores, artworks were displayed, and some of the most creative minds in America designed displays that were intended to present goods in ways that inspired people to buy them. The department store became a cultural primer telling people how they should dress, furnish their homes, and spend their leisure time (Leach 1993).

Advertising was another revolutionary development that influenced the creation of the consumer. The goal of advertisers was to aggressively shape consumer desires and create value in commodities by imbuing them with the power to transform the consumer into a more desirable person. Before the late 1880s, advertising was looked down on and associated with P. T. Barnum-style hokum. In 1880, only $30 million was invested in advertising in the United States; by 1910, new businesses, such as oil, food, electricity, and rubber, were spending $600 million, or 4 percent of the national income, on advertising. Today that figure has climbed to

Department store windows, such as this one at Saks Fifth Avenue in New York City, arouse consumers' desire for commodities.

well over $120 billion in the United States and to over $250 billion worldwide (Durning 1992:120).

By the early twentieth century national advertising campaigns were being initiated and celebrities were being hired to offer testimonials to their favorite commodities. Advertising cards, catalogs, and newspaper ads became a regular feature of American life. Outdoor advertising—billboards, signs, and posters—appeared everywhere. Electrical advertising—neon and flashing signs—were marketed, and Broadway became famous as the "Great White Way." Today advertising plays such a ubiquitous part in our lives that we scarcely notice it, even when it is engraved or embroidered on our clothing.

Another boon to merchandising was the idea of fashion: the stirring up of anxiety and restlessness over the possession of things that were not "new" or "up-to-date." Fashion pressured people to buy not out of need but for style—from a desire to conform to what others defined as "fashionable."

It is hardly surprising then that the garment industry in America led the way in the creation of fashion; its growth in the early 1900s was two or three times as great as any other industry. By 1915, it ranked only behind steel and oil in the United States. Fashion output in 1915 was in excess of one billion dollars; in New York alone, 15,000 establishments made women's clothes. New fashion magazines—*Vogue, Cosmopolitan,* and *The Delineator*—set fashion standards and defined what the socially conscious woman should wear, often using royalty, the wealthy, and celebrities as models. The fashion show was introduced in the United States by Ehrich Brothers in New York City in 1903; by 1915, it was an event in virtually every U.S. city and town. Relying on this popularity, the first modeling agency was founded in New York by John Powers in 1923 (Leach 1993:309). The entertainment industry contributed by making its own major fashion statements, as American women of 1920s sought to imitate stars such as Clara Bow.

Another addition to the marketing strategy was service, which included not only consumer credit (charge accounts and installment buying), but also a workforce to fawn over customers. Customers became guests.

William Leach suggested that service may have been one of the most important features of the new consumer society. It helped, he says, mask the inequality, poverty, and labor conflicts that were very much a part of the United States at this point in its history. If one wanted to understand how consumer society developed, Leach said, one could look at the rise of service. As economic inequality rose in America, and as labor conflict increased, Americans associated service with the "promise of America." Service conveyed to people the idea that everything was alright, that they had nothing to worry about, and that security and service awaited them. Service expressed what economists then and now would refer to as

> the "benevolent side" of capitalism, that is, the side of capitalism that gave to people in exchange for a dependable flow of profits—a better, more comfortable way of life. In this view, capitalism did not merely "strive for profits" but also sought "the satisfaction of the needs of others, by performing service efficiently." "Capital," said one turn-of-the-century economist, "reigns because it serves." (Leach 1993:146–147)

The second way in which American buying habits were changed was through a transformation of the major institutions of American society, each redefining its function to include the promotion of consumption. Educational and cultural institutions, governmental agencies, financial institutions, and even the family itself changed their meaning and function to promote the consumption of commodities. Before 1900, the contributions of universities to the capitalist economy largely dealt with how to "make" things, that is, with the production of commodities. Virtually no attention was paid to selling or keeping track of what was sold. For example, there was no systematic examination of mass retailing, credit systems, or banking offered by America's schools or universities. But in the twentieth century that began to change. For example, in New York City there was the good-design or arts-in-industry movement; schools such as the Pratt Institute and the New York School of Fine and Applied Arts (now Parsons School of Design) developed and began to prepare students to work in the emerging sales and design industries and in the large department stores. The University of Pennsylvania's Wharton School for Business and the Harvard School for Business introduced programs in accounting (virtually nonexistent before then), marketing, and sales. In 1919, New York

University's School of Retailing opened; in the mid-1920s, Harvard and Stanford established graduate business schools as did such schools as Northwestern, Michigan, California, and Wisconsin soon after.

Museums also redefined their missions to accommodate the growth of the consumer culture. The American Museum of National History and the Metropolitan Museum of Art in Manhattan, the Brooklyn Museum, and the Newark Museum, all heavily endowed by wealthy patrons such as J. P. Morgan, began to make alliances with business. Curators lectured to designers on Peruvian textiles or primitive decorative art. The head of the American Museum of Natural History, Morris D'Camp Crawford, assisted by the head of the anthropology department, Clark Wissler, urged businesspeople and designers to visit the museum. Special exhibits on the history of fashion and clothing were arranged, and Wissler even borrowed the window display techniques of New York department stores for his exhibits (as window display designers had borrowed the idea of the mannequin from anthropologist Franz Boas's display of foreign cultures at the 1893 World's Columbian Exposition in Chicago). The editor of *Women's Wear* magazine praised the museum for being "the most progressive force in the development of the designer" (Leach 1993:166).

The second set of institutions to aid in the development of consumer culture were agencies of the local and federal governments. The state, as an entity, had long taken a lively interest in commerce within its borders (as we'll see when we examine the history of global capitalist expansion in Chapter 3). But prior to the twentieth century, the state's concerns focused largely on the manufacture of commodities, the organization of business, the control of labor, and the movement of goods. It wasn't until the twentieth century that state agencies began to concern themselves with the consumption end of the business cycle. Thus in New York City, for example, merchants convinced the city government to widen streets, plant trees, and enact zoning legislation that segregated factories from retail areas so that shoppers would not have to confront factory workers on the workers' lunch breaks.

Nothing better represents the increasing role of the federal government in the promotion of consumption than the growth of the Commerce Department under Herbert Hoover, who served as its head from 1921 until his election as president in 1928. When the Commerce Building opened in Washington in 1932, it was the biggest office structure in the world (and was not surpassed in size until the Pentagon was built a decade later). At the time it brought together in one building virtually all the government departments that had anything to do with business, from the Patent Office to the Bureau of Foreign and Domestic Commerce (BFDC), then the most important agency of the department. From 1921 to 1930, the congressional appropriation for the BFDC rose from $100,000 to more than $8 million, an increase of 8,000 percent. The number of BFDC staff increased from 100 to 2,500.

Hoover clearly intended the Department of Commerce to serve as the handmaiden of American business, and its main goal was to help encourage the consumption of commodities. For example, between 1926 and 1928 the BDFC, under Hoover's direction, initiated the Census of Distribution (or "Census of Consumption," as it was sometimes called) to be carried out every ten years. (It was unique at that time; Britain and other countries did not initiate government-sponsored consumer research until the 1950s). It detailed where the consumers were and what quantities of goods they would consume; it pointed out areas where goods were "overdeveloped" and which goods were best carried by which stores. The Commerce Department endorsed retail and cooperative advertising and advised merchants on service devices, fashion, style, and display methods of all kinds. The agency advised retail establishments on the best ways to deliver goods to consumers, redevelop streets, build parking lots and underground transportation systems to attract consumers, use colored lights, and display merchandise in "tempting ways." The goal was to break down "all barriers between the consumers and commodities" (Leach 1993:366).

Hoover also emphasized individual home ownership. In his memoirs he wrote that "a primary right of every American family is the right to build a new house of its heart's desire at least once. Moreover, there is the instinct to own one's own house with one's own arrangement of gadgets, rooms, and surroundings" (cited Nash 1988:7). The Commerce Department flooded the country with public relations materials on "homebuying" ideas, producing a leaflet entitled *Own Your Own Home*, along with a film, *Home Sweet Home*. They advocated single-dwelling homes over multiunit dwellings and suburban over urban housing. The leaflet recommended a separate bedroom for each child, saying it was "undesirable for two children to occupy the same bed—whatever their age." Regardless of the reasons for these recommendations, the materials produced by the Commerce Department all promoted maximum consumption. Thus the government responded, as much as did educational institutions, to the need to promote the consumption of commodities.

Another step in creating a consumer economy was to give the worker more buying power. The advantage of this from an economic perspective is not easy to see. From the point of view of an industrialist or an employer, the ideal situation would be to pay as low a wage as possible in order to keep production costs down and increase profits. However, each producer of goods would like other producers to pay high wages, which would allow the other producers' workers to buy more products. The ideas that higher wages would serve an incentive for laborers to work harder or that higher wages might allow the worker to become a consumer occurred relatively late to factory owners and investors. The working class, they assumed, would work only as hard as they needed to get their basic subsistence, and to pay them more would only result in their working less. And when an occasional economic boom gave workers the spending power to consume at a higher level, the middle and upper classes would condemn them for their lack of thrift.

The economic power derived from turning workers into consumers was realized almost by accident. As industry attempted to increase efficiency, it developed new methods. Henry Ford introduced the assembly line, one of the apparently great innovations, to the manufacturing of automobiles. Workers occupied positions on the line from which they did not move ("Walking," Ford said, "is not a remunerative activity") and from which they would perform a single task. It was a process that required almost no training and that "the most stupid man could learn within two days," as Ford said. In essence, each worker had to repeat the same motion every ten seconds in a nine-hour workday.

Workers resisted this mind-numbing process. When Ford introduced his assembly line, absenteeism increased and worker turnover was enormous. In 1913, Ford required 13,000–14,000 workers to operate his plant, and in that year 50,000 quit. But Ford solved the problem: He raised wages from the industry standard of $2–3 per day to $5, and he reduced the working day to eight hours. Soon labor turnover fell to 5 percent, and waiting lines appeared at Ford hiring offices. Furthermore, production costs for Ford's Model T fell from $1,950 to $290, reducing the price to consumers. Most importantly, the rise in wages made Ford workers consumers of Ford automobiles, and, as other manufacturers followed suit, the automobile industry grew. By 1929, there were 23 million automobiles in the United States; by 1950 there were over 40 million. Today, including light trucks, there are almost 190 million vehicles.

In addition to the money coming from higher wages, buying power was increased by the expansion of credit. Credit, of course, is essential for economic growth and consumerism because it means that people, corporations, and governments can purchase goods and services with only a promise to pay for them at some future date. Furthermore, whenever credit is extended—whether it be by a store, a bank, a corporation, a person, or a government—in effect, money has been created, and more buying power has been introduced into the economy.

The increased ease of obtaining home mortgages was a key to the home building boom of the 1940s, 1950s, and 1960s, a boom that in turn fueled subsidiary industries—appliances, home furnishings, and road construction. Home mortgages had the further function of disciplining the workforce by forcing it to work to make credit payments. At the same time, homeowners gained a capital asset that served as a hedge against inflation. Automobile loans also added to consumer debt, and, similarly, fueled subsidiary economic growth—malls, highways, vacation travel, and so on. Credit cards gave holders a revolving line of credit with which to finance purchases. Americans currently owe $1.14 trillion in household debt not secured by real estate. This debt represents enormous confidence in the future of the economy because this money does not exist. Lenders in our economy simply assume that the money will exist when it comes time for people to repay their debts.

None of this would have been possible without a government financial policy that put limits on interest rates ("usury ceilings"), passed "truth in lending" laws, made it easier for certain groups (women and minorities) to borrow, and offered subsidized student loans. Thus credit increased consumer debt while creating a "mass market" for consumer goods that served further to stimulate economic growth (see Guttman 1994).

In addition to changes in the way workers were viewed and the expansion of credit, there had to be a change in the way retail establishments were organized. The emergence of the consumer was accompanied by an enormous growth in retail chain stores. Up until this point, distribution of goods was primarily controlled by small stores or large family-owned department stores. The 1920s saw the rise of the large retail conglomerates. In 1886, only 2 chains operated more than 5 stores; in

1912, 177 companies operated 2,235 stores; by 1929, nearly 1,500 companies were doing business in 70,000 outlets.

Finally, in addition to new marketing techniques and modified societal institutions that stimulated consumption, there had to be a change in spiritual and intellectual values from an emphasis on such values as thrift, modesty, and moderation toward a value system that encouraged spending and ostentatious display. T. J. Jackson Lears argued that from 1880 to 1930 the United States underwent a transformation of values from those that emphasized frugality and self-denial to those that sanctioned periodic leisure, compulsive spending, and individual fulfillment (Lears 1983). This shift in values, said Lears, was facilitated in American life by a new therapeutic ethos, an emphasis on physical and psychological health. This shift was promoted in part by the growth of the health professions and the popularity of psychology, along with the increasing autonomy and alienation felt by individuals as America ceased being a land of small towns and became increasingly urban. Advertisers capitalized on these changes by altering the way products were advertised; rather than emphasizing the nature of the product itself, they began to emphasize the alleged effects of the product and its promise of a richer, fuller life. Instead of just being good soap, shoes, or deodorant, a product would contribute to the buyer's psychological, physical, or social well-being (Lears 1983:19).

Clothing, perfumes, deodorant, and so on would provide the means of achieving love; alcoholic beverages would provide the route to friendship; the proper automobile tires or insurance policy would provide the means of meeting family responsibilities. Commodities would be the source of satisfaction and a vital means of self-expression. Ponder, for example, the following description by a 40-year-old man of the relationship between himself and his expensive Porsche:

> *Sometimes I test myself. We have an ancient, battered Peugeot, and I drive it for a week. It rarely breaks, and it gets great mileage. But when I pull up next to a beautiful woman, I am still the geek with glasses. Then I get back into my Porsche. It roars and tugs to get moving. It accelerates even going uphill at 80. It leadeth trashy women…to make pouting looks at me at stoplights. It makes me feel like a tomcat on the prowl…. Nothing in my life compares—except driving along Sunset at night in the 928, with the sodium vapor lamps reflecting off the wine-red finish, with the air inside reeking of tan glove-leather upholstery and the…Blaupunkt playing the Shirelles so loud that it makes my hairs vibrate. And with the girls I will never see again pulling up next to me, giving the car a once-over and looking at me as if I was a cool guy, not worried, instead of a 40-year-old schnook writer. (cited Belk 1988:148)*

In the late nineteenth century, a series of religious movements emerged that became known as *mind cure religions.* Henry James, in his classic 1902 book, *Varieties of Religious Experience,* drew attention to the mind cure movements, although he was not the first to use the term. These movements—New Thought, Unity, Christian Science, and Theosophy, among others—maintained that people could simply, by an act of will and conviction cure their own illnesses and create heaven on earth.

These movements were, as William Leach (1993:225) phrased it, "wish-oriented, optimistic, sunny, the epitome of cheer and self-confidence, and completely lacking in anything resembling a tragic view of life." There was no sin, no evil, no darkness, only, as one mind curer said, "the sunlight of health."

These movements held that salvation would occur in this life and not in the afterlife. Mind cure dismissed the ideas of sin and guilt. God became a divine force, a healing power. Proponents argued that Americans should banish ideas of duty and self-denial. As one early twentieth-century advocate said,

> [i]f you want to get the most out of life, just make up your mind that you were made to be happy, that you are a happiness machine, as well as a work machine. Cut off the past, and do not touch the morrow until it comes, but extract every possibility from the present. Think positive, creative, happy thoughts, and your harvest of good things will be abundant. (cited Leach 1993:229)

These new religions made fashionable the idea that in the world of goods men and women could find a paradise free from pain and suffering; they could find, as one historian of religion put it, the "good" through "goods."

Popular culture also promoted the mind cure ideology. As examples, there were L. Frank Baum's *The Wonderful Wizard of Oz*, which Leach characterized as "perhaps the best mind cure text ever written," and the Billikens doll, a squat Buddha-like figure, sometimes male and sometimes female, which represented the "god of things as they ought to be." Its success was without parallel in the toy trade and helped incite the doll craze in America. Billikens, it was said, would drive away petty annoyances and cares. One contemporary put it this way: "An atmosphere of gorged content pervades Billikens. No one can look at him [or her] and worry."

The popularity of the Billikens doll signaled change in spiritual values: it was now permissible to seek self-fulfillment in this life and find elements of satisfaction in manufactured commodities. The world was a good place: There was no misery; poverty, injustice, and inequities were only in the mind. There was enough for everyone.

These changes were not unique to America. Many of the same changes occurred in other nations, most notably Great Britain, Germany, and France (Carrier 1995). The consumer revolution of the early twentieth century was not the first of its kind either; but it happened with the most intensity and rapidity in America.

Thus by the 1930s, the consumer was well entrenched in the United States, complete with a spiritual framework and an intellectual rationalization that glorified the continued consumption of commodities as personally fulfilling and economically desirable, and a moral imperative that would end poverty and injustice. The creation of the consumer did not stop in 1930. Since that time the institutions of our society, particularly those of corporate America, have become increasingly more adept at creating sandpaintings in which people inhabit worlds whose very nature requires the continuous consumption of goods. Furthermore our culture has become skilled at hiding the negative consequences of our patterns of behavior, consequences such as labor exploitation, environmental damage, poverty, and growing inequities in the distribution of wealth. The ways through which the consequences

Tickle Me Elmo is a direct descendent of the Billikins Doll, a figure designed to drive away worries and cares and convey to people that the world was a good place with plenty for everyone.

of our patterns of consumption, labor, and capital accumulation are hidden from us are perhaps best illustrated by the appropriation of childhood in the service of commodity consumption. An investigation of this process will not only help us understand how culture functions to define our universe and our place in it, but also will reveal how power in the culture of capitalism can be used to mask from us some of the consequences of our own culturally defined modes of behavior.

Kinderculture in America: The Child as Consumer

The Role of Children in Capitalism

Anthropology teaches us that, much like the rest of our culture, childhood is socially created. That is, childhood and the ways that it is defined vary from society to society and from era to era. Childhood in nineteenth-century America was very different from what it is today. Prior to the nineteenth century, the major role of children in a capitalist economy was as workers (Lasch 1977:14ff). There were few industries that did not employ children at some level, and there were few families whose children did not contribute economically through either farm or factory labor. In twentieth-century America, this began to change. Social movements that for decades worked to restrict child labor finally convinced state and federal legislatures to pass laws making child labor illegal. These developments signaled a transformation of children from workers to consumers. Although this may not have been the intent of the reformers, children were to contribute far more to the national economy as consumers than they ever did as laborers.

It wasn't until the beginning of the twentieth century that retailers began to target children as a discrete group of consumers. As late as 1890, there was not a children's market worth considering; children ate, wore, and played with what their parents made for them. Germany was by far the largest producer of children's toys, and there were few, if any, factories in the United States producing children's clothing. Nor was there any market for infants' or children's foods. Yet by 1915, the baby clothing industry was one of the largest in the United States, with seventy-five factories operating in New York state alone. Toy production increased by 1,300 percent between 1905 and 1920. One reason was the destruction of the German toy industry during World War I. Another was the development of new toys in the United States that became international sensations, such as the racist Alabama Coon Jigger, a laughing, prancing, mechanical Negro male. But, most importantly, retailers were beginning to appreciate the profits that could be made from children's commodities.

Retailers also began to take note of psychologists' discovery of the "natural desire" of "little people" for goods and toys, heeding the psychologists' advice that "every attention shown the child binds the mother to the store," or the observation that if they cultivated consumers "as kids [they would] have them as customers for a lifetime." Santa Claus became one of the major vehicles for selling toys; his commercialization hit its peak in the 1920s.

Child psychologists and home economists also advised parents that children needed toys for exercise and toys to relax; children, they said, should have their own playrooms. These same experts lectured at department stores, advising parents of the educational values of toys. With this new emphasis on the child as consumer, by 1926, America had become the greatest producer of toys and playthings in the world. There were toys for the backyard, camping, the beach, and the "little private room which every child desperately needs to fulfill his or her individuality." Play, said the experts, "is the child's business; toys the material with which he works" (Leach 1993:328).

The federal government played a major role in redefining childhood. In 1929, Herbert Hoover sponsored a White House Conference on Child Health and Protection. The conference report, *The Home and the Child*, concluded that children were independent beings with particular concerns of their own. The child, the report said,

> *is often an alien in his home when it comes to any consideration of his special needs in the furnishings and equipment of the home. He belongs nowhere. He must ac-*

commodate himself to an adult environment—chairs and tables are too big and too high for him; there is no suitable place for his books and his toys. He moves in a misfit world with nothing apportioned to his needs. Often this results in retarding his physical, mental, and social development. (White House 1931)

The report advised parents to give their children their own "furniture and eating equipment" suitable to each child's age and size; it further advised parents to provide playrooms inside the house and fill the backyard with "toys, velocipedes, sawhorses, wagons, and wheelbarrows, slides and places to keep pets." "Generally a sleeping room for each person is desirable," it noted. As a child grows "older and becomes more social he wants games and toys that he can share with his friends." When the family decides on "the purchase of a piece of furniture or a musical instrument" of common interest, it is important to consult the children. Take them shopping for their own "things and let them pick them out by themselves."

*Through such experiences personality develops… [These] experiences have the advantage also of creating in the child a sense of personal as well as family pride in ownership, and eventually **teaching him that his personality can be expressed through things.** (White House 1931, [emphasis added]; see also Leach 1993:371–372)*

Thus in the space of some thirty years the role of children in American life changed dramatically; they became, and remain, pillars of the consumer economy, with economic power rivaling that of adults. Children have become a main target of advertisers; as one marketing specialist told the *Wall Street Journal*, "Even two-year-olds are concerned about their brand of clothes, and by the age of six are full-out consumers" (Durning 1992:120). Teenagers account for 30 percent of all shoe sales in the United States today. By 1990, children from ages five to twelve annually spent $4.2 billion of their own money. They influence household spending to the tune of another $131 billion each year, of which $82 billion goes to food and drinks (Kincheloe 1997: 225). Advertisers devise all sorts of campaigns to appeal to children and are often criticized for the messages they communicate. But some advertising executives are quite candid in their objectives. As one said, "No one's really worrying about what it's teaching impressionable youth. Hey, I'm in the business of convincing people to buy things they don't need" (*Business Week,* August 11, 1997:35).

The Social Construction of Childhood

Retail establishments in the early part of the twentieth century, particularly the new department stores, took the lead in redefining the world of children. They produced their own radio programs for children and put on elaborate shows. Macy's, which by the late 1920s had the largest toy department in the world, put on playlets for children in makeshift theaters or in store auditoriums. The most popular department store show was *The Wizard of Oz;* when the show was put on at Field's in Chicago, the children wore green-tinted glasses better to appreciate the "Emerald City."

In this era, the event that most symbolized the reconstruction of childhood was Christmas. Christmas only became a time of toy giving in America in the 1840s. The Christmas holiday was appropriated by retail establishments as a way to sell goods by the 1870s; people at that time had already begun to complain that Christmas was becoming overcommercialized (Carrier 1995:189). But it wasn't until the early twentieth century that retail establishments turned Christmas into a spectacle that appealed to children especially. By the mid-1920s, nearly every city in America had its own "radio" Santa Claus. Gimbel's in New York received thousands of letters addressed to Santa Claus; each was carefully answered by staff and signed "Santa," with the name of each child carefully indexed for future use (Leach 1993:330). In 1924, Macy's inaugurated its Thanksgiving Day parade, which ran from 145th Street to West 34th Street and culminated with the appearance of Santa Claus standing on Macy's 34th Street marquee waving to the throngs below.

Thanksgiving also came to mark the beginning of the Christmas buying season, a time when Americans spend some 4 percent of their income on Christmas gifts, and when department stores sell 40 percent of their yearly total of toys and 25 percent of their candy, cosmetics, toiletries, stationery, greeting cards, and books. (By the early 1990s, Americans were spending about $37 billion on Christmas gifts, a sum greater than the gross national product (GNP) of all but forty-five countries in the world [see Restad 1995:160].) The government did its part in defining the Christmas buying season when Fred Lazaus Jr., who was to become president of Ohio's Federated Department Stores, persuaded President Franklin Roosevelt in 1939 to move Thanksgiving Day from November 30, its traditional date, to November 23 to add one more week to the Christmas buying season. Congress made that official in 1941 when it moved the Thanksgiving celebration from the last Thursday in November to the fourth Thursday. The state thus assured that it could fall no later than November 28, guaranteeing a minimum four-week shopping spree (Restad 1995:162).

Santa Claus represents one of the more elaborate ways in which the culture of capitalism shields its members, particularly children, from some of its less savory features. The story of Santa Claus represented a world in which consumer, capitalist, and laborer were idealized: Commodities (toys) were manufactured by happy elves, working in Santa's workshop (no factories at the North Pole, and certainly no Chinese assembly plants) and distributed, free of charge, to good boys and girls by a corpulent, grandfatherly male in fur-trimmed clothes. It is perhaps ironic that when political cartoonist Thomas Nast created what has become the contemporary image of Santa Claus in 1862, he modeled Santa's costume after the fur-trimmed clothes worn by the wealthy Astor family (Carrier 1995:189).

Nast also created Santa's workshop, perhaps in nostalgic remembrance of prefactory production. Writers as early as the 1870s recognized the irony of this idealized version of Christmas and toy production. One magazine editorial in 1873, commenting on a picture of Santa's elves working gaily in some magical workplace, turning out dolls, boats, tops, and toy soldiers, compared it with the reality of the poor, working six days a week in factories (Restad 1995:149). William Waits in his book, *The Modern Christmas in America* (1992), suggested that Santa's major role was to "decontaminate" Christmas gifts, removing the stigma of factory industry (p. 25).

Others, of course, played a major role in transforming childhood, but we can do no better than to trace the trajectory of this transformation from its beginning—L. Frank Baum and his Emerald City—to its logical culmination in Walt Disney World.

Appropriation of Childhood, Part I, Baum's Emerald City

Pre-1900 children's stories were very different from those common today. The most famous were the stories of Jacob and Wilhelm Grimm. The Grimm brothers took traditional European folktales, most of which contained fairly gruesome and bizarre plots (cannibalism, incest, murder, etc.), and rewrote them so that they could be used as tools for the socialization of children. Each rewritten tale contained a moral lesson. But, as with nineteenth-century religion, government, and economic institutions, these stories lacked the power to produce the necessary mind cure impulse to consume. Consequently there emerged new kinds of stories in which the world was cleansed of the darkness of the Grimm's stories and presented as a happy place full of desirable things. The leader in this reconstruction of the child's universe was Baum.

Baum came from a well-to-do New York State family and had moved with his wife Maud Gage (whose mother, Matilda Joslyn Gage, was a leading nineteenth-century feminist leader) in the late 1880s to Aberdeen, South Dakota, where he opened a large retail store (Baum's Bazaar). In 1891, economic depression hit Aberdeen, and Baum went broke. He moved his family to Chicago, where he began to write the stories that would make him famous. In addition he took a lively interest in the art of window display, becoming an advisor to some of the largest department stores in the city.

Baum had always loved the theater, and he combined that with his interest in business to make window displays into theatrical productions, showing off retail goods to their best advantage. The quality of the goods mattered little to Baum; how they looked, their "selling power" was what mattered. He soon founded the National Association of Window Trimmers and developed a manual and later a journal, *The Show Window,* devoted to window displays. (The journal changed its title to *Display World* in the 1920s; it exists today as *Visual Merchandising.*) Baum's general message was to "use the best art to arouse in the observer the cupidity and longing to possess the goods" (Leach 1993:60).

Baum's personal philosophy was compatible with the various mind cure movements of the late nineteenth and early twentieth centuries. "People do not sin and should not feel guilt," he wrote in 1890 in the *Aberdeen Saturday Pioneer,* "the good things in life are given to be used." The "rainy day" theory of saving was all right, according to Baum, as long as it wasn't used as an excuse to deny oneself comforts. Who, he asked,

> *will be the gainer when Death calls him to the last account—the man who can say "I have lived!" or the man who can say "I have saved"? ... To gain all the meat from*

the nut of life is the essence of wisdom. Therefore, "eat, drink, and be merry— tomorrow *you die." (cited Leach 1993:247)*

Baum's books were filled with goods and mechanical inventions, landscapes of edible fruits, cakes, cookies, all intended to assure readers that the world was a good place. They were, said William Leach, affirmative, Americanized fairy tales. In fact Baum's explicit goal was to revolutionize children's literature. In his introduction to the first edition of *The Wonderful Wizard of Oz,* Baum wrote,

[t]he time has come for a series of newer "wonder tales" in which the stereotyped genie, dwarf and fairy are eliminated, together with all the horrible and bloodcurdling incidents devised by their authors to point to a fearsome moral to each tale.... The Wonderful Wizard of Oz *was written solely to please children of today. It aspires to being a modernized fairy tale, in which the wonderment and joy are retained and the heartaches and nightmares are left out. (cited Leach 1993:251)*

The story of the Wizard of Oz can be interpreted as a tribute to our ability to create illusions and magic, to make people believe in spite of themselves. In Baum's

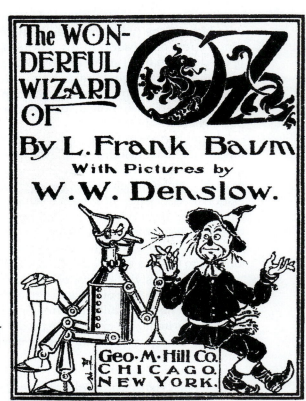

The Wonderful Wizard of Oz, *similar to the store display windows that Baum designed, was filled with all the good things in life, assuring the reader that the world is full of things to consume and enjoy.*

stories the Wizard is exposed as a charlatan, a "common man" with no special powers; but he is powerful because he can make others do what he wants, make them believe in the unbelievable. He is a confidence man. People adored him even as he escaped from Oz in a balloon and was remembered as the man who "built for us this beautiful Emerald City." Baum, said William Leach, created a benign trickster, consumer society's version of the capitalist. *The Wizard of Oz* represented a new spiritual-ethical climate that modeled itself on a version of the child's world in which dreams of self-fulfillment through consumption were legitimized and any negative consequences of consumption were banished. In brief, Baum's work represented but one of the sandpaintings of capitalism, one that appropriates childhood to represent a world in which the purpose of life is to consume.

Yet as sophisticated as Baum was in creating an ethos that encouraged people to buy, the master of the art was to be Walt Disney.

The Appropriation of Childhood, Part II,
Walt Disney and the Creation of Disney World

It is difficult to say when the child's universe, created to turn children into consumers, began to be used to entice adults. Perhaps the glorification of "youth" in advertising and the upward extension of childhood to include the teens were manifestation of this phenomenon. Regardless, the appropriation of childhood as a vehicle to encourage consumption at all ages and rationalize capitalism culminated in the creation of Walt Disney World. Disney and other major American corporations have created what Shirley Steinberg and Joseph Kincheloe (1997) call *kinderculture,* the promotion of an ethos of pleasure for the purpose of enticing adults as well as children to consume.

Walt Disney World is the ultimate sandpainting of the culture of capitalism. Instead of a single sandpainter using bits of colored sand and grain to create a picture barely large enough to contain a single person, a corporation has used millions of tons of concrete, wood, plastic, and glass to create the "home of childhood," a miniature universe that promotes innocence and trust, that allows people to leave the "real world" behind, and that encourages (in fact, insists) that participants put themselves in the hands of Disney. However, as Stephen Fjellman (1992:13) warned,

> [t]hese hands bear watching, for in their shaping of things lies danger. It is not just that our movements are constrained with the promise, usually fulfilled, of rewards. What is important is that our thoughts are constrained. They are channeled not only in the interests of Disney itself, but also in the interests of the large corporations with which Disney has allied itself, the system of power they maintain, and the world of commodities that is their life's blood.

Like the work of the sandpainters, Walt Disney World is a kind of ritual setting where participants are returned to childhood to be reborn as Disney adults. It is a respite from the anxieties and fears of everyday life; at Walt Disney World we

Walt Disney World represents, like the Navajo sandpainting, a miniature universe that, in this case, serves to define for its visitors their place in a world as consumers of commodities.

can walk in the roads, the place is clean, it is safe, everyone is polite, it is air-conditioned, and the trains run on time.

But if we look beyond the pleasantries, said Fjellman, we find that the environment is totally controlled and that there is a degree of discipline at work in this model world that rivals the discipline of a fascist state. And the control is real. In creating Walt Disney World, the Disney corporation secretly bought up forty square miles of central Florida real estate (twice the size of Manhattan) and was granted almost feudal powers over the land by the state. Disney World has its own government, it sets the rules, and it controls the message. *But what is the message of the Disney World sandpainting?* To answer this question, let's examine two aspects of Disney World: its depiction of American history and its representation of progress and the future.

History, or *distory*, as Mike Wallace (1985) called it, is everywhere at Walt Disney World, appropriated, like childhood, in the service of the Disney message. The history, of course, is highly idealized. Thus when Williamsburg was first opened, it omitted any reminder of the slaves who made up 50 percent of the colonial population. At Disney World historical figures are used as spokespersons for Disney, lending to its message the authority of their reputations. We meet presidents, listen to Thomas Edison and Davy Crockett. Benjamin Franklin and Mark Twain are tour guides. Fragments of Abraham Lincoln's speeches, most often taken out of context, are read to us by robots; and Leonardo Da Vinci, the Disney model of the prophetic visionary, is everywhere. At Disney World there is a conscious attempt to present the history of capitalism without the warts. Disney World designers are quite forthright and unapologetic about their intent. As one Disney spokesperson explained, "we are not telling history like it really was but as it should have been" (Fjellman 1992:31). Another Disney "imagineer," as the designers are called, explains "Disney realism" as a "sort of utopian nature, where we program out all the negative, unwanted elements and program in the positive elements" (cited Wallace 1985:35).

The center of Disney World (and the original Disneyland in California) is Main Street, a highly idealized, turn-of-the-century remodeling of life as it should have been, a consumer's paradise, scaled down to five-eighths of actual area. The street or square is filled with shops and taverns; people are defined by what they sell. Main Street cultivates a nostalgia for an imagined past without classes, crime, or conflict, a time of continuous consumption, "a supermarket of fun."

On one level Disney World is an extension of the shop windows designed by L. Frank Baum in the 1890s; on another it serves as an explicit model for the modern shopping mall. Urban planner James Rouse based a number of his town designs and historical shopping malls (Faneuil Hall in Boston, Harborplace in Baltimore, and South Street Seaport in New York) on Disney's Main Street (Wallace 1985:42; see also Kowinski 1985).

At the Hall of Presidents, Disney takes viewers through U.S. history in twenty-nine minutes flat. Disney does recognize, in a fashion, that U.S. history was not all that perfect. After all, the average adult visitor to Disney World is a well-educated professional who could not have been ignorant of the historical injustices in the United States's past. Consequently Disney World provides Frederick Douglass to speak to the oppression of Blacks, Chief Joseph represents indigenous peoples, Susan B. Anthony speaks about the concerns of women, and John Muir serves to remind visitors that progress often came at the expense of environmental disruption. However, each is a highly sanitized symbol of opposition to racism, sexism, and environmental devastation. In "distory" these figures do not remind us of persistent problems in the social fabric, rather they are presented as opportunities to overcome barriers. This is also bad, if not outright false, history.

For example, Disney appropriates for its version of indigenous people in American history the story of Chief Joseph and the Nez Percé. In 1877, the U.S. government, largely at the insistence of settlers who wanted the land, revised previous treaty commitments and attempted to settle all Nez Percé in the Walla Walla Valley of Washington on smaller reservations. One group, led by Chief Joseph and the war chief Looking Glass, refused and, after some young warriors killed a trader accused of selling bad whiskey to the Indians, fled the area, heading east into Idaho,

Wyoming, and Montana in an attempt to reach Canada. They were pursued by the command of General Oliver O. Howard, who Joseph's band defeated in battle or consistently outmaneuvered. The campaign, one of the most bloody and heroic of the Indian wars, ended when Joseph and the remnants of his band were finally surrounded by one of the three army commands that had set out to intercept them. In blizzard conditions on October 5, 1877, only forty miles from the Canadian border, Joseph met with the army's commanders to surrender. His surrender speech, among the most famous speeches in American history, was written down by an army lieutenant. At Walt Disney World Chief Joseph, in robot form, once again delivers his speech; the Disney version is as follows (cited Fjellman 1992:104):

> *Enough, enough of your words.*
> *Let your new dawn lead to the final sunset on my*
> *people's suffering.*
> *When I think of our condition, my heart is sick.*
> *I see men of my own race treated as outlaws, or shot*
> *down like animals.*
> *I pray that all of us may be brothers, with one country*
> *around us, and one government for all.*
> *From where the sun now stands, I will fight no more*
> *forever.*

However, except for the famous final line, that was not what Joseph said. Here is the original speech as recorded that day in 1877 (cited in Beal 1963:229):

> *Tell General Howard I know his heart. What he told me before I have in my heart.*
> *I am tired of fighting. Our chiefs are killed. Looking Glass is dead. The old men are*
> *all killed. It is the young men who say yes or no. He who led the young men is*
> *dead. It is cold and we have no blankets. The little children are freezing to death.*
> *My people some of them have run away to the hills and have no blankets, no food;*
> *no one knows where they are, perhaps freezing to death. I want time to look for my*
> *children and see how many of them I can find. Maybe I will find them among the*
> *dead. Hear me my chiefs, I am tired; my heart is sick and sad. From where the sun*
> *now stands, I will fight no more forever.*

There is obviously a significant difference between the Disney version and the one recorded on the battlefield. Instead of freezing children, the death of the elderly, and a military campaign that ended only after the deaths of hundreds of American and Nez Percé soldiers, Joseph's surrender speech has been turned by Disney into a testimonial to brotherhood and the nation-state.

In telling history "as it should have been," Disney paints a picture of an American past of which people can be proud, while subtly justifying whatever excesses may have been committed. As in the land of Oz, everything has happened for the better.

EPCOT (Experimental Prototypical Community of Tomorrow) is a more adult attraction than Fantasyland or some of the other venues of Disney World. EPCOT was Walt Disney's pet project until his death in December 1966. EPCOT was to be a utopian city of 20,000-plus residents that would attract urban planners and experimenters from all over the world. But Walt Disney died and corporate Disney turned the project into a gigantic, corporate advertisement, using the 1939 World's Fair in New York as its guide, and having pavilions depict the corporate version of the history of progress. Thus at EPCOT, Exxon presents the history of energy, while AT&T does communications. Transportation is presented by General Motors, the land by Kraft, the home by General Electric, and imagination by Kodak. Perhaps even more interesting, at the heart of each corporate pavilion is a ride, a setting much like a sandpainting, in which seated passengers travel through tunnels that open to huge dioramas filled with robots, videos, holograms, and other technological marvels.

Throughout the EPCOT pavilions there is this message: Technology equals progress, and progress is natural—and perhaps even American. There have been some problems along the way, the corporate exhibits tell us. "We" have made mistakes—but "we" (corporations) are working to solve those problems. "We" polluted the air, "we" abused the environment. Thus the imagineers admit that there were problems in the past, but reject corporate responsibility for them, putting the corporations at the forefront of the ecology movement. History is defined for us as "a record of the invention of commodities which allow man to master his environment" (Wallace 1985:44). Progress is defined as the availability of emancipatory consumer goods. The World of Tomorrow promotes capitalist development as inevitable, spreading the message that history was made by inventors and businesspeople, and that the corporations are the legatees of this past. It tells us, as Mike Wallace (1985:47) observed, that "citizens can sit back and consume."

But who is Disney World for? It is supposed to be for children, but it really represents the appropriation of childhood to encourage the consumption of commodities and, more important, once again to shield the consumer from the negative side of capitalism. Walt Disney World is now the single biggest tourist attraction in the entire world. Approximately one-tenth of the population of the U.S. travels there each year. But it is not a universal attraction. By and large it attracts people of relatively high incomes (median of $54,000 in 1998); three-quarters of them are professionals or managers. Only 3 percent are Black and 2 percent Hispanic. Seventy-one percent are from outside Florida.

As Wallace (1985:53) said,

> [a] *process of class self-affirmation seems to be at work. Certainly Disney World seems intent on providing reassurance to this class, on presenting it with its own pedigree. EPCOT's seventies-style liberal corporatism seems tailor-made for professionals and technocrats. It's calibrated to their concerns—nothing on labor, heavy on ecology, clean, well-managed, emphasis on individual solutions, good restaurants—and it provides just the right kind of past for their hippier sensibilities.* **Perhaps, therefore, professionals and managers (many of whom, after all, function**

as subalterns of capital) flock there because it ratifies their world [empha-
sis added]. Perhaps they don't want to know about reality—past or present—and
prefer comforting and plausible stereotypes.

Walt Disney World is only one manifestation of the tendency or necessity in capitalism to mask the unpleasant side effects of capitalist production and consumption. People may choose to do something that is harmful to others, but they do so according to a cultural logic that makes it the "right" choice. Our culture makes choosing even easier by masking the sometimes devastating consequences of our choices. Thus the process of insulating the consumer from truths that might reduce consumption is built into the culture of capitalism; denial is as much a part of it as is consumption. Furthermore, this denial—this part of the culture of capitalism—determines in many ways how we view the world. Put another way, the world as seen from the point of view of the consumer is very different from the world as seen from the perspective of worker, capitalist, or people of other cultures around the world. One of the tasks of this book is to try to help the reader appreciate these other points of view.

Conclusion

The culture of capitalism did not appear full-blown in December 1910 or at another date; it emerged as part of a historical process that required the creation of the laborer and the capitalist merchant, industrialist, and financier. It also required, as we have mentioned, a level of global integration unique in human history. It is important to understand how that integration occurred, and at what cost.

It is also important to understand the global consequences of the exporting of this culture to countries all over the world. William Leach (1993:388) summarized well one of the dilemmas: Capitalism, he said, had achieved a new level of strength and world influence, especially in the wake of the collapse of communism. It also, he concluded,

> *appears to have a nearly unchallenged hold over every aspect of American life,*
> *from politics to culture, so much so that the United States looks like a fashion ba-*
> *zaar to much of the rest of the world. For some Americans the continued power of*
> *consumerism has led to further degradation of what it means to be an American*
> *or of what America is all about. For others, this evolution has only enhanced the*
> *country's appeal, making it appear more than ever an Emerald City, a feast, a de-*
> *partment store to which everyone is invited and entitled. Just as cities in the*
> *United States once operated as generators of consumer desire for internal markets,*
> *today America functions similarly on a global scale.*

Chapter 2

The Laborer in the Culture of Capitalism

And thus do we gain all our wealth and estate
By many poor men that work early and late;
If it were not for them that do our labor full hard
We might go and hang ourselves without regard....
By these people's labor we fill our purse.
If trading grows dead, we will presently show it,
But if it grows good, they shall never know it.
—(SEVENTEENTH-CENTURY LABOR SONG)
FERNAND BRAUDEL, THE WHEELS OF COMMERCE

The capitalist system makes it very much easier for people not to realize
what they are doing, not to know about the danger and hardship, the
despair and humiliation, that their way of life implies for others.
—EDMUND WILSON, THE SHORES OF LIGHT

The consumer may drive the culture of capitalism, but without the laborer there would be no commodities to consume. Yet the emergence of the laborer—the person who survives by selling labor—is a recent historical phenomenon. In past centuries most people had access to land on which to grow their own food, selling whatever surplus they produced. Or they owned tools—implements for weaving, metalworking, or producing other objects for sale or trade. Thus to understand capitalism it is necessary to examine why people choose or are forced to sell their labor. Before beginning this examination it is necessary to have a fundamental understanding of the workings of the capitalist economy.

Capitalism is not an easy term to define. Pierre Proudhon, who first used it in 1861, called it "an economic and social regime in which capital, the source of income, does not generally belong to those who make it work through their labor" (cited Braudel 1982:237). The term *capitalism* does not appear in the writings of Karl

Russian laborers watch as the first Ford automobile assembled in the Soviet Union rolls off the assembly line in 1930.

Marx and did not gain currency until 1902, when the German economist Werner Sombart used it to denote the opposite of socialism. But definitions alone won't help us to understand fully the dynamics of something as complex as a capitalist economy. We need to understand the major characteristics of capitalism to appreciate how as an economic and a cultural system it has permeated our lives.

Few people will deny that the genius of capitalism lies in its ability to produce goods—commodities for people to buy and consume. Let's start our excursion into capitalism with a product, beginning with something nearly all of us buy at one point or another—sneakers—and examine, briefly, the largest manufacturer of sneakers, Nike, Inc. Today most of the sneakers—and clothes—we wear are assembled overseas because large corporations, such as Nike, have increasingly relocated assembly factories from their home countries to countries on the periphery. Consequently the clothes we wear; the TVs, stereos, and compact disks (CDs) we listen to; and the computers we use are at least partly produced by a person in another part of the world. This situation creates a clash of cultures that can be illuminating for what they tell us about other cultures and what they may tell us about ourselves. The effects that these factories have on other countries highlight the distinctive features of the capitalist economy and perhaps approximate the impact of early capitalism on our own society. But first let us digress briefly to an understanding of the economic logic of capitalism and particularly the role of labor within this economic system.

A Primer on the Economic Elements of Capitalism

Let's run through a quick primer on the economics of capitalism and its development. Briefly stated, the economics of capitalism grew out of the interactions of the following five items:

1. Commodities (C). There are basically two types of commodities: capital goods and consumer goods. Capital goods, such as land, raw materials, tools, machines, and factories, are used to produce consumer goods (e.g., television sets, VCRs, computers, houses) to be sold to others.
2. Money (M). Money is simply a standardized means of exchange. It serves to reduce all goods and commodities to a standard value. By putting a monetary value on something (e.g., a forest), it can be compared with any other commodity

Part of the genius of the culture of capitalism is its ability to produce vast quantities of goods, such as these Nike products, that consumers all over the world clamor to buy.

(e.g., government bonds). Money thus greatly facilitates the exchange of commodities.

3. Labor power (lp). Labor power is the work that is needed to transform one type of commodity into another (e.g., steel into an automobile).
4. Means of production (mp). Another term for capital goods, that is, the machines, the land, and the tools with which other commodities are produced.
5. Production (P). The combination of lp and mp to produce commodities.

In precapitalist societies or noncapitalist production, as in capitalist production, people either make or obtain commodities—food, clothing, shelter, and the like—to use. These commodities have what economists call *use value.* If someone needs a shirt, they make it; if they need food, they gather, hunt, or grow it. Occasionally they may trade for what they need or even buy it. Thus a farmer might barter some corn (C) in exchange for a shirt (C') or use money to purchase it, but the object is always to obtain something for use. We can diagram this type of exchange as follows:

$$C \longrightarrow C' \quad \text{or} \quad C \longrightarrow M \longrightarrow C'$$

In capitalism people produce or obtain goods not for their use, but for the purpose of exchange. That is, their object is to produce or obtain commodities (C) not to obtain another commodity (C') but to get capital or money (M). The goods have what is called *exchange value.* Thus in a business transaction when a person buys a commodity at one price and sells it at a higher price, the commodity is said to have an exchange value.

$$M \longrightarrow C \longrightarrow M'$$

Some people might argue that this exchange *is* capitalism, although most would call it *mercantile exchange,* suggesting that the formula for capitalism is incomplete. You still need one more development: to combine labor and the means of production in a unique way. From this perspective, fully developed capitalism looks like this:

$$M \longrightarrow C \longrightarrow P \longrightarrow C' \longrightarrow M'$$

or

$$M \longrightarrow C \longrightarrow \frac{mp}{lp} \longrightarrow C' \longrightarrow M'$$

Thus a manufacturer or producer has money (M) to buy commodities (C) (e.g., raw material, machines, labor) that are then combined (mp/lp) to manufacture commodities that carry a value greater than C (C'). The sale of these commodities permits the producer to receive a sum of money greater than M (M') that constitutes *profit.* Note that at this point, labor is considered a commodity to be purchased or rented, in the same ways that raw materials, machines, factories, or land are purchased or rented. Labor becomes a factor of production in the same way that raw materials, land, or machines are factors of production. In addition, at this point the accumulation of wealth comes to consist increasingly of productive capital (raw materials, machines, factories).

Let's apply the formula to our sample capitalist enterprise, the Nike Corporation. Nike invests money (M) to buy commodities (C), consisting of such things as leather, rubber, machines to make textile, and factories (mp), which they combine with labor (lp), the people who design, produce, and assemble the commodity—sneakers—(C') that they then sell for money (M'). The object of this entire process is to get M' to exceed M as much as possible. That constitutes the profit—the bottom line, so to speak.

And Nike doesn't just keep M'—it reinvests it in commodities and recombines it with mp and lp in order to repeat the process and earn/accumulate still more money and profits. (Figure 2.1 is a diagram of the cyclical nature of capitalist production.)

However, in the real world of finance there are other factors to consider. For example, producers of commodities do not often have the money (or capital) to start the production cycle on their own; they have to borrow money from banks or sell stock to investors to raise money to obtain the means of production and pay the labor power to produce goods. Consequently some of the profits take the form of principal and interest to repay investors' loans. The higher the rate of interest that the manufacturer offers investors, the easier it is to obtain loans. Moreover the producer, for example, Nike, doesn't have to put its profits back into producing more sneakers. It may invest that money elsewhere with the possibility of earning greater profits; in other words the manufacture and sale of sneakers may produce a profit of 10 percent, but if those profits can be reinvested elsewhere at 12 percent, so much the better.

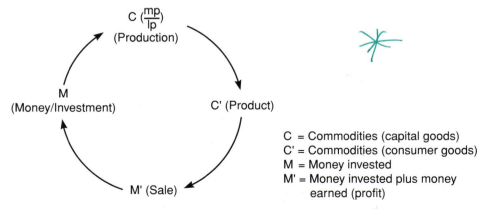

FIGURE 2.1   **Cycle of Capitalist Production**

And this reveals one dilemma that Nike and other producers of commodities face: making a profit is not enough. They must give their investors—the banks, stockholders, and so on—who supplied the money or capital to start the cycle of production enough of a return on their money so that they do not take it elsewhere. If they go elsewhere (and in today's world investors, as we shall see, have an enormous number of investment options), Nike may find it harder to locate investors and put together the money necessary to restart the cycle. Consequently they may have to pay higher interest rates and charge more for their products. In that case, however, they might not sell as many units, especially if Adidas or Reebok can sell their sneakers for less.

In order to make a profit it is imperative to keep the money spent on factories, machines (mp), and labor (lp) as low as possible. In fact, according to some economists, the ability to minimize the production costs of mp and lp, will determine the success or failure of the company. (We will return to that in a moment.)

It soon becomes apparent that the capitalist production process is very much a money-making game: Investors and manufacturers put money in at one end of the production process and get more money out of the other end in the form of profits or interest. It is very much like a hypothetical device that engineers call a "black box." Engineers assume that the black box produces something, but for the purposes of design and planning they do not concern themselves with how things are produced, that is, with the internal functioning of the box. They simply assume that if they put something into it—fuel, electricity, and so on—they will get something out (e.g., power, movement).

For most capitalist producers or investors, capitalism or capitalist enterprises, such as corporations, banks, bonds, or stocks, are like black boxes: You put money in one end and get more money out the other. (See Figure 2.2.) It is, of course, a highly complex business to know where to put the money, how much to invest, and so forth. But it is the amount of the return rather than the way that it is generated that is uppermost in importance.

Nevertheless it is in the black box that commodities are produced and consumed. It is also in the black box that we find the patterns of social, political, economic, ecological, and ideological life that either promote or inhibit the conversion of money into more money.

Thus capitalism is more than an economic system; its operation has far-reaching consequences for almost all aspects of our existence. Most of us order our lives in some way to produce and consume commodities that generate the profits and interest that make the capitalist system work. But although most people who invest

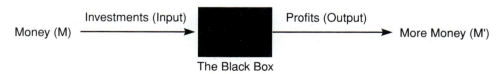

FIGURE 2.2   The Black Box

money do not concern themselves with how it is produced, others who are affected by this almost magical transformation often conceptualize the process in profound ways. For example, peasant farmers in Colombia have a way of conceptualizing capitalist exchange that may help us understand its essential elements and its cost: the baptism of money.

The Baptism of Money

After losing their land to large farmers and being forced to supplement their farming activities with wage labor, peasants in the lowlands of Colombia developed the practice of illicitly baptizing money in a Catholic church—instead of a newborn child. When presenting a child to the priest to be baptized, a peasant would hold a peso note that he believed received the priest's blessing instead of the child. The note, thus magically transformed and given the name of the child, will, it is believed, continually return to and enrich its owner by bringing with it other notes. In other words the note becomes interest-bearing capital that continues to generate more and more money. Peasants tell stories of such notes disappearing from cash registers, carrying with them all the other notes, and of the store owner who saved his money only because he heard two baptized notes fighting for possession of the drawer's contents.

The idea that money is animate, that it can magically bring back more money, may at first seem strange to us, but Michael Taussig (1977) argued that the Colombian view of money is very close to our own—the major difference having to do with their conception of the black box.

The major feature of capitalism is that money can be used to make more money. To do so the money must be invested in goods that must be sold, or invested in factories in which people work to make goods to be sold, and so on. Yet we often talk as if it is the money itself that makes the money, or as if money somehow has a life of its own. We speak of "the *sagging* dollar," "cash *flows*," or "putting our money to *work*." The news will report that "earnings have *surged* ahead," or that we have "*climbing* interest rates." Factories are even referred to as "*plants*" where our "*money grows*."

In other words our language conveys the notion that capital has an innate property of self-expansion. It is talked about as if it were a living being that reproduces itself (just as the Colombian peasant believes baptized money has a life of its own and can reproduce itself).

The belief that money has a life of its own is beautifully illustrated in Benjamin Franklin's classic work, *Advice to a Young Tradesman* (1748). Here is Franklin's advice:

> *Remember, that money is of the prolific, generating nature. Money can beget money, and its offspring can beget more, and so on. Five shillings turned is six, turned again it is seven and three pence and so on, till it becomes a hundred pounds. The more there is of it, the more it produces every turning, so that the*

profits rise quicker and quicker. He that kills a breeding-sow, destroys all her off-spring to the thousandth generation. (cited Taussig 1977:140)

The attitude expressed by Benjamin Franklin and expressed daily in our own lives is one that Karl Marx called *commodity fetishism*. Fetishism attributes life, autonomy, and power to inanimate objects—dolls, sticks, places, or, in capitalism, money or other commodities. But commodity fetishism also performs another function. By attributing animate life to money, by speaking of it as if the money itself produces money, we mask and hide the actual manner in which money begets money—the exploitation of labor, land, and people. In this magical way of thinking, we begin to think of money as being able to generate value and yield interest in the same way that pear trees bear fruit or pigs, piglets. The whole process of capital investment, making a profit, finding the cheapest labor, and so on, comes to appear natural, while the real source of profits and the noneconomic consequences of capitalism are largely hidden from view.

But money does not produce money by itself. It requires other things, and this is where the Colombian peasant belief about the baptism of money is quite profound. Colombian peasants' practice of baptizing money so that it brings back more money is a rational interpretation of our own view of money, but with one addition: for the Colombian peasant the process is immoral. It is immoral because it is money rather than the child that is baptized; profit can come only at the cost of the child's soul. In this way the Colombian peasant is offering a critique of the capitalism that has been imposed on his society in the past century by the expanding world system.

These peasants are also posing key questions: *How does capitalism perform its magic, converting money into more money, and do we pay a price for that conversion?*

The Construction and Anatomy of the Working Class

As noted in Chapter 1, capitalism involves interactions among three sets of people: consumers, laborers, and capitalists, each doing what it is supposed, indeed has, to do. The construction of the consumer took place largely in the twentieth century. The nineteenth century witnessed the development of the working class. Although the flowering of the consumer occurred largely in the United States, the laborer was largely a creation of the British economy, a creation that gradually migrated from Great Britain to the rest of the world.

Characteristics of the Working Class

The new working class was unlike any that had existed before. Four characteristics of this new category of persons stand out: (a) members of this class were by necessity mobile, free to move to wherever workers were needed, unhampered by property or family connections; (b) they were segmented or divided by race and ethnicity, age, and gender; (c) they were subject to new kinds of discipline and control; and

(d) they were militant, often protesting the conditions in which they were placed. Let's examine each of these characteristics in turn.

First, the new laborers were remarkably geographically mobile, moving temporarily or permanently to sources of employment. Most were mobile because they had been forced off their land or because the products they produced were no longer in demand. Take the situation of the Italian worker, for example. Beginning in the 1870s, the sale of public domain and church lands created a situation that allowed large landholders to add to their land, while small landholders were squeezed out as prices for agricultural products declined, in part because of the importation of Russian wheat. A blight destroyed many vineyards, and cheap imported goods disrupted local handicrafts. In the 1860s, some 16,000 people emigrated permanently; in the 1870s, the number grew to 360,000; between 1881 and 1901, the number rose to 2 million, 80 percent of whom were agricultural laborers.

The countries to which these immigrants scattered, including Australia, Canada, and most often the United States, quickly utilized the cheap labor in factories, railroads, mines, stockyards, and oil fields. In the period between 1820 and 1860, the main contingents of immigrants came from Ireland (2 million), southwestern Germany (1.5 million), and the British Isles (750,000). More English, Swedes, and Germans arrived between 1860 and 1890; again they were mainly displaced agriculturists

Geographic mobility is one characteristic of the laborer in the culture of capitalism. Here Chinese boys await medical examinations at Angel Island immigration station in San Francisco around 1910.

driven off their land by the importation of cheap American and Russian wheat (as Mexican farmers are currently being displaced by the importation of cheap American corn).

In 1890, the source of the new immigration shifted to southern and eastern Europe and consisted largely of displaced peasants from Italy, the Austro-Hungarian Empire, the Balkans, and Poland, along with Jews from Russia.

Coal miners in Pennsylvania had been British, Irish, and German prior to 1890. But after that time they were increasingly Poles, Slovaks, Italians, and Hungarians. The textile mills of New England that had been manned by French-Canadians, English, and Irish were, after 1890, manned by Portuguese, Greeks, Poles, and Syrians. In the garment trades Russians, Jews, and Italians replaced Germans, Czechs, and Irish.

Some 90,000 indentured Chinese laborers were sent to Peru between 1849 and 1874; more than 200,000 were sent to the United States between 1852 and 1875 where they were employed in fruit growing, processing and panning for gold, and railroad construction. Some 10,000–14,000 Chinese were used in the construction of the Central Pacific Railroad of California.

A second characteristic of the working class was that they were divided or segmented by race, religion, ethnicity, age, and gender. The new working class split into two broader categories: a labor aristocracy better able to defend its prerequisites through union organization and political influence, and workers who had to accept lower wages and less secure jobs. These divisions were often reinforced by the use of racial or ethnic distinctions that relegated certain groups such as Blacks and earlier in the century the Irish to only the lowest paying jobs. Capitalism did not create these racial and ethnic distinctions, but it did help in defining and reinforcing them and their economic consequences (Wolf 1982:380).

Ironically, the ethnic identities of new immigrants rarely coincided with their self-identification. They first thought of themselves as Hanoverians or Bavarians rather than Germans; as members of a village parish (*okolica*) rather than Poles; as Sicilians, Neapolitans, and Genoans rather than Italians; and as Tonga or Yao rather than "Nyasalanders." In effect, migrants had to be socialized to see themselves as members of particular ethnic groups. They were, as Wolf (1982:381) said, "historical products of labor market segmentation under the capitalistic mode."

The ethnic or racial groupings created or reinforced by capitalist culture often came into conflict with each other as they competed for scarce jobs and resources. The case of the Irish in England and the United States is telling. In the mid-nineteenth century, Karl Marx (1972:293–294) made the following observation about the relationship between English workers and newly arrived Irish laborers:

> *Every industrial and commercial center in England now possess a working class divided into two hostile camps, English proletarians and Irish proletarians. The ordinary English worker hates the Irish as a competitor who lowers his standard of life. In relation to the Irish worker he feels himself a member of the ruling nation and so turns himself into a tool of the aristocrats and capitalists of his own country against Ireland, thus strengthening their domination over himself. He cherishes*

religious, social, and national prejudices against the Irish worker. His attitude towards him is much the same as "poor whites" to the "niggers" of the former slave states of the USA. The Irishman pays him back with interest in his own money. He sees the English worker at once the accomplice and the stupid tool of the English domination in Ireland.... This antagonism is the secret of the impotence of the English working class, despite their organization.

In the United States the same degree of ethnic antagonism developed, particularly between Irish and Blacks. Irish leaders in the early nineteenth century generally were strong critics of slavery and supporters of its abolition. However, once the Irish emigrated to the United States, they, who in their own country were treated almost as badly by British rulers as African Americans were in the United States by Whites, became strongly pro-slavery and anti-Black. What accounted for this change in attitude?

Noel Ignatiev (1995), in his book, *How the Irish Became White,* maintained that during the first half of the nineteenth century in America, free African Americans competed successfully in the North for relatively good jobs. Before the Irish arrived in large numbers in the United States, the distinction between freedom and slavery was blurred by such intermediate conditions as chattel slavery, indentured servitude, and imprisonment for debt. But the American Revolution had eliminated these intermediate economic categories and reinforced the tendency to equate slavery with blackness and freedom with whiteness. If Blacks, then, were allowed to work in the same jobs as Irish, the Irish would be assigned to the same social category as Blacks. In fact the Irish risked being considered lower in status than Blacks, largely because as slaves Blacks had value that Irish did not. As one official of an Alabama stevedoring company put it, "The niggers are worth too much to be risked here; if the Paddies are knocked overboard, or get their backs broke, nobody loses anything" (Ignatiev 1995:109). Consequently the Irish did all they could to distance themselves from Blacks, including supporting slavery. But the major task of the Irish was to assure that Blacks did not have access to the same jobs that they did.

Gradually, by taking the menial jobs that had been done by Blacks, as they were encouraged to do by priests, the Irish began to dominate the ranks of the unskilled laborer—by 1855, the Irish made up 87 percent of New York City's 23,000 unskilled laborers. In 1851, *The African Repository,* a magazine devoted to African American concerns, wrote (cited Ignatiev 1995:111) that

in New York and other Eastern cities, the influx of white laborers has expelled the Negro almost en masse from the exercise of the ordinary branches of labor. You no longer see him work upon buildings, and rarely is he allowed to drive a cart or public conveyance. White men will not work with him.

"White men will not work with him," became the rallying cry of labor in elbowing out Blacks from jobs that were then taken over by Irish; as Frederick Douglass said, "In assuming our avocation [the Irishmen] has assumed our degradation."

But the key to the distinction between White and Black became work; White meant doing "White man's work," while Black meant doing "Black man's work." The distinction was arbitrary because many jobs that became White man's work when reserved for Irish had been performed by Blacks earlier. "White," Ignatiev pointed out, was not a physical description, but rather a term of social relations. This distinction resulted, then, in a situation in which to be "White" the Irish had to work in the jobs from which Blacks were excluded (Ignatiev 1995:111). Thus a division of labor was hardened into a distinction of race and ethnicity.

The workforce was segmented in other ways, most notably by gender and age, with women and children assigned to the lowest-paying and most menial jobs. (A discussion of that development in more detail follows later.)

The new working class was mobile and divided by race, ethnicity, gender, and age. In addition it had to be disciplined. Central to this process was the factory. The factory is a relatively recent historical phenomenon, having developed largely in the late eighteenth and early nineteenth centuries in Europe (although factory production in textiles may have existed as early as the fifteenth century). Prior to its development, most work (e.g., weaving, spinning, pottery making) was done in homes or small shops. The first factories were modeled on penal workhouses and prisons. Spinning mills were built and installed in brick buildings four or five stories high and employed several hundred workers. The iron and cast iron mills of the metal industry brought together several blast furnaces and forges and a large workforce (Beaud 1983:66). These settings may have increased the efficiency of production, but the new job discipline required of workers also created tensions between workers and their employers that, at various points in the years to follow, would result in situations approaching civil war.

The factory setting, for example, necessitated workers being disciplined to accept a new conception of time. Time, another of the things we take for granted, is subject to cultural definition. Our time is dictated, by and large, by our means of measuring it—clocks and watches. Time in other societies tends to be task-oriented or dictated by natural phenomena: in Madagascar, it might be measured by rice cooking (about one-half hour); in seventeenth-century Chile, the time needed to cook an egg was an Ave Maria said aloud; in Burma, monks rose when there was enough light to see the veins in their hands; in oceanside communities, the social patterning of time depends on the ebb and flow of tides. British anthropologist E. E. Evans-Pritchard (1940:103), in his classic account of the life of the Nuer of the Sudan, noted that

> the Nuer have no expression equivalent to "time" in our language, and they cannot, therefore, as we can, speak of time as though it were something actual, which passes, can be wasted, can be saved, and so forth. I don't think they ever experience the same feeling of fighting against time because their points of reference are mainly the activities themselves, which are generally of a leisurely character. Events follow a logical order, but they are not controlled by an abstract system, there being no autonomous points of reference to which activities have to conform with precision. Nuer are fortunate.

Time serves as one way to discipline the laborer as clocks, such as the time clock depicted above, control and record the arrival and departures of workers.

Historian E. P. Thompson (1967) noted that until the institution of modern notions of time, work patterns were characterized by alternating bouts of intense labor and idleness, at least whenever people were in control of their own working lives. He has even suggested that this pattern persists today, but only among some self-employed professionals, such as artists, writers, small farmers, and college students.

This is not to say that some preindustrial work was not difficult. Thompson (1967:8) described the typical day of a farm laborer in 1636: He rose at 4 A.M. and cared for the horses, ate breakfast at 6 A.M., plowed until 2 or 3 P.M., ate lunch, attended to the horses until 6 in the evening, ate supper, did other chores till 8 P.M., cared for the cattle, and then retired. However, this was during the height of the laboring year on the farm, and it was probably the laborer's wife, says Thompson, who labored the hardest.

It is difficult to say precisely when the Western concept of time and work began to change. Clocks were not widespread in Europe until the seventeenth century, although most towns probably had a church clock. But by the early 1800s, our present sense of time was well established.

Time was an entity that should not be wasted. "Time," as Benjamin Franklin wrote in *Poor Richard's Almanac*, "is money." At about the same period the idea that idleness was wicked began to gain currency. As *Youth's Monitor* phrased it in 1689, time "is too precious a commodity to be undervalued.... This is the golden chain on which hangs a massy eternity; the loss of time is insufferable, because irrecoverable" (quoted Thompson 1967:8). Leisure time, in general, was attacked; in some religious circles seeking amusement was seen as sinful. Anything that did not contribute to production was discouraged.

At about the same time the school was being used to teach a new time and work discipline. Social reformers in the late eighteenth century suggested that poor children be sent at the age of four to workhouses where they would work and be given two hours schooling each day. As one person said,

> [t]here is considerable use in their being somehow or other, constantly employed at least twelve hours a day, whether they can earn their living or not; for by these means, we hope that the rising generation will be so habituated to constant employment that it would at length prove agreeable and entertaining to them (cited Thompson 1967:84).

Thus by the middle of the nineteenth century, through the supervision of labor, fines, bells and clocks, money incentives, preaching, and schooling, a new time discipline was imposed on society at large and on the laborer in particular.

Finally, in addition to its mobility, segmentation, and discipline, the new working class was characterized by a new militancy that would lead to the closest thing the world has seen to a "world revolution." Early in 1848, the French political thinker and chronicler of American democracy, Alexis de Tocqueville, addressed the French Chamber of Deputies, saying what many Europeans feared. "We are sleeping," he said, "on a volcano.... Do you not see that the earth trembles anew? A wind of revolution blows, the storm is on the horizon" (cited Hobsbawm 1975:9).

At about the same time, the thirty-year-old Karl Marx and his twenty-eight-year-old friend Friedrich Engels were drafting the *Manifesto of the Communist Party*, which appeared in London in February 1848. Perhaps within days revolutionaries in France declared the establishment of a new republic; by March the revolution had moved into Germany, Hungary, and Italy; within weeks the governments of an area today encompassing France, Germany, Austria, Italy, Czechoslovakia, Hungary, part of Poland, Belgium, Switzerland, Denmark, and the old Yugoslavia were all overthrown. However, within six months of the outbreak the movement faltered and within eighteen months only the new government of France remained, and it was trying to put distance between itself and the insurrectionists. The only long-lasting change was the abolition of serfdom in what had been the Hapsburg Empire.

Although they had the support of moderates and liberals in the various countries, they were nevertheless "social revolutions of the labouring poor," as Hobsbaum (1975:15) put it. The revolutions were an expression of developing patterns of conflict between the rich and poor, each group developing its spokespersons. On the one side were people such as Jean-Baptiste Say in France and David Ricardo and Thomas Robert Malthus in England who argued that the poor had only themselves to blame for their condition. On the other side were those such as Karl Marx, Friedrich Engels, Robert Owen, Henri Saint-Simon, and Charles Fourier who blamed the exploitation of labor for poverty. The debate is not unlike the ones still being argued over such issues as welfare and the role of the state in alleviating poverty.

Malthus argued, for example, that

> *it is not in the power of the rich to supply the poor with an occupation and with bread, and consequently, the poor, by the very nature of things have no right to demand these things from the rich.... No possible contributions of sacrifices of the rich, particularly in money, could for any time prevent the recurrence of distress among the lower members of society. (cited Beaud 1983:78)*

It is a matter of morality, said Malthus, that

> *those who are poor must not produce children until they can adequately provide for them. To those who violate this rule, there should be no pity.*
>
> *To the punishment, therefore of nature he should be left, to the punishment of want. He has erred in the face of a most clear and precise warning, and can have no just reason to complain of any person but himself when he feels the consequences of his error. All parish assistance should be denied him; and he should be left to the uncertain support of private charity. He should be taught to know that the laws of nature, which are the laws of God, had doomed him and his family to suffer for disobeying their repeated admonitions.... It may appear to be hard that a mother and her children, who have been guilty of no particular crime themselves, should suffer for the ill conduct of the father; but this is one of the invariable laws of nature. (Malthus 1826:343)*

One French industrialist could write matter-of-factly that "the fate of the workers is not that bad: their labor is not excessive since it does not go beyond thirteen hours.... The manufacturer whose profits are poor is the one to be pitied" (cited in Baud 1983:101).

For others, such as Karl Marx and Friedrich Engels, society was being divided up into two hostile camps and classes, the bourgeoisie and the proletariat.

> *Masses of labourers, crowded into the factory, are organized like soldiers. As privates of the industrial army, they are placed under the command of a perfect hierarchy of officers and sergeants. Not only are they the slaves of the bourgeoisie class, and of the bourgeoisie State, they are daily and hourly enslaved by the machine,*

by the overlooker, and above all, by the individual bourgeoisie manufacturer him-self. The more openly this despotism proclaims gain to be its end and aim, the more petty, the more hateful and the more embittering it is. (Marx and Engels 1848/ 1941:14)

The proletariat must, said Marx and Engels, embody the suffering, rise against it, and produce a classless society free from the exploitation of one class by another. It must free itself, but only by transcending the inhumane conditions of present-day society. Marx had attempted in his writings to create a scientific theory of the fall of capitalism, in the same way that Adam Smith and David Ricardo had tried to create a scientific theory of the rise of capitalism. The results were not only a blueprint to be used by union organizers and revolutionaries, but also the creation of two utopian ideologies—that of capitalism and that of socialism—which would do battle into the twentieth century.

These, then, are some of the characteristics of the laborer and the relationship between labor and capital as established in the nineteenth century. There were other features as well, such as the increased vulnerability of the laborer to hardship and the greater likelihood of impoverishment. To understand better how the la-borer was constructed, let's turn to the contemporary world. In countries all over the world, the nineteenth-century processes through which the laborer was con-structed are being repeated. We can see this most clearly in the growth of overseas assembly plants.

The Growth of Overseas Assembly Plants

In capitalism, profits and interest depend on the difference between the cost of pro-ducing a product and the price at which it is sold. If someone has a monopoly on a product, and if people need it, producers can charge as much as they need to to maintain or increase profits. But if other companies produce the same merchan-dise, it is likely that the price a company can charge will be determined by what others charge. Thus Nike can charge one hundred dollars for its sneakers, but if its competitors are charging only forty dollars for the same product, Nike had better lower its price or face bankruptcy. Consequently profit must come not from in-creasing the price that people pay, but from controlling the cost of producing the product. Cost increase can be contained by controlling the cost of raw materials and machines—the means of production—or by controlling the price of labor.

The activity of work is common to all societies. In gathering and hunting soci-eties women and men spend a portion of their time gathering wild foods and hunt-ing game, in pastoral societies people spend time herding and caring for animals, and in agricultural societies they work at tending fields, harvesting and storing crops, and so on. But work in the black box of capitalism takes a different form. In fact some economists believe the key to understanding the way money creates more money is understanding the way labor figures in the production process. For them, profit comes directly from what they call the *surplus value of labor.*

As we noted earlier, to produce commodities for sale, labor must be purchased and combined with the means of production. For example, I might buy cloth and make shirts to sell. I may pay two dollars for the cloth and sell the shirt for ten, thereby making a profit of eight dollars. *Where does that profit come from?* One obvious place is the labor that went to convert the cloth into a shirt. In this case we might say the labor was worth eight dollars. But what if, instead of making the shirt myself, I paid someone else to do it, but paid them only two dollars, and still sold the shirt for ten. The value of the labor that went into making the shirt is still eight dollars, but the worker I hired received only two; I get to keep the other six dollars. It is this money that constitutes the surplus value of labor.

Obviously, then, one way for a company to maximize profits is to maximize the surplus value of labor and pay workers as little as possible. Another way to increase profits is to get the laborer to produce more in the same period of time. Thus if I paid my shirtmakers an hourly or daily wage, I could double my profits by getting them to produce two shirts in the time that they used to produce one shirt. This I could do by getting them to work faster or by improving the technology or process of shirt making to make it more efficient.

Companies that produce commodities such as textiles, electronic goods, and toys are labor-intensive; that is, they require human labor more than improved technology to manufacture their products and are consequently always trying to minimize what they pay workers. And given the economic logic of capitalism this makes perfectly good sense: The more they save on labor costs, and the less they charge for their product, the more they will attract consumers. Furthermore, the more they sell, the greater their profits and greater the return for investors and stock owners. Thus the role of labor in the black box is critical to our understanding of the amount of profit the box can generate.

Corporations in core countries, such as the United States, made much use of foreign labor in the nineteenth century. However, as we discussed above, most of that labor moved to the source of employment, traveling largely from Europe and Asia to work in American mines, railroad yards, and factories. However, once jobs were filled, the immigrants or their descendants who filled them were not anxious to see more immigrants arrive and compete for their jobs. Consequently they lobbied through unions, churches, and political parties for the government to pass restrictive immigration laws. When Chinese laborers were brought over to help build the transcontinental railroad, groups such as the Knights of Labor protested, even demanding that the Chinese get out of the laundry business. As a result the U.S. Congress passed the Chinese Exclusion Act of 1882, and anti-Chinese agitation broke out on the West Coast, marking one more stage in the emergence of racism in the United States.

Although importing laborers from overseas worked for a time, corporations soon found that they could more easily tap into pools of cheap labor by relocating their manufacturing processes when possible to countries on the periphery of the world system whose governments were committed to economic development through industrialization. For example, to facilitate the establishment of assembly plants, governments in Indonesia, Malaysia, Guatemala, and Mexico, among others, created in their countries *free trade zones*, areas in which large corporations were permitted to deliver goods to be assembled—cut cloth for wearing apparel, electronic components, and so on—and for which they were not required to pay tariffs, provided that the items were not then sold in the country in which they were assembled. In exchange, the multinational corporations, such as Nike, agreed to hire local workers. The home countries, such as the United States, contributed by passing legislation that allows corporations to transfer the assembled goods back to the United States, paying an import tariff only on the labor cost of each product rather than on the total value of the product. Thus the sneakers you wear were probably cut by machines in the United States, shipped to Indonesia or Vietnam to be assembled, and then shipped back to the United States to be distributed and sold there and elsewhere in the world.

As an economic arrangement, almost everyone seems to benefit from the growth of assembly plants.

- Nike and other companies are able to compete with other manufacturers by paying workers in Third World countries a fraction of what they would have to pay American workers.
- Workers in the Third World find employment.
- Consumers pay less for their clothes, electronic devices, toys, and so on.
- Investors get a higher return on their money.

It seems that the only ones who don't benefit are the American workers who lose their jobs (some half-million in the textile industry alone in the 1980s).

As a result the growth in assembly plants was dramatic. In 1970 there were an estimated 1,000 women working in manufacturing in Malaysia, for example; by 1980, there were 80,000 concentrated in textiles, electronics, and food processing. In Mexico the number of *maquiladoras,* as assembly plants are called, grew from virtually none in the 1960s to 1,279 employing 329,413 people in 1988, to over 1,600 plants employing almost 900,000 workers in 1997.

However, there are some problems. Critics have cited assembly plant workers' poor working conditions, their low pay, the actions of foreign governments in discouraging the formation of workers' unions, and the loose environmental regulations that have in some cases resulted in considerable environmental degradation around free trade zones.

For example, in 1995, American labor and children's rights groups called for a boycott of all garments assembled in Bangladesh to protest the estimated 25,000–30,000 children working in garment factories in Bangladesh. The United States is Bangladesh's biggest apparel customer, with nearly 50 percent of Bangladesh's $1.6 billion in garment exports arriving in the United States. In some assembly factories in El Salvador, where women earn $4.51 for the day, or 56 cents an hour, union organizers are often summarily dismissed, bathrooms are locked and can be used only with permission, and talking on the job is prohibited. In Guatemala workers are required to work overtime at a moment's notice and are dismissed if they refuse. There have been reports of systematic violence against union organizers in Mexico, El Salvador, and Guatemala. And, as we shall see, assembly plants have far-reaching consequences on the society and culture of the cities and countries in which they are located.

The Creation of Free Labor

One defining feature of capitalism is the creation of a class of people who are willing to sell their labor. There must be a working class and, subsequently, a demand for jobs. A key question then is, *why do people, particularly the workers, play the game of capitalism?* For example, if the pay is poor and working conditions harsh, *why do people work in assembly plants?* Although the United States is and has been largely a wage economy in which the vast majority of people, in effect, sell their labor to companies, we sometimes forget, as mentioned earlier, that the existence of a so-called working class is a recent development historically in the United States, and particularly in countries such as Malaysia and Mexico where, until recently, most people earned their living from the land or from what they themselves produced and sold. Thus to turn landed peasants and artisans into wage laborers required that they lose their land or sources of livelihood.

In Malaysia and Mexico, countries trying to industrialize and attract foreign manufacturers such as Nike, political developments in the nineteenth and early twentieth centuries led to the systematic dispossession of peasants from their land and to the increased importation of cheap products (e.g., textiles, iron implements) that put local artisans out of business. For example, up to the nineteenth century, Malaysia consisted of small states ruled over by sultans and so-called "big men," who extracted tribute from peasants. Peasants held use-rights to land and could pass on to children whatever land they worked, but no more than that. The center of life was the *kampung*, or village. But British colonialists took over the land and converted its use to the production of cash crops, leaving the unlanded population to seek labor on large plantations or migrate to cities in search of jobs. There was still more than enough land in Malaysia for everyone to farm, but it was used instead to produce crops, such as palm oil, for export rather than to produce food for the local population.

In Mexico a similar history has left most of the population without land to produce food. In the mid-nineteenth century the vast majority of the Mexican population lived in villages. The land was divided among the residents, but owned not by individuals but by the whole village. People were given the right to use land but not the right to sell it. Then, in the mid-nineteenth century, legislation was passed in Mexico declaring communally held lands to be illegal, giving peasants legal rights to their own land, which they could now also sell or mortgage to repay debts. The result was that wealthy persons—largely Americans—bought up huge tracts of land. By 1910, the year of the beginning of the Mexican Revolution, over 90 percent of the population was landless and forced to work on large agricultural estates or migrate to the cities in search of jobs. In the course of half a century, the vast majority of the Mexican population was transformed from an autonomous peasantry working their own land to a population of dependent wage laborers.

The process of land dispossession has continued to the present time (as will be discussed later), not only in Mexico and Malaysia but also in many other parts of the world, resulting in a large population of landless people with only their labor to sell. As a result the governments of these countries are under great pressure to facilitate the growth of jobs for the population. It is into these situations that

Young women, such as these uniformed workers at a Nike assembly in Indonesia, comprise the vast majority of workers at overseas assembly plants.

American, Japanese, German, and British corporations, among others, have come to build assembly plants.

But assembly factories involve a paradox. In countries such as Malaysia and Mexico it was the men who traditionally were the wage laborers, but it is women who are sought by corporations, such as Nike, as employees. It is the women, for some reason, who are willing to accept a wage level less than that needed for subsistence. Thus we need to ask *why are there jobs that pay less than a living wage and why do certain categories of people seem relegated to them?*

The Segmentation of the Workforce

One consequence of the establishment of offshore assembly growth was the entrance into the labor market of a new working population of young, single women between the ages of sixteen and twenty-four. *Why do the assembly plants choose to employ young women, and why is it that women choose to work under sometimes unpleasant conditions?* The answer to this question requires us to understand how and why labor is segmented into different levels.

Take, for example, the case of Malaysia. Aihwa Ong (1987) spent two years studying assembly plants in Malaysia owned by Japanese and American corporations. One of the first questions she asked was, why did the plants prefer to hire young women? Plant managers that she interviewed gave a number of reasons. One Japanese manager told Ong (1990:396–397) that "females [are] better able to concentrate on routine work," and "young girls [are] preferable than older persons, that is because of eyesight."

And another explained, "You cannot expect a man to do very fine work for eight hours [at a stretch]. Our work is designed for females…if we employ men, within one or two months they would have run away.… Girls [sic] below thirty are easier to train and easier to adapt to the job function."

The idea that women are somehow more suited biologically for assembly plant work is widespread in developing countries. For example, here is what a brochure designed to bring foreign investments into Malaysia says about its female workforce:

> *Her hands are small and she works fast with extreme care. Who, therefore, could be better qualified **by nature and inheritance** to contribute to the efficiency of a bench assembly production line than the oriental girl? [Ong 1987: 152, emphasis added]*

In Mexican *maquiladoras* the situation is much the same. María Patricia Fernández-Kelly (1983) was also interested in the effects of the assembly plants on women. To study these effects she found a job in a *maquiladora* to share the experiences of the workers and to meet the women and learn about their lives. She, too, found that companies preferred to hire young females because managers believed that women have higher skill levels, are more docile, and are more willing to comply to the monotonous, repetitive, and exhausting assignments. Men are described by managers as more restless or rebellious, less patient, more likely to unionize, and less tolerant of the working conditions. As one manager related to Fernández-Kelly (1983:181),

> *[w]e hire mostly women because they are more reliable than men, they have finer fingers, smaller muscles and unsurpassed manual dexterity. Also, women don't get tired of repeating the same operation nine hundred times a day.*

Assembly plants in both Malaysia and Mexico also preferred single women because managers believed that older, married women had too many other obligations, were often unwilling to work night shifts, and may have accumulated enough wage increments to be paid more than a new, young, single woman would earn.

There is also a large population of unemployed women that assembly factories can choose from. In Malaysia and Mexico there are three applicants for every available position. Thus one *maquiladora* manager could announce to a conference organized by the American Chamber of Commerce that the 30 percent unemployment rate in Ciudad Juárez allows for high employee selectivity. Moreover, village elders in Malaysia and family heads in Mexico are eager to send otherwise non-wage-earning women to work in the assembly plants.

But there is another reason for the employment practices of assembly plants, one that tells us even more about the black box of capitalism: You don't have to pay women and children as much as you have to pay men. Nor do you have to pay foreign workers as much as domestic workers. By extension you do not have to pay people of color as much as you pay Whites. That is, the contemporary labor force in peripheral countries such as Mexico and Malaysia is already segmented through various forms of social discrimination, as was the labor force in nineteenth-century North America and Europe. Whether capitalism creates this type of discrimination, reinforces it, or simply takes advantage of it where it exists is arguable. Regardless, there is no question that, at least to some extent, social discrimination and prejudice—sexism, racism, discrimination against immigrants—is profitable. It is an important part of the black box. But why?

Let's return to basic economics. Modern industries can be loosely divided into two types. There are *primary industries* whose markets are well defined, whose profits are relatively certain, whose capital investment is high, and who are able to pay good wages and ensure decent working conditions. These industries include automobile manufacturing, communications, and energy industries, to name a few. They require a well-paid, well-trained, and relatively content workforce.

Then there are *secondary industries* that include the fast-food industry, electronics, and, most notably, the clothing, garment and/or textile industries. There is intense competition, uncertain or changing demand, a lower profit margin, and a greater dependence on unskilled labor in these industries. They are the least desirable for workers, because to stay competitive companies must pay the lowest wages and yet maximize worker output. These are the industries most likely to expand operations to poorer countries. They are also the companies that are likely to hire the most vulnerable and the lowest-ranking members of a population. Traditionally these people have been women, children, or members of subjugated minorities. Thus when corporations locate assembly factories abroad, they are, in effect, expanding the secondary labor market.

Of course the hiring of women for low-paying, labor-intensive work has long been a feature of industrial capitalism. Women and children formed the bulk of the factory workforce at the beginnings of the industrial revolution in the late eighteenth and early nineteenth centuries. In 1851, 31 percent of the labor force in England consisted of women, 45 percent of whom were in manufacturing. In the English textile industry of 1840, over 75 percent of the workforce consisted of women and children. The locating of assembly plants overseas is simply the latest version of utilizing a socially vulnerable workforce to secure low-paid labor.

But this expansion of the secondary labor market abroad has had the following economic consequences for workers and corporations at home and abroad:

1. It has meant the transfer of jobs abroad and resulting unemployment at home.
2. It has widened the gap between primary and secondary labor in the United States.
3. From the perspective of workers in peripheral countries of the world system, it has meant the development of poorly paid, unstable jobs with little opportunity for promotion.

The process of targeting the most vulnerable segment of the population for low-wage jobs also affects the meaning that societies give to specific tasks. For example, the division between skilled and unskilled jobs is often not based on the nature of the work, as one would suppose; instead it is based on who is doing the work. In other words the work that women do in assembly factories is not necessarily less skilled than other work; it is considered unskilled because it is performed by women. Fernández-Kelly discovered this when she tried to learn the sewing techniques of women in Mexican garment *maquiladoras*. She could barely keep up with them; it required a skill level equal to or greater than many jobs that we call skilled. Thus work that women do is defined as "unskilled" because it is done by women, as work that Blacks or Irish did in the nineteenth century was defined as unskilled because it was done by Blacks or Irish.

However, from the standpoint of the corporation the transfer of secondary jobs to underdeveloped countries and the ensuing expansion of a cheap labor reserve pool affords corporate employers the greatest degree of political and economic control over workers. They are able to employ the most socially vulnerable sector of the working class, the people least likely to organize, demand better wages, or press for better working conditions. As one Mexican *maquiladora* worker put it, men are unwilling to perform the monotonous labor; women are more shy and submissive and are more used to following orders. They are more easily intimidated and forced to obey. They are the easiest to discipline.

In sum, for corporations women represent a major source of inexpensive, transient labor; thus women, while making up the vast majority of assembly plant workers throughout the world, occupy few skilled or managerial positions. And because they occupy the lowest positions, women can be hired and fired, depending on the overseas demand for such things as textiles, shoes, plastics, electrical appliances, and, increasingly, electronics.

However, in spite of the often poor pay and harsh working conditions that women working in assembly plants endure, some economists and public policy makers argue that such employment is necessary if women are ultimately to gain access to better positions and change their often subjugated positions in societies around the world. They argue that the money that women earn gives them control over resources that they would otherwise not have, that as families become dependent on the income that these women bring into their households, their positions in society will improve. Some also argue that the creation of this kind of work is a necessary stage of economic development and will eventually lead to better lives for all. We must remember, however, that if the labor market remains divided between primary and secondary industries, then someone must continue to do the low-paying work. Women may escape low-paying jobs, but only, as the Irish in the nineteenth century learned, if there is another group to take their places.

Control and Discipline

In nineteenth-century America, as young men and women sought work in the growing factory towns and cities, factory owners, as well as local citizens, faced a problem. These young people had been integrated into the social institutions of their hamlets and villages. As members of families and churches they were expected to conform to certain standards of behavior; deviance from those standards could bring condemnation, punishment, and even social ostracism. But in the towns and cities to which they moved, migrant workers often were freed from such constraints, free to experiment with behaviors previously denied to them. Consequently men often gained reputations as "rowdies," or "hoodlums," while women were labeled "immoral" or "loose." Thus the creation of free labor created a problem: *How do you control the labor force?*

For example, in turn-of-the-century New York City, thousands of young women found employment in factories and used their new-found freedom and the wages they earned for shopping, dating, dancing, or going on excursions to recreation areas, such as Coney Island. However, their behavior alarmed some people who saw it as immoral; consequently groups of social reformers organized and proposed ways to "protect" working women from these "temptations." Some of their solutions to the problem resulted in the formation of social and religious clubs and associations for young women, organizations such as the Young Women's Christian Association (YWCA).

But these organizations served another function as well; they relieved the fears of the parents of these young workers who otherwise might have been reluctant to allow them to migrate to cities and factory towns.

As in nineteenth-century America and Great Britain, employment in the new assembly plants of such countries as Malaysia and Mexico often requires young men and women to leave their homes and move to cities, freeing them from the traditional constraints imposed by family and church, freeing them to spend their leisure time in nontraditional activities. Take, for example, the situation of the largely female workforce in the new assembly plants of Malaysia. Most of the women are young, generally ranging from sixteen to twenty years old. In their villages they would have lived at home, perhaps attended school, and been involved in various household chores under the direction of their mothers. Dating would have been rare and, when it occurred, would have been carefully supervised by parents. Marriages were often arranged by parents. Factory work, however, allows these same young women to earn wages, a portion of which they control. Although most workers contribute one-half or more of their earnings to their families, they are free to spend the rest on themselves. Some use it for typing or academic classes to prepare for civil service jobs, in effect attempting to control their own job prospects and "careers." Some become consumers, taking shopping trips to town or to the movies, "making jolly with money," as they say. They exchange traditional *kampung* garb for tight T-shirts, jeans, and Avon makeup, trying to achieve what they call the "electric look."

Because working women are now expected to save money to contribute to their own wedding expenses—money that had been traditionally supplied by their families—they feel justified in choosing potential spouses. Sexual freedom may be increasing, as indicated by an increase in abortions, and women are beginning to cross social boundaries, having "illicit" relationships and marrying men of other ethnic groups (e.g., Chinese), something traditional family and church authorities would never have allowed.

But one consequence of the growth of the number of working women in Malaysia is a stream of criticism about the loose morals of factory girls, especially from Islamic fundamentalists. The Malay media portrays factory women as pleasure seekers and spendthrifts engulfed in Western consumer culture. A story about prostitution might promote sensational headlines, such as "Factory Girls in Sex Racket."

All of this has resulted in a call for greater control of working women, in spite of the fact that similar behavior, such as dating and movie going, among upper-class college students has not received the same notice. Even the academic community and religious and state officials have claimed to recognize the problem of declining morals of young women and proposed measures to arrest the decline, such as counseling and recreational activities. There have also been public calls for control of working women's leisure time, despite the fact that they tend to work about three hours per day more than women engaged primarily in traditional household chores.

In some ways the new-found freedom of factory workers is as welcome by businesspeople as it is by the young. Their new income—and their willingness to spend a portion of it on themselves—has turned young village men and women into consumers who buy many of the products they make. But the new freedoms create yet another problem. Capitalist enterprise requires a disciplined and reliable workforce; with old forms of discipline falling away new forms must be developed to replace them. The question is, *how is that done?*

Although family and church are largely absent from the lives of working young men and women, factory managers try to use these traditional institutions to control their workers. Malaysia is an Islamic country, and according to Islamic practice parents are obligated to care for their children up to age fifteen, while traditional customs decree that children must also care for their parents. Thus children, particularly women, are obligated to return to their parents the care that their parents gave them. One of the major appeals made to young women by factory owners and managers is that they use their wages to pay back part of what they owe their parents.

Factory managers also seek to maintain discipline by building relations with people in the women's home villages, thus enlisting their help in controlling workers. For example, managers make donations to community organizations in the villages that supply workers. They also devise regulations to help parents monitor the activities of their daughters. When workers commute from their villages to the factories, the managers deliver workers to their homes by bus, or they allow parents to see overtime forms so they know how much time their daughters were spending at work and at other activities. These efforts enhanced the prestige of managers in the eyes of village elders whose moral support could then be obtained for the social control of working daughters.

Corporations also use traditional family values to encourage workers to comply with company goals (Ong 1987:169). Thus managers tell workers that they are part of "one big family." One factory had posters proclaiming the company philosophy:

- To create one big family
- To train workers
- To increase loyalty to company, country, and fellow workers

Managers portray themselves as parent figures to the larger community from which women workers come, and, although workers complain of too much control, parents rarely tell their daughters to quit.

Religion is also used as a means of discipline (Ong 1987:185). Because it is an Islamic country, the Malaysian government includes special departments and agencies that have jurisdiction over the application of religious law. For example, under the current interpretation of religious law, Muslims may be arrested for *khalwat*, "close proximity" between a man and a woman who are not immediate relatives or married to each other. Those caught in situations that just suggest sexual intimacy, but not necessarily in the sex act, are fined or sentenced to jail for a few months. Muslims arrested for *zinah*, that is, illicit sexual intercourse, may be more severely punished. As a result of the increase in the number of young women working in assembly factories, there have been more raids by the government's Religious Department on the poor lodgings and cheap hotels used by the workers.

Then there is the factory discipline itself. We mentioned earlier that eighteenth- and nineteenth-century factories were modeled after prisons. Modern assembly plants have much the same character. In Malaysian assembly plants workers are sometimes watched through glass partitions. In one factory, for example, three supervisors and twelve foremen controlled 530 operators. Discipline was verbally enforced as women workers were scolded by overvigilant foremen for wanting to go to the prayer room, the clinic, or the toilet. Some foremen would even question workers in a humiliating manner about their menstrual problems or nonwork activities. Others were reported to have forced women to run laps around the assembly plant as a form of punishment for reporting late to work or not meeting their production quotas.

As in prisons, clothing can be used to instill discipline. Malaysian workers are required to wear factory overalls that they complain are too tight and which they are not allowed to unbutton. They are also required to wear heavy rubber boots. These clothes are very different from the loose-fitting clothes and sandals Malaysians traditionally wear while working.

Assembly plants also bring with them a Western, factory-oriented sense of the relationship between work and time to which contemporary assembly workers must adapt. Traditionally in Malaysia, for example, young girls carried out their household or farm tasks relatively free from modern time and work discipline; their activities were interspersed with social visits, usually free of female supervision and always free of male supervision. If there was anything to mark the passage of time, it was the cycle of daily Islamic prayer.

But female workers in the factories are clocked in daily for eight consecutive hours with two fifteen-minute breaks and a half-hour lunch break. Every month their work schedules are changed. Women begin to divide their lives into "work time" and "leisure time." They were watched over by overzealous foremen, screened before they could leave their work benches to go to the toilet, fined if they were late for work, in spite of the fact that pay was based on piecework, in vivid contrast to the traditional work routine where there was no distinction between work and life, and no conflict between labor and "passing the time of day."

People in Malaysia are aware of the shift from traditional social time to the capitalist clock time, and they have developed their own ways to critique it. Ong (1987:112) told the story of a married couple, Ahmad and Edah, driven, say their neighbors, by the acquisition of wealth to carefully spend their time on capital accumulation at the expense of social obligations. Their neighbors said their obsession with time was the result of a *toyal*, a spirit helper that they raised to filch money from neighbors. The *toyal*, they concluded, turned the tables on the couple by driving them even harder to use all their time to accumulate wealth.

Resistance and Rebellion

Capitalism requires a disciplined working class—people willing to work for wages that allow enterprises to make their necessary profit. But herein lies a problem: in general, people do not readily accept discipline and control and will seek a way to resist, either directly or indirectly.

Resistance to capitalist discipline can take direct forms, as in worker protests, formation of unions, and even revolution (subjects to be examined in later chapters). Resistance may also take the form of a moral critique, such as that of Colombian peasants who see capital accumulation represented in the baptism of money as the loss of a child's soul. Such indirect forms of resistance are not unique to the peoples of the periphery of the world system. For example, one of the stories that comes down to us from early industrial Europe is that of Rumpelstilskin. Folktales are more than just stories; they are statements about people's beliefs. Often they are morality tales that dramatize the consequences of proper or improper behavior. Jane Schneider (1989), for example, suggested that the meaning of the Rumpelstilskin tale lies in the development of the linen industry in early modern Europe. In fact, in many ways, it offers a critique of capitalist production not unlike that of the Colombian peasants.

In one version of the Rumpelstilskin story, a father brags that his daughter is able to spin straw into gold. The king, hearing of this boast, offers to take the girl as his wife if she is able to spin the straw in his castle into gold. The girl tries, fails, then enters into a pact with a strange dwarf who promises to spin the straw into gold for her, but only if she promises to give him her firstborn child. The girl accepts, Rumpelstilskin spins the gold, and she marries the king and has a child. The dwarf comes to claim his fee but is distressed by her tears and grief and offers her a way out. If she can guess his name, he will free her from the contract.

We have forgotten much of what this tale meant to sixteenth- and seventeenth-century European peasants. For example, one of the main industries of the period was linen production. Linen was produced by spinning flax straw into linen thread that was woven into a fabric that was sold for gold coins. So straw, in effect, really was spun into gold. Moreover the spinning process was performed largely by young women. A woman's spinning skill was not only a source of money, it was a quality men sought in wives—as the king sought in his future wife. Furthermore the story contains a pact with a demon, and the price is the firstborn. Thus, as in the Colombian baptism of money, we find the symbolic statement that the generation of wealth comes only with social and personal sacrifice, often of children or their souls.

Malaysian assembly plant workers have also found a subtle, generally symbolic means of expressing their resistance to capitalist discipline. It takes the form of spirit possession. Although Malaysia is a Muslim country, Islam exists side-by-side with indigenous beliefs about magic and spirits. Thus in the 1980s assembly plant managers in Malaysia—especially American and Japanese managers—were unexpectedly confronted with an epidemic of spirit possessions in their factories (Ong 1987:204). Forty Malaysian operators were possessed in one large American electronics plant; three years later in another incident 120 operators were possessed. The factory was shut down for three days while a spirit-healer (*bomoh*) was called in to sacrifice a goat to the possessing spirit on the premises.

Another American microelectronics factory was closed down when fifteen women were possessed. According to factory personnel officers, possessed girls began to sob and scream hysterically. When it looked as though the possession would spread, the other workers were immediately ushered out. The women explained that the factory was "dirty" and consequently haunted by a *datuk*.

The Malay universe is still full of spirits moving between the human and non-human domain. Spirit possession seemed to express themes of filth, angry spirits, and fierce struggles. Particularly prominent in the possession episodes were spirits, such as *toyol*, who help their masters gain wealth out of thin air; and the *pontianak*, who threaten the lives of newborn infants.

Aihwa Ong suggested that the women were not reacting to anything as abstract as industrial capitalism but against a sense of violation, of a dislocation in human relations, in much the same way the Colombian peasants reacted to wage labor with the notion of the baptism of money and the sacrifice of children's souls. Beliefs about the baptism of money in Colombia and spirit possession of factory workers in Malaysia are examples of the widespread critiques of capitalism that we find among people confronting capitalist production for the first time. They are ways that people find to express their sense that capitalist production brings a modicum of economic betterment at high social and personal costs.

Conclusion

A major assumption of this book is that it is impossible to understand the modern world and its problems—population growth, hunger, poverty, environmental degradation, health, war, religious fundamentalism, and so on—without an understanding of the capitalist economy that, with its goal of accumulating more and more wealth, has in the past four to five centuries redefined and created new social and cultural forms and altered traditional cultural institutions to serve its own purposes. Capitalism has been characterized here as a black box whose purpose it is to convert money into more money, to take monetary investments and convert them into profits and interest. For most people, this process is as magical as is the behavior of baptized money among Colombian peasants. They place money in banks, stocks, or other investments and expect to get more money back without ever questioning the process through which this conversion occurs.

We began to examine how the black box performs its conversion by looking at the growth of overseas assembly plants and the creation, segmentation, and disciplining of the labor force necessary for the box to function at its greatest efficiency. Historically free labor has been created by removing people from the land or destroying the small-scale industry that allowed them to support themselves. In different countries this was done in different ways, but the overall result has been the creation of populations whose sole means of support is in the sale of their labor. This is as true in industrialized countries as it is in developing or undeveloped countries. In fact all of us who depend on wage employment—from nuclear physicists to garment workers—constitute the pool of "free" labor. This labor pool is further divided along a continuum comprising at one end relatively well-paid, desirable jobs in industries or enterprises that require a well-trained workforce, and at the other end relatively low-paying, undesirable jobs in industries that are highly competitive and dependent on the existence of a cheap labor supply. Industries and enterprises that depend on a cheap labor supply are able to take advantage of social divisions and discrimination that generally follow lines of gender, race, age, and country of origin to minimize labor costs and control the labor force.

In creating or taking advantage of the increasing supply of cheap labor, the capitalist economy must also develop ways to maintain workforce discipline, which it does through the factory system, the redefinition of time, and the use of traditional institutions, such as the family and the church. Yet in spite of the new forms of discipline, workers offer resistance in the indirect form of masked criticism—as in the baptism of money, spirit possession, or moral tales such as that of Rumpelstilskin—or in the direct forms, protest and union organizing.

The mobility, segmentation, and disciplining of the workforce is, of course, only one feature of modern capitalism, and an examination of labor is only the beginning of an understanding of how the black box is able to transform money into more money. It is necessary to examine other components. In order to do so, let us turn to other major questions: How did the entire system develop historically? How did the black box evolve to where it is today? Most specifically, *how and why did the capitalist evolve from the merchant trader?*

$$Chapter\ 3$$

The Rise of the Merchant, Industrialist, and Capital Controller

From the fifteenth century on, European soldiers and sailors carried the flags of their rulers to the four corners of the globe, and European merchants established their storehouses from Vera Cruz to Nagasaki. Dominating the sea-lanes of the world, these merchants invaded existing networks of exchange and linked one to the other. In the service of "God and profit" they located sources of products desired in Europe and developed coercive systems for their delivery. In response, European craft shops, either singly or aggregated into manufactories, began to produce goods to provision the wide-ranging military and naval efforts and to furnish commodities to overseas suppliers in exchange for goods to be sold as commodities at home. The outcome was the creation of a commercial network of global scale.
—ERIC WOLF, PEOPLE WITHOUT HISTORY

When I think of Indonesia—a country on the Equator with 180 million people, a median age of 18, and a Moslem ban on alcohol—I feel I know what heaven looks like.
—DONALD R. KEOUGH, PRESIDENT OF COCA COLA

At no other time in human history has the world been a better place for capitalists. We live in a world full of investment opportunities—companies, banks, funds, bonds, securities, and even countries—into which we can put money and from which we can get more back. These money-making machines, such as the Nike Corporation, have a ready supply of cheap labor, capital, raw materials, and advanced technology to assist in making products that people all over the world

Fifteenth-century merchants in Paris display their wares and services.

clamor to buy. Moreover, governments compete for their presence, passing laws and making treaties to open markets, while maintaining infrastructures (roads, airports, power utilities, monetary systems, communication networks, etc.) that enable them to manufacture products or provide services cheaply and charge prices that remain competitive with other investments. Nation-states maintain armies to protect investments and see that markets remain open. Educational institutions devote themselves to producing knowledgeable, skilled, and disciplined workers, while researchers at colleges and universities develop new technologies to make even better and cheaper products. Our governments, educational institutions and mass media encourage people to consume more and more commodities. Citizens order their economic and social lives to accommodate work in the investment machines and to gain access to the commodities they produce. In return the investment machines churn out profits that are reinvested to manufacture more of their particular products or that can be invested in other enterprises, producing yet more goods and services.

But there are economic, environmental, and social consequences of doing business and making money. We live in a world in which the gap between the rich and poor is growing, a world that contains many wealthy and comfortable people but also contains almost one billion hungry people, one-fifth of its population. Then there are the environmental consequences of doing business: Production uses up the earth's energy resources and produces damaged environments in return. There are health consequences as well, not only from damaged environments but also because those too poor to afford health care often do without it. Finally there are the political consequences of governments' using their armed force to maintain conditions that they believe are favorable for business and investors.

In the long view of human history these conditions are very recent ones. For most of human history human beings have lived in small, relatively isolated settlements that rarely exceeded three or four hundred individuals. And until some ten thousand years ago virtually all of these people lived by gathering and hunting. Then in some areas of the world, instead of depending on the natural growth of plant foods and the natural growth and movements of animals, people began to plant and harvest crops and raise animals themselves. This was not necessarily an advance in human societies—in fact, in terms of labor, it required human beings to do the work that had been done largely by nature. The sole advantage of working harder was that the additional labor supported denser populations. Settlements grew in size until thousands rather than hundreds lived together in towns and cities. Occupational specialization developed, necessitating trade and communication between villages, towns, cities, and regions. Political complexity increased; chiefs became kings, and kings became emperors ruling over vast regions.

Then, approximately four or five hundred years ago, patterns of travel and communication contributed to the globalization of trade dominated by "a small peninsula off the landmass of Asia," as Eric Wolf called Europe. The domination by one region over others was not new in the world. There had existed prior to this time civilizations whose influence had spread to influence those around them—the Mayan civilization in Central America, Greek civilization of the fourth millennium B.C., Rome of the first and second centuries A.D., and Islamic civilization of the eighth and ninth centuries. But there was an important difference. The building of these empires was largely a political process of conquest and military domination, whereas the expansion of Europe, while certainly involving its share of militarism, was largely accomplished by economic means, by the expansion and control of trade.

Now let's shift our focus to the development of the *capitalist*—the merchant, industrialist, and financier—the person who controls the capital, employs the laborers, and profits from the consumption of commodities. This will be a long-term, historical look at this development, particularly because if we are to understand the global distribution of power and money that exists today and the origins of the culture of capitalism, knowledge of its history is crucial.

Assume for a time the role of a businessperson, a global merchant, or merchant adventurer, as they used to be called,[1] passing through the world of the last six hundred years. We'll begin searching the globe for ways to make money in the year 1400 and end our search in the year 2000, taking stock of the changes in the organization and distribution of capital that have occurred in that time. Because we are looking at the world through the eyes of a merchant, there is much that we will miss—many political developments, religious wars, revolutions, natural catastrophes, and the like. Because we overlook these events does not mean they did not affect how business was conducted—in many cases they had profound effects. But our prime concern is with the events that most directly influenced the way in which business was conducted on a day to day basis and how the pursuit of profit by merchant adventurers influenced the lives of people all over the world.

Our historical tour will concentrate on three areas:

1. An understanding of how capital came to be concentrated in so few hands and how the world came to be divided into rich and poor. There were certainly rich people and poor people in 1400, but today's vast global disparity between core and periphery did not exist then. *How did the distribution of wealth change, and how did one area of the world come to dominate the others economically?*

2. An understanding of the changes in business organizations and the organization of capital, that is, *who controlled the money?* In 1400, most business enterprises were small, generally family-organized institutions. Capital was controlled by these groups and state organizations. Today we live in an era of multinational corporations, many whose wealth exceeds that of most countries. We need to trace the evolution of the power of capital over our lives and the transformation of the merchant of 1400 into the industrialist of the eighteenth and nineteenth centuries then into the investor and capital controller of the late twentieth century. *How and why did these transformations in the organization of capital come about?*

3. The increase in the level of global economic integration. From your perspective as a merchant adventurer, you obviously want the fewest restraints possible on your ability to trade from one area of the world to another; the fewer restrictions, the greater the opportunity for profit. Such things as a global currency, agreement among nations on import and export regulations, ease of passage of money and goods from area to area, freedom to employ who you want and to pay the lowest possible wage are all to your advantage; furthermore, you want few or no government restrictions regarding the consequences of your business activities. *How did the level of global economic integration increase, and what were the consequences for the merchant adventurer, as well as others?*

With these questions in mind, let's go back to the world of 1400 and start trading.

---

[1]The name is taken from a sixteenth century English trading company, The Merchant Adventurers, cloth wholesalers trading to Holland and Germany with bases of operation in Antwerp and Bergen-op-Zoom, and, later, Hamburg. The company survived until 1809.

The Era of the Global Trader

A Trader's Tour of the World in 1400

If, as global merchants in 1400, we were searching for ways to make money, the best opportunities would be in long-distance trade, buying goods in one area of the world and selling them in another (see Braudel 1982:68). If we could choose which among the great cities of the world—Cairo, Malacca, Samarkand, Venice—to begin trading, our choice would probably be Hangchow, China. China in 1400 had a population of 100 million and was the most technologically developed country in the world. Paper was invented in China probably as early as A.D. 700 and block printing as early as 1050. China of 1400 had a thriving iron industry; enormous amounts of coal were burned to fuel the iron furnaces, equal in northern China alone to 70 percent of what metal workers in Great Britain used at the beginning of the eighteenth century. The explosive power of gunpowder was harnessed around 650 A.D. and by 1000 was used by Chinese armies for simple bombs and grenades. Cannons were in use by 1300, some mounted on the ships of the Chinese navy, and by the fourteenth century the Chinese were using a metaled-barreled gun that shot explosive pellets (Abu-Lughod 1989:322ff).

If you were to tour the Chinese countryside you would have been struck by the networks of canals and irrigation ditches that criss-crossed the landscape, maintained by wealthy landowners or the state. China was governed by a royal elite and administered largely by mandarins, people selected from the wealthy classes and who were exempt from paying taxes. State bureaucrats were also selected and promoted through civil service examinations open to all but those of the lowest rank of society (e.g., executioners, slaves, beggars, boatpeople, actors, laborers) (Hanson 1993:186). China produced some of the most desired trade goods in the world, particularly silk, spices, and porcelain.

The economic conditions in China also favored traders. There were guilds and associations of merchants such as jewelers, gilders, antique dealers, dealers in honey, ginger, and boots, money-changers, and doctors. China had its own currency system. In the Middle East and Europe governments issued money in the form of coins of precious metals whose value depended on their weight. In China there was not only copper coin, but paper money (cotton paper stamped with a government seal) to provide merchants with a convenient means of exchange. Paper money also allowed the state to control the flow of money in and out of the country. Precious metals, such as gold and silver, could not be used by foreigners in trade, so foreign traders were forced to exchange their gold or silver for paper money, which they then exchanged for gold and silver when they left. Since they had usually purchased Chinese commodities to sell elsewhere, they usually left with less gold and silver than when they arrived (Abu-Lughod 1989:334).

China was also politically stable. The rulers, members of the Ming Dynasty, had successfully rebelled against the Mongols 25 years earlier. The Mongols, nomadic horsemen who roamed the vast steppes of Central Asia, conquered China in 1276 and set up their own dynasty, the Yuan. The Mongols, eager to establish

The splendor and wealth of fifteenth- and sixteenth-century China is portrayed in this engraving of a Mandarin's terrace and garden.

trade with the rest of the world, had established relatively safe trade routes to the rest of Asia, the Middle East, and Europe. At least at first, the Ming appeared to want to maintain that trade, sending its impressive navy as emissaries to ports along the Indian Ocean.

The city of Hangchow was situated between the banks of the Che River leading to the sea and the shore of an enormous artificial lake. According to Ibn Battuta, an Arab trader who visited the city in the 1340s, the city extended over six to seven square miles and was surrounded by walls with five gateways through which canals passed. Thirteen monumental gates at which its great thoroughfares terminated, provided entry to the city. Situated on the hills overlooking the city were the imperial palace and homes of the wealthy state bureaucrats and merchants; at the opposite end of the city were the houses of the poor—crowded, narrow-fronted, three- to five-story houses with workshops on the ground floors. The main thoroughfare, the Imperial Way, was three miles long and 180 feet wide, crowded with carriages drawn by men or tiny horses.

The city was a trader's paradise. Inside the city were ten markets as well as tea houses and restaurants where traders could meet and arrange their business. Outside the city were a fish market and wholesale markets. Ibn Battuta said it was "the largest city on the face of the earth." Sections of the cities contained concentrations of merchants from all over the world. Jewish and Christian traders from Europe in one; Muslim traders in another, with bazaars and mosques, and muezzins calling Muslims to noon prayer. The bazaars of Chinese merchants and artisans were in yet another section. In brief, Hangchow would have been an ideal place to sell merchandise from Europe, the Middle East, or other parts of Asia and to purchase goods, such as spices and silks, that were in demand in other parts of the world.

Silk was particularly desired by foreign traders because its light weight and compactness made it easy to transport, and because China had a virtual monopoly in the silk trade. Syrian traders had smuggled silk worms out of China in the thirteenth century, and in 1400 one could purchase silk in India and Italy; but the quality of Chinese silk was superior. Since the production of silk was likely in the hands of Chinese merchants, you would have purchased it directly from them. You might also purchase Chinese porcelain, especially if you planned to travel by ship, since porcelain could be used as ballast by ships returning to the Middle East or Europe (see Figure 3.1).

Your next task would be to arrange to transport your goods to where you planned to sell them. Let's assume you had orders from merchants in cities such as Venice, Cairo, and Bruges, where Chinese goods were in demand. Your first task is to get your goods to the Mediterranean. You could go overland through China, through central Asia to Northern India, or to ports on the Black Sea, then travel to

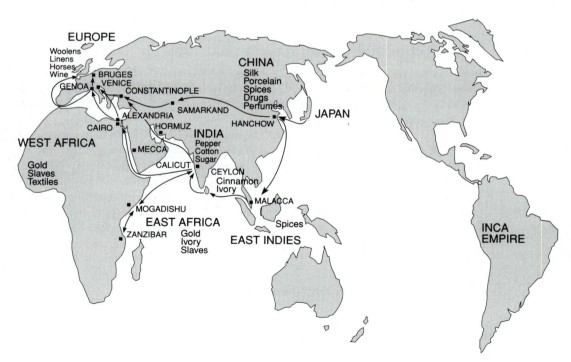

FIGURE 3.1   Major Trade Routes in 1400

European ports such as Venice and Naples. The trip overland through Asia to Europe would take you at least 275 days using pack trains—camels over the deserts, mules through the mountains, ox carts where roads existed, human carriers, and boats. The overland route was popular in the thirteenth and fourteenth centuries, when the Mongols had through their conquests unified Central Asia and issued safe conduct passes to traders. In 1400, however, with the Empire fragmented, you may have risked raiding by nomadic bands of Mongol horsemen.

A safer route in 1400 would have been the sea route, down the East Coast of China, through the Strait of Malacca to Southern India, and then either through the Persian Gulf to Iran and overland, through Baghdad to the Mediterranean, or through the Red Sea to Cairo, and finally by ship to Italy.

Traveling through the Strait of Malacca and into Southeast Asia, you would have found powerful elites ruling states from their royal palaces, surrounded by armed retainers, kin, artisans, and specialists. Beyond this was a peasantry producing rice to support themselves and the elites. These were the civilizations that built Angkor Thom and Angkor Wat in Cambodia. You would likely have been more at home, however, in the seaports that dotted the Strait of Malacca which owed their existence to trade. Occasionally these ports would merge with inland kingdoms such as Madjapahit in Java. The main city of the area in 1400 was Malacca, founded by pirates led in rebellion twenty years earlier by a prince from Madjapahit. The prince converted to Islam, attracting to Malacca wealthy Muslim merchants, and by 1400 Malacca was a city of forty to fifty thousand people with sixty-one nations represented in trade. The Portuguese Tomé Pires, writing a century later, said "Whoever is lord of Malacca has his hands on the throat of Venice" (cited Wolf 1982:58). While in Malacca, you likely would have obtained additional trade goods to take West. Spices, particularly cinnamon (at one time in Egypt considered more valuable than gold), were highly valued because they were easy to transport and brought high profits in the Middle East and Europe.

From Malacca you probably would have traveled along the coast of Southeast Asia and on to India, whose wealth in 1400 rivaled that of China. Southeast India had a thriving textile industry. Farmers grew cotton and passed it on to spinners, who made thread for the weavers. There is some evidence that merchants provided cotton and thread to spinners and weavers and paid the artisans for what they produced. There was a sophisticated technology: a vertical loom, block printing, and the spinning wheel, probably introduced from Turkey. But cotton and textiles were not the only items you might have obtained in India for trade; there were also dyes, tannins, spices, oil seed, narcotics, lumber, honey, and ivory (see Wolf 1982).

From India you might travel to East Africa, where from Bantu-speaking peoples you might have obtained slaves, ivory, leopard skins, gold from Zimbabwe, and rhinoceros horns (still believed in some parts of the world to be an aphrodisiac).

Leaving East Africa you would have journeyed up the coast through the Red Sea to Cairo or through the Persian Gulf, through Iraq to Baghdad, and on to Constantinople and the Eastern Mediterranean. You would have found the Islamic countries of the Middle East favorable to business, with a sophisticated body of law regulating trade, including rules for the formation of trading partnerships and the extension of credit. One law allowed people to pay for merchandise at a later date at a higher price, a convenient way around the Islamic prohibition of lending money at interest. Bags of gold coin whose value was printed on the outside, and whose contents were apparently never checked, served as money. There were bankers who changed money, took deposits, and issued promissory notes, another way of extending credit and making loans. Merchants kept their accounts by listing credits and debits. Thus all the rudiments of a sophisticated economy—capital, credit, banking, money, and account keeping—were present in Islamic trade (Abu-Lughod 1989:216ff).

From Cairo you could join a caravan to go south through the Sahara to West Africa, where textile goods were in demand and where you might obtain slaves or gold. Virtually two-thirds of the gold circulating in Europe and the Middle East came from West Africa. Or you might travel a short way to Alexandria, still a major city. From there you would travel by ship on the Mediterranean to one of the city-states of Italy, such as Venice or Genoa. Italy was the center of European and Mediterranean trade. At European fairs Italian traders would set up a bench (*banco,* from which *bank* is derived) with their scales and coins, enabling traders to exchange currency from one area of the world for another. Italian bankers monopolized the international exchange of money and credit, and it was they who pioneered the *bill of exchange.* This was a document in which a buyer agreed to deliver payment to a seller at another time and place in the seller's home currency. In the absence of any widely recognized currency, the bill of exchange greatly facilitated foreign trade (Abu-Lughod 1989:93).

You might then join other merchants from Genoa, Pisa, and Milan who formed caravans to take goods such as silks and spices from the Orient or the Middle East, alum, wax, leather, and fur from Africa, dates, figs, and honey from Spain, and pepper, feathers, and brazilwood from the Middle East, over the Alps to the fairs and markets of Western and Northern Europe, a trip taking five weeks. Or you could send your goods by ship, through the Mediterranean and the North Sea to trading centers such as Bruges.

Once you reached Northern or Western Europe, you had already left the wealthiest part of the world. After the decline of the Roman Empire Western Europe was a backward area, exploited for its iron, lumber, and slaves. Urban areas had declined and artisan activity retreated to rural areas. Moreover, Europe had been devastated in the fourteenth century by bubonic plague: In the mid-fourteenth century Europe's population was about eighty million (Abu-Lughod 1989:94). By 1400 plague had reduced it by 45 percent, to between forty and fifty million. The plague likely originated in Central Asia or China. It traveled the trade routes, stricking Chinese cities as early as 1320 and first striking Europe in Caffa, on the Black Sea, in 1346. It arrived in Alexandria in 1347, probably from Italian ports on the Black Sea. At its height in Alexandria it killed 10,000 people a day, finally killing 200,000 of the city's half million people. It struck Italy in 1348, appeared in France and Britain the same year, and reached Germany and Scandinavia a year later.

Feudalism was still the main form of political and economic organization in Europe. Kings bestowed lands, or *fiefs,* to subjects in return for their loyalty and service. Lords "rented" land to peasants, generally for a share of the produce, which they used to pay tribute to the kings and to finance their own expenses.

Woolen textiles were the most important products of Northern and Western Europe in 1400. Flanders (Western Belgium and Northwest France), the textile center of Northern Europe, had virtually monopolized the purchase of raw wool from England, and woolen textiles from Flanders were in demand throughout Europe and in other parts of the world.

Let's assume you have sold the commodities you brought from China and realized a handsome profit. The question is *what to do with your capital and profits?* You might buy Flemish textiles in Bruges or, depending on the political circumstances, travel to England to buy textiles. You might buy land or finance other traders in return for a share of their profits. If, however, you decided to undergo another trade circuit, returning east would be your likely alternative. The Americas were probably unknown, and certainly unreachable. You might have traveled down the European coast to West Africa, where European textiles were in great demand and where you could obtain slaves and gold. But while the wind patterns of the Eastern Atlantic would have carried your ship to West Africa, they made it impossible, given the sailing technology, to return by sea, and you would be forced to return overland across Northern Africa. Your likely trade route, then, would have been back to Italy and east through the Mediterranean to India, the East Indies, and China.

What if you had been able to cross the sea to the Americas? What would you have found in 1400? No one left a written record of life in the New World just prior to the arrival of Europeans. Archaeologists, however, have created a record from what was left behind. You would have discovered elaborate trade routes extending from South America into North America and the remains of great civilizations in Central Mexico and the Yucatan Peninsula.

The Inca were just beginning their expansion which would produce the Andean Empire confronted by Pizarro in 1532. Inca society in 1400 was dominated by the Inca dynasty, an aristocracy consisting of relatives of the ruling group, local rulers who submitted to Inca rule. Men of local rank headed endogamous patrilineal clans, or *ayllus,* groups who traced descent to a common male ancestor and who were required to marry within their clan. These groups paid tribute to the Inca aristocracy by working on public projects or in military service. Women spent much of their time weaving cloth that was used to repay faithful subjects and was imbued with extraordinary ritual and ceremonial value. The state expanded by colonizing new agricultural lands to grow maize. It maintained irrigation systems, roads, and a postal service in which runners carried information from one end of the empire to another. Groups that rebelled against Inca rule were usually relocated far from their homeland (Wolf 1982:62–63).

If you had traveled into the Brazilian rainforests you might have encountered peoples such as the Tupinambá, who lived on small garden plots while gathering and hunting in the forests. Sixteenth-century traveler Calvinist pastor Jean de Léry concluded that the Tupinambá lived more comfortably than ordinary people in France (cited Maybury-Lewis 1997:13).

In Mexico in 1400 the Aztecs were twenty years from establishing their vast empire with its capital at Tenochtitlán. In the Caribbean there were complex chieftainships with linkages to the civilizations of Mesoamerica and the Andes. A merchant of 1400 would have been able to follow trade routes that spread from Mexico into the southeastern and northeastern United States, encountering descendants of those who archaeologists called the Mississippians. In this society goods and commodities were used to indicate status and rank. A trader would have encountered towns or ceremonial centers focused on great terraced, earthen platforms. The Mississippians relied on the cultivation of maize, beans, and squash, called "the three sisters" by the Iroquois. You might have met the Iroquois at the headwaters of the Ohio River, the Cherokee in the southern Appalachians, the Natchez on the lower Mississippi River, and the Pawnee and the Mandan on the Missouri River. On the surrounding prairies your would have encountered the peoples of the Northwest, the buffalo hunters of the plains (the horse, often associated with the Plains Indians, wouldn't arrive for another century), and the Inuit hunters of the Arctic and subarctic. These civilizations and cultures might in later centuries have provided a lucrative market for the sale and purchase of goods, had not other events led to their devastation.

As we complete our global tour, the barriers to commerce are striking. For example, most political rulers were not yet committed to encouraging trade. While states might value trade for the taxes, tolls, and rents they could extract from traders, merchants were still looked down upon. Rulers generally viewed trade only as a way to gain profit from traders and merchants, and some states even attempted to control some trade themselves. In China, for example, trade in salt was monopolized by the government. Religious authorities in Europe, the Middle East, and China discouraged trade by extracting high taxes or forbidding loans at interest.

Geography was obviously a major barrier: trade circuits might take years to complete. Roads were few and ships relatively small and at the mercy of winds and tides. Security was a problem: a merchants' goods were liable to be seized or stolen, or merchants might be forced to pay tribute to rulers along the way.

Economically there were various restrictions. We were a long way in 1400 from anything resembling a consumer economy. Most of the world's population lived on a subsistence economy, that is, produced themselves whatever they needed to exist. In Europe, for example, where 90 percent of the population was rural, people might buy an iron plow, some pots, and textile products, but that was all. Consumers tended to be the urban dwellers, largely the clergy, aristocracy, and the small middle class consisting of artisans, merchants, and bureaucrats. Furthermore, if people wanted to buy more, there was virtually no currency with which to do it; even if all the gold and silver of Europe had been in circulation, it would have amounted to only about two dollars per person (Weatherford 1988:14).

Thus, overall the world of 1400 seemed little affected by trade. China and India were probably the richest countries in the world, and there is little doubt that royal rulers controlled most of the wealth, largely through the extraction of tribute from peasants, artisans, and traders. Much of this they redistributed in the form of gifts, feasts, and charity. Moreover, the people who worked the soil, as those who remained gathering and hunting at the fringes and outside the world system, had ready access to food. Though there is evidence of periodic famine in which thousands perished, it is unlikely that, as now, one-fifth of the world's population in 1400 was hungry. Thus while a growing system of trade was beginning to link more of the world's people together, there had yet to develop the worldwide inequities that exist today. This, however, would rapidly begin to change over the next one hundred years.

The Economic Rise of Europe and Its Impact on Africa and the Americas

Two events dominate the story of the expansion of trade after 1400: the increased withdrawal of China from world trade networks, and the voyage of Vasco da Gama around the southern tip of Africa. These events resulted in a shift in the balance of economic dominance from a country of one hundred million occupying most of Asia to a country of one million occupying an area just slightly larger than the state of Maine.

The reason for China's withdrawal from its position of commercial dominance is something of a mystery. The ruling dynasty moved the capital of China inland and allowed its powerful navy gradually to disintegrate. Regardless of the reasons for these actions, they resulted in a diminished role for China in global trade and Portugal, with the most powerful navy in the world, was quick to fill the vacuum left by China in the East Indies. Portugal used its navy to dominate trade and supplemented trading activities with raiding (Abu-Lughod 1989:243).

Japan also took the opportunity after China's withdrawal to expand its trading activity in Southeast Asia. Japan, like England, was in the fifteenth century a feudal society divided into an upper nobility, the *daimyo,* or great lords; and the *samurai,* vassals of the *daimyo;* and the *chonin,* or merchants, who were looked down on by the nobility. There was contact between Japan and Europe by the mid-sixteenth century, and Christian missionaries soon established themselves in Japan. But around 1500 Japan was involved in heavy trade with China, trading refined copper, sulfur, folding fans, painted scrolls, and, most important, swords. One trade expedition carried ten thousand swords to China and returned with strings of cash, raw silk, porcelains, paintings, medicines, and books. Thus in the fifteenth century, Japan was beginning economic expansion to areas vacated by China (Sanderson 1995:154).

Technological advances in boat building were partially responsible for Portugal's power. Around 1400 European boat builders combined the European square rigger with the lateen rig of the Arabs, the square rig giving ships speed when running and the lateen rig allowing the boat to sail closer to the wind. They also equipped their ships with cannons on the main deck and upper decks by cutting holes in the hull. The result was a speedy and maneuverable galleon, half warship and half merchantman (Wolf 1982:235).

Equally important for Portugal was location. Prior to the fifteenth century, Portugal was at the edge of the world system. The Mediterranean was controlled by the city-states of Italy and by Islamic powers. The Americas were seemingly out of reach, even if traders were aware of them. The west coast of Africa was inaccessible by boat unless one sailed south down the coast and returned overland. But once the route east to India and China was restricted, action shifted to the Atlantic, and as Africa and the Americas became readily accessible, Portugal was suddenly at the center of world trade.

It was the era of discovery and conquest, of the voyages of Columbus, of efforts to find alternative routes to China and the East Indies. Columbus believed he had discovered China or Ciangu (Japan), and as late as 1638 the fur trader Jean Nicolet, on meeting Winnebago Indians in the shores of Lake Michigan, wore a Chinese robe he brought to wear when meeting the Great Kahn of China (Wolf 1982:232).

Much is made in popular culture and history books of the spirit of adventure of early "explorers" such as Marco Polo, Vasco da Gama, and Christopher Columbus. But they were less explorers than merchant sailors. Their motivation was largely economic; they were seeking alternative ways to the riches of China and the East Indies. One might say that European economic domination, to the extent it was fueled by the wealth of the Americas, was due to the accidental discovery of two continents that happened to be in the way of their attempts to find alternative routes to China, Japan, and India.

If you were a global trader in the sixteenth century and if your starting point was Lisbon, Portugal, you had a choice of trade routes. You could go east to the Middle East, India, or Southeast Asia, all kept open to Portuguese traders by Portugal's navy. You could go south along the African coast, or follow Columbus's route to the New World. Or you could simply trade into the rest of Europe. All routes could prove profitable. In our reincarnation as a Portuguese trader, let's first go south to Africa.

Let's assume you have the capital to hire a ship to carry yourself and your goods to Africa. You would probably be carrying Mediterranean wine, iron weapons, perhaps horses, much in demand in Africa, and a consignment of textiles consisting perhaps of Egyptian linen and cotton. *What sort of commodities would you acquire in Africa for trade in Europe?*

Africans were already producing the same things as Europeans—iron and steel (possibly the best in the world at the time), elaborate textiles, and other goods. As a trader, you would have been interested in the textiles made in Africa, which were in demand in Europe. You would also have been anxious to trade in gold mined in West Africa, the source until that time of most of the gold in Europe and the Middle East. But your real interest would likely have been slaves.

The institution of slavery goes back well into antiquity. The ancient Greeks kept slaves, and slave labor was used throughout the Middle East and Europe in 1500. Moslems enslaved Christians, Christians enslaved Muslims, and Europeans enslaved Slavs and Greeks. Coal miners in Scotland were enslaved into the seventeenth and eighteenth centuries, and indentured servitude was widespread in Europe.

However, there was about to be a huge surge in the demand for slave labor from the new colonies being established in the Americas.

The nature of the slave trade has long been a contentious issue among historians. Many believe the slave trade was forced on Africa, if not by direct military intervention then by economic extortion, Europeans offering guns and horses needed by rulers to maintain their authority in exchange for slaves. But there is increasing evidence that the slave trade was largely an African institution that Europeans and others were only too happy to tap into. Slavery in Africa was different from slavery in Europe, however, and different from what it was to become in the Americas.

Slaves were regarded traditionally in Africa as subordinate family members, as they were in Europe going back to Aristotle's time. Thus slaves in Africa could be found doing any duties a subordinate family member might do. To understand the African institution of slavery it is also necessary to understand that among people in African states there was little notion of private property; for example, land was owned by "corporate kinship groups," networks of related individuals who together owned land in common. People were given the right to use land but not to own it. Slaves comprised the only form of private, revenue-producing property recognized in African law. Slaves could produce revenue because if you had the labor in the form of family members, wives, or slaves, you could claim the use of more land. African conceptions of property are reflected also in the fact that, whereas in Europe taxes were paid on land, in Africa taxes were paid on people, "by the head" (Thornton 1992).

The size of African states may have reflected the lack of concern with land as property. John Thornton (1992:106) estimated that only 30 percent of Atlantic Africa contained states larger than fifty thousand square kilometers (roughly the size of New York State), and more than half the total area contained states of five hundred to one thousand square kilometers. Africans went to war generally not to acquire land, as in Europe, but to acquire slaves, with which more land could be worked.

Given these attitudes toward land and toward labor, there existed in Africa at the time of European arrival a large slave population and a thriving slave market. Slaves were a major form of investment; a wealthy African could not buy land but could acquire slaves and, as long as land was available, claim more land to use. Moreover, slaves, since they were property, could be inherited by individuals, whereas land, since it belonged to the corporate kin group, could not. Investing in slaves would have been the wealthy African's equivalent of a European investing in land, and if you were not using slaves you could sell them (Thornton 1992:87). Thus European traders found ready sources of slaves, not because Africans were inveterate slave traders but because in Africa the legal basis for wealth revolved around the idea of transferring ownership of people (Thornton 1992:95).

Once you obtained the slaves, you might have obtained a special ship to transport them back to Europe or to one of the Atlantic islands, where they were in demand as workers on the expanding sugar plantations. Sugar in the sixteenth century was still a luxury item, used by the wealthy to decorate food or as medicine.

The primary areas of supply were around the Mediterranean—Egypt, Italy, Spain, and Greece. But with the opening of the Atlantic, sugar plantations were established first on the Canary Islands and the Azores and later in the Caribbean. Sugar production was a labor-intensive activity, and slaves from Africa supplied much of that labor. From 1451 to 1600 some 275,000 slaves were sent from West Africa to America and Europe. In the seventeenth and eighteenth centuries sugar would begin to play a major role in the world economy, but in the sixteenth century its possibilities were only beginning to be recognized.

Let's assume that after buying slaves in Africa and selling them in the new sugar plantations of the Azores, you resume your journey and go west to the Americas. The opening of the Americas brought into Portugal and Spain vast amounts of gold and silver plundered from the Inca and Aztec Empires and extracted from mines by slave and indentured labor. When Pizarro invaded Peru and seized Atahualpa in 1532, he demanded and received a ransom of a roomful of gold and killed the emperor anyway. When Cortes conquered the Aztec he demanded gold; after the Aztec's counterattack Cortes's fleeing men carried so much loot that one-quarter drowned as they fell from a causeway into a lake, so burdened down were they by their cargo (Weatherford 1988:7).

At the time of the conquest of the Americas, there was approximately $200 million worth of gold and silver in Europe; by 1600 that had increased eight times. Some 180–200 tons of gold, with a contemporary value of $2.8 billion, flowed into Europe, much of it still visible in the robes, statuary, and sacred objects of European churches (Weatherford 1988:14).

Most of the silver came from San Luis Potosí. Cerro Rico ("rich hill" in Spanish), the mountain above Potosí in Bolivia, is the richest mountain ever discovered, virtually a mountain of silver. In 1545 slaves and indentured laborers recruited from the indigenous population began digging silver out of the mountain, forming it into bars and coins, and sending it to Spain. By 1603 there were 58,800 Indian workers in Potosí, 43,200 free day laborers, 10,500 contract laborers, and 5,100 labor draftees. By 1650, Potosí rivaled London and Paris in size, with a population of 160,000 (Wolf 1982:136).

The amount of currency in circulation worldwide increased enormously, enriching Europe but eroding the wealth of other areas, and helping Europe expand into an international market system. China reopened its trading links to Europe and took in so much silver that by the mid-eighteenth century its value had declined to one-fifth what it had been prior to the discovery of America. The gold from the Americas also had the effect of destroying the African gold trade (Weatherford 1988).

Gold and silver were not the only wealth extracted from the New World. Spain imported cochineal, a red dye made from insects (it took 70,000 dried insects to produce one pound of cochineal), indigo (blue dye), and cocoa. Portuguese traders established sugar plantations on the Northeast coast of Brazil.

The cost of the European expansion of trade to the Americas, at least to the people of the Americas, was enormous. It resulted in the demographic collapse of the New World, what Eric Wolf called "the great dying" (1982:133).

There is broad disagreement about the population of the Americas at the time of the European conquest. In 1939 Alfred E. Kroeber, one of the founders of American anthropology, estimated that the total population of the Americas was about 8.4 million of which 900,000 were in North America. Harold Herbert Spinden, relying on archeological evidence, suggested there were 50–75 million people in the Americas in A.D. 1200. Henry F. Dobyns, working with archeological evidence, estimates of the carrying capacity of given environments, and historical documents, estimated 90–112 million in the hemisphere and 12.5 million in the area north of Mexico. The disagreement reflected in these numbers is not unimportant, for it involves an important legal question: *Did the "discovery" of the New World permit Europeans to move on to unoccupied wilderness, or did they displace and destroy a settled indigenous population?* If the latter is the case, then European claims of legal ownership of the land based on the doctrine of *terra nullius*—land belonging to no one—would be legally invalid.

There is little doubt, we think, that the higher estimates are closer to the actual population of the Americas. In 1500, Europe, a fraction the size of the Americas, had a population of 45 million; France alone had a population of 20 million, and tiny Portugal 1 million. And this was after the bubonic plague epidemics. There seems little doubt that the environment and societies of the Americas were capable of supporting large populations. The peoples of the Americas built empires, palisaded settlements, temples, great pyramids, and irrigation complexes. There was certainly an adequate supply of foodstuffs to support a large population; most of our diet today comes from plants domesticated first in the New World, including corn, potatoes, yams, sweet potatoes, tomatoes, squash, pumpkins, most varieties of beans, pepper (except black), amaranth, manioc, mustard, some types of rice, pecans, pineapples, bread fruit, passion fruit, melons, cranberries, blueberries, blackberries, coffee, vanilla, chocolate, and cocoa.

In 1496 Bartolomé Colón, Christopher's brother, authorized a headcount of adults of Española, the present-day Haiti and Dominican Republic, then the most populous of the Caribbean Islands. The people of the island, the Tainos, created a culture that extended over most of the Caribbean. Colón arrived at a count of 1.1 million working adults; if we add children and the elderly, and consider that disease and murder had already diminished the population, there must have been at least 2 million and as many as 8 million on that island alone (Sale 1991:160–161). Thus it is hardly unreasonable to suppose that the population of the Americas as a whole was upwards of 50–100 million people.

The scale of death after the arrival of the Europeans is difficult to conceive and rivals any estimate made for the demographic consequences of a nuclear holocaust today. When the Spanish surveyed Española in 1508, 1510, 1514, and 1518, they found a population of under one hundred thousand. The most detailed of the surveys, taken in 1514, listed just 22,000 adults, which anthropologists Sherburne Cook and Woodrow Borah estimated to represent a total population of 27,800 (Cook and Borah, 1960). Thus in just over twenty years there was a decline from at least 2 million to 27,800 people. Bartolomé de Las Casas, the major chronicler of the effects of the Spanish invasion, said that by 1542 there were just two hundred

In the early 1600s an epidemic (possibly smallpox) killed some 90 percent of the Wampanoags of Massachusetts.

indigenous Tainos left, and within a decade they were extinct. Cook and Borah concluded that in Central America an estimated population of 25.3 million was reduced by 97 percent in a little over a century. In all, it is estimated that 95–98 percent of the indigenous population of the Americas died as a consequence of European contact.

Many died in battles with the invaders; others were murdered by European occupiers desperate to maintain control over a threatening population; and still others died as a result of slavery and forced labor. But the vast majority died of diseases introduced by Europeans to which the indigenous peoples had no immunity.

The most deadly of the diseases was smallpox. It arrived sometime between 1520 and 1524 with a European soldier or sailor and quickly spread across the continent, ahead of the advancing Europeans. When Pizarro reached the Inca in 1532, his defeat of a divided Empire was made possible by the death from smallpox of the ruler and the crown prince. When a Spanish expedition set out from Florida for the Pacific in 1535, they found evidence of the epidemic in West Texas. Dobyns (1983) assumed that virtually all the inhabitants of the hemisphere were exposed to smallpox during that one epidemic. *What would the mortality rate have been from this one pathogen alone?*

Dobyns (1983:13–14; see also Stiffarm and Lane 1992) estimated that in the epidemic of 1520–1524 virtually all indigenous peoples—certainly those in large population areas—would have been exposed to smallpox, and since there would have been no immunity the death rate, judging by known death rates among other Native American populations, must have been at least 60–70 percent. Spanish reports of the time that half of the native population died, said Dobyns, most certainly were underestimates.

And this was not the only smallpox epidemic. Dobyns calculated that there were forty-one smallpox epidemics in North America from 1520 to 1899, seventeen measles epidemics from 1531 to 1892, ten major influenza epidemics from 1559 to 1918, and four plague epidemics from 1545 to 1707, to name a few. In all, he said, a serious epidemic invaded indigenous populations on average every four years and two and half months during the years 1520–1900.

Dobyns estimated that the population of Florida at the time of European contact was over 700,000. There was a smallpox epidemic in 1519, gastrointestinal infection in 1528, measles from 1528 to 1533 and an epidemic in 1535–1538, bubonic plague in 1545–1548, typhus in 1549, mumps in 1550, influenza in 1559, unidentified epidemics from 1564 to 1570 and 1585, Cape Verde fever in 1586, measles in 1596, and Bubonic plague from 1613 to 1617. During that time, the population declined from 700,000 to 36,450. The remainder perished in the centuries that followed, marking the disappearance of all populations that inhabited Florida at the time of the first Spanish voyage.

Thus the occupation of the New World by Europeans was not so much an act of conquest as it was an act of replacing a population ravaged by pathogens that Europeans carried with them. Depopulation was not the only consequence of the economic expansion of Europe into the Americas. The deaths of indigenous peoples proved a boon to the slave trade, as Europeans transported millions of Africans to the plantations and mines to replace the dying indigenous laborers. Much of the remaining native population gathered around mining communities and Spanish agricultural estates, providing a surplus labor supply, producing cheap crafts and agricultural products, and paying tribute and taxes to the colonizers (Wolf 1982:149). Their descendants today still suffer economic and social discrimination at the hands of descendants of European and indigenous unions.

The environment did not escape the consequences of the expansion of trade in the sixteenth century. Columbus imported to the New World the livestock-raising *ranchero* system from Castile, complete with what was to become our own "cowboy" tradition—roundups, lassos, open ranges, branding, and cowboys on horseback. The stock depleted native grasses, compacted the tropical soil, and stripped the ground cover that had prevented soil erosion, implanting the system, said historian Kirkpatrick Sale, of a red meat-dependent society that ensured future environmental destruction (Sale 1991:164).

In 1776, Adam Smith, in *Wealth of Nations*, which was to become the bible of capitalism, wrote, "The discovery of America, and that of a passage to the East Indies by the Cape of Good Hope, are the two greatest and most important events recorded in the history of mankind" (cited Crosby 1986 vii).

A decade later there was a debate among the *savants* of France over whether the discovery of the New World was a blessing or a curse. Abbé Guillaume Reynal, author of a four-volume study of trade between Europe and the East and West Indies, wrote a paper to answer this question. In it he listed the gains that Europe had received and discussed the costs to the peoples of Asia and the Americas. He concluded:

> *Let us stop here, and consider ourselves as existing at the time when America and India were unknown. Let me suppose that I address myself to the most cruel of the Europeans in the following terms. There exist regions which will furnish you with rich metals, agreeable clothing, and delicious food. But read this history, and behold at what price the discovery is promised to you. Do you wish or not that it should be made? Is it to be imagined that there exists a being infernal enough to answer this question in the affirmative! Let it be remembered that there will not be a single instant in futurity when my question will not have the same force. (cited Sale 1991:366–367)*

The Rise of the Trading Companies

The expansion of trade into the Americas marked an important development in the control of global trade and commerce: states began to take a much more direct interest in commerce within their borders. For example, states controlled much of the trade with the Americas. Each year two fleets of the Spanish Crown would leave from Cadiz or Seville carrying European goods, one landing at Vera Cruz and the other, with goods bound for Peru, landing at Cartagena or Portobelo in Panama. From there mules carried the goods into the Andes, returning with silver and American goods for shipment home. The two fleets converged in Havana before returning to Spain (Wolf 1982:149).

The seventeenth century marked the era of what economists call *mercantilism*, as European states did all they could to protect, encourage, and expand industry and trade, not for its own sake but to prevent wealth, largely in the form of gold and silver, from leaving their countries. States enacted protective legislation to keep out foreign goods and to prevent gold and silver from leaving, and they subsidized the growth of selected industries by ensuring the existence of a cheap labor supply. Also during the seventeenth-century the so-called trading or joint stock company evolved, a joining of trade and armed force designed to ensure the continued extraction of wealth from areas around the world.

As a global merchant in 1700 your best chance of making profits would have been to join a trading company, by far the most sophisticated instrument of state-sponsored trade. The companies consisted of groups of traders, each of whom invested a certain amount of capital and were given charters by the state and presented with monopolistic trade privileges in a particular area of the world. Since other countries also gave monopolistic trading privileges to their companies, there was often armed conflict between them. For example, in 1600 the British crown

East India House, the corporate headquarters of the East India Company in Amsterdam, included offices, warehouses, and an arsenal for its fleet. Spices filled its cellars, and, in the rear, herds of cattle were slaughtered and the meat salted for ship provisions.

issued a royal charter to the Governor and the Company of Merchants of London trading with the East Indies, later known simply as the British East India Company. The company was formed to share in the East Indian spice trade but met with resistance from the Dutch, who in 1602 formed the Dutch East India Company to monopolize Asian trade.

The Dutch maintained political control over its posts in India with an army of ten to twelve thousand troops and a navy of forty to sixty ships. The company brought 10–12 million florins worth of goods to Europe each year, producing a profit of 25–30 percent (Braudel 1982). In 1623 the Dutch authorities in what is now Ambon, Indonesia, executed ten Englishmen, ten Japanese, and one Portuguese, believing that the English planned to attack the Dutch garrison when their ships arrived. In India, however, the British East India Company defeated Portuguese troops and gained trading concessions from the Mughal Empire. The British East India Company gradually extended its trade into Southeast Asia. In 1757 it defeated Indian troops and took control of all of Bengal, looting the Bengal treasury of some £5 million. Eventually its control expanded to most of India, and it became the managing agency for the British colonization of India.

Other trading companies granted charters by the British state include the Virginia Company in 1606, the English Amazon Company in 1619, the Massachusetts

Company in 1629, the Royal Adventurers into Africa in 1660, and the Hudson's Bay Company in 1670.

The Dutch were initially best able to exploit the new developments in trade, largely because of their large merchant fleet and the development of the *fluitschip*, a light and slender vessel that carried heavy cargoes. The availability of funds in financial centers such as Antwerp and Amsterdam, much of it originating in the gold and silver of the Americas, allowed builders to get the best woods and best craftsmen and employ foreign sailors. Gradually, however, England and its navy gained, and the English trading companies soon dominated world trade.

As a merchant adventurer in the first part of the eighteenth century you may have joined the Virginia Company and established a trading post, or "factory," in southern Appalachia, probably in a Cherokee village. The Cherokee were necessary to supply the commodities you would want to acquire for trade, items such as deerskins, ginseng and other herbs in demand in Europe as aphrodisiacs and cures for venereal disease, and war captives that you could sell as slaves. In exchange, you would supply the Cherokee with European goods such as guns, ammunition, iron utensils, and European clothing. Your normal business practice would be to advance these goods to the Cherokee, thus obligating them to repay you. But to succeed in making a profit, you would need the cooperation of the Cherokee. This is where the British government came in.

Prior to European contact the Cherokee lived in large towns in which land was owned communally, and subsistence activities consisted of hunting, fishing, gathering, and agriculture. The Cherokee population had been decimated by disease by the early eighteenth century, but they still retained most of their traditional culture. For example, Cherokee villages were relatively independent from each other, each having its own leaders and each relatively self-sufficient in food and production of necessities such as clothing, weapons, and cooking utensils. The independence of village leaders, however, made it difficult for the British government and traders to deal with the Cherokee. If there were overall leaders who could make agreements binding on large groups, with whom government and merchants could deal, it would be far easier to make treaties, collect trade debts, and engineer political alliances (Dunaway 1996:31). Consequently, using their military power and the threat of withdrawing trade, the British government appointed chiefs who they recognized as having the power to make agreements binding on the entire Cherokee nation whether or not their authority was recognized by other Cherokee. The British government also encouraged conflict between indigenous groups, reasoning, as the South Carolina governor reported in the 1730s, "...for in that consists our safety, being at War with one another prevents them from uniting against us"(Dunaway 1996:28).

Thus merchants, such as yourself, along with the Cherokee, became integrated into a global trade network in which slaves and deerskins were sent through Charleston, Virginia, to England, the northern colonies, and the West Indies. In return, Charleston received sugar and tobacco from the West Indies and rum from the northern colonies that was manufactured from molasses from the West Indies which the Northern colonies acquired in exchange for lumber and other provisions. In exchange for the deerskins sent to England, Charleston received goods manufactured in England, such as woolens, clothing, guns, and iron tools. The deerskins were converted in England into leather goods, which merchants in England traded for raw materials, luxury goods, and meat provisions from all over the world (Dunaway 1996:34).

For traders, these arrangements worked very well: by 1710 as many as 12,000 Indians had been exported as slaves and by 1730 some 255,000 deerskins were being shipped annually from British trading posts to England and other parts of the world (Dunaway 1996:32). Furthermore, with the help of the British military strength and diplomacy, traders were making a 500–600 percent profit on goods advanced to the Cherokee in exchange for deerskins, slaves, and herbs.

But what of the Cherokee? By becoming integrated into the global economy on terms dictated by British government officials and traders, the Cherokee economy was transformed from self-sufficient agricultural production to a "putting-out" system in which they were given the tools for production (e.g., guns) along with

In this early nineteenth-century engraving, rival fur trading companies are competing with each other to secure trade with indigenous peoples in Canada.

an advance of goods in exchange for their labor—an arrangement that destroyed traditional activities and stimulated debt peonage. To pay off debts accumulated to acquire European goods, communal Cherokee land was sold by chiefs appointed by the British: in little more than fifty years the British extinguished title to about 57 percent of the Cherokee traditional land (some 43.9 million acres).

In addition, the new economy brought profound changes in Cherokee social life. Trade was male-oriented, men being responsible for acquiring the items— slaves and deer—desired by the British. This removed men from traditional agricultural activities as well as incapacitating them with rum (Dunaway 1996:37). By the mid-1700s, British observers noted that "women alone do all the laborious tasks of agriculture," freeing men to hunt or go to war.

Furthermore, traditional crafts deteriorated with the increased consumption of European goods such as guns, axes, knives, beads, pottery, clothing and cooking utensils. By the mid-1700s the British could report that "the Indians by reason of our supplying them so cheap with every sort of goods, have forgotten the chief part of their ancient mechanical skill, so as not to be able now, at least for some years, to live independent from us" (Dunaway 1996:38). In 1751, the Cherokee chief Skiagonota would observe that "the clothes we wear we cannot make ourselves. They are made for us. We use their ammunition with which to kill deer. We cannot make our guns. Every necessity of life we have from the white people" (cited Dunaway 1996:39).

The Era of the Industrialist

By 1800, England had militarily, politically, and economically subdued her closest rivals of the early eighteenth century—France and Holland. British commerce thrived, fueled largely by the growth of industry, particularly textiles, and the related increase in the availability of cheap labor. And while the British lost her American colonies—politically if not economically—she gained in many ways a wealthier prize—India.

But the big news was the industrial development of England. From 1730 to 1760 iron production increased 50 percent; the first iron bridge was built in 1779 and the first iron boat in 1787. In 1783 Watt produced the double-effect steam engine. From 1740 to 1770 consumption of cotton rose 117 percent, and by 1800 mechanized factories were producing textiles at an unprecedented rate.

Social scientists often pose the related questions, *what made England take off?* and *why was there an industrial revolution at all?* These are more than academic questions. As planners in so-called economically undeveloped countries attempt to improve peoples' lives through economic development, they often look to the history of Great Britain to discover the key ingredients to economic success. England became, to a great extent, the model for economic development, the epitome of progress, so it was believed, particularly in Great Britain.

The reasons for the industrial revolution in England and the emergence of the capitalist economy are varied, and while analysts disagree on which were the most important, there is general agreement on those that played some part. They include the following (see Wallerstein 1989:22ff).

1. An increase in demand for goods. This demand may have been foreign or domestic, supplemented by increased demands for largely military products from the state. The textile industry was revolutionary also in its organization of labor and its relationship to the foreign market, on which it depended for both raw materials (in the case of cotton) and markets. Historian Eric Hobsbawm argued that there was room for only one world supplier, and that ended up being England.

2. The increase in the supply of capital. An increase in trade resulted in greater profits and more money, and these profits supplied the capital for investment in new technologies and businesses.

3. A growth in population. Population increased dramatically in England and Europe in the eighteenth century. From 1550 to 1680 the population of Western Europe grew by 18 percent and from 1680 to 1820 by 62 percent. From 1750 to 1850 England's population increased from 5.7 million to 16.5 million. Population increase was important because it increased the potential labor force and the number of potential consumers of commodities. But there is disagreement as to why population increased and the effects it had on industrialization.

Some account for the increase with lower mortality rates attributable to smallpox inoculation and an improved diet related to the introduction of new foodstuffs, such as the potato. Life expectancy at birth went from thirty-five to forty years (M. Guttmann 1988:130). Others attribute the rise in population to an increase in fertility. Indeed, families were larger in the eighteenth century. In England between 1680 and 1820 the gross reproduction rate (number of females born to each woman) went from two to nearly three and the average number of children per family from four to almost six. Later we will need to examine the relationship of population growth to industrialization because it is key to understanding the rapid growth of population today.

4. An expansion of agriculture. There was an expansion of agricultural production in England in the eighteenth century that some attribute to enclosure laws. These laws drove squatters and peasants from common lands and forests from which they had drawn a livelihood. The rationale was to turn those lands over to the gentry to make them more productive, but this also had the effect of producing a larger landless and propertyless population, dependent on whatever wage labor they might find. Regardless, some argue that the increased agricultural yields allowed the maintenance of a larger urban workforce.

5. A unique English culture or spirit. Some, notably sociologist Max Weber, attribute the rise of England to the development of an entrepreneurial spirit, such as the Protestant ethic, that motivated people to business success in the belief that it would reveal to them that they were among God's elect.

6. State support for trade. Some claim that a more liberal state structure imposed fewer taxes and regulations on businesses, thus allowing them to thrive. The state did take action to support trade and industry. There was continued political and military support for extending Britain's economy overseas, along with domestic legislation to protect merchants from labor protest. A law of 1769 made the destruction of machines and the buildings that housed them a capital crime. Troops were sent to put down labor riots in Lancaster in 1779 and in Yorkshire in 1796, and a law passed in 1799 outlawed worker associations that sought wage increases, reduction in the working day, "or any other improvement in the conditions of employment or work" (Beaud 1983:67).

7. The ascendence of the merchant class. Stephen Sanderson (1995) attributed the development of capitalism to an increase in the power of the merchant class. There has always been, he suggested, competition between merchants and the ruling elites, and while elites needed merchants to supply desired goods and services, they nevertheless looked down on them. But gradually the economic power of the merchant class grew until, in the seventeenth and eighteenth centuries, the merchant emerged as the most powerful member of Western, capitalist society. Capitalism, said Sanderson (1995:175–176), "was born of a class struggle. However, it was not, as the Marxists would have it, a struggle between landlords and peasants. Rather, it was a struggle between the landlord class and the merchants that was fundamental in the rise of capitalism."

8. A revolution in consumption. Finally, some attribute the rapid economic growth in England to a revolution in the patterns of retailing and consumption. There was a growth in the number of stores and shops and the beginning of a marketing revolution, led by the pottery industry and the entrepreneurial genius of Josiah Wedgewood, who named his pottery styles after members of the Royal Family to appeal to the fashion consciousness of the rising middle class.

Regardless of the reasons for England's rise and the so-called industrial revolution, there is little doubt that in addition to the traditional means of accumulating wealth—mercantile trade, extracting the surplus from peasant labor, pillage, forced labor, slavery, and taxes—a new form of capital formation increased in importance. It involved purchasing and combining the means of production and labor power to produce commodities, the form of wealth formation called capitalism that we diagramed earlier as follows: $M \rightarrow C \rightarrow \frac{mp}{lp} \rightarrow C' \rightarrow M'$ [Money is converted to commodities (capital goods) that are combined with the means of production and labor power to produce other commodities (consumer goods), that are then sold for a sum greater than the initial investment]. *How did this mode of production differ from what went before?*

Eric Wolf offered one of the more concise views. For capitalism to exist, he said, wealth or money must be able to purchase labor power. But as long as people have access to the means of production—land, raw materials, tools (e.g., weaving looms, mills)—there is no reason for them to sell their labor. They can still sell the product of their labor. For the capitalistic mode of production to exist, the tie between producers and the means of production must be cut; peasants must lose control of their land, artisans control of their tools. These people once denied access to the means of production must negotiate with those who control the means of production for permission to use the land and tools and receive a wage in return. Those who control the means of production also control the goods that are produced, and so those who labor to produce them must buy them back from those with the means of production. Thus the severing of persons from the means of production turns them not only into laborers, but into consumers of the product of their labor as well. Here is how Wolf (1982:78–79) summarized it:

> *Wealth in the hands of holders of wealth is not capital until it controls means of production, buys labor power, and puts it to work continuously expanding surpluses by intensifying production through an ever-rising curve of technological inputs. To this end capitalism must lay hold of production, must invade the productive process and ceaselessly alter the conditions of production themselves... Only where wealth has laid hold of the conditions of production in ways specified can we speak of the existence or dominance of a capitalistic mode. There is no such thing as mercantile of merchant capitalism, therefore. There is only mercantile wealth. Capitalism, to be capitalism, must be capitalism-in-production.*

Wolf (1982:100) added that the state is central in developing the capitalist mode of production because it must use its power to maintain and guarantee the ownership of the means of production by capitalists both at home and abroad and must support the organization and discipline of work. The state also has to provide the infrastructure, such as transportation, communication, judicial system, and education, required by capitalist production. Finally, the state must regulate conflicts between competing capitalists both at home and abroad, by diplomacy if possible, by war if necessary.

The major questions are *how did this industrially driven, capitalist mode of production evolve, and what consequences did it have in England, Europe, and the rest of the world?*

Textiles and the Rise of the Factory System

Assume once again your role as a textile merchant; let's examine the opportunities and problems confronting you as you conduct business. Typical textile merchants of the early eighteenth century purchased their wares from specialized weavers or part-time producers of cloth or from *drapers,* persons who organized the production of cloth but did not trade in it. The merchant then sold the cloth to a consumer or another merchant who sold it in other areas of Europe or elsewhere. The profit came from the difference between what the merchant paid the artisan or draper and what the customer paid. This is not a bad arrangement. It does not require a large capital outlay for the merchant, since the artisan has the tools and material he or she needs, and as long as there is a demand for the cloth there is someone who will buy it.

But as a merchant you face a couple of problems. First, the people who make the cloth you buy may not produce the quantity or quality that you need, especially as an expanding population begins to require more textiles. Moreover, the artisan may have trouble acquiring raw materials, such as wool or cotton, further disrupting the supply. What can you do?

One thing to do is to increase control over what is produced by "putting out"—supplying the drapers or weavers with the raw materials to produce the cloth—or, if you have the capital, buy tools—looms, spinning wheels, and so on—and give them to people to make the cloth, paying them for what they produce. Cottage industry of this sort was widespread throughout Europe as merchants began to take advantage of the cheaper labor in rural areas, rather than purchasing products from artisans in towns and cities. In England of the mid-eighteenth century there was probably plenty of labor, especially in rural areas, supplied by people who had been put off their land by enclosure legislation or because of failure to pay taxes or repay loans. In the land market of the eighteenth century, there were far more sellers than buyers (M. Guttmann 1988).

Another problem English textile merchants faced in the mid-eighteenth century was that the textile business, especially in cotton, faced stiff competition from India, whose calico cloth was extremely popular in England. *How do you meet this competition?* The first thing England did was to ban the import of Indian cloth and develop its own cotton industry to satisfy domestic demand. This not only helped protect the British textile industry, it virtually destroyed the Indian cotton industry, and before long India was buying British cotton textiles. The result was summed up in 1830 in testimony before the House of Commons by Charles Marjoribanks (cited Wallerstein 1989:150):

> *We have excluded the manufactures of India from England by high prohibitive duties and given every encouragement to the introduction of our own manufactures to India. By our selfish (I use the word invidiously) policy we have beat down the native manufactures of Dacca and other places and inundated their country with our goods.*

And in 1840, the chairman of Britain's East India and China association boasted that

> *[t]his Company has, in various ways, encouraged and assisted by our great manufacturing ingenuity and skill, succeeded in converting India from a manufacturing country into a country exporting raw materials (cited Wallerstein 1989:150).*

The next, and to some extent inevitable, stage in textile production was to bring together in one place as many of the production phases of textiles as possible: preparing the raw wool or cotton, spinning the cotton yarn and wool, weaving the cloth, and applying the finishing touches. This allowed the merchant or industrialist to control the quantity and quality of the product and control the use of materials and tools. The only drawback to the factory system is that it is capital-intensive; the merchant was now responsible for financing the entire process, while the workers supplied only their labor. Most of the increase in cost was a consequence of increased mechanization.

Power loom weaving in a cotton textile factory in 1834. Note that virtually all the workers are women.

Mechanization of the textile industry began with the invention by John Kay in 1733 of the flying shuttle, a device that allowed the weaver to strike the shuttle carrying the thread from one side of the loom to the other, rather than weaving it through by hand. This greatly speeded up the weaving process. However, when demand for textiles, particularly cotton, increased, the spinning of thread, still done on spinning wheels or spindles, could not keep up with weavers, and bottlenecks developed in production. To meet this need James Hargreaves introduced the spinning jenny in 1770. Later, Arkwright introduced the water frame, and in 1779 Crompton introduced his "mule" that allowed a single operator to work more than 1,000 spindles at once. In 1790 steam power was supplied. These technological developments increased textiles production enormously: the mechanical advantage of the earliest spinning jennies to hand spinning was twenty-four to one. The spinning wheel had become an antique in a decade (Landes 1969:85). The increase in the supply of yarn—twelve times as much cotton was consumed in 1800 than in 1770—required improvements in weaving, which then required more yarn, and so on.

But the revolution in production produced other problems. *Who was going to buy all the goods that were being produced, and where was the raw material for production to come from?*

The Age of Imperialism

The results of the industrial revolution in Europe were impressive. The period from 1800 to 1900 was perhaps one of the most dynamic in human history and, certainly until that time, the most favorable for accumulation of vast fortunes through trade and manufacture. Developments in transportation such as railroads and steamships revolutionized the transport of raw materials and finished commodities. The combination of new sources of power in water and steam, a disarmed and plentiful labor force, and control of the production and markets of much of the rest of the world resulted in dramatic increases in the level of production and wealth. These advances were most dramatic in England and later in the United States, France, and Germany. In England, for example, spun cotton increased from 250 million pounds in 1830 to 1,101 million pounds in 1870; coal production increased from 10 million tons in 1800 to 110 million tons in 1870. World steam power production went from 4 million horsepower in 1850 to 18.5 million horsepower twenty years later; coal production went from 15 million tons in 1800 to 132 million tons in 1860, and 701 million tons in 1900. The consumption of inanimate energy from coal, lignite, petroleum, natural gasoline, natural gas, and water power increased sixfold from 1860 to 1900; railway trackage went from 332 kilometers in 1831 to 300,000 kilometers in 1876. The Krupp iron works in Germany employed 72 workers in 1848; there were 12,000 by 1873.

There was also a revolution in shipping as ocean freight costs fell, first with the advent of the narrow-beamed American clipper ship and later with the introduction of the steamship. A clipper ship could carry 1,000 tons of freight and make the journey from the south coast of China to London in 120–130 days; in 1865 a steamship from the Blue Funnel Line with a capacity of 3,000 tons made the journey in 77 days. The construction of the Suez Canal, completed in 1869 with the labor of 20,000 conscripted Egyptian *fellaheen,* or peasants, cut the travel time from England to eastern Asia in half—although it bankrupted the Egyptian treasury and put the country under Anglo-French receivership. These events initiated a military revolt that the British stepped in to put down, consequently cementing the British hold on Egypt and much of the Middle East. Politically, the United States emerged as a world power, and Japan was building its economy and would be ready to challenge Russia. The Ottoman Empire was on its way to disintegrating as France, England, and Russia sought to gain control over the remnants.

But it was not all good news for the capitalist economy. There was organized worker resistance to low wages and impoverished conditions, resistance and rebellion in the periphery, and the development of capitalist business cycles that led to worldwide economic depressions. Thus while business thrived in much of the nineteenth century, it had also entered a world of great uncertainty. First, with the expansion of the scope of production, capital investments had increased enormously. It was no longer possible, as it had been in 1800 when a forty-spindle jenny cost £6, to invest in the factory production of textiles at fairly modest levels. Furthermore, there was increased competition, with factory production expanding dramatically in Holland, France, Germany, and the United States. There was the constant problem of overproduction, when supply outstripped demand and resulted in idle factories and unemployed workers. Unlike agricultural production—there seemed always to be a market for food—industrial production depends on the revolution in demand or, as Anne-Robert-Jacque Turgot put it, "a transformation of desires" (cited in Braudel 1982:183). Until the eighteenth century manufacturers launched their enterprises only when profit was guaranteed by subsidies, interest-free loans, and previously guaranteed monopolies. Now manufacturers just had to hope people would buy their products.

The Great Global Depression of 1873 that lasted essentially until 1895 was the first great manifestation of the capitalist business crisis. The depression was not the first economic crisis: For thousands of years there had been economic declines because of famine, war, and disease. But the financial collapse of 1873 revealed the degree of global economic integration, and how economic events in one part of the globe could reverberate in others. The economic depression began when banks failed in Germany and Austria because of the collapse of real estate speculation. At the same time, the price of cast iron in England fell by 27 percent because of a drop in demand. The drop in iron prices increased British unemployment, while European investors, needing to cover their losses from real estate, withdrew their money from American banks. This led to bank collapses in the United States. In England from 1872 to 1875, exports fell by 25 percent, the number of bankruptcies increased, and rail prices fell by 60 percent. In France, the Lyon stock market crashed in 1882; bank failures and rising unemployment followed. Competition among railroads decreased profits and led to the collapse of railroad securities in the United States (Beaud 1983:119–120; see also R. Guttmann 1994).

The Depression of 1873 revealed another big problem with capitalist expansion and perpetual growth: it can continue only as long as there is a ready supply of raw materials and an increasing demand for goods, along with ways to invest profits and capital. Given this situation, *if you were an American or European investor in 1873, where would you look for economic expansion?*

The obvious answer was to expand European and American power overseas, particularly into areas that remained relatively untouched by capitalist expansion—Africa, Asia, and the Pacific. Colonialism had become, in fact, a recognized solution to the need to expand markets, increase opportunities for investors, and ensure the supply of raw material. Cecil Rhodes, one of the great figures of England's colonization of Africa, recognized also the importance of overseas expansion for maintaining peace at home. In 1895 Rhodes said:

> *I was in the East End of London yesterday and attended a meeting of the unemployed. I listened to the wild speeches, which were just a cry for "bread," "bread," and on my way home I pondered over the scene and I became more than ever convinced of the importance of imperialism.... My cherished idea is a solution for the social problem, i.e., in order to save the 40,000,000 inhabitants of the United Kingdom from a bloody civil war, we colonial statesmen must acquire new lands for settling the surplus population, to provide new markets for the goods produced in the factories and mines. The Empire, as I have always said, is a bread and butter*

question. If you want to avoid civil war, you must become imperialists. (cited Beaud 1983:139–140)

P. Leroy-Beaulieu voiced the same sentiments in France when, to justify the conquest of foreign nations, he said:

It is neither natural nor just that the civilized people of the West should be indefinitely crowded together and stifled in the restricted spaces that were their first homes, that they should accumulate there the wonders of science, art, and civilization, that they should see, for lack of profitable jobs, the interest rate of capital fall further every day for them, and that they should leave perhaps half the world to small groups of ignorant men, who are powerless, who are truly retarded children dispersed over boundless territories, or else to decrepit populations without energy and without direction, truly old men incapable of any effort, of any organized and far-seeing action. (cited Beaud 1983: 140)

As a result of this cry for imperialist expansion, people all over the world were converted into producers of export crops as millions of subsistence farmers were forced to become wage laborers producing for the market and required to purchase from European and American merchants and industrialists, rather than supply for themselves, their basic needs. Nineteenth century British economist William Stanley Jevons (cited Kennedy 1993:9) summed up the situation when he boasted:

The plains of North America and Russia are our cornfields; Chicago and Odessa our granaries; Canada and the Baltic are our timber forests; Australasia contains our sheep farms, and in Argentina and on the western prairies of North America are our herds of oxen; Peru sends her silver, and the gold of South Africa and Australia flows to London; the Hindus and the Chinese grow tea for us, and our coffee, sugar, and spice plantations are all in the Indies. Spain and France are our vineyards and the Mediterranean our fruit garden, and our cotton grounds, which for long have occupied the Southern United States are now being extended everywhere in the warm regions of the earth.

Wheat became the great export crop of Russia, Argentina, and the United States, much of it produced in the United States on lands taken from the Native Americans. Rice became the great export of Southeast Asia, spurred by Great Britain's seizure of lower Burma in 1855 and its increase in rice production from one million to nine million acres. Argentina and Australia joined the United States as the major supplier of meat as cattle ranchers in Australia and the United States turned indigenous peoples into hired hands or hunted them to extermination, as did the ranchers in California into the late nineteenth century (see Meggitt 1962).

In 1871 a railroad promoter from the United States built a railroad in Costa Rica and experimented in banana production; out of this emerged in 1889 the

United Fruit Company that within thirty-five years was producing two billion bunches of bananas. The company reduced its risk by expanding into different countries and different environments and by acquiring far more land than it could use at any one time as a reserve against the future.

The demand for rubber that followed the discovery of vulcanization in 1839 led to foreign investments in areas such as Brazil, where one major supplier increased production from 27 tons in 1827 to an average of 20,000 tons per year at the end of the nineteenth century. The laborers who collected the rubber were workers who had lost their jobs with the decline in the sugar industries and Indians, who were sometimes held captive or tortured or killed if they didn't collect their quota of rubber, or whose wives and children would be killed if they didn't return (Taussig 1987).

In the nineteenth century palm oil became a substitute for tallow for making soap and a lubricant for machinery, resulting in European military expansion into West Africa and the conquest of the kingdoms of Asante, Dahomey, Oyo, and Benin.

Vast territories were turned over to the production of stimulants and drugs such as sugar, tea, coffee, tobacco, opium, and cocoa. In the Mexican state of Chiapas and in Guatemala legislation abolished communal ownership of land. Land could now be privately owned and subject to purchase, sale, and pawning, allowing non-Indians to buy unregistered land and foreclose mortgages on Indian borrowers (Wolf 1982:337). These lands were then turned to coffee production and, later, cattle ranching. In Ceylon, common land was turned into royal land and sold to tea planters. In 1866 diamonds and gold were discovered in the Orange Free State of West Africa. By 1874, 10,000 Africans were working in the European-owned diamond mines and by 1884 almost 100,000 were working in the gold mines. By 1910, 255,000 were working the mines, and by 1940 there were 444,000.

Colonization was not restricted to overseas areas; it occurred also within the borders of core states. In 1887 the U.S. Congress passed the General Allotment Act (the "Dawes Act") to break up the collective ownership of land on Indian reservations by assigning each family its own parcel, then opening unallotted land to non-Indian homesteaders, corporations, and the federal government. As a consequence, from 1887 to 1934 some 100 million acres of land assigned by treaty to Indian groups was appropriated by private interests or the government (Jaimes 1992:126).

At first glance it may seem that the growth in development of export goods such as coffee, cotton, sugar, and lumber, would be beneficial to the exporting country, since it brings in revenue. In fact, it represents a type of exploitation called *unequal exchange.* A country that exports raw or unprocessed materials may gain currency for their sale, but they then lose it if they import processed goods. The reason is that processed goods—goods that require additional labor—are more costly. Thus a country that exports lumber but does not have the capacity to process it must then re-import it in the form of finished lumber products, at a cost that is greater than the price it received for the raw product. The country that processes the materials gets the added revenue contributed by its laborers.

Then there is the story of tea and opium and trade in China. China, of course, was a huge prize, but the British and Western European nations had a problem with trade into China: Chinese products, notably tea, were in high demand, but there was little produced in England or the rest of Europe that the Chinese wanted or needed. However, there was a market in China for opium, virtually all of which was produced and controlled by the British East India Company. Opium was illegal in China, but the government seemed incapable of stopping the smuggling that was hugely profitable for British, American, and French merchants. When in 1839 the Chinese government tried to enforce laws against opium sales by seizing opium held by British merchants in warehouses in Canton, the British government sent in troops and effectively forced the Chinese government to stop enforcing opium laws. An analogy today might be the Colombian government sending troops to the United States to force acceptance of Colombian cocaine shipments. Moreover, using its military superiority, the British demanded and received additional trading rights into China, opening a market not only for opium but for British textiles as well.

The British-led opium trade from India to China had three consequences. First, it reversed the flow of money between China and the rest of the world; during the first decade of the nineteenth century, China still took in a surplus of $26 million dollars; by the third decade $34 million dollars left China to pay for opium. Second, it is estimated that by the end of the nineteenth century one out of every ten Chinese had become an opium addict. Finally, cotton exports to India and China had increased from 6 percent of total British exports in 1815 to 22 percent in 1840, 31 percent in 1850, and more than 50 percent after 1873 (Wolf 1982:255ff).

Thus as a merchant adventurer your economic fortune has been assured by your government's control over foreign economies. Not only could you make more money investing in foreign enterprises, but the wealth you accumulated through trade and manufacturing gained you entry into a new elite, one with increasing power in the core countries. Power was no longer evidenced solely in the ownership of land, but in the control of capital. In England, for example, the great families of high finance and international trade, businessmen, manufacturers, ship owners, bankers, parliamentarians, jurists, families of the aristocracy and gentry, all criss-crossed by ties of marriage and kinship, became the new ruling class. This new elite depended for their economic power on business and industry to a great extent: in the eighteenth century landed inheritance accounted for 63.7 percent of national wealth in Great Britain; toward the end of the nineteenth century that figure had decreased to 23.3 percent. Meanwhile, during the same period, wealth linked to capitalist development increased from 20.8 percent to almost 50.0 percent (Beaud 1983:93).

In the United States a new capitalist elite emerged during and after the Civil War, as people such as J. P. Morgan, Jay Gould, Jim Fisk, Cornelius Vanderbilt, and John D. Rockefeller—most of whom made their fortunes in dealings with the U.S. government—emerged as a new bourgeoisie. More important, they were the driving force behind the emergence of a relatively new form of capital organization—the multinational corporation.

The Era of the Corporation, the Multilateral Institution, and the Capital Controller

While the imperialist activities of the core powers allowed their economies to grow, they also created international conflict on a scale never before imagined. In 1900, each of the great powers sought to carve out a sphere of domination in Asia, Africa, and South and Central America that with the help of nationalism, racism, and xenophobia turned economic competition into political and military conflict. These conflicts fed on myths of national or racial superiority—British, French, American, White, and so on—and the supposed civilizing mission of the West (Beaud 1983:144). At the Berlin Conference of 1885, great European powers met to carve up zones of influence and domination in Africa, laying the groundwork for levels of colonialization from which Africa still has not recovered.

Attempts to extend or defend these zones of economic influence triggered what was until then the bloodiest war ever fought—World War I. Eight million people were killed. Britain lost 32 percent of its national wealth, France 30 percent, Germany 20 percent, and the United States 9 percent. Germany was forced to pay $33 billion in reparations. Industrial production fell in all countries except the United States. Then the Russian Revolution cut off huge markets for European and American products, while colonized countries demanded independence.

The United States emerged from World War I as the world's leading economic power: its national income doubled and coal, oil, and steel production soared. However, workers' real wages and the power of labor unions declined; new forms of factory organization led to greater fatigue—there were 20,000 fatal industrial accidents per year in the 1920s; and the courts blocked the formation of new unions and the application of social laws such as those prohibiting child labor. It was an era of the rise of a new, great economic power—the corporation.

The Rise of the Corporation

From your perspective as a merchant adventurer, the most important development of the early twentieth century was the merger frenzy in the United States that led to the concentration of wealth in fewer hands. Companies such as Ford, General Motors, and Chrysler in automobiles, General Electric and Westinghouse in electric, Dupont in chemicals, and Standard Oil in petroleum dominated the market. In 1929, the two hundred largest companies owned half of the country's non-banking wealth. Since then, of course, corporations have become one of the dominant governance units in the world. By 1992 there were 37,000 transnational corporations controlling one-third of the world's private wealth. From their foreign operations alone they generated about $5.5 trillion in sales. The largest corporations exceed in size, power, and wealth most of the world's nation-states and, directly or indirectly, define policy agendas of states and international bodies (Korten 1995:54). Since, as a merchant adventurer, you have now entered the corporate age, *what kind of institution is the corporation and how did it come to accumulate so much wealth and power?*

Technically a corporation is a social invention of the state; the corporate charter, granted by the state, ideally permits private financial resources to be used for a public purpose. At another level, it allows one or more individuals to apply massive economic and political power to accumulate private wealth while protected from legal liability for the public consequences. As a merchant adventurer, clearly you want to create an institution in which you can increase and protect your own profits from market uncertainties (Korten 1995:53–54).

The corporate charter goes back to the sixteenth century, when any debts accumulated by an individual were inherited by his or her descendants. Consequently, someone could be jailed for the debts of a father, mother, brother, or sister. If you, in your role as merchant adventurer, invested in a trading voyage and the goods were lost at sea, you and your descendants were responsible for the losses incurred. The law, as written, inhibited risky investments. The corporate charter solved this problem because it represented a grant from the crown that limited an investor's liability for losses to the amount of the investment, a right not accorded to individual citizens.

The early trading companies, such as the East India Company and the Hudson's Bay Company, were such corporations, and some of the American colonies themselves were founded as corporations—groups of investors granted monopoly powers over territory and industries. Consequently corporations gained enormous power and were able to influence trade policy. For example, in the eighteenth century the English parliament, composed of wealthy landowners, merchants, and manufacturers, passed laws requiring all goods sold in or from the colonies to go through England and be shipped on English ships with British crews. Furthermore, colonists were forbidden to produce their own caps, hats, and woolen or iron goods.

But suspicion of the power of corporations developed soon after their establishment. Even eighteenth century philosopher and economist Adam Smith, in *Wealth of Nations,* condemned corporations. He claimed corporations operated to evade the laws of the market by artificially inflating prices and controlling trade. American colonists shared Smith's suspicion of corporations and limited corporate charters to a specific number of years. If the charter was not renewed, the corporation was dissolved. But gradually American courts began to remove restrictions on corporations' operation. The U.S. Civil War was a turning point: corporations used their huge profits from the war, along with the subsequent political confusion and corruption, to buy legislation that gave them huge grants of land and money, much of which they used to build railroads. Abraham Lincoln (cited Korten 1995:58) saw what was happening, and just before his death observed:

> *Corporations have been enthroned.... An era of corruption in high places will follow and the money power will endeavor to prolong its reign by working on the prejudices of the people...until wealth is aggregated in a few hands...and the Republic is destroyed.*

Gradually corporations gained control of state legislatures, such as those in Delaware and New Jersey, lobbying for (and buying) legislation that granted char-

Painter Diego Rivera's depiction of the symbols of corporate wealth, as John D. Rockefeller (rear left), J. P. Morgan (rear right), Henry Ford (to Morgan's left), and others read a ticker tape while dining.

ters in perpetuity, limited the liabilities of corporate owners and managers, and gained the right of corporations to operate in any way not specifically prohibited by the law. For example, courts limited corporate liability for accidents to workers, an important development in the nineteenth century when fatal industrial accidents from 1888 to 1908 killed 700,000 workers, or roughly one hundred per day. Other favorable court rulings and legislation prohibited the state from setting minimum wage laws, limiting the number of hours a person could work, or setting minimum age requirements for workers.

But it was a Supreme Court ruling in 1886 that arguably set the stage for the full-scale development of the culture of capitalism, by handing to corporations the right to use their economic power in a way they never before had. Relying on the Fourteenth Amendment, added to the Constitution in 1868 to protect the rights of freed slaves, the Court ruled that a private corporation is a *natural person* under the U.S. Constitution, and consequently has the same rights and protection extended to persons by the Bill of Rights, including the right of free speech. Thus corporations were given the same "rights" to influence the government in their own interest as were extended to individual citizens, paving the way for corporations to use their wealth to dominate public thought and discourse. The debates in the United States in the 1990s over campaign finance reform, in which corporate bodies can "donate" millions of dollars to political candidates, stem from this ruling, although rarely if ever is that mentioned. Thus corporations, as "persons," were free to lobby legislatures, use the mass media, establish educational institutions such as the many business schools founded by corporate leaders in the early twentieth century, found charitable organizations to convince the public of their lofty intent, and in general construct an image that they believed would be in their best interests. All of this in the interest of "free speech."

Corporations used this power, of course, to create conditions in which they could make more money. But in a larger sense they used this power to define the ideology or ethos of the emerging culture of capitalism. This cultural and economic ideology is known as *neoclassical, neoliberal,* or *libertarian economics, market capitalism,* or *market liberalism* and is advocated in society primarily by three groups of spokespersons: economic rationalists, market liberals, and members of the corporate class. Their advocacy of these principles created what David Korten called *corporate libertarianism,* which places the rights and freedoms of corporations above the rights and freedoms of individuals—the corporation comes to exist as a separate entity with its own internal logic and rules. Some of the principles and assumptions of this ideology include the following.

1. Sustained *economic growth,* as measured by gross national product (GNP), is the path to human progress.
2. *Free markets,* unrestrained by government, generally result in the most efficient and socially optimal allocation of resources.
3. *Economic globalization,* achieved by removing barriers to the free flow of goods and money anywhere in the world, spurs competition, increases economic efficiency, creates jobs, lowers consumer prices, increases consumer choice, increases economic growth, and is generally beneficial to almost everyone.
4. *Privatization,* which moves functions and assets from governments to the private sector, improves efficiency.
5. The primary responsibility of government is to provide the infrastructure necessary to advance commerce and enforce the rule of law with respect to *property rights and contracts.*

However, hidden in these principles, said Korten, are a number of questionable assumptions. First, there is the assumption that humans are motivated by self-interest, which is expressed primarily through the quest for financial gain (or, people are by nature motivated primarily by greed). Second, there is the assumption that the action that yields the greatest financial return to the individual or firm is the one that is most beneficial to society (or, the drive to acquire is the highest expression of what it means to be human). Third, is the assumption that competitive behavior is more rational for the individual and the firm than cooperative behavior; consequently, societies should be built around the competitive motive (or, the relentless pursuit of greed and acquisition leads to socially optimal outcomes). Finally, there is the assumption that human progress is best measured by increases in the value of what the members of society consume, and ever-higher levels of consumer spending advance the well-being of society by stimulating greater economic output (or, it is in the best interest of human societies to encourage, honor, and reward the above values).

While corporate libertarianism has its detractors, from the standpoint of overall economic growth few can argue with its success on a global scale. World economic output has increased from $3.8 trillion in 1950 to $18.9 trillion in 1992 (constant 1987 dollars); economic growth in *each decade* of the last half of the twentieth century was greater than the economic output in all of human history up to 1950. World trade has increased from total exports of $308 billion in 1950 to $3,554 billion (1990 dollars) (Korten 1995:18).

However, there were still some problems for the merchant adventurer in the early twentieth century. As corporations rose to power in the 1920s and 1930s, political and business leaders were aware that corporations, by themselves, could not ensure the smooth running of the global economy. The worldwide economic depression of the 1930s and the economic disruptions caused by World War II illustrated that. That every country had its own currency and that it could rapidly rise or fall in value relative to others created barriers to trade. Tariffs and import or export laws inhibited the free flow of goods and capital. More important, there was the problem of bringing the ideology of corporate libertarianism, and the culture of capitalism in general, to the periphery, especially given the challenge of socialism and the increasing demands of colonized countries for independence. The solution to these problems was to emerge from a meeting in 1944 at a New Hampshire resort hotel.

Bretton Woods and the World Debt

In 1944 President Franklin D. Roosevelt gathered the government financial leaders of forty-four nations to a meeting at the Mt. Washington Hotel in Bretton Woods, New Hampshire. From your perspective as a merchant adventurer it was to be one of the most far-reaching events of the twentieth century. The meeting was called ostensibly to rebuild war-ravaged economies and to outline a global economic agenda for the last half of the twentieth century. Out of that meeting came the plan for the International Bank for Reconstruction and Development (The World Bank), the International Monetary Fund (IMF) to control currency exchange, and the framework for a worldwide trade organization that would lead to the establishment in 1948 of the General Agreement on Tariffs and Trade (GATT) to regulate trade between member countries. While GATT was not as comprehensive an agreement as many traders would have liked, its scope was widely enlarged on January 1, 1995, with the establishment of the World Trade Organization (WTO). The functions of these agencies are summarized in Table 3.1.

The IMF constituted an agreement by the major nations to allow their currency to be exchanged for other currencies with a minimum of restriction, to inform representatives of the IMF of changes in monetary and financial policies, and to adjust these policies to accommodate to other member nations when possible. The IMF also has funds that it can lend to member nations if they face a debt crisis. For example, if a member country finds it is importing goods at a much higher rate than it is exporting them, and if it doesn't have the money to make up the difference, the IMF will arrange a short-term loan (Driscoll 1992:5).

The World Bank was created to finance the reconstruction of Europe after the devastation of World War II, but the only European country to receive a loan was Holland, then engaged in trying to put down a rebellion of its Southeast Asian colonies. The World Bank then began to focus its attention on the periphery, lending funds to countries to foster economic development, with, as we shall see, mixed results.

The GATT has served as a forum for participating countries to negotiate trade policy. The goal was to establish a multilateral agency with the power to regulate and promote free trade among nations. However, since legislators and government officials in many countries, particularly the United States, objected to the idea of an international trade agency with the power to dictate government trade policy, the creation of such an agency did not occur until the WTO was finally established on January 1, 1995. In essence, the agency can react to claims by member nations that other nations are using unfair trade policies in order to give businesses in their country an unfair advantage (see Low 1993:42). There are also ongoing negotiations among the twenty-seven largest industrialized countries to formulate a Multilateral Investment Agreement (MIA) that would grant transnational investors the

TABLE 3.1   The Bretton Woods Institutions

Institution or Agency	Function
International Monetary Fund **(IMF)**	To make funds available for countries to meet short-term financial needs and to stabilize currency exchanges between countries
International Bank for Reconstruction and Development **(World Bank)**	To make loans for various development projects
General Agreement on Tariffs and Trade **(GATT)**	To ensure the free trade of commodities among countries

unrestricted right to invest their assets and buy, sell, and move businesses wherever and whenever they like.

The year 1994 marked the fiftieth anniversary of the Bretton Woods institutions, prompting a worldwide review of their successes and failures. Generally the reviews were not favorable, and even the World Bank's own evaluations were highly critical of its performance. In spite of lending some quarter of a trillion dollars to peripheral countries, one billion people in the world are desperately poor; furthermore, the disparity of wealth in the world between the core and periphery has doubled in the last thirty years. The richest 20 percent of the world's people now consume 150 times more of the world's goods than the poorest 20 percent (United Nations 1993:11).

One of the most profound consequences of the Bretton Woods meeting is the accumulation of the debt of peripheral countries; some consider this "debt crisis" the gravest one facing the world. The reasons for the debt crisis, and the possible impact it can have on everyone's lives, is complex but essential to understand. Overwhelming debt of peripheral countries is one of the major factors in many global problems that we will explore, including poverty, hunger, environmental devastation, the spread of disease, and political unrest.

Three things were particularly important in creating the debt crisis: the change over the last third of this century in the meaning of money; the amount of money lent by the World Bank to peripheral countries; and the oil boom of the early 1970s and the pressure for financial institutions to invest that money.

Money, as noted in Chapter 1, constitutes the focal point of capitalism. It is through money that we assign value to objects, behaviors, and even people. The fact that one item can, in various quantities, represent virtually any item or service, from a soft drink to an entire forest, is one of the most remarkable features of our lives. But it is not without its problems. The facts that different countries have different currencies and that currencies can rise or fall in value relative to the goods they can purchase has always been a barrier to unrestricted foreign trade and global economic integration. Furthermore, there have always been disputes concerning how to measure the value of money itself. Historically money has been tied to a specific valuable metal, generally gold. Thus money in any country could always be redeemed for a certain amount of gold, although the amount could vary according to the value of a specific country's currency.

While the meeting at Bretton Woods would not lead to the establishment of a global currency, the countries did agree to exchange their currency for U.S. dollars at a fixed rate, while the United States guaranteed that it would exchange money for gold stored at Fort Knox at thirty-five dollars per ounce. But in the 1960s, during the Vietnam War and the increase in U.S. government spending on health, education, and welfare programs, the United States was creating dollars far in excess of its gold supply, while at the same time guaranteeing all the rest of the money in the world. As a result, in 1971 the United States declared it would no longer redeem dollars on demand for gold. This totally divorced the American dollar and, effectively, all the other currencies in the world, from anything of value other than the expectation that people would accept dollars for things of value. Money became simply unsecured credit (see R. Guttmann 1994).

But since countries no longer needed to have a certain amount of gold in order to print money, money became more plentiful; the increase in the amount of money in circulation also meant there was more to lend, and this led banks and other lending institutions to lower their interest rates to attract borrowers. This proved to be a boon, not only for individual borrowers but also for peripheral countries seeking to develop their economies. The problems were that the interest on most loans was adjustable (could go up or down depending on economic circumstances) and that debts began to accumulate beyond what countries could repay.

The second factor that led to the debt crisis was the operation of the World Bank. The Bank itself had a problem. European countries, whose economies it was to help rebuild, didn't need the help. *With a lack of demand for their services, what could they do? How could the institution survive?* The Bank's solution was to lend money to peripheral countries to develop their economies. The plan was to help them industrialize by funding things such as large-scale hydroelectric projects, roads, and industrial parks. Furthermore, the bigger the project, the more the Bank could lend; thus in the 1950s and 1960s money suddenly poured into India, Mexico, Brazil, and Indonesia, the Bank's four largest borrowers. From 1950 to 1970, the Bank lent some $953 million. We should not overlook the fact that these loans also benefited wealthy core countries, who largely supplied the construction companies, engineers, equipment, and advisors needed to develop these projects.

But the success of the Bank in lending money created another problem—what economists call *net negative transfers;* borrowing nations collectively were soon paying more money into the Bank than the Bank was lending out. Put another way, the poor or peripheral nations were paying more money to the rich core nations than they were receiving from them. Aside from the consequences for poor countries, this would lead ultimately to the bank going out of business—its only purpose would be to collect the money it had already lent out. This is not a problem for regular banks because they can always recruit new customers, but the World Bank has a limited number of clients to which to lend money. Now what do you do? The Bank's solution was to lend still more. Robert McNamara, past chief of the Ford Motor Company and Secretary of Defense during the John F. Kennedy and Lyndon B. Johnson administrations, more than any one person, made the World Bank into what it is today. During his tenure from 1968 to 1981, the Bank increased lending from $953 million to $12.4 billion and increased staff from 1,574 to 5,201. The result was to leave many peripheral countries with a staggering debt burden. But there were other problems as well.

The third source of the debt crisis was the oil boom of the early 1970s. Oil producers were making huge profits ("petrodollars"). The problem was that this money needed to be invested, particularly by the banks into which it went and from which depositors expected interest payments. But banks and other investment agents had a problem finding investments. One of their solutions was to lend even more money to peripheral countries. The source of the debt crisis is illustrated in Figure 3.2.

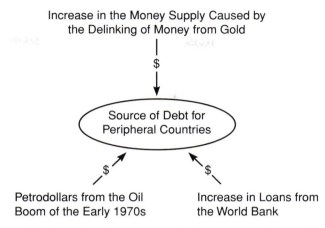

FIGURE 3.2   The Source of the Global Debt Crisis

Thus, by the late 1970s peripheral countries had borrowed huge sums of money and, with this infusion, were doing generally well. But then financial policies in the wealthy countries precipitated an economic collapse. With their own economies in recession because of the increase in oil prices in the 1970s, core governments reacted by raising interest rates. Countries such as Brazil, Mexico, and Indonesia that had borrowed large sums of money at adjustable, rather than fixed, interest rates suddenly found that they could no longer pay back what they owed. Many couldn't even pay back the interest on the loans. Furthermore, an economic recession in the core nations decreased the demand for whatever commodities peripheral countries had for sale, further undermining their economies.

This all sounds largely like an economic problem that would have little effect on people such as you or me, or on a peasant farmer in Mexico, craftsperson in Africa, or small merchant in Indonesia. But, in fact, it has had an enormous impact, and it illustrates how global problems are tied closely to today's merchant adventurers. It is estimated that the amount of money owed by peripheral countries increased from $100 billion in 1971 to $600 billion by 1981 (Caufield 1996:134). And the problem hasn't improved: the total owed by countries in the periphery increased in 1994 to well over $2 trillion (see World Development Report 1996:222). Table 3.2 on page 106 shows the increases in external debt for a few selected countries, along with the percentage of their yearly GNP (total of goods and services produced) that the debt represents. For example, Rwanda in 1980 owed $190 million, representing 16.3 percent of its GNP; by 1994 it owed $954 million, or 164.8 percent of its GNP. India in 1980 had an external debt of $20,582 million, or 11.9 percent of its GNP; by 1994 it owed $98,990 million, or 34.2 percent of its annual GNP.

This debt has not only created problems for the debtor countries; it has created a major problem for lending institutions and investors. There is an old joke that says that when an individual can't pay his or her bank debts, he or she is in trouble,

TABLE 3.2   **External Debt of Selected Countries, 1980 and 1994**

Country	Total External Debt (millions $)		External Debt as % of GNP	
	1980	1994	1980	1994
Bangladesh	4,327	16,569	33.4%	63.4%
Brazil	72,920	151,104	31.8%	27.9%
China	4,504	100,536	2.2%	19.3%
Ecuador	5,997	14,955	53.8%	96.6%
Egypt	19,131	33,358	89.2%	78.3%
India	20,582	98,990	11.9%	34.2%
Indonesia	20,944	96,500	28.0%	94.7%
Mexico	57,378	128,302	30.5%	35.2%
Nigeria	8,921	33,485	10.1%	102.5%
Pakistan	9,930	29,579	42.4%	56.6%
Peru	9,386	22,623	47.6%	46.2%
Philippines	17,417	39,302	53.7%	59.7%
Russian Federation	4,477	94,232	—	25.4%
Rwanda	190	954	16.3%	164.8%
Tanzania	2,616	7,441	—	229.5%

From World Development Report 1996:220–221.

but when a big borrower, such as a corporation or country, can't repay its debts, the bank is in trouble. This, in brief, was the dilemma posed by the global debt crisis for private lending institutions and the World Bank.

The World Bank and the IMF responded to the debt crisis by trying to reschedule the repayment of debts or extending short-term loans to debtor countries to help them meet the financial crises. However, to qualify for a rescheduling of a debt or loan payment a government had to agree to alter its fiscal policies to improve its balance-of-payments problems; that is, it had to try to take in more money and spend less. But how do you do that? There are various ways, all creating, in one way or another, serious problems. For example, countries had to promise to manage tax collecting better, sell government property, increase revenues by increasing exports, reduce government spending on social programs such as welfare, health, and education, promise to refrain from printing more money, and take steps to devalue their currency, thus making their goods cheaper for consumers in other countries but making them more expensive for their own citizens.

While these measures are rarely popular with their citizens, governments rarely refuse IMF requests to implement them because not only might they not receive a short-term loan, but agencies such as the World Bank and private capital controllers such as banks and foundations would also then refuse to make funds available. Yet structural adjustment programs (SAPs), as they are called, can have very detrimental effects on people in the country. Structural adjustment usually increases unemployment and increases the plight of the poor. In Zambia the number of children suffering from malnutrition increased after structural adjustment from one in twenty to one in five. In Brazil, the need to raise funds to pay back World Bank loans resulted in increased cutting of the rainforests, not only for lumber but to produce commodities, such as cattle, in high demand in the core nations. In Mexico, Guatemala, and other Central American countries, the need to produce crops for export resulted in the consolidation of peasant landholdings into large, capital-intensive farms.

Furthermore, structural adjustment and the need to repay loans and attract foreign capital forces countries to seek money from outside investors by persuading banks, corporations, mutual fund managers, and others who control capital that they will receive a higher rate of return if they invest money in their country rather than other countries. This competition for investors, as we shall see, has greatly increased the power of capital.

Finally there is the question, *where did all the money that was lent to peripheral countries go?* Since "capital flight"—money leaving the periphery—increased dramatically during the period of rising debt, the prevailing view is that loans were siphoned off by the elites in the periphery and invested back in the core. The World Bank estimates that between 1976 and 1984 capital flight from Latin America was equal to the area's whole external debt (Caufield 1996:132). Capital flight from Mexico alone from 1974 to 1982, invested in everything from condominiums to car dealerships, amounted to at least $35 billion. "The problem," joked one member of the U.S. Federal Reserve Board, "is not that Latin Americans don't have assets. They do. The problem is they are all in Miami"(Caufield 1996:133).

The Power of Capital Controllers

One of the enduring tensions in the culture of capitalism is the separation between political power and economic power; in a democracy, people grant the government power to act on their behalf. However, in capitalism, there are, in addition to elected leaders, capital controllers, individuals or groups who control economic resources that everyone depends on but who are accountable to virtually no one, except perhaps a few investors or stockholders. Their goals often conflict with state goals. As a merchant, industrialist, or investor your goals are simple: you want to attain the highest possible profit on your investment, you want to be certain your right to private property is protected, and you want to keep your financial risks to a minimum. As Jeffrey A. Winters (1996:x) suggested, if capital controllers, who are unelected, unappointed, and unaccountable, were all to wear yellow suits and meet weekly in huge halls to decide where, when, and how much of their capital (money) to invest, there would be little mystery in their power. But, of course, they don't. Collectively they make private decisions on where, when, and how to distribute their investments. Furthermore, under this system of private property, capital controllers are free to do whatever they wish with their capital: they can invest it, they can sit on it, or they can destroy it. States are virtually helpless to insist that private capital be used for anything other than what capital controllers want to do with it.

The anonymity of investors and the hidden power they hold (or that is hidden from us) present problems for political leaders: while the actions of capital controllers can greatly influence our lives, it is political leaders that we often hold responsible for the rise and fall of a country's financial fortunes. When unemployment increases, when prices rise, when taxes are raised or important services discontinued or decreased, we can fire our governmental representatives at the next election. However, we do not have the power to "fire" the board of General Motors or the investment counselors at Smith, Barney's or Chase Manhattan.

Though investors may not consciously coordinate their actions, their choices have enormous consequences for societies and state leaders. The reasons for this are obvious. States depend on revenue for their operation and maintenance. This revenue can come from various sources, including income taxes, corporate taxes, tariffs on imported goods, revenue from state-run enterprises (e.g., oil revenue),

Global investors and capital controllers remain virtually anonymous as they drive the worldwide flow of capital in such arenas as the Hong Kong Stock Exchange.

charges for state services (e.g., tolls), foreign aid, and credit, loans, or grants from abroad. In the case of peripheral countries, much of this money comes from international lending agencies. But money from international lending agencies represents only a small percentage of the money that flows into peripheral countries. Far more comes from *capital controllers,* those who control vast amounts of money that must be invested to ensure investors a competitive return. As a final stop on our historical tour as merchant adventurers, let's assume the role of capital controller. *You have substantial sums of money to invest; what do you do with it?*

During the last half of the twentieth century there has been enormous growth in the number of people with capital to invest. Many are the very wealthy, the elite 1 or 2 percent who control vast resources, such as the major corporations of the world. Others, as mentioned above, are responsible for deciding where to invest public moneys from multilateral organizations or state agencies. In addition, there are the less wealthy who save in banks and have pension funds or insurance policies. Investment capital from these different sources and held by capital controllers represents enormous power. Furthermore, with modern methods of communication most of this money is now extremely mobile: billions of dollars can be transferred from one place to another with the touch of a computer key. Capital was not always so mobile. For example, if you had money to invest fifty years ago in a textile plant, you might be constrained by import laws to build your factory in the country in which you wanted to sell your merchandise. In today's free trade environment, however, you can build your factory wherever you can get the cheapest labor.

With an increase in free trade, standardized currencies, and economic globalization in general, capital can move freely all over the world. This can greatly increase the power of the capital controller, because if more regions or countries compete to attract capital investment, you, as a capital controller, are more able to demand conditions that guarantee profits and minimize risk. If you could build a textile factory in a country with strong labor unions or one with weak ones, which would you choose? If one country had strong environmental laws that required you to control toxic waste, while another had few such regulations, where would you build? If one country had a high minimum wage, while another had none, where would you likely realize the highest profit? These issues have become subsumed under the term "competitiveness"; that is, to be competitive in a global economy, a country must institute policies that allow it to compete successfully for mobile capital with other countries.

This fact determines social, economic, and political policy in countries and regions all over the world, and it affects your life as well. The mobility of capital means that social systems that produce profitable investment climates will attract the most investment capital. *What constitutes a favorable investment climate? Investment climate* refers to the constellation of policies within a given jurisdiction (city, state, region, country) that either advance or inhibit the key goals of investors (profit, property guarantees, and low risk). A bad climate might involve the risk of the expropriation of private property, political instability, high taxes, strong worker's unions, strong environmental regulations, and social laws regarding minimum wage and child labor. A favorable climate can be created by low tax rates, tax holidays and other special incentives, weak unions, little environmental regulation, and few social regulations. Furthermore, capital (money) will flow away from locations (e.g., countries) that do not create profitable investment climates. This capital, constantly flowing in and out of communities, regions, or countries, represents what Winters (1996:x) calls "power in motion."

The amount of power in motion is difficult to measure; by 1992 the amount of direct foreign investment—money invested in such things as factories, equipment, and research facilities—reached $2 trillion. Furthermore, the amount being invested in peripheral countries has almost doubled since 1987 (Winters 1996:27). Thus, on an average day the volume of money transacted around the world amounted to close to $1 trillion. But the amount that flows into any given area can vary enormously; in 1995, for example, Africa received just 1.5 percent of the world's total.

The case of Indonesia offers a good example of what countries need to do to attract capital (Winters 1996). Indonesia fought for and gained independence from the Dutch in 1949. After a period of intense regional competition President Sukarno, the victor in this competition, instituted a policy to free the country from foreign influence, carefully trying to balance power between the army and a strong Communist Party. Among his actions, he began nationalizing foreign firms. With their property at risk, and no longer guaranteed by the state, companies and investors began to pull their money out of the country. Consequently, the economy collapsed. Then in 1965 the military, under General Suharto, put down an alleged coup by the PKI, the Indonesian communist party. The subsequent blood bath led to the slaughter of hundreds of thousands of Indonesians believed to be sympathetic to or members of the Communist Party and removal of Sukarno from power.

With little money, the new ruler, President Suharto, faced the problem of rebuilding an economy in ruins. To solve the problem Suharto turned to economics professors at the University of Jakarta and assigned them the task of designing a policy to attract foreign investors. The first thing they did was to send signals through the press that they were changing economic policies and appointing people to government offices known to be friendly to foreign investors. Next, they applied for loans from multilateral institutions such as the World Bank and the IMF, hoping their approval would build the confidence of foreign investors in their country. Then, to assure capital controllers that their country was politically stable, the government suppressed all political dissent and limited the power of workers to mobilize unions. Finally, the government modified their tax structure to favor foreign investors. The result was that foreign capital began to flow into the country, and in the late 1960s and early 1970s the Indonesian economy began to thrive.

But the story did not end there; what happened next illustrates how the power of capital controllers to create conditions favorable to investment is not absolute. Indonesia has large oil reserves, and when in the early 1970s oil revenue increased, Indonesia's need for foreign investment decreased. Since it had another source of money, the country became less friendly to foreign investors: taxes increased, preference was shown to domestic industries, and bureaucratic procedures became more cumbersome for foreigners wanting to do business in Indonesia. As a result, foreign investments decreased dramatically. As long as oil revenues were stable, Indonesia had no problem. But in the early 1980s, oil prices plunged, and once again the Indonesian economy was close to ruin. Once again, in response to domestic political pressure from those who were suffering from economic decline, the government, still under the control of President Suharto, found itself instituting the measures outlined above to attract capital investors once again.

Foreign investment did return to Indonesia, particularly in the growth of assembly plants; thus until late 1997, the economy was doing well. However the collapse of the value of Asian currencies in late 1997 left the Indonesian economy once again in ruin, its currency plummeting in value, unemployment spreading, and social unrest increasing. The government responded with greater social and political repression but ultimately Suharto resigned.

Nigeria offers an interesting counterexample to Indonesia; it illustrates that the conditions in which capital controllers operate can differ enormously in spite of similar needs (Winters 1996). Nigeria in the 1960s had as great a need for capital investors as did Indonesia, but because of internal conditions it was far less able to create a climate conducive to attracting capital controllers. One of the problems was the cultural and linguistic heterogeneity of Nigeria as opposed to Indonesia. Early in the process of decolonalization, Indonesia decided to adopt the neutral trade language of Malay-Indonesian. In Nigeria, on the other hand, there are hundreds of tribal languages. In addition, Indonesia gained its independence after a long military struggle with the Dutch, a struggle that served to unite the population and establish an effective military presence, one that evidences great solidarity. Nigeria, formed as a British colony in 1914, was "given" its independence in 1960 by Great Britain with little struggle, but in a way that heightened regional divisions which the British had created to ease the process of colonial governance. As a consequence of the lack of political centralization, there were, between 1960 and 1993, five successful military coups, at least four attempted coups, six different military leaders, and only nine years without soldiers in authority. Because of the cultural heterogeneity and political unrest it was virtually impossible for Nigeria to respond as did Indonesia to the demands of mobile capital controllers. As a result, it has been unable to attract needed capital investment.

In fact, virtually all countries today, core nations as well as those in the periphery, seek to create conditions to attract or keep capital investment, to create or keep jobs for the millions of people dependent on wage labor. To this end they work to maintain and promote the confidence of foreign banks and investors in the viability of their economy and the stability of their political regimes.

The major lesson of this analysis is that the economic goals of capital controllers—profit, a guarantee for private property, and little risk—can often conflict with larger societal goals, such as relative economic equality, environmental safety, equal access to medical care, and equal access to food. In other words, making the world safe for capital sometimes means making it unsafe for people. Many of the global problems that we will examine in later chapters—population growth, poverty, hunger, environmental devastation, disease, ethnic conflict, and the oppression of indigenous peoples—all, in one way or another, find their origins in the drive of capital to profit, to keep the profit, and to minimize the risks of capital investment. Having said that, we must also recognize that no other large-scale economic system has been able to do as well for so many, and that many of the vast gains in areas such as food production, technology and science, and medicine are directly attributable to the same economic drives. The important thing is to understand the dynamics of the system so that we can understand what we may need to give up and what we are able to maintain if we ever hope to solve global problems.

Conclusion

We began this chapter with the goal of trying to understand three historical developments that have had a profound influence on today's world and in the development of the culture of capitalism—the increase in the division of world wealth, changes in the organization of capital, and the increase in the level of economic globalization. We found that the division of wealth has grown enormously, between both countries and areas of the world. In 1995, over 1 billion people lived in absolute poverty, earning the equivalent of less than one dollar per day, while, according to the Maryland-based Bread for the World Institute, 358 billionaires listed by *Forbes* Magazine had a combined net worth equal to the combined income of the bottom 45 percent of the world's population (Dayal and Lobe, 1995).

The organization of capital has changed dramatically. We began our journey with capital largely in the hands of individual merchants, family groups, or limited partnerships and ended with the era of capital controllers, such as transnational corporations, multilateral institutions, and investment firms. In 1400, it might take a global merchant a year's journey from one area of the world to another to complete an investment cycle of buying and selling goods; today a capital controller can transfer billions from one area of the world to another without ever leaving the computer.

Finally, we have seen global economic integration increase to the extent that global trade is easier today than trade between adjacent towns was in 1400, as trade treaties dissolve regional and country boundaries, freeing capital to migrate where it is most likely to accumulate.

Chapter 4

The Nation-State in the Culture of Capitalism

> *...The mutual relationship of modern culture and state is something quite new, and springs, inevitably, from the requirements of a modern economy.*
> —*ERNEST GELLNER,* NATIONS AND NATIONALISM

> *Among the primary goals of the modern, post-Enlightenment state are assimilation, homogenization, and conformity within a fairly narrow ethnic and political range, as well as the creation of societal agreement about the kinds of people there are and the kinds there ought to be. The ideal state is one in which the illusion of a single nation-state is created and maintained and in which resistance is managed so that profound social upheaval, separatist activity, revolution, and coups d'état are unthinkable for most people most of the time.*
> —*CAROL NAGENGAST,* VIOLENCE, TERROR, AND THE CRISIS OF THE STATE

Imagine an alien from another planet who lands on Earth after a nuclear holocaust has destroyed all life but has left undamaged terrestrial libraries and archives. After consulting the archives, suggested Eric Hobsbawm, our observer would undoubtedly conclude that the last two centuries of human history are incomprehensible without an understanding of the term *nation* and the phenomenon of *nationalism.*

The nation-state, along with the consumer, laborer, and capitalist, comprise, we suggest, the essential elements of the culture of capitalism. It is the nation-state, as Eric Wolf (1982:100) suggested, that guarantees the ownership of private property and the means of production and provides support for disciplining the work force. The state also has to provide and maintain the economic infrastructure—

*The United Nations represents the global dominance of the
nation-state as the major form of political governance.*

transportation, communication, judicial systems, education, and so on—required
by capitalist production. The nation-state must regulate conflicts between competing capitalists at home and abroad, by diplomacy if possible, by war if necessary.
The state plays an essential role in creating conditions that inhibit or promote consumption, controls legislation that may force people off the land to seek wage labor, legislates to regulate or deregulate corporations, controls the money supply,
initiates economic, political, and social policies to attract capital, and controls the
legitimate use of force. Without the nation-state to regulate commerce and trade

within its own borders, there could be no effective global economic integration. But *how did the nation-state come to exist, and how does it succeed in binding together often disparate and conflicting groups?*

Virtually all people in the world consider themselves members of a nation-state. The notion of a person without a nation, said Ernest Gellner (1983:6), strains the imagination; a person must have a nationality as he or she must have a nose and two ears. We are Americans, Mexicans, Bolivians, Italians, Indonesians, Kenyans, or members of any of close to two hundred states that currently exist. We generally consider our country, whichever it is, as imbued with tradition, a history that glorifies its founding and makes heroes of those thought to have been instrumental in its creation. Symbols of the nation—flags, buildings, monuments—take on the aura of sacred relics.

The attainment of "nationhood" had become by the middle of the twentieth century a sign of progress and modernity. To be less than a nation—a tribe, an ethnic group, a regional bloc—was a sign of backwardness. Yet fewer than one-third of the states in the world are more than thirty years old; only a few go back to the nineteenth century; and virtually none go back in their present form beyond that. Before that time people identified themselves as members of kinship groups, villages, cities, or, perhaps, regions, but almost never as members of nations. For the most part, the agents of the state were resented, feared, or hated because of their demands for tribute, taxes, or army conscripts.

States existed, of course, and have existed for five to seven thousand years. But the idea of the nation-state, of a people sharing some bounded territory, united by a common culture or tradition, common language, or common race, is a product of nineteenth century Europe. Most historians see the French Revolution of 1789 as marking the beginning of the era of the nation-state. Yet in spite of the historical newness of the idea, for many people nationality forms a critical part of their personal identity. Some of the questions we need to explore are: *How did the nation-state come to have such importance in the world? Why did it develop as it did, and how do people come to identify themselves as members of such vague abstractions? Finally, why does the nation-state kill as often as it does?*

The question of killing is important, because today most killing and violence is either sanctioned by or carried out by the state. This should not surprise us: most definitions of the state, following Max Weber's (1947:124–135), revolve around its claim to a monopoly on the instruments of death and violence. "Stateness," as Elman Service (1975) put it, can be identified simply by locating "the power of force in addition to the power of authority." Killing by other than the state, as Morton Fried (1967) noted, will draw the punitive action of organized state force.

The use of force, however, is not the only characteristic anthropologists emphasize in identifying the state; social stratification—the division of societies into groups with differing access to wealth and other resources—is also paramount. Yet even here the state is seen as serving as an instrument of control to maintain the privileges of the ruling group, and this, too, generally requires a monopoly on the use of force (see Cohen and Service 1978; Lewellen 1983).

Thus to complete our description of the key features of the culture of capitalism we need to examine the origin and history of the state and its successor, the nation-state.

The Origin and History of the State

The Evolution of the State

States represent a form of social contract in which the public ostensibly has consented to assign to the state a monopoly on force and agreed that only it can constrain and coerce people (Nagengast 1994:1116). Philosophers and political thinkers have long been fascinated by the question of why the state developed. Seventeenth-century philosopher Thomas Hobbes assumed the state existed to maintain order, that without the state life would be, in Hobbes's famous description, "nasty, brutish, and short." However, anthropologists have long recognized that some societies do very well without anything approaching state organization; in fact "tribes without rulers," as they were called, represented until seven to eight thousand years ago the only form of political organization in the world. Government in these societies was relatively simple. There might be a chief or village leader, but their powers were limited. In gathering and hunting societies most decisions were probably made by consensus. Village or clan chiefs may have had more authority than others, but even they led more by example than by any force they might have had at their disposal. Power, the ability to control people, was generally diffused among many individuals or groups.

The state as a stratified society presided over by a ruling elite with the power to draw from and demand agricultural surpluses likely developed in the flood plains between the Tigris and Euphrates in what is now Iraq four to five thousand years ago. The fortified cities of Uruk and Ur, forming the state of Sumeria, had populations of forty thousand. States developed independently in Egypt, the Indus River Valley of India, the Yellow River Valley of China, and, later, Mesoamerica and Peru.

Anthropologists have long been concerned with the idea of the origin of the state (See Lewellen 1983). *Why didn't human aggregates remain organized into small units, or into villages or towns of 500–2,000 persons? What made the development of densely settled cities necessary? Why, after hundreds of thousands of years, did ruling elites with control of armed force emerge to dominate the human landscape?*

One theory is that as population increased and food production became more complex, a class of specialists emerged and created a stratified society. Who comprised this class or why they emerged is an open question. Karl Wittfogel (1957), in his "hydraulic theory" of state development, proposed that neolithic farmers in the area where states developed were dependent on flooding rivers, such as the Tigris, the Nile, and the Yellow Rivers, to water their fields and deposit new soil. But this happened only once each year, so to support an expanding population farmers began to build dikes, canals, and reservoirs to control water flow. As these irrigation systems became more complex, groups of specialists emerged to plan and direct these activities, and this group developed into an administrative elite that ruled over despotic, centralized states.

Others propose that an increase in population, especially where populations cannot easily disperse, requires more formal means of government and control and will lead to greater social stratification and inequality. These theories of state development emphasize the integrative function of the state and suggest that it evolved to maintain order and direct societal growth and development.

However, another framework emerges from the work of Marx and Engels. In this framework early societies were thought to be communistic, with resources shared equally among members and little or no notion of private property. However, technological development permitted production of a surplus of goods which could be expropriated and used by some persons to elevate their control or power in society. Asserting control permitted this elite to form an entrepreneurial class. To maintain their wealth and authority, they created structures of force.

The major criticism of this framework from anthropologists is that there is little evidence of this kind of entrepreneurial activity in prehistoric societies; moreover, it is difficult to apply notions such as "communism" and "capitalism" to early societies. However, Morton Fried (1967) proposed that differential access to wealth and resources creates stratification, and once stratification emerges it creates internal conflict that will lead to either disintegration of the group or to the elite imposing their authority by force.

Yet another view proposes that external conflict is the motivation for state development: Once a group united under a strong central authority develops, it could easily conquer smaller, less centralized groups and take captives, land, or property. Following this line of reasoning, if smaller groups were to protect themselves from predator states they too had to organize, the result being the emergence of competing states with the more powerful ones conquering the weaker ones and enlarging their boundaries. Robert Carneiro (1978) reasoned that war has served to promote consolidation of isolated, politically autonomous villages into chiefdoms of united villages and into states. At first war pits village against village, resulting in chiefdoms; then it pits chiefdom against chiefdom, resulting in states; and then it pits state against state, creating yet larger political units.

Elman R. Service (1975) proposed that social stratification will emerge out of the natural inequalities found in all societies, that some individuals will distinguish themselves and their special qualities, especially during times of need, will lead people to appreciate the advantages of having someone in control. In its earliest form, said Service, leadership is individual or charismatic, based on a particular person's special attributes, and cannot be passed on to others. However, because of the benefits of centralized leadership, societies institutionalize the role of chief, turning the charismatic chief into an institutionalized inequality and a ranked society. Thus states and hierarchy emerge as people, perhaps because of special circumstances, recognize the advantages of societal integration that formal leadership and bureaucracy can bring.

It should be clear that these theories are not mutually exclusive; the emergence of states may be a result of any one or a combination of factors. Thus, other theorists, such as Marvin Harris (1971) and Kent Flannery (1972, 1973), propose that the evolution of the state required the interaction of various factors such as control of birth rates, nature of food resources, and environmental factors.

Regardless of why the state emerged as a human institution, it is clear that by 1400 the world was very much divided into states and empires ruled by groups of elites who maintained their positions through the use of force. But the states of prehistoric times—the city-states of ancient Greece, the Roman Empire, the Chinese dynasties—were very different from the modern nation-state. It is doubtful that subjects of the Ming Dynasty or Roman Empire identified themselves as members of a state, let alone a nation. It is unlikely that a British or French soldier of the sixteenth or seventeenth century felt he owed allegiance to his "nation"—to his king or queen, perhaps, but not to anything so abstract as a "country." The nation-state is a very recent historical development, one we need to understand to appreciate its role in the culture of capitalism.

The History and Function of the Nation-State

The state as it exists today is obviously very different from the state that evolved seven thousand years ago or the state as it existed in the years 1500 or 1800. We have gone from being states to being *nations* or *nation-states*. The differences are important. A state is a political entity with identifiable components. If someone asked citizens of the United States to identify a constituent of the "state" they could point to federal buildings (e.g. the Congressional Office Building, the White House, federal courthouse), name federal bureaucracies (e.g. Congress, the Internal Revenue Service, the Department of Agriculture); they could list the things that the state requires of them—to pay taxes, register for social security, obtain citizenship, vote. However, if someone asked them what constituted the "nation," what, other then the flag, could they point to? Other than being "patriotic," what could they say is required of them by the "nation"? The American nation is a far more abstract concept than the American state; a nation, as Benedict Anderson (1991:5–6) put it, is "an imagined political community." Yet in the last two hundred years, states have evolved to nations or nation-states. But *why did a new form of political entity develop, and what function did it perform?*

The modern state, suggested Fernand Braudel (1982:515–516), has three tasks: to secure obedience and gain a monopoly on force with legitimate violence; to exert control over economic life to ensure the orderly circulation of goods and to take for itself a share of the national income to pay for its own expenditure, luxury, administration, or wars; and to participate in spiritual or religious life and derive additional strength by using religious values or establishing a state religion. We will examine later the use of violence by the state and the use of religious values. Let's first examine the state control of economic life.

The state has probably always been involved in its subjects' economic life in one way or another. The ancient state existed partly to protect the privileges of the elites by ensuring production of resources, offering protection from other elites, and extracting surplus wealth from a largely peasant population. Traders supplied wealth to the elite in the form of taxes, tributes, and fees required to do business. The state also performed some functions for the trader—it might mint coins and produce paper money, establish standards for weights and measures, protect the movement of merchants and goods, purchase goods, and create and maintain marketplaces where merchants could sell their products. But the ancient states probably did little actively to encourage trade, and in many ways they may have inhibited it. For example, they may have taxed the merchant to an extent that making a profit became difficult. The elite may have limited the goods that merchants could trade or limit the market for goods, for example by claiming exclusive rights to wear certain kinds of clothes or furs, hunt certain animals, eat certain foods, and inhabit certain sites.

It was in sixteenth- and seventeenth-century Europe and Japan that states began to take a truly active role in promoting and protecting trade, recognizing that the state's wealth depended on the success of its manufacturers and traders. They began to protect their manufacturers and traders by imposing protective tariffs on goods from other states, using military force to open markets in peripheral areas, and granting trading monopolies to firms within their borders. States created and maintained ports, built roads and canals, and, later, subsidized railroad construction.

The state was also involved in the consumption of goods, either by purchasing goods or, again, using its military or bargaining power to open up foreign markets to its merchants. One of the most lucrative sources of manufacturers' profits was (and still is) the sale to governments of weapons (some $40 billion in 1996) and other goods and services (food, clothing, and transportation) necessary to maintain the military and other government services. While ostensibly the military existed in core countries to protect the state against foreign invaders, it was far more often used to create and maintain colonies necessary for the success of domestic manufacture and trade, and to maintain domestic order. Finally, the state organized and directed financial institutions, such as banks, that ensured the ready availability of capital.

The nation-state, said Immanuel Wallerstein (1989:170), became the major building block of the global economy. To be part of the interstate system required that political entities transform themselves into states that followed the rules of the interstate system. This system required for its operation an integrated division of labor, along with guarantees regarding the flow of money, goods, and persons. States were free to impose constraints on these flows, but only within a set of rules enforced collectively by member states or, as it usually worked out, a few dominant states.

The general opinion of social and political analysts is that states not only had to exist but had to be of a minimum size to be economically and politically viable. Small countries or political entities should merge with others and even submerge their culture, language, and ethnicity if necessary. Small groups (Basques, Bretons, Scots) could not make it on their own, but only as members of a larger state (e.g., France or Britain). John Stuart Mill wrote:

Nobody can suppose that it is not more beneficial for a Breton or a Basque or French Navarre to be...a member of the French nationality, admitted on equal terms to all the privileges of French citizenship...than to sulk on his own rocks, the half-savage relic of past times, revolving in his own little mental orbit, without participation or interest in the general movement of the world. The same remark applies to the Welshman or the Scottish Highlander as members of the British nation. (cited Hobsbawm 1990:34)

One hundred years later, the same sentiments were echoed by academics and state officials; one African writer wrote in 1959 that in "three or four years, no one will remember the tribal, ethnic or religious rivalries which, in the recent past, caused so much damage to our country and its population (cited Young 1993:13). As recent African history shows, few prophesies have seemed so wrong.

At the beginning of the nineteenth century, the new capitalist state faced two problems. The first was political. With the downfall of the doctrine of the divine right of kings and the absolute state, political leaders faced a crisis of political legitimacy. *On what basis could they claim control of the state apparatus that had become so critical for the emergence and success of the "national economy"?* A second and related problem was economic: *How could the state promote the economic integration of all those within its borders?* While the English state could claim control over England, Scotland, and Wales and the French state over the regions of France (Bretagne, Picardie, Provence, Languedoc, etc.), the situation in the countryside did not reflect that control. At the beginning of the nineteenth century few residents of the British Isles would identify themselves as Britons; few residents of the state of France would identity themselves as French—at least 25 percent of them didn't even speak French. Germany and Italy, of course, didn't yet exist.

Thus the degree of economic integration of regions was weak or nonexistent. Not only did people speak different languages, they used different currencies, had different standards and measures, and were downright hostile to state officials. Wages and prices varied from area to area and standardized vocational training was virtually nonexistent. Furthermore, tastes in commodities differed; things manufactured or produced in one area might not appeal to people in other areas. Thus local economies existed either side-by-side with or independent of the so-called national economy. While countries such as England, France, and the Netherlands were busy incorporating territories in South and North America, Asia, Africa, and the Middle East into their national economies, they hadn't yet fully incorporated members of their own states.

There was, however, a single solution to both the political and the economic problem: to turn states into nations—groups of people who shared a common culture, language, and heritage and somehow belonged together (or thought they did), worked together, and shopped together. This was not easy to accomplish, since virtually all of the major European states in the eighteenth and nineteenth centuries were hodgepodges of languages, cultures, and religions. When Garibaldi united a group of provinces into what was to become Italy, less than 3 percent of the population spoke Italian as their native language. German became the language of Germany only because Joseph II arbitrarily decided it should be. Thus nations had to be created: Frenchmen, Italians, Germans, and Americans had to be manufactured by convincing them they had something in common, preferably loyalty and devotion to their respective states.

If members of a state would see themselves as sharing a common culture—a common heritage, language, and destiny—not only could state leaders claim to represent the "people," whoever they might be, but the people could be more easily integrated into the national economy. They would, ideally, accept the same wages, speak the same language, use the same currency, have similar skills, and similar economic expectations, and, even better, demand the same goods. The question is, *how do you go about constructing a nation?*

Constructing the Nation-State

It has been argued by some, especially ardent nationalists of various persuasions, that nation-states are expressions of preexisting cultural, linguistic, religious, ethnic, or historical features shared by people who make up or would make up a state. For many of the nineteenth-century German writers who were instrumental in creating the idea of the nation-state—Johann Gottfried von Herder, Johann Gottlieb Fichte, and Wilhelm Freiherr von Humboldt—nations were expressions of shared language, tradition, race, and state. Thus today we see some of the citizens of Quebec claiming that their cultural heritage and language differentiates them from the rest of Canada and entitles them to nationhood; Kurds aspiring to their own state on the basis of cultural unity; Bosnian Serbs demanding their own state on the basis of their ethnic purity; and Sikhs demanding their own state based on their mode of worship.

However, the more generally held view, certainly among scholars, is that nation-states are constructed through invention, and social engineering. Traditions, suggested Eric Hobsbawm, must be invented. People must be convinced that they share or must be forced to share certain features such as language, religion, ethnic group membership, or a common historical heritage, whether or not they really do. As Hobsbawm and Ranger (1983:1) put it,

> *"[i]nvented tradition" is taken to mean a set of practices, normally governed by overtly or tacitly accepted rules and of a ritual or symbolic nature, which seek to inculcate certain values and norms of behavior by repetition, which automatically implies continuity with the past. In fact, were it possible, they normally attempt to establish continuity with a suitable historic past.*

Creating the Other

An understanding of how the nation-state and, by extension, people's national identities are constructed is critical to understanding nationalism and ethnicity. Let's begin by examining some of the ways Great Britain and France, pioneers in nation building, went about the task. Linda Colley illustrated how this was done in Great Britain. Colley's book includes a painting by Sir David Wilkie, *Chelsea Pensioners Reading the Gazette of the Battle of Waterloo,* that caused a sensation when it was exhibited at the Royal Academy in 1822. The painting depicts a crowd celebrating the news of the British victory over Napoleon at Waterloo. The distinguishing feature of the painting is its clear identification of people from all over Britain. There are Welsh, Scottish, and Irish soldiers; women and children; rich and poor; even a Black military bandman. It is, Colley said, a celebration of patriotism that transcends boundaries of age, gender, class, ethnicity, and occupation. It is war, the painting suggests, that forged a nation by uniting this diverse group against a common enemy. Even the signs on the taverns celebrate past wars and victories. According to Colley, Wilkie recognized the importance of war in nation building, and that uniting diverse people and groups against outsiders is one of the most effective ways to create bonds among them (1992:366–367).

But outsiders can be used in more symbolic ways to build national unity. For example, Colley suggested that the making of the British nation from its culturally and linguistically diverse populations would have been impossible without a shared religion, that British Protestantism allowed the English, Scots, and Welsh to overcome their cultural divergence to identify themselves as a nation. However, that would not have been so effective had their religion not also distinguished them from their arch rival, Catholic France.

Sir David Wilkie's painting, Chelsea Pensioners Reading the Gazette of the Battle of Waterloo, *represents the power of the nation-state to transcend boundaries of age, gender, class, ethnicity, and occupation.*

Furthermore, the founding of a colonial empire created additional Others from whom members of the British nation could distinguish themselves. Britons thought the establishment of an empire proved Britain's providential destiny, that God had chosen them to rule over other peoples and to spread the Gospel. Contact with manifestly alien peoples fed Britons' belief about their superiority. They could favorably compare their treatment of women, their wealth, and their power. The building of a global empire corroborated not only Britain's blessings, but what Scottish socialist Keir Hardie called "the indomitable pluck and energy of the British people" (cited Colley 1992:369).

Thus one of the most effective ways to construct a nation is to create some Other against whom members of the nation-state can distinguish themselves. That Other needn't be a country; it may be a category of persons constructed out of largely arbitrary criteria such as physical characteristics or religion. Thus a group may insist that only people of a particular skin color or religion or who speak a particular language can be members of their nation. War, religion, and the creation of colonies full of subjugated peoples provided for Britons a sense of their collective identity as a people, allowing them to overcome their own significant differences in language, culture, and economic status. Of course people must find it in their own self-interest as well to proclaim their identity as members of a nation-state. As Colley pointed out, men and women became British patriots to obtain jobs in the state or to advertise their standing in the community. Some believed that British imperialism would benefit them economically or that a French victory would harm them. For some, being an active patriot served to provide them full citizenship and a voice in the running of the state.

Yet the creation of hated or feared Others through such means as war, religion, and empire building is probably not in itself sufficient to build loyalty and devotion to a nation. If it were, the nation-state would likely have emerged well before it did. Constructing a nation-state also requires a national, bureaucratic infrastructure that serves in various ways to unite people.

Language, Bureaucracy, and Education

Eugen Weber, in his book *Peasants into Frenchmen* (1976), provided a classic account of nation building; he documented how peoples in France were administratively molded into a nation by bringing the French language to the countryside, by increasing the ease of travel, by increasing access to national media, through military training, and, most important, through a national educational system. Weber (1976:486) compared the transformation of peasants into citizens of a French nation-state to the process of colonization and acculturation: unassimilated masses had to be integrated into a dominant culture. The process, he suggested, was akin to colonization, except it took place within the borders of the country rather than overseas. *What kind of transformation of national identity did take place in France in the nineteenth century?*

At the beginning of the nineteenth century, even after the French Revolution, a significant portion of rural France still lived in a world of their own. Few if any would have called themselves "French." The peasants of France were for the most part subsistence farmers, producing not for market or cash but for themselves and their families. People spent their lives in their villages. It is estimated that one-fourth of the residents of France did not speak French, including half the children who would reach adulthood in the last quarter of the nineteenth century. Arnold van Gennep would write as late as 1911 that "for peasants and workers, the mother tongue is patois, the foreign speech is French" (cited in Weber 1976:73).

State officials saw linguistic diversity as a threat not to administrative unity but to ideological unity, a shared notion of the interests of the republic, a oneness. Linguistic and cultural diversity came to be seen as imperfection, something to be remedied (Weber 1976:9). As a result, in the 1880s, at the insistence of the government, the French language began to infiltrate the countryside, a process more or less complete by 1914, although even in 1906 English travelers in France had problems communicating in French.

With the homogenization of language came the homogenization of culture. Local customs began to be replaced, dress and food preferences became standardized. While many aspects of local culture began to disappear, some were adopted as national symbols. The beret, worn only by Basques in 1920, became by 1930 a symbol of France; by 1932 some 23 million were manufactured, one for every French citizen.

Another sign of state integration and the decline of local traditions and values is the decay of popular feasts and rituals that celebrated the unity of local groups, and their replacement by private ceremonies and rituals along with a few national holidays. Communal celebrations such as Christmas, New Year, and Twelfth Night turned into family affairs. Where once they were public rituals, baptisms, first communions, and marriages became private ceremonies. Renewal ceremonies that glorified time (the season), work (harvest), or the community (through its patron saint) disappeared as the redistribution of goods once done through ritual at these ceremonies was now managed more efficiently (and more stringently) by the state (Weber 1976:398). The replacement of local holidays and festivals with national holidays also allowed these occasions to be turned into periods of massive consumption and gift giving, like Valentine's Day, Easter, Mother's Day, and Christmas in the United States (Schmidt 1995).

National unity in France was also evidenced by the growth of patriotism. In the early nineteenth century draft evasion in the provinces was high; for most, the military was a foreign institution. There was great tax resistance. Even toward the end of the nineteenth century some French citizens had never heard of Napoleon; national authority was embodied in the tax collector and the recruiting sergeant. This is not to say, as Weber (1976:114) pointed out, that the French were unpatriotic, only that they had no uniform conception of patriotism. As he said, "patriotic feelings on the national level, far from instinctive, had to be learned."

Thus in the nineteenth century people living within the boundaries of the French state gradually learned to be French. *But how did this happen; how were peasants turned into French citizens?* As with Great Britain, war and the struggle against outsiders certainly played a role in the conversion. The war against Prussia in

1870–1871 was a significant unifying event for most residents of France. The expansion of a colonial empire helped create Others to whom the French could feel superior. But more significant, as Weber pointed out, there were far-reaching changes in the infrastructure and bureaucracy of France.

New roads were built, connecting people to others to whom they had never been connected; the growth of the railroads further increased mobility and contact between people of different regions. The railroads helped to homogenize tastes. While we now associate the French with wine drinking, wine was not common in the countryside in the first half of the nineteenth century, becoming more available only with the railroads. The roads and railroads brought peasants into a national market; it allowed them to grow and sell crops they couldn't sell before and to stop growing those they could purchase more cheaply—bringing ruin to some local enterprises no longer protected by isolation. Fashions from the cities began to penetrate the countryside. And the roads and railroads set people on the move. If people migrated in the early part of the nineteenth century to find work, they almost always returned. This was no longer true by the end of the century.

As more people spoke French and became literate, they gained access to newspapers and journals, which in turn increased knowledge of national affairs and interests, demonstrating that events at the national level affected their lives. Military service increased identification with the state. Prior to the 1890s there was little sense of national identity in being a soldier; soldiers were either feared or thought to bring bad habits to their communities. Local men who joined the army were forced to conform when they returned to their villages lest their newly learned habits affect others. Many returned not even having learned to speak French. But the war with Prussia seemed to mark the beginning of a national identity in the rank and file of the military and among the peasants. The army began to become a school for the Fatherland. Furthermore, for most recruits life in the army was better than life at home; the army ate better, dressed better, and was healthier than the average French citizen, and toward the end of the century more and more soldiers did not return to their villages after finishing their military obligations.

But as important as all these agents of nation building were in France and other countries, perhaps none was as important as the school. Weber credited the school with being the ultimate source of acculturation that made the French people French.

At the beginning of the century educational conditions were abysmal in France, as in most countries; some teachers couldn't read, and some classes were conducted by nuns who could read only prayers. In 1864 a French school inspector commented that none of the children understood what they read, and when they could read they could not give an account of it. Furthermore, schooling in the countryside had little practical benefit; it could not improve the lives of students economically or socially. While improving education in the countryside had been a goal of the state since the 1830s, great changes occurred only in the 1880s, when the state began to subsidize education and every hamlet with twenty children or more was required to have a school.

It was clear to state officials that education was necessary as a "guarantee of order and social stability" (Weber 1976:331). "To instruct the people," one said, "is

Third graders in Palo Alto, California pledge their allegiance to their nation-state.

to condition them to understand and appreciate the beneficence of the government" (Weber 1976:331). Clearly there was an explicit link in the minds of state officials between education, nation building, national identity, and economic expansion. Following is a passage from a first-year civics textbook that helped students in "appreciating their condition."

> Society *(summary): (1) French society is ruled by just laws, because it is a democratic society. (2) All the French are equal in their rights: but there are inequalities between us that stem from nature or from wealth. (3) These inequalities cannot disappear. (4) Man works to become rich; if he lacked this hope, work would cease and France would decline. It is therefore necessary that each of us should be able to keep the money he has earned. (cited Weber 1976:331)*

Schooling was to be the great agent of nationalism. As one teacher said in 1861, it would teach national and patriotic sentiments, explain the benefits of the state and why taxes and military service were necessary, and illustrate for students their true interest in the fatherland. In 1881, another wrote that future instructors must be taught that "their first duty is to make [their charges] love and understand the fatherland." By the 1890s officials considered the school "an instrument of unity," an "answer to dangerous centrifugal tendencies," and the "keystone of national defense" (Weber 1976:332–333).

The best instrument of indoctrination, said school officials, was history, which, when properly taught, "is the only means of maintaining patriotism in the generation we are bringing up." In 1897 candidates for the *baccalauret moderne* were asked to define the purpose of history in education; 80 percent replied essentially that it was to exalt patriotism (Weber 1976:333).

Before 1870 few schools had maps of France; by 1881 few classrooms, no matter how small, were without one. By the end of the century the educational system seemed to be accomplishing its task, as evidenced by boys in rural France who began to enact the exploits of historical heroes.

Ernest Gellner (1983:34) drew the connection between nation building, education, and economic integration even more tightly. According to Gellner, work in industrial society no longer means working with things, rather it involves working with meanings, exchanging communications with other people, or manipulating the controls of machines, controls that need to be understood. It is easy to understand the workings of a shovel or a plow, it is another thing to understand the complex process through which a button or control activates a machine. As a consequence, a modern capitalistic economy requires a mobile division of labor and precise communication between strangers. It requires universal literacy, a high level of numerical, technical, and general sophistication, mobility where members must be prepared to shift from area to area and from task to task, an ability to communicate with people they don't know in a context-dependent form of communication, in a common, standardized language. To attain the standard of literacy and technical competence needed to be employable, people must be trained, not by members of their own local group but by specialists. This training could be provided only by something like a "national" education system. Gellner (1983:34) went so far as to suggest that education became the ultimate instrument of state power, that the professor and the classroom came to replace the executioner and the guillotine as the enforcer of national sovereignty, that a monopoly on legitimate education became more important than the monopoly on legitimate violence to build a common national identity and to provide the training necessary for the full integration of national economies.

Violence and Genocide

While creating a feared or hated Other, a national bureaucracy, and an educational system are essential in constructing the nation-state, violence remains one of the main tools of nation building. In fact there is a view, shared in anthropology by Pierre van den Berghe (1992), Leo Kuper (1990), Carol Nagengast (1994), and others, that the modern nation-state is essentially an agent of genocide and ethnocide (the suppression and destruction of minority cultures). Given the glorification of the nation-state as a vehicle of modernization, unity, and economic development, this seems a harsh accusation. Yet there exists ample evidence that one of the ways states have sought to create nations is to eliminate or terrorize into submission those within its borders who refuse to assimilate or who demand recognition of their status as a distinct ethnic or national group. In the United States the attempt first to kill all indigenous peoples then forcibly to assimilate those who remained, followed by a policy of "benign neglect," is but one example of state hostility to cultural variation, as we shall see. The claim that states are agents of death and oppression against minority or even majority groups (e.g., South Africa) is often provided in daily news reports.

Between 1975 and 1979, in one of the worst cases of state killing in the twentieth century, the government of Cambodia, the Khmer Rouge, systematically killed as many as two million of its seven million citizens. These killings were carried out in the name of a program to create a society without cities, money, families, markets, or commodity-money relations. Millions were disembowelled, had nails driven into the backs of their heads, or were beaten to death with hoes. This program involved destroying what the leaders saw as the enemy classes—imperialists (e.g., ethnic Vietnamese, ethnic Chinese, Muslim Chams), feudalists (the leaders of the old regime, Buddhist monks, intellectuals), and comprador capitalists (ethnic Chinese). The goal was as much nationalistic as it was socialistic—to return Cambodia and the Khmer race to its previous glory. They took over a country devastated by U.S. bombing during the Vietnam War and ended up by killing millions who they deemed didn't belong (Kuper 1990). But the killing of its citizens by the Khmer Rouge, while reaching an intensity matched by few states, was hardly an exception.

As Carol Nagengast (1994:119–120) wrote:

> *The numbers of people worldwide subjected to the violence of their own states are staggering. More than a quarter of a million Kurds and Turks in Turkey have been beaten or tortured by the military, police, and prison guards since 1980; tens of thousands of indigenous people in Peru and Guatemala, street children in Brazil and Guatemala, Palestinians in Kuwait, Kurds in Iraq, and Muslim women and girls in Bosnia have been similarly treated. Mutilated bodies turn up somewhere everyday. Some 6000 people in dozens of countries were legally shot, hung, electrocuted, gassed, or stoned to death by their respective states between 1985 and 1992 for political misdeeds: criticism of the state, membership in banned political parties or groups, or for adherence to the "wrong" religion; for moral deeds: adultery, prostitution, homosexuality, sodomy, or alcohol or drug use; for economic offenses: burglary, embezzling, and corruption; and for violent crimes: rape, assault, and murder.*

R. J. Rummel (1994), in a series of books on state killing, documented the carnage committed by states against their own citizens: 61 million Russians from 1917 to 1987; 20 million Germans from 1933 to 1945; 35 million Chinese killed by the Chinese communist government from 1923 to 1949 and 10 million killed by the Chinese nationalists; almost 2 million Turks from 1909 to 1918; and almost 1.5 million Mexicans from 1900 to 1920. In total, Rummel (1994:9) said, almost 170 million men, women, and children from 1900 to 1987

Remains of some 2,000 victims of the Khmer Rouge in a "killing field" in an abandoned schoolhouse outside Phnom Penh, Cambodia.

[h]ave been shot, beaten, tortured, knifed, burned, starved, frozen, crushed, or worked to death; buried alive, drowned, hung, bombed, or killed in any other of the myriad ways governments have inflicted death on unarmed, helpless citizens and foreigners. The dead could conceivably be nearly 360 million people. It is as though our species has been devastated by a modern Black Plague. And indeed it has, but a plague of Power not germs.

Rummel attributed state killing to power and its abuses, claiming it is largely totalitarian regimes that resort to democide, genocide, or ethnocide. Democracies also kill, as evidenced in the twentieth century by indiscriminate bombings of enemy civilians in war, the large-scale massacre of Filipinos during U.S. colonization of the Philippines at the turn of the century, deaths in British concentration camps during the Boer War in South Africa, civilian deaths in Germany as a result of the Allied blockade, the rape and murder of helpless Chinese in and around Peking in 1900, atrocities committed by Americans in Vietnam, the murder of helpless Algerians by the French during the Algerian War, and the deaths of German prisoners of war in French and U.S. prisoner of war camps after World War II. But Rummel said even these prove his point about power, for virtually all of these cases were committed in secret behind a trail of lies and deceit by agencies and power holders who were given the authority to operate autonomously and shielded from the press. Even attacks on German and Vietnamese cities were presented as attacks on military targets. He concluded that as we move from democratic through authoritarian and to totalitarian governments, the degree of state killing increases dramatically (Rummel 1994:17).

Pierre van den Berghe (1992:191) attributed state killing not to the misuse of authority but to nation building itself. Taking what he called a frankly anarchist position, he said

> *the process euphemistically described as nation-building is, in fact, mostly nation-killing; that the vast majority of so-called "nation-states" are nothing of the sort; and that modern nationalism is a blueprint for ethnocide at best, genocide at worst.*

Furthermore, van den Berghe argued, there is a strong pro-state bias in the social science literature that works to mask the genocidal character of nation-states. This bias, he said, promotes the myths that:

1. States are inevitable and you need them to keep the peace.
2. Stable political regimes must rest on legitimacy and not violence.
3. Large states are better because they are more economically viable.
4. States as the political organ of the nation should be taken for granted, with the distinction between nation and state best obscured by the designation nation-state.

Van den Berghe took exception to each of these claims. First, he said, states are not inevitable; people did without them until seven thousand years ago. States have been effective largely because they are effective at organizing coercive violence:

> *States are killing machines run by a few to steal from the many. A state is really a big gang or Mafia that extracts booty from its rivals and "protection money" from its own citizens through the use or the threat of violence. Conversely, gangs or Mafiosi are embryonic states. (van den Berghe 1992:192)*

To the claim that stable political regimes must rest on legitimacy, he said that legitimacy is simply a function of ideology and the extent to which people believe they are part of a state; legitimacy simply allows the state to economize on violence. "State power," he said, "rests on the last analysis on violence or the threat of violence" (1992:192).

Third, he rejected the idea that larger states are more economically viable than smaller states, in spite of arguments to the contrary. Some of the world's most economically powerful political entities—the city-states of Italy, Holland, England,

and Japan—were all relatively small. Finally he argued that most writers obscure the difference between nation and state by hyphenating them. There are, he said, few real nation-states; only Japan, Swaziland, and Somalia have citizens who speak the same language, share the same culture and history, and look on one another as a single ethnic group. Most so-called nation-states—Nigeria, Zaire, India, Canada, and so on—are multicultural, multiethnic, or multilinguistic. Furthermore, 42 percent of all the major ethnic blocs of the world (Basques, Kurds, Koreans, Ewe, Hutu, and others) are split between several states.

Van den Burghe said that the nation-state myth has been allowed to persist because international bodies such as the United Nations insist that internal killing is a state matter, a "gentlemen's agreement" between member states not to protest the butchering of their own citizens. Also, scholars perpetuate the myth with the use of nation-state designation. The result is to legitimize genocide in the interests of building nation-states that function to further economic and political integration.

Carol Nagengast (1994:122) proposed that state-sponsored violence serves to aid in the construction and maintenance of the nation-state. She examined not only state killing but also the institutionalization of torture, rape, and homosexual assault. The purpose of this state-sponsored violence is not to inflict pain but to create what Nagengast called "punishable categories of people," to create and maintain boundaries and legitimate or delegitimate specific groups. State violence against its own citizens, she suggested, is a way to create an Other, an ambiguous underclass that consists on the one hand of subhuman brutes and on the other hand of superhuman individuals capable of undermining the accepted order of society. Arrest and torture serves to stigmatize people and to mark them as people who no one wants to be. Arrest and torture become, in effect, a way of symbolically marking, disciplining, and stigmatizing those categories of people whose existence or demands threaten the idea, power, and legitimacy of the nation-state. Furthermore, since the torture and violence are committed only against "terrorists," "communists," or "separatists," it becomes legitimate. "We only beat bad people," said a Turkish prison official in 1984. "They are no good, they are worthless bums, they are subversives who think that communism will relieve them of the necessity of working." He revealed with apparent pride that he had "given orders that all prisoners should be struck with a truncheon below the waist on the rude parts, and warned not to come to prison again." "My aim," he said, "is to ensure discipline. That's not torture, for it is only the lazy, the idle, the vagabonds, the communists, the murderers who come to prison" (cited Nagengast 1994:121).

The Future of the Nation-State

The nation-state as currently conceived is two to three hundred years old. But what is its future? Some suggest that nation-states are no longer viable or necessary and will disintegrate into smaller, more culturally homogeneous units. Others (see, e.g., Smith 1995) suggest that the nation-state is still the most sensible solution to problems of social and economic order.

However, there are three developments that seem to threaten the integrity of nation-states: transnationalism—an increase in the number of people living and working in countries other than the one in which they hold citizenship; the growing power and influence of transnational corporations; and the growth in the number, and possibly influence, of nongovernmental organizations. Let's complete our examination of the nation-state by reviewing each of these developments.

Transnationalism and Migration

Lenin (1976) made the point that imperialism transported surplus capital from developed to undeveloped areas of the world and, as a consequence, destroyed local economies, replacing peasant farming and small-scale industry with wage labor. But the economies of underdeveloped areas are incapable of absorbing the labor it has created, and that labor is now spilling over into the core of the world capitalist economy. Currently 2 percent of the world's population—100 million people—live and work in countries of which they are not citizens.

Massive labor migration is not a new thing; in the last half of the nineteenth century and the first decades of the twentieth, as we saw in Chapter 2, millions of people migrated in search of land and wage labor. The migrations of the 1980s and 1990s, however, are different in at least two respects. First, labor migrants are maintaining or attempting to maintain close ties with their home countries, and home countries are also attempting to maintain those ties. Not only do Haitian migrants to the United States maintain close ties with their families in Haiti, but the Haitian government refers to those people as Le Dixième Département (*Dizyém Depatman-an* in Creole) of a country with nine geographical divisions or *Depatman*. It is as if Americans working abroad were referred to as a fifty-first state. Second, migrants are no longer as welcome in host core countries as they were in the nineteenth century, when there was an abundance of land and a shortage of labor. These two differences have created a very different view of migrants in their home countries and in the core countries in which they seek to work.

Linda Basch, Nina Glick Schiller, and Cristina Szanton Blanc (1994:7), in their book *Nations Unbound,* labeled the process where people's lives are stretched across national boundaries as transnationalism. They defined *transnationalism* as

> [t]he process by which immigrants forge and sustain multi-stranded social relations that link together their societies of origin and settlement. We call these processes transnationalism to emphasize that many immigrants today build social fields that cross geographic, cultural, and political borders.

Transnationalism, they suggested, requires a reconceptualization of the nation-state; whereas it was once thought of as people sharing a common territory, it now must include citizens who are physically dispersed among other states but who remain socially, politically, culturally, and sometimes economically part of the nation-state of their ancestors (Basch et al., 1994:8).

They believe transnational migrants are a product of global capitalism, as the debt of peripheral countries has created massive unemployment. The unemployed are vulnerable in their own countries because they cannot find work and in the countries to which they migrate because they cannot compete on an equal basis and often are used as scapegoats. It is because of this economic and political vulnerability that migrants construct a transnational existence seeking work in core countries while at the same time maintaining ties with family at home (Basch et al., 1994:27). Consequently, transmigrants are engaged in the nation-building process of two or more nation-states, the state of their origin and the one to which they have migrated in search of work.

Haitian migrants to the United States, for example, often send money and goods home both to aid their family and to advance their social position for their expected return home. One estimate is that in 1989, Haitian immigrants sent $99.5 million from New York to Haiti (Basch 1994:165). Many Haitians living in the United States build, buy, and maintain homes in Haiti and send home furnishings both for their own home and for their kin. Children are sent each year to visit or, in many cases, left in Haiti with kin because it is easier and cheaper to raise them there.

One motivation for maintaining ties arises from loyalty, sentiment, and emotional ties to Haiti. But there is also a sense of precariousness of rooting oneself in the United States, because of racism and discrimination, fear of unemployment, national chauvinism, the high cost of living, and, for some, the continued undocumented status that leaves them vulnerable to discovery and deportation. Marie Rose was born in Haiti but grew up in the United States, was educated in Brooklyn and received a masters of nursing, and became head of a nursing unit in a Brooklyn hospital. She continues to invest in her home in Haiti, where she spends two weekends each year. Her husband moved back to Haiti, taking with him the Mercedes Marie bought in the United States.

For the migrant's home country, migrants are valuable sources of foreign exchange. The home country's dilemma is how to take advantage of the money and goods that transnational migrants send home, while maintaining their identity and loyalty. For example, to promote transnationalism in the mid-1980s, Haitian leaders used Zionists as a model, Jews who were permanently part of U.S. political, social, and economic life but who were made to understand that they had a "homeland" in Israel. Father Jean Bertrand Aristide accelerated this process when he was elected president in 1991, going so far as to appoint to government posts Haitians who had become citizens of other countries. In his address to the United Nations, Aristide insisted his government had a right to intervene on behalf of Haitians living in other countries.

Viewed from the core, transnational migrants pose a different set of problems. The problem is that the often cheap labor supplied by the transnational migrant is desired, but the person who does the labor is not. The question is *how to keep the borders open to cheap transnational labor while at the same time maintaining the boundaries of the nation-state?* In the United States, for example, businesses want foreign labor, but the increase in the number of immigrants threatens some people's sense of their national identity; thus the increase in Spanish-speaking immigrants in the United States increased efforts to have Congress declare English the country's official language.

Michael Kearney (1991:58), examining the situation of the Mexican worker in the United States, suggested that immigration policy in core countries is largely directed to trying to separate the labor from the laborer: foreign labor is desired, but the person in which it is embodied is not. Consequently, the immigration policies of host countries must somehow separate labor from the person who supplies it, must "disembody the labor from the migrant worker."

One way to do this is to pass punitive antimigrant legislation that allows migrants to work in the United States but prohibits access to services, such as education for their children, welfare, and medical assistance. Thus American employers can obtain cheap labor, while the state can deny benefits accorded to citizen laborers. Another solution is to pass language laws that mark any non-English speaker as unqualified to be a member of the nation-state. Kearney pointed out also that even such things as border patrols function not so much to apprehend illegal migrants as to force them to accept low-paying jobs while not claiming benefits accorded to other laborers. He cited the example of migrant Mixtecs, who walk through the mountains in winter to find work and who because of their work ethic are desired by American employers. They don't understand why the *Migra* (border patrol) seek to apprehend them, forcing them to work harder and faster before they are apprehended, and forcing them to take whatever work at whatever wages they can. But, as Kearney (1991:61) pointed out, that is exactly the point of the *Migra;* it

Transnational migrants, such as these Haitian workers in a New York potato field, are desired as workers in the United States but not as persons with social rights.

is not intended to stop migrants from coming into the United States to work; rather it functions to discipline them to work harder and accept low wages.

Thus border areas become contested zones, manifestations of the dilemma of exploiting the laborer while denying the rights of the individual. Kearney noted that the border is as or more troubling to Mexico than it is to the United States. Given the economic situation in Mexico in the early 1990s, where income was dropping and unemployment was increasing, transmigration was highly valued. If Mexicans living and working in the United States were repatriated to Mexico, the increase in unemployment in Mexico would result in an impossible situation and possible social unrest. Furthermore, their return would mean the loss of Mexico's third or fourth most important source of foreign exchange (Kearney 1991:69).

The differences in wealth between the periphery and the core, the need of citizens of peripheral countries to find jobs wherever they are, and the desire in capitalist economies to seek the cheapest labor combine to create a dynamic that increases the number of transnational migrants working in core countries and threatens the boundaries between nation-states. Kearney suggested that boundary-maintaining activities such as language laws and punitive antimigrant legislation represent a sign of a threat to national boundaries. In the era of transnationalism, there is a dissolution of boundaries and a frantic attempt to deal with it by further defining, maintaining, and defending borders.

Will Corporations Rule the World?

Some see yet another entity as a threat to the power of the nation-state—the transnational corporation. In many ways this institution seems a natural development in a process of economic integration that began centuries ago. One of the major dynamics for the development of the nation-state, as mentioned above, is the need to integrate national economies. The growth of business and the creation of the consumer required standardized weights, measures, and currencies, common wages and prices, and a homogeneous consumer population such that a product produced in a given country would be desired by everyone in that country. The state was the main agency enforcing integration, through regulatory agencies, enforced wage and labor standards, and, perhaps most important, the development of state education and schools that would construct populations of Americans, French, English, Germans, Italians, and so on.

But as states required economic integration within their borders, the modern global economy requires global, not just state, integration. The institution best equipped to perform the task of global integration, some argue, is the transnational corporation. David Korten (1995:12) suggested that these entities represent a shift of power away from governments, which are ideally responsible for the public good, toward a few corporations and financial institutions, in which are concentrated massive economic and political power and whose sole motive is the quest for short-term financial gain. The corporation, Korten argued, has evolved from an institution with limited power to one that some claim is the dominant governance institution of the world and which exceeds most governments in size and power (see Table 4.1). One consequence is that corporate interest, as opposed to human interests, define the policy agendas of states and international agencies.

As we saw in Chapter 3, the corporate charter is a social invention that originally was supposed to promote the use of private financial resources for public purposes. It can be traced back to the sixteenth century. Since that time corporations have assumed enormous power and have advanced an ideology that Korten labeled *corporate libertarianism,* which places the rights and freedoms of corporations above the rights and freedoms of individuals. The question is, *how have corporations managed to convince governments of the worth of this ideology?* Perhaps more important, *how have they managed to convince the public that its interests are identical to those of the corporation?* Korten argued that corporations have advanced their interests by gaining control of various international and domestic agencies as well as social, political, and economic institutions (see Table 4.2 on page 138).

The first group of agencies that function to advance corporate interests, according to Korten, are the Council on Foreign Relations, the Bilderberg (named for the Hotel de Bilderberg of Oosterbeek, Holland), and the Trilateral Commission. These are private forums created to bring together people from government, business, the media, and academia to discuss the creation of public policy and create a consensus that aligns our most powerful institutions with the economic globalization agenda. For example, it was the Council on Foreign Relations and its journal, *Foreign Affairs,* that in the late 1930s recommended to President Roosevelt that he create a network of worldwide financial institutions to stabilize currencies and provide capital for the development of peripheral countries. This recommendation led to the conference in 1944 at Bretton Woods at which the World Bank and the International Monetary Fund were created. The Bilderberg began with informal meetings of North American and European leaders in 1954; participants have included virtually every major industrialist, financier, and government leader. The Trilateral Commission was formed in 1973 by David Rockefeller, chair of Chase Manhattan Bank, and Zbigniew Brzezinski, who was to be Secretary of State during the Carter administration. They describe themselves as a group of 325 distinguished citizens. Members have included heads of all the major corporations as well as American presidents (Carter, Bush, Clinton) and many who hold influential government posts. These institutions and others have brought together government, academic, and corporate leaders to create policy that directs the actions of governments and influential world agencies, such as the World Bank, the International Monetary Fund, and the United Nations, toward full integration of the world's capitalist economy.

In addition to these "informal" discussion groups, corporate libertarianism is evident in the working of the World Bank, which functions partly to control the financial links between corporations and borrowers. Thus the International Finance Corporation, one arm of the World Bank, functions to make government-guaranteed loans to private investors on projects deemed too risky for commercial banks.

Another way corporations sell their agenda is through lobbying groups and public relations efforts targeted to political leaders and the public. Until the 1970s this was done through straightforward lobbying groups, such as the Beer Institute

TABLE 4.1   The Top 100 Global Financial Entities

Rank	Country	1991 GNP (US$)	Rank	Country	1991 GNP (US$)
1	United States	5,686.0	51	**IBM**	64.8
2	Japan	3,337.2	52	**IRI**	64.1
3	Germany	1,516.8	53	**American Telephone & Telegraph**	63.3
4	France	1,167.7	54	**GE**	60.2
5	Italy	1,072.2	55	**Tomen**	60.2
6	United Kingdom	963.7	56	Israel	59.1
7	Canada	568.8	57	Portugal	58.5
8	Spain	486.6	58	**British Petroleum**	58.4
9	Russian Federation	479.5	59	**Daimler-Benz**	57.3
10	Brazil	447.3	60	**Sears Roebuck**	57.2
11	China	424.0	61	**Mobil**	56.9
12	Australia	287.8	62	**Hitachi**	56.1
13	India	284.7	63	Iraq (1988)	53.0
14	Netherlands	278.8	64	Venezuela	52.8
15	South Korea	274.5	65	Algeria	52.2
16	Mexico	252.4	66	**Nichimen**	49.9
17	Switzerland	225.9	67	**Cargill**	49.1
18	Sweden	218.9	68	**Matsutshita Electric Industrial**	48.6
19	Belgium	192.4	69	**British Gas**	48.5
20	Austria	157.5	70	**Nippon Telegraph and Telephone**	48.2
21	**ITOCHU**	157.0	71	**Philip Morris**	48.1
22	**Sumitomo**	150.8	72	**Fiat**	46.8
23	**Marubeni**	140.7	73	**Kanematsu**	46.6
24	**Mitsubishi**	136.3	74	Pakistan	46.1
25	**Mitsui & Co.**	133.8	75	Philippines	46.1
26	Iran	127.4	76	**Volkswagen**	46.0
27	**General Motors**	123.8	77	Malaysia	45.8
28	**Electricitéde France**	123.8	78	**Siemens**	44.9
29	Finland	122.0	79	**Kansai Electric Power**	44.6
30	Denmark	121.7	80	**WalMart Stores**	43.9
31	Ukraine	121.5	81	**Samsung Group**	43.7
32	Taiwan	118.9	82	**Nissan Motor**	42.9
33	Indonesia	111.4	83	**GTE**	42.4
34	Saudi Arabia	105.1	84	Colombia	41.9
35	Turkey	103.9	85	Kazakhstan	41.7
36	**Royal Dutch/Shell Group**	103.8	86	New Zealand	41.6
37	**Exxon**	103.2	87	**Unilever**	41.3
38	Norway	102.9	88	**ENI**	41.0
39	Argentina	91.2	89	Singapore	39.2
40	South Africa	91.0	90	**Telefonicode España**	38.8
41	**Stet**	90.3	91	Czechoslovakia	38.4
42	Thailand	89.5	92	Peru	38.3
43	**Ford Motor Co.**	89.0	93	**DuPont**	38.0
44	**Tokyo Electric Power**	87.5	94	**Texaco**	37.6
45	**Nissho Iwai**	86.4	95	**Ontario Hydro**	37.4
46	**Deutsche BundesposteTelekom**	85.3	96	Ireland	37.3
47	**Toyota Motor**	78.1	97	**British Telephone**	37.3
48	Poland	70.6	98	**Chevron**	36.8
49	Yugoslavia (former)	70.0	99	**Chubu Electric Power**	36.8
50	Greece	65.5	100	**Elf Aquitane**	36.3

TABLE 4.2   The Mechanisms of Corporate Control

Agency	Method of Control	Who It Controls
Trilateral Commission, Council on Foreign Relations, Bilderberg	Consensus building	Corporate, government, academic elites
World Bank	Financial control	National financial institutions
Public relations	Consensus building	Government leaders, voters, etc.
Advertising, media, and education	Consumers educational institutions, newspapers, TV, magazines, etc.	General population
World regulatory agencies	Political control	State agencies
Military force	State military organizations, private armies	Dissenters to corporate control and influence

and the National Coal Association. Today corporations try to mask their involvement by forming "citizen" groups, such as the National Wetlands Coalition (with its logo of a duck flying over a swamp), sponsored by oil and gas drilling companies and real estate developers fighting for lessening of restrictions on the conversion of wetlands to drilling sites and shopping malls. Keep America Green, sponsored by the bottling industry, argues for antilitter campaigns rather than mandatory recycling legislation.

Protected by the free speech provision of the First Amendment, corporations marshal huge public relations efforts on behalf of their agendas. In the United States the 170,000 public relations employees whose job it is to manipulate news, public opinion, and public policy in the interests of their clients outnumber news reporters by 40,000. A study in 1990 discovered that almost 40 percent of the news content of a typical U.S. newspaper originates as public relations press releases, story memos, and suggestions. The *Columbia Journalism Review* reported that more than half the news stories in the *Wall Street Journal* are based solely on corporate press releases (cited in Korter 1995:146). United States corporations spend almost half as much on advertising (approximately $120 per person) as the state spends on education ($207 per person). Korten (1995:146) suggested that the world outlined by George Orwell in *1984* has occurred, but it is the corporation rather than the state that is oppressing us: "We are ruled by an oppressive market, not an oppressive state."

Finally, in the 1980s and 1990s corporations gained formal control over international regulatory agencies. The assumption of this control began with the Bretton Woods initiative and culminated with the World Trade Organization. The WTO has the power to override rules and legislation passed by countries and local governments if its three-person panel, in private, decides that the rules "unfairly" inhibit free trade. Thus, the modern transnational corporation can use public policy forums, international financial agencies, public relations organizations, the media, schools, and world regulatory agencies to convince government leaders and the

The powers exercised by corporations through government, through private and public institutions, and through public relations specialists can often result in the voting public supporting actions that may not be in their best interest.

Reprinted with the permission of John Jonik.

public of courses of action that ensure profit making and reduce the risk of financial failure. Furthermore, to the extent that individual lives are influenced by corporate ideology, we may also be witnessing the increase of the authoritarian governance systems common to corporations.

It would seem that the only agency of control lacking in the corporation is armed force. Yet corporations have sometimes managed to co-opt the military of nation-states to serve their own ends or even, on occasion, to organize and equip their own private armies. Early in their development, corporations made use of armies, national guards, and sometimes even their own private military force to end strikes or punish or repress urban and rural protest. Even today corporations often become closely involved in state repression. In 1995 Shell Oil Corporation supplied arms to the Nigerian government as it sought to repress the Ogoni peoples, who were demanding that Shell cease polluting Ogoni lands. Shell earned worldwide condemnation for its involvement and possible acquiescence in the execution of Ogoni leader Ken Saro Wira. Oil companies such as Local 66 have lent direct or indirect support to the repressive regime in Myanmar (Burma), while other corporations appear to seek out relations with repressive regimes that ban labor organizing. We may be witnessing the birth of a new kind of war—"investor wars"—in which governments, to keep or attract foreign corporate investment, systematically repress and make war on minorities whose demands lend an impression of government instability that state leaders fear will scare away corporate investors.

Nongovernmental Organizations

Another set of global organizations that some claim presents an alternative to the nation-state is the nongovernmental organization (NGO). These organizations—also called the nonprofit sector, independent sector, volunteer sector, civic society, grassroots organizations (GROs), transnational social movement organizations, and nonstate actors—generally represent any organization, group, or institution that fulfills a public function but is not a part of the government or the territories in which it works. Nongovernmental organizations may be large transnational organizations, such as Amnesty International or the Red Cross, or small, local-level groups, such as a neighborhood group organized to provide day care. Generally it is the large international groups that some see as alternatives to nation-states.

There are various ways of conceptualizing the role of NGOs in relation to other political and economic bodies. Lester M. Salamon and Helmut K. Anheier (1996: 129) suggested that NGOs represent a third sector in global governance, the other two being the state and the corporation (or "market"). Marc Nerfin (1986) suggested that politically we can conceptualize NGOs using the metaphor of the prince, the merchant, and the people, with governmental power and the maintenance of public order the job of the prince; economic power and the production of goods and services the job of the merchant, and NGOs representing the citizen, the power of the people. In this framework, NGOs developed from citizen demands for accountability from the prince and merchant, competing with them for power and influence, and demands that neglected groups (e.g., the poor, children) be heard (see Weiss and Gordenker 1996:19; Korten 1990:95ff).

The NGO as we know it dates from the founding of the International Red Cross in Switzerland in 1865. Since that time there has been spectacular growth in the number of recognized NGOs, particularly in the 1980s and 1990s in the periphery. In 1909, for example, there were 176 international NGOs; by 1993 there were 28,900. In Nepal the number of registered NGOs rose from 220 in 1990 to 1,210 in 1993; in Bolivia from 100 in 1980 to 530 in 1992; in Tunisia from 1,886 in 1988 to 5,186 in 1991. Often NGOs in the periphery serve and employ thousands of people. In south Asia, for example, the Bangladesh Rural Advancement Committee (BRAC) delivers health, education, and credit services to almost 3 million people and employs 12,000. Some suggest (see, e.g., Edwards and Hulme 1995) that the development of NGOs may be as important in the last part of the twentieth century as the development of the nation-state was in the nineteenth.

Why have NGOs increased in importance? First, some suggest that the end of the Cold War made it easier for NGOs to operate without being drawn into the conflict between the West and the Communist Bloc. Second, revolutions in communication, particularly through the Internet, have helped create new global communities and bonds between like-minded people across state boundaries. Third, there are increased resources and a growing professionalism in NGOs. In 1994, 10 percent of public development aid ($8 billion) was channeled through NGOs, including 25 percent of U.S. assistance and 30 percent of projects funded by the International Bank for Reconstruction and Development. Nongovernmental organizations represent a major growth sector for people seeking employment. Fourth, there is the media's ability to inform more people about global problems. With this increased awareness, the public, particularly but not exclusively in core countries, demand that their governments take action. Finally, and perhaps most important, some people suggest that NGOs have developed as part of a larger, neoliberal economic and political agenda. Edwards and Hulme (1995:4), in *Non-Governmental Organizations*, maintained that the rise in importance of NGOs is neither an accident nor simply a response to local initiative or voluntary action. More important, they said, is the increasing support of NGOs from governments and official aid agencies acting in response to shifts in economic and political ideology.

Neoliberal economics assumes that markets and private initiative are the most efficient mechanisms for achieving economic growth and providing effective services. Governments, the theory assumes, should minimize their role because NGOs are more efficient in providing service. Thus NGOs are seen by nation-states themselves as the preferred way of delivering educational, welfare, and health services (Edwards and Hulme 1995:4). As a consequence, there is a good deal of evidence to suggest that NGOs are growing because of increased amounts of public funding. In recent years NGOs not dependent on state aid are the exception rather than the rule; furthermore, most of the aid has gone primarily to finance welfare services and development. Thus NGOs serve to replace, perhaps at a lower cost, the services in welfare, health, and education that peripheral countries are being forced to cut in exchange for World Bank loans, foreign investments, or loan restructuring.

There is plenty of evidence that the growth in size and number of NGOs is fed by increased governmental contributions along with greater contributions from multilateral developmental organizations such as the World Bank. On the one hand, these conditions have created additional monies for NGOs and GROs to develop; on the other hand, they risk becoming so dependent on governments that they have been co-opted and their independence threatened.

Regardless of the reasons for their increase there is little doubt of the continuing global influence of NGOs. As Lester M. Salamon and Helmut K. Anheier (1996:129) conclude:

> *Fundamental historical forces—a widespread loss of confidence in the state, expanding communications, the emergence of a more vibrant commercial and professional middle class, and increased demands for a wide range of specialized services—have come together in recent years to expand the role of private, non-profit organizations in virtually every part of the world. Such organizations enjoy distinctive advantages in delivering human services, responding to citizen pressure, and giving expression to citizen demands. As a consequence, the nonprofit sector has*

*come into its own as a major social and economic force, with substantial and grow-
ing employment and a significant share of the responsibility for responding to
public needs.*

Conclusion

The state emerged some seven to eight thousand years ago to politically integrate
largely heterogeneous peoples and cultures. Military conquest was the main vehicle for their creation and maintenance. Two to three hundred years ago, the nation-
state developed to fulfill a new need, that of economic integration. Military conquest as a device was not entirely abandoned, but new strategies of integration,
such as improved means of communication and transportation, national education
systems, and the ideology of nationalism, became preferred means of attaining
desired economic ends.

The nation-state helped create the type of people—laborers and consumers—
required to maintain and protect the interests of the capitalist. It created and maintained an unprecedented division of labor and imposed a shared culture that enabled workers to communicate with precision, while thirsting for the commodities
that labor produced and which served as the basis of the elite's wealth.

More important, terror and violence remained state instruments of integration,
serving to eliminate those who refused to assimilate into the new ideal of the nation-state or to mark as undesirable Others against whom the majority could unite.
As a consequence, millions have died as victims of their own governments.

But the need to integrate regions and territories economically is being replaced
by the need for global integration, while variations in the availability and price of
labor is leading to massive labor migrations that threaten state boundaries. In the
absence of a world government, organizations such as corporations and NGOs
have moved in to fulfill functions once thought the purview of the state, as other
organizations have developed to protect the rights of individuals and indigenous
groups—who, as we shall see, have suffered disproportionately in the drive to create the nation-state.

With this discussion of the nation-state, we conclude our outline of the culture
of capitalism and the origins of and relations among consumer, laborer, capitalist,
and nation-state. These relationships may seem complex but they are written on
virtually every commodity we possess. For example, sneakers were once for kids
or tennis or basketball players. Consumers for this commodity have been cleverly
created through massive advertising campaigns involving, among other things,
endorsements from popular sports figures, which not only make the shoes fashionable but allow Nike and other corporations to sell them for up to hundreds of dollars. To make the shoes Nike has, as they should do to please their investors,
sought out cheap sources of labor. The labor for a pair of Nike sneakers costs less
than $1 per pair, and the total amount Nike spends on labor is about the same as
that paid to sports figures for endorsements (see Figure 4.1). As a consequence,
Nike earns billions of dollars, returning much of it to banks and investors and using

DOONESBURY   Garry Trudeau

(continued)

FIGURE 4.1   The use of overseas assembly plants by corporations is a major
source of humor, as well as criticism; this is illustrated in this
series of Garry Trudeau cartoons that focus on the ethical
implications for male athletes who earn more for endorsing Nike
sneakers, than overseas assembly workers earn for making them.

(continued)

some to influence government legislation that would be favorable to its interests. To help generate this profit, nation-states support the entire operation by supporting and maintaining communication networks, financial institutions, and favorable labor legislation. Thus countries such as Vietnam and Indonesia offer tax breaks to Nike and control and discipline their labor force to ensure an inexpensive and docile work force, many of whom use their wages to purchase Nike products.

Thus while the historical, social, cultural, economic, political, and ideological factors that have helped create and maintain the culture of capitalism are in their totality complex, they can be identified in virtually every element of our culture, at least for those who care to look. Furthermore, as we shall see, these same factors contribute in one way or another to virtually every global issue that we discuss in the remainder of this book.

The Global Impact of the Culture of Capitalism

> *How can one deny the fascinating creativity of [capitalism] which in a few centuries has passed from mechanical looms powered by running water or steam to industrial robots capable of carrying out a series of complex operations; from printing to teletransmissions; from the discovery of America to the exploration of space? And how can one not be haunted by the destructive capacity of this dynamic at work?*
> —*MICHEL BEAUD*, A HISTORY OF CAPITALISM

Chapter **5**

The Problem of
Population Growth

*America and other rich nations have a clear choice today. They can continue
to ignore the population problem and their own massive contributions to it.
Then they will be trapped in a downward spiral that may well lead to the end of
civilization in a few decades. More frequent droughts, more damaged crops and
famines, more dying forests, more smog, more international conflicts, more epidemics, more gridlock, more drugs, more crime, more sewage swimming,
and other extreme unpleasantness will mark our course. It is a route
already traveled by too many of our less fortunate fellow human beings.*
—*PAUL EHRLICH AND ANNE EHRLICH,*
THE POPULATION EXPLOSION

*So why did the policies concerning population and family planning programs
change so drastically in the last [few] decade[s]? As in late eighteenth century
Britain, population has been growing rapidly. The expanding numbers of third
world people, who are no longer dutiful subjects toiling in their mines and fields
are not consumers either for an ever-expanding flow of manufactured products,
have become a burden for the industrial powers. They are not only a burden, but
also a threat, for, as in the time of Malthus, a great revolution is taking place.*
—*STEVEN POLGAR,* BIRTH PLANNING

Some modern research on the genetic structure of human populations suggests
that we are all descended from a relatively small number of individuals, and no
more than a few families, who lived in Central Africa as recently as 100,000–
200,000 years ago. By 15,000 years ago their progeny numbered 15 million (the
present population of Mexico City). The world population at the time of Christ had
increased to about 250 million (a little less than the present population of the
United States) and on the eve of the Industrial Revolution had tripled to about 700
million (a little less than the current population of Indonesia). In the following two

TABLE 5.1   Population, Annual Growth, and Doubling Time, 10,000 B.C. to 2000 A.D.

Year	10,000 B.C.	0	1750	1950	1990	2000 (projected)
Population (millions)	16	252	771	2530	5292	6100
Annual growth (%)	0.008	0.037	0.064	0.596	1.845	1.3000
Doubling time (years)	8369	1854	1083	116	38	25

centuries the population increased at an annual growth rate of 6 per 1,000, reaching 2.5 billion by 1950. In the following five decades it has more than doubled, at a growth rate of 18 per 1,000, today approaching 6 billion. In spite of signs that the growth rate is slowing, barring some demographic catastrophe, the world population will reach 8 to 10 billion by the year 2030 (Livi-Bacci 1992:31–32). Growth in world population is summarized in Table 5.1.

Listed below are some interesting facts and projections about world population growth:

- The rate of population increase, now approximately 1.7 percent per year, is expected to decline to a little less than 1 percent sometime during 2020–2025.
- Since the rate of population increase applies to an increasing population, the actual increase will be 88–97 million people per year in 1995–2000 before falling to 81 million per year in 2025.
- Developing countries will account for 95 percent of the world's population increase during 2000–2025.
- Between 1950 and 2025 the core countries' share of world population will have decreased from 33.1 percent to 15.9 percent; Europe's share will decrease from 15.6 percent to 6.1 percent.
- Also during 1950–2025, Latin America's share of the world's population will increase from 6.6 percent to 8.9 percent, Asia from 54.7 percent to 57.8 percent, and Africa's share from 8.9 percent to 18.8 percent.

The rapid rise in the rate of population growth has prompted concern that the world is poised on the brink of disaster, that we are running out of enough food to sustain the growing population and that population growth is responsible for poverty, environmental destruction, and social unrest. Moreover, so the argument goes, economic development in poor countries is impossible as long as populations continue to rise, because any increase in economic output must be used to sustain the increased population instead of being invested to create new jobs and wealth. These concerns have led to concerted efforts by international agencies and governments to control population growth, especially in peripheral countries where it is highest.

However, a number of people seriously question whether population growth is a problem. Some economists argue that population growth is a positive factor in economic development; some environmentalists claim that environmental destruction is a result of rapid industrialization and capitalist consumption patterns, not population growth; and some religious authorities are opposed to any form of birth control.

In 1994 the United Nations sponsored a conference in Cairo to examine the problem of population growth and propose measures to control it. The Cairo conference debated several approaches to controlling fertility; these included promoting modern contraception, promoting economic development, improving survival rate of infants and children, improving women's status, educating men, and various combinations of these. Except for the religious objections to promoting decreased fertility, few people questioned that there was a population problem, that it was a problem primarily of the poor nations, and that the solution required women to limit their fertility. Yet few if any of the assumptions underlying the issue of population growth and control were seriously questioned or examined. Some of these assumptions are as follows.

- Population growth contributes to economic decline and stagnation in the periphery and thus is responsible for global poverty, hunger, environmental devastation, and political unrest.
- Population increase in the periphery historically resulted from decreased mortality (death) rates, especially of infants, attributable to medical advancements, better nutrition, and improved sanitation.
- Population stability before the rapid population growth beginning in the eighteenth century was solely the result of a high mortality rate balanced by a high fertility rate.
- Efforts to control population growth in the periphery are hampered by religious beliefs that promote large families and lack of education for women.
- The only way to slow the birth rate is through birth control techniques and educational programs developed in Western countries.

These assumptions comprise part of the ideology of the culture of capitalism, which assumes that the problem of population growth is a problem of the periphery. This ideology drives not only public perception of the issue of population growth but also the policies of governments and international agencies such as the United Nations. Population growth, so the ideology goes, is a problem in Latin America, Africa, and Asia, and if the problem is to be solved these countries are the ones that must do it. These assumptions are given legitimacy by "scientific" theories that purport to explain population growth. Furthermore, this ideology leads us to "blame the victim," to assume the people who suffer from the supposed evils of population growth—hunger, poverty, environmental devastation, and political unrest—are the ones who have caused the problem.

However, as we shall see, the situation is more complex than that. To understand better the demographic and ideological issues involved in the population debate, we need first to examine the major frameworks used to explain population growth, the *Malthusian* or *neo-Malthusian* position, and the framework provided by *demographic transition theory*. We will try to show how they are seriously flawed, ethnocentric, and self-serving for core nations. Then we will examine some of the factors known to determine how many children are born and specifically examine what anthropology can contribute to the debate over population growth.

The Malthusians versus the Revisionists

Interest in the effects of increasing population date back at least as far as the Reverend Thomas Malthus's famous *Essay on the Principle of Population,* written in 1798, which outlines his well-known argument that while population "increases in a geometrical ratio," the resources for survival, especially food, "increase only in an arithmetical ratio" (see Livi-Bacci 1992:76). Without preventive checks to control fertility, such as "moral restraint" or "marriage postponement," argued Malthus, population will constantly increase, deplete resources, and bring into play "positive checks"—famine, disease, and war—that will return population to a balance with resources.

Malthus had some historical confirmation for his ideas. For example, he predicted that as population rose and the demand on resources increased, food prices (e.g., grain) would increase and result in increased mortality rates. Indeed, this seemed to have been the case in Europe in the seventeenth and eighteenth centuries. Likewise, he predicted that a decreased demand due to population decrease would result in lower prices, decreased mortality, and a subsequent rise in population, exactly as occurred in Europe after the plague epidemics of the fourteenth century.

Malthus predicted that disaster was imminent. What he failed to foresee was that in the face of increasing population, innovations in agricultural techniques would result in constantly increasing food production. Even though the world population today is at least six times what it was in 1800, there is still more than enough food produced worldwide to support the population.

In spite of his failed predictions, others have recently revived Malthus's message, arguing that while Malthus may have been wrong in his early projections no one could foresee the explosive growth of population in the past fifty years. Food production, they say, is now beginning to fall behind population growth, and even innovations that improve production are only stopgap measures. Neo-Malthusians may disagree on how close we are to disaster, but they unanimously agree that unless we take measures to reduce population growth, especially in the periphery, the whole planet faces ruin. The consequences of this population growth, they say, are now all around us in overcrowded cities, polluted environments, increased crime, and massive immigration. But their arguments have the most far-reaching implications in policies regarding economic development. It is impossible, according to Neo-Malthusians, for poor countries to escape poverty when their populations grow at a rate greater than 2 percent per year, because resources that could be used to increase living standards must instead go to maintaining the people added to the population. Thus any economic innovations will provide only temporary relief because the gains are quickly offset by the increase in population. They conclude that the only way economic development can provide benefits is for these countries to lower their birth rates. The governments of most countries must agree, since 127 countries, representing 94 percent of the world's population, express support for family planning.

Economist J. E. Meade (1967; see also Livi-Bacci 1992), provided a parable to illustrate what he saw as the folly of population growth. He tells of two imaginary countries, Sterilia and Fertilia. Sterilia is a coastal country with a democratic government and an ethnically mixed population. Fertilia, an inland country with a homogenous population, is ruled by upper-class landowners who have little contact with the outside world. Both countries were colonized; both received their independence at the same time and had similar demographic characteristics—high fertility (birth rate) and high mortality (death rate). Mortality, however, was sharply reduced in both countries by DDT spraying that eliminated malaria-bearing mosquitoes and penicillin that controlled disease.

Sterilia's government promoted economic development and to that end instituted a well-organized family planning program. The imperial elite of Fertilia, however, did little to control their growing population. Consequently, the surplus rural population flooded into the cites, and economic capital had to be used to support the growing number of poor, leaving little to invest in education, roads, communications, and health. People in Sterilia, on the other hand, began having smaller families and were able to save money which became capital for economic investment. Their well-fed, healthy, efficient workers produced and sold products and goods that earned more money to be invested in education, creating a still more efficient and profitable work force. Consequently, Sterilia surged ahead, with growing commerce, increasing literacy, and expanding health programs, whereas Fertilia became trapped in a spiral of increasing poverty. The moral of Meade's parable is clear: those countries that institute successful programs of birth control will prosper; those that do not will suffer economic and social decline. But is that really true?

The Case of India and China

We do have a real-life Sterilia and Fertilia—China and India, countries that together represent 38 percent of the population of the periphery. India, the Fertilia of our parable, has since the early 1950s promoted family planning programs, but with little success. When early attempts to convince couples to have fewer children failed, the government tried more coercive means, attempting to pass laws requiring sterilization after the third child (one province passed such a law but never enforced it). When that failed, the government attempted to convince women to use an intrauterine device, but this failed because of exaggerated rumors about the dangers of the devices. Oral contraceptives were never authorized for use in India. Consequently, the policy of population reduction has not been successful. While the birth rate fell from 5.97 children per woman in 1950 to 4.30 in 1990, increases in

A poster in India promoting birth control and family planning; the top figure represents a happy, Western-type nuclear family, while the bottom figure represents the alleged horrors befalling families with numerous children.

life expectancy pushed the population growth rate over the same period from 2.0 percent to 2.1 percent per year.

China, our real-life Sterilia, embarked on a concerted effort to control population growth in 1970, twenty years after India. In 1980 they developed a program to ensure that their population of 996 million would not exceed 1.2 billion by the year 2000. The government instituted policies to raise the age at marriage, increase birth intervals, and limit to two the number of children couples could have. Provincial leaders were assigned birth quotas and groups were formed to encourage the use of contraceptives, sterilization, and abortion, which was widespread, free, and did not require the husband's consent. Later, a one-child policy was encouraged by providing incentives for those complying (higher wages, larger houses, priority for children's education, and free medical care) and penalties for those not complying (wage cuts, smaller houses, lower priorities for education and medical care).

In spite of public resistance and a population with a large number of women of reproductive age, China has succeeded where India failed. Population growth fell from 2.2 percent in 1970 to 1.4 percent in 1990, and the number of children per woman fell from 5.99 in 1970 to 2.50 in 1990. Whereas India's population in 2025 will be four times what it was in 1950, China's population will have increased by a factor of less than three. One would predict, therefore, that the rate of economic growth will be higher in China than in India.

But that hasn't happened. In fact, both countries are beginning to improve economically, China ranking sixty-sixth in one measure of economic development and India sixty-ninth. Moreover, if we compare economic growth and standard of living as measured by the gross domestic product (GDP) of poor countries in general to population growth in those countries, there is no relationship. If we measure progress, as some have suggested, by an index of social freedom, India ranks well above China (see Livi-Bacci 1992:186–187). There are still significant differences between India and China: China has done notably better in improving the quality of life of the bulk of its population, ranking ahead of India in areas such as literacy, health care, life expectancy, and nutrition. But the reasons for these improvements are largely attributed to China's social policies and seem to have little to do with the rate of population growth.

Economists and demographers who have examined the connection between economic development and population growth in other countries have discovered little evidence that population growth inhibits economic development. In fact, historically, population growth correlates with economic prosperity, while population decline or stability is generally associated with economic stagnation or decline. For example, from 1820 to 1987, the population of the four leading Western nations (Great Britain, France, Germany, and the United States) grew by a factor of 5.5, while their combined GDP (in constant prices) increased by 93.0. In other words, while population increased five times production increased seventeenfold. Demographer Massimi Livi-Bacci (1992:145), after reviewing studies that examine the relationship between demographic and economic growth, concluded that during the past two centuries population growth has not hindered economic development and quite possibly the reverse is true, with the countries that experienced the greatest population increase assuming the leading role in the global economy.

Does the real-life failure of the parable of Fertilia and Sterilia mean there is no connection between population growth and economic development? That's difficult to say, but it does suggest that the connection is obscured by factors that probably cancel each other out. It also means population growth has not been an insurmountable obstacle to economic development.

The question is, then, *why doesn't population growth inhibit economic growth?* There are several possible reasons. First, predictions of decline in resources accompanying population growth have not been borne out. Resources—foodstuffs, raw materials, energy, and so on—are neither more scarce nor more expensive, and the efficiency with which we use resources has clearly improved. For example, in 1850 production of $1,000 worth of goods or services required the equivalent of 4.6 tons of petroleum equivalent; in 1900 this figure had dropped to 2.4 tons and in 1978 to 1.5 tons, a tripling of the ratio between cost and profit.

Second, neo-Malthusians tend to see people as consumers only; they fail to take into account that people also produce and that what they produce is often greater than what they consume. To some extent, they forget that human culture, unlike that of other animals, allows us to marshal additional energy sources.

To illustrate, economists at the United Nations developed a table based on the idea that people *consume* a certain amount of wealth and energy and that they also *produce* a certain amount, and that the amount produced and consumed varies by age. That is, at certain ages people consume more than they produce, while at others they produce more than they consume (see Table 5.2).

From birth to the age of twenty, and again beginning at age 65, people consume more than they produce. Between the ages of twenty and sixty-five, people produce more than they consume; that is, they contribute more to the economy than they detract from it. This means that as life expectancy of a population increases, the excess of production over consumption will also increase; that is, there is an excess in consumption when life expectancy is twenty or thirty years, while at a life expectancy of forty years output exceeds consumption. The table also suggests that societies whose members have life expectancies of fifty years or more produce the greatest excess of production over consumption, and this corresponds to the so-called economic "take-off" of several countries, including England, Wales, Sweden, and Japan (Omran 1971:532).

Of course, the table represents only a rough approximation of the relationship between life expectancy and productivity; productivity also varies according to

TABLE 5.2 Production and Consumption by Age

Age	Excesses in Consumption	Age	Excesses in Output
0–1	50	20–25	260
1–5	225	25–30	300
5–10	332	30–35	350
10–15	450	35–40	350
15–20	350	40–45	320
65–70	350	45–50	290
70–75	400	50–55	260
75–80	500	55–60	215
80+	650	60–65	85

See also A. Sauvy, *General Theory of Population,* New York: Basic Books, 1969.

available technology and the division of labor in a given society. In some areas of the world, for example, children contribute to household work or income as early as six or eight years old and are fully functioning members of the work force at thirteen. In those instances people are net economic contributors at earlier ages than in societies where members enter the work force in their twenties.

The third reason why population increase may not lead to economic decline is because of economies of scale; that is, the benefits of a resource multiply by their use. For example, a road's usefulness is clearly related to how heavily it is traveled. Since its function is to help trade, increase communication, and create a larger market, the more people who use it the more benefits it creates. Or if education is thought to stimulate growth, it follows that once schools are created, the more people who attend them the more benefits will accrue. Thus increases in population may make existing resources such as roads, schools, factories, and hospitals more economically profitable.

Fourth, since the consumption of commodities is what drives a capitalist economy, the more people there are, the greater, theoretically, is the demand for goods and services.

Finally, agricultural economist Ester Boserup (1965) suggested that human population growth can serve as a stimulus to agricultural and technological innovation. For example, in agricultural societies, as population increases people will farm more territory, farm the same territory more often, and use new technology, thus producing more food to support the growing population. This may require more work, but it will feed more people.

In sum, there is little evidence to indicate that economic growth is slowed by population increases. This does not necessarily mean there is no relationship, only that the evidence linking economic growth with population is far too tenuous to account for the alarms that Malthusians and neo-Malthusians have raised. But *isn't is possible that human beings are simply using up the space and resources allotted to them?*

The Issue of Carrying Capacity

Even if we accept the idea that population has not yet inhibited economic growth, *can we say, as many neo-Malthusians do, that while we haven't felt the impact yet, the reduced doubling time of the population will soon result in the human population exceeding the carrying capacity of the Earth?* Biologists use the term *carrying capacity* to denote the maximum number of organisms a given environment will support. For example, we can examine the types of food that sustain wolves in a specific environment and, by calculating how much of that food is available, estimate the number of wolves the environment will support. This is the kind of assumption Malthusians make about the human population: given food and other resources on the planet, how many people can survive before those resources are depleted?

The problem with applying the theory of carrying capacity to human beings is that our capacity for culture and symbolic thought enables us constantly to alter our diets and the way we exploit the environment for food. It is true, for example, that a given environment will support only so many people who live by gathering wild plants and hunting wild animals. But when a gathering and hunting people exceeded the population a given area could support and were restricted from migrating to another area, they could and did begin to plant and harvest their own plants and herd and breed their own animals. Later, when agricultural populations began to grow, they began to farm yet more land using techniques that allowed them to grow more food on the same land. Human beings are capable of constantly changing the rules of subsistence by altering their resource base. In fact, estimates of the Earth's carrying capacity vary widely, from 7.5 billion to 147.0 billion, depending on the technology employed to produce food (Livi-Bacci 1992:207; Cohen 1995). It is consequently difficult if not impossible to predict when our ability to provide for additional people will end, if ever. And that is one of the major arguments between Malthusians and Revisionists.

If we conclude that the alarms raised by neo-Malthusian arguments are unsubstantiated, it is fair to ask, *why do Malthusian alarms dominate the dialogue about the so-called problems of population growth?* More specifically, *why are their arguments so attractive to politicians and policy planners, and why do people so readily accept their assumptions?*

The Ideology of Malthusian Concerns

One of the important questions addressed by anthropologists concerns why people believe what they do about themselves and the world. That is, what social purpose or function does a particular belief serve? For example, if people believe that witches exist, and that they will punish people who harm others, the belief will serve to enforce proper social behavior. If people believe that gazing at someone with envy can harm that person, members of that society will be reluctant to flaunt their wealth, fearing it might attract an "evil eye." It is legitimate to examine the social function or purpose of any viewpoint, even those that are scientifically founded. Regardless of whether or not Malthusian assumptions are correct, it is legitimate to ask what social interests or purposes might be advanced by their acceptance (see Barnes 1974). Put another way, *do Malthusian arguments about population growth mask other concerns or social interests?*

For example, population growth was not, for Thomas Malthus, the major issue. What concerned him was the rising number of poor in England, why they should exist, and what should be done about them. Poverty, according to Malthus, was not a consequence of expanding industrialism, enclosure laws that evicted people from common lands, or the need of manufacturers for a source of inexpensive labor, but arose from the laws of nature, the discrepancy between the powers of reproduction and the ability to expand food production. People were poor because there were too many of them, and because they kept having children in spite of their poverty. Providing relief to the poor, argued Malthus, would simply encourage them to have more children. Instead, they should be forced to delay marriage (Malthus was opposed to all forms of birth control). In 1834, encouraged to a large extent by Malthus's writings, the British government revised the so-called

Poor Law, repealing various forms of relief that had been in place for centuries and leaving the destitute to decide whether their condition required their access to public shelters that were deliberately made into places of horror (Polgar 1975:86).

The Malthusian position assumes that if poverty exists it must be because of overpopulation, which is the fault of those people who, because of a lack of moral standards, refuse to change their reproductive behavior. There also may have been in the Malthusian position a fear that the army of the poor gathering in cities such as London would stimulate revolution, much as it did in France in 1787.

Malthus's ideas did not go unchallenged during the nineteenth century. Karl Marx, as we examined earlier, saw poverty not as a consequence of excess population but as a condition produced by the capitalist mode of production, which required a surplus of labor, an "industrial reserve army" condemned to compete for wages, with the losers doomed to unemployment and underemployment. It is their exclusion or partial exclusion from the economy and their dependence on wage labor, not their numbers, said Marx, that determined their impoverished condition.

Malthusian explanations for poverty and demographic theory were resurrected by neo-Malthusians after World War II. In his 1968 book *The Population Bomb*, biologist Paul Ehrlich, whose work is among the most influential in reviving Malthusian theory, described how he came to discover the significance of the population problem. It dawned on him, he said, "one stinking hot night in Delhi."

> *As we crawled through the city [in a taxi], we entered a crowded slum area. The temperature was well over 100 degrees and the air was a haze of dust and smoke. The streets seemed alive with people. People eating, people washing, people sleeping. People visiting, people arguing and screaming. People thrust their hands through the taxi window, begging. People defecating and urinating. People clinging to buses. People herding animals. People, people, people, people. As we moved slowly through the mob, hand horn squawking, the dust, noise, heat, and cooking fires gave the scene a hellish aspect. Would we ever get to our hotel? All three of us were, frankly, frightened...since that night I've know the* feel *of overpopulation. (Erlich 1968:15)*

As Indian sociologist Mahmood Mamdani (1972) pointed out, had Ehrlich been in Times Square in New York or Picadilly Circus in London he would have been in the midst of an even larger population, but those situations would not likely have led Ehrlich to fear overpopulation. Ehrlich was disturbed not by the number of people but by their poverty and the physical threat posed by a poor and potentially unruly populace.

In addition to those who blamed the poor for their poverty and targeted them for population reduction, Malthusian demographic and social theory also appealed to eugenicists, those who saw poverty as a consequence of faulty genes rather than national social or economic policy. Eugenic theory is rooted incorrectly in Charles Darwin's ideas about natural selection and "fitness." Eugenicists reason that Darwin's ideas can be applied to human populations, and that if people with defective genetic endowments had more offspring than those with superior genetic

Whether a place is perceived as "overpopulated" or not often depends on its degree of opulence; while these crowded streets of Seoul, South Korea are packed, few would see a "population problem." The poverty represented by this beggar's line in Varanasi, India, would more likely create concerns about "overpopulation."

endowments, the quality of the human race (or German "race," or British "race") would decline. Consequently, for eugenicists it makes sense to promote policies that discourage or prevent people with defective genes to reproduce, while encouraging people with superior genes to have as many offspring as possible. Clearly, they reason, people are poor because they have a faulty heredity.

Eugenics has long been discredited by most scientists, although it sometimes appears in modified forms, as it has recently in the debate over the inheritance of intelligence and IQ (see Cohen 1998; Robbins 1997:171ff). But in the heyday of eugenics in the 1920s, groups such as the Committee to Study and Report on the Best Means of Cutting Off the Defective Germ-Plasm of the United States concluded that "Society must look upon the germ-plasm as belonging to society and not merely to the individual who carries it" (cited Polgar 1975:189).

Another advocate of Malthusian demography, Garrett Hardin would write:

How can we reduce reproduction? ... But in the long run a purely voluntary system selects for its own failure: non cooperators outbreed cooperators. So what restraints shall we employ? A policeman under every bed? ... We need not titillate our minds with such horrors, for we already have at hand an acceptable technology— sterilization.... If parenthood is only a privilege, and if parents see themselves as trustees of the germ plasm and guardians of the rights of future generations, then there is hope for mankind. (cited Polgar 1975:190)

We will probably never know how many women in the world or in the United States were sterilized by those who felt they were ridding the population of "defective" genes. Allan Chase, in *The Legacy of Malthus* (1976), estimated that up to 1975 half of the one million sterilizations performed *yearly* in the United States were involuntary.

It should be apparent that it is difficult historically to separate advocates of birth control from racist and eugenic agendas. In the past, and perhaps today, programs to control or reduce population have often masked racist and sexist policies aimed at controlling the poor. Early concerns about population growth were directed at the poor in the core—the urban poor of England, Blacks and Native Americans in the United States, immigrants, and the rural poor. It was not until the 1950s that Western nations began to concern themselves with the fertility of people in the periphery. One question is, *why, in the 1950s and 1960s, did population growth in the periphery begin to concern Western governments?*

One reason may be the same as that for concern over poor populations in the core: it cost money to try to help them. Malthusians such as Paul Ehrlich embraced ideas such as those advocated by William and Paul Paddock, who in their 1967 book *Famine—1975* advocated using the military triage policy for food aid. The Paddocks recommended that the United States use its excess food production to halt starvation only in those countries that would submit to its power:

> *During the coming Age of Food that nation which has the most food will be, if it uses that food as a source of power, the strongest nation. This will be, then, clearly an era which the United States can dominate—if the United States picks up the challenge. (Paddock and Paddock 1967:232)*

Furthermore, advocates of population control share a concern for mass migration of the poor to their countries as well as for social unrest that could upset economic and political stability in the countries of the periphery. For example, a National Security Study memorandum produced in 1974 by the National Security Council at the request of U.S. Secretary of State Henry Kissinger concluded that population growth in the periphery is a threat to U.S. national security for four reasons: because larger nations will gain greater political power; because populous nations may deny the United States access to needed strategic materials; because a growing population will include a large number of young people who may be more likely to challenge global power structures; and because the growing population may threaten U.S. investors in those countries. The memorandum targets India, Brazil, Egypt, Nigeria, Indonesia, the Philippines, Bangladesh, Pakistan, Mexico, Thailand, Turkey, Ethiopia, and Colombia as the countries of greatest concern.[1]

Thus, as Steven Polgar (1972, 1975) suggested, U.S. foreign policy was driven less by a concern for overpopulation than by a concern that increasing population

---

[1]The original memorandum is available online at *Africa 2000* at http://www.africa2000.com/INDX/nssm200.htm. A link can also be found at the Web site for this book at http://www.plattsburgh.edu/legacy/

in the periphery hindered the possibility of raising the income level (and purchasing power) of people in the periphery and a concern that increased populations might represent a political and economic threat to the United States. Polgar said that population concerns in core countries stem not from a fear of overpopulation but from a change in the role of exploited countries. People in the periphery were needed at first for labor and later for markets. In fact, until the 1940s core countries not only were unconcerned with population growth in the periphery, but they complained it was too slow. Once the need for certain raw materials declined as synthetics were developed, and as the poverty of these people precluded their being turned into consumers, they ceased being useful, especially since they became potential revolutionaries, migrants, and criminals. "The subjects," as Polgar (1972: 197) put it, "have become burdens."

Not everyone who believes there is a population problem or that poverty is a consequence of overpopulation is a racist or an imperialist. But people have been far too ready to accept the basic Malthusian assumptions without question. The consequence is that Malthusian explanations for poverty, environmental destruction, disease, and social unrest may mask other, more pertinent, reasons for these problems and divert our attention from them. But it is not only Malthusian assumptions that have dominated the public discussions about population.

Demographic Transition Theory

The other framework that dominates discussions of the population problem is the *theory of demographic transition* (see Table 5.3). According to this theory, world population growth increased only very slowly from human beginnings to around 1750. This relatively steady state of population growth was maintained largely because high birth rates were offset by high death rates. Toward the end of the eighteenth century and the beginning of the nineteenth, mortality began to decline in developed countries because of advances in medicine and sanitation, while birth rates remained the same; consequently, population rose rapidly. Then, because of population pressures and the availability of contraception, birth rates declined to close to "replacement levels" and the rate of population growth stabilized, at least in the developed countries (see Coale 1974).

The population rise in the periphery came later, beginning in the mid-twentieth century, but was particularly explosive because mortality rates were reduced

TABLE 5.3   Stages of Demographic Transition

	Birth Rate	Mortality Rate	Population Growth
Stage 1	High	High	Stable
Stage 2	High	Low	Accelerated
Stage 3	Low	Low	Stable

much more quickly than in core countries, especially among children. Fertility rates in the periphery, according to demographic transition theory, are only now beginning to decline in response to population growth. This occurs when the increasing costs of education and child care in modernizing societies, along with the availability of modern forms of contraception, provide the incentives and means for people to reduce their family size.

The demographic transition model shares assumptions with neo-Malthusian theory: it, too, links lowered fertility with economic development. However, instead of arguing that economic development requires lower fertility, demographic transition theorists suggest that lowered fertility will result from economic development. The problem with this model is that it makes some decidedly ethnocentric assumptions.

First, it assumes that throughout history fertility rates have always been uniformly high. High fertility rates were necessary, reason demographic transition theorists, to balance the number of deaths that occurred because of the harsh living conditions of preindustrial peoples. Yet there was clearly an ethnocentric bias in this assumption; while demographic theorists recognized that fertility rates among preindustrial Europeans did vary depending on the age at which marriage occurred, as we'll see below, they assumed that preindustrial non-Europeans would not or could not control their fertility rates.

Second, the demographic transition model assumes that the only way of stabilizing population growth is to make available Western methods of birth control and contraception. As we shall see, the model significantly ignores variations in fertility that are due to various economic and social factors as well as the fact that preindustrial populations were significantly healthier than we give them credit for.

Third, it assumes that the resistance of people in poor countries to adopt Western standards of fertility is the result of irrational thinking, outmoded religious values, or traditional or fatalistic worldviews. Fertility control, in contrast, is consistently viewed as rational and modern (Caldwell 1982:119).

Finally, some claim that demographic transition theory has its own ideological bias, that its goal is to provide an alternative to Marx's idea of a surplus reserve of workers. As we noted earlier, Marx saw capitalism as creating a surplus population because competition for scarce jobs would allow merchants, manufacturers, and governments to keep wages as low as possible. If labor was scarce, on the other hand, employers would have to compete for laborers and wages would increase. If Marx was correct, one would have expected colonial governments to encourage population growth in the periphery, rather than restrict it. In fact, that is exactly what happened. In the early twentieth century, colonial governments in Africa worried about the *low* population and subsequent lack of laborers, and did everything they could to increase the birth rate.

Demographic transition theorists blame high population growth in the periphery on the people themselves, arguing that capitalist expansion, rather than causing the problem of population growth, can cure it. In other words, demographic transition models see economic development as an answer to the problem; Marx viewed economic development as a cause (O'Brien 1994).

Demographic transition theorists generally ignore the fact that human populations have consistently adjusted fertility rates to local economic and social conditions. Moreover, if that is so we can assume that high fertility in peripheral countries is not solely the result of a lack of ability to control births and that it is not, given the context of people's lives, irrational. That is, high fertility rates are not the result of ignorance, outmoded religious values, or lack of education but the result of social or economic factors that people, largely women, react to in order to adjust the size of their families. However, to understand how populations regulate their size without having access to modern means of birth control, we need to answer the question, *how have human societies historically controlled the size of their population?*

A Primer on the Determinants of Population Growth and Decline

At its simplest, worldwide population growth is a factor of only two things—births and deaths. If the rate of death is lower than the rate of birth, population increases. If deaths exceed births, population declines. In regional populations migration also contributes to population increases or declines, but for now let's focus on natural increases or decreases. The question is, *what economic, social, and cultural factors dictate birth and death rates?*

Fertility
Birth rates are a factor of the number of children born in a given population; this is determined by biological and social factors including the frequency of births during a woman's fecund period and the portion of the fecund period—between puberty and menopause—used for reproduction.

Frequency of births—the interval between births—is determined by a number of factors, including the following.

- Period of infertility after birth: There is a period after birth when ovulation does not occur.
- Time between ovulation and conception: While some women may conceive during the first ovulation after giving birth, others do not. The average is five to ten months.
- Average length of pregnancy (nine months)
- Fetal mortality: About one in five recognized pregnancies ends in miscarriage. (The actual number of interrupted pregnancies, including those that are unrecognized, may approach 80 percent.)
- Presence or absence of birth control techniques.

Of these factors, the length of time between births and the presence or absence of birth control techniques provide for most of the variation in birth rates. Length of time between births can be influenced by various cultural factors. For example, breast-feeding suppresses ovulation. In societies in which children are not weaned until the age of three, four, or five years, breast-feeding leads to greater intervals between births. Attitudes toward breast-feeding vary significantly: In some societies it is encouraged and expected; in others it is discouraged, perhaps because of concerns about body image or because it has sexual connotations.

Economic and consumption patterns may also influence breast-feeding. For example, breast-feeding in the periphery has markedly decreased in the past thirty to forty years because of increased advertising and sales of powdered infant formula. Thus, cultural or social factors that inhibit breast-feeding, especially in the absence of modern birth control methods, may result in shorter spacing between births and an increase in fertility and population growth.

Many societies practice a postpartum sexual taboo, a rule that women should not have sexual intercourse for a set period of time after the birth of a child. The period can vary from a few months to a few years, but regardless of the length, the taboo is likely to increase birth spacing.

Thus, even leaving aside the influence of modern birth control techniques, the spacing of births through so-called natural means may vary from eighteen to forty-five months (1.5–3.5 years).

A second major factor in fertility is the fecund period used for reproduction, or the number of years in which a woman can conceive. This, too, can vary considerably because of cultural, social, or economic factors. Biological fecundity is the period shortly after the onset of menses until the onset of menopause; this can vary from eleven years of age to over fifty years of age, although the average is fifteen years of age to forty years of age. More important, however, is cultural fecundity, the age at which a woman becomes sexually active. This is determined in most societies by age at marriage, which varies, on the average, from fifteen to twenty-five years of age.

Combining the minimum and maximum period between births attributable to natural factors with the minimum and maximum age at marriage produces two very different population growth scenarios (see Livi-Bacci 1992:13). Assuming a fifteen-year reproductive period (fecundity lasting from age twenty-five to age forty) with a maximum interval between births produces a fertility rate of 4.3 children per woman:

$$\frac{\text{15-year reproductive period}}{\text{3.5-year birth internal}} = 4.3 \text{ children}$$

However, assuming a reproductive period of twenty-five years (fecundity lasting from age fifteen to age forty) and minimum birth spacing of 1.5 years produces a fertility rate of 16.7 children per woman:

$$\frac{\text{25-year reproductive period}}{\text{1.5-year birth internal}} = 16.7 \text{ children}$$

The latter condition is not likely to be realized because it does not account for the increased risk of death or pathological conditions resulting from childbearing that may lower fecundity; in fact, the highest fertility rates recorded range from eleven to twelve children per woman. But the above projections provide some idea of the possible range of differences in fertility rates based solely on cultural factors such as age at marriage and age of weaning, independent of the availability and use of modern contraceptive techniques.

Anthropologists have also examined the extent to which other cultural practices, such as polygamy and monogamy, affect birth rates. For example, it has been predicted that polygyny—the practice of a man having more than one wife—might lower birth rates, since the frequency of intercourse with each wife would be lower than in a monogamous marriage. Studies, however, have been inconclusive. Frequency of sexual intercourse itself is another culturally determined variable that may affect fertility rates, but which also has not been shown to influence fertility rates significantly (see Nag 1975).

Death

A second major determinant of population growth is death, particularly the average life expectancy in a population. Most important is the percentage of the reproductive period realized in the life expectancy ranges. For example, in a population with a life expectancy of twenty years, the number of women who live through their full reproductive period is far less than in a population with a life expectancy of sixty years. In fact, demographers have calculated that with a life expectancy at birth of twenty years, only 29.2 percent of the potential reproductive period is lived, while with a life expectancy of eighty years, 98.2 percent of the potential fecund period is lived (Livi-Bacci 1992:19).

Most demographers have assumed that mortality rates in preindustrial societies were consistently high, but, as we shall see, that is probably mistaken. It seems we have consistently underestimated the general health levels of preindustrial societies.

The other major mortality factor in population growth is infant mortality, especially because this is where the greatest variation in life expectancy rates occur. It is also an area in which control on population growth can be exercised with the practice of infanticide and abortion. For example, one factor in death rates may be preference for male or female children, a preference that may be determined by economic needs. In societies that practice traditional agriculture there is evidence that boys and girls are equally valued as farm workers. In early industrial society, however, when wage labor began to be more prevalent, there was a preference for boys, a preference that gradually began to subside as women entered the factory work force (Harris and Ross 1987a:156).

Migration

Migration is another factor in population growth rates. While migration may not appear to influence world population, it can influence regional patterns of population growth and decline (and, consequently, influence global population) (see Manning 1990). For example, migration can affect reproductive rates: A population in which many people migrate may feel reduced population pressure, which may result in earlier marriages and rising birth rates. If more men migrate, fewer women may marry, causing the birth rate to decline. Migration rates may in turn be affected by cultural factors: In agricultural areas that practice impartible inheritance, in which land is passed on undivided to an older or younger child, those who do not inherit are more likely to migrate out; in agricultural societies that practice partible inheritance, in which land is divided among some or all children, people are less likely to leave.

Other factors can influence the rate of population growth, such as the percentage of a population of childbearing age and factors relating to environmental constraints. But what is important, and sometimes ignored by demographic transition theorists, is that populations have in the past been able to maintain population stability without modern methods of birth control; dramatic increases in population growth have sometimes occurred because of economic or social factors, not because modern health or sanitation practices reduced death rates. Since this is critical for understanding some of the biases in alarmist projections of population growth, let's examine a few historic cases of demographic transitions.

Some Examples of Demographic Change

To illustrate how the cultural and social factors outlined above can influence rates of population growth independent of modern birth control methods, let's look briefly at three cases of demographic change: the case of prehistoric gathering and hunting societies, the story of French Canadian fertility, and demographic changes in Ireland in the late eighteenth and early nineteenth centuries. We will see, as Marvin Harris and Eric Ross (1987a) noted, that historic populations did adjust their fertility rates to fit local economic and environmental conditions.

The First Demographic Transition

One of the assumptions of demographic transition theorists is that preagricultural peoples suffered from high mortality that was balanced by correspondingly high fertility to keep the population from dying out. Let's examine the first great demographic transition of 10,000–12,000 years ago, when human populations began to switch from gathering and hunting to agriculture.

We know from archeological evidence and research among gatherers and hunters that population growth rates before 10,000 B.C. were slow. However, chemical and anthropometric analysis of skeletal remains and ethnographic studies reveal that gatherers and hunters had fewer health problems than later agricultural and industrial peoples, and that the rate of infant mortality was comparable to or well below that of European rates up to the nineteenth century and below those of peripheral countries through the mid-twentieth century (Cohen 1994:281–282). Moreover, life expectancy was relatively high, around 30 years—higher than some nineteenth century Western countries, and higher than that in many peripheral countries until recently. If infant mortality was lower than many have assumed and life expectancy was higher yet the rate of population growth was low, then there must have been other means of controlling population size.

Assuming life expectancy varied from twenty-five to thirty-five years and that a woman's reproductive period extended from ages fourteen to twenty-nine, with birth spacing of twenty-three months, we would expect six births per woman; if three of these children survived, there would be a 50 percent increase in population for each generation. Since we know this did not occur, there must have been some limit placed on population growth. War and conflict between groups, given what we know about conflict among gatherers and hunters, cannot account for that much population loss, and episodic disasters would not have occurred with the frequency required to check population at that level.

The only other way population growth could have been limited is through a check on fertility. Research among contemporary gatherers and hunters, such as the Ju/wasi of Namibia studied by Nancy Howell (1979) shows that they have on average 4.7 children, well below the average in the periphery of six to eight. Howell suggested that the leanness characteristic of these populations is associated with late menarche, irregular ovulation, long postpartum amenorrhea (suppression of ovulation), and early menopause. She also suggested that an active physical life stimulated the contraceptive hormone prolactine in gathering and hunting populations, as does exercise in contemporary female athletes. Probably of greater influence is prolonged breast-feeding, which would have suppressed ovulation and resulted in greater birth spacing. Moreover, it is likely that abortion and infanticide played a major role in keeping population growth levels at near zero (Polgar 1972; Cohen 1994).

Regardless of the reason, gatherers and hunters do have lower fertility rates than sedentary neighbors, and research shows that their fertility levels increase when they settle. In other words, gathering and hunting peoples have traditionally been able to control fertility and adjust it to changing conditions.

The French Canadians

People have not only been able to maintain low fertility levels when conditions required it, they have also been able to increase their rate of growth. French Canadians represent a classic case of demographic success. In the seventeenth century 15,000 people migrated from France to what is now Quebec; some of these moved on, and in 1680 the population was about 10,000 people. In one hundred years, from 1684 to 1784, the population grew from 12,000 to 132,000—an elevenfold increase representing an annual growth rate of 2.4 percent. Since only approximately one-third of the original settlers established families, it is estimated that the vast majority of the current 80 million French Canadians are descended from some 1,425 women.

The demographic success of French Canadians was due not to declining death rates but to high birth rates resulting from early marriages. Probably because of a higher proportion of males in the population, women married at ages fifteen to sixteen; moreover, unlike women in France, widows in Quebec had little trouble remarrying and consequently giving birth to more children. Moreover, women in Quebec averaged only 25 months between pregnancies, compared to 29 months in France. Finally, there was a lower mortality rate and a life expectancy five years greater in Quebec than in France, perhaps because low population density kept down the spread of disease. Of the Quebec pioneers who began a family, each couple had 6.3 children, of whom 4.2 married; consequently, the population doubled in thirty years. The 4.2 children of each family in turn produced an average of 34

**TABLE 5.4   Fertility Rates of Women in Northwest France
Compared to Pioneer Women in Quebec
and Their Offspring**

Age at Marriage	No. of Offspring, NW France	No. of Offspring, Pioneer Women, Quebec	No. of Offspring, Daughters of Pioneers
15–19	9.5	10.1	11.4
20–24	7.6	8.1	9.5
25–29	5.6	5.7	6.3

See also Massimi Livi-Bacci, *A Concise History of World Population.* Cambridge: Blackwell, 1992.

offspring. That is, each original couple had more than 50 children and grandchildren. Moreover, daughters of pioneers had even higher fertility rates than their mothers and grandmothers, those marrying between fifteen and nineteen years of age having an average of 11.4 offspring, compared to 10.1 for the original pioneers marrying between the ages of fifteen and nineteen (which contrasted with 9.5 in northwest France, where most of the pioneers came from). Table 5.4 compares the number of offspring of women in the area from which the pioneers migrated with that for pioneer women and their offspring.

The fertility rate of French Canadians in the eighteenth century is among the highest ever recorded. Finally, some people assume religion was a factor in the fertility of Quebec women; however today, with Catholicism still the dominant religion in Quebec, as it was in the seventeenth and eighteenth centuries, the province has one of the lowest birth rates in the world.

The Case of Ireland
The case of Ireland reveals some of the mechanisms through which people can raise their fertility levels in response to local economic conditions and demands of colonial powers. At the beginning of the eighteenth century population growth in Ireland was relatively low. People married later, reducing the fecund period, and mortality was high, life expectancy generally being under thirty years. Then from 1780 to 1840 the population doubled, from 4 million to over 8 million. There seems little doubt that the reason was that women began to marry earlier, between ages fifteen and twenty, and in some areas even younger (Connell 1965:425). The question is, why were Irish women marrying earlier?

Marriages in Ireland were arranged, but only when the prospective bride and groom had access to land to farm. Before the late eighteenth century marriage was at a relatively late age—between twenty and twenty-five years for women—because there was not enough land to support early marriage. Two things happened that increased the availability of land and encouraged earlier marriages. Virtually all the farms in Ireland were owned by British landlords, who extracted rents from the

THE DAY AFTER THE EJECTMENT.

During the Irish potato famine of 1846–1847 thousands were evicted from their small farms for failure to pay their rents. This London Illustrated Times *portrayal of the famine is one of the most famous images of the disaster.*

tenants. Their profits rose when a new landholding was created, so they had a vested interest in increasing landholdings. In addition, population was rising in England in the late eighteenth century, increasing the demand for food, particularly corn. Landlords who increased their number of farms and the amount of land devoted to corn production could therefore realize greater profits. As a result, landlords subdivided farms into smaller and smaller plots, reclaimed swamps and extended farming into mountainous areas.

Families were able to subsist on smaller plots of land than before because of the potato. Introduced to Ireland in the sixteenth century, the potato had become the stable subsistence crop of the Irish farmer. Potato cultivation is very productive: an acre of potatoes can feed a family of six, including their livestock. A barrel of 280 pounds of potatoes can feed a family of five for a week at a daily consumption rate of eight pounds per person. Estimates are that people ate about 10 pounds a day, which, along with a liter of milk, would provide some 3800 calories along with all necessary nutrients. This allowed landlords to divide land into smaller parcels, providing a greater number of farms.

Thus from 1791 to 1831, the amount of agricultural land increased while the size of individual farming plots became smaller. The result was an increase in the number of farming plots, which permitted people to marry earlier, resulting in a rate of population increase of greater than 1 percent per year.

In 1845, a potato fungus struck, destroying the harvest of 1846 entirely and leading to the great famine of 1846–1847. This and epidemics resulted in 1.1–1.5 million deaths and an exodus from Ireland of 200,000 people per year. The average age at marriage increased from twenty-three to twenty-four in 1831–1841 to twenty-seven to twenty-eight by 1900, while one-fifth of the population never married. As a result, the population of Ireland decreased from 8.2 million in 1841 to 4.5 million in 1901.

In sum, the cases of the gatherers and hunters, Quebec pioneers, and Irish peasants reveal that, contrary to the assumptions of demographic transition theory, populations historically adjusted their fertility rates when they needed to adapt to local social and economic conditions, and they did so without the benefits of modern contraception. This raises the question *why are populations in the periphery not, for the most part, lowering their fertility rates in the face of increasing population and supposedly declining economic resources?*

Population Growth in the Periphery

Traditional demographic transition theory, and most public policy and government analysts, suggest that the rapid rise in population in the poor nations is due to lowered mortality, due itself to the importation of Western medical technology and public health measures. There is no question that life expectancy has increased remarkably in the periphery since 1950, and that a reduction in child mortality is the biggest factor in mortality decline.

However, population growth in the periphery began "exploding" well before the introduction of Western medicine and public health measures. Egyptian population grew in the nineteenth century from 2.5 million to 9.0 million, while the Mexican population grew from 5.8 million to 16.5 million. Cuba's population rose from 550,000 in 1800 to 5.8 million in 1953 (Wolf 1969:281). Furthermore, we saw how in Ireland the population increased not because of improvements in health but as a consequence of the economic demands of English landlords. The question is, *how and why did the economic expansion of the world capitalist economy change reproductive behaviors?*

The case of Java in the nineteenth century offers some clues. In 1830 the Dutch introduced into Indonesia the "Culture System" of colonial exploitation, requiring peasants to devote one-fifth of their land to Dutch-owned export crops (e.g., sugar, indigo, tea, tobacco) or to work sixty-six days on government-owned plantations or estates. In addition, as the Dutch demanded more land to produce export crops, thus taking land once used to grow subsistence crops, the remaining subsistence land had to be worked more intensively or subsistence production had to be extended to less productive land.

The introduction of the Culture System correlated closely with a rapid population increase in Java. In 1830 there were about 7 million people on Java; in 1840, 8.7 million; in 1850, 9.6 million; in 1860 12.7 million; in 1870, 16.2 million; in 1880, 19.5 million; in 1890, 23.6 million; and in 1900, 28.4 million—an average annual increase of approximately 2 percent for seventy years. It was during the era of the Culture System that people in Java began talking about the Dutch growing in wealth and the Javanese in number (Geertz 1963:70). Suggestions that these population increases can be attributed to better public health and sanitation facilities introduced by Europeans make little sense given the life expectancies of nineteenth century European urban dwellers; life expectancy in Amsterdam in 1800 was 25 years and for men in Manchester in the mid-nineteenth century was 24 years (Cohen 1989:202). Benjamin White (1973:224) suggested that the demand by Dutch colonialists for labor on Dutch estates or state projects removed men from subsistence agriculture, creating a labor shortage in the subsistence sector of the economy. Furthermore, subsistence production on less productive land required more work. Since the extended family unit both worked together to earn a living and controlled population growth, it was natural for them to react to the labor shortage by increasing family size.

Even when men began to be compensated for their labor with wages, according to White, it made sense to have more children. When the income of a production unit, in this case the family, depends on the wages brought in by each member, it makes good sense to maximize the size of the production unit. And this, apparently, is what the Javanese did. Moreover, the areas of Java that were most influenced by Dutch colonial policies were the areas with the greatest population increases (White 1973).

Other anthropologists, such as Carol R. Ember (1983), suggest that in general fertility increases with the intensification of agricultural activities (as occurred in Java and elsewhere). Ember pointed to evidence that women reduce birth spacing as agricultural activities intensify, partly to compensate for the increased domestic work for women when men increase their agricultural labors.

Thus it should be no surprise that populations grew under colonialism. As long as the production of commodities for export was essential to economic growth in the core, and as long as profits exceeded the costs of maintaining the colonies, policies that led to increases in the labor force served colonial aims (Polgar 1972:207). If there was any concern about population on the part of colonial rulers, it was that it was too low. One Frenchman complained in 1911 that Equatorial Africa lacked labor for its development (Cordell 1994:137). Women in Africa, like women in Java, responded to colonial economic pressures by increasing their fertility rates. For example, in villages in the Sudan, after the British established cotton growing in the 1920s to produce raw materials for its textile mills and increased the need for workers either to grow cotton or to replace those removed from subsistence agriculture, women began to wean their children earlier so they could become pregnant again (O'Brien 1994).

Wealth Flows Theory

It is clear, then, that people, particularly women, can and do adjust fertility in response to local economic and social conditions, and they do so without the assistance of Western methods of contraception. Yet fertility rates, while dropping in some counties, remain high in most. The question is, *why does the demand for children in developing countries remain high?* Among the reasons generally given are the following.

- The cost of raising children in rural areas is low, and in terms of cost children may represent a net gain economically.
- For security in old age. Surveys in Indonesia, the Koreas, Thailand, Turkey, and the Philippines reveal that 80–90 percent of parents expect economic assistance from children in their old age.
- Cultural factors encourage people to see children as an affirmation of family values, a guarantee of family continuity, and the expression of religious principles.

Demographer John Caldwell (1982), beginning with the idea that people in some societies resist attempts to limit fertility because of the economic benefits of children, formulated *wealth flows theory* to explain the reproductive decisions made by families. There are, according to Caldwell, only two types of reproductive strategies that families can adopt: one occurs where there is no economic gain to restricting fertility; the other occurs when there is an economic gain. Furthermore, where it is beneficial to have children people will maximize family size; where it is not economically beneficial people will minimize family size. In other words, when children contribute wealth to the family, when wealth flows from children to parents, parents will maximize the number of children they produce; when wealth flows from parents to children, parents will minimize family size. Caldwell defined "wealth" in broad terms to include not only money or wages but also economic security, labor assistance, prestige, the expansion of social and political networks, and so on.

The Yoruba of Nigeria, for example, desire large families because they increase the size of the security system in times of need, increase the number of cooperating individuals in less serious situations, and expand the range of economic and political contacts of family members. They also increase the number of political allies and the number of relatives who attend family ceremonies, both of which enhance prestige and status. For both urban and traditional Yoruba, family numbers are taken as signs of political strength and affluence. Moreover, a large family provides a springboard for success in the modern economy by supplying funds for education or personal connections to aid in finding jobs (Caldwell 1982:136). Children

Family form has much to do with family reproductive strategies. The many children in the extended Nigerian family pictured above are expected to contribute to its wealth, whereas the small number of dependents of the typical Western nuclear family, as this one in Boston, are expected to be a drain on family resources.

perform services not only by producing goods but by providing services that adults regard as children's work—carrying water, collecting fuel, messages, and goods, sweeping, looking after siblings, and caring for animals. Adult children help with labor and gifts and assist in making family contributions to community ceremonies, funerals, and birth ceremonies. Adult children also care for aging parents and contribute to farms and businesses in such a way that aged parents can still participate. Finally, parents can invest in training or education of children to maximize later returns. When surveyed, 80 percent of Yoruba said that children are better than wealth, and even that children *are* wealth. Only 6 percent said that children consume wealth. Caldwell (1982:140) concluded:

> *The key issue here, and, I will argue, the fundamental issue in demographic transition, is* the direction and magnitude of intergenerational wealth flows *or the net balance of the two flows—one from parents to children and the other from children to parents—over the period from when people become parents until they die.*

Furthermore, said Caldwell, for intergenerational wealth flow to change there must be a fundamental change in family structure; programs that simply emphasize family planning or increase the availability of contraception will not provide incentives to reduce fertility. Given these conclusions, the questions are, *what kinds of changes are required in family structure to reduce fertility, and if in some circumstances fertility decline is desirable, under what economic and social circumstances will families be motivated to have fewer children?*

The Social Implications of Wealth Flows Theory

Wealth flows theory highlights an area of research that demographers have tended to neglect—the relationship between family structure and fertility. Anthropologists have been traditionally concerned with kinship and family relations, because in small-scale and preindustrial societies kinship more than any other factor tends to define a person's relationship to everyone else. In small villages and towns, for example, it is not unusual for everyone to be related in some way to everyone else, and for everyone to know exactly what those relations are. In fact, in many societies, in the absence of kin a person is viewed with suspicion and hostility. Many anthropologists who have lived and done fieldwork in such communities have had the experience of being assigned some fictional kinship designation—the sister, brother, daughter, or son of someone in the community.

One of the major distinctions that anthropologists make about different types of families is the distinction between the so-called *nuclear family* and the so-called *extended family.* The nuclear family consists of a father, mother, and children. This is the standard family unit in most Western countries, and certainly in the United States. In other societies, extended families consisting of mothers and/or fathers and brothers, sisters, parents, grandparents, and others are the norm. Extended family structure can also vary considerably depending, for example, on whether a person is considered to be more strongly tied to his or her father and his kin (*patrilineal descent*), his or her mother and her kin (*matrilineal descent*), or equally to both (*bilateral descent*).

Whether a society emphasizes nuclear family ties or extended family ties can obviously have great significance on patterns of family relations. In nuclear families, for example, parents or siblings are clearly responsible for the care of children; in extended families, children may be cared for by parents, siblings, members of the mother's or father's family, grandparents, and so on. In nuclear families resources (income, possessions, etc.) are shared among mother, father, and children; in extended families resources may be shared and distributed among a far greater number of individuals.

Furthermore, emotional ties may vary considerably. In a patrilineal extended family a man may have closer ties to his brother than to his wife, or a woman closer ties to a brother or sister than to her husband. In nuclear families the main tie is between husband and wife, and their main obligation is to their children. The question is, *what implications do population control programs have for family structure and relations?*

If wealth flow is the main determinant of fertility in a society, then fertility behavior will change only if there is a shift from extended family structures, in which wealth almost always flows from children to parents, to nuclear family structures, in which wealth almost always flows from parents to children. In Nigeria, for example, government efforts at reducing fertility have met with almost no success, even among modernized urban families. This is because the extended family, even in the cities, remains the norm. In the few instances of so-called demographic innovators—those who have changed their fertility behavior—there has been a marked change in attitudes toward family and children to the emotional and economic patterns that resemble those found in nuclear families. These people have withdrawn emotionally from ancestors and extended family relatives and become more involved with their children and their children's future. They give more emotion and wealth to their children than they expect to get back. Caldwell (1982:149) speculated that those couples who have adopted the Western form of family, and consequently Western notions of family size, have probably done so not because of population control and family programs but because of the long-standing attempt by missionaries, colonial administrators, and educational authorities to persuade people to abandon their traditional family structure and adopt a Western family ideal.

To the extent that such efforts are successful and that population control and family planning programs contribute to these efforts, we will see a loss of extended families along with the patterns of emotional, economic, and social ties that characterize them, and the adoption of emotional, economic, and social characteristics of the Western family. In other words, fertility change requires a nucleation of obligations, expenditures, and emotions in which conjugal family ties take precedence over all external relationships and that foster the belief that what parents owe their children is more important than what children owe their parents. The Western nuclear family is also marked by a greater emphasis on the rights of individuals to act independently of the family, by, for example, choosing a spouse on the basis of mutual attraction, choosing a residence independent from one's parents, choosing a career, and making decisions together with a spouse about family size.

The Question of Gender and Power

Anthropologists suggest that relations between husbands and wives may be as important as the influences of extended and nuclear family structure in influencing fertility. In situations where there is high unemployment, where women have limited access to economic resources and must depend on men and children for economic contributions or economic security, fertility will be high. This is clearly revealed in the research of W. Penn Handwerker (1989) in Barbados.

In the 1950s, according to Handwerker, the West Indian family was characterized by weak conjugal bonds, a relative absence of stable nuclear units, weak bonds between fathers and children, and strong bonds between mothers and children. Family interactions among men, women, and children tended to take place in visiting relationships, consensual cohabitation, and legal marriage, which tended to occur late if at all. Consequently 80 percent of births occurred outside of marriage.

Historically, marriage patterns were a function of sugar production and the demand for sugar on the world market. The British freed their Barbados slaves in 1833, but the freed slaves were still dependent on wage labor in the sugarcane fields. Furthermore, to replace slaves who left, the British encouraged the migration of thousands of indentured laborers from India and the East Indies. As a result, the population of Barbados increased in the nineteenth century from 60,000 to 200,000. Since the sugar growers controlled the economy, and since there was a more than adequate work force competing for available jobs, wages were low. To get a job, a laborer often needed the patronage of someone connected to the sugar growers. As a result, living conditions for the bulk of the Black laborers were among the worst in the British West Indies. Infant mortality, for example, was 25 percent in the early 1900s and remained as high as 15 percent into the 1950s.

Handwerker claimed that the scarcity of jobs created severe competition among the poor for available work, such that men and women could optimize their resources only by exploiting each others' weaknesses. Since only men were employed on the sugar plantations, they earned most of the money, money they used to gain sexual conquests, rum, and unquestioned authority. Meanwhile, women exploited men's desire for sex, their absence from the home, and their distance from children to attach the children emotionally to themselves and distance them from their fathers.

This does not mean women didn't have jobs—60 percent worked from age fifteen to age fifty-five. But their work was low-paying manufacturing work, as seamstresses, domestics, and petty traders. Wages were so low that one women commented, "You are lucky if a daughter can earn enough to help herself, let alone help you" (Handwerker 1989:77). To survive, a women needed to supplement her income with that of a man.

These patterns of male-female relations resulted in a family pattern in which women attracted men as cohabitants, boyfriends, and, later, husbands in a unit in which men sought to dominate and control women. Men continued to meet their social obligations by working long hours, often at several jobs, providing an adequate material base for their wives and children; they exercised absolute authority in the home and spent free time with either men or other women. Women, needing men for economic support, submitted reluctantly, often complaining that their husbands or coresidents simply wanted a slave and expressing a desire to be treated as equals. Yet because of the pattern of outmigration of men, and the resulting greater number of women, men were able and expected to have extramarital affairs.

The result was a family in which men had minimal emotional attachments to their wives and children while women worked to maintain close ties to their children. Women used sex to cement the tie to men, and children, according to Handwerker's informants, were byproducts of the exchange. Moreover, older children were expected to help support their mothers and even to protect them from their fathers or stepfathers. As Handwerker (1989:88) said:

> Women could optimize or improve their resource control only by unrestricted childbearing. Getting pregnant and bearing children tended to be viewed as both a woman's duty and as her goal, and mothers generally took the view that their children owed them support for bringing the children into the world.

Even the belief system worked to enhance high fertility. Women believed that abstention from sex was unhealthy and that a woman who failed to bear all the children she was capable of bearing would suffer from high blood pressure and other diseases. "You have children until you can have no more," as one woman in her fifties put it. Thus patterns of economic exploitation created a family form in which women, acting according to the logic of their social and economic conditions, maximized the number of children they would have.

Beginning in the 1960s, however, family structure slowly began to change in response to changing economic conditions. The colonial sugar economy declined to the point that sugar represented only about 6 percent of domestic output and 10 percent of employment. Manufacturing and tourism grew, and with it the importance of education for access to jobs. Connections to people of influence mattered less. More important, women gained access to jobs unavailable to them before.

As a consequence, the Barbadian family of the 1980s was very different from the family of the 1960s and earlier. Women expect their husbands to be companions, and there have been equivalent expectations on the part of husbands. Although women still suffer from job discrimination, education provides them with access to better paying jobs as technical specialists, secretaries, receptionists, business executives, university academics, and lawyers. From 1950 to 1980 the percentage of women working in manufacturing increased from less than 15 percent to more than 50 percent. The competition for resources between men and women lessened and the exploitative pattern of relations decreased. Marriages came to resemble more the so-called companionate marriages that emerged in England in the nineteenth century (Stone 1976); men began to enjoy their families, and their lives began to center more on their wives and children.

This did not occur without conflict, however. Since the stronger emotional ties within the nuclear family required weakening to some extent ties outside the family, especially between sons and mothers, relations between wives and mothers-in-laws became strained as they competed for the affections of husbands. Regardless, the family of the 1980s came to resemble the idealized Western nuclear family. Women viewed children as a cost rather than as a future resource, and young Barbadian women explicitly denied owing anything to their parents.

With the change in family patterns there has been a dramatic decrease in fertility, from a birth rate of around 5.0 per woman in the 1950s to a low of about 2.0 in the 1980s. Handwerker (1989:210) concluded that changes in patterns of family relations, not large-scale population control programs of the sort advocated by the Cairo Population Conference, will determine fertility. It is not knowledge of contraceptive techniques or a population problem per se that inhibits women from having smaller families, but an issue of power relations. Family planning programs, said Handwerker:

> *Should not be expected to bring about fertility transition because they can neither create the jobs, nor provide the education necessary for many jobs that would permit women to achieve meaningful control over their own lives. The "right" to have*

a small family is not a real option for women who are dependent for basic material well-being on their children.

Problems and Prospects

Does all of the foregoing mean there is no population problem or that there should be a more concerted attempt to change family patterns in the periphery to a nuclear family type, to encourage reduced fertility and promote greater gender equality? Whether there is a population problem remains a moot question at best. There is no evidence that population increases in the periphery inhibit economic development, or that population increases are the major cause of poverty and environmental devastation. Poverty clearly is related to colonialism and the expansion of the capitalist world economy, and, as we shall see, population growth in the periphery is at best a minor factor in global pollution. This does not mean population regulation is universally undesirable, but it does mean fertility decisions are best made by women and men together based on local economic and social conditions, not by central planners whose ulterior motives may not be in the best interest of the people involved. It is foolhardy at best to expect a woman to have fewer children if they are her major source of economic security. And it is foolish to force families to reduce their size if the family's economic well-being depends on the size of the family production unit and its ability to supply labor or bring in additional wages.

Yet it is clear that smaller families can confer some benefits. Research suggests, for example, that educational opportunities for children, particularly women, decline in larger families. Thus if education is a condition for economic independence, limiting fertility is likely to be desirable (Birdsell 1994). Research also reveals that it is desireable to space births at least two years apart to limit the risk of infant death (Lloyd 1994:183). Thus in some situations, controlling the number and spacing of births is clearly beneficial.

Can we assume, then, that promoting the adoption of a Western-style nuclear family is desirable because it promotes greater equality of women? Possibly, although, as we shall see in Chapter 11, many researchers associate the nuclear family with the exploitation of women. Furthermore, extended families offer protection and security, so much so that in poor areas of the United States people "create" extended families through fictive or invented kinship ties to others and form reciprocal supportive relationships (see Stack 1974). Moreover, it is quite possible to have extended family relations in which women exercise as much power and authority as men, if not more.

In addition, few researchers have considered the negative features of nuclear family arrangements. Setting aside the obvious issues of broken families and concern and care for children and the elderly, we may be in danger of exporting the consumption patterns of Western families in addition to the social patterns. Nuclear family structure may tend to maximize consumption in various ways. For example, we noted in Chapter 1 how in the late 1940s and 1950s the American economy grew as a result of a home building boom and a boom in the consumption of all those items that go with home ownership—furniture, appliances, automobiles, and so on. *Will the nucleation of the extended family in peripheral countries result in similar patterns of consumption? Will that create an economic boom as in the United States? Will it result in increased environmental pollution and waste?*

Nuclear family structure, especially to the extent that it requires a reversal of wealth flow from children to parents, to parents to children, has created, again since the 1950s, a whole new class of consumers—twelve- to twenty-year-olds, with their own supply of wealth and their own consumer desires (and culture). *Will that create new markets and economic growth, or will it bring with it the same social problems that so-called youth culture creates in our own society?* Obviously it is difficult to predict, yet there has been virtually no discussion of the implications of changes in family structure that are required if we continue to promote fertility decline.

Conclusion

Western scientific and popular discussions of population growth have been dominated by two frameworks. The Malthusian perspective predicts that population growth threatens the world with starvation, poverty, environmental destruction, and social unrest. Demographic transition theory, while sharing the Malthusian concern over population growth, predicts that, as in the wealthy countries, population in poor countries will eventually stabilize if they adopt Western programs of economic development designed to bring them into the modern world. From an anthropological perspective, both views are faulty, both in their assumptions about the connections between population growth and economic development and in their ethnocentric assumptions about the reasons for population rise and decline in premodern societies. Furthermore, the Malthusian position has a clear class and perhaps ethnic bias in its tendency to blame the victims of poverty and environmental decline for their economic, social, and ecological state, ignoring the effects of the historical expansion of capitalism. The ethnocentrism of demographic transition theory is evident in its assumptions that modernization will result in lowered fertility because, somehow, modernity encourages rationality in choices about family size. However, as we have seen, there is nothing irrational about large families in societies where the family is a major source of economic support and security, and where the wealth received from children throughout one's life, far exceeds the wealth that flows to children.

We examined the relationship between fertility and family structure, describing John Caldwell's intergenerational wealth flows theory, and demonstrated that lowering fertility requires a change in family structure from an extended family pattern to a nuclear family pattern. We also noted that unless women also gain access to economic resources, it remains in their interest to maximize fertility. Yet, if fertility decline is a major priority for international agencies and countries, and if, as anthropological research indicates, such a decline requires the adoption of the Western nuclear family along with its values, attitudes, and consumption patterns, we need to examine the consequences of such a change. In particular we need to consider whether the social and economic effects of such a change are worth whatever might be gained by slowing population growth.

Chapter 6

Hunger, Poverty, and Economic Development

The persistence of widespread hunger is one of the most appalling features of the modern world. The fact that so many people continue to die each year from famines, and that many millions more go on perishing from persistent deprivation on a regular basis, is a calamity to which the world has, somewhat incredibly, got coolly accustomed.... Indeed, the subject often generates either cynicism ("not a lot can be done about it") or complacent irresponsibility ("don't blame me—it is not a problem for which I am answerable").
JEAN DRÉZE AND AMARTYA SEN,
HUNGER AND PUBLIC ACTION

Poverty is the main reason why babies are not vaccinated, why clean water and sanitation are not provided, why curative drugs and other treatments are unavailable and why mothers die in childbirth. It is the underlying cause of reduced life expectancy, handicaps, disability and starvation. Poverty is a major contributor to mental illness, stress, suicide, family disintegration and substance abuse. Every year in the developing world 12.2 million children under 5 years die, most of them from causes which could be prevented for just a few US cents per child. They die largely because of world indifference, but most of all they die because they are poor.
WORLD HEALTH REPORT (1995)

At the end of World War II public officials and scientists from all over the world predicted that with advances in modern technology it would be possible by the end of the century to end poverty, famine, and endemic hunger in the world. Freed from colonial domination and assisted by new global institutions such as the United Nations and the World Bank, the impoverished countries of Africa, Asia, and Latin America, people assumed, would follow the paths to economic development blazed by the core countries.

The efficiency of this dairy processing factory in the United States is a sharp contrast to the line of hungry people in Bangladesh waiting for a food distribution.

Today these optimistic projections have been replaced by hopelessness and resignation as perhaps one-fifth of the world's people live in absolute poverty, with incomes of less than $700 per year. Estimates of the number of people with insufficient food range from 600 million to over a billion, virtually one-fifth of the world's population. Children are particularly vulnerable; food aid organizations estimate that 250,000 children per week, almost 1,500 per hour, die from inadequate diets and the diseases that thrive on malnourished bodies. And hunger is not just a problem of the poor countries of the world. Estimates of the number of Americans living in hunger rose from 20 million in 1985 to 30 million in 1992, and with recent cutbacks in social assistance these numbers promise to become even greater.

Common misunderstandings about world hunger should be quickly dispelled. First, world hunger is not the result of insufficient food production. There is enough food in the world to feed 120 percent of the world's population on a vegetarian diet, although probably not enough to feed the world on the diet of the core countries. Even in countries where people are starving, there is either more than enough food for everyone or the capacity to produce it.

Second, famine is not the most common reason for hunger. While famines such as those in recent years in Ethiopia, Sudan, Somalia, and Chad receive the most press coverage, endemic hunger—daily insufficiencies in food—is far more common.

Third, famine itself is rarely caused by food insufficiency. When hundreds of thousands starved to death in Bangladesh in 1974, it was not because of lack of food. In fact, there was more food than there had been in the years leading up to the disaster and more food than was produced in the years following. The starvation resulted from massive unemployment brought on by flooded farmland and high food prices brought on by a fear of food shortages. People starved to death because they couldn't afford to buy food and had no land to grow their own.

Finally, hunger is not caused by overpopulation. While growing populations may require more food, there is no evidence that the food could not be produced and delivered if people had the means to pay for it. This does not mean population and food availability play no role in world hunger, but that the relationship is far more complex than it appears.

The questions, then, are *why do people continue to starve to death in the midst of plenty?* More important, *is it still possible to believe that poverty and hunger can be eliminated? If so, how?*

To answer these questions we need to know about the nature and history of food production and to understand the reasons why people are hungry. There is a prevailing view that hunger is inevitable, but that need not be the case. We will examine some possible solutions to world hunger, and how specific countries, some rich and some poor, have tried to ensure that people have adequate food.

The Evolution of Food Production: From the Neolithic to the Neocaloric

Until recently in world history virtually everyone lived on farms, grew their own food, and used whatever surplus they produced to pay tribute or taxes, to sell at local markets, and to keep for seed for the following year. Since the beginning of the Industrial Revolution people have left the land in increasing numbers, converging on cities and living on wages. As late as 1880, half of the U.S. population was engaged in agriculture; this figure decreased to 38 percent by 1900, and 18 percent by 1940. Today less than 2 percent of Americans feed the other 98 percent, as well as millions of others around the world who purchase the products of American agriculture (Schusky 1989:101). This shift of the population from farming to other sources of livelihood is intensifying all over the world. *Why do people leave the land on which they produce their own food to seek wage employment, which requires that they buy food from others?*

To answer this question we need to understand the history of agriculture, why food production has changed, and how economic and agricultural policies have resulted in increased poverty and hunger.

From Gathering and Hunting to the Neolithic

For most of their existence human beings produced food by gathering wild plants—nuts, roots, berries, grains—and hunting large and small game. Generally these people enjoyed a high quality of life. They devoted only about twenty hours per week to work, and archeological studies and research among contemporary gathering and hunting societies indicate that food was relatively plentiful and nutritious. Life span and health standards seem to have been better than those of later agriculturists. Consequently, a major question for anthropologists has been why human populations that lived by gathering and hunting began to plant and cultivate crops. Before 1960 anthropologists assumed that domesticating plants and animals provided more nourishment and food security than gathering and hunting. But when the research in the 1960s of Richard Lee and James Woodburn revealed that the food supply of gatherers and hunters was relatively secure and that the investment of energy in food production was small, speculation turned to the effects of population increase on food production. Mark Cohen (1977) suggested that increases in population densities may have required people to forage over larger areas in search of food, eventually making it more efficient to domesticate and cultivate their own rather than travel large distances in search of game and wild plants. Even then the shift from gathering and hunting to domestication of plants and animals must have been very gradual, emerging first on a large scale in Mesopotamia around 10,000 years ago, during the neolithic era. From that point until 5,000 years ago settlements domesticated such plants as wheat, barley, rye, millet, rice, and maize, and began to domesticate animals such as sheep, goats, pigs, camels, and cattle. Traditionally animals have served as a farmer's food reservoir, fed with surplus grains in good times and killed and eaten when grain became scarce. Some, such as sheep, goats, cattle, and camels, eat grasses that human beings cannot eat, thus converting cellulose to protein for human consumption in the form of meat and dairy products.

Slash and burn or *swidden agriculture* is the simplest way of cultivating crops; although it is highly efficient when practiced correctly it requires considerable knowledge of local habitats. In swidden agriculture a plot of land is cleared by cutting down the vegetation, spreading it over the area to be used for planting, and then burned. Seeds are planted and the plants cultivated and then harvested. After one to three years of use, the plot is more or less abandoned and a new area cut, burned, and planted. If there is sufficient land, the original plot lies fallow for ten years or more until bushes and trees reestablish themselves; then it is used again. Of the four major factors in agricultural production—land, water, labor, and energy—swidden agriculture is land-intensive only. It uses only natural rainfall and solar energy and requires about twenty-five hours per week of labor. Tools used are only an ax or machete and a hoe or digging stick.

Swidden agriculture is still practiced in much of the periphery, but only recently have researchers begun to appreciate its efficiency and sophistication. Burning vegetation, for example, once thought only to add nutrients in the form of ash to the soil, also kills pests, insects, and weeds. When practiced correctly, it is environmentally sound because it recreates the natural habitat. Swidden agriculturists must choose a site with the proper vegetation and desirable drainage and soil qualities. They must cut and spread the brush properly and evenly to maximize the burn and the heat. Cuttings that dry slowly must be cut earlier than those that dry quickly. Unlike in monoculture—the growing of a single crop—swidden plots are planted with a variety of foodstuffs as well as medicinal plants and other vegetable products. Swidden agriculturists must know when to abandon a plot so that grasses do not invade and prevent regeneration of brush and forest. Furthermore, abandoned plots are rarely truly abandoned, being used to grow tree crops or attract animals that are hunted for food.

Just as there is debate as to why gatherers and hunters began to practice agriculture, there is some question as to why swidden agriculturists began to practice the more labor-intensive *irrigation* or *plow agriculture.* These techniques do not necessarily produce a greater yield relative to the labor energy used; however, they do allow more efficient use of land by reducing or eliminating the fallow period. Land that in swidden agriculture would lie fallow is put into production. Irrigation agriculture also allows continual production on available land, sometimes allowing harvest of two or three crops in a year. Moreover, it permits the use of land that without irrigation could not be used for agriculture. Ester Boserup (1965) suggested that increasing population density required more frequent use of land, eliminating the possibility of allowing land to lie fallow to regain its fertility. Thus plow and irrigation agriculture, while requiring greater amounts of work, does produce more food.

The productivity comes at a cost, however. Of the four agricultural essentials—land, water, labor, and energy—irrigation requires more water, more labor, and more energy than swidden agriculture. In addition, irrigation generally requires a more complex social and political structure, with a highly centralized bureaucracy to direct the construction, maintenance, and oversight of the required canals, dikes, and, in some cases, dams. Furthermore, irrigation can be environmentally destructive, leading to salinization (excess salt buildup) of the soil and silting. For example, it is estimated that 50 percent of the irrigated land in Iraq and 30 percent in Egypt is waterlogged or salinized (Schusky 1989:72). Irrigated sites may also be used to dump sewage and often harbor disease-carrying parasites and insects, resulting in an increase in such diseases as cholera, typhoid, schistosomiasis, and malaria. Irrigated areas also serve as a haven for weeds. Finally, the shift to plow or irrigation agriculture changed the division of labor between men and women (Boserup 1970). Generally in swidden agriculture men clear the land and women burn the cuttings and care for the crops. In some areas today, such as sub-Saharan Africa, women do the majority of the agricultural labor. However, in plow or irrigation agriculture, women tend to do less of the labor. Women's labor shifts to domestic chores, and often the total amount of women's labor increases as their agricultural labor decreases (Ember 1983).

If we surveyed the world of 2,000 years ago, when virtually all of the food crops now in use were domesticated and in use somewhere, we would find centers of irrigation agriculture in China, Mesopotamia, Egypt, and India, with later developments coming in the Andes and Mesoamerica. Plow agriculture was practiced extensively in areas of the Middle East and Europe. But where agriculture was necessary, swidden agriculture, when population levels and state demands for tribute permitted, must have been by far the most common. Moreover, until the twentieth century there was little change or improvement in agricultural techniques.

Capitalism and Agriculture

The next great revolution in food production was a consequence of the growing importance of world trade in the sixteenth through eighteenth centuries and the gradual increase in the number of people living in cities and not engaged in food production. The expansion of trade and growth of the nonfarming population had at least four profound consequences for agricultural production.

First, food became a commodity that like any other commodity, such as silk, swords, or household furniture, could be produced, bought, and sold for profit. Second, the growth of trade and the number of people engaged in nonagricultural production created competition for labor between agricultural and industrial sectors of the economy. Third, the growth of the nonagricultural work force created greater vulnerability on the part of those who depended on others for food. The availability of food no longer depended solely on a farmer's ability to produce it, but also on people's wages, food prices, and an infrastructure required for the delivery, storage, and marketing of food products. Finally, the increasing role of food as a capitalist commodity resulted in the increased intervention of the state in food production. For example, food prices needed to be regulated; if they were too high not only might people starve but industrial wages would need to increase; if they were too low, agricultural producers might not bring their food to market. Import quotas or tariffs needed to be set to maximize food availability on the one hand and protect domestic food producers on the other. New lands needed to be colonized, not only to produce enough food but to keep food production profitable. The state might also regulate agricultural wages or, as in the United States, not regulate them. (While the United States has had a minimum wage for industrial workers since 1937, there is still no minimum wage for farm workers.)

As it turned out, the most important change in food production inspired by the transformation of food into a capitalist commodity was the continual reduction of the amount in human energy and labor involved directly in food production and the increase of the amount in nonhuman energy in the form of new technologies, such as tractors, reapers, and water delivery systems. The results of this trend continue to define the nature of agricultural production in most of the world.

Reducing labor demands in agriculture and increasing technology accomplishes a whole range of things that contribute to trade and profit in both the agricultural and industrial sectors. First, substituting technology for human labor and reducing the number of people involved in agriculture makes agriculture more profitable. Labor costs are reduced and agricultural wealth is concentrated in fewer hands. Increasing technology also creates a need for greater capital investments. As a result, those people with access to capital, that is the more affluent, are able to profit, forcing the less affluent to give up their farms. This further concentrates agricultural wealth. The increase in the need for capital also creates opportunities for investors (banks, multilateral organizations, commodity traders) to enter the agricultural sector, influence its operation by supplying and/or withholding capital, and profiting from it.

Second, reducing the number of people in agriculture and concentrating agricultural wealth to ensure profits of those who remain helps keep food prices and consequently industrial wages relatively low. This creates a danger of food monopolies and the potential for a rise in prices. For example, cereal production in the United States is controlled by only a few companies, and the prices of processed cereals such as corn flakes and oats are exorbitant. Yet as long as consumers are able to pay, the government is content not to intervene. As it is, food cost as a percentage of the cost of living in the United States is among the lowest in the world.

Third, reducing agricultural labor frees labor to work in industry and creates competition for industrial jobs, which helps keep wages low. That is, the more people who are dependent for their livelihood on jobs, the lower wages industry needs to pay.

Finally, to keep labor costs down and increase the amount of technology required for the maintenance of food production, the state must subsidize the agricultural sector. In the United States, for example, the government has financed irrigation and land reclamation projects, conducted agricultural research, and subsidized farm prices and/or energy costs. The U.S. government also subsidized agriculture by investing billions of dollars in Food Aid, buying surplus farm products and using them for foreign aid (although, as we shall see, the aim was not altruistic and the consequence for countries receiving the aid hardly benign.)

In sum, the results for the capitalist economy of the reduction of agricultural labor and the subsequent increase in technology are:

- A capital-intensive agricultural system, dependent on the use of subsidized energy
- The exploitation of domestic farm labor and of foreign land and labor to keep food prices low and agricultural and industrial profits high
- A large labor pool from which industry can draw workers, whose wages are kept down by competition for scarce jobs and the availability of cheap food

It is important to note that until the 1950s the technological intensification of agriculture did not substantially increase yield. That is, though an American corn farmer needed only one hundred hours of labor to produce one hectare (2.41 acres) of corn, the amount of corn produced was no greater than that produced by a Mexican swidden farmer, working ten times as many hours using only a machete and hoe. In other words, while mechanization made the American farm more economical by reducing labor energy and costs, it did not produce more food per hectare (Schusky 1989:115). One question we need to ask is *what happens when we export the American agricultural system to developing countries?*

The Neocaloric and the Green Revolution

The culmination of the development of capitalist agriculture, a system that is technologically intensive and substitutes nonhuman energy for human energy, was dubbed the *neocaloric revolution* by Ernest Schusky. For Schusky, the major characteristic of the neocaloric revolution has been the vast increase in nonhuman energy devoted to food production in the form of fertilizers, pesticides, herbicides, and machinery.

David and Marcia Pimentel (1979) provided a unique perspective on the neocaloric. Their idea was to measure the number of kilocalories[1] produced per crop

---

[1]A calorie or gram-calorie is the amount of heat needed to raise 1 gram of water 1° C to 15° C. The kilocalorie (kcal) of kilogram-calorie is 1,000 gram-calories or the amount of heat needed to raise 1 kg of water 1° C to 15° C. It can also be conceptualized as follows; 1 horsepower of energy is the same as 641 kilocalories; 1 gallon of gasoline contains 31,000 kilocalories; if used in a mechanical engine that works at 20 percent efficiency, 1 gallon of gasoline is equal to 6,200 kilocalories of work, or one horse working at capacity for a ten-hour day, or a man working eight hours per day, five days per week, for 2.5 weeks.

per hectare of land and compare it to the amount of both human and nonhuman energy expended in kilocalories to produce the crop. Their work dramatized both the efficiency of traditional forms of agriculture and the energy use required of modern capitalist agriculture.

For example, to produce a crop of corn a traditional Mexican swidden farmer clears land with an ax and machete to prepare it for burning and uses a hoe to plant and weed. Pimentel and Pimentel (1979:63) figured that crop care takes 143 days and the worker exerts about 4,120 kilocalories per day. Thus, labor for one hectare amounts to 589,160 kilocalories. Energy expended for ax, hoe, and seed is estimated at 53,178 kilocalories, for a total of 642,338 kilocalories. The corn crop produced yields about 6 million kilocalories, for an input-output ratio of 1 to 11; that is, for every kilocalorie expended, eleven are produced, a ratio that is about average for peasant farmers. Nonhuman energy used is minimal, consisting only in the fossil fuel (wood, coal, or oil) used in producing the hoe, ax, and machete.

Now let's examine plow agriculture with the use of an ox. One hour of ox time is equal to four hours of human time, so labor input for one hectare drops to 197,245 kilocalories from 589,160 kilocalories. But the ox requires 495,000 kilocalories to maintain. Moreover, the steel plow requires more energy in its manufacture, so fossil fuel energy used rises to 41,400, with energy for seeds remaining at 36,608, for a total of 573,008. However, the corn yield drops significantly, to half, so the input-output ratio drops to 1 to 4.3. The reason for the drop is likely the lowering of soil fertility. If leaves, compost, or manure is added to the soil yields might increase, but so would the energy required to gather and spread the fertilizer.

Finally, if we consider a corn farmer in the United States in 1980, we find that using modern farming machinery, herbicides, insecticides, fertilizers, transport, and irrigation, the farmer produces about 7,000 kilograms of corn per hectare, almost seven times that produced by the Mexican swidden farmer, but at a cost of almost 25 million kilocalories. Consequently, the input-output ratio is 1 to 3.5, far below the ratios of most "primitive" swidden farmers. In fact, in the United States the ratio of kilocalories used in crop production to kilocalories produced declined from 3.7 to 1 in 1945 to 2.8 to 1 in 1970. The question is, *why has modern agriculture become so energy intensive?*

The intensification of the use of technology in agriculture is largely the result of what has been called the *green revolution.* The green revolution began with research conducted in Mexico by American scientists in the 1940s and 1950s, sponsored by the Rockefeller Foundation. Their goal was to develop higher-yielding hybrid strains of corn and wheat suitable for Mexican agriculture. Soon the research produced dramatic results all over the world as farmers began using specially produced strains of crops such as wheat, corn, and rice called *high-yielding varieties* (HYVs). The productivity of the new seeds lay largely in their increased capacity for using fertilizer and water. Whereas increased use of fertilizer and water did not increase the yields of old varieties (in fact, it might harm them), it vastly increased the yields of the new varieties. Consequently, more and more farmers around the world adopted them. Use of these new varieties was encouraged by the petrochemical industry and fertilizer production plants, which sought to expand

Modern agriculture is capital and technologically intensive, requiring large tracts of land and a heavy investment in machines.

their markets. Thus, research efforts to develop HYV plants were expanded in India, the Philippines, and Taiwan, encouraged by the U. S. Agency for International Development (USAID) and the Rockefeller Foundation.

But the green revolution soon ran into some problems. First, the new plants required greater inputs of fertilizer and water. Because of the added energy costs farmers often skimped on fertilizer and water use, resulting in yields similar to those prior to the adoption of the new crops. Consequently, farmers returned to their previous crops and methods. Second, the OPEC oil embargo in 1973 raised oil prices, and since fertilizers, irrigation, and other tools of the green revolution were dependent on oil, costs rose even higher. Some people began to refer to high yielding varieties as *energy-intensive varieties* (EIVs).

The expense was increased further by the amount of water needed for fertilizers. Early adaptations of the new technology tended to be in areas rich in water sources; in fact, most of the early research on high-yielding varieties was done in areas where irrigation was available. When the techniques were applied to areas without water resources, the results were not nearly as dramatic. It also became apparent that the energy required for irrigation was as great in some cases as the energy required for fertilizer.

In addition, the green revolution requires much greater use of chemical pesticides. If farmers plant only a single crop or single variety of a crop it is more susceptible to the rapid spread of disease, which, because of the added expense, could create catastrophic financial losses. Consequently, pesticide use to control disease becomes crucial. Furthermore, since the crop is subject to threats from insect and animal pests at all stages of production—in the fields, in storage, in transportation, and in processing—pesticide costs rise even further.

Finally, the new fertilizers and irrigation favor the growth of weeds. Therefore herbicides must be applied, further increasing energy expenditure.

One result of the change from subsistence farming, in which the major investment was land, to a form of agriculture that is highly land-, water-, and energy-intensive is, as Ernest Schusky (1989:133) noted, to put the small farmer at a major disadvantage because of the difficulty in raising the capital to finance the modern technological complex. The result in the United States and elsewhere is the concentration of agricultural wealth in fewer hands and a constant reduction in the number of small family farms. (see Table 6.1.)

But it is in livestock production that the neocaloric really comes into focus. One innovation of the past hundred years in beef production was feeding grain to cattle. By 1975 the United States produced about 1,300 kilograms of grain for every person in the country. But 1,200 kilograms of that was fed to livestock. Dairy cows are relatively productive compared to beef cattle; it takes about 190 kilograms of protein to produce 60 kilograms of milk or about 36 kilocalories of fossil energy to produce one kilocalorie of milk protein. Beef get about 40 percent of their protein from grazing and 60 percent from grain. If we calculate the energy that goes into grain production and the operation of feedlots, the productive ratio is as low as 1 kilocalorie produced for every 78 kilocalories expended.

If we factor in processing, packaging, and delivery of food, the energy expenditure is even higher. For example, the aluminum tray on which a frozen TV dinner is served requires more calories to produce than the food on the tray. David Pimentel estimated that the American grain farmer using modern machinery, fertilizer, and pesticides uses 8 calories of energy for every 1 calorie produced. Transportation, storage, and processing consume another 8 fossil calories to produce 1 calorie (see Schusky 1989:102).

As Schusky said, in a world short on energy such production makes no sense but in a world of cheap energy, particularly oil, especially if it is subsidized by the

TABLE 6.1   Changes in Number of U.S. Farms by Size, 1950–1992

Size of Farm (Acres)	1992	1969	1950	% Change
1–259	1,310,000	1,944,224	4,606,497	–172%
260–499	255,000	419,421	478,170	–47%
500–999	186,000	215,659	182,297	+.08%
1,000 +	173,000	150,946	121,473	+58%
Total	1,925,000	2,730,250	5,388,437	–166%

Adapted from Eric Ross, *Beyond the Myths of Culture: Essays in Cultural Materialism*. New York, Academic Press, 1980.

nation-state, it is highly profitable. The real problem comes when agricultural production that substitutes fossil fuel energy for human energy is exported to developing countries. To begin with, there is simply not enough fossil energy to maintain this type of production for any length of time. One research project estimated that if the rest of the world used energy at the rate it is used in the United States, the world's petroleum resources would be exhausted on the food supply alone in the next ten to twelve years (Schusky 1989:119).

Furthermore, in countries with a large rural population the substitution of energy-intensive agriculture for labor-intensive agriculture will throw thousands off the land or out of work, resulting in more people fleeing to the cities in search of employment. And since modern agriculture is capital-intensive, the only farmers who can afford to remain will be those who are relatively wealthy, consequently leading to increasing income gaps in rural as well as urban areas. Where the green revolution has been successful, small farmers have been driven off the land to become day laborers or have fled to cities in search of jobs, as commercial investors bought up agricultural land. Or more wealthy farmers have bought up their neighbor's since only they had the capital to invest in fertilizers and irrigation.

This is not to say there have not been some successes in modernizing agriculture without creating greater social and economic inequality and depriving people of access to food. Murray Leaf (1984) described how one Indian village succeeded in increasing access to water, using chemical fertilizers, and increasing production while maintaining landholdings and building farm cooperatives and credit unions. In fact, some countries, including South Korea, Taiwan, and Cuba, have had notable successes in improving agriculture, alleviating poverty in the countryside, and promoting prosperity. But overall it is clear that we have developed a system of food production that is capital-intensive, favors large, state-subsidized agribusiness, minimizes the use of labor, and subsequently makes more people dependent on wage labor with which to obtain food. In the culture of capitalism, access to food is determined almost entirely by the ability to pay, not by the need to eat.

The Politics of Hunger

The obvious consequence of the reduction of labor needed for food production and the concentration of food production in fewer hands is that the world's population is more dependent on wage labor for access to food. People are consequently more vulnerable to hunger if opportunities for employment decrease, if wages fall, or if food prices rise and can starve even in the midst of food availability. This is not to say that lack of food is *never* a factor in hunger but it is rare for people to have economic resources and not be able to acquire food.

The role of food in a capitalist economy has other important consequences. For example, food production is not determined necessarily by the global *need* for food, it is determined by the *market* for food, that is how many people have the means to pay for it. That is why world food production is rarely at its maximum and why it is difficult to estimate how much food could be produced if the market demand existed. The problem is that not only are there not enough people with sufficient income to pay for all the food that could be produced, but so-called overproduction would result in lower prices and decreased profitability. For that reason, in many countries food production is discouraged. Furthermore, land that could be used to grow food crops is generally dedicated to nonfood crops (e.g., tobacco, cotton, sisal) or marginally nutritious crops (e.g., sugar, coffee, tea) for which there is a market. Finally, the kind of food that is produced is determined by the demands of those who have the money to pay for it. For example, meat is notoriously inefficient as a food source but as long as people in wealthy countries demand it, it will be produced in spite of the fact that the grain, land, and water required to produce it would feed far more people if devoted to vegetable crops. Thus people in Mexico go hungry because land is devoted to the production of beef, which few Mexicans can afford but which brings high prices in the United States.

In sum, we need to understand the economic, political, and social relations that connect people to food. Economist Amartya Sen (1990:374) suggested that people command food through *entitlements,* that is their socially defined rights to food resources. Entitlement might consist of the inheritance or purchase of land on which to grow food, employment to obtain wages with which to buy food, sociopolitical rights such as the religious or moral obligation of some to see that others have food, or state-run welfare or social security programs that guarantee adequate food to all. Not all of these kinds of entitlements exist in all societies but some exist in all. From this perspective, hunger is a failure of entitlement. The failure of entitlement may come from land dispossession, unemployment, high food prices, or lack or collapse of state-run food security programs, but the results are that people may starve to death in the midst of a food surplus.

Viewing hunger as a failure of entitlements also corrects ideological biases in the culture of capitalism, the tendency to overemphasize fast growth and production, the neglect of the problem of distribution, and hostility to government intervention in food distribution. Thus, rather than seeing hunger or famine as a failure of production (which it seems not to be), we can focus on a failure of distribution (see Vaughn 1987:158). Furthermore, we are able to appreciate the range of possible solutions to hunger. The goal is simply to establish, reestablish, or protect entitlements, the legitimate claim to food. Seeing hunger as a failure of entitlement also focuses on the kinds of public actions that are possible. For example, access to education and health care are seen in most core countries as basic entitlements that should be supplied by the state, not by a person's ability to pay. And most core countries see basic nutrition as a state-guaranteed entitlement, in spite of recent attempts in countries such as the United States to cut back on such entitlements. Thus by speaking of entitlements, we can focus on the importance of public action in dealing with world hunger.

To understand the range of solutions to hunger, we also need to distinguish between the more publicized instances of famine, generally caused by war, government miscalculations, civil conflict, or climatic disruptions; *food poverty,* in which a particular household cannot obtain sufficient food to meet the dietary requirements of its members; and *food deprivation,* in which individuals within the household do not get adequate dietary intake (Sen 1990:374).

To illustrate, let's take a look at two situations of hunger, first the more publicized instance of famine and then the less widely publicized endemic hunger.

The Anatomy of Famine

Famines have long been a part of history. Administrators in India as early as the fourth century B.C. wrote of measures to avert famines, and the people of India have been subject to massive famines throughout its history. China has also suffered major famines. The latest occurred in 1958–1961, when 15–30 million people starved to death.

Many historic famines were caused by crop failures, climatic disruptions, and war. Archaeologists have speculated that widespread climatic changes reduced the yields of Mayan agriculturists and resulted in the destruction of Mayan civilization. Yet it is clear that even historically famines resulted from entitlement failures rather than insufficient food (Newman 1990). Even during the Irish potato famine of 1846–47, when one-eighth of the population starved to death, shiploads of food, often protected from starving Irish by armed guards, sailed down the Shannon River, bound for English ports and consumers who could pay for it.

We can better appreciate the dynamics of famine and the importance of entitlements by examining a famine crisis in the African country of Malawi in 1949. It was by no means the most serious famine in Africa in the past fifty years, but Megan Vaughn (1987), in her analysis of it, provides answers to the key questions, *who starves and why?*

The famine began with a drought. The lack of rain was first noticed after Christmas 1948 and drew serious attention when in January, normally the wettest month of the year, there was no rain at all; it remained dry until some rain fell in March. In some areas the first and second plantings of maize, the main food crop, failed completely, and wild pigs, baboons, and hippos devastated the remaining crops. Old people who remembered the last famine in 1922 said there were signs of a major crisis, and within a few months it was apparent that people were starving. The British colonial government began to organize relief efforts, sending agricultural representatives into the countryside to organize the planting of root crops and replanting of crops that failed, and opening food distribution camps. By the time the rains came in October, there were reports of real malnutrition and of hundreds of children and adults starving to death. Many died, ironically, at the beginning of 1950 as the maize crop was being harvested, many from eating the crop before it ripened (Vaughn 1987:48).

According to Vaughn, women suffered most from the famine. The question is, *what happened to women's food entitlements that resulted in their being the most severely affected?* To answer this question we need to know a little about food production, the role of kinship in Malawi life, and the changing role of women in African economies.

Malawi at the time was under British control; agriculture was divided between cash crop agriculture—tobacco was the most important crop—and subsistence agriculture, the growing of such crops as maize, sorghum, and a few root vegetables. In addition, many people worked at wage labor, either in the formal employment

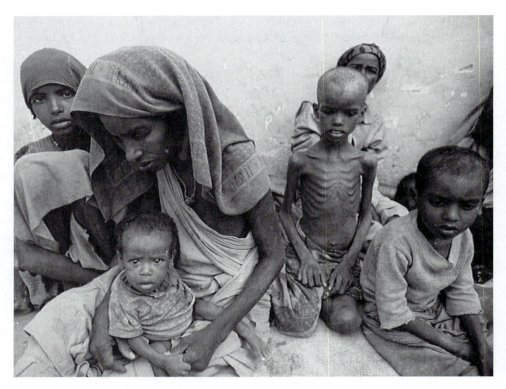

One of the images that emerged from the famine in Somalia in 1992.

sector, for European or Indian farmers or merchants, or the government, or in the informal employment sector, working on farms owned or worked by Africans. Cash could also be earned through migrant labor, almost exclusively a male domain, although women could earn money making and selling beer or liquor.

The predominant form of kinship structure was matrilineal, that is people traced relations in the female line. The most important kin tie was between brother and sister, and the basic social unit was a group of sisters headed by a brother. Under this system rights to land were passed through women, men gaining rights to land only through marriage. Traditionally, women would work their land with their husbands, who lived with their wives and children. In this system a woman's entitlement to food could come from various sources: her control of land and the food grown on it, sharing of food with matrilineal kin, wages she might earn selling beer or liquor or working occasionally for African farmers, or wages her husband or children might earn. In addition, during the famine the government established an emergency food distribution system from which women could theoretically obtain food. *What happened to those entitlements when the crops failed?*

Changes in the agricultural economy and the introduction of wage labor under European colonial rule had already undermined women's entitlements (Boserup

1970). The British colonial government was under pressure, as it was in other parts of Africa, to produce revenue to pay the cost of maintaining the colonies. Consequently they introduced cash crops, such as coffee, tea, cotton, and tobacco. The latter proved to be the most profitable in Malawi and was the major cash crop when the famine struck. But cash cropping was generally a male prerogative and provided wages for African men only when they worked for Europeans or Indians. Cash cropping by Europeans and Indians also took land that might have been used for food crops, contributing to a growing land shortage for Africans. Thus, in addition to providing new ways for men to gain economic power, European practices led to the decrease of women's power in the agricultural sector. This combination of changes in access to land, decreasing amounts of land available for Africans, and the growing importance of wage labor for men made women more dependent on men for their food entitlements when the famine struck.

When the famine became evident to the British authorities they took measures that further reduced women's entitlements. First, partly to conserve grain and partly because of a fear of social disorder, they forbade the making and sale of beer, removing a major source of income for women. Next, they assumed the family unit consisted of a husband, wife, and children, presided over by the husband, and refused to distribute food relief to married women, assuming they would obtain food from their husbands. However, many husbands were traveling to seek work elsewhere to buy food, and they might or might not send food or money home. Next, the government food distributions gave preference to those, mostly urban people who were employed in the formal economy by Europeans, Indians, or the government, neglecting those in the rural economy such as part-time women laborers. Furthermore, Europeans and Indians, who had ample food supplies during the famine, often shared with their workers who, again, were mostly men. Many of these men, of course, were conscientious husbands, fathers, brothers, and uncles and shared the food they received. But some did not, either keeping it for themselves or selling it at high prices on the black market.

To make matters worse, as the famine wore on social units began to fragment. This is a common feature of famines. Raymond Firth (1959) reported that during the early phases of a famine on the island of Tikopia, families recognized extended kin ties in the sharing of food, but as the famine wore on food was shared only within individual households. In Malawi the situation was even worse; at the beginning of the famine there seems to have been sharing within the main matrilineal kin group, but as it wore on the sharing unit became smaller and smaller until people ate secretly. Since one of a woman's entitlements consisted of food received from relatives, this would have further reduced the amount of food she received. Finally, divorce rates apparently increased significantly, particularly in families where the husband was a migrant laborer, further isolating women and reducing their food entitlements.

In sum, then, the most vulnerable portion of the population was women without male support but for whom the colonial authorities took no responsibility, married women whose husbands had abandoned them, and wives of long-term migrants who did not remit money (Vaughn 1987:147). In addition, of course, the children of these women suffered and died disproportionately.

The lesson of the Malawi famine is that starvation can be very selectively experienced within a population because of the distribution of food entitlements. Given the amount of food already available in the areas most affected by the famine and the food available through relief efforts, it is unlikely that anyone had to starve. But many did.

The Anatomy of Endemic Hunger

While famine as a cause of hunger has decreased, endemic hunger caused by poverty has increased. One problem with endemic hunger is that it goes largely unnoticed, by the press who prefer to cover the more spectacular instances of famine, and by governments whose economic and social policies might be held responsible for the hunger. Yet endemic hunger is a far more serious problem. India, for example, which has done an excellent job of famine prevention, has done poorly in solving the problem of endemic hunger. Consequently, every eight years, more Indians die as a result of hunger than Chinese died in the famine of 1958–1961. Yet the deaths in India do not receive nearly the public attention that is given to famine. One of the questions we need to ask is *how and why is endemic hunger ignored, unrecognized, and sometimes denied by state agencies, as well as by the hungry themselves?*

Governments often refuse to recognize hunger because it marks an admission of failure to provide adequately for its citizens. And hunger sometimes goes unrecognized because it is assumed to be a medical problem, rather than a problem of food entitlements. Doing anthropological fieldwork in Mali, Katherine A. Dettwyler (1994:71–73) encountered a little girl with swelling of the face, hands, feet, and abdomen, classic symptoms of kwashiorkor, a disease that results from a diet that is sufficient in calories but deficient in protein. The girl's mother said she had *funu bana,* "swelling sickness," and asked Dettwyler for medicine for her daughter, failing to recognize that what her daughter needed was extra meat or milk. When Dettwyler suggested just that, the mother responded by saying the little girl wasn't hungry and that she needed medicine. For the mother it continued to be a medical problem, not a food problem.

The denial of hunger prevents the development of programs to alleviate it. More insidiously, when hunger goes unrecognized or unacknowledged, problems that are a consequence of hunger, such as poor work performance, poor academic achievement, and stunted growth, are attributed to other factors, such as lack of motivation or cultural background.

To illustrate how social, economic, and cultural factors converge to produce hunger in the midst of plenty, as well as the complexity of identifying hunger and even admitting it exists, let's examine the problem of starvation in Brazil. Brazil is not a poor country, in fact it is among the top ten to fifteen economies in the world. During the period of great optimism following World War II, Brazil was one of the first of the so-called underdeveloped countries to embark on a concerted policy of economic and industrial development. A large number of Brazilians have become very wealthy, yet 40 percent of its population lives in poverty, and it has one of the highest rates of infant mortality in Latin America, with some regions having an infant mortality rate as high as those in impoverished countries of Africa. Exploring why this happened will help us understand the dynamics of world hunger.

Brazil set out to develop economically by imitating the pattern followed by core countries such as England, France, and the United States. The strategy was to build industry, export cash crops, and create jobs, with the idea that the wealth created would "trickle down" to others in society. However, to date that hasn't happened. Instead, peasants once able to secure a reasonable subsistence through simple agriculture are deprived of land, through either expropriation of land or privatization of communal land, and forced to work as wage laborers on the surviving farms or to flee to cities to seek work, often ending up in the shantytowns that surround the cities. Their wages are insufficient to buy food, and structural adjustment policies imposed by international lending institutions have forced the reduction of social support programs. One thing stands out: the vast majority of the population becomes dependent on others for food, food they must buy and which must be affordable. Unfortunately, in many cases, they do not have the means to buy food, or prices keep it out of reach. The problem of hunger and poverty is particularly severe in northeastern Brazil.

Sugar has dominated the economy of northeastern Brazil for over four hundred years. Fueled by a growing European demand for sugar, Portuguese colonists established plantations in the sixteenth century and imported slaves to grow and process sugarcane. The colonialization of Brazil and the nature of the economic relations created by sugar production created a pattern of class relations that remained largely intact through the mid-twentieth century. A plantation-owning elite ruled over a large peasant population that cut sugarcane for wages, using unused land to grow their own food crops. A few others worked for wages in the sugar mills and refineries. However, as the sugar industry expanded and as technological improvements were made in the 1950s and 1960s because of government policies to expand production for export, many peasants were evicted from the land, fleeing to the cities in search of jobs. Poverty was widespread, and even people with jobs did not make enough to meet family expenses. For example, in northeastern Brazil in 1989, the legal minimum monthly income was $40, while food expenses alone for a family of four were four times that amount.

To make matters worse, in the mid-1980s Brazil and other countries could not keep up their payments to the World Bank and other Western financial institutions from which they had borrowed to industrialize, and threatened to default on their loans. To help them avoid default, the World Bank allowed these countries to renegotiate their loans. These countries had to agree to change their economies by, among other things, reducing government spending on such things as public education, welfare, housing, and health, entitlement cutbacks that resulted in still greater hardships for the poorest portion of the population.

In 1982 Nancy Scheper-Hughes returned to a shantytown, Alto do Cruzeiro, located in the city of Bom Jesus da Mata, where she had worked as a Peace Corps volunteer in 1965. The shantytown consisted of five thousand rural workers, one-third of whom lived in straw huts. The vast majority of residents had no electricity, and water was collected by the women twice a day from a single spigot located in the center of the community. Most men and boys worked as sugarcane cutters during the harvest season. A few men and some women worked in the local slaughterhouse. Other than this part-time work, there was little employment. Many women found jobs as domestics among the middle- and upper-class families or sold what they could in the market. Many women and children worked in the cane fields as unregistered workers at less than minimum pay.

The economics of hunger in the shantytowns today is simple—there is not enough money to buy food. Because of the economic situation in Brazil, groceries cost twice in 1987–1988 what they cost in 1982. Furthermore, a basic subsistence costs one and a half times minimum wage. Many of the residents do not make minimum wage and are unemployed from February to September when there is no cane to cut. Furthermore, fresh vegetables that some used to grow or that were available from relatives in the countryside are no longer available because so many have been forced off the land by the sugarcane growers. In the 1960s brown beans cooked with slices of native squash, pumpkin, and onions were a staple; now the beans are cooked with only a little salt and flavoring. Dried beef was once available but is now prohibitively expensive and has been replaced by salted fish caught in the polluted river that passes through town. Even dried beans have become prohibitively expensive and dried cornmeal has taken its place.

With jobs scarce, available wages inadequate, land unavailable to grow food, and government assistance inadequate or nonexistent, residents of the shantytown scramble as best they can to acquire food. In fact, according to Scheper-Hughes, slow starvation is a primary motivating force in the social life of the shantytowns. People eat everyday, but the diet is so meager that they are left hungry. Women beg while their children wait for food, and children's growth is stunted by hunger and malnutrition. Children of one and two years of age cannot sit unaided and cannot or do not speak. Breastbones and ribs protrude from taut skin, flesh hangs in folds from arms, legs and buttocks, and sunken eyes stare vacantly. The plight of the rural worker and his or her family is, according to Scheper-Hughes (1992:146), "the slow starvation of a population trapped...in a veritable concentration camp for more than thirty million people."

Perhaps the most tragic result of hunger is the death of infants. Approximately 1 million children younger than five years of age die each year in Brazil. Northeastern Brazil, which accounts for 25 percent of child deaths, has an infant mortality rate of 116 of every 1000 live births, one of the highest in the world. And not all deaths are reported. In northeastern Brazil some estimate that two-thirds of infants who die, do so without a medical diagnosis.

Scheper-Hughes found that reliable statistics on infant mortality in the shantytowns were difficult to acquire. She finally obtained statistics for selected years in the 1970s, all of which indicated an infant mortality rate of 36 to 41 percent. From information she collected by combing public records, Scheper-Hughes found the following infant mortality rates for Bom Jesus da Mata: 49.3 percent in 1965; 40.9 percent in 1977; 17.4 percent in 1985; and 21.1 percent in 1987.

While the infant mortality rate in northeastern Brazil has generally declined, the decline, said Scheper-Hughes (1992:280), is misleading. Instead of a decline in infant

*A homeless mother and child trying to survive on the
streets of a Brazilian city.*

mortality there is a "modernization of child mortality," characterized by containing
child death to the poorest families and by a change in the major reported causes of
child death from the "old killers," diseases now controlled by immunization, to
"new killers," especially infant malnutrition and dehydration caused by diarrhea.

News reports and government studies about poverty in Brazil do mention the
problem of infant mortality, but they generally attribute it to malnutrition and disease. But Scheper-Hughes's study revealed a more basic problem: People, especially infants and children, are not just malnourished, a term that implies only a

poor diet, they are starving to death. Yet even medical authorities rarely mention starvation. When Scheper-Hughes examined medical records of children and infants who died she found that in 34.8 percent of cases the cause of death was cessation of heart beat and respiration; in 22.2 percent it was listed as dehydration. Only 3.4 percent were attributed to malnutrition and only 1.7 percent to diarrhea. One wonders, wrote Scheper-Hughes (1992:303),

> [a]mid the sea of froth and brine that carried away the infants and babies of the Alto do Cruzeiro, what kind of professional prudery it was that "failed to see" what every mother of the Alto do Cruzeiro knew without ever being told. "They die," said one woman going to the heart of the matter, "because their bodies turn to water."

One way to mask the evidence of starvation is to turn it into a medical problem; the *medicalization of hunger* is exactly what Scheper-Hughes discovered in Brazil. People interpret the symptoms of starvation, even in children, as conditions that require medical treatment rather than food.

One of the things anthropology teaches about the human capacity for culture is that people place experiences in systems of meaning that allow them to make sense of their experiences. Illness and disease are no exception; different people define differently what constitutes illness as opposed to something that is not illness. Moreover, people will define what constitutes a medical problem (e.g., infant diarrhea) as opposed to, say, a social problem (e.g. hunger). In northeastern Brazil hunger, a social problem, has been redefined as a medical problem. How and why this has been done reveals much about how human beings construct their own world of experience and how people construct systems of meaning that best enhance their social or political interests.

One of the major traditional illness syndromes in Brazil, and indeed in much of Latin America, is *nervos,* assumed to be a wasting sickness that leaves the victim weak, shaky, dizzy, tired, depressed, and disoriented. When someone is suffering from these symptoms, they say they are sick with *nervos.* People believe *nervos* is the result of an innately weak and nervous body. In years past when someone thought they suffered an attack of *nervos,* they drew on their traditional store of herbal medicines and the practical knowledge of elderly women in the household. Today they seek medical help from one of the local clinics; now *nervos,* a traditional disease category, is thought to be treatable by modern medicine.

But there was another more insidious change in how people defined their physical condition: symptoms associated with hunger began to be talked about as *nervos.* That is, hunger and *nervos* became synonymous. This was not always the case. Starvation and famine have long been a feature of life in northeastern Brazil; people frequently complained of *fome* (hunger) and its terrifying end, *delirio de fome,* the madness that signaled the end of life from starvation. But hunger is rarely mentioned today. If a person is weak, tired, or dizzy he or she will not complain of hunger and seek food but instead complain of *nervos* and seek medicine to cure it. In other words, people who may be suffering from hunger and who twenty years ago would have defined themselves as suffering from *fome* now define themselves as suffering from *nervos,* an illness separate from hunger that just happens or is the result of innate weakness. Moreover, if weakness, fatigue, dizziness, and other symptoms that may be related to slow starvation just happen, then no one is at fault and social causes of the problem can be ignored.

Nancy Scheper-Hughes (1992:174) said a hungry body represents a potent critique of the nation-state in which it exists, but a sick body implicates no one and conveys no blame, guilt, or responsibility. Sickness just happens. The sick person and the sick social system are let off the hook. A population suffering from starvation, however, represents a threat to the state that requires economic and social solutions—social programs, jobs, or land redistribution. *Nervos,* a sickness, is a personal and "psychological" problem that requires only medical intervention and faults no one, except perhaps the person suffering from it. Sickness requires little state action, other than supplying the occasional prescription of tranquilizers, vitamins, or sleeping pills. Instead of the responsible use of state power to relieve starvation and hunger, there is a misuse of medical knowledge to deny that there is a social problem at all.

Scheper-Hughes (1992:207) related the story of a young single mother who brought her nine-month-old child to the clinic, explaining that the baby suffered from *nervoso infantil.* She complained that the small, listless, and anemic child was irritable and fussy and disturbed the sleep of family members, especially the grandmother, who was the family's economic mainstay. Herbal teas did not work, and the grandmother threatened to throw them out if the child did not sleep. The doctor refused to give her sleeping pills for the child and instead wrote a prescription for vitamins. The doctor failed to acknowledge the mother's real distress, as well as the child's state of malnutrition, and the vitamins served virtually no purpose other than to redefine the infant's condition from starvation to sickness or malnutrition.

On other occasions children will be brought to doctors with severe diarrhea, a classic symptom of starvation. Simple rehydration therapy, feeding the child special fluids, will usually cure the diarrhea for a time. But the child is still returned to an environment where, with lack of food, the problem is likely to recur until after being "saved" perhaps a dozen times the child finally dies of hunger.

The question, said Scheper-Hughes, is *how do people come to see themselves as primarily nervous, and only secondarily hungry? How do they come to see themselves as weak, rather than exploited? How does overwork and exploitation come to be redefined as a sickness for which the appropriate cure is a tonic, vitamin A, a sugar injection? Why do chronically hungry people "eat" medicines and go without food?*

One reason is that since hungry people truly suffer from headaches, tremors, weakness, irritability, and other symptoms of nervous hunger, they look to doctors, healers, political leaders, and pharmacologists to "cure" them. They look for strong-acting medicines, so they line up at clinics and drug stores until they get them. One cannot, said Scheper-Hughes, underestimate the attractiveness of drugs to people who cannot read warning labels and who have a long tradition of "magical medicines."

Furthermore, she said, health is a political symbol subject to manipulation. Slogans such as "health for all by the year 2000," or "community health," filter down to poor, exploited communities where they serve as a cover for neglect and violence. There is power and domination to be obtained by defining a population as sick or nervous, and in need of the power of politicians and doctors:

> *The medicalization of hunger and childhood malnutrition in the clinics, pharmacies, and political chambers of Bom Jesus da Mata represents a macabre performance of distorted institutional and political relations. Gradually the people of Bom Jesus da Mata have come to believe that they desperately need what is readily given to them, and they have forgotten that what they need most is what is cleverly denied. (Scheper-Hughes 1992: 169–170)*

Conspiracy by medical workers is not necessary to effect this transformation. Doctors and clinic workers themselves accept the magical efficacy of cures; either that or they are demoralized to the extent that they prescribe drugs as the only solution they have to ills they are ill-prepared to solve but called on to treat. As one doctor (cited Scheper-Hughes 1992:204) said:

> *They come in with headaches, no appetite, tiredness, and they hurt all over. They present a whole body in pain or in crisis, with an ailment that attacks them everywhere! That's impossible! How am I to treat that? I'm a surgeon, not a magician! They say they are weak, that they are nervous. They say their head pounds, their heart is racing in their chest, their legs are shaking. It's a litany of complaints from head to toe. Yes, they all have worms, they all have amoebas, they all have parasites. But parasites can't explain everything. How am I supposed to make a diagnosis?*

Economic Development and Solutions to Hunger

What solutions are there to the problem of world hunger and the poverty that ultimately causes it? Is it best to focus on economic development or, as some call it, growth-mediated security systems, assuming so-called market mechanisms will improve people's lives? Or are famine and endemic hunger best addressed by public support systems in the form of state-financed food and nutrition programs, state-financed employment, or cash distribution programs? The answer to these questions are not easy. Some argue, for example, that state-run programs take money needed for economic development and divert it to programs that may in the short-run alleviate poverty and hunger but in the long-run will simply aggravate the problem by undercutting the growth of private enterprise. This is the position generally taken by multilateral organizations, such as the World Bank and IMF which insist on limitations or cutbacks in state spending as conditions for loans or structural adjustment programs to assist countries in debt. Others respond that state-run antipoverty programs represent an investment in the human capital necessary for economic development, that a population that is hungry, undernourished, and subject to disease is less productive.

To illustrate some of the problems involved in solving the problem of hunger, let's examine three cases of attempts to supply people with entitlements to food. The first is an example of foreign aid, having countries with food surpluses simply donate food to countries in need. The second is a case of successful economic development, the case of South Korea. The third example involves programs that target the most susceptible portion of the population—women.

Foreign Aid: PL 480

One way to alleviate hunger is through food aid, that is, the sale or donation, often at subsidized prices, of agricultural products by wealthy countries such as the United States to peripheral countries. One of the best examples of this kind of program is Food for Peace, or Public Law 480. The story of PL 480 (Agricultural Trade and Assistance Act of 1954) provides an excellent example of how state intervention promotes the growth of agricultural profits in the core while undermining growth in the periphery. In fact, the story is an agricultural parallel to the growth of industrial capitalism examined in Chapter 1. There we examined how in the late nineteenth century the efficiency of production threatened to flood the capitalist world with unsold commodities, and how this threat spurred the consumer revolution in core countries and an attempt to expand markets for core industries and corporations. Much the same thing happened with agriculture in the second half of the twentieth century.

With advances in technology, American farmers in the mid-1950s produced more food than Americans could eat. The government took various actions to solve this problem, including paying farmers *not* to grow crops and buying surplus produce and storing or destroying it. In addition, the government instituted PL 480, a program to subsidize the sale of American farm products to peripheral countries ostensibly in need of food or willing to purchase U.S. farm products. Under PL 480 countries can purchase U.S. agricultural products and stretch their payments out as long as forty years or may receive the food free to meet crisis situations such as earthquakes, hurricanes, civil conflict, droughts, and other natural disasters. Two-thirds of this food is distributed through nonprofit food agencies such as CARE, Catholic Relief Services, and Church World Service. The largest recipients of PL 480 assistance have been India ($6.2 billion), Pakistan ($2.3 billion), South Korea ($2.1 billion), Egypt ($2.8 billion), Vietnam ($1.5 billion), and Indonesia ($1.7 billion).

The program would seem to benefit almost everyone. American agribusiness can sell surplus products and even increase production and, more important, establish export markets through increased demand for their products. U.S. shippers profit from the increased exports since, according to the law, they must transport at least half of them. Peripheral countries get food on long-term credit that they can use to help needy people, while government officials can use it as patronage to distribute to political supporters. Nonprofit agencies depend on the products to support their operations, and, finally, people in peripheral countries get free or subsidized food. It sounds like the perfect program. Other than the U.S. taxpayer who must pay to purchase the surplus agricultural products produced by agribusiness, who suffers?

Critics of food aid claim that instead of helping the countries in which the food is distributed, it undermines local food growers by flooding the market with free produce (see Maren 1997). An analogy might be the flooding of peripheral countries with cheap, factory-made textiles, thus driving local artisans out of business. In other words, aid programs represent simply the dumping of core surplus into peripheral economies and calling it charity. Furthermore, once small farmers are driven out of business, the country becomes dependent on food imports, having to buy agricultural products from the same agribusinesses that, with U.S. government subsidies, helped undermine local farmers.

To make matters worse for producers in the periphery, those who continue to grow food crops (rice, wheat, corn) find that the same core countries that flood their countries with subsidized agricultural produce place strict limitations on the amount of food (e.g., tomatoes, sugar, rice) they will import. In other words, core countries help their farmers by subsidizing the sale of their products to peripheral countries while at the same time placing severe restrictions on what peripheral farmers can sell to core countries.

Some critics, such as Michael Maren, even accuse those who profit from food aid (agribusiness, relief agencies, and peripheral political leaders) of manufacturing news of food crises by exaggerating claims of famine and manipulating the press to further their own interests. Most aid, these critics say, ends up being stolen, sold, or simply stored by foreign governments or distributed to those who could purchase it if they had to.

The Case for Economic Development: South Korea

If redistributing food from food-rich countries to food-poor countries doesn't work, what other means are there to ensure food entitlements? An obvious solution is for countries to formulate policies to promote economic development and reduce poverty. However, as we've seen, historically the tendency in the globalization of the culture of capitalism is to increase discrepancies in wealth both worldwide and locally. Thus, as in Brazil, economic development vastly increases the wealth of the country but leaves millions more vulnerable to starvation than were before.

There have been cases of successful development, however. One of the most dramatic, and one that is often used as proof that peripheral countries can reduce hunger and poverty through economic growth, is in South Korea (Kennedy 1993). Often not discussed in the case of South Korea's "economic miracle" is the agricultural policy it adopted, one very different from that of Brazil and other countries that opted to intensify growing of cash crops at the expense of peasant production.

After World War II, South Korea planned to develop areas of society that would maximize its citizens' quality of life. They planned for 100 percent primary education and increased opportunity for secondary school and college, such that between 1960 and 1980 secondary school attendance increased from 27 to 76 percent and college attendance from 5 percent to 12 percent. Adult literacy increased from 76 percent to 93 percent. Infant mortality declined from 78 to 34 per 1,000, and life expectancy rose from 54 to 65 years of age. The population growth rate declined from 2.5 percent to 1.7 percent per year.

South Korea also had a unique opportunity to define rural agricultural policy. Before World War II, Japan occupied Korea and seized all the rice paddy land. After the war, with Japan defeated and the country divided among the communist-run government of North Korea and the more market-oriented South Korea, the South Korean government redistributed land retaken from the Japanese to the peasant population. By establishing a three hectare limit on the amount of land any one person could hold, the government ensured that anyone who wanted land to farm could have it. This policy worked to maximize equality in the countryside and maintain labor needs in agriculture. Furthermore, the small holdings did not lend themselves to the introduction of technology-intensive agriculture that would reduce the need for labor.

To stimulate industry, to keep industrial wages low to ensure that industrial products were competitive in the world market, and to make food accessible, the South Korean government established agricultural policies that until the 1970s kept food prices at less than half the world market value. While this helped the industrial economy, farmers did not receive market value for their labor. Thus the impetus for economic development came from agriculture or, as some would say, on the backs of farmers. Why farmers did not protest is an interesting question; Ernest Schusky (1989:161) suggested that the receipt of free land made them more amenable to lower economic returns.

In 1971, President Park introduced the Saemaul Movement, a government program that implored the population to devote themselves to the virtues of hard work and thrift, a movement that coincided with a marked improvement in rural life. The government let food prices rise until they were two or three times what they would have brought on the world market. As a consequence, food production increased noticeably in spite of a declining agricultural labor supply as more people moved to the cities. The increase in agricultural production was not a result of mechanization but of greater productivity (Schusky 1989:152).

Rural incomes were also increased through the introduction of wage work in village industries, such as the weaving of rice straw products and, later, textile and electronic industries. While the wages paid in villages lagged behind urban wages, household income, a combination of wages and agricultural income, was about the same. Consequently, fewer people left the countryside to move to the cities.

Farm income was increased even more by an increase in production of vegetables, animals, and fruits, most notably with the help of simple technology. South Korean farmers began to expand their growing season by planting seeds under sheets of vinyl stretched over frameworks of bamboo or metal. The earlier planting allows farmers to double-crop, producing a crop of lettuce, tomatoes, onions, or strawberries in the two or three months before June, when the land must be plowed for rice farming. Urban demand for these new crops has more than kept up with farm production, further increasing farm income and with little energy cost. In addition, animal crops such as beef, chicken, and dairy products are becoming popular in South Korea. Since urban dwellers spend about one-third of their income on food, equity in rural-urban income has been maintained.

Thus Korea managed, at least until the 1990s, to develop agriculture by allowing prices (and wages in the cities) to rise and using inexpensive technology. Equity in the countryside was maintained through land redistribution and limits on landholdings.

In other cases of growth-mediated development, such as that in Taiwan, economic development was not wholly driven by industry and market mechanisms. Public action in ensuring equitable land redistribution and placing limits on farm size in rural areas played a major role, as did investments in human capital in the form of education, health, and nutrition.

Targeting Vulnerable Populations: The Grameen Bank

As we saw in the case of the 1949 famine in Malawi, women are particularly vulnerable to hunger and poverty. This is true not only in peripheral countries, but in core countries as well. Two out of every three poor adults in the United States are women, including more than one-fourth of all women older than age sixty-five not living in families. The 16 percent of all American families headed by women represented 53 percent of the families officially classified as living below the poverty level.

There is evidence that small capital investments to women can provide opportunity for successful entrepreneurship and relief from poverty. The best evidence for this comes from the experiences of the Grameen Bank in Bangladesh, one of the poorest countries in the world. Unemployment is high, and women in Bangladesh suffer systematic discrimination revealed by, among other things, the 0.940 to 1 ratio of females to males in the population. Descent in Bangladesh is patrilineal and residence is patrilocal, that is women are expected to live with or near their husband's family after marriage. Most Bangladesh families also observe *purdah;* a system based on the belief that women must be isolated to protect them and ensure that they observe socially accepted standards of modesty and morality. *Purdah* effectively limits a woman's physical mobility to the area around her homestead and her social contacts to immediate family members. Consequently, girls learn to accept dependence on male family members and, later, husbands. Education for women is often considered irrelevant.

The Grameen Bank was founded by Mohammad Yunus, an economics professor at Chittagong University in Bangladesh. The simple premise of the Grameen Bank is that small loans (seventy-five dollars or less) to mostly poor women who, with no collateral, are unable to borrow from regular banks will enable them to establish small retail businesses (e.g., vegetable vendor, fruit seller, tea stall owner, lime seller, egg seller) or small manufacturing businesses (e.g., incense maker, plastic flower maker, wire bag maker, mat weaver, toy maker) whose income will enable them to pay back the loan with interest. The bank's philosophy is best expressed by Yunus (1994) himself in a speech before the International Rotary Convention in 1994. Credit,

The vast majority of borrowers from the Grameen Bank are women. Here a lender makes one of her regular loan payments.

he said, is the key to alleviating poverty. If people have only their labor to sell, they will remain poor. However, if their labor can be connected with capital, it is the one single thing that will allow them to overcome their poverty.

Yunus began by making small loans himself or by cosigning for formal bank loans; in 1983 he established the Grameen Bank as a formal financial institution. Today it has almost 1.5 million borrowers and a remarkable loan default rate of only 2 percent, compared to a default rate of 70–90 percent for commercial banks in Bangladesh. There are more than 1,000 branches in over 68,000 villages. The bank was profitable until 1992, when the government forced it to raise the wages of its workers, who many observers credit with the bank's success. The latest reports indicate that the bank is now breaking even.

The bank charges 20 percent interest, compared to compound interest rates of 13–16 percent at commercial banks, but principal is repaid first and interest calculated weekly on the remaining principal, making for an effective interest rate of 10–12 percent. Over 90 percent of the borrowers are women.

The Grameen Bank is unique also because it combines its lending activities with a regimented social program. Borrowers are required to organize themselves into groups of five and to meet regularly with bank staff. They are required to memorize the bank's sixteen decisions,[2] and pledge to observe the bank's four major principles—discipline, unity, courage, and hard work. They must also pledge to shun child marriage, keep families small, build and use pit latrines, and plant as many seedlings as possible during planting seasons. At meetings they are required to salute, recite the decisions, do physical drills, and sit in rows of five to mark their group affiliation.

The question we need to ask is *does extending financial credit to poor women serve to empower them economically, socially, or politically?* Research by social scientists suggests it does. Women borrowers report increases in days worked, income, and nutrition (Wahid 1994). Other ethnographic research (Schuler and Hashemi 1994) suggests that bank membership not only empowers women economically but significantly increases contraceptive use and fertility control. Anthropologists and economists suggest that the success of the bank in empowering women, raising their economic standards, and ensuring repayment of loans may be in large part due to the social ritual and regimentation of the program. The chanting, saluting, and other rituals help women create an identity outside the family, while the meetings give women legitimate reasons to associate with people outside their households. In addition, the chanting and recitation of bank principles may empower women who have been taught for most of their lives to be silent in front of strangers (Schuler and Hashemi 1994:73).

In the 1990s the bank expanded its lending and projects; began offering housing loans, and financed large-scale projects such as fish farming programs and textile production. The latter has allowed Bangladesh weavers to produce cloth that is successfully competing with imported textiles. The bank has also established its own health insurance program, members paying about $1.25 per year for insurance that then pays for their doctor's visits and discounted medicines. Recently the

---

[2]The Sixteen Decisions of Grameen Bank

1. We respect the four principles of the Grameen Bank—we are disciplined, united, courageous, and workers—and we apply them to all our lives.
2. We wish to give our families good living standards.
3. We will not live in dilapidated houses. We repair them and work to build new ones.
4. We cultivate vegetables the whole year round and sell the surplus.
5. During the season for planting, we pick out as many seedlings as possible.
6. We intend to have small families. We shall reduce our expenses to a minimum. We take care of our health.
7. We educate our children and see that they can earn enough money to finance their training.
8. We see to it that our children and homes are clean.
9. We build latrines and use them.
10. We only drink water drawn from a well. If not, we boil the water or we use alum.
11. We will not accept a marriage dowry for our son and we do not give one to our daughter at her marriage. Our centre is against this practice.
12. We cause harm to no one and we will not tolerate that anyone should do us harm.
13. To increase our income, we make important investments in common.
14. We are always ready to help each other. When someone is in difficulty, we all give a helping hand.
15. If we learn that discipline is not respected in a centre, we go along to help and restore order.
16. We are introducing physical culture in all centers. We take part in all social events.

World Bank has offered loans to allow the Grameen Bank to expand its operations to other countries, many of which have begun to establish lending programs similar to that of Grameen Bank.

Conclusion

It is apparent that hunger is not caused by a lack of food, but rather by some people's lack of entitlement to food. It is apparent, also, that the poverty that causes hunger is a consequence of global economic forces, such as the financial debt that peripheral countries accumulated in the 1970s. Other instances of hunger and famine are generally a consequence of political unrest. Even in relatively wealthy countries such as Brazil, the growing gap between rich and poor that has seemingly resulted from growing integration into the world economy results in thousands dying of starvation.

We have seen, furthermore, that economic policies of the wealthy countries are not designed to help the poor countries, but to further the interests of corporate and political agendas. Even food aid programs that are touted as evidence of humanitarian concern increase the profits of agribusiness and may do far more harm economically than good.

Finally we asked whether anything could be done to alleviate hunger and poverty in the periphery. We have seen how some countries have alleviated the threat of famine and ensured food entitlements for virtually all citizens. We also examined the role of women in development and examined programs and initiatives, such as the Grameen Bank, that, by improving the position and power of women, have reduced poverty and the threat of hunger.

Chapter 7

Environment and Consumption

If the life-supporting ecosystems of the planet are to survive for future generations, the consumer society will have to dramatically curtail its use of resources—partly by shifting to high-quality, low-input durable goods and partly by seeking fulfillment through leisure, human relationships, and other nonmaterial avenues.
—ALAN DURNING, HOW MUCH IS ENOUGH

A man is rich in proportion to the things he can afford to let alone.
—HENRY DAVID THOREAU, WALDEN

The first sweetened cup of hot tea to be drunk by an English worker was a significant historical event, because it prefigured the transformation of an entire society, a total remaking of its economic and social basis. We must struggle to understand fully the consequences of that and kindred events, for upon them was erected an entirely different conception of the relationship between producers and consumers, of the meaning of work, of the definition of self, of the nature of things.
—SIDNEY MINTZ, SWEETNESS AND POWER

All animals alter their environments as a condition of their existence. Human beings, in addition, alter their environments as a condition of their cultures, that is by the way they choose to obtain food, produce tools and products, and construct and arrange shelters. But culture, an essential part of human adaptation, can also threaten human existence when short-term goals lead to long-term consequences that are harmful to human life. Swidden agriculture alters the environment, but not as much as irrigation agriculture, and certainly not as much as modern agriculture with its use of chemical fertilizers, pesticides, and herbicides. Domesticated animals alter environments, but keeping a few cattle for farm work or cows for dairy products does far less damage than maintaining herds of thousands to supply a meat-centered diet.

The degree to which environments are altered and damaged is determined in part by population and in part by the technology in use. Obviously, the more people in a given area, the more potential there is for environmental disruption. Tractors and bulldozers alter the environment more than hoes or plows. But the greatest factor in environmental alteration—in the use of raw materials, the use of nonhuman energy, and the production of waste—is consumption. Because of our level of consumption, the average American child will do twice the environmental damage of a Swedish child, three times that of an Italian child, thirteen times that of a Brazilian child, thirty-five times that of an Indian child, and 280 times that of a Chadian or Haitian child (Kennedy 1993:32). In per capita production of energy alone, the United States leads other countries by a vast margin (see Table 7.1).

William Rees, an urban planner at the University of British Columbia, estimated that it requires four to six hectares of land to maintain the consumption level of the average person from a high-consumption country. The problem is that in 1990, worldwide there were only 1.7 hectares of ecologically productive land for each person. He concluded that the deficit is made up in core countries by drawing down the natural resources of their own countries and expropriating the resources, through trade, of peripheral countries. In other words, someone has to pay for our consumption levels, and it will either be our children or inhabitants of the periphery of the world system (Korten 1995:34).

Our consumption of goods obviously is a function of our culture. Only by producing and selling things and services does capitalism in its present form work, and the more that is produced and the more that is purchased the more we have

TABLE 7.1   Per Capita Consumption of Energy, Selected Countries, 1994

Country	Energy (kilograms of oil equivalent)
United States	7,819
Germany	4,128
Soviet Union	4,014
Japan	3,856
Mexico	1,561
Turkey	957
Brazil	718
China	664
Indonesia	366
India	248
Nigeria	162
Bangladesh	64

From World Development Report 1997: 228–29.

progress and prosperity. The single most important measure of economic growth is, after all, the gross national product (GNP), the sum total of goods and services produced by a given society in a given year. It is a measure of the success of a consumer society, obviously, to consume.

However, the production, processing, and consumption of commodities requires the extraction and use of natural resources (wood, ore, fossil fuels, and water); it requires the creation of factories and factory complexes whose operation creates toxic byproducts, while the use of commodities themselves (e.g., automobiles) creates pollutants and waste. Yet of the three factors environmentalists often point to as responsible for environmental pollution—population, technology, and consumption—consumption seems to get the least attention. One reason, no doubt, is that it may be the most difficult to change; our consumption patterns are so much a part of our lives that to change them would require a massive cultural overhaul, not to mention severe economic dislocation. A drop in demand for products, as economists note, brings on economic recession or even depression, along with massive unemployment.

The maintenance of perpetual growth and the cycle of production and consumption essential in the culture of capitalism does not bode well for the environment. At the beginning of Chapter 1 we mentioned that the consumer revolution of the late nineteenth and early twentieth centuries was caused in large part by a crisis in production; new technologies had resulted in production of more goods, but there were not enough people or money to buy them. Since production is such an essential part of the culture of capitalism, society quickly adapted to this crisis by convincing people to buy things, by altering basic institutions and even generating a new ideology of pleasure. The economic crisis of the late nineteenth century was solved, but at considerable expense to the environment in the additional waste that was created and resources that were consumed. At that time the world's population was about 1.6 billion and those caught up in the consumer frenzy was a fraction of that total.

The global economy today faces the same problem it faced one hundred years ago, except that the world population has almost quadrupled. Consequently it is even more important to understand how the interaction between capital, labor, and consumption in the culture of capitalism creates an overproduction of commodities and how this relates to environmental pollution. To illustrate, let's take a quick look at the present state of the global automobile industry.

In capitalism competition between companies for world markets requires that they constantly develop new and improved ways to produce things and lower costs. In some industries, such as textiles, as we saw in Chapter 2, competition requires seeking cheaper sources of labor; in others, such as the automobile industry, it means creating new technologies that replace people with machines to lower labor costs. Twenty years ago it took hundreds of hours of human labor to produce one automobile. Today a Lexus LS 400 requires only 18.4 hours of human labor, Ford Motor Company produces several cars with 20.0 hours of human labor, and General Motors lags behind at about 24.8 hours per car (Greider 1997:110–112).

Food production is one of the major sources of pollution. Here sugar cane fields are being burned in Hawaii prior to replanting.

In addition to reducing the number of jobs available to people, advanced productive technology creates the potential for producing ever more cars, regardless of whether there are people who want to buy them. In 1995 the automobile industry produced over 50 million automobiles, but there was a market for only 40 million. What can companies do? Obviously they can begin to close plants or cut back on production, which some do. In the 1980s some 180,000 American auto workers lost their jobs because of cutbacks and factory shutdowns. But each producer, of course, hopes the problem of selling this surplus is someone else's problem, so they continue to produce cars.

From the perspective of the automobile companies and their workers, the preferred solution to overproduction is to create a greater demand for automobiles. This is difficult in core countries, where the market is already saturated with cars. In the United States, for example, there is one car for every 1.7 persons. However, there are places in the world where there are few cars. In China, for example, there is only one car for every 680 people. Imagine the environmental impact if the consumption rate of automobiles in China, with a population of well over a billion people, even began to approach the consumption rate in the United States.

But that is exactly the goal of automotive manufacturers and the nation-states that operate to help them build and sell their products. Not only would automobile makers in the core like to enter the Chinese market, the Chinese themselves plan to build an automobile industry as large as that of the United States, to produce cars for their own market and compete in other markets as well. If China—or India, Indonesia, Brazil, or most of the rest of the periphery—even approached the consumption rate of automobiles common in the core, the increased environmental pollution would be staggering. There would be not only massive increases in hydrocarbon pollution but also vastly increased demands for raw materials, especially oil. And the overproduction dilemma is not unique to automobiles: the steel, aircraft, chemical, computer, consumer electronics, drug, and tire industries, among others, face the same dilemma.

The environmental problem could be alleviated if consumers simply said "enough is enough" and stopped consuming as much as they do. But, as noted above, any reduction of consumption would likely cause severe economic disruption. Furthermore, few are aware of how large our reduction would have to be to effect a change. A study by Friends of the Earth Netherlands asked what the consumption levels of the average Dutch person would have to be in the year 2010 if consumption levels over the world were equal and if resource consumption was sustainable. They found that consumption levels would have to be reduced dramatically. For example, to reduce global warming by the year 2010, people in the Netherlands would have to reduce carbon emission from the current 12 tons (it is 19.5 in the United States) to 4 tons; to accomplish that a Dutch person would have to limit the use of carbon-based fuel to one liter per day, thus limiting travel to 15.5 miles per day by car, 31 miles per day by bus, 40 miles per day by train, or 6.2 miles per day by plane. A trip from Amsterdam to Rio de Janeiro could be made only once every twenty years. (Korten 1995:34).

Thus it is unlikely that we will ever significantly change our consumption patterns. Consumption is as much a part of our culture as buffalo hunting was part of Plains Indian culture; it is a central and necessary element. Consequently there is no way to appreciate the problem of environmental destruction without understanding how people are turned into consumers, how luxuries are turned into necessities. That is, *why do people choose to consume what they do, how they do, and when they do?*

Take sugar, for example. In 1995, each American consumed in his or her soft drinks, tea, coffee, cocoa, pastries, breads, and other foods sixty-six pounds of sugar. Why? Liking the taste might be one answer. In fact, a predilection for sweets may be part of our biological makeup. But that doesn't explain why we consume it in the form of sugarcane and beet sugar and in the quantities we do. Then there is meat. Modern livestock production is one of the most environmentally damaging and wasteful forms of food production the world has known. Yet Americans eat more meat per capita than all but a few other peoples. Some environmentalists argue that we can change our destructive consumption patterns, if we desire. *But is our pattern of consumption only a matter of taste and of choice, or is it so deeply embedded in our culture as to be virtually impervious to change?*

To begin to answer this question, we shall examine the history of sugar and beef, commodities that figure largely in our lives, but involve environmental degradation. Sugar and beef is an appropriate combination for a number of reasons:

1. The production and processing of both degrade the environment; furthermore, the history of sugar production parallels that of a number of other things we consume, including coffee, tea, cocoa, and tobacco, that collectively have significant environmental effects.
2. Neither is terribly good for us, at least not in the quantities and form we consume them.
3. Both have histories that closely tie them to the growth and emergence of the capitalist world economy. They are powerful symbols of the rise and economic expansion of capitalism; indeed they are a result and a reason for it.
4. With the rise of the fast-food industry, beef and sugar, fat and sucrose have become the foundations of the American diet; indeed, they are foundation foods of the culture of capitalism symbolized in the hamburger and Coke, hot dog and soda, and topped with a fat and sucrose dessert—ice cream.

The Case of Sugar

The history of sugar reveals how private economic interests, along with economic policies of the nation-state and changes in the structure of society, combined to convert a commodity from a luxury good believed to have health benefits into a necessity with overall harmful health consequences. In the process, it vastly increased the exploitation of labor—first in the form of slavery, then in migrant labor—converted millions of acres of forest into sugar production—in the process expelling millions from their land—and changed the dietary habits of most of the world. It illustrates how our consumption patterns are determined in capitalism and why we engage in behavior that may be environmentally unsound and personally harmful. The story of sugar is an excellent case study of how the nation-state mediated interaction of the capitalist, the laborer, and the consumer produces some of our global problems.

Sugar Origins and Production

Sugarcane, until recently the major source of sugar, was first domesticated in New Guinea, then grown in India and the Middle East. The processing of sugarcane into sugar is complex and environmentally damaging. There are various kinds of sugar plant, most of which grow quickly after regenerating from cuttings left in the fields after harvests or from the controlled planting of cuttings. The stalk matures in nine to eighteen months and must be cut when the juice in the stalk contains the most sucrose. The juice must be extracted quickly, before it rots or ferments; it is squeezed from the cane by chopping, pressing, or pounding, then heated to evaporate the liquid, leaving crystals from which centrifugal machines extract most of the molasses. The molasses may be used as a sweetener or, more important, processed into rum. The raw sugar that remains after the molasses is extracted can be consumed as is, turned into a liquid syrup, or processed further to obtain the granular white sugar that most Americans and Europeans favor.

Sugar production alters the environment in a number of ways. Forests must be cleared to plant sugar; wood or fossil fuel must be burned in the evaporation process; waste water is produced in extracting sucrose from the sugarcane; and more fuel is burned in the refining process. When Spain sought to expand sugar production into the Atlantic in the sixteenth century, it colonized the Canary Islands, then inhabited by the Guanche. The Spaniards transformed the Canarian ecosystem, clearing the forests and hillsides to make way for cane fields and for fuel for the fires of the *ingenio,* or sugar house. Within a few decades wood was so scarce that the government tried, in vain, to protect the forests from the lumberjacks (Crosby 1986:96). The Guanche were also gone within a century. When sugar production expanded in the seventeenth century, the sugar refineries of Antwerp caused so much pollution that the city banned the use of coal. Contemporary sugar production in Hawaii not only has destroyed forests, but waste products from processing have severely damaged marine environments. "Big sugar," as the sugar industry is called in Florida, is largely responsible for the pollution, degradation, and virtual destruction of the Everglades.

Thus sugar, like virtually all commodities, comes to us at an environmental cost. Yet people did not always crave sugar. For that to happen, a luxury had to be converted into a necessity, a taste had to be created.

Uses of Sugar

By A.D. 1000, when sugar was grown in Europe and the Middle East, it was a highly valued trade item and a luxury. Sugar was used largely as a spice and a medicine and was available only to the wealthy. In Arabian medical works from the tenth and fourteenth centuries, for example, sugar was an ingredient in virtually every medicine. So useful was sugar as a medicine that one way of expressing desperation or helplessness was the saying "like an apothecary without sugar" (Mintz 1985:101). According to one source, "nice, white sugar" from the Atlantic Islands cleaned the blood and strengthened the chest, lungs, and throat; when used as a powder it was good for the eyes, and when smoked it was good for the common cold. Mixed with cinnamon, pomegranate, and quince juice, it was good for a cough and fever (Mintz 1985:103).

Sugar was also used for decoration, mixed with almonds (marzipan) and molded into all kinds of shapes, the decorations becoming central to celebrations and feasts. And it was used as a spice in cooking and, of course, as a sweetener. It was also used as preservative. We still use sugar to preserve ham, and it is often added to bread to increase its shelf life. But through the seventeenth century, even with its diverse uses, it was an expensive luxury item reserved for the upper classes.

The Development of the Sugar Complex

As a luxury item, sugar brought considerable profits for those who traded in it. In fact, it was the value of sugar as a trade item in the fifteenth and sixteenth centuries that led Spain and Portugal to extend sugarcane production, first to the Atlantic Islands, then to the Caribbean Islands, and finally to Brazil, from which, beginning in 1526, raw sugar was shipped to Lisbon for refining.

Modern economists like to talk about the spin-off effects of certain commodities, that is the extent to which their production results in the development of subsidiary industries. For example, production of automobiles requires road construction, oil and petroleum production, service stations, auto parts stores, and the like. Sugar production also produced subsidiary economic activities; these included slavery, the provisioning of the sugar producers, shipping, refining, storage, and wholesale and retail trade.

The slave trade was a major factor in the expansion of the sugar industries. Slaves from Europe and the Middle East were first used on the Spanish and Portuguese plantations of the Canary Islands and Madeira, but by the end of the fifteenth century slaves from West Africa were working the fields. The growing demand for and production of sugar created the plantation economy in the New World and was largely responsible for the expansion of the Atlantic slave trade in the sixteenth,

The increased demand for sugar in the eighteenth and nineteenth centuries represented a boon for West Indies sugar plantations and created a demand for more laborers, including slaves and children.

seventeenth, and eighteenth centuries. From 1701 to 1810 almost one million slaves were brought to Barbados and Jamaica to work the sugar plantations.

Money was to be made also from the shipment of raw sugar to European refineries, more yet from the wholesale and retail sale of sugar, and probably more yet from the sale by European merchants of necessary provisions to the plantation owners. Investors in Europe, especially England, put money into the sugar industry, either in the development of plantations, the sale of provisions to the colonial plantations, shipping, or the slave trade. Attorneys, grocers, drapers, and tailors invested small amounts to form partnerships to finance slave-buying expeditions to Africa and the subsequent resale of slaves to buyers from the sugar plantations of the New World. Thus it was during the sixteenth and seventeenth centuries that sugar became the focus of an industry, a sugar complex that combined the sugar plantations, the slave trade, long-distance shipping, wholesale and retail trade, and investment finance.

The Expansion of Sugar Consumption

Yet it was not until the late seventeenth century that sugar production and sales really began to influence sugar consumption in Europe. Sugar consumption increased fourfold in England and Wales from 1700 to 1740 and doubled in the next thirty-five years. From 1663 to 1775 consumption increased twentyfold. Sugar consumption rose more rapidly than that of bread, meat, and dairy products in the eighteenth century. While the per capita annual consumption in 1809 of eighteen pounds of sugar per person does not compare to our present consumption of almost seventy pounds, it was more than sufficient to generate large profits.

Why did people in England begin to consume sugar in greater and greater quantities? First, increased sugar production led to reduced prices, making it accessible to more people, although its use was still largely confined to the upper and emerging middle classes of English society. One reason prices remained as high as they did was the imposition of high import tariffs on sugar produced in other countries. Planters in the British West Indies and people who invested in their enterprises were a powerful force in English politics. To protect their profits, they lobbied and received protection from foreign competitors. They were also powerful enough to prevent British abolitionists from winning legislation to end the slave trade, at least until the beginning of the nineteenth century.

Second, the benefits of sugar were widely touted by various authorities, notably popular physicians. Dr. Frederick Slare found sugar a venerable cure-all. He recommend that women include at their breakfast bread, butter, milk, and sugar. Coffee, tea, and chocolate were similarly "endowed with uncommon virtues," he said, adding that his message would please the West Indian merchant and the grocer who became wealthy on the production of sugar. Slare also prescribed sugar as a dentifrice, a lotion, and a substitute for tobacco in the form of snuff and for babies. Sidney Mintz (1985:107–108) said of Slare that while his enthusiasm for sugar is suspect, it is more than a curiosity because it relates to so many aspects of what was then still a relatively new commodity; furthermore by stressing sugar's value as a medicine, food, and preservative, he was drawing additional attention to it.

Slare's enthusiasm for sugar was not an oddity; others shared his enthusiasm. No contemporary advertising executive could improve on the description of sugar by John Oldmixin, a contemporary of Slare:

> One of the most pleasant and useful Things in the World, for besides the advantage of it in Trade, Physicians, and Apothecaries cannot be without it, there being nearly three Hundred Medicines made up with sugar; almost all Confectionery Wares receive their Sweetness and Preservation from it, most Fruits would be pernicious without it; the finest pastries could not be made nor the rich Cordials that are in the Ladies' Closets, nor their Conserves; neither could the Dairy furnish us with such a variety of Dishes, as it does, but by their Assistance of this noble Juice. (cited Mintz 1985:108)

A third reason that sugar consumption increased in the eighteenth century was its use as a sweetener for three other substances, all bitter and all technically drugs (stimulants)—tea, coffee, and cocoa. All of these were used in their places of origin without sugar, in spite of their bitterness. All three initially were drinks for the wealthy; by the time they were used by others they were generally served hot and sweetened.

Fourth, sugar's reputation as a luxury good inspired the middle classes to use it to emulate the wealthy—sugar was a sign of status. The powerful used sugar for conspicuous consumption, as a symbol of hospitality and the like. When sugar was a luxury the poor could hardly emulate these uses, but as the price declined, as its use expanded, sugar became available to the poor to use in much the same way as their social betters.

Finally, sugar consumption increased because the government increased its purchase of sugar and sugar products. After the capture of Jamaica and its sugar plantations from the French in 1655, the British navy began to give its sailors rum rations, set in 1731 at half a pint per day and later increased to a pint per day for adult sailors. The government also purchased sugar to distribute to poorhouse residents.

Thus sugar production and consumption increased, as did the amount of land devoted to its production and the number of sugar mills and refineries, distilleries producing rum, and slaves employed in the whole process. Most important, the profits generated by the sugar trade increased dramatically.

The Mass Consumption of Sugar

By 1800, British sugar consumption had increased 2,500 percent since 1650 and 245,000 tons of sugar reached European consumers annually from the world market. By 1830 production had risen to 572,000 tons per year, an increase of more than

233 percent. By 1860, when beet sugar production was also rising, world production of sucrose increased another 233 percent to 1,373 million tons. Six million tons were produced by 1890, another 500 percent increase (Mintz 1985:73).

Two acts by the British government helped spur this massive increase in sugar production and consumption. First, the government removed tariffs on the imports of foreign sugar. This made foreign sugar more accessible to British consumers and forced domestic producers to lower their prices, making it affordable to virtually all levels of British society. Second, England abolished slavery during the years 1834–1838 (it had abolished the slave trade in 1807). This had the effect of forcing technological improvements, but it also spurred the creation of a labor pattern that exists to the present. The freed slaves were without land and tools and were dependent on whatever labor they could get. As Mintz (1985:176) noted, while freed from the discipline of slavery they were reduced to laborers by the discipline of hunger. The surplus supply of labor was increased when the British Foreign Office went to the aid of the planters in the West Indies by helping them import contracted laborers from India, China, and elsewhere. The freed slaves, unable to secure a livelihood independent of the sugar industry or to use collective bargaining, settled into obscurity until they reentered British consciousness as migrants to England more than a century later.

The lower price of sugar increased its use in tea and stimulated a dramatic rise in the production of preserves and chocolate. More important, it must have been apparent to sugar producers and sellers that there was a fortune to be made by increasing the availability of sugar to the working mass of England. Certainly there were those who worked hard to expand its availability.

Sidney Mintz's history of sugar reveals how much social, political, and economic power had to do with increased sugar consumption. Planters, slavers, shippers, bankers, refiners, grocers, and government officials, all profiting in one way or another from increased sugar consumption, exercised power to support the rights and prerogatives of planters, the maintenance of slavery, the availability of sugar and its products (molasses, rum, preserves) and products associated with it (tea, coffee, cocoa), and to supply it to the people at large at prices they could afford. Thus the consumption of sugar was hardly just a matter of taste—it had to do with investments, taxes, the dispensation of sugar through government agencies, and a desire to emulate the rich, among other things. It also had to do with convenience and the changes in household structure, labor, and diet that accompanied the Industrial Revolution.

Rural workers in England in the eighteenth and nineteenth centuries typically had diets that consisted of oatmeal, porridge, milk, homemade bread, and vegetable broth. While simple, the diet was relatively nutritious. In the industrial cities, however, it could be costly. Fresh food in general would have been more costly in the city, and food preparation, especially if it needed cooking, required fuel, which cost yet more money. Furthermore, urban women were, as noted earlier, also working in the factories twelve to fourteen hours per day, reducing the time they could spend on food preparation.

As a result, the diet of the urban working class and poor was transformed to one dominated by tea, sugar, store-bought white bread, and jam. Hot tea replaced vegetable broth. Jam (50–65 percent sugar) was cheaper than butter to put on bread, was easily stored, and could be left open on shelves for children to be spread on bread in the absence of adults. In other words, the cultural and social constraints of time and cost created in the urban, industrial setting combined with the convenience of sugar and the prodding of those who profited from its sale to shape the diet of the British working class. It was an ideal arrangement, for, as E. P. Thompson (1967) noted, after providing profits to plantation and refinery investors, sugar provided the bodily fuel for the working people of Britain. Sugar is also what Sidney Mintz referred to as a "drug food," a category that includes coffee, tea, cocoa, alcohol, and tobacco—foods that deaden hunger pangs and stimulate effort without providing nutrition, and do so cheaply. That is one reason why they were transformed from upper-class luxuries to working-class necessities.

Modern Sugar

Sidney Mintz (1985:180–181) suggested that the consumption of goods such as sugar is the result of profound changes in the lives of working people, changes that made new forms of foods and of eating seem "natural," as new work schedules, new sorts of labor, and new conditions of life became "natural." This does not mean that we lack a choice in what we consume, but that our choice is made within various constraints. We may have a choice between a McDonald's hamburger and a Colonel Sanders chicken leg during a half-hour lunch break. The time available acts to limit our choice, removing, for example, the option of a home-cooked vegetarian lunch.

Sugar has become, as it did for the nineteenth-century British laborer, a mainstay of the fast-food diet in the United States, the perfect complement to fat. Both fat and sugar are made more attractive by the clever use of language. The fat side of our diet is advertised with words like "juicy," "succulent," "hot," "luscious," "savory," and "finger-licking good." The sugar side is advertised as "crisp," "fresh," "invigorating," "wholesome," "refreshing," and "vibrant." And the sugar in soft drinks serves as the perfect complement to hamburgers and hot dogs, since it possesses what nutritionists call "go-away" qualities—removing the fat coating and the beef aftertaste from the mouth.

Thus sugar fits our budgets, our work schedules, and our psychological needs while at the same time generating monetary profits and growth. As Mintz (1985: 186) put it, sugar

> [s]erved to make a busy life seem less so; in the pause that refreshes, it eased, or seemed to ease, the changes back and forth from work to rest; it provided swifter sensations of fullness or satisfaction than complex carbohydrates did; it combines easily with many other foods, in some of which it was also used (tea and biscuit, coffee and bun, chocolate and jam-smeared bread)…No wonder the rich and powerful liked it so much, and no wonder the poor learned to love it.

The Story of Beef

The story of beef is very much like that of sugar, except that livestock breeding has been indicted for even greater environmental damage than sugar production, largely because of the vast amount of land needed to raise cattle. As an agricultural crop, sugar is quite efficient; while it has little nutritional value, it is possible to get about eight million calories from one acre of sugarcane; to get eight million calories of beef requires 135 acres. In addition, much of the beef we eat is grain-fed to produce the marbling of fat that makes it choice grade and brings the highest prices; as mentioned earlier, 80 percent of the grain produced in the United States is fed to livestock. In addition, two-thirds of U.S. grain exports go to feed livestock in other countries. Thus to the amount of land needed for rangeland, we must add the farm land devoted to animal feed; moreover, as we saw in Chapter 6, this grain production requires tons of chemical fertilizer, pesticides, and herbicides, all of which negatively alter the environment.

Cattle raising consumes a lot of water. Half the water consumed in the United States is used to grow grain to feed cattle; the amount of water used to produce ten pounds of steak equals the household consumption of a family for an entire year. Fifteen times more water is needed to produce a pound of beef protein than an equivalent amount of plant protein. There are also environmental problems associated with beef waste products; a feedlot steer produces forty-seven pounds of manure per hour (Ensminger 1991:187), not to mention the methane gases that contribute to the destruction of the ozone layer. Even more pollution is produced by the slaughter, refrigeration, transport, and cooking of beef.

Cattle raising has also been criticized for its role in the destruction of tropical forests. Hundreds of thousands of acres of tropical forests in Brazil, Guatemala, Costa Rica, and Honduras, to name just a few countries, have been leveled to create pasture for cattle. Since most of the forest is cleared by burning, the extension of cattle pasture also creates carbon dioxide and, according to some environmentalists, contributes significantly to global warming. In addition, with increasing amounts of fossil fuel needed to produce grain, it now takes a gallon of gasoline to produce a pound of grain-fed beef.

Much of the rangeland of the United States has been devastated by livestock herding to the point that it has become desert. Currently two to three million cattle graze on 306 million acres of public land. According to the General Accounting Office (GAO) more plant species are being threatened by cattle grazing than by any other single factor, and populations of pronghorn, antelope, and elk have virtually disappeared from western rangelands. Much of this is a consequence of government policy. For example, the Bureau of Land Management, responsible for allotting land for livestock use, in one district in Oregon allots about 252 million pounds of herbage to livestock and 8 million pounds to wildlife. The government also participates in the killing of thousands of coyotes and other so-called predator animals each year, largely at the insistence of ranchers in order to protect their livestock as well as animals such as bison and deer that may carry disease. It is not surprising that the Bureau of Land Management reported that almost 95 million acres of

The Chicago stockyards in 1948. Before being slaughtered, cattle are fattened with grain grown on the American prairies.

rangelands are in "unsatisfactory condition," a condition attributed by researchers to overgrazing (Rifkin 1992:211).

The same problems are occurring in areas of Africa that have a long tradition of cattle raising. When cattle populations were managed by traditional means and for traditional consumption, there was little environmental damage. When attempts were made to introduce Western livestock raising practices and technologies to increase the number of cattle and develop a larger beef export industry, pasture has turned to desert and wild animals have disappeared, largely because of overgrazing by cattle (Rifkin 1992:216).

In addition, beef is terribly inefficient as a source of food. By the time a feedlot steer in the United States is ready for slaughter, it has consumed 2,700 pounds of grain and weighs approximately 1,050 pounds; 157 million metric tons of cereal and vegetable protein is used to produce 28 metric tons of animal protein. Finally, beef in the quantities that Americans consume it is unhealthy, being linked to cardiovascular disease, colon cancer, breast cancer, and osteoporosis.

Yet Americans are among the highest meat consumers in the world and the highest consumers of beef. Over 6.7 billion hamburgers are sold each year at fast-food restaurants alone. Furthermore, we are exporting our taste for beef to other parts of the world. The Japanese, who in the past consumed only one-tenth the amount of meat consumed by Americans, are increasing their consumption of beef. McDonald's sells more hamburgers in Tokyo than it does in New York City.

Marvin Harris (1986) suggested that "animal foods play a special role in the nutritional physiology of our species." He pointed out that studies of gathering and hunting societies reveal that 35 percent of the diet comes from meat, more than even Americans eat, and that this dietary pattern has existed for hundreds of thousands years. Many cultures have a special term for "meat hunger." The Ju/wasi of Botswana, for example, say "hunger is grabbing me," not just because they haven't eaten but because they haven't eaten meat. Harris pointed out that it is also an especially efficient protein source and that when people can afford it, they eat more meat.

However, it is worth noting that historically few societies have made meat the center of their diet. If we look around the world, we find that most diets center on some complex carbohydrate—rice, wheat, manioc, yams, taro—or something made from these—bread, pasta, tortillas, and so on. To these are added some spice, vegetables, meat, or fish, the combination giving each culture's food its distinctive flavor. But meat and fish are generally at the edge, not the center, of the meal (Mintz 1985). Moreover, whether or not we just like meat, *why do American preferences run to beef?* Anthropologists Marvin Harris and Eric Ross (1987b) have some interesting answers that may help us understand why, in spite of the environmental damage our beef consumption causes, we continue to eat it in such quantities. The answers involve understanding the relationships among Spanish cattle, British colonialism, the American government, the American bison, indigenous peoples, the automobile, the hamburger, and the fast-food restaurant.

The Ascendancy of Beef

The story of the American preference for beef begins with the Spanish colonization of the New World. The Spanish, as noted earlier, introduced the so-called cattle complex to the New World, where it became established in Argentina, areas of Central America, particularly Northern Mexico, and Texas. By the 1540s, cattle were so numerous around Mexico City that the Spaniards had to train Indians to handle them. Fortunes were made in cattle in the sixteenth century on meat and leather.

In Argentina, the number of feral cattle increased so rapidly on the pampas that by the seventeenth century meat was eaten three times a day, and animals were killed for their hides and the meat left to rot. One seventeenth-century traveler wrote of Argentina,

> [a]ll the wealth of these inhabitants consists in their animals, which multiply so prodigiously that the plains are covered with them…in such numbers that were it not for the dogs that devoured the calves…they would devastate the country. (cited Rifkin 1992:49)

TABLE 7.2   U.S. per Capita Meat
Consumption, 1900–1994
(in pounds)

Year	Beef	Pork
1994	63.6	49.5
1993	61.5	48.9
1990	64.0	46.4
1977	125.9	61.6
1976	129.4	58.2
1975	120.1	54.8
1970	113.7	66.4
1960	85.1	64.9
1950	63.4	69.2
1940	54.9	73.5
1920	59.1	63.5
1900	67.1	71.9

See also Ross 1980:191; AlSO U.S. Bureau of the Census 1990,
1993, 1994.

In colonial America, however, pigs, not beef, were the meat of choice. Eric Ross (1980) pointed out that the preference for beef or pork is related in part to environmental factors. Pigs tend to be raised in forested areas and can be maintained in areas of relatively dense populations since they eat the same food as human beings. In densely populated West Germany in 1960, the ratio of cattle to hogs was 0.06 to 1, while in sparsely populated Argentina, with its large tracts of range land, it was 11.2 to 1.0. Another reason pork was preferred in America was that the preservation process—smoking, salting, and pickling—improved the flavor of the meat, whereas for beef it did not. In fact, pork was the meat of choice in the United States until the 1960s, when beef overtook it. While meat consumption in the United States has declined since the 1970s, beef is still preferred (see Table 7.2).

The Emergence of the American Beef Industry

On the eve of the Industrial Revolution, England was the beef-eating capital of the world, with 100,000 head of cattle slaughtered annually in London. But in the nineteenth century, with its population increasing and more people migrating to the factory towns and cities, England began to look toward its colonies and ex-colonies for food, especially meat. Eric Ross (1980) suggested that the motivation was not simply to get food but to keep meat prices low in order to keep wages low and allow industry in Great Britain to remain competitive with industries in other countries. As we saw earlier, the British increased cattle production in Ireland by increasing the amount of land devoted to pasture, pushing people onto smaller plots of land and increasing dependence on the potato. When the potato blight hit Ireland in 1846–1847 and millions starved, the export of Irish grain and livestock intensified. In fact, because of the massive outmigrations caused by the famine, English landlords were able to intensify cattle production even more; from 1846 to 1874 the number of Irish cattle exported to England climbed from 202,000 to 558,000, and more than 50 percent of the total land mass of Ireland was devoted to cattle raising.

England next turned to Argentina, where the development of the refrigerated steamer permitted the shipment of fresh beef to England. In the 1870s English, Scottish, and Irish colonists already owned 45 percent of the sheep and 20 percent of the cattle herds in Argentina, and English demand and English capital helped develop the Argentine beef business. One of the greatest nineteenth-century fortunes made in England, that of the Vesteys, was made by dominating the Argentine meat market.

Who was eating all this meat? It was not the working class, whose breakfast consisted of little more than bread, butter or jam, and tea with sugar and whose dinner might include a meat byproduct, such as Liebig's extract (made from hides and other residue), or inferior cuts. The gentry, however, apparently consumed vast quantities. Beef, in fact, had been for some time the choice of the British well-to-do. For example, in 1735 a group of men formed the Sublime Society of Beef Steaks, most renowned for the invention of the sandwich by one of its members. The society consisted largely of members of the British elite but also included painters, merchants, and theatrical managers. It existed until 1866. Twice a year the group would meet for dinner, at which, according to the society's charter, "beef steaks shall be the only meat for dinner" (Lincoln 1989:85).

Here is one description, dating from 1887, of a typical breakfast table of the British nobility (Harris and Ross 1987b:35–36):

> *In a country house, which contains, probably, a sprinkling of good and bad appetites and digestions, breakfasts should consist of a variety to suit all tastes, viz.: fish, poultry, or game, if in season; sausages, and one meat of some sort, such as mutton cutlets, or fillets of beef; omelets, and eggs served in a variety of ways; bread of both kinds, white and brown, and fancy bread of as many kinds as can conveniently be served; two or three kinds of jam, orange marmalade, and fruits when in season; and on the side table, cold meats such as ham, tongue, cold game, of game pie, galantines, and in winter a round of spiced beef.*

The army and navy consumed enormous amounts of meat, each sailor and soldier getting by regulation three-fourths of a pound of meat daily; in fact, the diet of the military was vastly superior to that of the bulk of the population. Between 1813 and 1835 the British War Office contracted for 69.6 million pounds of Irish salted beef and 77.9 million pounds of Irish salt pork; as Harris and Ross (1987:37–38) noted, Irishmen were able to eat the meat of their own country only by joining the army of the country that had colonized theirs. Furthermore, the British military, by distributing rum and meat to their men, helped to subsidize both the sugar and meat industries.

Laying largely untapped in the latter half of the nineteenth century, by either the British or the Americans, were the American Great Plains and the vast herds of Texas longhorns. The longhorn was the remnant of the Spanish herds that ran wild. It was uniquely adapted to the extremes of heat and cold of the prairies; it could eat almost anything, including leaves and prickly pear, and by the 1830s and 1840s cowboys began to round up the strays and herd them to New Orleans. In the 1830s there were 100,000 head of cattle roaming Texas; by 1860 there were over 3.5 million.

But cattle traders faced three problems in trying to make a profit from long-horn cattle. The first problem was shipping cattle to areas in the Midwest from where they could be distributed. They could be driven overland, but that was too costly. The second problem was the availability of rangeland; in the 1860s the plains were occupied by indigenous peoples and their major food source, the buffalo (bison). Finally, there was the quality of the beef; longhorn beef was too lean and tough for British tastes. The solutions to these problems would define the American taste for beef and a good part of the history of the American West.

The problem of transporting cattle to the Midwest and East was solved by a young entrepreneur, Joseph McCoy, who convinced the Union Pacific Railway to construct a siding and cattle pen at its remote depot in Abilene, Kansas, and pay him a commission on every animal he delivered for shipment. The animals would be driven from Texas to Abilene on the Chisholm trail. McCoy first needed and got the governor of Kansas to lift a quarantine on Texas cattle that had been imposed because of the spread of Texas fever; then he persuaded the Illinois legislature to allow his shipment of cattle into their state. On September 5, 1867, McCoy shipped twenty railway cars of cattle east from Abilene. By 1871 he was shipping 700,000 cattle annually. Through the 1870s the Chisholm Trail was traveled by herd after herd headed for the slaughterhouses, tables, and leatherworks of the East.

But as the demand for meat, leather, and tallow grew, more land was needed for cattle; the plains, once considered the Great American Desert, were being promoted as a land of a "fairy-tale" grass that required no rain and could support millions of head of cattle (Rifkin 1992:73). Only two things stood in the way of its use—buffalo and Indians.

Cattlemen, Eastern bankers, the railroads, and the U.S. Army believed the solution to both problems could be effected by the extermination of the buffalo, and they joined in a systematic campaign to that end. In a period of about a decade, from 1870 to 1880, in one of the world's greatest ecological disasters, buffalo hunters ended 15,000 years of continuous existence on the plains of the American bison, reducing herds of millions to virtual extinction. Stationed in Kansas, Colonel Richard Henry Dodge wrote that in 1871 buffalo around the post were virtually limitless; by the fall of 1873 "there was now myriads of carcasses. The air was foul with a sickening stench, and the vast plain, which only a short twelve months before teemed with animal life, was a dead, solitary, putrid desert" (cited Rifkin 1992:74).

Buffalo hunters were getting one to three dollars a hide, and heroes such as William F. Cody (Buffalo Bill) were entertaining European royalty on buffalo hunts, while railroad passengers, armed with rifles provided by the conductors, shot the animals from the moving trains. Not everyone approved of the slaughter, and some newspaper editorials condemned it, but to no avail. Even the bones were ground up for fertilizer and sold for eight dollars a ton. The "white harvest," as it was called, even engaged indigenous groups, who would bring the bones in wagons for sale at the railroad depots; meat met sugar as "fresher bones" were made into char and used in the refining process to remove the brownish coloration of sugar. In a speech to the Texas legislature in 1877, General Phillip Sheridan said of the buffalo hunters:

> *These men have done…more to settle the vexed Indian question than the entire regular army has done in the last thirty years. They are destroying the Indians' commissary; and it is a well-known fact that an army losing its base of supplies is placed at a great disadvantage. Send them powder and lead if you will; but for the sake of lasting peace let them kill, skin, and sell until the buffalo is exterminated. Then your prairies can be covered with speckled cattle and the festive cowboy who follows the hunter as a second forerunner of an advanced civilization. (cited Wallace and Hoebel 1952:66)*

With the buffalo went the Indians of the Plains. Their major food and source of ritual and spiritual power removed, they were soon vanquished and confined to reservations, land granted to them in earlier treaties with the U.S. government taken away.

The American bison was the staple food of the indigenous peoples of the American plains, but the presence of both inhibited the conversion of the plains to cattle raising.

In one of the great ironies of history, cattlemen made fortunes selling beef to the U.S. government for distribution to Indians forced onto reservations and hungry because of the buffalo slaughter. Furthermore, cattlemen grazed their animals on what remained of Indian land, paying them in beef or cash only a fraction of what the grazing rights were worth.

The final problem in the story of England and the Texas longhorn involved the toughness or leanness of plains cattle. The British liked their beef generously marbled with fat. This problem was solved by a historic bargain; western cattle would be transported to the midwestern farmbelt and fed corn until their meat was speckled with fat, then shipped by rail and steamer to English ports (Rifkin 1992:58–59). The integration of the plains and the prairie, rangeland and farmland, was so complete that to this day the price of corn is closely linked to the demand for and price of cattle.

As a consequence of the merger of cattle and corn in the 1870s, British banks were pouring millions into the American West. They formed the Anglo-American Cattle Company Ltd. with £70,000 of capital; then the Colorado Mortgage and Investment Company of London, buying 10,000 acres of rangeland north of Denver; then the Prairie Cattle Company Ltd. and the Texas Land and Cattle Company, Ltd. The Scottish-American Company invested £220,000 in land in Wyoming and the Dakotas. Cattlemen associations were formed that controlled millions of acres and often became spokespersons for foreign cattle barons. In all, the British invested some $45 million in western real estate, and by the 1880s America was responsible for 90 percent of beef imported to England (Harris and Ross 1987b:38). By the mid-1880s, 43,136 tons of fresh beef were being shipped yearly to Great Britain (Rifkin 1992:95).

The takeover of the West by the British so alarmed some Americans that in the 1884 presidential election, both parties included planks that would limit "alien holdings" in the United States. The Republican campaign slogan of 1884, "America for Americans," was directed not at poor Latin Americans or Asian migrants or European minorities, as it would be later, but the British elite. But the British invasion of the American cattle industry had one other long-lasting effect: it defined for the next one hundred years the American taste in beef.

In response to both British tastes and midwestern farm interests, the U.S. Department of Agriculture developed a system of grading beef that awarded the highest grade—prime—to the beef with the most fat content, choice grade to the next fattiest, select grade to the next, and so on. Thus the state participated in creating a system that inspired cattle raisers to feed cattle grain and add fat because it brought the best price, while at the same time communicating to the consumer that since it was most expensive the most marbled cuts of beef must be the best.

The federal inspection and grading standards also aided another important sector of the beef industry, the meat packers. Beef packers wanted to centralize their operations, to bring live animals to one area to be butchered, but most states had laws that required inspection of live animals twenty-four hours before slaughter. Butchers were opposed to the centralized slaughter of beef because, since most animals were slaughtered and butchered locally, centralizing the operation would put many of them out of business. The beef packing industry lobbied successfully to convince Congress to pass a federal meat inspection system that, unlike state inspection systems, would not affect out-of-state centralized operations (Harris and Ross 1987b:202).

Aided by the government, the meat packing business proceeded to dominate the production and distribution of beef. Refrigeration technology and the new federal inspection standards allowed individuals such as George H. Hammond in 1871, Gustavus Swift in 1877, and Philip and Simeon Armour in 1882 to slaughter beef in one area of the country—Chicago—and ship it fresh to any other area of the country. Their growth and domination of the meat packing industry resulted in the concentration of production in five companies that by World War I handled two-thirds of all meat packing in the United States. By 1935 Armour and Swift controlled 61 percent of meat sales in the United States.

One of the great technological innovations in meat packing was the assembly (or, as Jeremy Rifkin [1992] called it, "disassembly") line. Henry Ford is generally credited with developing assembly line technology in the construction of his Model T Ford in 1913. However, even Ford said that he got his idea from watching cattle hung on conveyor belts passing from worker to worker, each assigned a specific series of cuts until the entire animal was dismembered. The working conditions in the meat packing industry were then and remain among the worst of any industry in the country. At the turn of the century they prompted Upton Sinclair to produce his quasi-fictional account, *The Jungle,* (1906) whose descriptions of the slaughterhouses promoted such public outrage that the government acted to regulate the meat packing industry.

The state has also heavily subsidized our taste in beef by allowing cattlemen to graze cattle on public lands at a fraction of market costs for grazing on private land, thus making beef more affordable and encouraging its consumption. As early as the 1880s, cattlemen were fencing millions of acres of public land, to which they had no title, with the newly invented barbed wire. In fact, at that time most of the cattle companies grazing their cattle on public land were British. After objections to the practice were raised, the government passed the Desert Land Act of 1887, which awarded land to anyone who improved it. The Union Cattle Company of Cheyenne dug a thirty-five-mile-long ditch, called it an irrigation canal, and claimed 33,000 acres of public land (Skaggs 1976:62).

In 1934 Congress passed the Taylor Grazing Act, which transferred millions of acres of public land to ranchers if they took responsibility for improving it. In 1990, some 30,000 cattle ranchers in eleven western states grazed their cattle on 300 million acres of public land, an area equal to the fourteen East Coast states stretching from Maine to Florida (Rifkin 1992:105–106). These permit holders pay a third to a quarter less than they would pay on private lands.

But the victory of beef was not yet complete. To appreciate the story of American beef consumption, we need to understand the role of the American government in creating the legal definition of a hamburger and the infrastructure that encouraged the spread of the automobile.

Legend has it that the hamburger was invented by accident when an Ohio restaurant owner ran out of pork sausages at the Ohio Fair in 1892 and substituted ground beef on his buns. The hamburger was the rage of the St. Louis World's Fair of 1904, and by 1921 White Castle had opened its hamburger chain in Kansas City. But the hamburger still needed an assist, and it got it from the automobile and the government.

Henry Ford's Model T began the American romance with the automobile, and the number of Americans with cars has grown enormously in the twentieth century. There are now as many automobiles as there are licensed drivers in the United States. But it was the surge in highway construction after World War II (a $350 billion project to construct a network of 41,000 miles of superhighways) that made the automobile boom possible. This led to the growth of the suburbs and the fast-food restaurants that were to make beef, and particularly the hamburger, king.

Pork, as mentioned earlier, had always competed with beef for priority in American meat tastes. While beef was more popular in the Northeast and the West, pork was the meat of choice in the South, whereas in the Mid-Atlantic states and the Midwest they were relatively evenly matched. But by the 1960s beef clearly became the meat of choice for most Americans.

One advantage of beef was its suitability for the outdoor grill, which became more popular as people moved into the suburbs. Suburban cooks soon discovered that pork patties crumbled and fell through the grill, whereas beef patties held together better. In addition, since the U.S. Department of Agriculture (USDA) does not inspect pork for trichinosis because the procedure would be too expensive, it recommended cooking pork until it was gray; but that makes pork very tough. Barbecued spare ribs are one pork alternative, but they are messier, have less meat, and can't be put on a bun.

In 1946 the USDA issued a statute that defined the hamburger:

Hamburger. *"Hamburger" shall consist of chopped fresh and/or frozen beef with or without the addition of beef fat as such and/or seasonings, shall not contain more than 30 percent fat, and shall not contain added water, phosphates, binders, or extenders. Beef cheek (trimmed Beef cheeks) may be used in the preparation of hamburgers only in accordance with the conditions prescribed in paragraph (a) of this section. (Harris 1987:125)*

Marvin Harris (1987:125–126) noted that we can eat ground pork and ground beef, but we can't combine them, at least if we are to call it a hamburger. Even when lean, grass-fed beef is used for hamburger and fat must be added to bind it, the fat must come from beef scraps, not from vegetables or a different animal. This definition of the hamburger protects not only the beef industry but also the corn farmer, whose income is linked to cattle production. Moreover, it helps the fast-food industry, because the definition of hamburger allows it to use inexpensive scraps of fat from slaughtered beef to make, in fact, 30 percent of its hamburger.

The row of fast-food restaurants that line streets in virtually every American town and city represents not only the union of sugar and fat, but also the fast-paced lives required in a consumer-oriented society.

Thus an international beef patty was created that overcame what Harris called the "pig's natural superiority as a converter of grain to flesh."

The fast-food restaurant, made possible by the popularity of the automobile, put the final touch on the ascendancy of beef. Ray Kroc, the founder of McDonald's, tapped into the new temporal and work routines of American labor. With more women working outside the home, time and efficiency were wed to each other as prepared foods, snacks, and the frozen hamburger patty became more popular. In many ways, the fast-food restaurant and the beef patty on a bun were to the American working woman of the 1970s and 1980s what sugar, hot tea, and preserves were to the English female factory worker of the latter half of the nineteenth century. They both offered ease of preparation and convenience at a time when increasing numbers of women worked outside the home.

Thus, as with sugar, our "taste" for beef goes well beyond our supposed individual food preferences. It is a consequence of a culture in which food as a commodity takes a form defined by economic, political, and social relationships. We can, as many have done, refuse beef. But to do so requires a real effort, as those who try to follow a strictly vegetarian diet can attest.

In addition, as with much of what Americans do, the matter of beef does not stop in the United States. The United States produces about 9 percent of the world's beef but consumes 28 percent of it. In 1995, Americans consumed 25,461,000 pounds of beef, and while consumption per capita is declining the total amount of beef consumed is increasing. The consumption of beef in core countries is having more of an impact on countries in the periphery, and this is likely to worsen as other countries, such as Japan and China, begin to emulate American and European dietary patterns. Let's look at just one example, in Costa Rica, of peripheral countries converting their forests into grazing land for cattle to profit from the core's demand for beef.

The Internationalization of the Hamburger

In the 1960s, with the help of the World Bank, governments in South and Central America began to convert tropical forest into pasture to raise beef for the international market. The case of Costa Rica, analyzed by Mark Endelmann (1987), is illustrative. The United States began to purchase beef from Central America in the 1950s, largely because prices were about 40 percent lower than in the United States.

The state plays a role in the production and importation of foreign beef. Foreign beef suppliers must meet USDA certification of their herds and packing facilities and are subject to import quotas that are more informal than formal, since the quotas themselves are in violation of GATT. Therefore, countries from whom we import beef must "voluntarily" restrict sales to the United States.

International financial agencies, such as the World Bank, also play a role in promoting cattle production by financing and requiring the establishment of a cattle infrastructure. For example, international lending institutions required Costa Rica's Central Bank to add a cattle technical extension division and the Banco Nacional de Costa Rica to add animal husbandry and veterinary sections to the branches of the bank located in cattle ranching areas. The loans themselves were used for such things as road building in cattle-raising regions and livestock improvement. In fact, the International Development Bank devoted 21 percent of its loans in the 1960s to the cattle sector of the economy. Furthermore, USAID (U.S. Agency for International Development) helped develop roads and livestock-related extension and research agencies for Costa Rican cattle farmers.

A powerful livestock lobby developed in Costa Rica. The "chambers of cattlemen" is a national federation that placed spokespersons in the legislative assembly, banks, ministries, and major political parties. This lobby convinced the government to increase exports, which had the effect of drastically reducing beef available for local consumption. Only inferior beef that would be rejected by USDA inspectors was made available for domestic consumption.

The increase in cattle production also had environmental consequences for Costa Rica. From 1950 to 1973 the area of pasture in Costa Rica doubled from 622,402 hectares to 1,558,053 hectares. Since brushland is also used, it may be that as much as 89.9 percent of the country's productive land is used for livestock. It has also resulted in widespread destruction of the forests. In 1950, 72 percent of Costa

Rica consisted of rainforest; by 1973 only 49 percent of the country was forested, and by 1978 this had decreased to only 34 percent (Endelmann 1987:554).

The expansion of cattle raising often occurred at the expense of peasant subsistence agriculture, as cattleman evicted or forced peasants off their land or bought the land. Since cattle raising uses far less labor than agriculture, the peasants were forced into the cities, where unemployment was already high. And since cattle raising is profitable only on a large scale, the expansion led to further concentrations of wealth.

Yet if countries such as Costa Rica can escape the poverty discussed in Chapter 6, *is it fair to expect them to reduce their cattle production because of concerns in core countries about rainforest destruction? Might there be ways for countries such as Costa Rica and Mexico to raise beef, reduce environmental destruction, and assist the poor?* Let's examine one example of how anthropologists, working with agricultural specialists, can supply some answers.

Environmentally Sustainable Cattle Raising

Is it possible to develop ways of producing cattle that are not environmentally destructive? This is a question that some anthropologists are examining. Ronald Nigh, for example, has developed a project in Mexico in which indigenous methods of agriculture and stock raising are being applied not only to raise crops but to regenerate rainforests destroyed by stock breeding.

Mexico, along with most Central American countries, has lost vast amounts of its rainforests. At the beginning of the century Mexico had 13 million hectares (31 million acres) of rainforest. Today only 2.4 million hectares remain. Of the total destroyed, 5.5 million hectares were converted to pasture, and over half of that is in an advanced stage of degradation and erosion. Furthermore, while 60 percent of Mexico's productive land is devoted to pasture or forage for animals, more than 50 percent of its population never consumes animal products.

Nigh (1995) maintains that the destruction of the rainforest by cattle grazing is largely the result of the importation of what he called the *factory model* of agricultural production. The factory model is designed to produce a single product (corn, soy, beef, pork, etc.) in as short a time as possible. It tends to be technology-intensive and environmentally damaging. Furthermore, it tends to convert whole regions to a single type of agricultural production—cattle in one area, corn in another, wheat in another, and so on. In Central America the factory model of cattle raising has required clearing large tracts of land with fire and herbicides and reseeding with grasses that are not well-suited to the environment. The result is degradedation of the land by uncontrolled grazing and its eventual abandonment and return to secondary vegetation.

Nigh suggested that it is far more productive and far less damaging to the environment to look at agriculture as an ecological, rather than a manufacturing, process, to adopt what S. R. Gleissman (1988; see also Posey et al. 1984) referred to as an *agroecological approach.* One foundation of this approach is to combine indigenous practices that have produced food yet preserved the environment with contemporary agricultural research. The major difference between a factory approach and an agroecological approach is that the latter creates a polyculture—the production of multiple crops and animals—rather than a monoculture—the growth or production of a single crop or animal. Indigenous methods of production in the rainforest create a system that enhances regeneration of land, flora, and fauna.

For example, there are sites of secondary vegetation in the Mexican rainforest left by Mayan farmers who practice swidden agriculture. The farmers clear a site, use it to grow corn for five to eight years, and then move on. These sites may soon look like the land abandoned by cattle ranchers, but Mayan farmers do not abandon the sites. They continue to work the garden, perhaps planting fruit trees, and use the site to attract mammals and birds to hunt. In fact, the area is designed to attract an animal crop and the Maya refer to it as "garden hunting" (Nigh 1995). Since, unlike the factory model, no herbicides are used to clear the land, plant and animal life can regenerate. Thus traditional agriculture creates an environment that mixes fields, forests, and brushlands.

The idea is to create productive modules, each a mosaic of productive spaces. The agroecological model, drawing as it does on indigenous systems developed over centuries, creates an ecologically sustainable system of production modeled after natural systems, rather than a system that displaces natural ones.

Rather than demonizing cattle, Nigh said, it is possible to design an agricultural system modeled after indigenous systems in which cattle are integrated into an agroecological model, one in which diversity rather than uniformity is emphasized. For example, one area would be used for annual crops such as corn, squash, root crops, spices, and legumes. Secondary areas, including those previously degraded by overgrazing, can be used for fruit trees, forage, and so on. Other secondary areas, using specially selected animal breeds and grasses, can be devoted to intensive grazing. In his project, for example, they selected a breed developed in New Zealand that is small but a high milk producer. Intensive grazing frees up tropical rainforest land that should never have been converted to pasture to begin with. Nigh maintains that by using only organic fertilizers and controlled grazing, it is possible to recover aquatic areas (ponds, rivers, and lakes) and take advantage of water resources such as fish, mollusks, turtles, and birds.

Exporting Pollution

We can now see how economic, political, and social factors contribute to our patterns of consumption. The same analysis can be applied to many other commodities that we consume in great numbers which have a detrimental effect on the environment. Some examples are large houses, electronic devices, and appliances. Furthermore, there are the host of environmental problems caused by industrial pollution, the use, storage, and disposal of nuclear energy, the mountains of garbage that are accumulating as packaging becomes as much of a problem as the commodities they enclose. But there is a paradox here: While the consumption patterns of core countries are the primary cause of environmental pollution, resource depletion and destruction, and the production of toxic substances, the core countries suffer far less from environmental problems than peripheral countries. The United States, for example, while having its share of environmental problems, enjoys relatively cleaner air, cleaner water, and more open spaces than peripheral countries whose people consume and produce a fraction of what Americans do. *How do we explain the spread of environmental destruction to the periphery?*

On December 12, 1991, Lawrence Summers, then chief economist of the World Bank and later Undersecretary of Treasury in the Clinton administration, sent a memorandum to some of his colleagues, intending only, the World Bank later said, to provoke discussion. The memo, in brief, argued that it made perfectly good economic sense for the United States to export its pollution and toxic waste to poor countries. The memo then appeared in *The Economist*, the prestigious British publication, under the headline, "Let Them Eat Pollution."

Summers argued that the World Bank should encourage the movement of "dirty industries" from core countries to less developed countries. He based his argument on three things: first, from an economic point of view, the cost of illness associated with pollution measured in working days lost is cheapest in the country with the lowest wages; second, underdeveloped countries are "underpolluted," and consequently the initial increases in pollution will have a relatively low cost; finally, since people in less developed countries have a lower life expectancy, pollutants that cause diseases of the more elderly, such as prostate cancer, are less of a concern. In sum, Summers argued that a clean environment is worth more to the inhabitants of rich countries than to those of poor countries, therefore the cost of pollution is less in poor countries than in rich countries; consequently, it makes perfect economic sense to export "dirty" industries to the less developed countries (Foster 1993).

The reaction to the memo from most environmentalists was scathing. José Lutzenberger, Brazil's Secretary of the Environment, issued a response in which he said, among other things,

> [i]t was almost a pleasant surprise to me to read reports in our papers and then receive [a] copy of your memorandum supporting the export of pollution to Third World countries and the arguments you present for justifying it. Your reasoning is perfectly logical but totally insane. (cited Rich 1994:246–248)

Yet, John Bellamy Foster (1993:12) said, there was little in the memo that has not been stated in other terms many times, largely by economists and public policy analysts. The memo was a perfect expression of the view of the environment and of people that emerges logically from the culture of capitalism. From an anthropological perspective, the memo is illustrative of our culture's cosmology, its view of the person and the environment. The premises of Summers's argument include:

1. The lives of people in the Third World, judged by "foregone earnings" from illness and death, are worth less—hundreds of times less—than those of individuals in advanced capitalist countries where wages are hundreds of times

higher. Therefore it makes sense to deposit toxic wastes in less developed countries.

2. Third World environments are underpolluted compared to places such as Los Angeles and Mexico City (where children had to be kept home from school for a month in 1989 because of air pollution).

3. A clean environment, in effect, is a luxury good pursued by rich countries because of the aesthetic and health standards in those countries. Thus the world-wide costs of pollution could decrease if waste was transferred to poor countries where a clean environment is "worth" less, rather than polluting environments of the rich where a clean environment is "worth" more.

Essentially, the memo expresses a perspective in which a monetary value can be put on both human life, based on wage prospects, and the environment, based on the value people place on a clean environment. It reveals the tendency of the culture of capitalism to commodify virtually everything, including human life and the environment. As Foster (1993:12) said, Summers's memo is not an aberration; in his role as chief economist for the World Bank, Summers's job was to help create conditions for the accumulation of profit and to ensure economic growth. The welfare of the world's population, the health of the environment, "nor even the fate of individual capitalists themselves—can be allowed to stand in the way of this single-minded goal."

The Economist, in fact, went on to defend Summers, saying that governments constantly make decisions in regard to health, education, working conditions, housing, and the environment that are based on differential valuations of certain people over others. For example, in the 1980s the U.S. Office of Management and Budget (OMB) sponsored a number of studies that concluded that the value of a human life was between $500,000 and $2 million, then used those figures to argue that some forms of pollution control were cost-effective and others were not. Other economists have argued that the value of a human life should be based on earning power, thus a woman is worth less than a man, a Black's life worth less than a White's.

As shocking as that may sound, that is exactly how we, for the most part, operate. For example, three out of four off-site commercial hazardous landfills in southern states were located primarily in African American communities, although African Americans represent only 20 percent of the population. The core countries already ship 20 million tons of waste annually to the periphery. In 1987 dioxin-laden industrial waste was shipped from Philadelphia to Guinea and Haiti; in 1988, 4,000 tons of PCB-contaminated chemical waste from Italy was found leaking from drums in Nigeria.

Economists like Summers argue that it is more important to build an economic infrastructure for future generations than to protect against global warming. They compare the cost of rainforest destruction with the economic cost of conserving it, without recognizing that rainforest destruction is irrevocable. They argue that rather than halting economic development because of global warming, countries will be able to use their newly developed riches to build retaining walls to hold back the rising sea; furthermore they argue that money spent to halt carbon dioxide output could be better spent dealing with population growth (Foster 1993:16).

Foster concluded that capitalism will never sacrifice economic growth and capital accumulation for environmental reform. Its internal logic will always be "let them eat pollution." Opposition will develop, as we shall see in a later chapter, and some changes made, as have been made in the United States over the past thirty years, but environmental concerns will never be allowed to threaten the system itself. This is clearly evident if we turn again to the latest developments in the American automobile industry.

The latest development in American tastes for automobiles is the preference for so-called utility vehicles. In 1997 they constituted one of every two family vehicles sold (65 million in all). These vehicles emit 57 percent more carbon dioxide than standard automobiles, are the fastest-growing source of global warming gases in the United States, and use 50–100 percent more gasoline than ordinary passenger automobiles (Bradsher 1997). Because they were used primarily on farms and construction sites they were classified in the 1970s as light trucks, and pollution emission standards and minimum mileage requirements that applied to other vehicles did not and do not apply to them. These vehicles are highly profitable; not only do the profit margins exceed those for other vehicles, but the American automobile industry is protected by high import tariffs on light trucks made overseas (because of a trade war with Germany in 1964) that do not apply to other foreign-made automobiles. For this reason, automobile manufacturers and workers' unions have lobbied heavily to prevent Congress from extending pollution and gasoline consumption standards to utility vehicles. As Foster concluded (1993:19):

> *Where radical change is called for little is accomplished within the system and the underlying crisis intensifies over time. Today this is particularly evident in the ecological realm. For the nature of the global environmental crisis is such that the fate of the entire planet and social and ecological issues of enormous complexity are involved, all traceable to the forms of production now prevalent. It is impossible to prevent the world's environmental crisis from getting progressively worse unless root problems of production, distribution, technology, and growth are dealt with on a global scale. And the more that such questions are raised, the more it becomes evident that capitalism is unsustainable—ecologically, economically, politically, and morally—and must be superseded.*

Conclusion

We began this chapter by asking why people choose to consume what they do, how they do, and when they do. We concluded that our tastes are largely culturally constructed, and that they tend to serve the process of capital accumulation. There is no "natural" reason why we engage in consumption patterns that do harm to the environment. Furthermore, we suggested that of all the contributing factors to environmental pollution, the most difficult to "fix" is our consumption behavior, since it serves as the foundation of our culture.

To illustrate we examined how the American taste for sugar and fat was historically constructed largely to serve the interests of sugar and beef producers. We examined how anthropological research is trying to help peripheral countries in their effort to meet western demands for products such as beef without destroying their environmental resources.

We also examined how core countries are attempting to maintain their culture by exporting their by-products—pollution and resource depletion, and how from some perspectives that seems to make perfect sense.

Most important, we examined the historical and cultural dynamic that drives the consumption of specific commodities and our attitudes about the environmental damage that results, and concluded that it is not an aberration, but an intrinsic part of our way of life.

Chapter 8

Disease

Cities...were microbe heavens, or, as British microbiologist John Cairns put it, "graveyards of mankind." The most devastating scourges of the past attained horrific proportions only when the microbes reached urban centers, where population density instantaneously magnified any minor contagion that might have originated in the provinces. Any microbes successfully exploited the new urban ecologies to create altogether novel disease threats.
LAURIE GARRETT, THE COMING PLAGUE

A thorough understanding of the AIDS pandemic demands a commitment to the concerns of history and political economy: HIV...has run along the fault lines of economic structures long in the making.
PAUL FARMER, AIDS AND ACCUSATION

In the halcyon days after World War II, when everything seemed possible and the advance of science and economic prosperity inspired government leaders and leading academics to predict a coming era of worldwide peace and prosperity, medical professionals were predicting the end of infectious disease. Universal health was set as a realistic and achievable goal. The U.S. Surgeon General in 1967 said it was time to close the door on infectious disease. There was some reason for this optimism. As a result of a worldwide vaccination campaign, smallpox had been completely eliminated, the last case in the world being diagnosed in 1979. Malaria, one of the world's major killers, had been reduced worldwide and even eliminated in some areas by controlling the vector—the mosquito—that spread the disease and through the development and massive distribution of curative drugs. Tuberculosis, the major killer of the nineteenth century, was disappearing. The U.S. Surgeon General declared that measles would be eliminated by 1982 with an aggressive immunization campaign. Jonas Salk had discovered a cure for poliomyelitis, the scourge of childhood, and the development of antibiotics promised to rid us of every infirmary from pneumonia to bad breath. Then, in the space of a decade, everything changed.

AIDS has become the signature disease of the culture of capitalism, striking particularly hard in the poor countries of the periphery, such as Gambia where this sign advises condom use.

AIDS was one of the shocks that changed universal optimism to what Marc Lappé (1994) called "therapeutic nihilism," an attitude common today among hospital personnel that nothing will work to cure patients. But there were other reasons for the change: the emergence of antibiotic-resistant strains of disease; the reemergence of malaria, cholera, and tuberculosis in even deadlier forms; the emergence of other new diseases, particularly Lyme disease, dengue-2, and hemorrhagic fevers such as eboli that result in massive internal bleeding and have mortality rates of up to 90 percent. Measles, supposed to be eradicated from the United States in 1982, was ten times more prevalent in 1993 than 1983. These developments and others have required medical researchers in biology, epidemiology, and anthropology, among others, to reexamine the relationship between human beings and the microbial world, particularly those pathogens that cause disease. It is clear that we underestimated the ingenuity of microbes to adapt to our adaptations to them, and failed to appreciate how our patterns of social, political, and economic relations affect the emergence and transmission of disease.

Each age, it seems, has its signature disease. Bubonic plague in the fourteenth and fifteenth centuries emerged as a result of the opening of trade routes to Asia, carried by merchants and warriors from the middle of the then world system west to Europe and east to China. Syphilis spread in the sixteenth and seventeenth centuries through increased sexual contact of people in towns and cities. Tuberculosis was the disease of the nineteenth century, spread through the air in the densely packed cities and slums of Europe, the United States, and the periphery.

As we shall see, AIDS is very much the signature disease of the latter quarter of the twentieth century, serving as a marker for the increasing disparities in wealth between core and periphery and the accompanying disparity in susceptibility to disease. More than 98 percent of deaths from communicable disease (16.3 million a year) occur in the periphery. Worldwide 32 percent of all deaths are caused by infectious disease, but in the periphery infectious disease is responsible for 42 percent of all deaths, compared to 1.2 percent in industrial countries (Platt 1996:11).

Table 8.1 summarizes the major diseases afflicting the world today, the number of people affected, annual mortality, and whether the disease is on the rise, declining, or stable.

The fact that each historical epoch has its characteristic illness reveals clearly that how we live—the social and cultural patterns at any point in time and space—largely define the kinds and frequencies of diseases to which human beings are susceptible. The questions we need to ask are; *what do we do that exposes us to disease? What do we do that exposes others to disease? How do we create the conditions for unique interactions between pathogens, their environments, and their hosts? Furthermore, what features of human societies make pathogens more or less lethal?*

Many of the things we discussed in previous chapters are relevant. For example, increases in population density clearly relate to the emergence and frequency of disease, as does the division of the world into rich and poor. The crowding into cities of rural workers and peasants as agricultural land becomes concentrated in the hands of a few influences disease susceptibility. Public policy that makes economic growth a priority and neglects health programs encourages the spread of disease, as do International Monetary Fund structural adjustment programs in peripheral countries that demand the cutting of health, sanitation, and education programs. The alteration of the environment has enormous consequences for the spread and emergence of disease.

Infectious disease, of course, is not the only health problem we face. Environmental pollutants, often a direct outgrowth of industrialization, cause sickness. For example, asthma, often aggravated by industrial pollutants, is on the rise. Millions of people face malnutrition and starvation, conditions that further expose them to disease. Commercially promoted products such as alcoholic beverages and tobacco endanger health. Of the estimated 1.1 billion smokers in the world today, 800 million are in the periphery. The World Health Organization reports that smoking-related deaths in the periphery will rise from 1 million per year in the early 1990s to 2 million by the year 2000 (World Health Organization, The Tobacco Epidemic, 1995). Furthermore, as cigarette sales continue to fall in the core in response to antismoking campaigns and state legislation, cigarette companies, with the support of core governments, have intensified their efforts to sell their products to people in other countries, particularly to women and the young. For example, the United

TABLE 8.1   **Characteristics of Major Infectious Diseases, 1993 Estimates by Death Counts**

Disease	Incidence (millions)	Deaths (millions)	Trend	Vector	Symptoms
Acute respiratory infections	248.0	4.1	Stable	Bacterium and virus, airborne	Cold, sore throat, influenza, pneumonia, and bronchitis
Diarrhea	1,800.0	3.0	Down	Bacterium and virus, water- and food-borne	Frequent liquid stools, sometimes bloody
Tuberculosis	8.8	2.7	Up	Bacterium, airborne	Severe coughing, sometimes with blood, chest pain, exhaustion, weight loss, and night sweats
Malaria	400.0	2.0	Up	Protozoan, mosquito-borne	Fever, headache, nausea, vomiting, diarrhea, malaise, enlarged spleen, liver, renal and respiratory failure, shock, pulmonary and cerebral edema
Measles	45.0	1.2	Down	Virus, airborne	Rash, fever, encephalitis in rare cases
Hepatitis B	4.2	1.0	Up	Virus, sexual contact	Anorexia, abdominal pain, sometimes rash, jaundice, cirrhosis of liver (chronic infection)
AIDS	(AIDS) 0.6 (HIV) 4.0	0.7	Up	Virus, HIV types 1 and 2, sexual contact, shared hypodermic needles	Autoimmune dysfunction progresses from asymptomatic to lethal; any organ system can be targeted. Initially, fever, weight loss, diarrhea, fatigue, cough, skin lesions, opportunistic infections such as cancer and tuberculosis
Whooping cough	4.3	0.4	Down	Bacterium, airborne	Hacking cough, respiratory tract infection, sometimes pneumonia, brain damage, death
Meningitis	1.2	0.2	Stable	Bacterium and virus, airborne	Inflammation of meninges of brain and spinal cord
Schistosomiasis	200.0	0.2	Up	Protozoan, snail-borne	Cirrhosis of liver, anemia
Leishmaniasis	13.0	0.2	Up	Protozoan, sandfly	Skin lesions, inflammation and crusting, skin ulcers, tissue destruction in nose and mouth

From Anne E. Platt. *Infecting Ourselves: How Environmental and Social Disruption Trigger Disease.* Washington, DC: Worldwatch Institute, 1996. With permission.

States has used free trade arguments to pressure other nations—Thailand, Taiwan, and South Korea—with economic sanctions to open their markets to American cigarettes. In such cases it is easy to see a direct connection between the capitalist world system and the onset of disease. However, the relation that exists between the culture of capitalism and infectious pathogens is often more subtle and hidden.

A Primer on How to Die of an Infectious Disease

Human beings swim in a sea of microbes; we eat them, breathe them, absorb them through skin openings and membranes. Most do us no harm, and many are useful. Millions of bacteria live in our intestinal system to aid digestion and in nature serve as catalysts for decomposition of material that can then be reused by plants and animals. Many we never meet, as they exist in distant parts of the world. Some microbes, however, do harm us. Harmful or pathogenic microbes include bacteria, viruses, and parasites that invade our bodies and cause illness and, in some cases, death. The question we need to ask is *what determines the relationships that we have with the infectious pathogens whose world we share?*

To answer this question let's ask what it requires for a pathogen to kill us; that is, *what does it take for us to die of an infectious disease?* At least four things have to happen. First, we must come into contact with the pathogen or a vector—such as a mosquito, tick, flea, or snail—that carries it. Second, the pathogen must be virulent, that is, have the capacity to kill us. Third, if we come into contact with a deadly pathogen, it must evade our body's immune system. Finally, the pathogen must be able to circumvent whatever measures our society has developed to prevent it from doing harm. As we shall see, human actions are critical in each step.

First, *what actions of human beings increase their likelihood of coming into contact with an infectious pathogen?* Various behaviors may serve to expose an organism to an infectious agent. For example, carnivorous animals create an opportunity for pathogens to spread when they eat the flesh of other animals; animals that congregate create opportunities for the spread of pathogens by physical contact. Since human behavior is dictated largely by our culture, cultural patterns that characterize human populations play a major role in creating or inhibiting opportunities for pathogens to spread. Actions that change the environment or change the size, density, and distribution of human settlement patterns increase or decrease the likelihood of our meeting an infectious parasite or influence the size of the parasite population. The emergence of Lyme disease is a good example of many of these factors.

Lyme disease was first reported in 1975, when two women, in Old Lyme and Haddam, Connecticut, reported to a Yale physician that their children had strange symptoms, including aching bones, malaise, and neurological symptoms such as poor memory and concentration. Study revealed that the disease, now spread throughout much of the United States, is carried by four varieties of ticks. The question is, *why did it quite suddenly become a major health problem?* The reason ap-

Human beings coexist with all kinds of bacteria, viruses, and parasites that can cause illness. Whether or not we contract the disease, and whether it is fatal, is determined largely by our way of life.

parently has to do with human alterations of the environment along with human settlement and recreational patterns.

In the seventeenth and eighteenth centuries much of the New England forest was cleared for farming. As farming declined the forests grew back, but with a very different ecology than the one that existed originally: Gone were certain species of animals, such as wolves, bears, and mountain lions, and populations of deer and mice, once controlled by these predators, increased dramatically. Also increasing were the populations of ticks associated with deer and mice and, with the ticks, the

Borrelia organism, a pathogen they carried in their salivary gland. As human beings built settlements (suburbs) along the forests and ventured into them for recreational activities, they were exposed to the tick. The result was Lyme disease.

As noted above, coming into contact with a pathogen is not, in itself, sufficient to kill us. The pathogen itself must be virulent enough to disrupt critical bodily functions or reproduce so extensively in the body that the damages it causes will result in death. There is obviously a big difference between "catching" a cold, and "catching" HIV. We seem to take for granted that some diseases are more severe than others, but the reality is far more complex. A pathogen that is harmless to one host may be lethal in another. There is a herpes virus, for example, that has evolved to survive, spread, and do no harm in one type of monkey but is 100 percent lethal when it infects another type (Garrett 1994:573).

Generally, it is not in the best interest of a parasite, bacteria, or virus to harm its host; it is far better to allow the host to survive, to provide an environment for the pathogen to reproduce and spread. Furthermore, it is a distinct advantage to the pathogen if the host remains mobile to help the pathogen spread to new hosts. The rhinoviruses that cause the common cold, for example, reproduce in the cells that line the nasal passages; they are shed by sneezing or a runny nose. If a person with a cold wipes the nose with a finger and then touches the finger of another person, the exposed person may inhale the contaminated air or touch the finger to his or her mouth. However the pathogen is spread, it requires the host to move, so killing or disabling the host is counterproductive.

Thus most microbes that we come into contact with and even those that infect us do us little or no harm. However, there are certain exceptions to the rule that microbes should not harm their host. First, the newer the disease, the more deadly it is likely to be, since microbe and host will not have had sufficient time to adapt to each other. Anything that human beings do that exposes them to diseases they haven't been previously exposed to increases the likelihood that the disease can kill them. The destruction of the peoples of North, South, and Central America in the sixteenth and seventeenth centuries, as we saw in Chapter 3, is a case in point. Having never been exposed to such diseases as smallpox, measles, influenza, and even, in some cases, a common cold, millions died. Something as simple as increased travel can bring people into contact with a disease that is far more lethal for them than for the people who share their environment with the pathogen. Intestinal illnesses that are the bane of travelers are but one example; the traveler can be devastated by a pathogen that people native to the area harbor in their bodies with little or no effect. HIV-2 is carried in the bodies of African green monkeys with apparently little effect, but when it "crossed over" to human beings the result was fatal.

A second exception to the rule that pathogens should do no harm is when the disease is carried and spread by a vector. When a disease is spread from human to human by another species, such as the mosquito, flea, or tick, and does not depend on human beings for its existence, reproduction, or transmission, the pathogen is under no selective pressure to spare human beings and can be as virulent as it likes.

In fact, extensive multiplication in the human host might be beneficial, because it increases the likelihood of the vector picking it up and continuing the microbe's reproductive cycle. It might be even better for the host to be disabled if, for example, the host would be less able to protect itself from the vector. As we might expect, pathogens are generally very kind to vectors, generally causing them no harm whatsoever (Lappé 1994:25). What this means is that anything that human beings do to increase their exposure to vector-borne pathogens will increase their likelihood of contracting a deadly disease.

A third exception to the "do no harm" rule is when a pathogen is spread by contaminated water or another external medium. For example, diarrheal diseases tend to be more virulent if they are spread by water systems and do not require person-to-person contact. The reason, suggested biologist Paul Ewald (1993:88), is that diseases that are spread by contaminated water lose nothing by incapacitating their host, but they gain a great deal by reproducing extensively in the host. Their large numbers make it more likely that they can contaminate water supplies through the washing of sheets or clothing or through bodily wastes. Thus human activities that create contaminated water supplies are likely to create more virulent forms of diseases.

Finally, the fact that diseases are spread by vectors or external mediums suggests that the virulence of a disease is affected also by the ease of transmission: the easier a disease is to transmit, the more virulent it is likely to be, or, conversely, the more difficult a pathogen is to transmit, the less virulent it will be. If a disease is difficult to transmit, the microbe that can lurk in the body without harming it, thus allowing the host to survive until an opportunity arises to jump to another host, has a decided advantage over a microbe that quickly kills or disables its host. Thus chronic diseases such as tuberculosis can lie dormant for years without doing damage to the host, waiting for an opportunity first to infect the host and then to spread to another. However, reasoned Ewald, if the disease is easy to transmit, then it is under no selective pressure to spare the host. Diseases such as ebola, for example, reproduce so rapidly in the body, and infect virtually every organ, that anyone who comes into contact with any of the victim's bodily fluids is likely to contract the disease.

The notion that diseases that are difficult to transmit are likely to be less lethal has interesting implications. For example, sexually transmitted diseases in generally monogamous populations should be less virulent, according to Ewald, because the pathogens have to wait longer to be transmitted from host to host. If sexual activity increases, however, it is to the pathogen's advantage to increase rapidly in the body to take advantage of the increased likelihood of transmission. This seems to fit with some developments with HIV, the virus that causes AIDS. In populations in which transmission was more difficult because people had fewer sex partners or were more likely to use condoms, the disease evolved into a less virulent form (Garrett 1994: 587).

Even if Ewald's hypothesis that diseases that are easier to transmit are more lethal does not apply universally, its implications are striking. It means, as Ewald

(1993:93) suggested, that we should be able to make a pathogen less lethal by increasing the price it pays for transmission; in other words, by making the pathogen more difficult to transmit, we should be able to force it to evolve toward a less lethal form. Thus by cleaning up water supplies, protecting ourselves from mosquitoes, reducing the likelihood of the spread of sexually transmitted diseases, we are working not only to prevent the disease but to make it less deadly when it does occur.

Having examined how human actions bring us into contact with a pathogen and help determine how lethal it is, let's move on to the next step toward our death. Let's assume we have come into contact with a pathogen that is highly virulent to human beings. Is there anything that can save us? Fortunately, the human body has evolved a highly sophisticated immune system that generally prevents microbes from harming us. When a microbe infects the body, specific cells of the immune system, T cells, attach themselves to the invader, signaling other cells, macrophages, to envelop and destroy it. Once destroyed, other cells of the immune system call off the attack, lest the system overreact and destroy its own cells.

It is an ingenious system and, under stable conditions, one that will hold in check most microscopic invaders. However, if an immune system is weakened, for example by hunger, it is less able to fight off disease. Furthermore, in unstable conditions, when the opportunity exists for rapid changes in the number and type of microbes, the microbes have a decided advantage. Microbes are extremely adept at evolving ways to escape the body's immune system. The reason is that viruses and bacteria mutate and reproduce at a much faster rate than larger organisms such as human beings. Consequently, if a microbe evolves that can somehow get around the immune system, that particular variety of microbe will have a distinct adaptive advantage, and more of its offspring will survive. Ultimately this will lead to the emergence of a microbe for which our bodies have no defense.

Simple arithmetic demonstrates how quickly microbes can adapt to changed or threatening environments. Let's assume that a variety of an organism—let's call it X—emerges with a characteristic that gives it only a 1 percent reproductive advantage over another variety—Y—of the same organism. That means that 101 of the X variety will survive in each generation to only 100 of Y. Arithmetically this means that X will become the dominant form of the organism in only thirty generations. In human terms thirty generations is a long time—700–800 years. But for microorganisms thirty generations is a very short time—for bacteria that reproduce every twenty to thirty minutes, thirty generations can elapse in a day, at the end of which two bacteria have produced 1 billion.

Because of this ability to adapt so quickly, some microbes have developed the ability to evade the immune system. The bacterium that causes dengue hemorrhagic fever has evolved to use the immune system to spread from the blood systems to the vital organs. The virus that causes influenza changes so rapidly that infection by one strain does not confer any immunity to subsequent strains. The AIDS viruses evolved to attack and destroy the body's immune system, not only allowing the virus to survive and spread but creating the opportunity for other diseases, such as tuberculosis, to take root and thrive. In fact, one of the major threats of AIDS is that the rapid change in its genetic structure, about 1 percent per year in some varieties, will allow it to evolve resistance to whatever defenses the body or medical researchers may develop.

Assuming, then, that we have met a lethal pathogen and that the body's immune system is unable to destroy it, what next? As far as we know, human beings have always sought to cure whatever illness afflicted them. Ritual and ceremonial cures are known in societies throughout the world, as are the use of plants and other natural resources. However, there is little question that one of the major success stories of the culture of capitalism is the development of measures to protect people from and cure them of infectious disease. The discoveries of the causes of infectious disease and then the development, manufacture, and distribution of vaccines and antibiotics has, in general, extended the human life span in societies throughout the world. Worldwide, life expectancy at birth was 48 years in 1955; 59 years in 1975; and 65 years in 1995 (World Health Report 1997).

Unfortunately, just as microbes can quickly adapt and evade the natural defenses of our immune system, they can also quickly evolve to render modern drugs useless. When antibiotics are overused or used incorrectly, or prescribed for viral infections against which they are useless, new varieties that are resistant to existing antibiotics may evolve. Some researchers claim that half of the 150 million antibiotic prescriptions written by American doctors each year are misprescribed or misused in this way. Patients take a portion of the prescribed dosage and, once they feel better, neglect to take the rest. This results in killing the bacteria most susceptible to the antibiotic, but may leave unaffected those that are more resistant. Those resistant bacteria then gradually become the dominant strain of the microbe; even if 99.9 percent of the original strain is destroyed, the survivor is likely to be a superstrain on which existing antibiotics have no effect (Platt 1996:54).

Furthermore, half of the antibiotics used in the United States are used for livestock, aquaculture, and other biological industries. Monocultural farming is a major source of the problem. When only one kind of animal or one kind of crop is grown, a disease outbreak can decimate a business. A commercial chicken farm, for example, may have 100,000 chickens; an aquaculture facility may have thousands of salmon. To protect themselves, growers use antibiotics to fend off disease, creating an opportunity for evolution of drug-resistant strains of pathogens, some of which may be capable of infecting people.

Anne E. Platt (1996:52) summed up the problem when she wrote:

> *Today, almost all disease-causing bacteria are on the pathway to complete drug resistance. More than a half century after the discovery of antibiotics, humanity is at risk of losing these valuable weapons and reverting to the pre-antibiotic era.*

Thus we get some idea of how human actions can influence the relationship between infectious pathogens and human bodies, and what it takes in a general sense for us to die of an infectious disease. Next let's examine how this translates to the relationship between disease and culture, and more specifically, how people's behavior in the culture of capitalism contributes to the creation and transmission of infectious disease.

The Relationships between Culture and Disease

As we have seen, our world is filled with organisms that can cause us harm. Whether or not we come into contact with them, how deadly they are for us, and whether or not we can help the body fight them off or reach a mutually beneficial arrangement is greatly influenced by the kinds of lives we lead or, more specifically, the cultures and patterns of social relations that we construct, maintain, and reproduce. Let's examine this a little further and identify some of the specific cultural adaptations of human beings that either encourage or inhibit disease. One of the questions we want to consider is, *how has the emergence of consumer capitalism influenced the spread of disease?* Put another way, *how does the behavior appropriate to our culture expose people to the risk of disease or create opportunities for the creation and spread of infectious pathogens?* To illustrate the relationship between culture and disease, between our behavioral choices and how they affect our relationships with the world of microbes, let's examine what happened to disease during another great cultural transformation in human history, the shift from gathering and hunting to agriculture.

Gathering and Hunting to Early Agriculture

Members of early gathering and hunting societies were likely afflicted by a range of diseases far different from our own. Small, geographically scattered human populations did not afford infectious diseases the same opportunity for infection and transmission as do large, densely populated modern societies. Most pathogens in early human societies must have depended for their survival on nonhuman hosts. When they infected human beings it was when people got in the way of the reproductive cycle of the nonhuman host, not because the microbe depended on human beings for their survival.

Contact with wild animals likely exposed early human societies to such diseases as rabies, anthrax, salmonellosis, botulism, and tetanus (Cohen 1989:33). Worm parasites that infested animals' bodies would have been encountered by hunters. Malaria and yellow fever were transmitted by mosquitoes and other diseases by ticks. As Mark Cohen noted in *Health and the Rise of Civilization* (1989), these diseases strike rarely, cannot spread directly from person to person, and do not claim many victims. But since human beings would not have built up an immunity to these diseases, and since the offending microbes would not have depended on human transmission, the diseases were often fatal.

There were also categories of disease that could be transmitted from person to person; these would have had to live in hosts for a long time to have the opportunity to spread, and must have been transmitted fairly easily by touch, breathing, sneezing, or coughing and in food or other shared items. Yaws was probably one such disease, as may have been the herpes virus and a variety of intestinal illness (Cohen 1989:37). Since diseases tend to evolve toward less virulent forms the longer they coexist with a population, diseases that we recognize today as mild may have been more serious in earlier human populations.

However, it was during the transition of human societies from gatherers and hunters to sedentary agriculturists that began some 10,000 years ago that whole new relationships developed between culture and disease. By remaining sedentary people probably came into contact with fewer pathogens, and by remaining in one place people likely developed greater immunities to localized bacteria, viruses, and parasitic infection. Sedentariness also makes it easier to care for the sick. But, as Cohen pointed out, sedentariness also has some major disadvantages. First, sedentary societies are more likely to engage in long-distance trade, which may increase contact between groups and, as a consequence, spread disease from one group to another. Sedentary populations also create more favorable conditions for pathogens to spread; permanent shelters attract vermin—insects and rodents— that may carry disease, while the buildup of garbage and human waste may serve in sedentary societies to harbor and spread microbes, especially if water sources are infected with human waste.

Alteration of the landscape through horticulture, animal husbandry, and agriculture exposed people to new disease. Malaria-bearing mosquitoes would have thrived in the ponds and bodies of stagnant water created by human environmental intervention. Ponds and irrigation ditches would have provided opportunities for expansion of the snail that carried schistosomiasis.

Improvements in cooking technology, particularly pottery, may have helped cook food more thoroughly and destroyed disease-carrying microbes, but porous pots may have encouraged the growth of some bacteria. Storage of food for extended periods increased the possibility of bacteria buildup and fungal contamination and attracted disease-carrying vermin.

Finally, regular contact with domesticated animals exposed human populations to additional infections. Living in close contact with animals gives parasites such as tapeworm an opportunity to involve human hosts in their life cycle as they pass between humans and domestic animals. There is evidence that most human respiratory disease arose after animals were domesticated, and a whole range of disease now common in human beings—measles, smallpox, influenza, and diphtheria—are thought to have their origins in domestic animals (Cohen 1989).

"Graveyards of Mankind"

Much as agriculture changed the relationship between microbes and humans, the voluntary or involuntary decisions of people to move to cities greatly favored the spread of infectious disease. Simply put, the more people per square mile, the more easily an infectious agent could pass from one person to another. For example, as early as 2,000–4,000 years ago writers told of infestations of lice, bedbugs, and ticks that they associated with dense housing conditions and the onset of disease. The chances of a citizen of ancient Rome living to the age of thirty years was one in three, whereas 70 percent of rural residents survived until thirty (Garrett 1994:236). In 430 B.C. an epidemic of an unknown disease in Athens killed half the population.

But while cities have existed since at least 6,000–7,000 years ago, they began increasing dramatically in size during the expansion of the capitalist world system, Cities became the hubs of financial activities and were themselves one of the main reasons for the growth of trade, city residents relying on food from rural agricultural areas and trade items from distant places. Cities also grew as a consequence of the commercialization or capitalization of agriculture, as more people were pushed off the land and forced to seek sustenance in the cities of the core and then the periphery.

Five diseases in particular seem to have benefited from the expansion of urban environments—bubonic plague, leprosy (Hansen's disease), cholera, tuberculosis, and syphilis. Bubonic plague, as we saw in Chapter 3, was spread in the fourteenth century by traders and invaders from central Asia west into Europe and east into China and periodically reemerged, with disastrous demographic, economic, and social consequences. Cities tried to protect themselves by banning travelers from entering and by finding scapegoats on which to blame the disease. Tens of thousands of Jews and alleged devil worshippers were slaughtered for this reason, the city of Strasbourg alone killing 16,000 of its Jewish residents. The Brotherhood of Flagellants, a society of Christian men, beat themselves with leather straps embedded with iron spikes to drive out the sins they believed responsible for the disease (Garrett 1994:238). In 1665 the plague hit London, killing as many as 3,000 people per day.

Leprosy is a particularly good example of an apparent adaption of a parasite. The disease swept over Europe in 1200, aided by the growing density of cities, disdain for bathing, wool clothing, and sharing of bedding with others to stay warm. The disease is caused by a bacterium passed by human contact that attacks the nerves of the extremities, causing them to go numb. Since there is no feeling in the fingers, toes, and other extremities, injuries go unnoticed by the victim, leading to the characteristic disfigurement and stigmatization of victims. By 1980, most of the world's five billion people had antibodies to the bacteria, indicating they had been harmlessly exposed to the disease (Garrett 1994:239).

Cholera struck the world's cities in four devastating pandemics between 1830 and 1896, spreading through contaminated water and sewage systems. In St. Louis in 1849 10 percent of the population perished; in the city of Mecca in 1847 some 15,000 residents and Muslim pilgrims died, and another 30,000 died in 1865; in London in 1847 53,000 died. Since the disease seemed to affect the most impoverished segments of the population, those in power assumed it was due to lower-class "immorality." It was not until 1849 that London physician John Snow demonstrated that the disease was transmitted via water supplies. Snow removed the handle of a pump that was the sole water supply for a cholera-ridden neighborhood, and the local epidemic ended. Yet it was years before authorities were convinced that the disease was transmitted through the water supply and took measures to protect it.

Tuberculosis was the most deadly disease of the nineteenth century. Like others, the bacteria responsible for the disease *Mycobacterium tuberculin,* was ancient, dating back to at least 5000 B.C. Tuberculosis is a slow-growing disease, causing illness only after months or years of infection, and then ultimately killing the host;

An illustration from a St. Louis newspaper of 1868 depicts the horror of a cholera epidemic.

however, only about 10 percent of those infected actually develop the disease. It is transmitted through microscopic droplets exhaled by victims, making people who inhabited densely populated, closed spaces—the kind typical of urban slums—particularly susceptible.

The effect of population density on the incidence of tuberculosis is evident in its history in the United States. In 1830, Boston had a crude death rate from tuberculosis of 21 per 1,000, half that of London which had a far larger population. By 1850, when Boston's population had grown, the death rate was 38 per 1,000. In Massachusetts in general tuberculosis rates increased by 40 percent from 1834 to 1853. Then, toward the end of the nineteenth century, for unknown reasons, tuberculosis rates began to decline. In 1900, tuberculosis killed about 200 of every 100,000 Americans; by 1940, before the advent of antibiotic therapy, the rate was 60 per 100,000.

A number of hypotheses have been offered in the ensuing debate over why tuberculosis death rates declined. Some claim that better nutrition enabled people better to withstand infection. Reni Dubos, whose 1952 book *The White Plague* pioneered the study of the connection between human behavior and disease, claimed that the elimination of the deplorable working conditions of men, women, and children during the Industrial Revolution along with improved housing resulted in the decline.

Laurie Garrett (1994:244) suggested that a clue to the decline in tuberculosis can be found in the experience of South Africa. Even with the increased availability of antibiotics and an understanding of the transmission of the disease, death rates for tuberculosis rose 88 percent from 1938 to 1945. Cape Town saw a rise of 100 percent, Durban 172 percent, and Johannesburg 140 percent. Urban rates of infection were as high as 7 percent of the total population, while in rural areas, despite poverty and hunger, the rates were less than 1.4 percent. Virtually all cases struck the Black and Asian or "colored" population.

Housing, according to Garrett (1994:245), seemed the most likely culprit responsible for the outbreak. During that period South Africa had its own industrial revolution and, as in Europe in the eighteenth and nineteenth centuries, required inexpensive labor. Blacks and colored, by far the major source of cheap labor, were required by law to live in areas designated by the government and to carry identity cards that stipulated where they could and could not go. The government subsidized housing for the White population, but government-sponsored housing projects for Blacks actually declined during this period of expansion by 471 percent, resulting in abysmal living conditions. The South African medical authorities blamed the outbreak on an imagined genetic susceptibility of Blacks, thus blaming the victim for an affliction caused by the expansion of the capitalist economy.

Cities also seemed to provide ideal conditions for the emergence of sexually transmitted diseases such as syphilis. The density of population, anonymity of urban life, and influx of single people, especially men, in search of work, promoted greater sexual activity, experimentation, and prostitution.

There is some debate over the origins of syphilis (see Baker and Armelagos 1988). It is carried by a bacterium transmitted in sexual intercourse or at birth from an infected woman to her child. It was first reported in Europe in 1495 among French soldiers (explaining its early designation as the "French disease") fighting against Naples and within two years had spread throughout the world, apparently existing in a deadlier form than it does today. Since the outbreak of the disease coincided with the return of Columbus's sailors from the New World, many scholars believe its origin lay in the Americas, from which it was spread by European conquerors to the rest of the world. Others argue that the rate at which the disease killed indigenous people of the New World suggested a lack of any immunity that would have likely have been conferred if the disease were native to that area of the world. Still others (see Hudson 1965) suggest that syphilis is caused by the same bacterium that causes yaws, a common but easily cured childhood skin disease with a worldwide distribution, and that local sanitary conditions determined whether the disease manifested itself as yaws or syphilis. Regardless of its origins, it spread throughout European cities from the sixteenth through the twentieth centuries.

The pace of urbanization from the fifteenth to the nineteenth centuries that created conditions for diseases such as plague, leprosy, cholera, tuberculosis, and syphilis to spread has dramatically increased in the twentieth century, especially in the periphery. In 1950 there were only two megacities—urban areas with ten million or more people—New York and London. By 1980 there were ten: Buenos Aires, Rio de Janeiro, São Paulo, Mexico City, Los Angeles, New York, Beijing, Shanghai, Tokyo, and London. Demographers predict that by the year 2000, 3.1 billion people will be living in cities. Some of these will be born in cities, but many will be migrants from rural areas flocking to cities, as they have for centuries, in search of jobs, often after being forced off their land by the continuing concentration of agricultural production and wealth in a few hands and by government policies that function to create cheap labor to fuel economic growth. These densely packed populations will continue, as they have for centuries, to be prime breeding grounds for the creation and dissemination of disease.

When New York and London were reaching megacity status, they were doing so in countries that were the richest in the world. That wealth allowed them to adjust to their growth by building sanitation services, public health networks, and medical services to accommodate not only growing numbers of people but the special problems created by increasing population density. The new megacities, with the exception of some in East Asia, for the most part lack that luxury. Not only have they grown at unprecedented rates, but they are in countries on the brink of economic ruin. The international debt of countries such as Brazil, Egypt, Mexico, and India prevents them from building facilities to accommodate the growing urban populations. Residents live in hastily constructed shantytowns and slums that rival any of those in eighteenth- and nineteenth-century Europe and America for the extent of poverty and disease. Even the richer cities cannot keep up with the growth; in Tokyo in 1985 less than 40 percent of dwellings were connected to proper sewage, and tons of untreated human waste was dumped into the ocean. Hong Kong, another of the more wealthy cities, was dumping one million tons of untreated waste each day into the China Sea. In the poor cities, of course, the situation is far worse. In 1980, 88 percent of Manila's population lived in squatter settlements with houses built of scrap wood, cardboard, tin, or bamboo. Nairobi's slums, where 40 percent of the population lived, were deliberately left off official maps of the city (Garrett 1994:251).

A United Nations report reveals that the average child growing up in one of the urban slums of the periphery is forty times more likely to die before her or his fifth birthday of a preventable infectious disease than a rural child in the same country. No country is immune; the extent of neglect of inner city children in the United States was underscored in 1993 when the World Health Organization announced that the United States had fallen behind Albania, Mexico, and China in childhood vaccination rates, largely because of the collapse of health services to inner city poor (Garrett 1994:512).

Thus human demographic patterns, largely a consequence of labor movement and commerce, continue to generate environments that not only harbor pathogens and provide ample opportunity for their spread, but help opportunistic pathogens expand their base of operations. A case in point is cysticercosis, a disease produced by tapeworms found in undercooked pork and other animal flesh which in some forms can infect the brain. Epidemiologists observed that in Mexico City people were being infected not from eating undercooked pork—those infected could not afford to eat meat—but from the water of the Tula River, highly polluted and the city's primary water source. Tens of thousands of people living in shantytowns downriver from the city's sewage system were being infected. Once a parasite adapts to a new environment, it may easily spread. By 1980 this pathogen had found its way to Los Angeles, carried back by a traveler to Mexico, immigrants, or visitors to the United States.

Diseases of Environmental Change

Urban centers emerged as a natural outgrowth of the expansion of commerce, increased industrialization, and the need for financial hubs to serve as links between commercial and industrial centers. However, the environmental and social changes of the past fifty years that have influenced the spread of disease have been more methodical and controlled. We carefully plan and build massive hydroelectric projects that result in the flooding of millions of acres, in the process creating new environments for water-borne infectious parasites. We methodically destroy millions of acres of rainforests, in the process creating new habitats to be exploited by disease vectors. We plan and build roads that bring people into areas where they have never been, thus exposing them to new pathogens. We expand habitats, consequently changing the delicate ecological balances and promoting evolution of microbes that once infected only nonhuman species to infect human beings. We knowingly dump raw sewage into our oceans and waterways, not only spreading disease worldwide but creating a massive evolutionary medium for new pathogens to develop. In modern warfare we devastate environments in ways that past armies were incapable of doing, in the process creating opportunity for pathogens to thrive.

For example, in 1985 the Daima Dam was built on the Senegal River by the Mauritanian, Senegalese, and Malian governments. The dam made possible the irrigation of 10,000 hectares of desert soil, converting it into fields of sugarcane, potatoes, mint, and rice. As a result of agricultural expansion, a few members of a local tribe became millionaires (Platt 1996:45). But with the dam came infectious disease. Sanitation in the area is poor, and the irrigation canals, from which people drink, bathe, and wash their clothes, have become infected with strains of diarrheal bacteria. The dam also halted the flow of saltwater that once penetrated up to 200 kilometers inland. The salt water had kept the snail population in check, but the dam created ideal conditions for an epidemic of snail-borne schistosomiasis. The first cases were detected in 1988, and by 1990 60 percent of the population exhibited symptoms. In one village that had profited from growing mint, 91 percent of the people were infected.

Schistosomiasis is an ancient disease. Egyptian mummies have evidence of infection and the disease was common in China around 200 B.C. during a time of expanding rice cultivation. Today it ranks second only to malaria among diseases in tropical regions. It infects farmers and fishers who wade in shallow water infested with the snails that carry the disease. It is transmitted when people defecate the larvae of the parasite, which then travels through water supplies and infects other snails and people (Platt 1996:47).

In some areas the disease is so prevalent that it goes unrecognized. Katherine A. Dettwyler (1994:46) was doing anthropological work on disease in Mali and taking urine samples; she received one from a young boy that appeared to be full of blood. The urine contained over 500 *Schistosoma* eggs per milliliter, the highest count measurable with the technique she used. When she gave him a look of consternation, he asked, "What's the matter?" "Does your urine always look like this?" she asked. "Yes," he replied, "Isn't it supposed to? Doesn't everyone's?" She later learned that in some communities the first appearance of red urine in boys was believed to be equivalent to the onset of menstruation in girls, and was thought to indicate sexual maturity. In some communities celebratory rites of passage were held when boys reached this milestone.

When Brazil completed its highway through the Amazon a new disease, *oropouche,* began to strike residents of Belém; it affected 11,000 people. It seems that when settlers cleared the forest for cacao planting, they disturbed the habitat of a midge that harbored the virus that caused the disease. Discarded cacao shells provided a new breeding ground for the insect, and the explosion of their population in association with human settlements created the opportunity for disease spread.

One reason forest, especially rainforest, destruction unleashes disease is because of the variety of species that exist in forests. A single hectare of rainforest contains more insect species than the entire New England area or all of Great Britain. When human beings destroy that habitat, it brings them into contact with insects and pathogens that are then searching for new habitats and new hosts.

Dengue is an example of how new, more deadly diseases can emerge as a consequence of environmental damage and population movement. Dengue is a virus, a cousin of the yellow fever microbe and generally spread by the female *Aedes aegypti* mosquito. In any one of its four forms dengue was not life-threatening, and it had virtually disappeared by 1950 after worldwide campaigns to eradicate the carrier mosquito. But in 1953 a new variant, dengue-2, struck in Manila in the Philippines. Dengue-2, or dengue hemorrhagic fever, was far worse than any of the other forms of the disease, causing internal hemorrhaging, shock, and soaring fevers. In 1958 it hit Bangkok, Thailand, infecting 2,297 people, mostly children, and killing 240; within five years 10,367 people were infected and 694 had died.

Researchers discovered two clues to the origins of the disease: first, it was carried by *A. aegypti;* second, all of the victims had at some time been exposed to one of the milder forms of dengue. While the earlier disease did no damage, the immune systems of those afflicted had created antibodies to the disease. The researchers discovered that dengue-2 had developed a remarkable method to use those antibodies to its own advantage. As mentioned earlier, when a foreign body enters the human bloodstream, antibodies attach themselves to it, largely to identify it for other parts of the immune system that will then attack and destroy it. Antibodies attached themselves to the dengue-2 virus, signaling the macrophage cells to envelop the invading microbe and destroy it. But the dengue-2 virus had developed the ability to take over the immune system's primary killer cells, not only allowing it to evade the immune system's response but giving it access to every organ of the body, producing fevers as high as 107°F, convulsions, shock, and death.

Dengue-2 spread through East and South Asia with ever-expanding populations of *A. aegypti* and *Aedes albopictus*, better known as the tiger mosquito, probably named for its aggressive behavior. The disease spread to the Americas, likely in ships carrying the mosquitoes. When mosquito abatement programs were cut in various countries to reduce government expenses, an opportunity was created for the disease to spread. Dengue-2 made its appearance in 1981 in Havana, Cuba, where an epidemic that raged for six months caused 340,000 illnesses and 158 deaths.

The Cuban epidemic sent shockwaves through the U.S. public health community, because in 1980 two residents of Laredo, Texas, had developed dengue hemorrhagic fever. In 1982 an epidemic in New Delhi, India, sickened 20 percent of the population, and by 1990 the disease would be endemic in Latin America. To make matters worse, a shipment of used tires from Japan to Houston, Texas, for retreading contained tiger mosquitoes, creating the likelihood of this aggressive mosquito invading urban environments and outcompeting the less aggressive mosquito. Unlike *A. aegypti,* which feeds only on humans, the tiger mosquito feeds on virtually any animal, raising the possibility that it can harbor and transmit viruses from other animals.

The question is, *what led to the creation of dengue hemorrhagic fever?* Tom Monath of the Centers for Disease Control and Prevention in Atlanta, Georgia, examined historical and laboratory evidence and concluded that World War II was responsible (see Garrett 1994: 257). He surmised that the massive bombings, the population movements and dislocations, and wartime disruptions of mosquito abatement programs resulted in a surge in the population of *A. aegypti.* Then rapid troop movements brought into the Philippines people who, perhaps without knowing it, had been infected by one of the existing dengue varieties. American troops who arrived may already have been to dengue-infested areas such as Burma, Thailand, Indonesia, the Pacific Islands, and China. Thus all four varieties of dengue, each adapted to its specific environment, were brought together in one place and rapidly passed between people and mosquitoes, creating the cycle necessary for the ultimate mutation of one variety into dengue-2. The expansion of commercial travel and possibly the Korean and Vietnam Wars created further opportunities for cross-fertilization and spread of the disease to the slums of Latin America.

By 1981, when dengue-2 hit Havana, it had become an annual feature of the urban Philippines. There, when the mosquitoes emerged in full force after every rainy season, dengue-2 arrived like clockwork, infecting tens of thousands of children and killing 15 percent of those infected. Nonexistent before World War II, by 1980 dengue-2 was one of the major childhood killers in Asia.

The kinds of connections operative in the creation of dengue hemorrhagic fever, between microbes, disease vectors such as mosquitoes, and the movement and activities of human beings, can be enormously complex. New outbreaks of cholera in the 1990s involved not only microbes, vectors, and human beings, but such diverse events as global warming, the spread of oceanic algae, breakdown of sanitation, and the eating habits of the people of Peru. Cholera also provides an example of the interconnectedness of people in the creation and transmission of disease.

Much of the pollution that human beings pour into the oceans—raw sewage, fertilizers, pesticides, and other chemical waste—serves as nutrients for algae blooms, thus increasing their size and frequency. Researchers discovered in the 1970s that a cholera vibrio which they labeled El Tor could live inside algae, taking a form that allowed it to lie dormant for weeks, months, and perhaps years. It was further discovered that El Tor is immune to a whole range of antibiotics.

El Tor is common in South Asia, particularly off the coast of Bangladesh. It is believed to have been picked up in algae by a Chinese freighter, which then dumped the cholera-carrying algae off the coast of Lima, Peru. The vibrio then infected shellfish in the area. The shellfish was used in making ceviche, mixed raw fish and shellfish in lime juice, a national delicacy of Peru. The ocean waters carried the algae up and down the South American coast, and by the end of 1991 cholera had struck at least 336,554 people, killing 3,538. By 1993 at least 900,000 people were reported infected, and 8,000 died. Tests showed that the cholera recovered from patients was identical to that in the algae.

Then in 1992 a whole new strain of cholera emerged off the coast of India. Dubbed Bengal cholera, it was unaffected by the antigens developed by the immune systems of people afflicted with either classical cholera or El Tor, thus leaving everyone open to reinfection.

Scientists trying to determine the cause of the outbreaks and the reason for the emergence of new strains of cholera hypothesized that algae blooms have exploded in size and frequency, fed by nutrients from fertilizer, garbage, and fecal waste incubated in the hotter waters resulting from global warming. The expanded algae blooms become giant floating gene pools in which bacteria, viruses, algae, and terrestrial microbes from human waste and runoff float around, possibly mutating rapidly because of the increased ultraviolet radiation caused by the damage from industrial pollutants to the atmosphere. The algae spread rapidly to different parts of the world, bringing new and more deadly variants of disease (Garrett 1994:563–567).

Anne E. Platt, in *Infecting Ourselves*, examined many of the social, political, and economic activities that result in higher risks for infectious disease (see Table 8.2 on page 258).

AIDS and the Culture of Capitalism

We mentioned earlier that AIDS is very much the signature disease of our age. By this we mean the conditions for its development and spread were essentially created by our patterns of beliefs, attitudes, and behaviors. AIDS burst upon the world in 1981, when physicians in San Francisco and New York began to encounter symptoms in young men that either had been seen previously in older men or were so rare most physicians had never seen them. They turned out to be opportunistic

TABLE 8.2   Causes of Infectious Disease Emergence and Representative Disease Examples

Cause of Emergence	Infectious Disease
Changing environmental conditions	
Deforestation	Malaria, hemorrhagic fever, rabies, Lyme disease
Agriculture and irrigation	Argentine hemorrhagic fever, Japanese encephalitis, Bolivian hemorrhagic fever, schistosomiasis, influenza (pandemic)
Dam building, road building	Schistosomiasis, malaria, Rift Valley fever
Poor sanitation and hygiene	Diarrheal diseases, malaria, schistosomiasis, lymphatic filariasis, river blindness, dengue, yellow fever, cholera, Guinea worm disease, Japanese encephalitis, salmonella, hemolytic uremic syndrome, cryptosporidiosis, giardiasis
Climate change	Hanta virus, plague, malaria, schistosomiasis, other vector-borne disease
Demographic changes	
Urbanization	Yellow fever, malaria, dengue, acute respiratory illness, plague, cholera
Increased trade, travel, migration	Cholera, yellow fever, influenza, dengue, dengue hemorrhagic fever, pneumonia, HIV/AIDS, influenza
Deteriorating social conditions	
Breakdown in public health services	Measles, diphtheria, pertussis, tuberculosis, cholera, influenza, HIV/AIDS, other sexually transmitted diseases
War and civil disorder	Malaria, cholera, diphtheria, waterborne diseases
Increased sexual activity	Hepatitis B and C, HIV/AIDS, other sexually transmitted diseases
Intravenous drug use	HIV/AIDS
Overuse of antibiotics	Antibiotic-resistant malaria, tuberculosis, staphylococci, pneumococci, enterococci, gonorrhea, others
Other	
Air conditioning systems	Legionnaire's disease
Ultra-absorbent tampons	Toxic shock syndrome
Unknown	Streptococcus Group A, ebola

From Anne E. Platt. *Infecting Ourselves: How Environmental and Social Disruption Trigger Disease.* Washington, DC: Worldwatch Institute, 1996. With permission.

infections, such as rare forms of pneumonia, cancer, and other diseases that attacked bodies whose immune systems had been destroyed. The new disease was first called gay-related immunodeficiency disease (GRID) because of its early diagnosis among gay men, but when it was acknowledged to occur in heterosexual populations the name was changed in 1982 to acquired autoimmune-deficiency disease (AIDS). In 1983 the disease appeared in Zaire, and some European researchers thought they had unearthed cases in European hospitals as early as 1967, and possibly 1959.

The early 1980s was a turbulent time for AIDS. Researchers were competing to be the first to isolate and identify the virus. Researchers in Europe and Africa could not publish their articles in the leading medical journals because the peer review panels did not believe the disease was transmitted heterosexually and claimed the researchers had missed some other mode of transmission. The Reagan administration, which had made millions of dollars available for research in Legionnaires' disease, was reluctant to release funds for AIDS research, education, and services. Leaders of the religious right in the United States opposed using federal funds for a disease they claimed was God's judgment against immorality and corruption. Pat Robertson, a Baptist minister, founder of the Christian Broadcasting Network, and presidential candidate in 1988, claimed scientists were "frankly lying" when they said AIDS could be spread heterosexually and that condoms would prevent infection. In the meantime, AIDS continued to spread among heterosexuals, gay men, intravenous drug users, and hemophiliacs given HIV-infected transfusions (Garrett 1994:469).

At the end of 1997, the Joint United Nations Programme on HIV/AIDS (UN-AIDS) and the World Health Organization reported that as of 1997, 30 million people worldwide are infected with HIV, or one out of every one hundred sexually active adults (see UNAIDS/WHO 1997). Transmission rates in 1997 amounted to 16,000 new infections each day. If those rates of transmission continue, 40 million people would be affected by the year 2000. Of those infected, 90 percent live in the periphery; since there are few facilities for testing, it is estimated that nine out of every ten people who are HIV-positive have no idea they are infected. In 1997, 2.3 million people died of AIDS, a 50 percent increase over the 1996 death rate. Nearly half of those who died were women, and 460,000 were children.

Sub-Saharan Africa has the highest infection rate, with 7.4 percent of all people between the ages of fifteen and forty-nine thought to be infected. In Botswana, 25–30 percent of all adults are thought to be infected, and in Zimbabwe seven out of every ten pregnant women tested were HIV-positive. In Botswana, where life expectancy rose from forty-three years in 1955 to sixty-one years in 1990, life expectancy has reverted to the level of the late 1960s. India, where 1 percent of the population is infected, there are 3–5 million people living with HIV. In Cambodia, one in every twenty pregnant women and one in every sixteen soldiers or policemen test positive for HIV. In areas of Brazil 3 percent of all pregnant women test positive, as do 8 percent of all pregnant women in Haiti. It is estimated that since the beginning of the epidemic, 3.8 million children under the age of 15 have been infected and over 2.7 million have died. In North America there have been 1–2 million cases of HIV. This total is heavily skewed toward the poorest segments of the population; in 1995 the incidence of AIDS was 6.5 times greater for Blacks and 4.0 times greater for Hispanics than for Whites.

We now think we know the origin of AIDS, that it likely crossed over from non-human primates in central and west Africa sometime after World War II, infecting only a few people until the late 1970s, when it made its breakthrough worldwide. But there are many questions we need to explore to understand the effects of human culture on the disease. For example, *What features of global culture influenced the spread of the disease? What features of our culture determined the people most at risk for AIDS? How did our culture influence the way people choose to react to the epidemic and those affected by it?*

How Did the Disease Spread?

AIDS reveals the extent to which we are interconnected in global space. We live in a world, as geographer Peter Gould (1993:66–69) noted, in which New York is closer to San Francisco than it is to towns 200 miles away; in which Los Angeles is closer to Miami and Houston than it is to towns in Nevada; in which Kinshasa, Zaire, is closer to Paris than to villages in the center of the country. Gould meant by this that people located at the hubs of the capitalist world system, those cities connected by rapid air travel, are more likely to come into contact with each other than they are with people located spacially much closer to them. Viewed another way, patterns of contact are characterized by what Gould called "hierarchical diffusion" rather than "spacially contiguous diffusion." In the hierarchical diffusion that characterizes AIDS, or "AIDS space," as Gould called it, the disease jumps from travel hub to travel hub.

This is not the first time global space has been redefined by revolutions in trade and travel. In the earlier eras of sea travel seaports became economic hubs as well as the major points of distribution for disease. Today, with rapid air travel, economic centers such as Tokyo, New York, Paris, Jakarta, San Francisco, London, São Paulo, Bombay, Johannesburg, and Moscow form the geographic center of the world system and, as a consequence, the epicenters of the spread of AIDS.

With the exception of infected blood supplies, AIDS has to be carried from place to place by people and transmitted directly. There is no vector involved in AIDS as in plague, malaria, or dengue. But human travel provides an effective means of transmission. Therefore, to understand the spread of AIDS, we need to ask *why in the culture of capitalism do people travel?* Generally they travel for one of four reasons: tourism, business, labor migration, and war, all of which have had a major role in the spread and distribution of AIDS.

Tourism is essentially a product of industrial capitalism of the nineteenth century. While the wealthy of Europe had their country estates and cottages for centuries, travel and tourism were relatively new phenomena for the emerging middle class (Hobsbawm 1975:203). Made possible by the development of steamboats and railways, the tourist industry grew throughout the nineteenth and early twentieth centuries. For the British middle class holiday travel became a serious enterprise in the 1860s and 1870s; this transformed the British coastlines with promenades and piers. In Europe mountain resorts, such as Biarritz, were becoming fashionable. Tours through Europe became popular, creating an industry and a form of travel that was probably unique. For the poor, day trips dominated; American resorts such as Coney Island in New York became popular for new immigrants to the United States. In the twentieth century tourism evolved into a major industry, and few people, certainly in the core, have not at one time or another been tourists. In 1995, receipts from international travel reached $372 billion; the World Trade Organization estimates that by the year 2010 one billion people a year will be tourists (Scherer 1996).

Tourism has always been associated with disease, as any traveler can tell you who has sampled food and water laden with bacteria to which his or her system had no resistance. It is likely that such perils have confronted travelers for centuries. But in the age of AIDS it is not only the traveler who is at risk; the people in the host country are equally susceptible.

We have no figures on the number of people who have contracted AIDS as a consequence of tourist travel, but researchers suggest that it has had a major impact on at least two countries hardest hit by the epidemic, Haiti and Thailand. One reason for their susceptibility is that both were targeted for "sex tours."

Anthropologist and physician Paul Farmer (1992) suggested that the history of HIV/AIDS in Haiti is linked to its history as a tourist destination. In the 1970s, Haiti, the poorest country in the Western Hemisphere, became a major tourist attraction with the closing of Cuba in 1959 to American tourists. Tourist visits to Haiti increased to 100,000 per year by 1970 and 143,538 by 1979. (Later, the tourist industry was a casualty of the Haitian AIDS epidemic: tourist visits dropped to 75,000 in the winter of 1981–1982 and under 10,000 the following winter.)

Tourism in Haiti brought with it an increase in institutionalized prostitution. Poverty and 60–80 percent unemployment rates made prostitution for males and females one of the only economic alternatives available. The country, particularly the Carrefour area of the capital city Port-au-Prince, gained a reputation for cheap sex. Travel guides published for homosexual men recommended Haiti to tourists.

Whether AIDS was brought to Haiti by American tourists, as some researchers suggest, or in some other fashion is a matter of debate, but it is clear that tourism accelerated the spread of the disease among Haitians and, probably, among tourists. By the late 1980s the rate of HIV in hotel workers catering to tourists was 12 percent, and Haiti had one of the highest rates of infection in the world. But even when Haitian workers became aware of AIDS, they seemed to treat it as just an "occupational hazard" (Farmer 1992:145).

In Thailand, also, tourism played a major role in the spread of AIDS. HIV/AIDS was relatively late in arriving in Thailand, with the first recorded death in 1984, a gay man who had spent time in the United States. By 1987 the rate climbed in months from 15 percent to 43 percent among intravenous drugs users. The group hit hardest by AIDS was the commercial sex workers. Among Chaing Mai prostitutes the rate of infection went from 0.04 percent in 1989 to 70 percent 20 months later (Garrett 1994:489).

Thailand had for years an active trade in both drugs and prostitution, trades that accelerated when Thailand became a major rest and recreation zone for American

*Advertisements for sex tours, such as this one for
Thailand, attract tourists from Europe, North America,
and other parts of Asia and create fertile breeding grounds
for the AIDS virus and other sexually transmitted diseases.*

military personnel during the Vietnam War. Both drugs and prostitution were, and continue to be, major sources of foreign exchange for Thailand's economy. By 1990, Thailand was attracting 5.3 million tourists a year, with a high proportion of single men from Malaysia, Japan, and Taiwan and with special "sex tours" arriving in Bangkok from Japan, the Middle East, and Europe, particularly Germany. As a consequence of the growth in the sex industry, there are 500,000–800,000 prostitutes representing some 10 percent of the female population between the ages of fifteen and twenty-four. In some areas of Bangkok in the early 1990s there was an AIDS infection rate of 90 percent.

Probably because of the economic importance of the sex industry, particularly for attracting tourists, government authorities in Thailand were slow to respond to the threatened epidemic. As cases began to increase in 1987, the government decided not to launch an anti-AIDS campaign for fear of "inciting panic." By 1989, 0.5 percent of all pregnant women were HIV-seropositive, with some northern provinces reporting rates of 3 percent. In 1991 the government reevaluated its policy and noted again that they did not want to create panic. A Bangkok newspaper reported that HIV/AIDS was spread only by anal sex and intravenous drug use, when in fact there were forty times more heterosexual cases than homosexual cases reported. The World Health Organization estimated that by 1992, 450,000 people in Thailand were infected.

Another form of travel that characterizes the capitalist culture is labor migration. At least since the increase in slave trade in the seventeenth and eighteenth centuries, the world economy has required massive shifts of laborers from one area to another. While it is difficult to determine exactly the extent of the worldwide transmission of AIDS by migrating workers, there is considerable evidence that this type of travel was a major cause of AIDS transmission in Africa. Male workers travel from rural areas to urban areas in search of work, visit prostitutes whose infection rate in some areas approach 90 percent, and bring the disease back to their rural villages.

Commercial and business travel were also instrumental in the spread of AIDS. The routes of infection in Africa travel along well-traveled truck and commercial transportation routes. The north-south alignment of AIDS starts at Djibouti at the mouth of the Red Sea, the port city and railway terminal for the city of Addis Ababa, the capital of Ethiopia, to which goods, and AIDS, flow. In 1991 some 50–60 percent of prostitutes and 1 percent of the general population were reported infected with HIV. In the Sudan 80 percent of the "bar girls" were seropositive for HIV-1. From Uganda to Mozambique, samples of truck drivers indicate that 30–80 percent are infected. Estimates are that Tanzania has 800,000 infected people, of a total population of 18 million, and Uganda 1.3 million out of 12 million. Malawi may have the highest rate of infection in the world, with over 30 percent of the adult population infected. The highway between Malawi and Durban, South Africa, is known as the "Highway of Death," truckers having an infection rate of 90 percent (Gould 1993:75).

Patterns of AIDS distribution seem to follow commercial routes in North America as well. Paul Farmer (1992:149) noted that the incidence of AIDS in the Caribbean correlates with the degree to which a country is economically integrated into the "West Atlantic system." Excluding Puerto Rico because it is not an independent country, the countries with the highest rates of AIDS—the Dominican Republic, the Bahamas, Trinidad/Tobago, Mexico, and Haiti—are also the countries most dependent on trade with the United States and most linked to the American economy. The country with the highest rates of AIDS—Haiti—was most dependent on U.S. exports.

Finally, the movement of soldiers and refugees precipitated by conflict played a role in the spread of AIDS. Researchers speculating about the origins of AIDS and the factors that may have contributed to its breakout in central and East Africa concluded that something dramatic must have happened around 1975 to cause the emergence of the epidemic. The period of 1970–1975 was characterized by guerrilla warfare, civil war, tribal conflicts, mass refugee migrations, and striking dictatorial atrocities. Laurie Garrett suggested that such social upheaval may have affected the course of AIDS both directly and indirectly. For example, most African conflict was characterized by rival forces trying to cripple each other economically, politically, socially, spiritually, and militarily. In such conflicts, civilian casualties are high. In any number of military campaigns of the past two to three decades in central Africa rape was used (as it was in Bosnia) systematically to terrorize and dominate the enemy. Some armies have tested up to 50 percent HIV-positive. Other human activities resulting from social disruption, including increased multiple partner sexual activity, famine and malnutrition that further stressed immune systems, large-scale migrations and concentrations of people in refugee camps, increased prostitution, and destruction of health care services, could have further spread the disease (Garrett 1994:367–368).

Who Gets Infected with AIDS?

Reni Dubos (1968) wrote in the 1950s and 1960s of the special vulnerability of the poor to infections; malnutrition, substandard housing, dense population, and lack of access to health care all promote the spread of infectious disease. Certainly poverty played a role in the spread of tuberculosis, cholera, and syphilis. But AIDS has affected not only the economically marginalized, but also those who are socially and politically marginalized—homosexuals, women, and children.

Public and governmental responses to the AIDS epidemic, especially in the United States, was greatly influenced by the mistaken assumption that it was a disease of homosexual men, in spite of the fact that there was clear evidence of heterosexual transmission in the United States, Europe, and particularly Africa, where it was almost exclusively transmitted by heterosexual relations. We may never know to what extent the association of the disease with a socially marginalized portion of American society delayed research and education efforts, but it is clear that it didn't help.

It is also clear that the poor, globally and in the United States, have been the most frequent victims of the disease. Africa, the poorest area of the world, has by far the highest incidence of AIDS, with Malawi, the poorest country in Africa, having the highest rates. Poor countries in other areas of the world are the others most affected. For a particularly apt illustration of a poor and socially marginalized country that suffers disproportionately with AIDS, let's return to Haiti.

Haiti itself is very much a creation of the capitalist world system. In the sixteenth and seventeenth centuries the indigenous population (the Taino) were exterminated and the country resettled with African slaves ruled by a European elite. Haiti passed from Spain to France in 1697 and was renamed Saint-Dominique. In 1804 a slave revolt led by Toussaint L'Ouverture succeeded in defeating the French, establishing the country of Haiti, the first, as Paul Farmer referred to it, of the Third World countries.

The new country found itself in a world hostile to the idea of self-governing Blacks, a nightmare to every country in which slavery endured, particularly the United States. Every effort was made to undermine Black rule in Haiti. The French demanded that Haiti compensate planters for the loss of land, and periodically in the nineteenth century European gunboats would appear in Haitian ports demanding compensation. By 1900, 80 percent of national revenue was going to pay off international debts, and by the late 1920s Haiti was being advertised in *Financial America* as a place where "easily directed" Haitian labor could be had for 20¢ per day, as opposed to $3 per day in Panama.

American domination has continued throughout the twentieth century, as Haiti has lived with a series of despotic rulers supported by the United States. This history left Haiti in 1983 with an annual per capita income of $315 overall and $100 in the countryside. The agricultural situation was so bad that Haiti was a net importer of food, even sugar. Even when Haiti had promise as a recreational playground for other North Americans, the tourist industry collapsed because of Haiti's reputation as the originator of AIDS. There were few avenues out of poverty in Haiti. The 60 percent unemployment rate combined with the country's dependence on the United States set the stage for what Farmer (1992:189–190) called the "West Atlantic pandemic."

AIDS is not only a marker of poverty, it is becoming a marker of gender and age as well. We saw in our discussion of famine and hunger that women and children are particularly at risk. In the instance of AIDS, women worldwide represent the majority of all reported cases. The fact that women, who were at the fringe of the epidemic in the mid-1980s, have frequently become victims reflects the role of women in global capitalist culture. Women seem to become infected at a younger age; in many countries 60 percent of new AIDS infections are among women between the ages of fifteen and twenty-four; in surveys of several African and Asian countries, women under twenty-five account for 30 percent of new AIDS cases, compared to fifteen for men under twenty-five.

Women contract the disease largely through heterosexual intercourse; many of these cases are among women who are monogamous but have male partners who are not. This is due in part to the sexual subordination of women in many countries where men initiate sexual relations and women, especially wives, have little say. The attitudes toward women and sex in many countries inhibits conversation about sexual matters and virtually prohibits AIDS educational campaigns directed toward women. Furthermore, education is hampered by the higher illiteracy rates among women in many countries. Even in countries with well-developed campaigns to educate women about the risk of AIDS, men still often resist condom use because of decreased sensitivity, ignorance about how to use them, or fear that their use will cause sterility.

Women also contract the disease through prostitution, itself a reflection of the limited options available to women, especially in poor countries. As Laurie Garrett (1994:368) said about AIDS and prostitution in Uganda,

> [a]s a business, prostitution was second only to the black market. For most women there were only two choices in life: have babies and grow food without assistance from men, livestock, or machinery, or exchange sex for money at black-market rates.

Finally, the more women are infected with AIDS, the more likely children will be infected. Children are not only at risk of acquiring the disease at birth. AIDS can be transmitted by infected hypodermic needles, yet many countries that depend on intravenous drugs are too poor to afford new needles. In some African countries needles are reused. Intravenous transmission of AIDS to children is not solely a problem of the periphery. In Russia, the collapse of communism and the social and economic chaos that followed virtually destroyed the country's health care system. Syringes were simply not available, and medical personnel, especially in rural

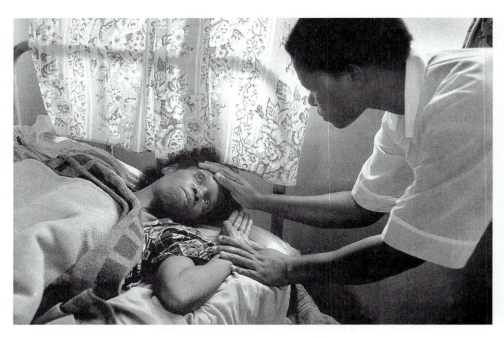

Women, particularly in Africa, comprise the majority of AIDS victims.

areas, were forced to use the same syringes again and again, up to 400 times in some cases. In 1988 AIDS emerged in Elistya, capital of the Kalmyk Republic on the Caspian Sea. A baby had been infected by its mother. The baby was treated by staff who used the same syringes to draw blood samples and administer drugs to all the babies in the hospital's nursery for three months; HIV was unknowingly injected into all the babies on the ward and some of their mothers (Garrett 1994:501).

Socially marginalized members of the capitalist world system face another danger: once infected with HIV they are the ones least likely to receive treatment or to receive information to enable them to take measures to avoid the onset of AIDS. As AIDS researcher Renée Sabatier (cited Garrett 1994:475) noted in reference to AIDS education campaigns,

> *I think there is a very real danger that we're going to end up as a [world] society divided between those who were able to inform themselves first and those who were informed late. Those who have access to information and health care, and those who don't. Those who are able to change, and those who aren't. I think there is a real danger of half of us turning into AIDS voyeurs, standing around watching others die.*

The announcement in the summer of 1996 of a new drug treatment that restores the body's immune system and holds the AIDS virus at bay is a further development in the ghettoization of AIDS. While the announcement was greeted with great enthusiasm, the treatment costs at least $10,000–20,000 per year and is therefore beyond the reach of the world's poor.

Who Gets Blamed?

We saw the phenomenon of blaming the victim when we examined population growth, poverty, hunger, and environmental degradation. Problems generated by core exploitation of the periphery are blamed on the periphery itself. However, nowhere is the phenomenon of blaming the victim more clearly illustrated than in the case of HIV/AIDS, and nowhere was that more clear than in the case of Haiti. When the AIDS epidemic was identified, Haitians with AIDS were a "wild card": they didn't fit the categories of homosexuals, hemophiliacs, and heroin users. So they were added as a whole category, thus completing the early four-H club (homosexuals, hemophiliacs, heroin users, and Haitians). But this was clearly racist: there was no reason, based on some thirty-four cases, to place all Haitians in a risk group. This would be analogous to claiming that all San Franciscans or all New Yorkers were at special risk to contract and spread the disease. Risk designation was akin to being labeled a carrier. Then, in a leap that surprised few Haitians, AIDS was said to have originated in Haiti.

Bruce Chabner of the National Cancer Institute was quoted in 1982 as saying, "Homosexuals in New York take vacations in Haiti, and we suspect that this may be an epidemic Haitian virus that was brought back to the homosexual population in the United States" (cited in Farmer 1992: 201). This epidemic of blame led to widespread discrimination against Haitians in job hiring and a rapid decline in the Haitian tourist industry.

The Haitian government was angry with the Centers for Disease Control because, even when it became evident that the rate of infection was higher in other Caribbean Islands and most U.S. cities, the CDC refused to abandoned the designation of Haitians as a high-risk group. In 1985 the CDC finally removed the designation, but without comment, refusing to admit it made an error. Then in 1990, the FDA ruled that Haitians could not donate blood. It was an absurd ruling; as one Boston newspaper editorial pointed out, if the FDA was consistent it would have banned donations from all San Franciscans, New Yorkers, Bostonians, and emigrants from other Caribbean Islands, some of whom had rates of AIDS/HIV as much as ten times greater than Haiti's. (see Farmer 1992; 220)

Why was Haiti singled out? Largely, according to Paul Farmer, because the U.S. folk model of Haitians included images of superstitious natives, Blacks, immigrants, and the like that symbolized the stigma associated with AIDS. The model was driven to some extent by the media. The *New York Times* wrote that "Haitian voodooists may be unsuspectingly infected with AIDS by ingestion, inhalation, or dermal contact with contaminated ritual substances, as well as by sexual activity"(cited Farmer 1992:3). This view was furthered by the medical community. Jeffrey Viera, senior author of the paper that put Haitians at risk, blamed the media for stigmatizing Haitians but himself made reference to voodoo rituals, the drinking of menstrual blood, and the like. An article in the *Journal of the American Medical Association* entitled "Night of the Living Dead" considered these voodoo origin theories, asking whether necromantic zombies transmit HTLV-III/LAV (Farmer 1992:3). Blaming Haiti for AIDS was a classic case of blaming the victim.

The view from the periphery concerning the origins of AIDS was quite different than the view from the core. As researchers focused on Africa as the origin of the disease, African officials became sensitive to what they saw as a Western campaign to blame their countries for the epidemic. One result was official government denials that there was any AIDS in African countries, even after the epidemic had clearly become established. One African health minister was fired after admitting to international health agencies that AIDS was present in his country. Not surprisingly, conspiracy theories abounded. One theory was that the American CIA had introduced the disease; another, popular also in core countries, was that AIDS was the result of American germ warfare experiments gone awry.

Haitians saw AIDS as a disease visited on them by resentful Americans. As one Haitian school teacher (cited Farmer 1992:232) put it, "The Americans have always resented Haiti, ever since 1804. Being strong, they can punish us, humiliate us. The AIDS thing was a perfect tool."

Haitian teenagers in the United States, when asked if they thought the U.S. did what they did on purpose, almost universally said yes. Others said that AIDS was created in U.S. laboratories.

Paul Farmer (1992:58), in *AIDS and Accusation,* concluded that questions asked by Haitians and Americans such as

> *Is AIDS a product of North American imperialism? Can one person send an AIDS death to another through sorcery? Are Haitians a special AIDS risk group? Are 'boat people' disease-ridden and a risk to the health of U.S. citizens? ... underscore several of the West Atlantic pandemic's central dynamics—blame, search for accountability, accusation, and racism—that have shaped both responses to AIDS and the epidemiology of a new virus.*

Conclusion

The disease factors that we examined in this chapter have practical consequences. For example, knowledge of the effects of culturally defined human behavior can help us predict as well as treat disease. Might more careful application of this principal have made a difference? Could we have anticipated the emergence of AIDS, as many medical anthropologists once posited? Would we have let multidrug-resistant tuberculosis get out of hand? Would we have allowed so many antibiotic-resistant strains of disease to develop or relied so much on antibiotics? Would drug-resistant malaria be out of control? Would new diseases such as Lyme disease spread so quickly?

Even if we were to predict, as some scientists did, the dangers of overuse of antibiotics and other things, could we really have done something about it? Even knowing the dangers of AIDS, the U.S. government moved slowly in releasing research funds. Even when it was known that anal sex was responsible for AIDS, many in the homosexual community refused to heed advice for safe sex, believing AIDS was just a scare tactic to discredit their life style.

We continue to create "disease sinks," populations of poor and marginalized people among whom infectious pathogens thrive and who may serve as breeding grounds for new diseases. If there was some omnipotent microbe responsible for the survival and spread of all infectious pathogens, it could hardly improve on the actions of human beings in the culture of capitalism whose cumulative behavioral choices relegate some of their numbers to these sinks.

The lesson is that while we must be aware of how our behavior puts us in danger of contracting disease, we must also be aware of the factors that promote adoption or rejection of therapeutic regimes necessary to lower our risk of becoming ill, cure us, or inhibit the creation of new and more deadly strains of disease. If biologist Paul Ewald is correct and diseases become more lethal the more easily they are spread, then given the increase in travel, the increase in the number of poor, the cutback of medical and public health services for structural adjustment programs, the ecological destruction of habitats such as rainforests, and the emergence of drug-resistant strains of new and old killers, we are truly on the verge of a pandemic on a scale of that which struck the peoples of North and South America in the sixteenth and seventeenth centuries.

What can be done? That is difficult to say, but it seems that political, religious, and social associations that can marshal forces against largely imaginary social, political, and religious enemies certainly could rally populations to cope with the pathogens that threaten to overwhelm us.

Chapter 9

Indigenous People, Ethnic Groups, and the Nation-State

At the present time indigenous societies that believe it is immoral not to share with one's kin or with those less fortunate than oneself are...considered backward, for this surely hampers capital accumulation and therefore "progress" as the modern world defines it.
—DAVID MAYBURY-LEWIS, INDIGENOUS PEOPLES, ETHNIC GROUPS, AND THE STATE

Official statements frequently justify the extension of government control over tribal populations as an effort to bring them peace, health, happiness, and other benefits of civilization... But, undoubtedly, the extension of government control was directly related to protecting the economic interests of nonindigenous peoples moving into formerly exclusive tribal areas.
—JOHN BODLEY, VICTIMS OF PROGRESS

There is a museum exhibit in Jakarta, Indonesia, of a Javanese wedding; the guests are arranged around the bride and groom, each dressed to represent a different Indonesian ethnic group, of which there are hundreds. The exhibit is reminiscent of a early nineteenth-century painting mentioned earlier by the British painter Sir David Wilkie, *Chelsea Pensioners Reading the Gazette of the Battle of Waterloo,* in which all the various groups that made up the British nation-state and empire—Welsh, Scottish, Irish, Black, and so on—are depicted together reading of Wellington's victory over Napoleon. Indonesia is one of the most culturally diverse countries in the world. It is also one of the most officially tolerant toward ethnic diversity. Ethnic tolerance is incorporated into education programs and "hate speech" is a crime. But it is a tolerance with definite limits. Java is the dominant island in Indonesia, and the museum exhibit suggests, said Anna Lowenhaupt Tsing (1993:24), that

While Indonesia officially recognizes and celebrates cultural diversity, the dominant culture is still Javanese, represented here in the wedding of the son of Indonesian ex-President Suharto (on the far left), Hutomo "Tommy" Mandala Putra (third from left) and his bride, Ardhia "Tata" Pramesti Rigita Cahyani (fourth from left).

minority groups are "invited" into the nation, but only as long as they bow to Javanese standards.

One of the casualties of the expansion of the culture of capitalism is cultural diversity. As noted in Chapter 4, one of the functions of the nation-state is to integrate, peacefully if possible, violently if necessary, the diverse peoples within its borders into a common culture. At best, minority cultures are integrated into the larger culture in superficial ways—dress, art, dance, music, and food are maintained and represented as the culture itself. At worst, however, policies of the nation-state may lead to ethnocide, the destruction of culture, or, in more extreme instances, genocide, the destruction of a people.

The dilemma of minority groups in the modern nation-state is particularly evident in Indonesia because it officially recognizes and celebrates diversity but this does not stop the nation-state from systematically destroying the culture of indigenous peoples. Anna Lowenhaupt Tsing, in her book *In the Realm of the Diamond Queen,* described the fate of the Meratus Dyak, who subsist on swidden agriculture and gathering and hunting, and, while relatively isolated in the Meratus mountains, frequently trade with other groups. Their culture requires that they frequently move to establish new garden plots. Individuals also travel to maintain political contact with other Meratus groups, travel being a source of prestige.

However, according to Tsing (1993:41), the Indonesian government sees the Meratus as uncivilized, stuck in a timeless, archaic condition outside modern history. Furthermore, the government attributes their condition to their mobility and travel across the forest landscape. From the state's perspective, Meratus mobility constitutes "seminomadism" and labels them as runaways from state discipline and a threat to national security. For the Meratus, however, mobility is a sign of personal autonomy.

In Indonesia, there are over 1.5 million members of what the government calls "isolated populations." Most, like the Meratus, live in small, scattered mountain settlements. To transform these societies into forms acceptable to the Indonesian government, they established the Management of Isolated Populations Project, which operates, to quote one official document, to guide "the direction of their social, economic, cultural and religious arrangements in accord with the norms that operate for the Indonesian people" (Tsing 1993:92). To meet the goals of the project the government devised various strategies that function largely to attempts to discipline these populations and bring them under government control. One strategy is resettlement. The government builds clustered housing and moves isolated populations to them. The state justifies this housing by saying it is more modern, but in fact it makes everyone visible, keeps them in one place, enables government control, and in some cases creates settlements designed specifically to ensure military security. The Meratus quickly caught on to the government's game and built their villages with clustered housing so they would "look good if the government comes to visit" (Tsing 1993:93).

The government also initiated nutrition programs to reorganize the eating habits of isolated populations. The Meratus were given a demonstration in which locally unavailable meats and vegetables were prepared "the right way." The Meratus were considered unordered in their eating habits; as one village head explained: "[Indonesians] drink in the morning," referring to the typical morning diet of coffee or tea and a pastry, "and then have two meals during the day. We [Meratus] sometimes eat five times a day and sometimes once a day. It's not ordered." (cites Tsing 1993:93) But eating habits are dictated by work schedules, and in farming or hunting communities one can eat at very different times. For government planners even the way food is prepared is supposed to follow national standards; one government official complained that the Meratus butchered a chicken but cooked it without sour spices or chili peppers. To please government authorities the Meratus leaders now see to it that the chickens are cooked "properly when authorities visit."

The government also exercised control over isolated populations by introducing family planning programs. Once again, there was a distinct difference in how the government saw the program and how the Meratus viewed it. The program was essentially an attempt by the nation-state to discipline the population into following state-mandated views of family form and reproductive practices. In the early 1980s the state began a program to encourage women to use IUDs or take birth control pills. To advance the program the government encouraged a local male leader, Pa'an Tinito, to enroll women in the program. He signed up women, but it became apparent that they had little idea of what the program was about, and were dismayed when Tinito explained the purpose of contraception. The men were shocked; how could the government possibly want them to limit the size of their population? Weren't communities already too small and weak? The program was ridiculous and there must be some mistake. Pa'an Tinito responded that the government only wanted a *list* of women; nothing was said about limiting repro- duction. When the supply of oral contraceptives arrived some months later, Pa'an Tinito brought them back to his house and hung them in the rafters, where they stayed (Tsing 1993:109).

In developing relocation, nutrition, and family planning programs, the nation- state was, in effect, imposing its standards of social structure and family authority. There should be a fixed and stable "village" consisting of individual families, each with a family "head," generally a man. For the government, to get to women one must go through men. But this is not the way the Meratus were organized, nor was it the way the Meratus saw the situation. Their view of the world differed signifi- cantly from that of the nation-state in which they are subjects. The dilemma faced by the Meratus, as well as other indigenous and ethnic groups, is whether one can be simultaneously outside and inside the nation-state. As Tsing (1993:26) put it,

> *Marginals stand outside the state by tying themselves to it; they constitute the state locally by fleeing from it. As culturally different subjects they can never be citizens; as culturally different 'subjects,' they can never escape citizenship.*

In this chapter we will examine the dilemma of minority cultures—indigenous and ethnic groups—in the nation-state. We need to ask *why were indigenous cultures destroyed? How did their destroyers justify their actions? What is likely to be the fate of the indigenous cultures and ethnic groups that remain in the world? What is the cause of eth- nic conflict?*

The Fate of Indigenous Peoples

Who are indigenous or tribal peoples? They certainly include the aboriginal peoples of Australia, the Indians of North, South, and Central America, and the peoples of most of the African continent. At the second general assembly of the World Coun- cil of Indigenous peoples, indigenous peoples were defined as follows (Bodley 1990:153):

> *Indigenous people shall be people living in countries which have populations com- posed of different ethnic or racial groups who are descendants of the earliest pop- ulations which survive in the area, and who do not, as a group, control the national government of the countries within which they live.*

The difficulty with this definition, said David Maybury-Lewis (1997:7), is that it assumes that should indigenous people gain control of the government they would no longer be indigenous; however, it is clear they are native to the countries they inhabit and that they claim they were there first and have rights of prior occupancy to their lands. They also have been conquered by peoples racially, ethnically, or culturally different from themselves; they generally maintain their own language and, most important, "are marginal to or dominated by the states that claim jurisdiction over them." That is, indigenous peoples are defined largely by their relationship to the state. Maybury-Lewis (1997:55) concluded that

> *[m]any people are stigmatized as "tribal...because they reject the authority of the state and do not wish to adopt the culture of the mainstream population that the state represents. They are in fact stigmatized as being "tribal" because they insist on being marginal.*

Maybury-Lewis estimated that approximately 5 percent of the world's population fit the description of indigenous peoples; these are the descendants of peoples who have been marginalized in the global capitalist economy.

One of the problems faced by indigenous peoples, as we saw with the Meratus, is that their cultures often conflict with the culture of capitalism. Consequently, the first question we need to explore is *how is the culture of indigenous peoples incompatible with the culture of capitalism?*

Some Characteristics of Indigenous Peoples

The cultures of indigenous peoples are vulnerable to destruction from capitalist expansion partly because their way of life differs so significantly from that in the culture of capitalism. While there are significant differences among these cultures, they do tend to share certain characteristics. For example, they tend to be mobile; they may be nomads who threaten state integrity by traversing international boundaries or shifting agriculturists who require large tracts of land or whose frequent movements make them difficult to control.

A second characteristic of small-scale indigenous societies, and one that is quickly undermined by capitalist culture, is their communal ownership of valuable resources, particularly land. Communality creates all kinds of problems in the culture of capitalism. For example, communally held land is not as readily sold or purchased, requiring group consensus. Financial institutions cannot use communally-held land as collateral for individual's debts, since it cannot be repossessed. Furthermore, contrary to some writers' view (see Hardin 1968; Hardin & Baden 1997), communally-held lands tend to be more subject to conservation measures and less subject to exploitation for short-term financial gain. Finally, communal resources and discoveries that are not legally incorporated cannot be protected from capitalist exploitation. For example, the Urueu-Wau-Wau peoples of the Amazon developed from plant extracts an anticoagulant that Merck Pharmaceuticals "discovered" and is attempting to develop, yet no benefits accrue to the Urueu-Wau-Wau, who are threatened with extinction. Thus, as Darrell Posey (1996:7) noted, traditional and communal knowledge that would be recognized as property if held by an individual or a legally designated "natural person," such as a corporation, is deemed in the culture of capitalism to be free for the taking.

A third characteristic of small-scale indigenous groups that is incompatible with capitalist culture is kinship-based social structure. In small-scale societies most relationships are defined by a person's kin links with others, and the primary social unit tends to be the extended family. The large network of relations that each person can call on for help promotes the sharing of resources and reduces the need to consume and to work to make money. The small, socially isolated nature of family units such as the nuclear family make them more susceptible to state control and discipline. As we shall see, one of the first features of indigenous societies to come under attack is the pattern of kinship relations. This does not mean kinship cannot be used as a basis for control and accumulation of capital; early business enterprises were family-based, as noted in Chapter 3, and small family businesses still thrive. Yet, perhaps because of the need for a mobile and socially unattached labor force, extended family units do not do well in the culture of capitalism.

Fourth, most small-scale indigenous societies tend to be relatively egalitarian. As John Bodley (1990:4) noted, equality in social relations reduces the incentive and need to consume, since people have far less need to use material possessions to mark their status. Furthermore, nation-states require a political hierarchy to govern effectively. Without a recognized local leader with the power to make decisions, who, for example, will collect the taxes? Who will enforce government directives? Who will ensure that the laws of the nation-state are enforced? As we shall see, one of the first things that nation-states do to control indigenous peoples is to impose a new pattern of authority.

Finally, and perhaps most important, indigenous peoples tend to control resources or occupy land desired by members of the capitalist nation-state or the nation-state itself. Thus, as John Bodley (1990:4) wrote:

> *The struggle between tribes and states has been over conflicting systems of resources management and internal social organization. Tribes represent small–scale, classless societies, with decentralized, communal, long-term resource management strategies, whereas states are class-based societies, with centralized management systems that extract resources for the short-term profit of special interest groups. Understandably, then, the political conquest of tribal areas often brings rapid environmental deterioration and may impoverish tribal peoples.*

The Process of Ethnocide

In *Victims of Progress*, Bodley described the various ways nation-states acted to transfer the rights of resources from indigenous peoples to settlers wishing to exploit the resources for themselves. The process occurs in stages, generally beginning with the establishment of a frontier situation and advancing through military intervention, the extension of government control, and the gradual destruction of indigenous culture through land takeovers, cultural modification, and economic development. Bodley's analysis provides insight into why indigenous peoples have disappeared and gives ample evidence that their "integration" into the modern world was neither voluntary nor beneficial to them.

The Frontier Situation

Often the destruction of an indigenous culture begins with the establishment of a frontier, an area perceived to be abundant in natural resources that can be easily exploited but seems not to be controlled by a nation-state. Prior ownership rights and interests of indigenous peoples are considered irrelevant by both the nation-state and by invading settlers. For example, in 1909 the London magazine *Truth* published the account of a young American engineer, Walter Hardenburg, describing the brutality of the managers of a British and Peruvian-owned rubber company in the Putumayo River region separating Peru and Colombia (see Taussig 1987). The article, which described the enslavement, torture, and killing of Indian rubber gatherers, caused a sensation and led the British government to send Roger Casement, then a consular representative in Rio de Janeiro, to Brazil to investigate the charges. Casement had already written a report describing the horrors inflicted by rubber traders on native workers in the Congo, horrors depicted in Joseph Conrad's fictional account, *Heart of Darkness* (1972/1902).

In his report to Sir Edward Grey, head of the British Foreign Service, Casement described again and again the horrors inflicted on the indigenous peoples of the Putumayo region, accounts that he collected from Black workers recruited by the rubber companies from Barbados, who themselves, under threat of death, had inflicted the horrors. For example, he wrote to Grey of the fate of Indians who did not fill the quota of rubber allotted to them (cited Taussig 1987:35):

> *The Indian is so humble, that as soon as he sees that the needle of the scale does not mark the ten kilos, he himself stretches out his hands and throws himself on the ground to receive the punishment. Then the chief [of the rubber station] or a subordinate advances, bends down, takes the Indian by his hair, strikes him, raises his head, drops it face downwards on the ground, and, after the face is beaten and kicked and covered with blood, the Indian is scourged. This is when they are treated best, for often they cut them to pieces with machetes.*

Casement said that 90 percent of the Indians he saw carried scars from floggings. He described other ways the company managers disciplined and controlled their Indian workers, including deliberately starving them, burning alive those who tried to run away, killing children, and inflicting virtually every form of torture imaginable. Casement's report became the centerpiece of a British House of Commons Select Committee called to investigate the charges against British-owned rubber companies operating in the Putumayo region. Yet virtually nothing was done to change the situation, partly because the British could not assert political

A rubber plantation owner in Liberia in 1930 watches over a native worker cutting grooves in the tree to release the latex.

control over the region; in fact, one of the most brutal of the company managers later became a head of state.

The kinds of frontier situations described by Hardenburg and Casement almost a century ago, common in most areas of the periphery, still exist today. For example, consider what is happening to the Yanomami Indians of Brazil. Yanomami is the name given the Indians who live along the border between Brazil and Venezuela; in 1980 there were 10,000 Yanomami. They were protected somewhat by their isolation until the 1970s, when the Brazilian military government built a road that passed through Yanomami territory. The highway was never finished, but the traffic it brought to Yanomami country carried with it disease, starvation, and death. The highway brought gold miners, who forced some Yanomami out of their villages and massacred others; federal police were unable or unwilling to expel the miners, and the governor of the area refused to take judicial action against the murderers. Even the Brazilian Indian Service (FUNAI) was literally under attack by uniformed gunmen hired by the miners.

In 1986 the military enlarged a small airstrip that had been used by FUNAI and missionaries, ostensibly to protect the borders against drug trafficking and subversion, but resulting in intensification of the gold rush into Yanomami territory. As a result, by 1988 at least one-fourth of the Yanomami had died and the majority of survivors were sick and starving. When the situation caused an international outcry, the president of Brazil declared that it was impossible to expel the miners from the territory and even proposed demarcating three reserves in the area, not for the Yanomami but for the miners (Maybury-Lewis 1997:27). Alcida Ramos (1995:312) in a recent book on the situation among one Yanomami, the Sanumá, concluded:

> *I didn't expect to be around, only ten years after my immersion into an autonomous and healthy culture such as I found among the Sanumá, to see one of the worst examples of cultural devastation in the recent history of Brazilian Indigenism.*

Military Intervention

Military force was another means of destroying indigenous populations. Clearly the superiority of European weaponry made the difference in their confrontation with indigenous cultures, although not without some notable losses and defeats at the hands of less well-armed peoples. In 1860, when the Maori resisted the work of a survey team subdividing a large block of their land, the governor declared martial law and sent in the military to subdue them. The Maori managed to fight for twelve years against a force that at one time numbered 22,000 soldiers, costing the colony 500 people and 1.3 million pounds (Bodley 1990:50).

It was military intervention, of course, that finally subdued the Indians on the American Plains in the period from around 1850 to 1880. When Plains nations resisted takeover by Euro-Americans of their land and resources, the U.S. government sent in the military to control them, succeeding, as noted in Chapter 7, only after they destroyed the buffalo herds on which the Indian nations depended.

The Extension of Government Control

Once indigenous nations were militarily subdued, the next step in the process of cultural transformation was the extension of government control. When the nation-state is able to extend its authority, the indigenous society ceases being an autonomous "nation" and becomes incorporated into the state. In most cases rulers of the nation-state justified control as bringing to indigenous peoples the benefits of civilization. As John Bodley (1990:58) noted, however, it was directly related to protecting the economic interests of nonindigenous peoples moving into indigenous territory.

Various techniques were used to establish political control. One was simply *direct rule,* in which a person from the dominant group was appointed, after the military had subdued a population, to administer the subjugated group. The French did this in Africa, appointing French commissioners or heads. More common, and probably more effective, was the technique pioneered by the British in Africa, called *indirect rule.* This involved maintaining and strengthening the role of traditional leaders, or creating them when they did not exist, and governing through them (Bodley 1990:71).

The base camp program used by Australia to extend governmental control in Papua New Guinea proved to be particularly effective. The territory of Papua New Guinea was relatively isolated; even into the 1940s there were indigenous groups that had never been in direct contact with outside areas. To extend their control the Australian government would send an armed patrol with trade goods to establish a base camp in an area already under government influence. While the patrol was in camp, they offered highly prized trade goods such as salt, steel tools, and cloth to visitors to establish contact with surrounding villagers. Then they would move out to the villages and ask permission to build a rest house to allow longer visits by the patrol. While these requests were not always welcome, the villagers would generally be convinced by native interpreters. Then more distant villagers would come for trade goods, and the officer would agree to give them, but only if the villagers would build a road for him. When new villagers were visited, gifts would be distributed and perhaps a government-sponsored feast would be given. Peace agreements were drawn up and native police were strategically placed, after which village chiefs were appointed to act as intermediaries between the village and the government. Then annual visits by patrols were made. The Australian government considered the efforts at pacification successful when labor recruiters seeking workers for coastal plantations were allowed to operate freely in a village. In areas where resistance was more determined and where villagers might desert their homes when patrols were in the area, the patrols might kidnap old people left behind in the village until communications were established with resisters.

This process of peaceful penetration began in the 1920s and has continued uninterrupted, except during World War II, to the present. In 1950, for example, 168,350 square kilometers were not yet fully controlled. By 1970 only 1,735 square kilometers remained uncontrolled (Bodley 1990:66).

Land Policies

The policies of nation-states toward land ownership are one of the more delicate issues in the process of incorporating indigenous peoples or the resources they control into the nation-state. International law, and most governments, generally recognize that aboriginal inhabitants possess rights to the lands they use. For example, in 1787 the U.S. government declared in the Ordinance for the Government of the Northwest Territory (Fey and McNickle 1970:56),

> [t]he utmost good faith shall always be observed towards the Indians; their lands and property shall never be taken from them without their consent; and in their property rights and liberty, they never shall be invaded or disturbed, unless in just and lawful wars authorized by congress.

However, that policy was honored only so long as the Native Americans had a viable political presence and only so long as there was land that Euro-Americans did not want. Most early treaties recognized Indian rights to land and designated large areas in the West as Indian land. However, as European migration increased and as Indian land became desired, the government pressed to renegotiate old treaties, generally finding someone to negotiate with who would sign such treaties. However, even treaties could not protect Indian land from the U.S. Congress, as we saw in Chapter 3; in 1887 Congress passed the Indian Allotment Act (Dawes Act), which led to the appropriation of almost 100 million acres of Indian land (Jaimes 1992:126).

Cultural Modification Policies

After destroying the autonomy of indigenous peoples and gaining control of their lands and resources, the next step for the nation-state is to modify the culture. Any native custom considered immoral, offensive, or threatening was abolished. Indigenous kinship systems and social organization were particularly threatening to colonists. At various times such things as the payment of bride price, infant betrothal, polygamy, levirate (a man marrying his brother's widow), secret societies, and traditional kinship duties and obligations in general were attacked or banned. The extended family was particularly criticized by economic development agents even into the 1960s as a "drag on economic development and a serious obstacle to economic progress" (cited in Bodley 1990:96).

Unfortunately, in retrospect anthropologists played an important role, unwittingly or not, in the efforts to modify indigenous cultures and incorporate them into the nation-state. Even Margaret Mead (1961:19–20), one of the great spokespersons for tolerance and understanding of indigenous peoples, was convinced that tribal peoples she worked with wanted to "modernize": "We do not conceive of people being forcibly changed by other human beings. We conceive of them as seeing a light and following it freely."

Development theorists (Goulet 1971:25–26) suggested that "traditional people must be shocked into the realization that they are living in abnormal, inhuman conditions as psychological preparation for modernization."

Ward Goodenough (1963:219), one of the most respected figures in anthropology, noted in his book *Cooperation in Change*, that

> [t]he problem that faces development agents…is to find ways of stimulating in others a desire for change in such a way that the desire is theirs independent of further prompting from outside. Restated, the problem is one of creating in another a sufficient dissatisfaction with his present condition of self so that he wants to change it. This calls for some kind of experience that leads him to reappraise his self-image and reevaluate his self-esteem.

Education for Progress

One of the most effective ways indigenous cultures have been modified, as we noted in Chapter 4, is through formal education. As the French, British, German, and American governments used it to integrate those within their borders, so they used it to integrate colonial peoples. As John Bodley (1990:103) said,

In many countries schooling has been the prime coercive instrument of cultural modification and has proved to be a highly effective means of destroying self-esteem, fostering new needs, creating dissatisfactions, and generally disrupting traditional cultures.

Formal education often conflicted with indigenous teachings and served to undermine them. The schools established by the French in its African colonies taught two subjects, the French language and "morale," meaning ideals of "good habits" such as order, politeness, respect, and obedience. In Italian East Africa, boys were taught to farm and make crafts while girls were taught to cook native foods. Textbooks (see Bodley 1990:104) contained such passages as

I am happy to be subject to the Italian government and I love Italy with the affection of a son.

or

Help me, oh God, to become a good Italian.

Often the first efforts at education were controlled by missionaries. It was a useful partnership for both the church and the nation-state. The missionaries educated indigenous children in the ways of the nation-state while at the same time converting them to whatever religious faith they represented. Thus French Jesuit missionaries opened schools along the St. Lawrence River in 1611 with a government edict to "educate the Indians in the French manner"(cited Noriega 1992:371).

In the United States missionaries and church groups played a major role in indigenous education and were paid by the government to develop educational programs. One of the earliest models for missionary schools was the Methodist Episcopal Society, established in 1839 in Leavenworth, Kansas. The school was modeled on a rigid, military-style regimen. Indian students worked a 400-acre farm to raise money to pay for their education; since there were no labor costs, the school succeeded and became a model for hundreds more missionary-run manual labor schools. Soon separate schools were opened for girls. These schools remained missionary-controlled until the end of the nineteenth century.

By the end of the 1860s attendance at these schools was mandatory on many Indian reservations. However, it soon became apparent to government observers that day schools on the reservations left students too close to their family and culture. Consequently the government initiated a program of Indian boarding schools to isolate Indian students from the "contaminating" influences of their own society. In its final form the boarding school drew heavily from the penal procedures used to break the wills of indigenous resistance leaders, and owed much to the efforts of Richard H. Pratt. Pratt was an army captain who believed he could turn Native Americans into Whites; he convinced the government to allow him to run an educational program at the prison at St. Augustine, Florida, where captured

Indigenous students, carefully dressed in required Western-style clothing, attend class at the Carlisle Indian School. In this class, photographed in 1900, they are debating the resolution "that the Negroes of the South should not be denied the right of citizenship." The American government did not grant full citizenship to indigenous people until 1924.

Cheyenne leaders were held. He founded his first Indian boarding school in Carlisle, Pennsylvania; the school combined the manual labor model perfected by the missionaries with the penal model Pratt perfected in St. Augustine. Carlisle then served as the model for a national network of Indian boarding schools.

Indian children in boarding schools were isolated, given short haircuts, dressed in military-style uniforms, forced to maintain silence during meals, and forbidden to speak in their own language. Family visits were restricted and children were not allowed to return home, even during vacations. It was not unusual for a child who began at the school at the age of six not to see his or her home or family until the age of seventeen or eighteen. The boarding school program created individuals who, stripped of their own culture and language, did not fit into their culture of origin but were not accepted by the larger society.

People resisted. The Hopi, for example, hid their children from roving Mormon missionaries who wanted to gather the children and send them to the Intermountain School in Utah. Eventually the local Indian agent called in troops who assisted in the roundup, but not until they were bombarded with rocks from the tops of the mesas and forced to retreat temporarily. Although the boarding schools were gradually phased out, as late as 1973 of the 52,000 Indian children over whom the Bureau of Indian Affairs had control, 35,000 were in boarding schools.

As Jorge Noriega (1992:381) noted,

[t]he whole procedure conforms to one of the criteria—the forced transfer of children from a targeted racial, ethnic, national or religious group to be reared and absorbed by a physically dominating group—specified as a Crime Against Humanity under the United Nations 1948 Convention on Punishment and Prevention of the Crime of Genocide.

Economic Development

The next step in the destruction of indigenous cultures was integrating them into the national economy. This was sometimes achieved through violence, as in slavery and forced labor, and was sometimes far more subtle, coming under the rubric of "economic development." As Bodley (1990:114) pointed out, "development" is a highly ethnocentric term denoting growth, inevitability, and progress; "transformation" is a far more appropriate term in this context.

Initially the most common way of incorporating indigenous people into the capitalist economy was through forced labor. Settlers and colonial governments found that many people didn't want or need to work for wages—their consumption needs were modest and they met their basic needs by growing their own crops or sharing products among kinspersons or other groups. In French West Africa, conscript labor forces were required to spend three years working on highways, railroads, and irrigation projects. In some forced labor situations the death rate ranged up to 60 percent per year (Bodley 1990:116). Forced labor, common throughout colonized areas, was not internationally outlawed until 1957.

Another technique for forcing indigenous peoples into the capitalist economy was through taxation; forcing people to pay taxes (head taxes, poll taxes, etc.) in cash forced them to labor on White plantations, work in mines, or raise cash crops to pay the taxes. These measures were staunchly defended as necessary to "civilize the savages." U.S. legal authority Alpheus Snow (cited Bodley 1990:118) wrote in 1921 that "natives simply lack the acquisitive drive characteristic of civilized man, and doing virtually anything that will correct this mental deficiency is permissible and even a moral duty of the state."

Economic change was also fostered through technological development. A good example is the Zande Development Scheme. The Azande were a large population of hunters and shifting cultivators living in scattered homesteads in the southwest corner of Sudan. The British assumed administrative control in 1905 and proceeded to outlaw features of Azande culture that they found threatening, such as shield making, warrior societies, and even iron smelting. In 1911 the entire population was relocated along roads built by conscripted Azande labor and prevented from locating their farm plots in favored places in the forests or along streams. A head tax was introduced in the 1920s to force people to seek wage labor, and importation of British trade goods was encouraged. But the isolation of the area, the self-sufficiency of the population, and the lack of any resource in demand in the rest of the world inhibited the economic integration of the Azande into nation-state. Then in the 1930s, the government decided on an "economic development" program to introduce cotton as a cash crop. The agricultural development expert appointed to study the feasibility of the project called for a conversion of the Azande into

> *[h]appy, prosperous, literate communities...participating in the benefits of civilization through the cultivation of cotton and the establishment of factories to produce exportable products on the spot. (cited Bodley 1990:123)*

In 1944 the government justified the project, saying "We have a moral obligation to redeem its [the southern Sudan's] inhabitants from ignorance, superstition, poverty, malnutrition, etc." (cited Bodley 1990:123). By 1946 the project was underway with the building of a small complex that included facilities for spinning, weaving, and soap making and employing some 1500 Azande workers under European supervision. Every man in the district was required to work at least one month per year at $0.85–$1.30 per month. Furthermore, to facilitate development 50,000 Azande families, some 170,000 people, were removed from their roadside homes, where they had been forcibly resettled thirty years earlier, and relocated into geometrically arranged settlements and on to arbitrarily selected sites, without consideration of individual desires to be near kin.

The key to the project was the cotton growing, but the Azande had no desire to plant cotton; frustrated officials said the Azande had no "realization of what money could do for them." One solution was to force anyone who refused to grow cotton to do a month's labor on the roads as punishment. Yet, as remarkable as it seems, said Bodley (1990:124–125), the planners really did seem to have been driven by the best of intentions, "to bring progress, prosperity, and the reasonable decencies and amenities of human existence to the Azande." According to one district commissioner, "The object throughout has been to interfere as little as possible with the people's own way of life."

In 1965, twenty years after the project began, one Sudanese journalist

> *[r]eported enthusiastically that the standard of living in Zandeland was higher: consumption of sugar had doubled in just nine years; there were no naked people left; Azande women were dressed in the fashionable northern Sudanese style; and everyone had bicycles and lived in clean houses equipped with beds and mattresses... best of all, there were now swarms of children everywhere! (cited in Bodley 1990: 125)*

By the 1980s, the decline of the cotton market and a civil war in Sudan had left the Azande economy in virtual ruin.

These kinds of projects, of course, are common today. Governments in the periphery turn to areas occupied by the few remaining indigenous cultures in order to raise cash to pay off the debts they accumulated in the 1970s and 1980s. The results, as we shall see, continue to be devastating.

The Guaraní: The Economics of Ethnocide

It is difficult for any member of the culture of capitalism to take an unbiased view of indigenous peoples, that is not to view such groups as backward, undeveloped, economically depressed, and in need of civilizing. This, of course, is the way indigenous peoples have been portrayed for centuries. Theodore Roosevelt (cited Maybury-Lewis 1997:4), famous for his campaign to conserve nature, said "The settler and pioneer have at bottom had justice on their side; this great continent could not have been kept as nothing but a game preserve for squalid savages."

In the nineteenth century, "scientific" theories of evolution and racial superiority allowed people to rationalize the enslavement, confinement, or destruction of indigenous peoples. As late as the 1940s, British anthropologist Lord Fitzroy Raglan (cited Bodley 1990:11), who was to become president of the Royal Anthropological Institute, said that tribal beliefs in magic were a chief cause of folly and unhappiness. Existing tribes were plague spots: "We should bring to them our justice, our education, and our science. Few will deny that these are better than anything which savages have got." While many of these attitudes have changed, indigenous peoples still tend to be seen as needy dependents or victims, largely incapable of helping themselves. We tend to see their destruction as a consequence of their weakness, rather than of patterns of behavior and exploitation built into the culture of capitalism.

It may help to change that view if instead of seeing indigenous peoples as needy dependents living largely outmoded ways of life we consider the resemblance between indigenous societies and a modern, socially responsible corporation that carefully manages its resources, provides well for its workers, and plans for the long term rather than the short term. Looking at indigenous societies in this way may help us better appreciate why they don't survive. The fact is that environmentally and socially responsible corporations do not fare well in the capitalist world; they fail not because of any inherent weakness but because they become targets for takeovers by individuals or groups who, after taking the corporation over, quickly sell off the carefully managed resources solely to make a quick profit, leaving the corporation in ruin and its workers unemployed.

Take the fate of the Pacific Lumber Company. The family-owned company was known as one of the most environmentally and economically sound companies in the United States. It pioneered the practice of sustainable logging on its large holdings of redwoods and was generous to its employees, even overfunding its pension plan to ensure that it could meet its commitments. Furthermore, to ensure the security of its employees, it had a no-layoff policy. Unfortunately, the very features that made the company a model of environmental and social responsibility also made it a prime target for corporate raiders. After they took control of the company in the late 1980s they doubled the cutting rate on company lands, drained $55 million of the $93 million pension plan, and invested the remaining $38 million in a life insurance company that ultimately failed (Korten 1995:210). And the fate of Pacific Lumber is not unique.

Indigenous peoples possess all the characteristics that make them prime targets for takeovers. Like responsible corporations, they have managed their resources so well that those same resources (e.g. lumber, animals, farmlands) become targets for those who have used up theirs or who wish to make a quick profit. The indigenous peoples themselves become expendable, or themselves become resources to be exploited. To illustrate let's look at the case of the Guaraní as described by Richard Reed (1997).

History and Background

Most of the 15,000 Guaraní are settled in the rainforests of eastern Paraguay; they live in 114 communities ranging from three to four houses to over one hundred families. They are a minority population in a country in which most citizens are *mestizo* or *criollos,* descendants of Europeans who married Guaraní.

When Europeans arrived, over one million Guaraní and related groups lived in the area stretching from the Andes to the Atlantic Ocean. The Guaraní welcomed the first conquistadors, joining them in carving out trade routes to the Andes. The earliest reports of travelers indicate that the Guaraní system of production and standard of living were successful. In 1541 the region's first governor, Cabeza de Vaca (cited Reed 1997:8), noted that the Guaraní

> [a]re the richest people of all the land and province both for agriculture and stock
> raising. They rear plenty of fowl and geese and other birds, and have an abundance
> of game, such as boar, deer, and dantes (anta), partridge, quail and pheasants; and
> they have great fisheries in the river. They grow plenty of maize, potatoes, cassava,
> peanuts and many other fruits; and from the trees they collect a great deal of honey.

In addition to their economic success, the Guaraní were a relatively egalitarian society in which a person's place in society was determined by kinship. Leadership was usually determined by age, although political leaders had little or no power of coercion over others.

The Guaraní engaged European markets soon after contact, managing to combine their traditional subsistence activities of swidden agriculture and hunting and gathering with the collection of commercial products from the forests such as yerba mate, a naturally growing tea, animal skins, and honey. Anthropologists call this combination of productive activities *agroforestry,* the active management of forest resources for long-term production.

To understand agroforestry as practiced by the Guaraní, we need to understand a little about the nature of tropical rainforests. They are the most diverse biosystems on Earth, containing half the recorded species in the world, although only about 15 percent of these species have even been discovered. They are also among the most fragile ecosystems. A rainforest is a layered system, the top layer, or canopy, provided by large trees protecting the layers underneath it, with each species of plant or animal in lower layers dependent on the other's, and all surviving on a very thin layer of soil.

Guaraní agroforestry focuses on three activities: horticulture, hunting and gathering, and commercial tree cropping. The agriculture is shifting or swidden agriculture, in which small areas of the forests are cut and burned, the ash providing a thin layer of nutrients for the soil. These areas are planted until spreading weeds and decreased yields force the farmer to move to a new plot. The old plot is not abandoned but planted with banana trees and manioc, crops that need little care and which produce for up to four years. In this way land is gradually recycled back into tropical forest. Furthermore, these plots provide forage for deer, peccary, and other animals, which the Guaraní trap or shoot.

Fishing is another source of protein. Usually the Guaraní fish with poison. They crush the bark of the timbo tree and wash it through the water, leaving a thin seal on top of the water. They wait for the water to be depleted of oxygen and the stunned fish float to the surface. The Guaraní also fish with hook and lines. Other food sources include honey, fruit, the hearts of palm trees, and roots gathered from the forest floor.

Finally, to earn cash, the Guaraní collect yerba mate leaves, animal skins, oils, and food. In these activities the Guaraní use the forest extensively but not intensively. For example, they will cut leaves from all yerba trees but take only the mature leaves from each tree every three years, thus promoting the plants' survival. In addition, since the Guaraní harvest from a number of ecological niches and since their consumption needs are modest, they never overexploit a commodity to earn cash.

Thus the Guaraní use the forest to supplement their other subsistence activities, integrating this resource into their production system. It is a production system that is modeled after that of the rainforest itself; by incorporating trees the system preserves or recreates the forest canopy necessary for the survival of plants and animals below it. The surviving diversity of crops and animals ensures the recycling of nutrients necessary for their maintenance. In fact, as Richard Reed (1997:15) noted, "agroforestry often increases ecological diversity."

Agroforestry differs markedly from the typical exploitive forest activities in the culture of capitalism, such as intensive agriculture, lumbering, and cattle raising, activities modeled after factory production. First, indigenous production systems are diverse, allowing forest residents to exploit various niches in the forest without overexploiting any one niche. Second, unlike intensive agriculture, lumbering, or cattle raising, the Guaraní production system depends on the resources of plants and animals themselves rather than on the nutrients of the forest soils. Thus by moderate use of the soils, water, canopy, and fauna of the forest the Guaraní ensure that the whole system continues to flourish. Third, Guaraní production techniques lend themselves to a pattern of social relations in which individual autonomy is respected and in which activities do not lend themselves to a division of labor that lends itself to status hierarchy. The basic work unit is the family, with both men and women involved in productive labor—farming, gathering food, and collecting commercial products—and reproductive labor—child care, food preparation, and the construction and maintenance of shelters.

Fourth, unlike the activities of the culture of capitalism, the Guaraní mode of production is neither technology- nor labor-intensive. The Guaraní spend about 18 percent of their time in productive activities; one-third of that is devoted to horticulture, slightly less to forest subsistence activities, and about 40 percent to commercial activities. Another 27 percent of their time is devoted to household labor. In all, about half their daylight time is spent working; the rest is devoted to leisure and socializing. Reed said that the Guaraní workday is approximately half that of a typical European worker.

Finally, unlike capitalist production, which is tightly integrated into the global system, Guaraní production allows them a great deal of autonomy from the larger society. When prices for their products are too low, the Guaraní stop selling; if prices on store goods are too high, the Guaraní stop buying. Thus they do not have to rely on commercial markets; their stability is in their gardens, not their labor.

This autonomy can be attributed in part to the Guaraní's modest consumption needs. Food accounts for about 40 percent of the average family's monthly market basket—about two kilograms of rice, pasta, and flour; one kilogram of meat, a half liter of cooking oil, and a little salt. Cloth and clothing is the next most important purchase, perhaps a new shirt or pants (but not both) each year. Another one-fifth of the budget is spent on tools, such as machetes and axes, and an occasional luxury, such as tobacco, alcohol, or a tape recorder. Thus, as Reed (1997:75) noted, the Guaraní engage the global economic system without becoming dependent on it.

Contemporary Development and Guaraní Communities

Guaraní culture and their system of adaptation are, however, being threatened. Since the 1970s the rate of forest destruction in Paraguay has increased dramatically as forests are cleared to make way for monocultural agriculture and cattle ranching. As a result, Guaraní house lots stand exposed on open landscapes and families are being forced to settle on the fringes of mestizo towns. Reed made the point that it is not market contact or interethnic relations that are destroying the Guaraní; they have participated in the market and interacted with mestizo townspeople for centuries. Rather, it is a new kind of economic development spawned by the needs of the global economy.

After decades of little economic growth, in the 1970s the Paraguayan economy began to grow at the rate of 10 percent per year. This growth was fueled by enormous expansion of agricultural production, particularly cotton, soy, and wheat. Most of this growth came at the expense of huge tracts of rainforest felled to make way for the new cultivation. As Reed said, since 1970 every effort has been made to convert the land of eastern Paraguay into fields for commodity production. A number of things contributed to rainforest destruction.

First, roads built into the forests for military defense against Brazil contributed to the influx of settlers into the rainforest. Second, large-scale, energy-intensive agriculture displaced small farmers, who flooded to the cities in search of work.

This created pressures on these populations to find work or land, but rather than redistribute the vast tracts of cleared land held by wealthy cattle ranchers to peasants, the government chose to entice poor peasants into the forests with land distribution programs. Between 1963 and 1973, 42,000 families had been given land; between 1973 and 1976, 48,000 families were given a total of four million hectares of land.

A third factor was international finance. The oil boom of the 1970s, along with changes in currency, allowed core institutions to go on a lending spree as people sought ways to reinvest their profits. Like most other peripheral countries, Paraguay borrowed heavily in the 1970s to build roads, hydroelectric projects, and other things they believed necessary to build an industrial economy. The money that came into the country from the World Bank and other financial institutions needed to be reinvested by Paraguayan financiers, and some invested in farms and cattle ranches in the forests. Finally, to repay the loans, the country needed to raise funds, which it did by expanding agricultural growth in export crops, putting further demands on the rainforest.

The process of environmental destruction soon followed. For example, the Guaraní group Reed worked with (the Itanaramí) suffered their first major incursion in 1972, when the government cut a road into their forest. It was built partly to control the border with Brazil, but it also allowed logging in what had been impenetrable forests. Loggers brought in bulldozers to cut road directly to the hardwood trees. Lumber mills were positioned along the roads and the cut lumber was trucked to the capital city, where it was shipped to the United States, Argentina, and Japan. As Reed (1997:85) said, the forests that had provided the Guaraní with shelter and subsistence were cut down so that consumers in the United States, Europe, and Japan could enjoy furniture and parquet floors.

The roads also brought into the Guaraní forest impoverished Paraguayan families in search of land that they illegally cut to create fields in the forests, fields that will bear crops only for a short time before losing their fragile fertility. To complicate matters, Brazilian peasants, many displaced by large-scale agricultural projects in their own country, crossed the border seeking land on which to survive. The area even became home to a Mennonite community seeking to escape the pressures and problems of the larger world.

On the heels of these colonists came agribusiness concerns clearing more forest on which to raise soy and cotton. Within months of their arrival, thousands of hectares of forest were cut down and replaced by fields of cash crops. The road that had brought in the military, loggers, and peasant colonists was now used to haul out produce for foreign markets and for cattle drives to deliver meat to consumers across South and North America.

Thus in the same way that corporate raiders seize responsible corporations to turn a quick profit, often destroying them in the process, people seeking a profit from the lands of the Guaraní quickly destroyed the forest. The logging companies cut the trees that provided the canopy for the forests as well as the trunks on which vines such as orchids and philodendron climbed. Without the protective cover of the large trees, the enormous diversity of life that thrived beneath the canopy, was

A landless Guaraní family in Brazil living in roadside tents.

no longer viable. Faunal populations declined immediately because their habitat was being destroyed and because they were being hunted to extinction by the new settlers. With the flora and fauna decimated, all that remained was a fragile layer of topsoil, which the harsh sunlight and rains quickly reduced to its clay base.

The rate of forest destruction was enormous. From 1970 to 1976, Paraguayan forests were reduced from 6.8 million to 4.2 million hectares. Half of the remaining forest was cut by 1984 and each year thereafter another 150,000–200,000 hectares has fallen to axes and bulldozers. At this rate, the Paraguayan forests will be gone by the year 2025.

More to the point for this discussion, with the rainforest went the way of life of the Guaraní. When Reed first began working with the Itanaramí in 1981 they were isolated in the forest, living largely as they had for centuries. By 1995 they were on a small island of forest in an "ocean of agricultural fields."

The Guaraní had no legal title to the land they have inhabited for centuries, such title being claimed by the nation-state; those who bought the land from the government assume they have both a legal and moral right to remove any people occupying the land. Even when Guaraní were allowed to retain their houseplots their traditional system of agroforestry was impossible because their forest was being destroyed and they were forced to seek new and smaller plots. Furthermore, the settlers destroyed their hunting stock, so the Guaraní quickly came to depend for meat on the occasional steer slaughtered by ranchers in the towns, for which the Guaraní had to pay cash. But the ranchers destroyed the stands of yerba mate, a source of cash for the Guaraní, that they had cultivated for centuries.

Gradually, with their traditional production system destroyed, the Guaraní were forced to enter the market economy as cotton or tobacco growers or as wage laborers on the lands they had sustained for centuries. Those who entered the agricultural sector found that the new system of farming was capital-intensive and required inputs of fertilizers, herbicides, and insecticides. Families went into debt becoming dependent on mestizo merchants and lenders. Those who chose to work found that wages were often too low to support a family, forcing several or all family members to work. Furthermore, labor required people to travel outside their communities so that even those families who managed to gain access to land on which to garden had little time for it. Since wage labor demands the strongest workers, it is often the youngest and strongest who must leave their communities.

There are other effects. Illness and disease became more prevalent. Suicide, virtually unknown previously in Guaraní communities, increased from a total of six in 1989 to three suicides per month in the first half of 1995. The leadership system collapsed, as religious leaders who earned their authority through their ability to mediate disputes found themselves helpless to mediate the new problems that arose between Guaraní and mestizo or government bureaucrats. Today the government appoints community leaders, to make it easier for them to control and negotiate with Guaraní communities. These new leaders derive their power from assistance programs that funnel resources to the Guaraní, but which many leaders use to reward friends and relatives and punish non-kin and enemies.

In sum, the debt assumed by the Paraguayan government to foster economic expansion and the resulting expansion of capital-intensive farming and cattle ranching in the 1980s disrupted Guaraní society more than had four centuries of contact; as a result its members are dispersing and assimilating into the larger society. It would be easy to condemn the Paraguayan government, and other governments whose indigenous peoples are being destroyed. Yet the nation-states are only doing what capital controllers are supposed to do: they are choosing modes of production and ways of life that will bring the greatest immediate monetary return.

Ethnic Violence and the Question of Political Sovereignty

Indigenous peoples are not the only ones to suffer at the hands of the nation-state. Ethnic groups have also been subject to persecution and violence. Few if any nation-states do not have within their borders groups of people who, because of some characteristic—common language, religion, skin color, geographic origin, or mode of livelihood—claim to share, or are said by others to have, a sense of relatedness that resembles kinship (Maybury-Lewis 1997:60). However, ethnic groups, like nation-states, are socially created; thus whether a particular group chooses to emphasize or ignore its own or another's distinctiveness is a social decision. Very often ethnicity is used as a political tool by "ethnic entrepreneurs" to rally support for their own cause (Maybury-Lewis 1997); in other cases it is used to stigmatize groups so that others may gain an economic or social advantage. But however ethnicity is defined, it has proved to be a major factor in global conflict, particularly in violence by nation-states against its own citizens.

There are all kinds of rules and regulations established by the Geneva Convention on how citizens of one country may treat those of another country, and while they are frequently ignored they serve to some extent to limit arbitrary interstate brutality. However, other than the unenforceable Universal Declaration of Human Rights of the United Nations Charter, there are no internationally agreed on conventions on how individual states can treat their citizens, particularly those who are defined or who define themselves as somehow distinct. Yet of the ninety-four wars recorded since the end of World War II, sixty-nine were intra-state conflicts, resulting in the death of 17–30 million people, most of them civilians. Numbers such as these stagger the imagination and mask the individuality of the horror and the means of death.

After the U.S.-sponsored military overthrow of an elected government in Guatemala in 1954, the country went through almost 35 years of civil war. During this time military governments tried to assert their control over a reluctant citizenry while protecting the property rights of an entrenched elite, including those of various American corporations, the biggest being the United Fruit Company. During the most violent period of the 1980s, some 200,000 people, mostly Mayan Indians, were murdered by the state. One of those was the sixteen-year-old brother of Nobel Peace Prize Winner, Rigoberta Menchú (1984:172ff). Arrested by the military on suspicion of being a "subversive," he was tortured by being forced to run after having his testicles tied behind him. Then his captives cut off his fingernails, fingers, and parts of his skin. The skin on his head was pulled down over his face, while the fleshy part of his face was cut off. After sixteen days of such torture he was brought, along with other captives, to the center of a village. In an event announced in advance by the soldiers and in front of his mother and sister, Petrocinio Menchú Tum, unrecognizable to all but his mother, was exhibited naked by an army captain who explained in graphic detail what was done to the captives, warning others of the same fate. Then, along with the other captives, he was doused with gasoline and burned alive. Multiply the terror, suffering, and grieving of that one death by the millions of members of minority ethnic groups killed by state-sanctioned violence, and you begin to get an idea of the inhumanity of state-sponsored death.

Why does ethnic violence happen? Why would Hutu want to slaughter Tutsi, some of whom were their neighbors, friends, even relatives? Why would Bosnian Serbs want to massacre and rape Bosnian Muslims after centuries of coexistence? Blaming such violence on "ancient hatreds" doesn't make much sense when these groups had lived together peacefully for centuries. That's like blaming ancient hatreds for gang violence between Irish and Italian or between African-American and Hispanic youngsters in New York.

A funeral procession in Guatemala in the early 1980s for men killed by the military and exhumed from a mass grave.

If we examine cases of purported ethnic conflict we generally find that it involves more than ancient hatred; even the "hatreds" we find are relatively recent, and constructed by those ethnic entrepreneurs taking advantage of situations rooted in colonial domination and fed by neocolonial exploitation. In this regard, the case of Rwanda is instructive.

Genocide in Rwanda

Perhaps there is no better case than Rwanda of state killing in which colonial history and global economic integration combined to produce genocide. It is also a case where the causes of the killing were carefully obscured by Western governmental and journalistic sources and blamed instead on the victims and ancient tribal hatreds.

A country the size of Belgium, with a population of 7 million people (overpopulated according to most reports, but Belgium supports over 10 million people),

Rwanda experienced in 1994 one of the worst genocides of the twentieth century. Some 800,000 people, mostly but not exclusively Tutsis, were slaughtered by the Hutu-run state. Contrary to media and many government reports, the genocide was largely the result of Rwanda's political and economic position in the capitalist world system. It involved such global factors as its colonial history, the price of coffee, World Bank and International Monetary Fund policies, the global interests of Western nations, particularly France, the interests of international aid agencies, and Western attitudes toward Africa (Shalom 1996).

Archeological evidence suggests that the area that is now Rwanda was first inhabited by Twa-speaking hunters and gatherers, who dominated the area until around A.D. 1000. Hutu speakers then began to settle in the area, setting up farms and a clan-based system of monarchies that dominated the Twa. Around the sixteenth century, new immigrants from the Horn of Africa, the cattle-raising Tutsi, arrived and set up their own monarchy in Rwanda, establishing a system in which Hutu were tied economically as "clients" to Tutsi "patrons." In reality, it was rarely possible based on physical characteristics to tell who was Hutu and who was Tutsi. Tutsi became a term applied to lineages that controlled wealth in the form of cattle, while Hutu were those without wealth and who were not tied to powerful people. The political system was not unlike that which existed in many other parts of Africa and which still exists today in some countries. The Hutus maintained their own chiefs, intermarriage was not uncommon, and many Hutus could attain power and influence virtually equal to that of Tutsi chiefs. In fact, a poor Tutsi could slide into becoming a Hutu and a wealthy Hutu lineage could become Tutsi (Maybury-Lewis 1997:101).

When the Germans assumed control of the area after the Berlin Conference of 1884, they applied their racist ideology and assumed that the generally taller, lighter-skinned Tutsis were the more "natural" rulers, while the Hutus were destined to serve them. Consequently the Germans increased Tutsi influence.

After the defeat of Germany in World War I, Belgium took over colonial control of Rwanda, and further intensified the split between Tutsi and Hutu by institutionalizing racist doctrines. They replaced all Hutu chiefs with Tutsis and issued identity cards that noted ethnic identity, making the division between Hutu and Tutsi far more rigid than it had been before colonial control. They also gave the Tutsi elite the responsibility to collect taxes and administer the justice system. The Tutsi chiefs used this new power granted them by Belgian rule to gain Hutu land. However, excluding the wealth and status of Tutsi chiefs, the average financial situation of Hutus and Tutsis was about the same.

Both groups were subject to the harsh colonial rule of Belgium in which forced labor was common, taxes were increased, and the beating of peasants by Belgian colonists became standard practice. Furthermore, the colonial rulers transformed the economy, requiring peasants to shift their activities from subsistence or food crops to export crops, such as coffee. Coffee production had the effect of extending the amount of arable land, since it required volcanic soil that was not productive for other, particularly food, crops. As we shall see, this had far-reaching consequences and would contribute to the conditions that precipitated the genocide.

In the 1950s the Tutsis began to campaign for independence from their colonial rulers. Since Belgians believed the Hutu would be easier to control, they shifted their support to them and began to replace Tutsi chiefs with Hutu. In 1959, when clashes between Hutu and Tutsi broke out, the Belgians allowed Hutus to burn down Tutsis houses. Belgium then allowed the Hutu elite to engineer a coup, and independence was granted to Rwanda on July 1, 1962. It is unclear how many Tutsis were killed in the actions preceding independence, but estimates vary from 10,000 to 100,000. In addition, 120,000–500,000 Tutsis fled the country to neighboring countries such as Burundi and Zaire, from which Tutsi guerrillas engineered raids into Rwanda. Within Rwanda, the Hutu rulers established ethnic quotas limiting Tutsi access to education and government employment.

In 1973 a military coup d'état brought to power Juvenal Habyarimana, who promised to establish "national unity." To this end he installed one-party political rule of the National Revolutionary Movement for Development (MRND) and made Rwanda a one-party state. While the government or party was clearly totalitarian in nature, foreign powers appreciated the fact that Habyarimana "ran a tight ship," even requiring all Rwandans to participate in collective labor on Saturday. In fact, Habyarimana achieved many needed reforms: the civil service was modernized, clean water was made available to virtually everyone, per capita income rose, and money flowed in from Western donors. However, some projects, often imposed by multilateral organizations, were fiascoes and probably contributed to Hutu–Tutsi enmity. For example, in 1974 the World Bank financed a project to establish cattle ranches over an area of 51,000 hectares. The bank hired a Belgian anthropologist, René Lemarchand, to appraise the project; he warned that the Hutu were using the project to establish a system of patronage and spoils that served to reduce the size of Tutsi herds and grazing areas and to increase Tutsi economic and political dependence on the Hutu, and that the project was aggravating Hutu–Tutsi conflicts. Lemarchand's warnings were ignored (Rich 1994:93).

Soon, whatever progress Rwanda was making to climb out of the pit of its colonial past was undermined by the collapse of the value of its export commodities—tin and, more important, coffee. Until 1989, when coffee prices collapsed, coffee was, after oil, the second most traded commodity in the world. In 1989, negotiations over the extension of the International Coffee Agreement, a multinational attempt to regulate the price paid to coffee producers, collapsed when the United States, under pressure from large trading companies, withdrew, preferring to let market forces determine coffee prices. This resulted in coffee producers glutting the market with coffee and forcing coffee prices to their lowest level since the 1930s. While this did little to affect coffee buyers and sellers in wealthy countries, it was devastating to the producing countries, such as Rwanda, and to the small farmers who produced the coffee.

If you are a coffee consumer, especially one who likes the new premium, fresh-roasted varieties, you will pay between eight to ten dollars per pound. Of that, fifty to seventy cents represents the world market price, of which thirty to fifty cents goes to the farmer who produced the coffee. The remainder goes to mid-level buyers, exporters, importers, and the processing plants that sell and market the coffee.

For Rwanda, the consequences of the collapse of coffee prices meant a 50 percent drop in export earnings between 1989 and 1991. Furthermore, since the soil in which coffee was grown is useless for most other crops (except coca, the source of cocaine), farmers could not shift production to other crops.

The sudden drop in income for small farmers resulted in widespread famine, as farmers no longer had income with which to purchase food. The consequence for the Rwandan state elite was just as devastating; the money required to maintain the position of the rulers had come from coffee, tin, and foreign aid. With the first two gone, foreign aid became even more critical, so the Rwandan elite needed more than ever to maintain state power in order to maintain access to that aid.

However, maintaining access to aid, particularly from multilateral organizations, required agreeing to financial reforms imposed by those organizations. In September 1990, the IMF imposed a structural adjustment program on Rwanda that devalued the Rwandan franc and further impoverished the already devastated Rwandan farmers and workers. The prices of fuel and consumer necessities were increased, and the austerity program imposed by the IMF led to a collapse in the education and health system. Severe child "malnutrition" increased dramatically, and malaria cases increased 21 percent due largely to the unavailability of antimalarial drugs in the health centers. In 1992, the IMF imposed another devaluation, further raising the prices of essentials to Rwandans. Peasants uprooted 300,000 coffee trees in an attempt to grow food crops, partly to raise money, but the market for local food crops was undermined by cheap food imports and food aid from the wealthy countries.

While the economy was collapsing, the Rwandan Patriotic Front (RPF), a group of Tutsi refugees from Uganda, invaded the country to overthrow the Habyarimana regime. Thus the state was confronted with crisis from two directions: economic collapse precipitated by the fall in coffee prices and military attacks from Tutsis who had been forced out of the country by ethnic rivalries fueled by colonial rulers. Fortunately, the Habyarimana regime was able to parley the invasion by the RPF into more foreign aid. The French, anxious to maintain their influence in Africa, began providing weapons and support to the Rwandan government, and the army grew from 5,000 to 40,000 from October 1990 to mid-1992. A French military officer took command of a counterinsurgency operation. Habyarimana used the actions by the RPF to arrest 10,000 political opponents and permitted the massacre of some 350 Tutsis in the countryside.

In spite of increased state oppression and the French-supported buildup of the armed forces, in January 50,000 Rwandans marched in a prodemocracy demonstration in Kigali, the country's capital. Hutu extremists in Habyarimana's government argued to crush the opposition on a massive scale, but instead, he introduced democratic reform and allowed the political opposition to assume government posts, including that of prime minister. However, he also authorized the establishment of death squads within the military—the *Interahamwe*, ("those who attack together") and the *Impuzamugambi* ("those with a single purpose")—who were trained, armed, and indoctrinated in racial hatred toward Tutsis. These were the groups that would control most of the killing that was to follow.

Hutus being trained by the French military. Formed into special brigades, units such as this were largely responsible for the deaths of hundreds of thousands Tutsis and politically moderate Hutus.

By this time, the coming crisis was becoming evident; human rights groups were warning about the existence of the death squads, and members of Habyarimana's inner circle set up a new radio station—a potent source of power in a country that is 60 percent illiterate—using it to denounce attempts to forge a peace agreement between the government and the RPF and inciting racial hatred. Acts of violence against Tutsis increased after the president of neighboring Burundi was killed in an attempted coup by Tutsi army officers. Hutus were incited to kill Tutsis, and the RPF responded by killing Hutus: some 50,000 peasants were reported killed, slightly more Tutsis than Hutus.

As Habyarimana continued to negotiate with the opposition under international pressure to reach a settlement, his plane (a gift from President Mitterrand of France) was shot down, killing him and everyone on board. The identity of the persons who fired the missile has never been proved, but most independent analysts agree it must have been Hutu extremists close to Habyarimana. Within an hour of Habyarimana's death, roadblocks were put up throughout Kigali as militia and death squads preceded to kill moderate Hutus, including the prime minister, whose names were on prepared lists. Then the death squads went after every Tutsi they could find, inciting virtually everyone in the civil service to join in the killing. The Hutu extremists set up an interim government committed to genocide. Yet, even when it was clear to most people that the genocide was orchestrated by an authoritarian state, journalists as well as U.N. Secretary General Boutros Boutros-Ghali would characterize the slaughter as "Hutus killing Tutsis and Tutsis killing Hutus." Building on Western stereotypes of savage Africans, Mayor Ed Koch, of New York City, characterized the genocide as "tribal warfare involving those without the veneer of Western civilization."

As long as the killing could be characterized as interethnic violence, the core states, whose actions had created the situation for the killings and whose economic policies precipitated the violence, could distance themselves from the conflict. It wasn't until months later, after some 800,000 Tutsis had been killed, that government leaders in the West began to acknowledge the genocide.

The slaughter did not end until the RPF finally defeated the government's armies and took control of the country. But the dying didn't stop. The fleeing Hutu elite used radio broadcasts to incite fear in the Hutu populace that to remain in the country meant certain retaliation from Tutsi survivors and the victorious RPF. Consequently, millions of Hutus fled the country, gathering in refugee camps in neighboring countries and becoming a country in exile for the Hutu extremists who fled with them, using their control over the fleeing army to maintain control of the Hutus in refugee camps. The press and media coverage of the refugees also served as a fund-raising bonanza for foreign aid organizations, although some 80,000 Hutus died in cholera epidemics in the camps. It was not until 1996 that Hutu refugees began to return to Rwanda and to the government of reconciliation established by the RPF.

In sum, the Rwandan disaster was hardly a simple matter of tribal warfare or ancient hatreds. It was the case of an excolonial, core-supported state threatened with core-initiated economic collapse and internal and external dissension resorting to genocide to remove the opposition that included, in this case, both Tutsis and moderate Hutus.

Rights of Self-Determination

One of the features of the modern world are the many ethnic and indigenous groups arguing, sometimes violently, for greater recognition, autonomy, and control over economic resources claimed by the nation-state. Some even demand the right to their own nation-state. The nation-state of which they are a part often responds with political repression and violence. The multiethnic Indonesian state is busy suppressing East Timorese who were unwillingly included in the Indonesian state given its independence by the Dutch. The Russians recently fought an independence movement in Chechynia, while the Ethiopian government battles its own independence movement. Almost half of the residents of Quebec want some kind of independence from the rest of Canada, while Native Americans in Guatemala, Mexico, El Salvador, Peru, Canada, the United States, and elsewhere demand independence or better representation. Tamils fight for independence in Sri Lanka, and the British try to control the independence aspirations of Catholics in Northern Ireland. In fact, there are probably few nation-states in which there is not some group striving for greater representation and which are not answering those demands with force or the threat of force. This raises some crucial questions: *What are the rights of a people, however defined, for independence or the right to form their own government?* More specifically, *does there exist a person who, by virtue of his or her humanity, enjoys a set of specific rights above and beyond the entitlements granted by the nation-state?* (Nagengast 1994:128).

Article One of the Universal Declaration of Human Rights of the United Nations seems to be unambiguous in making political self-determination a basic human right. Yet while it recognizes the rights of individuals to self-determination, it does not give that right to societies or groups. The United Nations extends that right only in very specific cases in which there is also a territorial basis to the claim.

One way out of this problem has been to recognize limited rights of indigenous or ethnic groups within a state, rights to certain kinds of education, social affairs, culture, while defense, international trade relations, and diplomatic affairs are left to the central state. But the question of self-determination can lead to some strange situations.

For example, in 1994 the people of Quebec voted in a referendum whether or not to begin negotiations with the federal government to secede from Canada and establish their own nation-state. The referendum was defeated but by less than 1 percent of the vote; it is likely there will be another in the years to come. The dilemma has to do with the indigenous people of Quebec, the Cree, Montagnais, Inuit, Naskapi, and Innu. If Quebec has the right to secede because of its claim to be a "distinct society," then surely the indigenous peoples have the same right. Yet when faced with the question of rights of self-determination of indigenous peoples in Quebec, Lucien Bouchard, Premier of Quebec, replied that the right of self-determination belonged to the "Quebec people" but not to the Indians (cited Coon Come 1996). *On what ground can the Quebec government justify its claim to sovereignty on the basis of its distinct language, culture, and history, and at the same time deny the right to Cree, Montagnais, Naskapi, Inuit, and Innu?*

Matthew Coon Come (1996), then Grand Chief of the Cree Nation, in a 1996 speech at the Harvard Center for International Affairs and Kennedy School of Government observed that

> *[t]he Quebec government has pursued an odious solution in its quest for absolute sovereignty over the corner of America they call their own. This solution is the systematic minimization and denial of our status as a people and of our Aboriginal, treaty and constitutional rights. The secessionists' double standards with regard to our rights have now reached new and disturbing depths—so low that they challenge basic principles of decolonization and universal human rights.*

The issue of sovereignty and human rights raises the question: *What are the rights of individuals vis-à-vis the nation-state? Is it possible for individuals to make appeals to justice above and often against their own state?*

During the past fifty years there has been some recognition that individuals because of their ethnic group membership or political views can appeal to international agencies or groups for physical and judicial protection. Most influential are groups such as Amnesty International, the United Nations, Cultural Survival, and Watch Committees. Amnesty International, for example, was launched in 1961 by British lawyer Peter Benenson with a newspaper appeal, "The Forgotten Prisoners," published worldwide in May 1961. The appeal marshaled an international campaign to support human rights. Within a year the organization had sent delegates to four countries to represent prisoners in 210 cases. Today Amnesty International has more than 1 million members, subscribers, and donors representing over 190 countries and territories, as well as 4,341 local Amnesty International groups registered with the International Secretariat, plus several thousand school, university, professional, and other groups in 93 countries. The central office, in London, has a permanent staff of 300 and 95 volunteers from over 50 countries.

Amnesty International has a precise mandate outlined in an international statute: to free all prisoners of conscience, that is people detained anywhere for their beliefs or because of their ethnic origin, sex, color, or language, who have not advocated or used violence. Its members and staff also work to ensure fair and prompt trials for political prisoners and to abolish torture, capital punishment, and cruel treatment of prisoners, along with extrajudicial executions and "disappearances."

As an international conscience for human rights and to protect individuals from the violence of their own states, Amnesty International not only sends representatives to investigate reports of government abuse but also attempts to enlist the commitment of states themselves to end abuses. One of its most powerful weapons is its ability to marshal international support, largely by publicizing what it deems to be human rights violations. For example, in its 1996 annual report Amnesty International documents human rights violations in 146 countries. This includes extrajudicial executions in 63 countries including Burundi, Colombia, Brazil, India, Russia, and Rwanda; 10,000 cases of prisoners subject to torture in 114 countries including Indonesia, Iran, Mexico, and Sudan; 4,500 cases of death by torture in 54 countries including Kenya, Egypt, Myanmar, and Turkey; 46,000 people held in jail without being charged in 43 countries including Israel, Azerbaijan, and Paraguay; 5,500 people under sentence of death in 31 countries, including Japan, Kenya, and the United States, where 56 people were executed in 1995, the highest number since 1977.

Thousands of people are held as prisoners of conscience, charged because they spoke out against the ruling government; Amnesty International lists 2,200 in China, over 1,000 in India, 1,000 in Afghanistan, and 300 in Sri Lanka. Thousands of people have been reported "disappeared," while paramilitary groups or death squads supported and sometimes trained and equipped by their government carry out the dirty work, allowing those in power to deny responsibility for human rights violations. In Colombia, for example, more than 150 people disappeared after being held by the military, police, or paramilitary forces. Amnesty International notes deaths in the United States of people in police custody in disputed circumstances, and widespread allegations of torture and ill treatment by police and prison officials.

Anthropologists have been particularly active in seeking to end abuses against indigenous peoples and ethnic groups. Cultural Survival, founded in 1972 by David Maybury-Lewis to defend the rights of indigenous peoples, has been one of the leaders. It sponsors research, advocacy, and publications, such as *Cultural Survival Quarterly,* that examine situations that threaten indigenous groups, makes suggestions to solve conflicts, and attempts to marshal international support to pressure nation-states to observe the rights of individuals and groups.

The American Anthropological Association, the major professional association of anthropologists, has adopted a more activist role in situations that threaten the integrity of indigenous people. One example is the letter written by the association's president, Yolanda Moses (now president of City College of New York) to Brazil's president, Fernando Henrique Cardoso, protesting his government's plan to reopen to land claims the reserves of some 344 indigenous groups in the Amazon basin.

The extent to which these efforts will affect the policies of nation-states is questionable. We have reviewed the extent to which the power of capital drives the actions of the nation-states, along with the growing power of multinational corporations, whose interests almost always conflict with those of indigenous peoples and ethnic groups seeking to protect their resources and culture or claiming greater self-determination. Yet, as we shall see in Part III, protest against nation-states or the culture of capitalism itself is far more widespread than most people realize.

Conclusion

We observed at the beginning of the chapter that one of the casualties of the expansion of the culture of capitalism is cultural diversity. There are a number of reasons, including profound cultural incompatibilities between indigenous peoples and the culture of capitalism and the need of the nation-state to ensure their political authority and control over economic resources desired by corporations or the nation-state itself. We also observed that the very features that make indigenous peoples excellent custodians of the environment make them susceptible to takeover and destruction.

Furthermore, we concluded that conflict between groups within nation-states, often characterized as ethnic violence, has more to do with the economic consequences of the expansion of consumer capitalism and the actions of the nation-state. Finally, we examined the issue of national self-determination and the rights of individuals in the nation-state and the actions of groups such as Amnesty International and Cultural Survival.

Related to all of these issues is whether the incorporation of indigenous peoples or ethnic groups into nation-states and the culture of capitalism is beneficial or harmful to them. That is, as John Bodley (1990:138) asked, *does entry into consumer capitalism increase or decrease a given culture's ability to satisfy the physical and psychological needs of its population or its stability?*

Bodley (1990:138–139) concluded that a careful examination of the conditions of indigenous peoples before and after their incorporation into the world market economy,

> *[l]eads to the conclusion that their standard of living is* lowered, *not raised, by economic progress—and often to a dramatic decline.* This is perhaps the most outstanding and inescapable fact to emerge from the years of research that anthropologists have devoted to the study of culture change and modernization. *(emphasis added)*

Part III

Resistance and Rebellion

People resist exploitation. They resist it as actively as they can, as passively as they must.
IMMANUEL WALLERSTEIN, ANTISYSTEMIC MOVEMENTS

Chapter 10

Peasant Protest, Rebellion,
and Resistance

The bourgeoisie cannot exist without constantly revolutionizing the instruments of production, and thereby the relations of production, and with them the whole relations of society.
KARL MARX AND FREDERICK ENGELS,
MANIFESTO OF THE COMMUNIST PARTY

The cruelties of property and privilege are always more ferocious than the revenges of poverty and oppression.
C. L. R. JAMES, THE BLACK JACOBINS

On January 1, 1994, the Zapatista Army of Liberation (EZLN) announced its existence by briefly occupying highland towns in the state of Chiapas in Mexico. In its declaration of war against the government, the Zapatistas claimed to represent the indigenous people of Mexico. It is unlikely that the Zapatistas, a group of poorly armed peasant farmers, had any hope of fighting and winning a revolution against a Mexican military equipped with modern weapons supplied in large part by the United States, but they did threaten a guerrilla war in one of the most inaccessible areas of the country.

The Zapatista protest, which we will examine in more detail below, is but one example of social resistance, protest, and rebellion that mark the expanding culture of capitalism. Social protest in the form of marches, worker's strikes, religious and social movements, terrorism, and revolution seems an endemic feature of our emerging global culture. There are few days that one cannot find media reports of people protesting against a perceived injustice at the hands of some group, corporation, or state. It is difficult to say whether our period of history is more prone than others to nonviolent and violent protest. Historians Charles, Louise, and Richard

Tilly (1975) referred to the years 1830–1930 in Europe as the "rebellious century," and historian Eric Hobsbawm (1964) called the period including and following the French Revolution the Age of Revolution. But our own period of history has its own claim to these titles.

Many people in the United States are actively involved in or support some protest movement: a civil rights organization, an organization protesting religious, gender, or ethnic discrimination, a group protesting against corporations and the state for environmental destruction, a militia group protesting what they see as illegal government actions, a religious group protesting the increasing secularization of society or what they see as threats to the traditional family, and so on. If we add to this people's day-to-day acts of resistance, even just symbolical ones, against what they consider oppressive conditions or excessive demands made by others in such everyday settings as the workplace and school, we begin to appreciate how much of our lives involve, in one way or another, social protest.

How can we begin to make sense of these actions? Who is protesting? Against whom is the protest directed? What are the conditions that are being objected to? What form does the protest take? Finally, what is the reaction to the protest?

One way to make sense of social protest, at least from a global perspective, is to examine the extent to which it is a consequence of the globalization of capitalist culture. We have already seen how many people have benefited from the spread and expansion of capitalistic trade. Some people enjoy lives that were unthinkable 600, 300, even 100 years ago. But not all people benefited from the development and expansion of trade. Farmers and peasants who lost their land and were made dependent on sporadic wage labor are not better off; women, certainly in the periphery, may not be better off; the quality of the lives of children in many countries declined with the globalization of the economy; indigenous peoples have not fared well; those condemned to live in conditions in which disease thrives, those suffering because of environmental degradation, and those forced by the segmentation of labor to work for less than a living wage cannot be said to be better off.

In many ways, the central role of trade in the culture of capitalism has increased the gap between the rich and the poor, creating conditions ripe for the emergence of social protest. Thus conflict and protest represent not an occasional tear in the fabric of capitalist culture; protest is woven into the fabric as an intrinsic part of the way of life. As Karl Marx and Frederick Engels suggested, it is capitalism that is revolutionary, constantly changing patterns of work and social relations in search of profit and producing protest against those changes.

What leads people to protest, riot, or even revolt? There has been a tendency for social scientists and others to see in these actions a breakdown of some sort in the social order. So-called functional theories of protest assumed that in the normal workings of society protest is unnecessary and unhealthy. Order, rather than conflict, is the normal state of affairs. According to this popular framework, when protest, especially violent protest, is present, we will find uprooted, marginal, and disorganized people. This framework has often been applied in U.S. government-sponsored reports about the urban riots of the 1960s and 1970s. The reports concluded that the disruptions were the result of the marginalization of the poor, of the breakdown of social order.

However, another perspective suggests that the constant changes inherent in capitalist production, distribution, and consumption makes conflict inevitable: there are always changes taking place in modes of production and organization of labor, in market mechanisms, technological innovation, and so forth. Since all such changes bring some form of social and economic dislocation, we can expect protest to be the "normal" state of affairs. Furthermore, protests are not spontaneous uprisings but movements that bring together in organized fashion people who share certain interests, and who organize to express those interests. Generally, these movements develop from sustained resistance of some sort. Finally, when such movements involve violence, the violence is generally initiated by those against whom the protest is directed (Tilly et al. 1975:243). Thus while a labor strike may turn violent, in most cases the violence is initiated by the government, company or private militia, or police.

In this and the next two chapters we will examine the phenomenon of social protest, the different forms it takes, and the groups it most affects. In this chapter we will focus on peasant protest. Small-scale agriculturists have been among the groups most affected by the expansion of capitalism. As agriculture becomes more mechanized and landholdings concentrated in the hands of a few, more peasants have been driven off the land and forced to seek wage labor on the larger farms or in urban areas. Many resist this change in their living conditions. The question is, *how are we to understand the actions of peasant farmers who wish to resist or take up arms against a heavily armed and obviously superior opponent? Can they hope to win?*

History, of course, is full of successful and unsuccessful peasant revolutions. Eric Wolf (1969) examined successful peasant-inspired revolutions in Mexico, Russia, China, Algeria, and Vietnam. China, Russia, and England were the scene of thousands of peasant uprisings from the twelfth century onward. Yet in the vast majority of such rebellions, the rebels gain little. And we rarely see the more subtle forms of everyday resistance that serves to protect peasant interests and prevent excessive exploitation. For example, in many societies, peasants could protest simply by moving to a new landholding or abandoning farming.

Peasant societies have long been a major focus of anthropological study. It was societies of small-scale agriculturists that generally preceded the emergence of industrialization around the world, and peasant societies today are still being modified by globalization of the capitalist economy. Billions still try to survive by growing their own food, and the balance of their lives is often precarious. We can get an idea of how peasant farms work by looking at a typical medieval German farm. A forty-acre farm in northeast Germany in 1400 produced 10,200 pounds of grain crops. Of this 3,400 pounds was set aside for seed and 2,800 pounds went to feed working livestock. This is referred to as the *replacement fund,* the output needed to continue the cycle of agricultural production. Of the remaining 4,000 pounds, 2,700 pounds was paid to the lord who held domain over the land. This constituted the *fund of rent.* Thus of the 10,200 pounds produced, only 1,600 pounds of grain remained to sustain the farmer's family. With an average-sized family that amounted to only 1,600 calories per day (Wolf 1967:9). Consequently, the family needed to seek other food sources, perhaps a garden or livestock kept for food. In addition, some of what is produced often goes into what Eric Wolf called a *ceremonial fund,* produce that is

An idealized depiction of a feudal economy in France, with peasants dutifully plowing the fields. In reality, there were thousands of peasant revolts in Europe and Great Britain throughout the early modern era.

shared, generally at ritual occasions, with others in the community. The ceremonial fund may be used to give dinners or feasts or to contribute to community-wide celebrations.

While there is wide variation in the structure of peasant societies, the division of produce on medieval German farms into replacement funds, ceremonial funds, and funds of rent gives us a good idea of what is required of the produce of the farm. It also demonstrates the centrality of land to peasant life; obviously what is produced depends largely on the amount and quality of land available for production. For this reason virtually all peasant protest focuses in some way on the struggle over land. How the protest is conducted, the form of protest, and whether it involves collective and/or violent action depends on a number of factors.

Let's examine three twentieth-century cases of peasant protest, all focusing on land and changes in the peasants' relationship to it. In a case of contemporary peasant protest in Malaysia we will examine nonviolent resistance and the ways poor peasants try to deal with the impact on their lives of the green revolution. We will examine a case of violent rebellion in Kenya inspired largely by British colonial policies during the first half of the twentieth century. Finally, in a case of peasant protest in Chiapas, we can appreciate how the globalization of the world economy can affect the lives of peasant farmers and precipitate a revolution. In all three cases the protest was clearly related to global factors: the protest of Malaysian peasants was a consequence of the spread of high-technology agriculture, the Mau Mau revolt in Kenya a result of British imperialist expansion of the late nineteenth century, and the protest in Chiapas a direct consequence of the globalization of the modern economy.

Malaysia and the Weapons of the Weak

In his study of the plight of poor Malaysian peasants, James Scott (1985) made the point that we have for too long focused on violent forms of protest and have neglected to study everyday resistance to oppression or just excessive demands. *How do the relatively powerless resist oppression by the relatively powerful?* Because open revolt and resistance can be foolhardy, people find more subtle ways of resistance. We can see this in our everyday behavior. Anthropologists who have studied the culture of grade school and college classrooms have noted the different ways that students resist classroom discipline. For example, students may slump in the chairs designed to force their bodies into positions of upright compliance, refuse to participate, talk to other students, or read or sleep in class as forms of resistance to what they perceive as attempts at cultural domination (Alpert 1991).

Subtle and nonconfrontational forms of protest are common in situations where those with little power want to register their resistance to what is forced on them. In the context of peasant society, Scott (1985:29) referred to these kinds of actions as the "weapons of the weak." This resistance stops short of any kind of collective defiance; it is more likely to consist of such things as foot dragging, dissimulation, false compliance, pilfering, feigned ignorance, slander, arson, sabotage, and so forth. These actions, like those of the slouching, nonattentive student, require no planning or collective effort and avoid direct conflict with authority. But, said Scott, it is important to understand these *weapons of the weak* if we are to understand peasant resistance and begin to understand under what conditions these forms of resistance give way to outright rebellion.

Malaysian Peasants and the Green Revolution

Malaysia of the 1990s was, until the Asian economic collapse of 1997–1998, an excellent case of a country doing well economically. Its revenues from tropical hardwoods, oil, tin, rubber, and palm oil led to an annual economic growth rate of 3.9 percent from 1960 to 1976 and a per capita income twice as high as any other Southeast Asian country. But as in most Asian countries, the income is unevenly distributed, with agricultural incomes declining and many peasants finding their livelihood threatened. Ironically, one of the reasons for the growing inequality of income is agricultural changes wrought by the green revolution. In 1966 Malaysia, with the help of the World Bank, began the Mudra irrigation project on the Kedah Plain. It involved building two large dams that increased irrigation, permitting peasants to plant and harvest twice each year rather than once. Double-cropping of rice was extended to 260,000 acres. By 1974 the project was declared an unqualified success by the World Bank; it more than doubled production, reduced unemployment, and raised the rate of return on investments from 10 percent to 18 percent. There is little doubt that collectively the Malay peasantry is better off than before, and little doubt that if one wishes to be a rice farmer in Southeast Asia, the Kedah Plain is the place to be.

Scott said the changes in villages since the new prosperity are striking: there are new shops, roads, motorcycles, and mosques, and corrugated tin and plank siding has replaced attap roofs and siding. Peasants with the smallest plots can grow enough rice to feed their families. Infant mortality and malnutrition were cut by half. With securer incomes, fewer peasants have lost their land, and ownership has stabilized. Thus there was much good news following the green revolution in Malaysia.

But there is bad news as well, largely in the growing inequities in land access and income. The rich in the village (most still poor by greater Malaysia's standards) were getting richer and the poor poorer. *What does it mean to be poor and held in little regard by others in a peasant village?* One of the poorest villagers in Sedaka was Razak. His home was so decrepit that he avoided asking people inside. His children were poorly fed, and one died while Scott resided in the village. Others in the village avoided and ridiculed Razak, and Scott was regaled with the stories of Razak's unabashed begging, his fraudulent dealings (e.g., selling a pile of wood to two people), and his seeming lack of concern with village gossip about him.

The plight of poor villagers such as Razak was worsening because the traditional ties of dependence between rich and poor were being eroded by the green revolution. In the past, land-owning peasants could not farm all their land, so they rented it to land-poor tenants who worked the land for a rent. While the rents may have been exploitative, they were negotiated after a harvest; after a bad harvest the rents could be negotiated downwards, and after a good harvest rents would be higher.

In addition, traditionally the landowners needed the labor of the poorer farmers for plowing, transplanting the young rice plants, gathering the rice, and thrashing rice grains from the stalks. While the wages were low, land-poor villagers could count on the income to supplement whatever they could grow themselves.

Finally, the land-rich and the land-poor farmers were bound together by gift giving and ceremonial exchange, with the rich expected to give gifts and charity to the poor. There were traditionally three forms of ritual giving in Sedaka: the Islamic *zakat,* alms that are given voluntarily; sharing of wealth by the rich with the poor, to cleanse the poor of envy, hatred, and resentment; and *derma* gifts and ritual feasts. Gift giving was a reciprocal arrangement: the recipient was obliged to return the gift at some later date. Since the poor were not expected to return charity, they repaid the rich with loyalty and an obligation to help with the labor of planting and harvesting.

In the past, then, the well-to-do villagers had justified their superior positions by claiming they benefited the poor; they rented land to them, paid them for their labor, and distributed gifts and gave feasts for the whole village. In effect, they legitimized their superior position by citing their services to the poor and claimed in return the poor's gratitude, respect, and deference. These traditional arrangements of dependency were disrupted by the agricultural changes that occurred in Sedaka, which operated virtually to make poor peasants superfluous.

First, the introduction of double-cropping and increased yield made the land more valuable. One effect of this was to change the conditions of land rental and tenancy. Because land was more valuable people from outside the community offered to rent it at higher prices than local land-poor peasants could pay. Moreover, since the land was more profitable many richer peasants chose to farm it themselves or gave it to family members rather than renting it. To make matters worse, rent began to be paid in advance, not after the harvest, and there was no longer rent adjustment in the event of a poor harvest. As a result, the poor peasants of Sedaka found their access to land much reduced after the introduction of double-cropping.

Second, with the increase in the value of land rich farmers were able to take advantage of new technologies, specifically mechanical harvesters and broadcast sowing. The harvesters, which could bring in the rice harvest quicker and with little or no increase in cost compared with human labor, greatly reduced the number of jobs available to poor farmers and their family members.

Third, in addition to the loss of land and labor, the poor found that traditional gift giving and charity of the richer members of the community declined. The motivation for gift giving was always the need of the rich to cement the obligations of the poor so the rich could call on them for labor when it was needed. With mechanical harvesters available to do most of the work, farmers were no longer dependent on local labor.

Thus in the course of a few years, the poor peasants of Sedaka saw their opportunities for land, jobs, and charity dramatically decreased. The social and economic ties that bound different levels of the community to each other began to unravel, and bonds of exploitation that tied the poor to the rich were freed, but, as Scott (1985:77) noted, "this is the freedom of the unemployed, the redundant."

The wealthier farmers, of course, were simply playing the economic game as it is played throughout the world. They took advantage of the increased value of land by raising rents, saving money and time with the use of mechanical harvesters, and redistributing less of their profit to others in the form of charity, gift giving, and ritual feasting. The problem is that their new behavior violated the old norms of the society, in which they were expected to rent land at prices people could afford, hire the poor to plant, harvest, and thresh the rice, and give charity, gifts, and feasts. These norms were once the basis of their authority. One of the accusations of the poor that rich must defend against is that they are failing to live up to their traditional obligations (Scott 1985:184).

In sum, advances in agricultural production wrought by the double-cropping of rice, made possible by the green revolution and the World Bank, increased the gap between rich and poor and, more important, weakened the social and economic ties between the various economic classes of the village. One solution available to poor peasants was flight; they could simply leave the village and migrate to another village or, more likely, to the urban centers to search for jobs. But for those unable to flee, there were few choices.

The question is, *what could the poor do to alleviate their condition? Was it possible to gain back what was lost?*

Fighting Back

The first question we might ask is, *what is resistance?* Scott (1985:290) defined it as

> [a]ny *act(s) by member(s) of a subordinate class that is or are* intended *to either mitigate or deny claims (for example, rents, taxes, prestige) made on that class by superordinate classes (for example, landlords, large farmers, the state) or to advance its own claims (for example, work, land, charity, respect) vis-à-vis those superordinate classes.*

Traditionally peasants have found various ways to express their sense of being exploited or to resist directly what they see as excessive demands placed on them by landlords, the state, or others. As Scott (1985:300) pointed out, much of the folk culture of peasant societies legitimates resistance. Peasant folklore, for example, is full of stories of evasiveness and cunning, represented in Malaysia by the figure of *Sang Kancil,* a mouse deer figure—a small, weak being who survives and triumphs over more powerful figures using only wits and cunning. In the United States there is the figure of Br'er Rabbit. The myth and folklore of virtually every peasant society has a Robin Hood figure, a local hero who defends the peasant from the elite or represents the peasant who is willing and able to fight back. As Eric Hobsbawm (1959) pointed out, the bandit is almost always someone who is wrongly accused and convicted of a crime who then attempts to shield the peasants from their oppressors. In these ways peasant culture underwrites and legitimizes resistance.

But, as James Scott (1985:301) pointed out, the goals of peasant resistance are generally modest.

> *The goal of most resistance is not necessarily to overthrow a system of oppression or domination, but, rather, to survive. The usual goal of peasants, as Hobsbawm has so aptly put it, is* "working the system to their minimum disadvantage."

One of the ways the poor of Sedaka worked the system to their "minimum disadvantage" was through gossip, or character assault. But the gossip was of a particular sort, essentially an accusation against the rich that they were not living up to the rules of behavior the rich themselves had previously used to justify and legitimate their social position. It attempted to emphasize the apparent hypocrisy of the rich, much as American civil rights advocates of the 1950s and 1960s highlighted the ethical contradictions of racial segregation in a supposedly free society or as Solidarity members in Poland of the 1970s used the existence of worker repression in a supposedly worker state.

Poor peasants in Sedaka used Islamic law and traditional relations between rich and poor to put pressure on the rich to live up to their obligations to those less fortunate. For example, in Sedaka Haj Broom was notorious as a miser who, some people say, acquired his land and wealth through shady business dealings. For the poor of Sedaka, his name was synonymous with greed and arrogance, and the low esteem in which he was privately (never publicly) held served as a warning to other wealthy farmers of behaviors to avoid. Put another way, gossip represented an appeal by the poor to previously held norms of tenancy, generosity, charity, employment, and feasts taken for granted before double-cropping (Scott 1985:282). Gossip chipped away at the reputations of wealthy farmers much as theft chips away at their wealth. Gossip is also a relatively safe vehicle of protest, since its author is generally unknown. The rich responded to these attacks by blaming the poor for their own plight, often using Razak as their example of the poor. Gossip, said Scott (1985:22–23), functions like propaganda and embodies whole stories. The mention of Razak's name by the rich conjured up visions of grasping and dishonest poor; the mention of Haj Broom by the poor incited visions of the "greedy, penny-pinching rich." The former represented to the rich where the poor were heading, as the latter represented to the poor the increasing violation of village standards by the rich.

In addition to gossip and an appeal to tradition, there were other ways the poor of Sedaka resisted their condition, such as theft. While not as frequent as it once was, when rustlers stole water buffalo, theft was relatively common. Stolen items included water bottles left out to be filled by the government water truck, bicycles, motorcycles, fruit from trees, and, fairly commonly, sacks of rice left out in the fields. Most of the theft was believed to be done by the local poor, and the victims were almost without exception the wealthier members of the community.

There is some evidence that the poor viewed such theft, especially of rice, as a substitute for the charity that was less forthcoming than in the past. And while the losses were not great for wealthier farmers, the gain by the poor was, for them, substantial. The wealthy farmers reacted to theft with a combination of fear and anger, yet no rice theft has ever been reported to the local police. And people didn't report a theft from a neighbor even if they knew the identity of the thief, for fear of having their own rice stolen in retaliation. Another act of resistance was the killing of livestock of the rich by the poor, especially when the livestock posed a nuisance, as when they pecked open a rice sack and ate the rice.

Sabotage was a weapon of the poor used in Sedaka, specifically against the mechanical harvesters that were taking their jobs. Combine parts were smashed, sand and dirt were put in gas tanks, trees felled to block their progress. The owners of the combines, generally Chinese businessmen from urban areas, occasionally posted watchmen to guard the harvesters when they were left in the fields, but in one incident a watchman was forced to climb down while protesters set the harvester afire.

Most of the protest in Sedaka was the acts of individuals, but there was some collective action, mostly by the women of the village. Women in Sedaka worked in crews that were hired by farmers to plant and transplant rice seedlings, something the combines could not do. While the women would not openly tell a farmer that they would not be available to transplant if he used a combine to harvest, they could "let it be known," as they said, that they were upset at the loss of work. If they did "strike," they would not call it that; they would simply tell the offending farmer they had other work that had to be completed before they could get to his fields. In this way, the women avoided any open confrontation that might result in their loss of jobs while putting pressure on farmers to abandon the mechanical combines. The farmers retaliated by threatening to bring in outside laborers to transplant, and some in fact did so, and the threatened boycott collapsed. Farmers in other villages faced similar strikes that created a worker shortage, and women from Sedaka would go there to transplant fields. This "strike breaking" behavior undermined the larger effort, but made a point to the women's immediate bosses.

Thus the people of Sedaka attempted to register their protest to the changes that affected their lives. *Were their protests effective?* To some extent they were. Some farmers hired people rather than use machines, even though they might have gotten their crops in quicker with the harvester; other farmers continued to lease their land to the poor when they could probably have gotten more money by renting it to outsiders or by farming it themselves. And some farmers still gave ritual feasts, thus honoring the traditional norms of the village rather than seeking to maximize their monetary gains.

Obstacles to Resistance

While their income was declining in the face of agricultural change, there was little the peasants of Sedaka could do other than make use of the weapons of the weak. There were obstacles to more open resistance, not the least of which was a fear of losing what little was left. The rich were still powerful enough that gossip about them had to be done behind their backs. Moreover, the rich still had enough control over labor to maintain a viable threat. Thus when the women "let it be known" that they wouldn't harvest unless wages were raised, the richer farmers, in turn, "let it be known" that they would bring in outsiders.

Furthermore, the change wrought by the green revolution was relatively slow. Changes in land tenure and technique did not hit all the poor and did not hit at once. For example, landlords began to collect rents before rather than after the harvest only gradually, the complete change taking several seasons. Had it been done by one landlord to many tenants, there might have been open protest. The loss of tenancies to landlords who wanted to rent to outsiders, to farm themselves, or to give to children happened gradually, as did the raising of rents. The only thing that happened quickly was the use of combines to harvest, but that was an ambiguous change and many middle-class peasants took advantage of the speed, as did even a few of the poor. Even they were torn between getting the crops in fast and the loss of some wage labor for themselves or their children.

Moreover, the changes did not involve more exploitation of the poor, it meant cutting off relations with them. Thus wages weren't reduced, they were done away with altogether; the poor were removed from the productive process rather than being directly exploited. In fact, it removed points of conflict: there was no longer a need to haggle over the end of harvest rent or over wages for harvesting or transplanting. And once the struggle in the realm of production is severed, so is the conflict in the realm of ritual. As Scott (1985:243) suggested, if the rich had increased their profits by demanding more from their tenants, rather than just dismissing them, the protest would have been far more dramatic. The sites where class conflict had historically occurred had been bulldozed. The plight of the Malaysian peasants, Scott (1985:243) said, is analogous to that of the recently fired American factory worker who remarked, "The only thing worse than being exploited is *not* being exploited."

Finally, in addition to normal constraints against openly protesting or resisting, such as the fear of losing work, tenancy, and charity, there is the routine repression of arrest and persecution. While the situation in Malaysia is not nearly as bad as in neighboring Indonesia, where killings, arrests, and repression from paramilitary units are more routine, there is in Malaysia still the real threat of arrests and persecution initiated by local political leaders.

Protest and Change

One of the great strengths of the modern capitalist economy is its adaptability, its ability to seek out sources of capital accumulation, that is, ways to make profit. However, while this may strengthen national economies and provide better lives for some, it can also disrupt the lives of others. We see this in the United States as thousands of people are thrown out of work by factory closings as corporations take advantage of cheaper labor in other countries. While this provides jobs for others and lower-priced goods for American consumers, it creates hardship for those whose jobs have been replaced. We see the same thing happening to the poor villagers of Sedaka. Capitalist agriculture may grow more rice and make greater profits for some landowners and farmers, but it also undermines the economic base of others. Whether their lives or the lives of their children will be improved as a result is, of course, another question. It is the disruptions of the short-term that the poor are attempting to resist. Thus, from the perspective of the poor, while they might have been exploited under the traditional system of land tenancy, labor, and charity, now they have been cut adrift into uncertainty.

The precapitalist norms of the village emphasized relations between rich and poor that involved what might be called a "politics of reputation." The rich employed the poor, rented their land to them, gave them charity and gifts; in return the poor supplied their labor and their respect. It was a system in which the rich benefited more than the poor, and which they had a major hand in constructing. But this is the very system the rich have had to violate to take advantage of new opportunities. Put another way, it is the capitalization of agriculture that has revolutionized life in Sedaka; the poor, rather than being revolutionary in their resistance, find themselves trying to resist a revolutionary social and economic order. Again, as Scott (1985:346) said,

> [i]t has been capitalism *that has historically transformed societies and broken apart existing relations of production. Even a casual glance at the record will show that capitalist development continually requires the violation of the previous "social contract" which in most cases it had earlier helped to create and sustain...The history of capitalism could, in fact, be written along just such lines. The enclosures, the introduction of agricultural machinery, the invention of the factory system, the use of steam power, the development of the assembly line, and today the computer revolution and robotics have all had massive material and social consequences that undermined previous understandings about work, equity, security, obligation, and rights.*

In the case of Sedaka, we see peasant farmers trying not to change a system but rather to defend and maintain a social order that, while exploitative, nevertheless looked better than what the green revolution ushered in. Whether they were correct is another matter. It may be that as they lose access to land and labor, they will find something better. But the point is that their efforts at resistance were largely conservative, an attempt to preserve or return to previous forms of dependence. They accused the rich not of making excessive profits but of violating the very behaviors that the rich previously used to exploit the poor.

Kikuyu and the Mau Mau Rebellion

The everyday resistance of Malaysian peasants to their worsening economic situation was largely individual resistance, and it was generally nonviolent. But peasant protest sometimes involves collective action and sometimes results in violent conflict. We need to ask *at what point does resistance take on a more collective form, and what are the conditions that result in peasant protest turning violent? Furthermore, what is the reaction to protest?* The case of the Kikuyu in Kenya is instructive.

From 1952 to 1956 the British struggled to repress a rebellion by mostly Kikuyu peasant farmers. By the end of the revolt they had taken the lives of over 11,000 rebels and had forcibly detained nearly 100,000 people, while 200 Europeans and some 2,000 Africans loyal to the British were killed by the rebels. The Mau Mau rebellion was only one of hundreds that took place as Europeans attempted to assert colonial control over peoples of Africa, Asia, and the Americas, but it serves as a good example of the conditions under which a group is willing and able to go from passive resistance to active and even violent resistance. The Mau Mau rebellion also reveals the psychology of oppressors as they struggle to understand why they are objects of protest. Finally, it is important because it has been considered the first great African liberation movement and, according to Robert Edgerton (1989), was probably the most serious crisis of Britain's African colonies.

The British in East Africa

Toward the end of the nineteenth century most of East Africa became an economic battleground between Germany and England, each attempting to control the resources of the area. To avoid conflict, the two countries met in Berlin in 1884 to carve up much of East Africa among themselves. Kenya was to be included among Great Britain's "sphere of influence." Their efforts to control the economic life of East Africa were, of course, often resisted by Africans, sometimes violently. But British military actions, often ruthless, soon subdued most resistance (Edgerton 1989:4). Kenyans not only had to deal with the British invasion, they also were decimated by plagues of locusts, prolonged drought, cattle disease, and an epidemic of smallpox. Contemporary estimates of the number of Kenyan deaths during that period range from 50 percent to 95 percent of the population. When white settlers, at the encouragement of the British, arrived in 1902 to claim land, much of the territory seemed to them to be empty.

The Kikuyu, the largest cultural group in Kenya, reacted to the invasion by attacking settlers, prompting further British military expeditions and more Kikuyu deaths. In their rage, in early September 1902 the Kikuyu seized a white settler, pegged him to the ground, and wedged his mouth open with a stick; then an entire village urinated into his mouth until he drowned (Edgerton 1989:5). They cut off his genitals, disemboweled him, and defecated on his body. The British reacted by surrounding the village at night and massacring everyone, including old men and women, sparing only the children who had hidden in the forest.

The Kikuyu in many ways had the most to lose from the British occupation. They subsisted on a combination of horticulture and livestock-raising on communally owned land, governed by a councils of elders soon to be replaced by the British with appointed chiefs. Consequently the Kikuyu continued fighting the British, using spears and poisoned arrows. Their courage greatly impressed British officers, but by 1904 the resistance had ended. Other groups in Kenya, such as the Luo, Kamba, and Nandi, fought the British but with no more success than the Kikuyu. The cattle-herding Maasi, considered the most imposing warriors in Africa, fought alongside the British against the Kikuyu.

British officials made little effort to hide their intent to seize African land, confine the Africans to reserves, and use them as cheap labor. There was some protest registered in England to British actions and intents in East Africa. Sir William Harcourt (cited Edgerton 1989:3), a past professor of international law, exclaimed that "Every act of force you commit against a native within a sphere of influence is an unlawful assault; every acre of land you take is robbery; every native you kill is murder."

But settlement continued, advertisements appearing in British newspapers at home and in British colonies describing the economic virtues of Kenyan settlements. Many of the settlers were South African, others came directly from Britain, traveling by ship to Mombassa, then taking the newly built Uganda Railroad to Nairobi, where they went by oxcart with their belongings to the farmland they had claimed. Many of the settlers were offspring of wealthy British lords send to Kenya

The British perfected the system of indirect rule, in which they appointed and maintained, militarily if necessary, indigenous rulers sympathetic to their colonial aims.

to make their fortune, some receiving title to over 100,000 acres. Even people of limited means, such as the father of British writer and aviatrix Beryl Markham, were able to save enough by working for the wealthy to buy a thousand-acre farm. The often elaborate lifestyles of the white elite, especially in a part of the highlands called "Happy Valley," consisted of well-publicized drinking and drug parties, polo matches, and sexual escapades. A standard joke in Britain at the time was, "Are you married or are you from Kenya?" (cited Edgerton 1989:17).

But to succeed settlers both rich and poor needed African labor, and the Africans were not anxious to work for wages, and those who did hardly displayed the work ethic and discipline the settlers had hoped for. The Kikuyu soon learned the value of money and would walk 300 miles to Mombassa to work, but the settlers were not willing to pay the wages available in Mombassa.

To solve the problem of getting the Africans to work for settlers the government introduced a hut and poll tax that forced Africans to work for wages to pay the taxes; at the same time, they prohibited them from growing cash crops, such as coffee, sisal, and maize. Africans were also forced to carry a pass (*kipande*) that bore their name, tribal affiliation, fingerprints, work history, and, later, photograph. The *kipande* had to be worn around the neck in a metal container (Edgerton 1989:15). Any White could virtually ruin an African's prospect for employment by writing such descriptions as "lazy" or "arrogant" on their pass.

To administer their colonial holdings the British developed a system that became known as indirect rule. They assumed, wrongly, that every African group must have a ruling chief, so they appointed someone from each group to the position of paramount chief and to serve as an intermediary between colonial administrators and his group. The Kikuyu, for example, had no paramount chief. The major ruling body among the Kikuyu was the *ciama*, or council of elderly and respected people, who dealt with all aspects of life from settling disputes to circumcision (required for both boys and girls), marriage, and other rituals. They had the power to levy fines on wrong-doers and force them to pay compensation to victims, usually the sacrifice of a goat that would be eaten by the members of the council. The British practice of appointing paramount chiefs had the effect of creating a ruling elite with special access to the wealth and privilege that the colonial government had the power to bestow. Thus the power of the chiefs originated in and depended on the armed might of the British. They used this authority to extort money from whoever they could, whenever they could, appropriating livestock, demanding land, and ordering women to have sex with them. If anyone protested the chief's behavior, he or she was killed. A chief could cane a person who did not remove his hat and bow to him or arrest someone who coughed while he was speaking at a meeting.

The British also selected and trained Africans to staff, under white officers, the police and their African army. These people also became part of an African elite generally loyal to the British.

The Mau Mau rebellion began in 1952, led largely by peasant agriculturists evicted from lands that they had worked, along with a disenfranchised urban group and others restricted to reserves that were soon unable to hold the growing African population. Probably the biggest role was played by peasants who had lived in the White Highlands, an area of fertile agricultural land on which British settlers were given farms.

The White Highlands

To take advantage of their domination of Kenya the British seized land held by Kikuyu in some of the most fertile areas of the country, such as the White Highlands, and distributed it to British settlers. The settlers were required to pay the sum of three rupees (approximately one dollar) per acre to the Kikuyu owners. Since the settlers required laborers to work the land for them, and since the peasants required income to pay the newly imposed taxes, the people from whom the land was forcibly purchased were urged to remain in the Highlands and work for the new settlers. In exchange for three to five months of labor per year, each family was given six to seven acres (much of which had been theirs) on which to grow their own crops and graze their cattle and sheep (Kanogo 1987). They were also given a small wage, rarely exceeding fourteen shillings (about fourteen American cents at the time) per month. By way of comparison, the poll tax was twenty shillings and a cheap shirt cost four shillings.

At first the Kikuyu who remained in the White Highlands working for the settlers adapted quickly to their situation. The squatters, as they were called, were free to raise crops, cattle, and sheep and to support family members, many of whom did not work for the settlers. If a settler tried to limit the amount of land a squatter worked or to evict relatives who were not workers, the squatter was free to move to the land of another settler. The labor demands were relatively meager and could be met by a man's wife, children, or relatives. Moreover, the squatters could favorably compare their lives with those of other Africans working on farms for wages only.

More important for the Kikuyu, their livestock herds—cattle, goats, and sheep—thrived. Cattle and goats were particularly important for the Kikuyu. They represented wealth and were used in all kinds of ceremonial and economic exchanges. They served as bridewealth, presentations made by a groom's family to the bride's family at marriage. They were important in ritual observances and constituted a financial reserve that could be sold for cash to pay taxes or school fees or purchase consumer goods.

The squatter arrangement worked also for many of the European settlers. While many were wealthy, a large number had little capital to pay workers but could acquire land cheaply enough to exchange for the labor they needed. In addition, many settlers allowed Africans to work land in exchange for cash or a portion of the produce, thus securing crops that they themselves might be having trouble growing. Thus within twenty years of the British takeover of the White Highlands many Kikuyu had been converted from land-owning peasants to squatters working the same land in exchange for their labor and, occasionally, a portion of their produce. The squatters were able to sell their surplus produce and build up sizable herds of cattle and sheep.

But the settlers were not content with this arrangement; they wanted to limit squatter cultivation and livestock raising to what the squatters needed for subsistence. In effect, the settlers wanted to reduce the Kikuyu to dependent laborers by removing the peasant option. Thus the period from 1920 to 1950 was marked by repeated attempts by the settlers to reduce the amount of land and livestock available to Kikuyu squatters. For example, by 1920 the settlers had convinced the colonial government to pass legislation requiring squatters to work for Europeans 180 days per year and allowing settlers to call on the labor of women and children during times of peak labor demand. In 1930 the government, at the settlers' urging, initiated what the Kikuyu called *kifagio,* or "sweeping away," when squatter stock was reduced from an average of several hundred head for each laborer to about five per family with no corresponding increase in wages. The losses in wealth to the squatters was considerable; some squatters had accumulated as many as one thousand goats.

In 1937 the colonial government passed legislation that, in effect, gave the settlers the authority to reduce or eliminate squatter livestock and regulate the number of working days required of each squatter. The settlers reacted to this new authority by increasing the number of working days to 240 and then 270 per year. They passed regulations regarding the livestock squatters were legally able to keep; these regulations eliminated all cattle and goats, allowing each family to keep only fifteen to twenty sheep. The settlers enacted these regulations without increasing wages (which remained at about fourteen shillings per month) and against the advice of the colonial government (Kanogo 1987:63).

In addition to reducing the land and livestock held by squatters, there were other forms of squatter oppression. A settler might graze his animals on the African's fields or just destroy the crop, or might evict the squatter before he could harvest his crop, keeping it for himself. Thus as the squatters struggled to remain economically viable and relatively independent, the settlers did all they could to turn them into dependent wage laborers.

The Kikuyu resisted the constant modifications of their relationship to the land and livestock and, consequently, each other in ways peasants had always resisted oppression. They failed to show up for work, settled illegally on unused land, tried to organize strikes, killed or maimed settlers' livestock, or fled to the forests, reserves, or the cities. But the campaign to drive the Kikuyu off the land was highly successful. By 1948, three thousand Europeans owned more arable land in the highlands than was available to the more than one million Kikuyu on their reserves.

The Roots of the Rebellion

Organized political resistance to British colonization of Kenya began in 1922, when a Kikuyu named Harry Thuku organized the Young Kikuyu Association to protest the poll tax and *kipande* identity containers and preached that the British had stolen Kikuyu land. He was quickly arrested, and a crowd that included the future first president of Kenya, Jomo Kenyatta, surrounded the jail. When a woman named Mary Nyanjira raised her dress over her head and insulted the manhood of the guards facing the crowd, they fired, killing her and 25–250 people, depending on whose accounts you believe. It was reported that Europeans dining on a verandah opposite the jail also fired into the fleeing crowd. Thuku was never put on trial, but he was exiled for nine years.

In 1925 the Kikuyu Central Association (KCA) was formed, and Jomo Kenyatta became its general secretary. Kenyatta was sent by the KCA to England to be educated because they saw him as a future leader. He traveled to Russia, became a skilled orator in English, married an English woman (in spite of a pledge to the KCA that he would never marry a European), studied anthropology under noted anthropologist Bronislaw Malinowski, and wrote a competent, if idealized, ethnography of the Kikuyu, *Facing Mount Kenya* (1962). He is pictured on the cover holding a spear.

Realizing that a successful movement would need to involve more than just the Kikuyu, Kenyatta organized the Kenyan African Union (KAU). To assure the loyalty of members and to establish a sense of solidarity and purpose, he used a traditional Kikuyu device, an oath. Oaths among the Kikuyu were common and used to prove one's innocence in legal cases, to pledge loyalty before going to war, to show devotion during religious services, or to prove they had not impregnated a particular woman. The Kikuyu believed the violation of an oath, like lying after swearing on a bible, could kill you; the KAU oath (cited Edgerton 1989:48) stated simply:

> If you ever argue when you are called
> If you ever disobey your leader,
> If called upon in the night and you fail to come
> May this oath kill you

Seemingly typical of colonial regimes, the British either did not recognize or refused to admit that their African subjects wanted to drive them out. Even on the eve of the Mau Mau revolt the retiring British Governor of Kenya, Sir Phillip Mitchell, announced in 1952 that all was well in Kenya.

But all was not well. First, the peasant squatters were continually being squeezed by the settlers. The colonial government had tried to help by opening a resettlement area called Olegurone for Kikuyu who were evicted from the highlands and who had settled on Maasi land, sometimes marrying with Maasi. But the government insisted that the land was owned by the government and could only be used, not owned, by the Kikuyu. Furthermore the government dictated inheritance patterns of anyone on the land, allowing a man to pass along his right as tenant only to the eldest son of the eldest wife, instead of dividing the land among children as Kikuyu had done traditionally. They also set strict rules over what could be planted, where it could be planted, and how it was to be farmed. When most Kikuyu refused to accept British directives on the control of land and agricultural activities, they were evicted and sent back to the reserves.

But the reserves were another flashpoint for revolt. Ignored and virtually never entered by settlers, the reserves had become overpopulated, and the resultant overplanting had eroded most of the land. Hunger was widespread, as the British should have realized since they rejected 90 percent of Kikuyu recruits for the British Army at the start of World War II because of malnutrition. When the government introduced modern agricultural methods to the reserves, they never bothered to consult with the Kikuyu. One of the colonial government's pet projects was terracing the land to prevent erosion. This project required the chiefs to round up laborers, mainly women, to do the work. Not only did the Kikuyu not understand the need for terracing, many assumed the work was being done to prepare it for British settlers.

As a result of the situation on the reserves, thousands of landless Africans fled to the cities in search of jobs. Few found them, and the cities became home to thousands of unemployed people. In Nairobi, the fortunate few who found shelter were living fourteen to a room, four to a bed; the less fortunate slept under buses, cars, or wherever they could find shelter. In Nairobi many Kikuyu organized themselves into gangs that roamed the streets, robbing non-Kikuyu Africans and Asians. The most powerful Kikuyu gang, called the Forty Group because most of its members were circumcised and initiated in 1940, controlled prostitution. But they also had decided that all Europeans had to be driven out of Kenya, and some took a secret oath to obey orders and kill if asked. One prominent gang leader was Fred Kubai, who would play a major role in the development of Mau Mau and later claim it was his brainchild (Edgerton 1989:35).

In addition to the poverty and the loss of land, the Kikuyu were split between those who benefited from and those who suffered under colonial rule. In fact, in many ways the coming rebellion resembled a Kikuyu civil war, with the rebels directing much of their rage against those who remained loyal to the British and continued to profit from the patronage they received.

Finally, another reason for protest was the color bar and racism. The British, especially the settlers, considered Africans to be one step removed from savagery, saved only by the thin veneer of civilization brought to them by the British. Settlers considered Africans to have the intelligence of twelve-year-olds, claimed they did not feel pain as Europeans did, and believed they could even will themselves to die. While beating and killing of Africans by Whites was not uncommon, it was not until 1959, after the rebellion, that a White was convicted of killing an African, and even that conviction shocked and outraged the White community.

The Rebellion

The Africans resisted these conditions as best they could. For example, women refused to work on new agricultural projects imposed by the colonial government; the labor unions in the cities called strikes, and more and more people began to take the Mau Mau oath. The oath had become more demanding over the years and was accompanied by an elaborate ceremony. Fred Kubai was in charge of administering the oath and executing anyone who violated it (cited Edgerton 1989:52–53):

> If you ever disagree with your nation or sell it, may you die of this oath.
> If a member of this Society ever calls on you in the night and you refuse to
>   open your hut to him, may you die of this oath.
> If you ever sell a Kikuyu woman to a foreigner, may you die of this oath.
> If you ever leave a member of this Society in trouble, may you die of
>   this oath.
> If you ever report a member of this Society to the government, may you
>   die of this oath.

The ceremony was patterned after the Kikuyu male initiation ceremony; it involved slaughtering a male goat of one solid color if possible and collecting its blood in a gourd bowl and cutting out its chest. Those who took the oath were cut seven times and their blood mixed with that of the goat. (This cutting was later stopped because the scars were conclusive evidence to colonial authorities that a person had taken the oath.) The initiate was asked, "What are you?" After answering "I am Kikuyu," a cross standing for Kikuyu and Mumbi, the mythical parents of the Kikuyu people, was made on the initiate's forehead with the blood. Then the initiate ate the goat's meat, which was dipped into the blood seven times; taken into a hut; and lectured about the oath and the "movement" (Edgerton 1989:53).

Later, when the violence was about to begin, the rituals became more elaborate and the oath included promises to kill Whites and steal their guns and valuables and to kill anyone opposed to the movement. The British found out about the oath and reacted with horror. The secretary of state (cited Edgerton 1989:61), on hearing it, said,

The Mau Mau oath is the most bestial, filthy, nauseating incantation which per-verted minds can ever have brewed. I am not unduly squeamish, but when I first read it I was so revolted that it got between me and my appetite...I can recall no instance when I have felt the forces of evil to be so near and so strong.

The British government knew of Mau Mau but thought it was a religious move-ment. But, as we shall see, the oath obsessed Kenyan Whites, and they believed, or wanted to believe, that it was responsible for the entire rebellion.

As the rebellion was about to occur, as thousands of Kikuyu were fleeing the reserves for the Kenyan forests that were to become the rebel base, and as hun-dreds of thousands of Kikuyu were taking the Mau Mau oath, Jomo Kenyatta was kept ignorant about the Mau Mau plans. The militants in the Kenyan African Union, which included most of the Mau Mau leaders, did not trust Kenyatta; they knew he was opposed to violence and that the British had sworn to arrest him if he did not publicly denounce Mau Mau. Yet Whites in Kenya never doubted that Ken-yatta was the "evil genius" behind Mau Mau, its "puppet master," as writer Els-peth Huxley called him (cited Edgerton 1989:55).

Members of the movement did not call it Mau Mau, and there is no agreement on where the term originated. They called themselves "the movement," "the Afri-can government," or other native names, but the term "Land and Freedom Army" became the most common and survived the end of the rebellion. The British prob-ably maintained the term Mau Mau because it conjured up images of a secret soci-ety and hid the fact that it was a rational political organization fighting for land and freedom. The British government and the police did everything they could to make sure Mau Mau was depicted to the world media as a group of criminals lead-ing an irrational attack against the forces of law and order.

But the rebellion had been carefully planned. The central planning committee consisted of twelve members. Another group of thirty members directed the tak-ing of oathes and shielded the central committee from the police. The committee was in charge of recruiting government employees who could provide information on British plans, setting up networks for food and provisions for the rebels in the forests, and acquiring weapons. This proved particularly difficult. The British had long banned Africans from owning guns, and those owned by Whites were locked in "gun safes" when not in use. One method of obtaining guns was to attack police officers, steal their weapons, and dismember and hide their bodies. This worked so well that the British thought that the disappeared police officers had just gone home, until they discovered the dismembered foot and boot of one victim. Later the rebels secured arms by raiding police stations and army posts of the government's African soldiers. Rarely did they attack the well-armed British soldiers sent in to quell the rebellion.

Kikuyu women were to play a major role in the revolt. Women had already organized district committees to fight for land and become active in political processes. While Kikuyu women traditionally never administered oaths, before and during the rebellion women became oath givers (Presley 1992:129). It was largely women who organized and ran the networks that supplied the rebels in the forests with food, medicine, guns, ammunition, and information. And while only about 5 percent of the rebel forces in the forest were women, many took active roles in military actions.

"State of Emergency"

Isolated attacks against Whites and Africans loyal to the British began in September 1952, but the act that precipitated the British declaration of a "state of emergency" was the assassination in October 1952 of Senior Chief Waruhiu when he left the Native court where he presided. The sixty-two-year-old chief was with two friends in his Hudson sedan when it was stopped by three men wearing police uniforms; one approached and asked if Senior Chief Waruhiu was in the car; when the chief identified himself the man shot him in the mouth and three times in the body, leaving the two friends and the driver unharmed. One of the first government acts after the emergency was declared was to arrest Jomo Kenyatta, certain he was the mastermind and believing his arrest would end the rebellion.

The leaders of the movement targeted Kikuyu such as Chief Waruhiu who had cooperated with and, in some cases, benefited greatly from collaboration with the British. They also targeted settlers, causing outrage when they killed Roger Ruck, his wife Esme, a doctor, and their six-year-old son Michael. Kenyan and international newspapers gave great attention to the details of the killings, and Kenyans were particularly horrified when the man who confessed turned out to be one of Ruck's Kikuyu servants who had cared for Michael. International press reports about rebel attacks on settlers and Kikuyu loyal to the government appeared under headlines about "helpless," or "heroic" Whites being slaughtered by "fanatical," "bestial," "degraded," or "satanic" "gangsters" or "terrorists." Unreported were the stories of Kikuyu captives who were stripped of their clothing and possessions and machine-gunned to death as White officers looked on (Edgerton 1989:80).

By 1953 there were 30,000 young men and women assembled in the forest, with the active army consisting of 3,000 men. There was little coordination to Mau Mau operations; rebel actions consisted largely of hit-and-run attacks, often on symbolic targets such as the Royal Sagana Lodge where Queen Elizabeth had stayed the previous year on her visit to Kenya. The rebels did not have sufficient weapons to mount a concerted attack on well-armed British positions. Few of the leaders had any education; perhaps as a caricature of British titles, they gave themselves such names as General China, General Russia, and General Hitler. Dedan Kimathi, the leader of the rebels in the forest whose capture virtually ended the rebellion, called himself Field Marshall Sir Dedan Kimathi, later adding the title Prime Minister. Most of the rebels were young men and women who joined the rebellion in the forest with the enthusiastic belief that they would drive the British out of Kenya and receive land on which to farm.

By the end of 1953, 3,064 of the Mau Mau had been killed and 1,000 captured; almost 100,000 Mau Mau supporters had been arrested and 64,000 brought to trial. Nevertheless, the fight did not go well for the British army. They were ill-prepared for forest warfare; they made noise, shot at phantoms, feared attacks from elephants and rhinoceros, and fared poorly in the high altitude of the mountain forests. Soon the British soldiers sent to fight were patrolling the periphery of the forest while African soldiers recruited after the emergency was declared for the "Home Guard" fought in the forest.

Mau Mau activity spread to neighboring Uganda and Tanganyika, and Mau Mau agitating in Nairobi was widespread. Theft of money and guns increased, and Kikuyu gangs forbade Africans in the cities to engage in such European practices as smoking European tobacco, drinking European beer, wearing hats, and riding city buses. They set up courts and were essentially running the city.

To end resistance in Nairobi, the British surrounded the city and went through it section by section, rounding up Kikuyu and others and sending them to detention camps or reserves. When 3,000 women and 6,000 children were rounded up to be sent back to the reserve on trains, the women threw the food given them at railway staff and out windows while singing Mau Mau songs. Thereafter the British put screens on the train windows to "protect the railway staff."

But finally British power wore down the rebels. They had destroyed the urban base and cut off most communication with the reserves by building a fifty-mile-long ditch between the forests and the reserve with sympathetic Kikuyu. The ditch was ten feet deep and sixteen feet wide in places, filled with barbed wire and sharpened bamboo stakes. It was dug by forced Kikuyu labor—women, children, and the elderly working from 6 A.M. to 6 P.M. under orders of loyalist chiefs. The British bombed the forests, often with nineteen-pound bombs from small Pipers and Cessnas; before the emergency was over they had dropped 50,000 tons of bombs on the forests and fired two million rounds of ammunition on strafing runs. Finally, the British relocated one million Kikuyu from their scattered homesteads into villages surrounded with barbed wire, where thousands died from hunger and disease. Dedan Kimathi's capture in October 1956 marked the end of the organized resistance.

The Mau Mau rebellion shook the British, but more interesting was the reaction to Mau Mau violence. There is no question that the rebels committed atrocities, especially against Africans loyal to the British. But if the atrocities committed by the rebels were awful, those committed by the settlers and the African police were far worse. Prisoners were routinely tortured and suspects killed with impunity. Settlers advocated killing all Kikuyu and even using an atomic bomb. Trials were rigged. When Kenyatta was tried on the charge of being the Mau Mau leader, the British judge, carefully selected by the governor of the colony, guaranteed a conviction in exchange for a payment of 20,000 pounds on which he could retire to

England. He received it. When the sole witness against Kenyatta admitted afterward that he had been bribed with the promise of an English university education, he was promptly arrested for perjury. Settlers openly "hunted" Kikuyu, others bragging that they had killed hundreds. Edgerton provided a particularly graphic account concerning two Kikuyu boys who were stopped by settlers reacting to a report of Mau Mau activity in the area. Unable to tell the settlers what they wanted to know, the boys were tied by the ankles to back of a land rover and dragged until their faces had been torn off. The men left them in the road and returned home, laughing, to drink brandy. Police came upon one group of Kikuyu and killed them all, later discovering they were loyalist Kikuyu who had huddled together for protection against the rebels. But the most gruesome charges were to come later because of atrocities committed against Kikuyu held in detention camps.

The Oath and the Detention Camps

One of the questions we asked at the beginning of this discussion was how those against whom protest is directed react. Obviously the British and the settlers reacted brutally. Edgerton (1989:242) compared their reaction to that of the terrible vengeance wrought by White slaveholders in response to slave revolts. White Kenyans, he said, always feared a violent uprising but masked their fear with assurances that Africans were loyal, docile, and cowardly. When this illusion was shattered, they felt betrayed and tried to regain their pride, as well as their wealth and privilege, by reacting with torture, massacre, and mutilation, all to try to demonstrate the futility of protest.

So difficult was it for the British government and the settlers to understand the revolt that they attributed it almost entirely to the Mau Mau oath. They could understand no other reason why loyal retainers might be compelled to take up violence, why "decent, trusted servants" could turn into what they assumed were inhuman monsters. So fearful were they of the oath that of the first 1,015 Mau Mau who were hanged during the Emergency, 222 were found guilty of no crime except administering oaths (Edgerton 1989:174). Thus, ignoring their expropriation of Kikuyu land, their racism, and the legislation that required Africans to carry identification cards, ignoring the conditions on the reserve, the poverty and destitution in the cities, and the destruction of Kikuyu livestock, they assumed that if they could wipe out the effects of the oath they could once more convert the savages into loyal workers and retainers. A thirty-one-year-old settler who was born in Kenya expressed the following sentiment (cited Edgerton 1989:241):

> *I was raised with Africans, you know. Kyukes mostly. I thought I knew what they were like but when the Mau Mau terrorism began I realized I didn't know them at all. They weren't like us. They weren't even like animals—animals are understandable. They're natural. The Mau Mau were... what's the word? Perverted, I guess. It was the oath you see. Once they took it, life didn't mean anything to them. If we couldn't drive the [Mau Mau] poison out of them by getting them to confess, all we could do was kill them.*

Suspected Mau Mau rebels detained by the British army in 1953. By the end of the rebellion, the British had arrested almost 100,000 Kikuyu.

Statements such as this echo the European witch trials of the fifteenth through seventeenth centuries, when it was believed that only by getting a witch to confess could they be cured.

Following the advice of British psychiatrists in Kenya, the British assumed the way to resolve African protest was to reeducate Kikuyu, and the place to do so was the detention camps. By 1959, 80,000 suspected Mau Mau, Mau Mau sympathizers, or simply oath takers were imprisoned and subjected to everything from Christian schooling to beatings, mutilation, and torture. While the horrendous conditions in the camps—starvation rations, electric shocks, torture, castration, rape, and the like—were reported little was done until eleven men were killed in a savage attack by prison guards resulting from a plan initiated by a senior superintendent of prisons.

Since the British believed the oath prevented Mau Mau from working for Europeans, the superintendent reasoned that if he could force Mau Mau leaders to work, their violation of the oath would release them from its hold. In 1959 he had an officer in charge of one camp at Hola march 85 men into the fields surrounded by 111 African guards to force them to work. Despite their willingness to work, the prisoners were set upon again and again by the guards, until 11 were beaten to death. The officer in charged later claimed they died from drinking polluted water, not knowing that an autopsy was in progress and that the results would be made public. The outcry, especially in England, over indisputable proof of the conditions in the detention camps caused a political scandal that not only led to canceling the emergency and releasing all detainees, but set into motion a process that would lead to Kenyan independence four years later. What the deaths of over eleven thousand Mau Mau rebels could not accomplish was accomplished by the deaths of the eleven detainees.

Independence

At the time of the Mau Mau rebellion colonial rule was being threatened elsewhere in Africa. The French were involved in a long and costly rebellion in Algeria, Ghana had achieved independence in 1960, and Belgium was leaving the Congo. White settlers in Kenya still thought independence and Black rule was at least a decade or two off. But in Great Britain, the government, weakened by economic decline and in no condition to defend the colonies, developed a plan to turn Kenya into a parliamentary democracy and give Africans full participation in the government. Kenyatta was released from detention and soon became the head of the Kenyan African National Union (KANU). The British permitted elections and suffrage, and in a ceremony on December 12, 1963, with Jomo Kenyatta and Prince Phillip representing the Royal family standing side-by-side, the British flag was lowered and the new Kenyan flag raised.

Whites began to leave. Those who remained did so largely because they could not sell their land, but Kenyatta did everything he could to allay their fears, proclaiming a doctrine of "forgive and forget" for both Africans and Whites and trying to steer a course through the fear of civil war among Africans of different ethnic groups such as the one that had erupted in the Congo. We must remember that the European agreements that had carved up Africa into states paid little attention to cultural and ethnic boundaries and ethnic groups had little opportunity or need to form political alliances or accommodations under repressive colonial rule. Thus Kenyatta had to mold diverse ethnic groups—Luo, Kikuyu, Lao, Kanga, Maasi— into one government modeled after European states. Think of countries such as Canada, which has been trying for hundreds of years with mixed success to accommodate only two linguistic groups—English and French—and you get an idea of the problems of African states with far greater cultural and linguistic divisions.

Kenyatta granted political office to one person who had tried to kill him while in prison and appointed judges who had been responsible for his detention. But he also largely ignored the sacrifices of the Mau Mau rebels and the allegiance of loyalists to the British. For example, Ian Henderson, a Kikuyu-speaking police officer who had interrogated and tortured General China in 1954 after his capture, was retained as an officer in the Kenya police. General China was denied a commission in the Kenyan army, being forced instead to enlist as a private and to endure basic training under the command of British officers who had been retained to train the army. In fact, those Africans who fought with the British against the Mau Mau fared far better than those who had fought against the British. Mau Mau veterans claimed they deserved free land and recognition for their sacrifices and even formed a political party to advance their demands, but to little effect. For this Kenyatta was severely criticized. He was also attacked for the wealth that he, his family, and his backers accumulated, earning them the nickname "The Royal Family."

Bitter stories surfaced, such as that of Wanjohi Mung'au, who was imprisoned for ten years by the colonial government. After his release he attempted to organize Mau Mau veterans into cooperatives to force Europeans off their land; he was imprisoned by Kenyatta's government for another seven years. Solomon Memia (cited Edgerton 1989:234), a Mau Mau veteran living in the Nairobi slums said,

> *I regret to state that those of us who fought for freedom were never given a chance to participate in the present government. The majority of ex-freedom fighters are among those who live here in these shanties, because they have nowhere else to go. We weren't given jobs because it was alleged we were uneducated. The young who were in school during the freedom struggle are the ones who have the say in our government, and they are not concerned with our affairs.*

Yet Kenya ultimately thrived, as many Whites stayed, with many American Whites joining them. Tourism boomed, and the economy did relatively well. But most Kenyans remain poor, and, with the population now five times what it was when the British arrived, land is scarce.

By 1988, a vast gap had opened between the African elite and the bulk of the Kenyan population. Here is Edgerton's (1989:231) summary:

> *The Kenya elite live luxuriously in the same neighborhoods that were once reserved for whites. They drive expensive cars, vacation in Europe, and send their children to private schools, and have their needs taken care of by servants. Their life-style resembles those of the wealthy whites who used to live in the same large houses, except that they hire more guards, have embedded more broken glass on top of the walls that surround their estates, and spend more money on electronic security systems. There are many more desperately poor people in Nairobi today than ever before, and they often burglarize and sometimes kill the wealthy "Black Europeans" (or "Benzi," as they are often called after the Mercedes-Benz cars they often drive). There are even more poor people in rural areas, many of whom remain landless. Only about 25 percent of Kenya's land is arable, and the fertile land that was once plentiful enough for six million people must now support four times that number. But the vast "white highlands" that were once a symbol of injustice and dispossession, are now almost entirely in African hands. Wealthy Africans are the new targets of discontent.*

In 1989 there was a popular insurrection against the Kenyan government that resulted in some reforms, but unrest and protest continues, often met with violence by the nation-state.

On the left is Emiliano Zapata, Mexican revolutionary leader, from whom the present-day Zapatistas took their name. On the right is the leader of the present Zapatista rebellion in Chiapas, Sub-Commandante Marcos, and one of his officers.

The Rebellion in Chiapas

We saw in the cases of Malaysia and Kenya how global economic developments—the green revolution in the case of Malaysia, nineteenth-century British imperial expansion in the case of Kenya—created conditions that spurred peasant protest. In the case of the Zapatistas, the revolt is clearly related to globalization of the economy. Not coincidentally, January 1, 1994, the day the Zapatistas declared their revolt, was also the day that marked Mexico's entrance into the North American Free Trade Alliance (NAFTA), a free trade treaty between Mexico, the United States, and Canada that would gradually phase out protective tariffs in all three countries. That the events were not unrelated in the eyes of the Zapatistas was made clear by the masked Zapatista leader, Sub-Commandant Marcos, when he said, "NAFTA was the death certificate of the indigenous peoples of Mexico."

The Zapatista army was named for Emiliano Zapata, one of the heroes of the Mexican Revolution of 1910. Zapata led the army of the state of Morelos against the sugar plantation owners in an attempt to gain land for landless peasants. Prior to 1860 most Indian land in Mexico was owned collectively by village communities, but legislation passed under the leadership of Mexico's first president, Benito Juarez, gave individuals title to village land. The legislation was intended to free Indians from the domain of their community and give them control of their own property. But the right to own also included the right to sell, and over the course of the next fifty years two million acres of communally held land was absorbed into large haciendas or landholdings. In many cases it was pawned to meet living expenses and the expenses of sponsoring religious feasts, from which people gained respect and prestige (Wolf 1969:17).

The succeeding government of Porfiro Díaz, which ruled Mexico from 1876 to 1910, sold huge tracts of state land, mostly to American corporations to attract foreign capital. The result of these changes in land ownership was that by 1910, the year the Mexican Revolution began, the vast majority of the Mexican population was landless. For example, in 1910, in the northern state of Chihuahua, where rebel leader Pancho Villa operated with his revolutionary army, seventeen persons owned two-fifths of the state and 95.5 percent of family heads owned no land at all (Wolf 1969:33).

The Mexican Revolution of 1910 was fought to regain the land that was lost, and the government installed by the victorious rebel armies lost little time in writing into the Constitution of 1917 a law (Article 27) that provided for the redistribution of land held by the state and private owners to landless peasants. The major provision for redistribution required at least twenty people to present a petition to the government for contiguous landholdings (*eijidos*) that they would receive collectively, with the stipulations that they work the land and they could not sell or mortgage it. Thus the Constitution of 1917 reestablished, in part, the collective ownership of land that the government had done away with in the mid-nineteenth century.

Part of the paradox of the Zapatista rebellion of 1994 was that it occurred in a country whose constitution included a provision for land redistribution. To understand this apparent contradiction, it is necessary to know a little more about Chiapas, the Mayan Indian population, the globalization of the world's economy, and the Mexican government's altering in 1992 of Article 27 of the Constitution.

Poverty and Inequality in Chiapas

Chiapas is the southernmost state in Mexico, bordering Guatemala to the south and the Pacific Ocean to the west. It is the poorest state in Mexico, with the highest malnutrition and illiteracy rates; 28 percent of the population consists of Mayan Indians. The Mayans are the second largest indigenous group in the Western Hemisphere, second in number only to the Quechua-speaking descendants of the Inca.

Chiapas is a highly stratified society, with a few wealthy landowners at the top, a small middle tier consisting of merchants, small-scale farmers, coffee growers, government bureaucrats, and political leaders, and a large poor population of small landholders, wage laborers, artisans, and unemployed. In 1994 almost 20 percent of the population had no income and another 40 percent had an income less than the minimum wage.

The societies of Chiapas were always stratified to some degree. Mayan society had its elite, and when the Spanish conquered Mexico they maintained a two-tier society that remains in place today, with themselves and later their Ladino descendants on top and the indigenous people on the bottom. This division is particularly evident in the tropical forests of Chiapas, the area from which the Zapatistas have drawn most of their active support.

While Zapata and Pancho Villa were fighting at the beginning of the twentieth century for land for peasants in the north, ranchers in Chiapas created private armies, the *mapaches* ("raccoons," so-called because of their habit of raiding fresh corn from Indian corn fields) to suppress any movement for land reform on the part of the Indians of Chiapas. These ranchers controlled huge landholdings and terrorized the local population, hanging virtually the entire male population (500 people) in one local church during the Mexican Revolution to demonstrate their power. *Mapache* officers received landholdings in exchange for their services. In 1916 the federal army moved into Chiapas to initiate land reform, but those officers and soldiers who did not take land themselves were driven back by the *mapaches*, whose acts are still celebrated by Chiapas ranchers. In 1916, 8,000 private land-holders owned 3 million hectares (7.4 million acres), virtually all of the good land in the state; by 1993 the number of private landholders was reduced to 6,000, while the Indian population had grown ten times to 2 million (Nigh 1994:9).

As in the case of Malaysia and Kenya, the Zapatista protest concerned relation-ships within local communities and the divisions of power and wealth. There is in Chiapas a clear economic and political hierarchy, even in Mayan communities, with those at the top supporting the government and the ruling political party, the PLN, and the bottom supporting or at least sympathizing with the Zapatistas. Vil-lages, towns, and cities in Chiapas are generally governed by political bosses (*ca-ciques*) whose authority comes from their position in the ruling party. The *caciques* generally control such sources of wealth as soft drink and beer distributorships and trucking and communication services. These divisions within Mayan commu-nities were clearly evident after the Zapatista began their rebellion and the army moved in to occupy the area. Representatives of human rights organizations reported seeing homes flying white flags, signaling the occupants' support for the army, while many homes without flags were empty. In addition, some Maya formed local vigi-lante groups, which, along with the private armies of the ranchers, the *guardias blan-cas* ("white guards"), attacked and harassed Zapatista supporters and sympathizers. Thus, as with Malaysian villages and Kikuyu settlements and reserves, there was a clear division between the well-to-do and the poor and, as in the case of the Mau Mau rebellion, community members who sympathized with the rebels and those loyal to the government. The question is, *how did this inequality develop?*

The Zapatista base is largely in eastern Chiapas, in the foothills of the central highlands and the Lancandon rainforest that borders Guatemala. Until the 1950s the rainforest was largely unoccupied. The Chol and Cholti Maya who inhabited the area in the sixteenth and seventeenth centuries were either killed by military and missionary expeditions or relocated to work on Spanish haciendas (Nations 1994:31). In the 1950s the government encouraged settlement in the rainforest by Tzeltal and Tzotzil Mayans from the overpopulated central highlands. There the Mayan colonists competed with loggers and ranchers for land. A pattern devel-oped whereby loggers would build roads into the rainforests, take whatever timber they wanted, and be followed by Mayans practicing slash and burn agriculture. However, because of poor planning and limited support from the government, along with the lack of relevant agricultural skills by the new settlers, the soil was soon denuded, and Mayan settlers found it necessary to move to other areas of the forest where the same cycle was repeated (Duncan 1994:28).

Furthermore, the government never issued clear land titles to the Mayan farmers, paving the way for cattle ranchers to graze their stock on the cleared forest. As a result of this pattern, two-thirds of the Selva Lancandona has been cleared, leaving only the Montes Azules Biosphere Reserve with its original vegetation. In addition, the area's population increased from 6,000 in 1960 to over 300,000 in 1994. While some of the Maya in the rainforest have received title to land (and the leaders of their communities quickly declared their loyalty to the government), the vast majority have not and have continually been harassed by the *guardias blancas* to move off the land.

Another category of Zapatista supporters are Protestant converts who were evicted from their villages in the 1970s and 1980s. They were expelled ostensibly because they undermined the traditional religious practices of the largely Catholic population, but most were forced to move because they challenged the traditional political system of local bosses, refused to pay taxes to support traditional religious ceremonies, and refused to consume liquor or beer, an important source of income for town officials (Gossen 1994:19).

In addition to the Mayans who moved into the area in the 1950s and 1960s and the religious and political refugees, there are others that the government encouraged to settle in the rainforests to serve as a buffer against the Mayans from Guatemala, who were streaming across the border to escape the Guatemalan army.

Economic inequality was aggravated by the economic boom of the 1960s and 1970s in Mexico. During that time Mexico borrowed heavily from world financial organizations to invest in energy. Much of the investment went for oil exploration and drilling and hydroelectric projects in Chiapas. While Chiapas supplies fully 50 percent of Mexico's electricity, almost 35 percent of Chiapas homes have no electricity. The jobs and wealth that came into Chiapas in the 1960s and 1970s were not equally distributed, and one consequence was increased village conflict. Furthermore, as some members of the population were earning large sums working on government projects, others were losing their land to cattle and dairy ranchers and to the flooding created by the hydroelectric dams.

June Nash (1994), who did field work in a Chiapas village in the 1960s, reported that some poor peasants assumed that the rich had accummulated their wealth through the use of witchcraft, while others believed the wealth was given to the rich by cave dwellers in exchange for their souls. She also reports that interpersonal conflict that took the form of witchcraft accusations or expressions of envy—the evil eye—were settled by homicide.

Thus the rebels likely consisted of representatives of different Mayan groups, some religious and political victims of more prosperous Maya, along with some Ladinos. The question is, *why did they join in or support the revolt?*

The Rebellion and the Global Economy

One of the major reasons for the plight of poor Chiapas peasants is the decline in support for small-scale agriculture in Mexico. The debate over whether Mexico needed peasant agriculture at all increased in 1982 when the debt crisis (Mexico had a $96 million foreign debt) forced Mexico to adopt an austerity budget in exchange for a restructuring of the debt. One of the measures adopted that affected Chiapas peasants was the removal of the subsidy for fertilizer (Collier 1994:16). Cooperatives were formed, and the Indians began to agitate for political and economic reform. They were met by brutal repression from the *guardias blancas*. Next, believing the world coffee market had stabilized, Mexico ended coffee price supports for farmers. Coffee production was the major cash crop of Chiapas peasants. As soon as Mexico cut its price support, the world market price for coffee plunged, further damaging the livelihood of peasants in the Chiapas lowlands and throwing many into bankruptcy (Nations 1994:33).

Then, in the clearest sign of the government's withdrawal of support for small-scale agriculture, they modified Article 27 of the Mexican Constitution so that if landholders agreed, *ejido* land could be sold. In addition, the government let it be known that there was no more land to redistribute. This ended the land redistribution program, leaving Chiapas peasants without land or without title to land on which they were squatting.

Finally, NAFTA was negotiated and approved. Free trade in itself might not have damaged the economic prospects of Chiapas's peasants. They might have done well with their agricultural, forest, and handicraft products, but it was clear there was little or no support from the government. Furthermore, with NAFTA signed and dreams of an increase in American beef imports, ranchers in Chiapas began talking openly of expanding their cattle production, which clearly would have required taking over additional peasant land. This meant increased confrontations with the *guardias blancas*. In fact, many peasants had reportedly begun arming themselves before the revolt to protect themselves from the ranchers' private armies.

Thus, as James D. Nations (1994:33) put it, it is little wonder that some Chiapas farmers began to feel they were victims of a conspiracy, with no market for their crops and no land to grow them on anyway:

> It is not difficult to imagine a Tzeltal or Tojolbal farmer sizing up his choices: he can move to San Cristobal de las Casas and sell popsicles from a pushcart, he can work for a cattleman punching cows, or he can rebel against a situation that seems to have him trapped. That hundreds of farmers chose to rebel should come as no surprise.

The Revolt and the Reaction of the Mexican Government

James Scott pointed out that poor farmers in Malaysia were protesting not so much their traditional position in their villages, but rather the worsening of that position as a consequence of technological change. The Kikuyu in Kenya were not protesting the initial seizing of land by the British; they had adapted quite well as squatters. Their protest was against the constant worsening of their economic position as British settlers tried to increase their economic domination. The rebellion occurred only after the settlers destroyed African livestock and evicted people en masse from their farms. Likewise, the peasants in Chiapas had adapted to voluntarily or involuntarily leaving their villages in search of land in the rainforests of the Chiapas lowlands. Resistance occurred only after a whole series of changes by the Mexican government, culminating in the altering of Article 27 and NAFTA, as it tried to adapt to changes in the global economy.

The Chiapas rebellion reveals another feature of resistance that we saw in Sedaka as well as in Kenya: the attempt of those resisting oppression to use the past ideals and rhetoric of their oppressors against them. In Chiapas, the Zapatistas used the rhetoric and principles that gave the Mexican government and the ruling political party, the PRI, its original legitimacy, much as the peasants in Malaysia fight the rich with the ideology the rich once used to justify their legitimacy in the traditional social order. The Zapatistas made it clear that the government betrayed the very principles that gave it legitimacy in the beginning, even going so far as to negate the very laws and rationale that the Mexican Revolution was fought for and reinstituting the land alienation that created the conditions for the Mexican revolution to begin with.

Two aspects of the government's reaction are worth noting. First, they seem to have been relatively restrained in their reaction, due in part, no doubt, to the skilled handling of the media and the Internet by the Zapatistas, whose supporters maintained a Web site (http://www.utexas.edu/ftp/student/nave/zapatismo.html) to report the Zapatistas's version of events. With the story making international headlines and the Zapatistas compared with Mexican heroes of the revolution, the government could not move to crush the rebellion militarily. Certainly given the effectiveness of the Guatemalan genocide against its Mayan population, the Mexican army, at least as well equipped as the Guatemalan military, could have, and may yet still, do the same. The Zapatistas also made skilled use of the Internet to distribute its communiqués and report moves of the Mexican military and the *guardias blancas.* Zapatista communiqués are available at http://www.utexas.edu/ftp/student/nave/zapatismo.html and http://lanic.utexas.edu70.

The second interesting feature of the revolt is the reaction of the world's financial community. One of the fears created by the Zapatista rebellion is that it would undermine investor confidence in the Mexican government and investors would either pull their money out of Mexico, causing a further collapse of the Mexican economy, or dissuade them from putting money into the Mexican economy. These concerns were clearly voiced by an advisor to the Chase Bank; Riordan Roett, in an internal memo, advised that if the Mexican government was to retain investor confidence it must "eliminate the Zapatistas" (Silverstein and Cockburn 1995). Whether by coincidence or not, within three weeks of the memo's circulation, the Mexican military moved offensively against the Zapatistas.

James Nations (1994) suggested that there are some real problems for the Mexican government, problems that any government faces if confronted by peasant resistance. First, if the government does react with financial aid it may become just more political patronage and reach only those loyal to the PRI. In addition, if the media—which has served to limit the violence of the government response and prevent it from mounting a genocidal campaign as in Guatemala—loses interest, massive repression may result. Some 50,000 Guatemalan refugees still in Chiapas may become targets of violence. Furthermore, the factions have been arming themselves. Arms sales have increased and groups are forming to defend traditional rights and powers, reminiscent of the death squads formed by eastern Chiapas ranchers. This factional conflict exploded on December 22, 1997 with the massacre of 45 unarmed Indian sympathizers of the Zapatistas, including four pregnant women and 18 children. The killers were apparently pro-government gunman armed with AK-47 combat rifles distributed by a local PRI official (Preston 1998). Finally, the government must find some way to provide additional income and employment, but to do so by increasing the land under cultivation would mean taking land from cattlemen or from the Mayan farmers in the rainforest.

Conclusion

The central dilemma of peasants in the expanding capitalist world, according to Duncan Earle (1994:27), is whether or not small-scale agriculture has any place in the modern world. The option is the American system, where 2 percent of the population supplies food for the other 98 percent. Earle made the point that peasant farmers do and can make a profit, that it is a far more sustainable form of production, and that it does not degrade the rainforest, especially if it is based on coffee production that substitutes coffee plants for bushes under the rainforest canopy. But even coffee production is changing to a factory-type model, in which it is grown in vast open fields devoid of tree cover. The Mexican government and other governments around the world have taken actions that indicate that their answer is no, there is no place for peasants, and that the major question is whether it is best for peasants to move into the cities already burdened with millions living in squatter settlements or to have them in the countryside as laborers.

These three examples of peasant protest and rebellion reveal some of the factors that produce discontent in peasant populations. Peasant protest, however, will likely disappear as the need and opportunity for small farmers disappears. It would take a major overhaul of the world economy to reverse the concentration of agricultural wealth that exists today. However, there remain other sources of discontent, much of it coming from those people or their descendants who were the peasant farmers of past generations.

Chapter 11

Antisystemic Protest

The paranoid scapegoating process at a time of social change, when people are experiencing a sense of compulsion to live up to old moral obligations even when they are ignoring them in day-to-day behavior, is a common human event. It accompanies many social movements and is apt to flare up when law and order lapse.
ANTHONY F. C. WALLACE, ST. CLAIR

That man over there says that women need to be helped into carriages, and lifted over ditches, and have to have the best place everywhere. Nobody helps me into carriages, or over mudpuddles, or gives me any best place! And ain't I a woman? Look at me! Look at my arm! I have ploughed and planted and gathered into barns, and no man could head me! And ain't I a woman? I could work as much and eat as much as a man—when I could get it—and bear the lash as well! And ain't I a woman? I have born thirteen children, and seen most of them sold into slavery, and when I cried out with my mother's grief, none but Jesus heard me! And ain't I a woman?... If the first woman God every made was strong enough to turn the world upside down all alone, these women together ought to be able to turn it back, and get it right side up again.
SOJOURNER TRUTH, CITED SILVERBLATT, WOMEN IN STATES

The rebellions of peasants in Malaysia, Kenya, and Mexico resemble the peasant rebellions of centuries ago against landlords, nobles, elites, or whoever controlled their land and whose demands became excessive or who threatened peasant survival. The major difference between the revolts we examined and those of centuries ago are that the conditions which today's peasants protest clearly are a consequence of the globalization of the capitalist economy and the resulting social and economic transformations. But what of other forms of protest, such as workers organizations and strikes, national liberation, civil rights, feminist, militia, environmental, and fundamentalist religious movements? Is there any relationship among the diverse groups of people involved in these protests, and is there a way to conceptualize them as a whole? That is, can we place these movements in any sort of global perspective?

There is a school of thought in anthropology, sociology, history, geography, and political science that attributes these protests to the expansion of the capitalist world system. For that reason they term these *antisystemic protest* (Amin et al. 1990).

Capitalism requires constant change—new modes of production, new organizations of labor, the expansion of markets, new technology, and the like. It requires a society of perpetual growth. On the one hand this allows a capitalist economy enormous adaptability and flexibility. It allows business to take advantage of new technologies, to create new products and jobs, to pursue new markets, to experiment with new forms of financing, to abandon unprofitable products, forms of labor, or markets. On the other hand, this flexibility often has far-reaching effects on patterns of social and political relations.

The invention and development of the automobile revolutionized American society; it created millions of jobs and new industries and provided salaries for people to buy homes, appliances, and more automobiles. But the revolution wrought by the new technology also created pollution, dependence on petroleum, and industries that, in search of profit, open and close plants, first creating jobs and prosperity and then leaving unemployment and depression. Other innovations, such as the computer, revolutionized the workplace, possibly improved efficiency, created new modes of communication, and made vast stores of information available at a finger's touch. But the computer also made thousands of management jobs obsolete, just as agricultural changes made millions of peasants obsolete. While marveling over a technological innovation we often neglect to consider those whose livelihood is endangered. In our fascination with the benefits of the automobile, we rarely remember those whose living depended on horse-drawn transportation.

One can argue, as many have, that in the long run these innovations will benefit everyone. We can, as some economists do, demonstrate that in the long run business fluctuations eventually balance out. But the ups and downs of the economist's growth chart are experienced by people as alternative phases of prosperity and crisis (Guttmann 1994:14). The economy may seek equilibrium in the long run, but people do not live in the long run; having a job and an income is an everyday concern.

In this chapter we will examine the protests of those who claim that the culture of capitalism has had a detrimental effect on their lives or the lives of others. These protests can be seen as emerging from what world system theorists identify as the two world revolutions, in 1848 and 1968. We will look at labor protest associated with the revolution of 1848, feminist protest whose origins can also be said to lie in 1848, and environmental protest that, while originating in the nineteenth century, took on new meaning as a result of the revolution of 1968.

Protest as Antisystemic: The Two World Revolutions

The first world revolution, suggested Immanual Wallerstein (1990), occurred in 1848, when workers, peasants, and others staged rebellions in eleven European countries. The series of revolts that began in France were all put down within a few months, but they succeeded in setting an agenda for protest that ultimately led to most of the reforms called for by protesters. The second world revolution occurred in 1968, when workers, students, peasants, and others in the United States, France, Italy, Czechoslovakia, Japan, and Mexico participated in popular uprisings. These movements also failed to gain the immediate objectives of the protesters, but they, too, set the agenda for reforms—civil rights, gay rights, women's rights, indigenous rights, environmental reform, among others—that have defined the goals of social movements since.

The Revolution of 1848

The revolution of 1848 began in France when on February 24 workers declared a new republic based on universal suffrage; within a month it had spread to southwest Germany, Bavaria, Berlin, and most of Italy. Within weeks the governments of most of continental Europe had been overthrown; the revolution even incited a rebellion in Brazil and another revolution a year later in Colombia (Hobsbawm 1975:10). Within a year and a half, however, the revolution was defeated and, except in France, previous regimes restored to power. But while workers failed to gain their immediate objectives, the revolution of 1848 defined two sets of social movements: worker movements protesting the oppression of laborers originating in industrial revolution; and movements of national liberation motivated by a desire of peripheral countries to gain freedom from imperialism and colonial oppression. Both types of movements were, say world system theorists, modeled after the French Revolution of 1789 and its call for "liberty, equality, and fraternity." The year 1848 did not, of course, mark the beginning of such movements; organized worker protests against the abuses of industrialization go back at least to the seventeenth century in Europe, and the movements for national liberation includes the American Revolution and the successful revolt against the French by Haitian slaves in 1802. But by 1848 the general guidelines and issues involved in the protests were clearly formulated.

Worker Movements

The revolution of 1848 marked the first time a proletariat-based political group tried to achieve political power. While they failed, said Wallerstein (1990), the revolution began an intense debate among labor rights advocates over the best way of improving the situation of the growing number of industrial workers. One option was to organize unions and gain the right to strike. The problem was that the nation-states of Europe and the Americas outlawed worker unions and made strikes a criminal offense. Another option was to fight for the right to vote and form political parties to represent workers' rights. If suffrage—the right to vote—was extended to more of the electorate, and since the workers comprised a majority of the population, then they could simply assume power through the ballot box. Others argued that the governing elite would never let itself be voted out of power and that violent revolution was the only solution. The result was that two competing strategies emerged in Europe and the United States to improve the condition of workers, one

*Citizens and workers in Paris, France barricade the streets
in the Revolution of 1848.*

led by social democratic parties seeking political power through the vote, the other
by communist organizations advocating revolution.

By 1945 unions and labor-led political parties arose in the United States, England,
France, and much of Western Europe, resulting in a vast improvement in the conditions of the working class. Most core countries recognized the rights of workers
to strike and bargain collectively, developed programs of social insurance (e.g., social
security programs, unemployment programs, workers compensation programs,
health programs, education programs), and extended the vote to the poor, ethnic
minorities, and women. From the mid-nineteenth to the mid-twentieth century the
number of people in poverty in the United States and Western Europe decreased
dramatically. By 1948 most American and Western European workers enjoyed a
level of prosperity that few would have dreamed of in 1848.

At the same time, workers in revolutionary states, including Russia and most of eastern Europe, achieved their goals under communist regimes, and while they were not as prosperous as their Western counterparts, they probably enjoyed greater guarantees of basic needs (e.g. jobs, food, shelter). Thus, within a century workers enjoyed benefits fought for in the revolution of 1848.

Nationalist Antisystemic Movements

As working-class movements in Europe and the United States were struggling to improve their lives, national liberation movements were occurring on the periphery. While the social democratic and communist movements in the core were led by the industrial proletariat, the nationalist movements in the periphery were initiated by the middle class and intelligentsia reaching out to other anticapitalist segments of their populations. Thus virtually all the countries of Latin America gained their independence in the nineteenth century. The countries of Asia and Africa under European colonial rule gained their independence after World War II. By 1968, with the exception of the continuing struggle in Vietnam and continued colonial domination in a few African states, colonial powers had been forced to abandon politically their nineteenth- and early twentieth-century empires and ostensibly hand over power to indigenous elites.

The enormous world economic growth that followed World War II created an illusion. In the West, people thought they had found the solutions to the problems of economic depression and unemployment and that their world had entered a period of perpetual prosperity and growth; world hunger would be erased, infectious diseases would be eradicated, and class conflict would be a thing of the past. In the communist countries people believed they had discovered the economic formula for economic security; Russian Premier Nikita Khrushchev would in 1960 boast that by 1980 the U.S.S.R. would have overtaken and surpassed the United States in providing for its citizens. In the Third World the leaders of national liberation movements, such as the one we examined in Kenya, felt that their mixtures of socialism and capitalism would enable them to develop economically and begin to achieve the prosperity of the West. In sum, as Samir Amin et al. (1990:96) suggested, in the period after 1945 in a majority of countries the ostensible objectives of the antisystemic movements of the nineteenth century had come to pass as workers' or other popular movements gained control of major nation-states (Wallerstein 1990:33).

Each of the movements that emerged out of the revolution of 1848, according to Wallerstein, can take credit for one fundamental reform. The social democrats of the West claimed to have transformed the core states into welfare states with social insurance and an increase in real wages, a compromise Wallerstein called "Fordism." Conservative forces acceded to these reforms because they subdued protest without endangering capital accumulation; furthermore, they made good economic sense. However, conservative forces still sought to whittle away at the welfare state and the reforms embedded in them. In the communist countries, the socialization of the means of production was the great reform, along with social insurance and welfare, but at a lower level than in the West, albeit with a higher degree of security and employment. The great achievement of the national liberation movements was not an increase in wages or social security nor the socialization of the means of production, but the increased participation of indigenous people in government and the creation of an indigenous elite, such as we saw in Kenya, Mexico, and Malaysia.

Yet 1968 would see the beginning of another world revolution, this time against states that were controlled by or contained representation of the very groups that had initiated the revolution of 1848. The labor-oriented Democratic Party was in power in the United States, the labor party ruled in Britain, socialists controlled France and Italy, and Eastern European countries, at least in theory, were ruled by the workers through national communist parties. The question is *why, when so many of the objectives of the first world revolution were realized, did another revolution occur?*

The Revolution of 1968

The revolution of 1968 was marked in the United States by student protests over Vietnam, demonstrations at the Democratic National Convention in Chicago, and campus demonstrations that led to the killing of students at Jackson State and Kent State Universities by state militia. In France workers and students barricaded the streets of Paris; similar demonstrations occurred in Japan, Mexico, and elsewhere.

From a world system perspective, 1968 was as much a turning point as 1848. The "old" movements had attained state power or at least a voice in the state, so that the popular uprisings in 1968—in the United States, France, Italy, Czechoslovakia, Japan, Mexico—were not so much uprisings against the existing world system as they were protests against the "old" antisystemic movements in power in the world system. The 1968 revolution was triggered by the conviction that the old movements had not fulfilled their objectives, that they had become "part of the problem." However, the 1968 revolution also represented a protest by groups who felt they were not sharing in the system (Wallerstein 1990:27).

In the United States people protested against the government's attempt to suppress the nationalistic objectives of the Vietnam peoples; in Russia and Eastern Europe people learned about the brutalities of Stalin and witnessed the repression of freedom movements in Hungry and Czechoslovakia; in the periphery the dream of economic development turned into a nightmare of poverty, government repression, and corruption. These developments combined to leave those who had failed to gain relief with no place to turn. Thus in the midst of a continuing and unpopular war in Vietnam and a growing "counterculture" protesting consumerism and the growing gap in wealth between the core and the periphery, the dissidents could turn to neither the social democrats nor the communists to express their discontent. Instead, new social movements were created that focused on "identity issues" such as civil rights, women's rights, gay and lesbian rights, indigenous people's rights, and handicapped rights (Wallerstein 1990:41). For a time, there was a sense of mutual solidarity among these movements expressed in the idea of a "rainbow coalition."

Demonstrators outside the Democratic National Convention in Chicago in 1968 are attacked by police.

While in the West the theme was the forgotten people—minorities, women, and gays—in the East the struggle was directed against the bureaucrats of the communist states, a protest that would culminate in what some claim was the world revolution of 1989 that toppled the communist regimes of Eastern Europe (Wagar 1991:102). In the periphery it was not that social and economic reforms failed to help half the people or that reforms created as many privileged people as they removed. Rather, it was that those in power promoted or at least acquiesced in adopting economic reforms and practices that resulted in continuing (often worsening) economic conditions, neocolonial subordination, and the emergence of a new elite.

Thus in 1968 the antisystemic movements born in 1848 faced the new antisystemic movements born in 1968. Yet, as Immanual Wallerstein (1990:45) suggested,

> [w]hen all is said and done, all these movements (as movements) emerged out of a rejection of the injustices of the existing world-system, the capitalist world-

economy. Each in its own way was seeking to fulfill the slogan of the French rev-
olution: more liberty, more equality, more fraternity.

A range of antisystemic movements emerged out of the two world revolutions. Our assumption is that each of these we examine in this chapter represents protest against various features of the culture of capitalism. This is not to suggest that all the movements conceptualized their protest in that way; often they did not. Members of the militia movements in the United States, for example, do not focus on capitalism in their protests; their targets include the United Nations, Jews, Blacks, the World Trade Organization, and other agencies or groups that they blame for their economic distress. Yet on closer analysis, it is clearly the globalization of trade, the loss of manufacturing jobs to overseas assembly plants, the decline of small farmers and ranchers that caused them economic harm (see Beeman 1997; Junas 1995).

The Protests of Labor: Coal Miners in Nineteenth-Century Pennsylvania

In *St. Clair,* Anthony F. C. Wallace (1987) offered an intimate glimpse of life in the nineteenth-century Pennsylvania coal town of St. Clair and the conditions that led to labor protest, and the efforts of mine owners and operators to suppress it. For various reasons, coal mining was not economically viable in much of Pennsylvania, yet mine operators persisted in their efforts to make a profit, scrimping on safety and workers, wages and then blaming the workers for their lack of success. As we shall see, the workers responded with labor protest met with systematic repression.

The Coal Industry and the Worker's Life

In the 1820s and 1830s investors from Philadelphia and New York turned their attention to the coal fields of Pennsylvania, investing heavily in land they thought would yield high profits in coal. The landowners generally did not run the mining operations themselves but rented or leased the land to coal mine operators. The operators expected to make a profit because of the need for coal to provide warmth in homes and fuel for the furnaces of what they hoped would be a thriving U.S. iron industry. Labor for the mines came from new immigrants from England, Germany, Ireland, and Wales.

Coal mining in the anthracite region of southeastern Pennsylvania entailed digging shafts underground to locate the veins of coal, building tracks or hoists in the shafts to haul coal and transport men and equipment to and from the surface, and constructing pumps to drain the water shafts. Above ground was a series of conveyer devices called breakers that broke the large pieces of coal into desired sizes and loaded the coal onto railroad cars or canal barges for shipment to its destination.

Each mine in southeastern Pennsylvania, where St. Clair is located, employed 200–300 persons. Work organization, as it is in most industries, was hierarchical and divided between those who worked below ground in the mines and those who worked above ground. The lowest-level worker in the mines was boys eight to twelve years of age who worked the ventilation doors that controlled air flow in the mine as men, mules, and equipment passed back and forth. Next were the teen-age boys who drove the mules that pulled the carts filled with coal. Next in the underground hierarchy were the miners' helpers, and next were the contract min-ers, who were paid according to the amount of coal they loaded. Toward the top of the worker's hierarchy were the craftsmen—masons, carpenters, blacksmiths, and pumpmen—who worked underground. In charge of this group were the mine boss and the fire boss, whose main duty was to inspect the mine each morning to ensure that it was safe from methane gas produced by the coal, rock falls, and flooding. Above ground the bottom of the hierarchy consisted of the slatepickers, who picked debris out of the coal before it was loaded for shipment and who might be as young as four years of age and other unskilled workers doing a variety of loading chores. Higher up in the above ground hierarchy were the highly skilled workers such as engineers, machinists, carpenters, and teamsters.

The work force in the mine was also divided by ethnic group; the top jobs were held by migrants from areas with a coal mining tradition—England, Wales, and Germany; at the bottom were migrants from Ireland, who had little or no mining experience. The place of the Irish at the bottom of the hierarchy was also a conse-quence of their reputation for rowdiness, drunkenness, and unsafe conduct in the mines.

Mining grew significantly in the St. Clair area from the 1840s through the 1870s, in spite of the fact that few people were making any money and many were losing a great deal. The costs to operators of mining a ton of coal seemed to vary from $1.56 to $3.16. These figures did not include township taxes, canal or railroad shipping costs, or commissions to sales agents, nor depreciation on property or interest on loans. Railroad shipping costs varied, climbing or falling from an aver-age of about $1.60 per ton. In sum, the actual cost of mining a ton of coal must have been at least $3.16 to $4.16, although, given the absence of accounting procedures it is unlikely mine operators knew their full production costs. However, depending on the competition, the time of year, the supply, and other factors, the price of coal to customers averaged only about $2.75 per ton. Moreover, there were frequent interruptions to mining operations caused by accidents, breakdowns, overproduc-tion, and flooding.

Wallace suggested that one reasons people continued to mine despite losing money was the inadequacy of their accounting procedures: by the time they real-ized that they were losing money it was too late to do anything about it. Wallace (1987:25) estimated that 95 percent of all collieries failed from 1820 to 1875, and the median survival time of a company was less than one year.

Why was coal mining unprofitable in St. Clair and the surrounding area? Appar-ently there were two reasons: the geology of the area and the frequent work stop-pages caused by accidents.

Veins of coal are stratified deposits of decomposed organic materials trans-formed underground by pressure and heat into masses of carbon-rich materials. Movements of the Earth's crust sometimes brings these veins to the surface, so that they form vertical or diagonal deposits. The size and directions of these deposits determine how easy or difficult they are to mine. Those veins brought to the surface are obviously the easiest to mine, and these deposits were the first to be exploited. Other deposits can be reached only by digging underground. For these the ease of mining depends on the size of the vein and the depth to which one had to dig to reach it. The problem in the St. Clair area was that the nature of the coal deposits required a lot of digging to reach veins that were often small or of poor quality.

Apparently coal mine operators could have avoided their losses if they had taken seriously the reports of geologists who concluded that mining in the area would not be profitable. But the landowners and the mine operators chose to ignore those reports, believing instead those who attacked the scientists' findings and claimed that the investments that had already been made could prove profitable.

The second reason the mines failed to make money—the frequency of work stoppages due to accidents—was related to the first; given the small profit margin to be made mining coal in the anthracite district, mine operators had to save money on operations, and one way they did that was by scrimping on safety. Coal mining is dangerous. In addition to cave-ins, flooding caused by pump failures, and the risks of working around the conveyor belts of the breakers, there was the constant danger of explosions. Coal produces methane gas, and when the amount of methane reaches a 5–12 percent mixture with oxygen any flame or spark will ignite it. Since miners of the period carried open-flame lamps attached to their helmets, the possibility of explosion was very great. One way to prevent the critical buildup of methane was to construct ventilation systems that ensured constant air flow through the shafts. Such systems were costly, however, and since the profit margins were so small most mine operators invested a minimum in such systems. Moreover, there were no state or federal safety standards that the mine operators had to follow. The costs of neglecting safety were high to both miners and mine operators: miners lost lives and limbs in accidents and explosions, and operators lost money in the destruction of equipment.

The mine owners failed to recognize or admit that the geology of the coal fields made it uneconomical to mine: They blamed their economic failure not on the geology or their business practices, but on the federal government for not putting a high enough tariff on British iron being imported into the country. Coal mining profits were closely tied to the rise and fall of the American iron industry; if the iron industry did not expand, the coal industry could not grow. But British iron was cheaper, and perhaps better, than American iron. If British iron was made more expensive by high import tariffs, both the American iron industry and the coal industry would expand and profit.

Accidents and work stoppages, however, could not be blamed on the British or the government. Mine operators and owners, instead of recognizing their own culpability, blamed careless workers. When Wallace reviewed accident reports for the period, he found that in almost every case the accident was blamed on miner negligence. This not only absolved the mine owner of blame for the economic losses, it also relieved the mine operator of any financial liability for the accident.

The accident and death rates due to inadequate ventilation and lack of emergency tunnels to allow miners to escape from explosions or cave-ins were appalling.

An artist's rendition of a Pennsylvania coal mine disaster in the nineteenth century. A mining employee had less than an even chance of surviving for twelve years, and he could expect to be killed or crippled for life in six.

It is difficult to get reliable figures on injuries and deaths in the mines from 1850 to 1880. After examining fatality rates from 1870 to 1884, Wallace estimated that fatality rates varied from 2.3 percent to 6.8 percent of the work force per year—and this was after the passage of a mine safety law in 1869 in Pennsylvania. We do know that the numbers killed in Pennsylvania mines were far higher than in Great Britain; there was one fatality for every 33,433 tons mined in Pennsylvania as opposed to one fatality per 103,000 tons in Great Britain.

Before the passage of the mine safety law in 1869 no one kept consistent records, but by using reports in the *Miner's Journal,* the major publication for the mining industry, Wallace concluded that each year 6 percent of people employed in mining, including those who worked above ground, were killed, another 6 percent were crippled for life, while yet another 6 percent were seriously injured. Thus a mining employee had less than an even chance of surviving for twelve years, and he could expect to be killed or crippled for life in six. (Wallace 1987:253) Since mine operators continued to see the accidents as caused by careless miners, and since the courts absolved them of any responsibility for death or accidents, there was little need for them to change their practices.

Given the difficulty of making a profit in coal mining, mine operators not only cut costs on safety but also minimized the pay of miners. It was a buyer's market for labor. The transformation of agriculture in Europe, as we saw in Chapter 2, created millions of landless peasants, while the fluctuations in demand for such products as textiles, iron, and coal resulted in great economic insecurity for those dependent on jobs for their livelihood.

Mine managers made $1.95 per day, foreman $1.25 per day, blacksmiths $1.08 per day, and miners $1.16 per day if they worked twenty-four days in the four-week pay period (or about $28 per month). Contract miners were a different category and were paid by the wagon load, or by the yard if they were cutting tunnels. But out of this the contract miner had to pay his helpers and other expenses, such as lamps and wicks. Helpers generally earned $0.85–0.95 per day, which meant the contract miner had to earn about $50 per month just to earn as much as he paid his helper.

The income was above subsistence level for the time, but that assumed no work stoppages, no illness, and no layoffs—all three of which were likely at some point. This was compensated for, in some respects, by the fact that most households had more than one wage earner; a household with one worker might make $150–200 per year. Some households took in boarders and some women worked as seamstresses, cooks, and maids.

Food was cheap; corn was $0.50 per bushel, eggs $0.11 per dozen, flour $5.00 per barrel, butter $0.18 per pound, bacon $0.07 per pound, beef $0.08 per pound. Housing was also cheap. Thus a laborer with a wife and two children who earned on the average $20 per month could subsist and even save a little; families with more than two children would have required income from other family members, but children could be put to work by the time they were eight or nine. The problem was that work was often not steady—strikes, floods, and accidents often closed down the mines or disabled the miner.

Furthermore, working in the mines took a devastating toll on the miner's health. Coal mining produced not only methane gas but tiny particles of coal dust that worked its way into the lungs. The rates of disability and death due to "miner's asthma," or black lung disease, were extremely high. As one mine inspector (cited Wallace 1987:257) of the time wrote,

[a]fter six years' labor in a badly ventilated mine—that is a mine where a man with a good constitution may from habit be able to work everyday for several years—the lungs begin to change to a bluish color. After twelve years they are densely black, not a vestige of natural color remaining, and are little better than carbon itself. The miner dies at thirty-five of coal miner's consumption.

Worker Resistance and Protest

How could the laborers protect their interests, and formally or informally protest the dangers they faced in the mines and the economic insecurity brought about by low wages, layoffs, and work stoppages?

Miners protested their low wages and dangerous work conditions in various ways; there were spontaneous work stoppages, acts of sabotage against the mines, demonstrations and marches, and probably work slowdowns. Many of these acts were met with force from the police or state militia. The first regional strike in the region occurred in 1858, when lower coal prices resulted in wage cuts. Miners closed down the mines and marched through the streets banging drums and waving flags. The sheriff called out the militia, and men were arrested on riot charges.

The first effective strike occurred in 1868, when the Pennsylvania legislature passed a law making eight hours a legal workday, although it also meant a cut in wages. Miners began a strike, demanding that the eight-hour day be instituted with no cut in wages, resulting, in effect, in a 20 percent pay raise. The dispute was settled after the miners closed down the mines, with workers obtaining a 10 percent wage increase.

While unions were illegal, the miners formed the Workingmen's Benevolent Association of St. Clair in 1868, the forerunner of the United Mine Workers of America. Although the mine owners and operators refused to recognize the association as the bargaining agent for mine workers, it was effective in lobbying for safety legislation and improved living conditions, as well as in organizing strikes.

Also central to Irish protest against discrimination, both on the job and off, were the Molly Maguires. The term *Molly Maguires* originated in the south of Ireland and was applied to groups of peasants who organized to retaliate against landlords, magistrates, and others guilty of injustices to poor, Irish families. The name was suggested by the practice of young men who disguised themselves by blackening their faces with burnt cork and dressing in women's clothing. In these disguises they beat or killed gamekeepers, servers of eviction notices, cottage wrecking crews, or others responsible for oppressing Irish families. It was Benjamin Bannan, in his *Miner's Journal,* who began to articulate the idea of Irish Catholics and the Molly Maguires in the role of conspirators, calling it a secret Roman Catholic organization that aims to control the political process and the Democratic Party.

To what extent the Molly Maguires were a formal secret society or an imagined conspiracy is a moot question. There is no question, however, that Irish Catholics organized to protect themselves and to retaliate, sometimes with violence, against discrimination or what they perceived as injustice. Organizations such as the Molly Maguires are not uncommon in social situations in which there is little effective public order or among groups that view the state authorities as hostile to them. These groups become institutionalized systems of law outside the official law, a parallel government outside the official government. Eric Hobsbawm (1959:6) referred to such groups as *mafia,* seeing them as a form of organized rebellion again hostile groups or public authorities.

The main importance of the Molly Maguires in the struggle between Irish mine workers and the mine owners and operators was that they became the focus of the owners' and operators' attempts to destroy the miners association and to link it, as well as other worker organizations, with an international conspiracy. In many ways, the Molly Maguires represented to the mine owners what the Mau Mau oath

An artist's rendition of a meeting of Irish miners identified as Molly Maguires during a coal miners strike in 1874.

represented to the British in Kenya. It also represents attempts by nation-states or capitalist enterprises to associate social protest with activities defined as illegal and to label such protest as criminal or terrorist activity.

   Whether there was a secret society operating in the coal fields of Pennsylvania, or whether the name Molly Maguires was applied to any group seeking retributive justice is unclear. It was clear that there were individuals who did not hesitate to use violence on those who they felt inflicted injustice on the Irish or whose injustice went unpunished by the courts. Furthermore, labor violence was real enough: there were attacks on strike breakers, sabotage at the mines, and physical attacks on mine operators or their agents, and the workers' association often used the language of violence. Furthermore, many believed that the parent organization of the Molly Maguires was the Ancient Order of Hibernians, an Irish Catholic Benevolent association modeled after fraternal organizations such as the Knights of Columbus, from which Irish were excluded.

   In September 1875 there was an epidemic of murders and attempted murders; the victims had been guilty of attacks on Irish or of firing or blacklisting Irish workers. As Wallace (1987:374) said, those who were called Molly Maguires acted on "the demand for retributive justice in an atmosphere of ethnic discrimination by the authorities and bitter resentment by those who felt that they had systematically been denied their rights."

The punishments dealt out by the Molly Maguires were carefully weighted according to the crime. Capital offenses included killing an Irishman and being acquitted by the court, trying to kill an Irishman and not being arrested, and depriving an Irishman of his livelihood. Verbally threatening an Irishman called for a severe beating. The victims were always selected because they were the ones who committed the injury, and never attacked as random targets; women and children were never targeted, even if they were witnesses (Wallace 1987:359). Defense funds were established for Mollies, as Irishmen believed, with some justification, that they were being discriminated against and could not expect justice from the courts or police.

Thus workers had various means to protest their treatment by mine owners and operators, other miners, and state or local authorities. They ranged from informal and spontaneous acts, to formal labor organizing, to organized violence, much of which originated in ethnic discrimination, as it did in labor protest. But labor and ethnic discrimination were tied together by the mine owners and operators in their attempts to destroy the workers' organizations.

Destroying Worker Resistance

Mine owners and operators were vehemently opposed to any legislation that either increased safety in the mines or recognized workers' rights to collective bargaining. Additional safety measures, they argued, would make the mines uneconomical, and collective bargaining would give the workers too great a say in mine operation. The Pennsylvania legislature did pass safety legislation in 1869, but only five months later a mine explosion at Avondale, Pennsylvania, killed 108 people, most of whom were asphyxiated by gases while waiting to be rescued because there was no escape tunnel.

The owners also tried to destroy the Ancient Order of Hibernians, claiming it was simply a front for the Molly Maguires. But the ultimate goal of the mine operators was to destroy the union and other miner organizations. The leader of the attack was John Gowen, an ex-coal operator and attorney for the Philadelphia and Reading Coal and Iron Company, which by 1885 came to dominate the anthracite coal district.

Gowen's strategy was to portray the Workingmen's Benevolent Association and the Ancient Order of Hibernians as extensions of the Molly Maguires, in effect scapegoating worker organizations for real or imagined offenses of the Molly Maguires. First he hired the Pinkerton Detective Agency to infiltrate the Workingmen's Benevolent Association to uncover connections between it and the Ancient Order of Hiberbians and the Molly Maguires. The operative could find no evidence of any connection between the union and any secret organization.

Gowen then hired another agent to infiltrate the Ancient Order of Hibernians. The agent reported only that many people were leaving the organization because of the attempt to connect it to the Molly Maguires. In fact, the smear campaign against the Order was so effective that some Irish clergy had condemned it, even threatening to excommunicate any Catholic who remained a member.

Gowen finally got his chance to destroy the Order in a case of attempted murder of a Welshman, M. "Bully Bill" Thomas. Thomas, a prizefighter, had gotten involved in a melee between the Welsh and Irish fire companies, both of which arrived to put out the same fire; shots were fired, a man was killed, and a young Irishman named Daniel Dougherty was charged with murder. Dougherty was acquitted, and this time the avengers were Welshmen, not Irish. "Bully Bill" Thomas and others made an attempt on Dougherty's life, and local members of the Ancient Order of Hibernians planned a retaliation. Thomas was attacked and shot but survived; based on his complaint and evidence from the Pinkerton agent, arrests were made. Gowen put the Ancient Order of Hibernians and the Workingmen's Benevolent Association on trial, painting them in such sinister terms that being a member was tantamount to having a bad reputation. A succession of trials resulted in the hanging of twenty men convicted of conspiracy to murder. The trial, in effect, succeeded in scapegoating the miners and their organizations for the economic failure of the coal fields.

In fact, according to Wallace, there was little or no connection between the Workingmen's Benevolent Association and the Ancient Order of Hibernians, although there is little doubt that the Molly Maguires served as a mechanism for Irish Catholics to achieve retributive justice in a hostile world. More interesting, the reaction of Gowen and others is reminiscent of the reaction of the British to the Mau Mau, refusing to recognize any real oppression and blaming instead oath taking and secret ritual. The end result was to discredit an already broken union and fix the blame for the problems of the coal trade on forces outside the trade, such as the absence of protective tariffs on British iron and the workers themselves.

Wallace's story of St. Clair also provides some insights into the origin of labor conflict, a story being repeated today in industries all over the world. In St. Clair we found a marginally profitably industry trying to squeeze a profit by lowering wages and scrimping on safety measures, creating conditions ripe for labor protest. Today we find marginally profitable, highly competitive industries, such as textiles, electronics, and toys, cutting labor costs by moving into countries whose lack of labor legislation mirrors the labor situation in Pennsylvania in the nineteenth century. Workers in these countries face the same problems of low wages and unsafe working conditions that workers in the Pennsylvania coal fields of the nineteenth century faced.

These conditions have led to attempts to organize, attempts generally met with legal repression or violence by industry owners or managers and the state. For example, the International Confederation of Free Trade Unions in 1997 documented union rights violations in 108 countries. Trade unionists were threatened and attacked in Guatemala; trade unions are banned in Burma; ninety-eight union organizers were killed in Colombia, twenty-four in Brazil, and nine in Bolivia. In Cambodia trade union protests led to the arrests of 4,264 people and the dismissal of 153,494 workers. In 1993, Masinah, a young female worker at a watch factory in Indonesia, was abducted, gang-raped, and murdered for leading a strike to add a $0.25 meal allowance to an $0.84 per day salary. Even in the United States, claims the ICFTU, at least one in ten workers campaigning for unionization is illegally fired.

Global Feminist Resistance

In September 1995, representatives from nongovernmental organizations all over the world gathered in Beijing, China, at the Fourth World Conference on Women, to develop what conference participants called "strategic sisterhood," an international strategy to unite the causes of women in the periphery with those in the core. The model for present-day protests about the rights of women can be traced to the world revolution of 1848. In that year 400 participants gathered in Seneca Falls, New York, to plan their strategy to fight for the abolition of slavery. At the meeting Elizabeth Cady Stanton, one of the leading social activists of the nineteenth century, introduced a resolution that women be given the right to vote. Such an idea was radical even in that setting, and it passed only after Frederick Douglass, the most prominent African American of the nineteenth century, supported the resolution. The resolution was greeted with contempt by most Americans: one newspaper called it an insurrection, another accused the women of being Amazons. And while Black men were given the right to vote in 1869, women, with the exception of those in a few western states such as Wyoming, Colorado, Idaho, and Utah, were not allowed to vote until 1920. Yet, though it took over seventy years, the right for women to vote was one of the changes that emerged out of the revolutionary mood of 1848.

While the modern feminist movement has helped raise the status of women, at least in the West, women remain among the most economically, politically, and socially marginalized members of global society. As Martha Ward noted in *A World Full of Women* (1996:221), the major occupations of women worldwide are "street-selling, factory assembly lines, piecework, cash-cropping, and commercial agriculture, prostitution or sex work, and service in domestic settings, like maids who change the sheets on hotel beds."

At the same time that women produce 75 to 90 percent of food crops in the world, they are responsible for the running of households. According to the United Nations, in no country in the world do men come anywhere close to women in the amount of time spent in housework. Furthermore, despite the efforts of feminist movements, women in the core still suffer disproportionately, leading to what sociologists refer to as the "feminization of poverty," where two out of every three poor adults are women. The informal slogan of the Decade of Women became "Women do two-thirds of the world's work, receive 10 percent of the world's income and own 1 percent of the means of production" (cited Ward 1996:224).

These conditions have incited feminist protest in virtually every country of the world. In India, dowry—the money and gifts a bride brought with her to her husband's household—became an object of protest in the 1970s when a young woman was killed by her in-laws because her parents could not meet the in-laws' increasing demands for dowry. Apparently this was not uncommon; there were other reports of in-laws dowsing daughters-in-law with kerosene and setting them on fire. These were often classed by authorities as suicide and passed off as family affairs of no concern to the state (Kumar 1995). In Bangladesh, women organized to gain access to employment and fair wages and to revise inheritance laws that favored men (Jahan 1995). In the Philippines, women organized to gain labor rights

Women in New Delhi marching to protest high food prices in 1973.

after the imposition in 1972 of martial law by President Ferdinand Marcos, a movement that contributed to the election of Corazon Aquino as the first woman president of the Philippines. In South Africa, women have organized to protest sexual abuse, economic inequality, and the exclusion of women from public policy decision making (Kemp et al. 1995). In Kenya, women's groups have proliferated to support the entry of women into business, community projects, and revolving loan programs (Oduol and Kabira 1995).

The women's movements that proliferated in the 1970s have had significant effects in some areas. In Peru, for example, it would have been unusual twenty years ago to see, as one can now, a woman conducting the national symphony orchestra, working in politics, or running a business. Twenty years ago Peruvian women's lives centered on their family and the home (Blondet 1995).

In spite of some gains, however, the economic position of women in global society remains, as a whole, marginal to that of men. For example, women represent about 60 percent of the billion or so people earning $1.00 or less per day. We need to ask *what are the factors that contribute to the inferior position of women in the world, and what are some of the strategies that can be employed to improve their position?*

Gender Relations in the Culture of Capitalism

Eleanor Leacock, who has studied the role of women in capitalism around the world, concluded that some women hold some measure of influence and power (1986:107). But the degree of power varies with the gender system of their culture, the status of the race, religious group, or class to which they belong, the political system under which they live, and their personal attributes and life histories. Leacock agreed with Karl Marx and Friedrich Engels that capitalism is patriarchal and paternalistic, that the mode of production which creates a hierarchy of labor and a family structure that relegates women to domestic work inevitably leads to the oppression of women. The question is, *what evidence is there that the marginalization of women and the protest that it inspires, particularly in the periphery, is a consequence of the expansion of the culture of capitalism?*

Four developments that accompanied the expansion of the culture of capitalism helped define its system of gender relations: the loss of control by women over valuable and productive resources; the transformation of extended families into male-dominated nuclear families; the expansion of industry into the periphery; and the imposition on peripheral countries by multilateral institutions of structural adjustment programs. Let's examine each of these developments.

In the eighteenth and nineteenth centuries capitalist expansion altered two sets of social relations in societies into which it spread. First, capitalism resulted in the loss of control by most members of societies of the means of production, making them dependent for survival on the sale of their labor. Second, capitalism undermined large, extended family groups, isolating people into individual or nuclear families, each a separate economic unit ruled over by male household heads. In these developments, said Leacock (1983:268), lie the origins of the modern suppression of women. For example, women among the Cherokee and Iroquois in North America were equals or near equals of men. Women generally controlled the production of food crops and played a major role in public decision making; among the Iroquois, women chose the political leaders and could decide themselves to terminate a marriage. Colonists initiated changes by negotiating or trading only with men and by introducing a European model economy to replace horticulture and hunting. This undermined the authority of extended kin groups, in which women played a major role, thus creating a society based on male-dominated agriculture. Among the Montagnais-Naskspi of Labrador, cooking, cleaning, and housework did not become institutionalized as women's work until women became dependent on fur-trapping husbands and individual households of husbands, wives, and children replaced family lodges. In this way, said Leacock (1986:117), women's productive activities and decision-making authority shifted from the larger kin groups and the fields to the household domain, while their social status was redefined as subservient to and dependent on male household heads.

Missionaries further undermined women's authority, especially in societies where women had important ritual responsibilities, by refusing to deal with women and by using their power to undermine traditional family arrangements. The missionaries believed the patriarchal nuclear family was ordained by God and taught that a woman's role was to provide loving care for husband and children. As a result, women's unpaid household labor became, for all practical purposes, a gift to plantation or mine owners, manufacturers, or traders who realized their profit from the work of husbands and sons (Leacock 1983:271).

An 1835 engraving depicting the work of indigenous women in the eastern United States in 1835.

In her survey of Africa, Ester Boserup (1970:277) noted much the same process: the economic and social policies of British, German, Dutch, Portuguese, and French colonizers undercut the traditional role of women as farmers, merchants, and participants in the political process of families by undermining the power of extended families or clans, taking away women's rights to land, and relegating women to the household or low-paid wage labor. We saw the consequences of this in Chapter 6 in the case of the famine in Malawi.

Karen Sacks (1979) summarized these changes in Africa by contrasting the roles of "sisters" with the roles of "wives." "Sisterhood," Sacks argued, is shorthand for a relationship in which women have access to valuable resources (land, livestock, and money) based on their membership in the extended kin group of brothers and sisters. Sisterhood connotes autonomy, adulthood, and the possibilities of gender equality. Wife or "wifehood," on the other hand, connotes a relationship of dependency. According to Sacks, the development of nation-states in the culture of capitalism undermined women's status by dismantling the larger, family-based institutions on which "sister" relations rested, turning women into dependent wives.

The works of such writers as Leacock, Boserup, and Sacks raise an interesting issue (see Silverblatt 1988). Modernization theorists who argue about the benefits and sometimes the inevitability of modernization generally point to the decline of the extended family and the emergence of the nuclear family as the basic unit of society as a major example of progress. Most feminist theorists propose that the nuclear family is partly responsible for the inferior position of women. Since we propose that this change has little to do with "modernization" and more to do with the emergence and expansion of the culture of capitalism we need to ask *why was the extended family not compatible with other elements of capitalist culture?*

We examined, in Chapter 1 why the nuclear family promoted consumption by requiring each small unit to purchase and consume commodities that in extended family units could easily be shared. In Chapter 9, we examined why communal property held by extended families is problematic to the economic and legal relations in capitalism. But there are other reasons why small nuclear family units are preferred in the culture of capitalism. For example, the extended family, as a political entity, conflicts with the needs of the nation-state to educate and control its citizens. Members of large extended families are more difficult to control than are members of small, isolated, nuclear families. In addition, the demands for a flexible and mobile labor supply make the extended family impractical. It is far better for capitalism to reduce people's social and emotional ties to others, to make it easier for them to relocate to where labor is needed. If we assume that it is the preferred family unit in the culture of capitalism, how does the nuclear family lend itself to the relegation of women to an inferior position?

First, the emergence of the nuclear family tended to release men from the ties to the extended family and make them more autonomous, giving them greater control over resources and over the members of their households. In societies where women retain close ties to their families, such control is rarely present. Furthermore, recognition of the male as head of the household conveys to male household heads control of those resources.

Second, the nuclear family and the patrilocality of the work force serves to separate adult women from their peers, therefore reducing the potential for the social support of other women and for building class consciousness among women. The classic example, of course, is the nuclear family with a mother who does not work outside the home (Tétreault 1994:10). In some cases, as in Japan and China, the young bride is brought into the patriarchal home and virtually isolated from outside society.

A third feature of the nuclear family that supports the subservient position of women is the prevalent form of marriage. The nuclear family is traditionally composed of a larger, older, better-educated, richer, more sexually experienced, and generally legally favored man who is married to a smaller, younger, less well educated, propertyless, inexperienced and socially less well-protected woman. While this form of marriage is not restricted to the culture of capitalism, its historic prevalence in European cultures and its spread through economic colonization and missionary activity to the periphery certainly helped sustain or create households of dominant men and subservient women (Tétreault 1994:9–10).

In addition to removing from women access to the means of production and making the male-dominated nuclear family the main social unit of society, the expansion of industrial production from the core to the periphery served to marginalize women economically. The growth of assembly plants in countries such as Mexico, Haiti, Guatemala, and Indonesia beginning in the 1960s and 1970s depended on a disproportionately female work force in low-paying jobs. While some have argued that such work expanded women's economic options, the fact remains that as global capital spread women worked harder, either in and from their homes or in assembly plants. Yet the work is economically marginal, temporary, or low-paying. Globally, two-thirds of all part-time workers and 60 percent of all temporary workers are women. Furthermore, while working for pennies an hour, women remained responsible for all or most of the household labor necessary to sustain their families (Eisenstein 1997).

The global economic trends of the 1990s have further undermined women as nation-states, at the urgings of such groups as the International Monetary Fund and the World Bank, terminate social services intended to alleviate the conditions of people living in poverty, a disproportionate number of whom are women and children (Basu 1995:6). Thus the withdrawal or reduction by the state of its support of workplace legislation, social service programs, job programs, health programs, and education programs disproportionately affects the position of women in society (Eisenstein 1997).

In sum, feminist protest arises from conditions that relegate women to the private or domestic sphere, that offer only low-paying jobs, and that undermine public policies geared to protect women and children from the widespread poverty that exists in the periphery. The question is, *what are some of the ways people can resist the marginalization and subjugation of women globally?*

Strategies of Protest

Clearly, to the extent that the inferior status of women is linked to the nature of the economy, family, and the nation-state, it becomes difficult, if not impossible, to change. For this reason some have suggested that the revolutionary overthrow of capitalist nation-states is the only solution to female oppression. Historically, this may help explain the prominent role of women in revolutionary programs. We saw in Chapter 10 the prominent role played by women in the protests of peasants in Malaysia, the Mau Mau revolt in Kenya, and the revolt in Chiapas. Women were given prominent places, at least initially, in the communist revolutions in Russia, China, and Cuba. Yet it is arguable how much these revolutions improved the status of women.

One of the first acts of the Chinese government after its victory in 1949 was to establish the All-China Women's Federation to further the status of women. The communist government banned the Chinese custom of foot binding of women, built a system of universal health care, and dramatically improved women's health.

Yet today some of the worst cases of female labor exploitation are found in China. In an incident reminiscent of the notorious 1911 Triangle Shirtwaist factory fire in New York City that killed 145 garment workers and prompted new labor legislation, a fire in November 1993 killed eighty-four female workers in a toy factory in Shenzhen in south China. They were prevented from escaping by doors and windows barred to prevent stealing. Furthermore, the Chinese government repeatedly cracks down on the formation of independent labor unions whose work, while not specifically aimed at improving the condition of women, would greatly benefit women laborers.

After the socialist revolution of 1959 in Cuba, Fidel Castro's government moved to integrate women better into the public spheres of government and labor. In 1960 the government formed the Federation of Cuban Women (FMC) to consolidate existing women's institutions in support of the revolution and integrate women into the work force. While only 13.7 percent of the potential female work force was active in 1953, by 1990 45 percent of working-age women were employed. Yet in spite of such apparent gains, "motherhood" remains at the heart of the official view of women in Cuba; child care and domestic duties remain at the core of the female role, and Cuban women continue to bear the brunt of domestic labor—housework and child care (Lutjens 1994).

While the goals of socialist revolutions to improve the status of women clearly did not live up to their promise, clearly the fall of communism in Eastern Europe has worsened the condition of women. Seventy-three percent of Russia's unemployed are women, half of whom have college educations. The overwhelming number of peddlers on the streets of Moscow are old women and young mothers. Without the protection of the socialist nation-state, the traditional view of women as housewives has reemerged. Gennady Melikyan, Russia's labor minister, made this clear when he said, "Why should we employ women when men are unemployed? It's better that men work and women take care of children and do the housework"(Eisentstein 1997).

In Western countries women's movements have focused on affirmative action, reproductive rights, and greater access of women to education. At the Fourth World Conference on Women in Beijing, there was a strong movement for women in the periphery to begin to adopt the strategies employed by feminists in the core. Yet many women and women's groups in the periphery are wary of Western forms of feminist protest. Many women's groups in the periphery or the ex-communist countries of Eastern Europe see attempts to export Western feminism as a new form of colonialism or imperialism. In Muslim countries, in particular, many women reject what they see as the "man-hating" feminism of Western women's movements.

Anthropologists, such as Aihwa Ong (1997), have warned against the tendency of Western feminists to impose their value system of individual autonomy on women's movements in peripheral countries. Ong noted that male leaders in Asian countries, such as China, Indonesia, and Malaysia, have argued that women's rights are not simply about individual rights but about culture, community, and the nation-state. They counter accusations that they are exploiting female labor in assembly plants by arguing for their right to develop economically and for the obligation of all members of the community or nation to contribute to that development in any way they can, that the right to develop is also a "human right." Asian leaders claim that the family, state, or nation is the primary unit of advancement, not the individual. The problem, said Ong, is *how can women's movements in the periphery counter these arguments that in their cultural context are so persuasive?*

Insufficient attention has been given to cultural and religious differences between core and peripheral countries regarding the role of women and the place of political protest (Ong 1997). Feminists must be sensitive to "othering," wherein Westerners gain their sense of being liberated by defining others, particularly women from the periphery, as being backward and oppressed. For example, when delegates at the conference from Catholic and Muslim countries argued for a strategy that recognized a "separate but equal" status for women, they were accused of being traditional and marginalized by Western representatives.

Ong suggested that it would be more fruitful for women's movements in the core to be more receptive to an exchange of ideas and to consider the idea that strategies for improving the status of women must recognize cultural differences and the nature of power relations in different societies. We must, said Ong, "analyze the ways women and men in different societies struggle over cultural meanings that structure their lives."

To illustrate, Ong related the story of the Sisters in Islam, a group of Western-educated feminists who are trying to change gender relations in Malaysia, not by employing Western feminist methods but within the context of their own culture through the reinterpretation of Islamic texts. Islam, particularly Islamic fundamentalism, has been targeted by Western feminists and human rights advocates as being particularly oppressive toward females. Islam permits polygyny, restricts the inheritance rights of females to half that of males, restricts the movements of women, and, in extreme cases, denies women an education or any position outside the home.

Sisters in Islam, instead of condemning Islamic belief, argue that women should be afforded the same access to religious education as men, and with this education they should enter into debate with the almost exclusively male Muslim clerics about the meaning of sacred texts such as the Qur'an and their interpretation of the role of women in society. Using newspaper columns to reach the public, the Sisters in Islam argue that the interpretation of the sacred texts must put Qur'anic recommendations in historical context. For example, male clerics justify Islam's approval of polygyny by claiming the Qur'an justified polygyny because the male sex drive made them "adulterous by nature." The Sisters of Islam counter this interpretation by pointing out that the Qur'an does not give men a blanket right to more than one wife; the sanctioning of polygyny in the Qur'an must be understood in the historical context in which the death of men through wars left women and children without male support. Allah thus sanctioned polygyny, they argue, not because of any intrinsic difference in the sex drive of men and women, but because it helped alleviate the problem of war orphans and widows, by allowing widows to remarry men who already had a wife or wives.

The Sisters of Islam also argue against the stringent dress codes that male clerics say are demanded by the Qur'an. Citing verses of the sacred texts, the Sisters of Islam argue that "[c]oercion is contrary to the spirit of the Qur'an which states that there is no compulsion in [Islamic] religion"(cited Ong 1997) and that it is wrong to try to enforce faith through authority. The proper way to protect women, they say, is through decent and respectful treatment. Coercive dress policy, "in fact, runs counter to Islam's emancipatory emphasis upon reason [and] freedom as the basis of human morality" (cited in Ong 1997).

Groups such as the Sisters of Islam have produced results. One Malaysian official (cited Ong 1997:89) who is now chair of the U.N. Commission for Human Rights noted:

> *Malaysia used to be a male-dominated society.... In the old days, there was no talk of women's rights, but through the gradual process of politicization, women...are able to assert themselves. Compared with ten years ago, there is much more publicity, consciousness, and more sensitivity on questions of women's rights.*

Malaysia is still a male-dominated society, but by entering into a dialogue with Muslim clerics on their own terms, the Sisters of Islam have produced what Ong called a kind of "feminist communitarianism" that combines the liberal right to question authority, certainly recognized in the Qur'an, with the cultural norms of their own community. These kinds of movements, said Ong, should not be dismissed by Western feminists; rather, the idea of women's rights makes sense only in the context of specific cultural communities.

Ecological Resistance Movements

There is little question, as we have seen, that the culture of capitalism is environmentally destructive and that the need for perpetual economic growth requires perpetual environmental exploitation. But, as in changes in other areas of life, such as agriculture, technology, and family structure, not everyone suffers equally. It is true that everyone may be affected by global warming and the increase in acid rain, but not everyone is affected by the flooding of farmland or hunting territories, disposal of waste products, or pollution of water supplies. These problems are disproportionally borne by people who inhabit the margins and periphery of the culture of capitalism. It is peasants, gatherers and hunters, and the poor in general who lose their livelihood when huge hydroelectric projects dam rivers and flood land, when demand for lumber destroys the forests, when nuclear and other waste is disposed of in or near poor communities or shipped to peripheral countries. Furthermore, some people benefit far more than others from the economic activities that affect the environment and, for that reason, are far less likely to object or protest. But at some point environmental damage does and will affect everyone.

Earthfirst!

Most contemporary ecological resistance movements, as Bron Taylor (1995) called them, originated in the 1960s, although concerns about environmental alterations go back to the nineteenth century. Many of these movements seek, as do most peasant, labor, and feminist movements, somehow to limit the detrimental effects of capitalist economic expansion. Others seek to revolutionize the culture they see as responsible for environmental devastation. Activists in these movements attribute environmental destruction to an ideology associated with capitalism that human beings must dominate and "tame" nature; they argue furthermore that this belief emerges directly out of the domination of human beings of other human beings. Consequently, as long as human beings seek domination of others, so will they seek domination over nature and, eventually, destroy the planet. One of these movements is Earthfirst!

Earthfirst! originated in the early 1980s, beginning with humorous protests, such as unfurling a plastic "crack" down the face of the Glen Canyon Dam, symbolically freeing the Colorado River. Protests became more confrontational when members blockaded logging roads, conducted "tree-sits," or resorted to "ecotage" or "monkeywrenching," by vandalizing equipment or driving metal, ceramic, or quartz stakes into trees to make their harvest dangerous and, hence, unprofitable. Earthfirst! clearly promotes an ideology that attributes to the nonhuman world an animate force, expressed in the slogan "I am the rainforest, recently emerged into consciousness, defending myself." Some events held for Earthfirst! members mythic significance, such as biologist Aldo Leopold's story of watching the "green fire" die in the eyes of a wolf he had just shot, or in Paul Watson's description of the intelligence he saw in the eyes of a harpooned whale he was trying to save, an "intelligence... that spoke wordlessly of compassion...that communicated [that he knew] what we had tried to do"(cited Taylor 1995:15).

Earthfirst! closely identifies with the social protests of indigenous peoples. One of their first symbolic acts was to create a memorial to Apache chief Victorio, whose armed resistance to the European conquest marked for them the effort to preserve the environment (Taylor 1995:18). They have supported and identified with the struggles of indigenous people in the Amazon to protect the forests and stop destructive oil exploitation. They raised funds for the Ecuadorian Huaorani to clear three- to four-meter-wide corridors through the rainforest and plant palm trees to demarcate territory allotted them by the government and prevent "accidental" colonization of their land. They organized boycotts against lumber from the Sarawak Rainforest to support the resistance of the Penan and Iban tribes. They allied themselves with the Kalinga and the Bontoc peoples of the Philippines to prevent the construction of a dam that would have inundated their villages and

An Earthfirst! protest against the cutting of pecan trees as part of a flood control program.

burial grounds. In North America they have allied themselves with indigenous groups such as the Apache Survival Coalition and the Coalition for Nitassian comprised of Innu and Cree Indians and others, who hope to stop Hydro Quebec's hydroelectric dam projects that would flood thousands of acres of Innu and Cree hunting grounds.

The ties between ecological resistance movements and indigenous protest reveal the extent to which antisystemic protests are intertwined, often bringing together peasants, indigenous peoples, women, and others in common cause. One of the more interesting movements that contains strands of different types of protest is *Chipko,* the attempt to save the forests of India. It is particularly interesting because it emerged out of a peasant protest over the conversion of common lands to state control and private exploitation, and it resulted in the questioning of one of the central arguments over environmental destruction, the idea of "the tragedy of the commons."

Chipko and the Tragedy of the Commons

In his often cited 1968 article, "Tragedy of the Commons," Garrett Hardin implied that land held in common is more likely to be abused and exploited than land held privately. Hardin based his argument on the premise that what each person gains individually by exploiting the commons for his or her own ends is far greater than what they individually lose. For example, if a pasture is held in common by a community, each person, said Hardin, has more to gain from adding one more sheep to his or her herd than what they lose individually by their exploitation of the pasture. People are motivated, therefore, to exploit the commons as much as possible, and if each person follows his or her own individual interests by adding more sheep, the commons will soon be destroyed. If each person, however, controlled his or her individual plot, people would be less motivated to damage it since what they gain is clearly offset by what they lose. A contemporary example might ask what each of us has to gain by purchasing an automobile, as opposed to what we lose from the pollution our individual car adds to the environment. Since we gain a lot by having a car, but individually increase pollution only slightly, we are motivated, as is everyone else, to buy cars.

Hardin's argument is logically ingenious, but empirically flawed. Anthropologists, particularly, have argued that communally held land, especially in the periphery, tends to be better preserved and regulated than privately owned resources (see McCay and Fortmann 1996). A good example is that of the forests in northern India, and the Chipko movement.

Chipko (literally "to hug") originated in nineteenth-century peasant protests over the destruction of the forests of northern India that were once described by British colonial officials as "inexhaustible." The peasants in the area lived largely on small-scale agriculture, livestock herding, and gathering and hunting in the surrounding forests. The society was organized into castes, that is hereditary occupational groups into which each person married.

Agricultural land in most villages was owned by the people who worked it, with a portion of what they produced serving as their share of village revenue payable in tribute or taxes to area rulers or British colonial authorities. The surrounding forests were managed collectively. The forests were a necessary feature of economic life as a place for grazing animals, for medicinal herbs, and for food. Moreover, the forests held spiritual significance as a place of deities and shrines. There were particularly magnificent species of trees, and while there was no formal management, protection of the forests was secured by the ritual significance of areas and by rules that abusers of the forests would suffer boycott or exclusion from the forest (Guha 1990:33–34).

The isolation of the area left it largely untouched until 1878, when the colonial government passed regulations closing segments of the forest to peasant use and designating some areas for lease to private developers. The government was particularly interested in certain trees suitable for the construction of railway sleeper cars for the expanding Indian railway. British colonial regulations fixed the amount of building timber the peasantry could use, restricted grazing rights to certain types of forests within a five-mile radius of the villages, and even specified where dry grass could be gathered. The government also banned burning of the forest floors that peasants had used to grow and gather wild grass.

Peasants protested their exclusion from portions of the forests; they ignored the regulations, continuing to graze their animals and cut wood for their own use. They also burned the underbrush in the forests where new saplings had been planted by lumber interests for later harvesting. But the most violent form of protest was incendiarism, the deliberate setting of fires in the forests. In 1919–1920 there were 13,457 breaches of the fire laws in one area of northern India.

Restrictions on peasant use of the forests, exploitation of lumber, and peasant protest continued after India gained its independence from Great Britain in 1947 because the new Indian government, faced with the need to raise revenue, continued the forestry policies of the British colonial government. The results were continuing forest destruction, alienation of the peasants from the forests they had protected for centuries, and continuing protest. In 1962 a new road was built into the forest with funding from the World Bank, further increasing forest exploitation. Satellite photographs reveal that of the 34,042 square kilometers of land declared as forests in the area, only 6.6 percent has good tree cover, and another 22.5 percent has medium tree cover, and another 13.8 percent has poor tree cover. Over half the land classified as forest has no tree cover at all (Guha 1990:146).

Two events triggered the emergence of an organized environmental protest movement. First, floods in the foothills in 1970 resulted in the loss of life and property; the population recognized that losses were greater in villages that lay below land on which forests had been destroyed. The second thing that triggered Chipko was the awarding of rights to a cricket bat manufacturer to cut trees after a peasant cooperative had been denied rights to cut trees in the same forest to make farm implements. It was then that organizers thought of wrapping themselves around (hugging) trees to prevent their being cut. Women gained prominence in the movement because of an attempt by the government to deceive one village by calling the men of the village to a meeting, while they sent in laborers to cut the forest; however, the women of the village, alerted by a young girl, placed themselves between the laborers and the trees and forced the laborers to leave. In another area, 5,000 trees were marked for cutting, and villagers camped out in the forests until men hired by a private company were forced to withdraw.

Chipko has become just one of many such protests against forest destruction in the Himalayan foothills, but it is by far the most publicized and gained broad international appeal as both an environmental and a women's movement. Often forgotten, however, is the peasant roots of the protest: it began as a struggle for subsistence before it emerged as a movement for environmental preservation.

Ramachandra Guha, in *The Unquiet Woods* (1990), noted some other interesting lessons in Chipko that relate to social protest in general and peasant protest in particular. First, Chipko reveals how, as in the cases of Kenya and Mexico, policies of "economic development," or "modernization" formulated at the top levels of states, corporations, and international financial institutions are often experienced by lower levels—such as peasants, women, and laborers—as exploitation. In the strategies of economic development, indigenous peoples, landless peasants, and women are expected to bear the brunt of industrialization; such problems as disease, social unrest, food scarcity, and land hunger testify to the impact of this process (Guha 1990:195). Moreover, while the negative social and economic consequences on the poor in the periphery of programs of economic development are well documented, often ignored is the impact on the environment and the social protest that is likely to ensue. Guha (1990:195–196) concluded,

> [f]rom an ecological perspective, therefore, peasant movements like Chipko are not merely a defense of the little community and its values, but also an affirmation of a way of life more harmoniously adjusted with natural processes. At one level they are defensive, seeking to escape the tentacles of the commercial economy and the centralizing state; at yet another level they are assertive, actively challenging the ruling-class vision of a homogenizing urban-industrial culture.... Far from being the dying wail of a class about to drop down the trapdoor of history, the call of Chipko represents one of the most innovative responses to the ecological and cultural crisis of modern society. It is a message we may neglect at our own peril.

Conclusion

We suggested in this chapter that rebellion and protest that seems endemic to the culture of capitalism is largely antisystemic, consisting of responses of groups who at some time were socially or economically marginalized or who have suffered disproportionately in the expansion of capitalism into the periphery. However, it is important to note that in only a few cases is protest directed explicitly at the culture of capitalism itself. Rather, protesters select as objects of their protest groups or individuals who they hold individually responsible. We saw in the case of the protests of poor Malaysian peasants that the object of their ire was peasants who were richer than themselves, rather than the green revolution or the institutions, such as the World Bank, that ultimately were responsible for their distress. Likewise, laborers in the coal mines of Pennsylvania blamed mine operators, many of whom made virtually no profit from their efforts, rather than the system that drove them and the mine operators to try to accumulate capital in a failing industry. In other words, rarely do social protest movements specifically attack the system that is the source of their distress, instead focusing on real or symbolic figures who, for them, embody their oppression.

Chapter 12

Religion and Antisystemic Protest

Religious distress is at the same time the expression of real distress and the protest *against real distress. Religion is the sigh of the oppressed creature, the heart*
of a heartless world, just as it is the spirit of spiritless conditions.
—*KARL MARX*, CRITIQUE OF HEGEL'S
"PHILOSOPHY OF RIGHT"

We are living in a society today that is quite sophisticated and very educated.
Ours is indeed a clever generation, but one that is suffering because men are
doing what is right in their own eyes and disregarding God's immutable laws. If
a person is not a Christian, he is inherently a failure.
—*JERRY FALLWELL, cited AMMERMAN*,
NORTH AMERICAN PROTESTANT FUNDAMENTALISM

The rebellions and movements that we examined in Chapters 10 and 11 each
sought, in their own way, to reform what participants saw as the excesses of capitalism. Few of these movements, however, offered a radical cultural alternative;
that is, while they decried the constant economic and social change, the uneven
distribution of wealth, the exploitation and marginalization of selected groups,
or the environmental damage fostered by the culture of capitalism, none actively
sought to replace it with another. Peasants seek land, not the overthrow of the society that displaces them; laborers seek higher wages and better working conditions
within the culture of capitalism from which, in their other roles as consumers and
capitalists, they benefit; women and minorities seek improved status within the
existing society; indigenous groups struggle to be left alone; and environmental
protesters, with the exception of those who offer a largely undefined spiritual alternative, seek only greater environmental safeguards.

Jerry Falwell, one of the leaders of the Protestant Fundamentalist movement in the United States, speaks at a Jesus rally in 1996.

Communism was often depicted as a major challenger to capitalism, yet communism and its authors—Lenin, Stalin, and Mao—never rejected the larger nineteenth-century culture of industrial capitalism. They sought largely to modify the nation-state to give workers greater influence and to obtain a more equitable distribution of wealth within a system of production, distribution, and consumption that differed little, if at all, from that of capitalism. They simply wanted to replace private capitalism with state capitalism. Even Marx and Engels did not call for overthrow of the industrial order; their solution was to seize the nation-state and raise the power of labor above or at least equal to the power of capital (the power of people over the power of money). The views of Marx and Engels (like those of many early nineteenth-century industrialists) were utopian; they called for the end of private property, recognition of the equality of women, dismantling of the patriarchal nuclear family, and discarding of organized religion. But the only groups to attempt to follow that or a similar agenda were the small utopian or intentional communities that proliferated in the first half of the nineteenth century, such as New Harmony, the Oneida Community, and Amana, and later, following the political unrest of 1968, Twin Oaks and the many small communal groups that thrived in late 1960s and early 1970s, a few of which survive today (Kanter 1972; Erasmus 1972; Oved 1988).

While the peasant, labor, feminist, indigenous, and environmental protests and rebellions did not seek to change the basic tenets of the culture of capitalism, there were and are movements to overthrow and replace it. Most of these are religious in character; through some spiritual agency these groups seek either the removal or destruction of what they believe is an immoral culture, a withdrawal from it, or the forceful or voluntary adoption of a new way of life.

Religion has always had a revolutionary element; most religions began as a rebellion against one or another established order. Christianity began as a Jewish protest against behaviors and beliefs that the protesters felt were violations of God's word. The gospels of the New Testament are clearly revolutionary in intent, as we shall see when we examine the emergence of liberation theology, while the Old Testament documents the struggles of people against what they believe is illegitimate authority.

Yet the fact that religion is often the source of antisystemic protest should not obscure the role of religion in legitimizing some of the basic premises of the culture of capitalism. Certainly there was a good deal of cooperation between the church and the state in the early expansion of the world system. Missionaries accompanied the conquerors and explorers and helped pacify populations, convert them to one or another brand of Christianity, and transform them into willing laborers for the global economy. Missionaries served as a vanguard of capitalism by introducing their converts to Western concepts of time, space, and the person embedded in the culture of capitalism. As Jean Comaroff (1985:27) observed,

> [t]he mission was an essential medium of, and forerunner to, colonial articulation; it was the significant agent of ideological innovation, a first instance in the confrontation between the local system and the global forces of international capitalism. The coherent cultural scheme of the mission—its concepts of civilization, person, property, work, and time—was made up of categories which anticipated and laid the ground for the process of proletarianization.

In his classic work, *The Protestant Ethic and the Spirit of Capitalism*, Max Weber (1958) suggested that the Protestant Reformation provided an ideological basis for capitalism as well as a motivation for making a profit by equating material success with personal salvation and a sign of God's blessing. Historians have seen in religion of the nineteenth century a replacement for the moral restraints that had been provided by family and community but destroyed by the explosive growth of cities and the mobility of labor. Anthony F. C. Wallace (1987), for example, pointed out how Irish immigrants in Pennsylvania confronted in the local Catholic Church a replacement for behavioral restraints that had been provided by extended families in Ireland, a moral restraint very much welcomed by mine owners, business people, and others. Paul E. Johnson (1978) traced the religious revival in the United States in the 1830s and 1840s to the need for religion to replace the moral guidelines and social constraints that had been provided in small rural communities by the family but absent in the newly industrialized cities of the Northeast. As we saw in Chapter 1, most religious leaders in the early twentieth century had little difficulty accommodating to the shift from an ideology of self-denial to one of self-fulfillment and indulgence. Nevertheless, while religion has served to buttress the assumptions of the culture of capitalism, it has served in some forms also to resist them.

The goal of this chapter is to ask the questions, *to what extent have religious movements been expressions of antisystemic sentiments? That is, how have religious movements served as a means of protest against the expansion, both in the core and in the periphery, of the culture of capitalism?* To answer these questions we will first examine some religious movements in the periphery, and then turn our attention to the large-scale protests that have emerged from the world's major religions.

Indigenous Religious Movements as Protest

Central in anthropology to the idea of religious change is Anthony F. C. Wallace's concept of *revitalization movement*. Wallace (1966:30) suggested that religious beliefs and practices start from situations of social and cultural stress as "conscious, organized effort by members of a society to construct a more satisfying culture." All religion, he said, originates in a revitalization process. The origins of all the major religions lay in reactions to social and/or cultural systems that the founders found unsatisfying; anthropologists, historians, and sociologists have documented hundreds of instances of religious movements around the world that originated in protest over people's conditions, and have used the idea of revitalization to conceptualize everything from Melanesian Cargo Cults to the militia movements in the United States (Beeman 1997).

However, as useful as the concept of revitalization has been in furthering our understanding of religious change and protest, it has a basic weakness. As applied to religious movements of the past two hundred years, it has failed to consider the fact that virtually all such movements have been reactions to a single phenomenon—the development and expansion of industrial or consumer capitalism. Generally, revitalization movements, such as the cargo cults of Melanesia and New Guinea, the Ghost Dance among the Indians of the American Plains, and large-scale religious movements that have emerged from Islam, Christianity, Judaism, and others, have been as much antisystemic protest as they have been revitalization. That is, the attempt to construct a more "satisfying culture," as Wallace put it, has generally been a protest against the negative effects of capitalist expansion. For this reason, it may be more fruitful to view these movements as expressions of antisystemic protest rather than solely attempts at revitalization.

To illustrate, let's examine three religious movements of peoples in the periphery, the Ghost Dance, the cargo cults, and the Zionism movement in South Africa. Each was an expression of protest against economic and social conditions emerging from capitalist expansion, but with important differences: they varied in the degree to which they used the trappings of core religions as opposed to indigenous belief and ritual. Furthermore, they varied in the extent to which they expressed overt hostility to the nation-state and consequently the extent to which they prompted oppressive and violent retaliation by the nation-state.

The Ghost Dance

In 1889 a missionary-educated Paiute Indian named Wovoka had a vision (Mooney 1965). He had been taken up to heaven where, he said, he met God; he also met Indians who had died and who were in heaven living their traditional life. God, he

The Ghost Dance that spread among indigenous groups in the United States in 1889 and 1890 was one of many spiritual resistance movements through which indigenous peoples protested the destruction of their culture and way of life.

said, instructed him to return to Earth and tell people that they must live in peace with Whites and with each other. He was also given instructions for a ritual dance that, if performed for five days and five nights, would reunite people on Earth with friends and relatives in the other world. Converts carried Wovoka's message from Nevada to indigenous groups throughout the United States and Canada, where it was often embellished in various ways. In some versions Whites and Indians would live in harmony; in others the world would be destroyed and only Indigenous people brought back to life. In other versions the buffalo would return, and people would live as they had before the invasion of European peoples.

The message of the Ghost Dance, as it became known, was carried by representatives sent by rail by indigenous groups to meet with Wovoka and spread to groups throughout the American Plains and beyond to peoples seeking a revival of a way of life disrupted by capitalist expansion. The message of the Ghost Dance was particularly attractive to groups such as the Lakota who had been systematically deprived through treaty and deceit of most of their land and confined to reservations where they were dependent on government provisions that were often not delivered. However, the Ghost Dance, which held the promise to the Lakota of a revival of their traditional culture, ended in one of the great military tragedies in American history.

Alarmed that the Ghost Dance might presage an open rebellion by the Lakota, an Indian agent assigned to one of the Lakota reservations called in the military. Frightened that they might be attacked, some of the Lakota fled; they were pursued by the Seventh Cavalry, George Armstrong Custer's old command that had been defeated by a combined force of Lakota and Cheyenne in 1876. The army caught up to the Lakota at a place called Wounded Knee. With cannon and rifles surrounding the Lakota, a surrender was arranged. As soldiers rummaged through Lakota shelters searching for guns, a shot was fired. The army responded by pouring cannon and rifle shot into the encampment, killing hundreds of men, women, and children, some of whom had sought shelter from the barrage hundreds of yards away.

In many ways, the Ghost Dance is a prototype of a form of religious resistance that parallels the "weapons of the weak" we discussed in Chapter 10. They are religious movements that serve, if only symbolically, to protest economic, social, or political oppression. When they result in violence, it is almost always violence initiated by the nation-state or their representatives, either against whole groups, as in the massacre at Wounded Knee, or against leaders of the movements who the agents of the nation-state fear are leading or are capable of leading a general revolt. It was probably not a coincidence that days before Wounded Knee, the Lakota spiritual leader Sitting Bull was assassinated by Lakota police as they tried to arrest him.

The Cargo Cults

Among the most dramatic of the indigenous religious protests were the cargo cults of Melanesia and New Guinea. These movements arose in the late nineteenth century and early twentieth century as core nations sought to exploit the resources in the Pacific Islands. Cargo cults generally began when a prophet announced the imminence of a cataclysm that would destroy the world, at which point the ancestors, God, or some other liberating power would appear and deliver the cargo—commodities possessed by Europeans—and bring a reign of eternal bliss. People prepared themselves to receive the cargo by building storehouses, jetties, and plane runways, sometimes abandoning their gardens, destroying their livestock, eating all their food, or throwing away their money. Cargo cults represent a paradoxical response to capitalist expansion. On the one hand, they evidence themselves in a passionate desire to possess the commodities thought to be in abundance in the dominant culture; on the other hand, they tend to reject the power and influence of the Westerners who bring the cargo.

The story of European exploitation and the effects on indigenous peoples of the Pacific closely followed the patterns we examined in Chapter 9. Cargo cults were a response to the excesses of colonial exploitation and were documented by Peter Worsley (1968) in his classic analysis, *The Trumpets Shall Sound*. Capitalist expansion came to Fiji in the eighteenth century, for example, as Europeans sought sandalwood to supply the Chinese market with material for joss sticks and incense for religious services. By 1813 the supply of trees on Fiji was exhausted.

By the 1860s there was a large influx of European settlers to Fiji, which resulted in a vastly increased alienation of land from Fijians as well as increased lawlessness in the European community, which local governments were unable to control. There was also an increase in the need for native laborers to supply the growing coconut plantations. Colonial powers countered the reluctance of indigenous peoples to work on the plantations by introducing tax laws, forcing them to work to earn cash when they could have easily subsisted on their own produce. Treatment of native laborers, as in other areas, was harsh. In New Guinea colonial governments sanctioned various forms of punishment such as flogging or hanging by the wrists for laborers whose efforts did not satisfy labor supervisors. Equally harsh were the economic dislocations, ill understood by indigenous peoples, that were part of the global economy. Prices for coconuts, oil, and other cash crops rose and fell with the vagaries of the market, creating either new demands for labor or widespread unemployment.

Missionary activity was also a major factor in the development of the cargo cults. Missionaries played a major part in the colonial process in the South Pacific, comprising 15 percent of the European population in most areas. The missionaries divided up territories among themselves, often leading Natives to question why rivalries existed between the different denominations. Religion was one area of European life that the Natives did not reject. In fact, religion was thought by those participating in the cargo cults to be the source of the magical power that created the goods. Native peoples had no knowledge of the material reality of European society and the production process that created commodities, and the Europeans they knew apparently did not work for the goods they possessed; with their missionary education the natives concluded that secret magical power was the key to European wealth, power they wished to obtain (Worsley 1968).

It was in response to these conditions that the cargo cults flourished. A good example was the "Vailala madness" first reported in Papua New Guinea in 1919. The most obvious manifestation of the Vailala madness was the trancelike state or possession that adherents fell into. The movement occurred in an environment of colonial exploitation; oil had been discovered and plantations were being built. Most followers had been indentured laborers, often in conditions of severe discipline and illness. In June 1910, for example, in the Lakekamu gold fields, 225 of 1,100 workers died of dysentery and other causes.

The originator of Vailala madness was said to be an old man named Evara, who fell into a trance when he disappeared for four days. He said that a sorcerer had "ripped up his belly." He prophesied the coming of a steamer carrying spirits of dead ancestors who would bring the cargo with them. Rifles were among the expected goods. Cargo would be contained in crates, each identified according the village to which it would be delivered. The spirits, said Evara, revealed that all the flour, rice, tobacco, and other trade belonged to Papuans, not Whites, and that the Whites would be driven away (Worsley 1968:81).

The hostility to Whites in Papua New Guinea was not surprising. One plantation manager used his whip to silence the lamentations of some "boys" mourning for a dead friend; another said "I want the nigger to work for me so I can make my pile and leave this so-and-so country" (cited Worsley 1968:82). While the movement evidenced hostility to Whites, people believed also that the ancestors would be White. Some Whites were actually followed around by Natives who believed they were their deceased relatives.

Ceremony and ritual accompanied the movement. People had visions of heaven in which food was abundant and people wore long, flowing robes. Many claimed to receive messages from Jesus Christ or God. Villagers set up tables and decorated them with flowers in beer bottles, bowls of rice, betel, and coconut husks; relatives of the dead who were thought to be returning sat around these tables feasting, while other villagers sat silently, their backs to the tables, awaiting the arrival of the cargo. Temples were built that resembled mission churches, and a flagpole was erected that was thought to be the medium through which people could communicate with the dead ancestors. There was a strict moral code that encouraged the giving of feasts for the ancestors, abandoning adultery and theft, and observing the Sabbath. There was also the idea that all native paraphernalia should be destroyed and gardens should be abandoned.

The movement lasted twelve years before it ceased spreading; by the time it ended, in the 1930s, people claimed the prophesies had been fulfilled; that they had seen the steamers, that messages had been received from flagpoles, and that tracks of the dead were seen on beaches. Furthermore, the cargo had been delivered as more and more people gained access to the European commodities they so much desired.

Zionism in South Africa

Both the Ghost Dance and cargo cult movements were influenced to some extent by missionary activity. This should not be surprising: the message of the Bible, particularly the New Testament, must have been very appealing to participants in the movements: the equality of all under God, the favored divine status of the weak, the common stewardship over God's earthly domain are all messages designed to appeal to an oppressed people. Furthermore, if indigenous religious movements derived, at least in part, from missionary teachings, participants in the movement might expect them to be sanctioned by political authorities. Missionary activity was tolerated by European and American colonizers, indeed welcomed, but only to the extent that it contributed to the maintenance of a disciplined and submissive population. Thus the degree of the protest and resistance contained in indigenous religious movements had to be carefully measured against the likelihood of government retaliation.

One of the most repressive nation-states to emerge out of the culture of capitalism was the apartheid government of South Africa, whose military power made open rebellion by Africans virtually impossible. In that setting religious protest was often the only way to express resistance. Let's examine one such movement, the Full Witness Apostolic Church in Zion described by Jean Comaroff (1985) in her work on the Tshidi of South Africa, *Body of Power, Spirit of Resistance.*

The Tshidi are representative of many of the peoples of South Africa who lived primarily by a combination of agriculture and herding. The takeover of South Africa by the British resulted in African people being confined to theoretically self-governing protectorates or homelands. Agricultural and livestock production declined because of such factors as cattle disease and drought, but also because agricultural labor was being drained by the demand for labor in the diamond mines, gold fields, factories, and White farms.

The result for people such as the Tshidi was the underdevelopment of their rural base and the emergence of a system in which they were dependent on the sale of their labor for their survival. By 1970 over half the women were employed outside the home for extended periods and over three-quarters of the men were working away from home for at least nine months each year. Labor on the farms was left to the remaining women and children, who were prevented by South African law from accompanying their husbands and fathers to industrial centers. Furthermore, the passage of Blacks between the town and countryside was carefully regulated by the apartheid government; movement outside the homelands required a pass, strict curfews were imposed, and the African population was carefully watched by uniformed police and bureaucrats. Thus the Tshidi came to realize their state of oppression in the brutal mine compounds and in the degrading rituals of apartheid.

Suppression of African resistance has long been a feature of the South African landscape. Only in the past few years has the degree of violence—assassinations, kidnapping, and torture—used by the South African government to suppress dissent become public. Consequently resistance needed to be more subtle. People could not directly challenge the mechanisms of political, social, and economic domination of the apartheid South African government; instead they contested the logic of the system on which it is based and of which they are a part. Resistance was to be symbolic.

To appreciate this kind of resistance we might think back to the means of resistance used by Malaysian peasants, the weapons of the weak, as James Scott (1985) called them. Or we might consider symbols of resistance and independence used by American youth—the clothing, music, and other activities used to contest the discipline imposed by schools, parents, and the larger community. The Tshidi used as their vehicle a religious movement imported from the core, the Full Witness Apostolic Church in Zion. Comaroff sees the Zionist movement as a means by which Tshidi members protested their marginality to and the affects of the capitalist world system. The protest is expressed in dress, in ritual, and in ideology.

The Christian Catholic Apostolic Church of Zion (CCACZ) was founded in 1847 by a Scotsman, Alexander Dowie, who came to North America in 1888. In 1899 he built his Zion City on 6,500 acres on Lake Michigan, forty-two miles north of Chicago. Within a year the "city" boasted a population of several thousand, a bank, brickyard, stores, small factories, schools, and a printing press.

Zion City was to be a haven from the sinful environment represented by the city of Chicago. The majority of its members were clerics, self-employed artisans, struggling small businessmen—mostly poor and working class. This was a population marginal to the nineteenth-century capitalist take-off who rejected much of the emerging capitalist culture, which they found alienating (Comaroff 1985:179).

Zionists conceptualized the alienation they felt as an uncoupling of man and God; they expressed it in metaphors of sickness and health, which replaced the established doctrines of damnation and salvation. Through the metaphor of healing, Zionists sought to cast out disease and the influence of Satan by reintegrating body, soul, and spirit. As Zionism was exported to the periphery, it seemed to draw together everything that the experience of colonialization and wage labor had driven apart, offering the possibility of rebuilding a holistic community from which the culture of capitalism could be resisted.

The first representative of the CCACZ to South Africa arrived in Johannesburg in 1904, largely at the invitation of a Dutch Reformed missionary. Zionism was introduced to the Tshidi by returning migrant laborers or lone itinerant prophets searching for a local following. At that time most Tshidi had converted to Methodism, the dominant colonial religion in the area, although Black and White churches were carefully separated, but by the 1970s the CCACZ had made considerable inroads. According to Comaroff, 4,750 people were still members of the orthodox churches, but at least 3,750 had converted to Zionism, while another 1,000 were members of other independent churches.

The Full Witness Apostolic Church in Zion was founded in 1956 by Bishop N, a Zulu contract worker in the Johannesburg mines. The church itself is a 240-square-foot mudbrick structure. Followers dress distinctively in a white robe, green tunic, and white headscarf with red, black, and white yarn cords that are never removed.

Typical Sunday services begin with a meal; when all have eaten the bishop's senior wife signals the start of hymn singing, clapping, and drumming. Church members dance and the men sink to their knees facing east, the direction of the rising sun. The Spirit seizes several women and people begin to testify. The testimony contains themes of oppression, often contrasting the outside world (wage labor, the city, strangers) with the inside world (home, the congregation). Central to the act of testifying is the idea of healing (Comaroff 1985:210).

The Full Witness Apostolic Church in Zion represents what anthropologists refer to as a "cult of affliction," a community of sufferers, a solitary band of "wounded healers," whose bodies reflect their oppressed social state. Indeed, many converts, Comaroff noted, come to the church with real organic distress. The ritual of testimony involves a healing process that dramatizes the difference between the corruption of the outside world and the healing spirit of the congregation.

The Zionist church also serves to ritually cleanse the commodities that Tshidi must purchase, at the same time rejecting the culture in which they originate. Members bring all their purchased commodities, such as foodstuffs, shoes, and blankets, and place them on a table located in the center of the church; during the service they are sprinkled with holy water. Thus the cargo of the rejected system is not itself repudiated; rather it is reformed and cleansed through a ritual act. As Comaroff (1985:218–219) said, "as alienated products are given a new social and spiritual identity, the experience of alienation is reversed."

In the same way that Zionists rework commodities through ritual, they also rework the body in dress. Members of the church clothe themselves in a combination

The white robes worn by members of the Zionist Church in South Africa contrast sharply with the drab khaki, black, or tight-fitting uniforms required of workers.

of Protestant and indigenous garb to recreate an order that rejects the one prevailing in their lives. Their white robes, flowing hair, and colored tunics contrast sharply with the drab, often threadbare clothing worn by the majority of rural Tshidi, clearly communicating their "otherness," dress that combines the biblical appearance of the world of the Christian mission with hints of a precolonial Tshidi past. These clothes also contrast in color and form with the drab khaki or black, tight-fitting uniforms of the military, mine, mission, or domestic service.

Comaroff noted that dissenting movements in the periphery seem to adopt these "side alleys" of Western culture, such as faith healing and occultism. But despite often diverse origins, these symbolic orders share an opposition to the culture of capitalism and seek to subvert the structures of colonial societies. The Zionist Church, like other small-scale religious movements, serves as a refuge and emblem for those who are marginalized by the expansion of capitalist culture. As Comaroff (1985:254) said,

> *Zionism is part of a second global culture; a culture lying in the shadow of the first, whose distinct but similar symbolic orders are the imaginative constructions of the resistant periphery of the world system.*

The Global Challenge of Antisystemic Religious Protest

Religious movements such as the Zionist protest, of which there are probably thousands in the world, cannot hope to challenge the domination of global capitalism. Instead they offer a respite from the feelings of hopelessness and alienation felt by those at the economic periphery of capitalist culture. The rituals, services, and gatherings represent periods of withdrawal from the system during which members can collectively regain their integrity and identity. They are not unlike the various utopian or alternative communities that flourished after the revolutions of 1848 and 1968, which sought to create alternative worlds within tightly bounded, sometimes physically isolated communities that gain public attention only when their members commit an illegal or seemingly irrational act.

Far more prominent are the large-scale religious protests represented by "fundamentalist movements" that have gained public attention in the past three decades. Rather than small-scale, isolated instances of religious protest, these movements are offshoots of the world's major religions, contain millions of participants, and have serious designs on the control of the nation-state. The cultures represented by these movements remain the only legitimate challengers to the global domination of capitalist culture.

In many ways these movements are difficult to characterize. They are called fundamentalist movements by the media, government analysts, and many religious scholars, but the designation has been criticized by some as containing derogatory connotations. Mark Juergensmeyer (1993; 1996) suggested calling them "nationalist religious movements." However that implies that the movements are primarily political in nature, while they seem to be protesting a much greater range of cultural features. For that reason, perhaps antisystemic is a more accurate phrase, although we will retain the term fundamentalism, largely because of its widespread use.

To explore the extent to which large-scale religious protests represent antisystemic movements, we will examine the rise of Islamic fundamentalism in the Middle East, the role of Protestant fundamentalism in the United States, and the interplay between Protestant fundamentalism and liberation theology in Latin America. Each Fundamentalism arose out of discontents with specific features of the industrial revolution and modern life, and each claims to provide a formula for transforming modern culture and society. While each of the movements is rooted in a particular cultural tradition, and often in local conditions, they share some features in common.

1. Contrary to impressions left by the mass media that these are recent movements, most had their origins in the nineteenth century, as a reaction to the secularization of religion in modern life or as a reaction to the expansion of the world economy and/or domination by colonial powers.

2. Each is historically oriented and interprets contemporary global events (the debt crisis, war and ethnic strife, disease) as divine portents that validate their central doctrines. Furthermore, each attributes what it perceives as the relative decline or lack of prominence of its country in global affairs to a loss or lack of faith in whatever religious principles it espouses.

3. Each contemporary fundamentalism has designs on state power and has, in one form or another, adopted contemporary political structures (e.g., political parties, youth organizations, modern communication techniques) to attain that end. In some cases they seek control over established nation-states, while in others they wish to establish their own, independent state.

4. All insist that while converting others to their world view is a central goal, believers should keep themselves separate from nonbelievers.

5. Each makes and has a strong appeal to young people, particularly college students, and has developed organizations to reach them.

6. While each has attempted to reach its goals by socially approved methods, each has a militant segment, such as Hizbullah in Lebanon, Operation Rescue in the United States, and Gush Emunim in Israel, that challenges the power of the secular state by disobeying secular law with violent and/or nonviolent means in what they claim is a call to a higher law.

7. Most religious fundamentalisms stress the importance of the family in social life, claiming that the family as an institution has been undermined by the secular nation-state. Some place a striking emphasis on the duty of women to embody tradition, with the home being for men a sanctified retreat from the world of work, where they can relax and assert their authority.

8. While none of the fundamentalisms has a well-developed economic agenda to replace the corporate libertarianism of capitalism, they do have in common certain criticisms of it. They feel that capitalism has replaced the fraternal atmosphere of the premodern economy with ruthless economic competition and bitter competition over public resources (Kuran 1993:290–291). They all believe that the economic problems of today are caused by moral degeneration. Modern economics, they say, sees human wants and consequently human demands as unbounded; the supply can never catch up with demand. Most fundamentalisms, however, reject this amoral approach; instead of seeing human wants as unbounded, they see them as evidence of modern civilization's inability to control individual acquisitiveness. Individuals can be persuaded against pursuing an immoral lifestyle (Kuran 1993:295).

The redistribution of wealth is a common theme in religious fundamentalisms, although not all deal with it in the same way. All encourage the wealthy to aid the poor, but none insists on full equality. Islamic fundamentalists encourage the state to enforce traditional Qur'anic rules on a religious tax whose proceeds go to help the poor. Christian fundamentalists are generally opposed to economic redistribution, advocating instead the end to transfer programs, arguing that obeying God's commands will alleviate poverty and inequality.

Islamic Fundamentalism

Islamic fundamentalism gained international prominence with the Iranian Revolution, Iran's transformation into an Islamic state and the return from state-imposed exile of the Ayatollah Khomeini in 1979. The media has paid much attention to the fundamentalist resurgence, as have the leaders of nation-states with sizable Muslim populations. There has also been much media attention to so-called Islamic terrorist organizations, attention that has often bordered on bigotry. Thus when the Oklahoma federal building was blown up by American militia sympathizers in 1995, the media first reported the presence of "Middle Eastern-looking" men in the area of the blast. There has also been a tendency in the Western media to assume that the beliefs, goals, and organizational methods of Islamic fundamentalists are everywhere the same, thus ignoring important local differences.

The general thrust of Islamic fundamentalist belief is that Muslims have strayed from the moral life that the Qur'an dictates, and that true Muslims must return to a life of piety and faith. Fundamentalists believe that the early success of Islamic civilization was due to their faith and that the decline of Islamic influence over the past centuries is due to their straying from that faith. If Muslims can return to their previous religious idealism, they can eliminate the social, political, economic, and moral problems afflicting the Muslim people and create an ethical order on Earth (Sachedina 1991:406).

Muslims attribute the decline of Islamic piety to the influence of the West on their societies in general, and on colonial and economic domination and the rise of Western secular influence in particular. Islamic fundamentalists are not opposed to modernization; rather, they argue that the Qur'an could provide the foundation for appropriate social institutions and social ethics in a modern, technical age. Islamic fundamentalists see a conflict between the religion that God ordained and the historical development of the world He controls. Consequently they have tried to prevent further erosion in what they see as the true faith, at the same time resisting what they see as alien domination in any form over Muslim societies.

Islamic fundamentalists in different countries attribute the ills of their country—poverty, loss of influence, conflict—to a straying from true Muslim belief and behavior and to some degree blame the West, or modernization in general, for their political, economic, and social problems. In Egypt, for example, fundamentalists believe that their defeat at the hand of Israel in the Six Days War in 1968 was a sign from God that they had strayed from the true faith. National good fortune, on the other hand, is attributed to maintenance of the faith; the discovery of offshore oil in Malaysia, for example, was attributed by Muslims to their faith.

While Islamic fundamentalists in different countries share certain beliefs and goals, there are significant differences among them. In Egypt, for example, fundamentalists believe that creating an Islamic society will help people compensate for the loss of family relationships incurred as people find it necessary to leave villages and become more independent of their families. For that reason, suggested Andrea B. Rugh (1993), the most militant are the young people, especially those who, despite having a college education, can find no jobs and who consequently see in Islam a non-Western alternative. The dominant feature of Islamic fundamentalism in Malaysia is the dakwah movement. The dakwah is a small religious group or commune that separates itself from the larger society to lead lives that members believe are based on Muslim law as given in the Qur'an. Manning Nash noted that dakwah is a youth movement of largely university-educated men and women. Members of dakwah express discontent with what they see as the modern, urban, pluralistic, and secular world. They see it as sensual, corrupt, neurotic, and trivial (Nash 1991:695). They read Islamic literature, carefully evaluating their behavior according to passages from the Qur'an. Women wear ankle-length dresses and, in public, the *chador* or a version of it. Members of the dakwah try to maintain small businesses or stalls or bake items to sell locally. Another unique feature of Islamic fundamentalism in Malaysia is its ethnic character and its appeal to Malays as opposed to other ethnic groups, such as Indians and Chinese. To some extent, it is a nationalist protest against the influence of Indians and Chinese who gained economic prominence in Malaysia during the British colonial period. It also relies heavily on anti-Western, antimodern rhetoric. The West, wrote Nash (1991:731),

> *[i]s seen primarily as the threatening "other," personified variously by the United States and Western Europe—a chaotic power, lacking in discipline, in morality, and indeed in simple human decency. Thus, for most dakwah organizations, the West remains the principle enemy, an aggressor who through its educational systems and its mastery of science has been successful in implanting atheism, materialism, and moral decadence in the heart of Malaysian Islam.*

Islamic Fundamentalism in Iran

The Islamic revolution in Iran has all the characteristics of an antisystemic movement. Iran was controlled by core states—Russia, Great Britain, and the United States—for over a century. The secular government of the Shah was put in power by an American CIA-engineered coup in 1953 against an elected government and was rapidly industrializing, led by the sale of its plentiful oil supplies to core nations. The Islamic revolutionary government quickly acted to reverse what they saw as the imposition of a foreign culture on their own. It's important, therefore, to understand the social and historical background of this revolution.

Iran was the center of the Ottoman Empire that began to rise to prominence in the Middle East in the sixteenth century. As the Ottoman polity began to break up in the nineteenth century, both England and Russia inflicted military defeats on Iran and gained concessions to exploit various resources such as tobacco. But the tobacco concessions so angered merchants and the Islamic religious leaders, the *ulama*, that they forced the government to rescind the concession to the British. A leader in this revolt was Jamal al-Din al-Afghani, who preached against Western imperialism and became one of the central figures in Islamic resurgence at the turn of the century in both Iran and Egypt. Thus the protest against Western influence hardly began with the overthrow of the shah in 1979; it extends well back into the nineteenth century.

The British gained economic control over Iran when the Russians withdrew after the Bolshevik revolution in 1917. Because of the weakness of the Iranian central government there were various revolts, the most serious being the Jangali revolt of 1917–1921 led by Kuchik Khan—referred to by one English writer as the Robin Hoods of the Caspian Marshes—which financed their revolt by stealing from wealthy landlords (Munson 1988). Reza Kahn defeated the Jangali by gaining the support of the merchants and the army. Reza wanted to establish a republic but the *ulama* objected, so Reza had himself declared shah and established the Pahlavi dynasty. With the support of the British, he rapidly secularized the country, clearly trying to westernize it; he forced men to wear European clothes, including brimmed hats, and forbade women from wearing the *chador* or veil, analogous to requiring European women to go bare-breasted. Public protests followed. More important, trade and commerce under the shah was monopolized by Europeans.

The gradual withdrawal of the British from Iran after World War II allowed the *ulama* to regain some of their authority and led to the democratic election in 1951 of Mohammad Mosaddeq as prime minister. One of Mosaddeq's first acts was to nationalize the Anglo-Iranian Oil Company. He also banned a militant religious group, the *Fada'iyan-e Islam,* led by Ayatollah Kashani. These two acts ultimately led to his downfall in a coup arranged by the American CIA to install the son of Reza Kahn as shah. After the coup, the shah banned the parties that had helped put him in power and began the period of American domination of Iran and continued westernization of the country. When the shah announced that women would be allowed to vote there was a religious protest in Qum, the religious center of Iran, to

An anti-American protest by Islamic women in Teheran.

which the shah responded by attacking the seminary. With the help of the CIA, the shah set up a security apparatus, SAVAK, to suppress domestic opposition.

The revolution of 1979 that overthrew the shah and brought Ayatollah Khomeini to power represented a joining together of the *ulamas*, the merchants, and the intellectuals in reaction to the shah's policies, the repressions, and the killings. The stage was set for the return of Khomeini on February 1, 1979, aboard a jet from France.

We can see in this history the interplay between, on the one hand, British and American attempts to control political events in Iran and consequently the vast Iranian oil fields and on the other hand, Islamic leaders who objected largely to the secularization of Iran that seemingly arose from British and then American influences. But the fundamentalist revolution in Iran was neither sudden nor surprising. There were many factors involved in the revolution, including the poverty of the majority of Iranian peasants, the violent repression of dissent led by SAVAK, and the economic excesses of the leaders who took great pains to flaunt the wealth gained by oil sales to the West. It also marked the continued resistance by many Iranians to the assimilation of their country into the culture of capitalism.

Protestant Fundamentalism in North America

Protestant fundamentalism has gained almost as high a profile in the United States as Islamic fundamentalism has in Arab and Southeast Asian countries. While it is difficult to estimate precisely how many people in the United State are fundamentalists, it is clear that many people share the same beliefs. For example, 72 percent of Americans say the Bible is the word of God and 39 percent say the Bible is literally true. Two-thirds say that Jesus Christ rose from the dead, and 44 percent are creationists who agree that God created the world in pretty much its present form within the last 10,000 years (Ammerman 1991).

It is also clear that Protestant fundamentalism has gained a strong voice in the political process in the United States, demanding that political candidates adhere to certain fundamentalist principles, including support for the banning of abortion, support for school prayer, and support for laws controlling what can appear in the mass media.

Foundations of Protestant Fundamentalism

There are three basic tenets held by people who consider themselves to be Protestant fundamentalists. First, they are evangelicals; that is, they begin with the fact that they are saved. Not all evangelicals are fundamentalists, but this is one point on which evangelicals and fundamentalists agree. Second, they believe in the inerrancy of the Bible; they believe the Bible to be true, even when it says things they don't like. Furthermore they believe it provides an accurate view of history and science, as well as God-given moral guidelines. Theologians may argue about what different passages mean, but through prayer and study the truth evident in the Bible will be revealed. Third, they believe in premillennialism, the doctrine of Rapture. Fundamentalists, like other Christians, believe in the End Times, a point in history when the present world ends and the thousand-year reign of Christ on Earth begins. But fundamentalists also believe that prior to that, Jesus Christ will appear and to the blare of heavenly trumpets lift his bride, the (true) church, up to heaven. This is the Rapture. Then begins the Tribulation, a seven-year period when all unfilled Bible prophesies are fulfilled, when God, Satan, Christ, and Anti-Christ meet in the final battle of Armageddon in Israel, and when Christ returns with his army of believers to begin his millennial reign on earth. Christians have no role in the playing out of these events, and nothing that anyone can do will change the date of the Rapture; that date was set by God at the beginning of time (Harding 1991:61). However, it is possible, through careful observation of world events, to predict the coming of the Rapture.

There are some variations in Protestant fundamentalist belief and practice, but the essentials are relatively consistent. The question is, *what was the stimulus for the rise of Protestant fundamentalism, and how can we account for its recent resurgence?*

The Emergence of Fundamentalism in North America

Fundamentalist belief began to form in the mid-nineteenth century, largely in reaction to the modernization and secularization of Protestant churches and as a response to the challenge to religion of nineteenth-century science, technology, and culture. Darwin's theory of evolution was one of the most threatening scientific developments, but others, such as sociologist Emile Durkheim's ideas about the power of social forces to shape individual behavior, Sigmund Freud's theories of sexuality, and the works of anthropologist Franz Boas that attacked ethnocentrism and absolutism, struck at some of the basic beliefs and the truth of the Bible. Fundamentalists were particularly offended when biblical scholars turned a scientific eye to the scripture itself, claiming the Bible is neither unique nor the "word of God" and comparing biblical stories with the myths of other societies.

But it was not only the work of academics who threatened the inerrancy of the Bible that triggered a fundamentalist reaction; there was the change in American culture itself. There were new attitudes and values that accompanied the shift from a primarily agrarian society to an urban industrial society. From the end of the Civil War to the beginning of the twentieth century the industrial work force quadrupled, and inventions such as the telegraph, electricity, and telephones were transforming the country. It was to science and technology that people began to look for improvements in their lives.

In addition, immigration and urbanization were changing where people lived and with whom they lived and worked. All of these changes prompted religious reactions. Some of those who were religiously inclined joined the Social Gospel movement, which sought to alleviate the ills caused by urban crowding and poverty; others became Adventists or Jehovah's Witnesses, carrying on the early nineteenth-century prophesies of William Miller and Charles Russell that the world was about to end. Or people became possessed by the Holy Spirit and joined Pentecostal movements. Those who were fundamentalists, however, differed in that they rejected any compromise with those who no longer saw the Bible as the word of God (Ammerman 1991:14).

Inerrancy of the Bible became the centerpiece of the fundamentalist movement in the early twentieth century. Theologians attacked the works of German scholars who claimed the Bible was an historic document composed by many authors. Fundamentalists argued that if the Bible claimed to be divinely inspired then, since it was the word of God, it must be inspired. Those trying to show that the Bible was in error, fundamentalists said, had to "prove" that a disputed fact was in the original texts—those unsullied by copying and transmission—and that it really meant what the critic said it meant and was really in conflict with a proven fact of science. Given such a standard, it was virtually impossible to prove the Bible wrong.

After World War I fundamentalists interpreted Germany's defeat as punishment for the work of German scholars trying to examine the Bible scientifically and for the acceptance of Darwin's theory of evolution, while they saw the League of Nations as the world government that they believed would appear just prior to the Tribulation. Thus, as Christian fundamentalists do today, they interpreted world events in terms of their religious beliefs.

Early twentieth-century fundamentalists focused their early protests on schools and the teaching of Darwin's theory of evolution. There is some misunderstanding about fundamentalist objections to Darwin's theory of evolution. Most theologians had little problem accommodating Darwin's theory to religious doctrine. The real problem, at least for fundamentalists, was not so much Darwin's biology but the application of his theory to the interpretation of social life, and the idea that the "strong" were destined to replace the "weak." If this were true, said fundamentalists, then war on one's neighbors became natural. Furthermore, the application of Darwin's theories to the workings of society legitimated the then very popular doctrine of eugenics, the idea that the state should enact laws to ensure that only the "fittest" bred. This, of course, further imposed human will on a divinely guided universe.

The protest over the teaching of evolution in American schools may never have received the prominence it did had not William Jennings Bryan volunteered to prosecute John Scopes, a Tennessee high school teacher charged under Tennessee law with illegally teaching the theory of evolution. Bryan was a major American figure, three-time presidential candidate, advisor to presidents, crusader for women's rights, and defender of the Bible. To counter Bryan the American Civil Liberties Union sent a team of lawyers headed by Clarance Darrow to defend Scopes. Darrow, in his way, was as imposing a public figure as Bryan, and probably the most famous lawyer of his time.

Darrow succeeded in turning the case into a science versus religion contest, and the issue of using the theory of evolution to interpret social history never received a hearing. Bryan won the case; Scopes was convicted. But the public ridicule of fundamentalist arguments of the inerrancy of the Bible resulted in American public opinion overwhelmingly supporting Scopes.

After the Scopes trial and the public reaction to it, Protestant fundamentalists were convinced that American culture had come under the sway of "secular humanism," a godless view of the world that substituted human action and wisdom for divine action and guidance. Since they could not transform society, they turned

The Scopes Trial in Tennessee in 1925 was turned into a battle between religion and science by Clarance Darrow (standing in front of the table) in his defense of John T. Scopes (to the immediate right of Darrow, staring straight ahead).

to saving individual souls. Most fundamentalist churches broke away from their parent churches and formed their own organizations, such as the American Council of Christian Churches founded in 1941 by Carl McIntire. Fundamentalists joined missionary organizations and there was enormous growth in Bible colleges and institutes as well as expansion into publishing and radio and television broadcasting. Charles Fuller's "Old Fashioned Revival Hour," which appeared in 1934, became one of the most popular shows on radio, followed on television by the enormously popular Oral Roberts and Rex Humbard.

There was also a growth in political radicalism; Gerald Winrod wrote in his journal of seeing the End times, a Jewish Anti-Christ, and a Jewish conspiracy to rule the world. In the 1950s, fundamentalists took up the banner of anticommunism, with Carl McIntire arguing that the Revised Standard Version of the Bible was a communist plot, and that Jews and Blacks constituted the main threat to White Christian civilization. But it was the revolution of 1968, the civil rights movement, the feminist movement, and the antiwar movement with its slogan "question authority" that seemed to provide evidence for fundamentalists that society was disintegrating and the Rapture must be near.

Burned-out hippies and disenchanted liberals, along with other seekers who had failed in the 1968 revolution to transform society, began to join fundamentalist churches. As one hippie-turned-fundamentalist said (cited Ammerman 1991:39),

> [o]ne person tells you to do one thing, and the next person tells you to do the opposite. "Get a job, get a haircut." Or "Turn on, tune in, drop out." Or "Support the President," and someone else says "Impeach Nixon" or 'Stop the War,' or whatever it is, you know. It makes you crazy. What do you do? It's typical of the world. You're in confusion. In the Lord the Word shows you what to do, and you can rest in it. You don't have to be gray.

Fundamentalists were also concerned about America's role in the world; in spite of their condemnation of what was happening to American culture, America was still the fundamentalists "city on a hill"; moreover, America's military strength and economic influence provided the entree into other countries for fundamentalist missionizing; there was a fear that "the light of the gospel might go out because it would have no great chosen nation to carry it" (cited in Ammerman 1991:40).

Finally, there were a series of changes that seemed to be challenging fundamentalists to come out of their political isolation. Among them was the Equal Rights Amendment to the constitution; fundamentalists feared it would prevent women from fulfilling their biblical role as submissive wives. They saw laws promoted by governmental and private social agencies that sought to define the limits of a parent's right to punish their children as an attack on parental authority as it was defined in the Bible. They saw the extension of the civil rights movement to homosexuals, whose lives seemed to fundamentalists grossly immoral, as a direct attack on biblical injunction. They fought against the prevention of prayer in school. And, finally, they saw behind *Roe v. Wade* and the legalization of abortion all the forces that were trying to destroy the family and Christian morality.

The defense against the scientific attack on the inerrancy of the Bible did not go away; it resurfaced in the doctrine of scientific creationism, the use of the tools and language of science to prove that the world was indeed created in 4004 B.C. But where the inerrancy of the Bible was the major issue one hundred years ago, today the focus of fundamentalist interest is the protection of the traditional family—a legally married man and woman with their children preferably supported by the husband's work—as the basic unit of society (Ammerman 1991:45). From this flows the fundamentalist opposition to pornography, gay and lesbian rights, the Equal Rights Amendment, and laws designed to protect abused wives and children. And at the centerpiece of this agenda is the opposition to abortion.

With these agendas, and the active participation of Protestant fundamentalists in politics, there has been a resurgence of fundamentalist influence in American life. One of the clearest indications of this is the enormous growth in church schools and home schooling. From 1965 to 1983 enrollment in evangelical schools rose sixfold, and the number of schools approached 10,000. As many as 100,000 fundamentalist children were being taught at home. While some of this was due to desegregation, it is also largely a religious issue.

Some of these positions have served to unite fundamentalists with other groups with whom they have, at one time or another, been vehemently opposed. Their opposition to abortion with Catholics; their opposition to pornography with the feminist movement; their opposition to the ERA with Mormons; and their support of Israel with Jews. But it has also created splits with those who decried such alliances.

Variations in Doctrine

There are also new variations of Protestant fundamentalist belief, most markedly the Christian reconstructionists, probably the most clearly antisystemic fundamentalist group. Christian reconstructionists seek to replace the "modern bureaucratic state" with a Christian state modeled after the Bible; their ideal is the seventeenth-century Puritans of Massachusetts. They argue that people must submit to the rule of God and follow a doctrine they call "theonomy."

The economics of Christian fundamentalists are more complex and varied than generally supposed (Iannaccone 1993; Kuran 1993). Most people associate Christian fundamentalists with support of the free market economy, opposition to government redistribution programs, defense of private property, and opposition to any form of socialism. Yet little is made of economics in the writings of most Christian fundamentalists, and many fundamentalist colleges or universities do not even have an economics department. Jerry Fallwell is the most outspoken of the Christian fundamentalist leaders when it comes to the defense of the free market, but the Christian reconstructionists are the only group to systematize a conservative economic agenda, arguing that the Bible dictates that private property should be regulated only by the family and the religious community, not by the state. The Bible, they say, imposes a flat tax of 10 percent and argues against any kind of centrally planned economy. Metallic currency is the only kind permitted, and income redistribution violates the eighth commandment, "Thou shalt not steal," and is simply institutionalized theft.

There is also an evangelical left which argues that the Bible teaches that God is on the side of the poor. Best represented by the writings of Jim Wallis (1984) (*Agenda for a Biblical People*), they draw attention to the vast disparities in wealth that exist in the modern world and argue that "overconsumption is theft from the poor," that the wealth of the core comes only at the expense of the poor of the nonindustrial world. The biblical solution, they argue, is redistribution. Christians should consume less, they say, and contribute more to the poor. Influenced by the secular left, the counterculture of the 1960s, and communitarian Christian groups such as the Amish, Mennonites, and Hutterites, said Laurence R. Iannaccone (1993:350) the evangelical left argues that

> [t]he system which creates and sustains much of the hunger, underdevelopment, and other social ills in the world today is capitalism. Capitalism is by its very

nature a system which promotes individualism, competition, and profit-making with little or no regard for social costs. It puts profits and private gain before social service and human needs. As such it is an unjust system and should be replaced.

The Militants of Protestant Fundamentalism

Protestant fundamentalism also has its more militant activists, perhaps best represented by Operation Rescue. Operation Rescue was begun in Binghamton, New York, in 1988 by Randall Terry. Its goal was to protest legal abortion by barricading abortion clinics, blocking women's access to clinics, confronting women entering and leaving the clinics, and harassing them verbally and physically, even following them or tracing their license plate numbers and calling them at home. Operation Rescue picketed clinics and the homes of clinic physicians, sent threatening letters, and made threatening phone calls. By 1990 Operation Rescue reported that 35,000 of their protesters had been arrested, while another 16,000 risked arrests in what the group called "rescues" (Ginsburg 1993).

The ultimate goal, however, was more than simply stopping abortion. Rather they intended to use the opposition to abortion, in the words of evangelical Protestant leader Francis Schaeffer (cited Ginsburg 1993:558), "as a way for evangelicals to challenge the entire legitimacy of the secular modern state, withholding allegiance until the nation returns to its religious roots in matters like public prayer and religious education." As Faye Ginsburg (1993:558) noted, the opposition to abortion is the means protesters use to return America to "traditional Christian values."

Operation Rescue was not the first group to use violence to protest abortion. The right-to-life movement goes back to the 1973 Supreme Court ruling in *Roe v. Wade* that recognized a woman's right to abortion. Some groups had already adopted confrontational tactics of blocking the entrances to clinics and harassing abortion providers. The National Abortion Federation keeps a record of "violent incidents" against abortion providers that includes invasions of clinics, vandalism, murders, death threats, bomb threats, bombings, assaults, arson attempts, arson, and kidnapping attempts. From 1977 through December of 1997 they have documented a total of 2,167 violent incidents including 5 murders, 38 bombings, and 148 cases of arson, 71 cases of attempted arson or bombings, and 355 cases of invasion. They have also documented 33,809 arrests of abortion protesters (see National Abortion Federation 1997).

The state's official reaction to the violence is ambiguous. In an influential anti-abortion essay in 1983, President Ronald Reagan, an opponent of abortion, said the increase in attacks on abortion clinics did not constitute terrorism because they were not carried out by an organized group; he did reverse himself in 1985, speaking out against these "violent anarchistic activities."

It is clear that Randall Terry's agenda is to refashion what he sees as a godless society according to the beliefs and values of his version of Christian fundamentalism. Thus as Ginsburg (1993:579) said, it is a mistake to look at Operation Rescue only in the context of the abortion debate; rather its intent is to impose on Ameri-

An Operation Rescue, antiabortion protest outside a women's clinic in Little Rock, Arkansas in 1994.

can society its version of Christian culture: "For 'rescuers,' fighting abortion is simply a first step in reversing America's 'moral decline,' much as opposition to the teaching of evolution was considered a way to fight secularization in the 1920s."

Others have interpreted the movement by emphasizing its heavily male makeup. Susan Faludi depicted these fundamentalist men of the "late baby-boom generation" as sociologically identical to Randall Terry, carrying a grudge against "careerist women." They missed out on the political engagement of the 1960s and were also cheated out of the economic bounty of that era, fearing that they will earn less than their fathers, be unable to buy homes, and be unable to support a family. They see themselves losing ground as women are gaining it (Ginsburg 1993:577).

Yet it seems something of an oversimplification to see the militancy of Operation Rescue in particular, and Protestant fundamentalism in general, as a reaction to the improvement in the position of women. To begin with, the position of women has not improved that dramatically, as we noted in Chapter 11. Furthermore, as Ginsburg noted, the aims of the movement are far broader, seeking to replace the culture of capitalism with a society modeled on the Bible.

This takes us back to the question *to what extent can religious fundamentalisms be said to be antisystemic?* Certainly Islamic fundamentalism with its opposition to Western influence contains antisystemic elements, although some would argue that they are more nationalistic than antisystemic. The case of Protestant fundamentalism is even more ambiguous. It, too, contains strong antisystemic elements, with its opposition to the power of the nation-state and condemnation of the very features that define the culture of capitalism, particularly the self-indulgent consumerism that is one of its key elements. Yet some elements of Protestant fundamentalism clearly seem to be reactionary, founded in opposition to the agenda of the revolution of 1968, including the women's movement and the gay and lesbian rights movements. Protestant fundamentalists have been adamant in their defense of the patriarchal family. Yet even here there is ambiguity: Randall Terry claims he was strongly influenced by the political events of the 1960s and considers himself a "young rebel"(Ginsburg 1993:577).

Yet if there is ambiguity in the extent to which Protestant fundamentalism is a protest against the culture of capitalism, the position of Protestant fundamentalism in Latin America is even more difficult to characterize.

The Contest between Liberation Theology and Protestant Fundamentalism in Latin America

When General August Pinochet led a CIA-supported coup against the democratically elected government of Salvadore Allende in 1973, the Methodist Pentecostal Church in Santiago, Chile issued a statement praising Pinochet. They claimed the coup was an act of God protecting the people from the evil and darkness of Marxism, in the same statement rejecting United Nations findings of repeated instances of torture and brutality by coup leaders.

From 1982 to 1983, General Efrain Ríos Montt held the presidency of Guatemala, and each Sunday, dressed in civilian clothes, in his position of elder of El Verbo Church, a mission of California-based Gospel Outreach, he preached a sermon broadcast on state radio. At the same time, his military was carrying out a repressive antiinsurgency campaign against Mayan peasants marked by thousands of violations of civil and human rights. According to Amnesty International, 2,700 people were killed in purges in the first five months of his rule (Deiron 1991:143).

The active support for militaristic regimes is only one paradox of the phenomenal growth in fundamentalist, evangelical, pentecostal churches in Latin America. In El Salvador from 1980 to 1985 membership in Assemblies of God churches grew from 20,000 to 80,000; in Guatemala 25 percent of the population are Protestant, and it is predicted that by the end of the 1990s half the population will be Protestant. The loser in the conversions is Roman Catholicism. But the battle involves more than religion; it is also political. Catholics in Latin America have become associated in the past three decades with liberation theology, while Protestant churches represent those with more conservative, decidedly pro-capitalist political views. In some instances, particularly in Guatemala, the conversion to Protestant denominations was an explicit attempt by Guatemalan Catholics to distance themselves from the doctrine of liberation theology, in some cases to protect their lives.

The Growth and Development of Liberation Theology

Roman Catholicism has dominated the lives of the peoples of Latin America since the time of the Spanish and Portuguese conquests. Catholic missionaries accompanied the early expeditions and, in populations decimated by war, slavery, and disease, found fertile ground for their teachings. Throughout most of its history in Latin America, the Catholic Church either was apolitical or actively supported whatever regime was in power. Only in the past thirty years, and with minimal support from the Catholic hierarchy, have clergy begun to take an activist political role in the lives of church members. A number of factors pushed the Catholic Church to a more activist political role in the periphery.

First, the Catholic Church is being transformed from a core to a peripheral entity. In 1900, 70 percent of all Catholics lived in Europe and the United States; in the year 2000, 70 percent will live in the poor countries of the periphery. Moreover, the leadership is changing: in 1951 there were 2 African bishops and 31 Asian bishops; by 1981 there were 293 African bishops and 408 Asian bishops.

Second, the experiences of clergy in their often impoverished rural and urban parishes forced them into a more activist role. In the wave of authoritarian repression that swept through Latin America in the 1960s and 1970s, the Church found itself in the uncharacteristic position of opposing the military. The disappearances, tortures, arrests, and killings affected church personnel, solidifying their commitment to the poor. There was, as some people called it, a "conversion of the bishops," as once conservative church leaders, as a consequence of the experiences of their clergy, began to oppose repressive regimes. It was the murder of a priest working with the poor that sparked Oscar Romero's conversion from an Episcopal conservative to San Salvador's champion of the poor, and ultimately led to his assassination. Another once conservative Brazilian bishop excommunicated the governor of a Brazilian state, along with other officials and leaders of a landowners group, after the deaths of those advocating a land redistribution scheme.

Third, at the 1968 meeting of the Latin American Bishops Conference (CELAM) in Medellin, Colombia, the bishops issued a document that called for the end of institutionalized violence and the building of a social order that defends the poor and oppressed.

Fourth, there seemed initially to be support for a more activist role by clergy from the Vatican. Pope John Paul II went so far as to lump Western capitalism with Marxist collectivism as promoting forms of labor organization and control of the means of production antithetical to Christian principles.

Fifth, the Third World debt and the declining services, rising food and energy prices, and rising unemployment that it has inspired began to push the Catholic Church toward an anticapitalistic position. Two Bolivian ordinaries went so far as to say it was immoral for Bolivia to pay its external debt. All of this increased church hostility to capitalism; the increased suffering of the poor, the role of institutions such as the International Monetary Fund, the political machinations, graft and corruption emerging with capitalism affected how all levels of the Catholic hierarchy viewed their economic system (Budde 1992:49).

Finally, the challenge posed by Protestant missionary groups working with the poor, and their growing success at gaining converts, pushed many in the Catholic Church to work more closely with the poor and seek to empower them to improve their conditions.

Thus liberation theology grew out of experiences that forced the Church to rethink its role in society and politics. The poor, instead of being objects hoping for a better life after death or objects of charity, became objects of empowerment and participants in religious, political, and economic institutions. The idea that the poor shall inherit the earth takes on more immediate and activist tones with con-

Liberation theology meetings, such as this one in Brazil, marked one response of the Catholic church to poverty and oppression in Latin America.

crete efforts to enhance the role of poor people as legitimate participants in religion, society, and politics (Levine 1986).

The result was that Catholic churches became centers for the defense of human rights and attacks against government repression. Church leaders in Latin America attacked inequality and injustice and began to participate in forming organizations and social movements to give the poor a political and economic voice. Most prominent were the formation of Christian base communities. These were influenced by the writings of Paulo Freire (e.g. 1970, 1998) and promoted *conscientization,* a sense of class and oppression, egalitarian and democratic internal values. It was an attempt, as some put it, to apply the Gospel to everyday life in the hope that these efforts would ultimately replace the old order of things.

While traditional Christians considered these communities outrageous innovations and military regimes closely monitored them, they grew rapidly; some three million Catholics in Latin America take part in them (Deiron 1991:158). Thus the Church began to cut its ties to authoritarian governments and became a critic of the established order, consequently reordering both the cultural and political landscape of Latin America.

Growing Opposition to Liberation Theology

More recently, however, the optimism over the possibilities of liberation theology to promote real social and economic change have been replaced by doubts from activists, scholars, and journalists over whether liberation theology has any future at all. Growing opposition from the Church hierarchy, the collapse of socialism in Europe, the loss of the poor constituency to evangelical Protestant movements, growing opposition from North American and European Catholics, and governments in both the core and the periphery have all served to weaken the appeal of liberation theology. Opponents of liberation theology were quick to label it a Marxist ideology and to minimize its similarity to the message of the Gospels.

The opposition of core Catholics has been reinforced by official opposition from the U.S. government (see Budde 1992). In 1969 a fact-finding report by Nelson Rockefeller to Richard Nixon warned that the Catholic Church in Latin America, once a reliable ally of the United States, is now open to "subversive penetration." In 1980 a Reagan policy team concluded that opposition to liberation theology must be an important part of U.S. policy in Latin America. The document warned that liberation theologists "use the church as a political arm against private property and productive capitalism" and recommended countermeasures. At a conference of American military chief of staffs in 1989 the two items on the agenda were subversion and drug trafficking on the one hand, and the subversive quality of liberation theology on the other; a confidential document leaked two years later said that the international communist movement has used the religious front to gain power. Thus the United States pressured Pope John Paul II to take an anti-Sandinista line in Nicaragua, found common cause with church conservatives, and used such conservative evangelicals as Jimmy Swaggert, Pat Robertson, and Jose Efrain Ríos Montt to advance U.S. interests in Latin America (Budde 1992).

The Growth of the Evangelical Movement in Latin America: The Case of Guatemala

While some scholars, journalists, and government officials question whether liberation theology is dead, few question the health of Protestantism in Latin America, especially in countries such as Guatemala that have experienced a mass of Protestant conversions in the past two decades. Protestant missionizing in Guatemala began in the nineteenth century and for the few converts offered an alternative to the domination of the conservative Catholic Church, which was resisting the growing modernization of the Guatemalan elite. But it was not until the second half of the twentieth century that Protestantism began to make inroads among the Guatemalan peasantry.

Catholic opposition to the Guatemalan government began when the American CIA orchestrated the overthrow in 1954 of the democratically elected government of Jacobo Arbenz Guzmán in order to protect U.S. investors, in particular the United Fruit Company for which Guatemala was a virtual colony. The United States installed a series of repressive military regimes that drew the Catholic hierarchy into criticizing the human rights violations of the government. The Guatemalan government reacted by attacking the Catholic Church. They accused the Church of harboring communists and caches of guns, and claimed that priests were leading bands of guerrillas in the peasant revolt in the Guatemalan highlands. The government also retaliated politically and militarily, harassing and arresting church leaders and killing more than a dozen priests and hundreds of lay leaders (Stoll 1994:103).

One of the reactions of the peasantry and the elite to government repression and killing was to flock to Protestant churches. These churches, not necessarily fundamentalist in the same sense as the North America Protestant churches, share the devotion to the Bible and the conviction that members are "saved" or "born again." But unlike other fundamentalist movements, the Guatemalan *evangélicos*, as they call themselves, do not want to go back to their roots; instead they reject the past, claiming, for example, that the Spanish conquest created a society in which one group, the ladino—mixed descendants of the Spanish and indigenous populations—dominated and despised the other—the indigenous people. They blame Guatemala's impoverished state on its Hispanic Catholic heritage and want to remake themselves in the image of the society they idealize—the United States. In some fashion, the evangelical movement in Guatemala resembles the cargo cults of the South Pacific, religious movements that promised converts the deliverance of the precious cargo of European and American colonizers—refrigerators, automobiles, home furnishings, and the like.

Who in Guatemala is converting? Certainly the vast majority are poor. Others join simply to distance themselves from the Catholic Church's criticism of the government and to protect themselves from state-sponsored death squads. Yet as many as 5 percent of the elite have also joined evangelical churches. Evangelical religion in Guatemala received an enormous boost when in 1982 the army put into power General Ríos Montt without knowing that months before he had joined a California-based evangelical religious sect, Church of the Word. Montt did not claim, as past military rulers did, that he had been put in power to restore stability; instead he claimed that he was put in power by God. He was replaced by the military after sixteen months in office, but he was so popular he likely would have won the 1990 presidential election had he not been disqualified by a law that banned from state leadership people who had previously been installed by a coup d'état (Stoll 1994: 102).

Other members of the upper class in Guatemala are answering the appeals of North American missionizing groups, such as the Full Gospel Business Men's Fellowship, an international network of men's clubs with fifty-nine clubs in Guatemala alone by 1990. Dressed in business suits and meeting for lunch in restaurants and hotels, they suddenly break into a hymn or jump up to hug each other, and listen to a member testify how he was saved from drink, corruption, or philandering by the lord (Stoll 1994:105). Groups such as this have proved receptive to the appeals of the North American religious right and the electronic evangelicals such as Pat Robertson and Jimmy Swaggert.

What is the attraction of evangelical groups? As mentioned above, they were for the poor a sanctuary from the death squads. But that accounts for only a part of their appeal. Given the shortage of priests in the Catholic Church, there was a real appeal of a religion in which any person could start a church. Evangelical religion met the needs for new places of worship, while schisms within the churches led to constant splitting and forming of new congregations. Furthermore, the demands and control of worship were not so rigorous that church members could not continue to consider themselves Catholics, a tendency made easier by the Catholic Church's increased tolerance for charismatic practices as a way of decreasing defections.

The elite were attracted by the "health and wealth" message of evangelical churches, the doctrine that God wants people to enjoy the good things in life, and that repentance from sin—drinking, smoking, sexual philandering, and so on—will bring affluence. One might see in evangelical Protestantism in Latin America a similarity to the mind cure religions of the early twentieth-century United States that paved the way for the growth of consumerism, which we discussed in Chapter 1.

But both rich and poor may have been attracted by the belief in the power of prayer to transform society. David Stoll made the point that most nonreligious people (as well as most anthropological and sociological theories of religion) view prayer as an act or a stage of religious thought in which the believer feels helpless to influence events in his or her life, and so turns to prayer as a last resort. Yet, he said, to the believer, prayer is a form of social activism, a form of spiritual warfare against the powers of Satan. As one pastor explained to David Stoll (1994:109):

> *If God controls the universe and I pray to him, he can work in several ways. He can change the hearts of people, for example. There is a great quantity of Christians who do not live as such. They don't pay their taxes, they don't stop at traffic lights, they don't reject bribes. What would this country be like if they started behaving like Christians?*

The goals and the attraction of evangelical religion lie in the assumption that if you can change individual behavior, if you can bring morality to the people, you can transform the entire society and bring a reformation in public morality. They take prayer campaigns such as "Jesus is the Lord of Guatemala" and turn them into ways of interpreting the crisis in Guatemala, arguing that if they can cast demons out of the individual, they can cast them out of the country.

Of course by emphasizing changes in the individual as a way to transform society, evangelicals are also able to avoid talking about needed social and economic reforms and government and military abuse of power, subjects considered *delicado*, critiques that could bring a visit from the death squads. Evangelicals explain that it is not their mission to examine the historical, social, and economic causes of Guatemala's civil war; rather their task is to accomplish "silent social work" to transform Guatemalan society from the ground up. Even when Stoll brought up the subject of human rights with some of the few military converts, they simply referred him to Old Testament justifications for the slaughter of old men, women, and children along with combatants (Stoll 1994:114).

Can evangelical movements actually succeed in implementing social and economic reform in Latin America, as opposed to, say, liberation theology or violent revolution? Some American sociologists suggest they can; by forming small, private congregations that promote equality, they say, evangelicals are modeling change for the larger society in the same way nineteenth-century dissident churches did in England, in the process paving the way for "democratic capitalism." But David Stoll (1994:118–119) questioned the analogy of evangelicalism in Guatemala with Protestant-inspired change in England. Given the control of the country by the military and the resistance of the privileged elite to any real social and economic change, there is little opportunity to speak out, let along effect any real change:

> *Like other Latin Americans, Guatemalans are also being caught in deeper and more disadvantageous forms of dependency on the global capitalist economy. With the country becoming a free trade area for transnational giants, competitive forces are likely to undermine the kind of small-scale entrepreneurialism which Protestantism is supposed to promote but which in fact is already well established in Latin America.*

Conclusion

We began this chapter by asking to what extent religious movements have been expressions of antisystemic sentiments and how they have served as a means of protest against the expansion, both in the core and in the periphery, of the culture of capitalism. It is clear, we believe, that in the case of small-scale religious protests, such as the Ghost Dance, the cargo cults, and the attraction of Western religious movements such as Zionism, participants are responding to the effects of the expansion of the culture of capitalism. It is less clear, however, in the case of the various fundamentalisms that have gained popularity in the latter part of the twentieth century. These cultural movements oppose what they call modernization, secular humanism, or, in the periphery, Westernization, seemingly synonyms for capitalism. Yet they contain elements, particularly in their view of women and the family and opposition to alternative lifestyles, that suggest that they are more reactions to the antisystemic revolution of 1968 than protests to capitalism. Certainly the rise of Protestant fundamentalism in Latin America bears some resemblance to the religious changes that accompanied the rise of capitalism in early twentieth-century America. The emphasis on individual salvation and health seems to mirror the mind cure movements that set the stage in the United States for the seeking of happiness through commodities.

Yet we should remember that antisystemic movements rarely specifically target the whole culture of which they are a part. Rather, they select some element and blame it for the source of their distress. Poor Malaysian peasants blamed slightly less poor peasants for their plight; Kikuyu in Kenya blamed other Kikuyu; coal miners blamed coal mine operators, who in turn blamed the U.S. government; while fundamentalists blame academics, women, and homosexuals.

Regardless of the object of their protest, we must remember that in seeking to transform capitalism by using the Qu'ran, the Old Testament, the New Testament, the teachings of Budda, or some other cultural alternative, fundamentalisms represent, with the exception of small-scale secular and religious movements, the only viable alternative to the culture of capitalism and, in the event of a global economic collapse, the only cultures prepared, politically and ideologically, to replace it.

C o n c l u s i o n

Global Futures

The great triumph of humanity I had dreamed of now took a different shape in my mind. It had been no triumph of universal education and general cooperation, such as I had imagined at first. Instead, I saw a real aristocracy, armed with perfected science and working out to a logical conclusion the industrial system of today. The triumph of the overworld humanity had not been simply a triumph over nature, but a triumph over nature and their fellow men.
—H. G. WELLS, THE TIME MACHINE

In H. G. Wells's novel *The Time Machine,* the Time Traveler arrives in the future to find the human beings having evolved into two distinct species: the beautiful and delicate Eloi who live above ground, and the apelike Morlocks who live underground and whose labors made possible the leisurely life of the Eloi, but who now prey on them. It was, said the Time Traveler, the logical extension into the future of life in nineteenth-century industrial Britain. *The Time Machine* was to be the first of many, and some would say, the most prescient, of Wells's excursions into the future. Certainly all indications are that one of the dominant characteristics of the culture of capitalism is to increase the economic gap between rich and poor, both within core countries and between the core and the periphery. In 1990, the poorest 70 percent of the world's people earned 7 percent of its income, while the remaining 30 percent earned 93 percent (Wagar 1991:79). Economist Lester Thurow (1996) argued that the gap between rich and poor can only increase, since future income depends on present income. In other words, in market economies future wealth depends on present investments; only those with money now will have more later; wealth leads to wealth, poverty to poverty. Unless we find a way to link democracy and capitalism symbiotically, he said, the numbers of poor and disaffected must increase, and with their increase comes the danger of violent upheaval.

Not everyone has such a pessimistic view of the world to come. In fact, our view of the future depends largely on our view of the past and present. If we believe the culture of capitalism has succeeded in solving many world problems and bettering our lives, then we will no doubt believe that it continue to do so in the future. If we believe the culture of capitalism is responsible for most of the problems, then we can only conclude that they will continue to accumulate.

W. Warren Wagar, in his book *The Next Three Futures* (1991), outlined three paradigms or scenarios of the future, each dictated by the view of the past and present of their respective advocates. First there is the paradigm of those he calls *technoliberals,* who have abiding faith in the ability of technology and capitalist managers to solve the world's problems and preserve democracy (Wagar 1991:36). The vast majority of people who concern themselves with predicting the future, particularly those who work for government and industry, said Wagar, are technoliberals. The technoliberal is well aware of the problems in the world but is convinced that these problems can be solved through capitalism and some combination of free market mechanisms and the state-directed redistribution of wealth. Technoliberals, for example, tend to believe that the population problem (and they believe that there is one) can be solved through rigorous population control programs, particularly in the periphery. Technoliberals maintain that the environment can be preserved through technological remedies; they credit capitalism with bringing democracy to more and more countries and an increased standard of living to most of the world's people, often pointing to the worldwide increase in life expectancy as proof of their claims. For technoliberals the future of capitalism is bright, not only for capitalists but for everyone else also. Capitalism works because it motivates people.

The second major vision of the future is shared by those who hold to the *radical,* or "socialist," "social democratic," or "Marxist" paradigm or scenario. For radicals the culture of capitalism represents the problem, not the solution. Radicals hope for the demise of the capitalist world system and the injustices that it creates and seek to replace it with some kind of socialist worker's commonwealth (Wagar 1991:38) Radicals, like technoliberals, believe there is a profound problem with population growth and poverty, but radicals are convinced it can be solved only by land reform and the adoption of more appropriate agricultural methods and technologies. Radicals blame corporate greed for environmental problems and reject the idea that corporations who caused the problem can help solve it. Radicals, while recognizing the material gains made in the past few centuries, attribute these gains to the exploitation of labor and peoples of the periphery; they point to the widening gap in wealth between classes and between nations, and predict this will lead to a violent revolution.

For radicals capitalism must fail because it ultimately concentrates wealth in the hands of a few, playing havoc with peoples' lives for the sake of profit. While technoliberals point to the growth of democracy with capitalism, radicals hold capitalism responsible for the failure of democratization and the rise of repressive regimes in such countries as Indonesia, Nigeria, Guatemala, Peru, and most countries of the periphery. They see corporate power leading only to a decline of democracy and the increasing concentration of power in the hands of corporate monopolies. They argue that Western bourgeois democracy, in which power is concentrated in the hands of those who control the media, the schools, and the workplace, should not be confused with real democracy. Consequently, if the culture of capitalism is not overthrown, democracy will rapidly decline.

The third view of the future is that of the *counterculturalists.* Counterculturalists reject one of the central tenets of both technoliberialism and radicalism—the desirability or need for a greater centralization of power. Instead counterculturalists argue for decentralism, a downscaling of things, a view best illustrated in E. F. Schumacher's *Small Is Beautiful: Economics as If People Mattered* (1975). In essence, the counterculturalists attack one of the central features of the culture of capitalism—the desirability or need for perpetual growth. Economically they argue for a shift from capital-intensive technology to simpler labor-intensive technologies, the replacement of nonrenewable energy resources such as coal and oil with renewable sources such as solar or wind energy, and the replacement of the multinational corporation with locally based cooperatives. Counterculturalists argue that it is the materialistic value system of our culture that is responsible for environmental destruction, and that it must be revised. Unlike technoliberals, whose vision of the good life is manifested in Walt Disney World's Tomorrowland, counterculturalists are particularly concerned with the future quality of life, arguing that the emphasis on work must be replaced with a greater emphasis on income security, part-time employment, along with a rebirth of the extended family to enable retired people to spend more time with children and grandchildren. Counterculturalists, said Wagar, "rarely make a wholesale assault on capitalism, as such, but it is difficult to imagine how capitalism could survive, much less thrive, in a world tailored to their specifications" (1991:43).

In his fictional work, *A Brief History of the Future,* Wagar offered a future in which all three scenarios are played out. The capitalism of the technoliberals thrives into the twenty-first century when, in 2044, the countries of the world are thrown into a war in which 70 percent of the earth's population is destroyed. With the capitalist world system in shambles, a socialist world government, the Commonwealth, emerges, governed by a global People's Congress and dedicated to the eradication of the three intolerable evils of the old order: tribalism—the sovereignty of nation and race; capitalism—production for profit and creation of classes; and sexism—male dominance (Wagar 1992:145). The Commonwealth succeeds in eradicating poverty, expanding education (teacher–student ratios of no more than 1 to 5), and rebuilding the environment. But in the end, bureaucratism becomes a horror, and new political parties emerge advocating the miniaturization of society and arguing for greater freedoms for local communities. In the year 2147 the Small Party gains a majority of seats in the People's Congress, and the Commonwealth is peacefully dissolved.

Perhaps the only scenario Wagar neglected is that of religious fundamentalisms. While he examined the role of religion in the possible formation of future ideologies (1991:139–140) and recognized the contribution of religious groups to the dissolution of his fictional Commonwealth (1992:218), he neglected the possibility that religious fundamentalisms of various persuasions may dominate our futures. Technoliberals, radicals, and counterculturalists tend to underestimate the role of religion and belief in our lives, often dismissing it as a relic of the past. Yet it may be fair to say that in the event that radicals and counterculturalists are correct in their assessment that the cultural of capitalism, with its tendencies to exploit people and the environment, and its need for perpetual growth, cannot persist, then of all the cultures poised to replace it those of religious fundamentalisms seem the most prepared. In the past, certainly, periods of economic decline have been characterized by surges in religious conviction and activity. *Is it unlikely, then, that in the event of the total collapse of the culture of capitalism, existing fundamentalisms will emerge to dominate our cultural landscape?*

References

Abu-Lughod, Janet L. 1989. *Before European Hegemony: The World-System A.D. 1250–1350.* New York: Oxford University Press.

Alpert, Bracha. 1991. Student's Resistance in the Classroom. *Anthropology and Education Quarterly* 22:350–366.

Amin, Samir. 1990. The Social Movement in the Periphery: An End to National Liberation. In *Transforming the Revolution: Social Movements and the World-System,* edited by Samir Amin, Girovanni Arrighi, Andre Gunder Frank, and Immanuel Wallerstein. New York: Monthly Review Press.

Amin, Samir, Girovanni Arrighi, Andre Gunder Frank, and Immanuel Wallerstein. 1990. *Transforming the Revolution: Social Movements and the World-System.* New York: Monthly Review Press.

Ammerman, Nancy T. 1991. North American Protestant Fundamentalism. In *Fundamentalisms Observed,* edited by Martin E. Marty and R. Scott Appleby (Fundamentalism Project, volume 1). Chicago: University of Chicago Press.

Anderson, Benedict R. O'G. 1991. *Imagined Communities: Reflections on the Origin & Spread of Nationalism.* New York: Verso.

Baker, Brenda J. and George Armelagos. 1988. The Origin and Antiquity of Syphilis. *Current Anthropology* 29:703–721.

Barnes, Barry. 1974. *Scientific Knowledge and Sociological Theory.* London: Routledge & Kegan Paul.

Basch, Linda, Nina Glick Schiller, and Cristina Szanton Blanc. 1994. *Nations Unbound: Transnational Projects, Postcolonial Predicaments, and Deterritorialized Nation-State.* Amsterdam: Gordon & Breach.

Basu, Amrita. 1995. Introduction. In *The Challenge of Local Feminisms: Women's Movements in Global Perspective,* edited by Amrita Basu. Boulder: Westview Press.

Beal, Merrill D. 1963. *"I Will Fight No More Forever": Chief Joseph and the Nez Perce War.* Seattle: University of Washington Press.

Beaud, Michel. 1983. *A History of Capitalism 1500–1980.* Translated by Tom Dickman and Anny Lefebvre. New York: Monthly Review Press.

Beeman, William O. 1997. Revitalization Drives American Militias. In *Conformity and Conflict: Readings in Cultural Anthropology,* 9th ed., edited by James Spradley and David W. McCurdy. New York: Longman.

Belk, R. W. 1988. Possession and the Extended Self. *Journal of Consumer Research* 15: 140–158.

Birdsall, Nancy. 1994. Government, Population, and Poverty: A Win-Win Tale. In *Population and Development: Old Debates, New Conclusions,* edited by Robert Cassen. New Brunswick: Transaction.

Blondet, Cecilia. 1995. Out of the Kitchens and onto the Streets: Women's Activism in Peru. In *The Challenge of Local Feminisms: Women's Movements in Global Perspective,* edited by Amrita Basu. Boulder: Westview Press.

Bodley, John H. 1985. *Anthropology and Contemporary Human Problems,* 2nd ed. Mountain View: Mayfield Publishing.

Bodley, John H. 1990. *Victims of Progress,* 3rd ed. Mountain View: Mayfield Publishing.

Boserup, Ester. 1965. *The Conditions of Agricultural Growth.* Chicago: Aldine.

Boserup, Ester. 1970. *Women's Role in Economic Development.* New York: St. Martin's Press.

Bradsher, Keith. 1997. License to Pollute: Light Trucks, Darlings of Drivers, Are Favored by the Law, Too. *New York Times,* November 30; http://www.nytimes.com

Braudel, Fernand. [1979] 1982. *Civilization and Capitalism 15th–18th Century: Vol II, The Wheels of Commerce.* (Translated by Siân Reynolds. New York: Harper and Row.

Budde, Michael L. 1992. *The Two Churches: Catholicism and Capitalism in the World-System.* Durham: Duke University Press.

Business Week. 1997. Gen X Ads: Two for Me, None for You. August 11.

Caldwell, John C. 1982. *Theory of Fertility Decline.* New York: Academic Press.

Carneiro, Robert. 1978. Political Expansion as an Expression of the Principle of Competitive Exclusion. In *Origins of the State,* edited by Ronald Cohn and Elman Service. Philadelphia: Institute for the Study of Human Issues.

Carrier, James G. 1995. *Gifts and Commodities: Exchange and Western Capitalism Since 1700.* London: Routledge.

Caufield, Catherine. 1996. *Masters of Illusion: The World Bank and the Poverty of Nations.* New York: Henry Holt.

Chase, Allan. 1977. *The Legacy of Malthus: The Social Costs of the New Scientific Racism.* New York: Alfred A. Knopf.

Coale, Ansley. 1974. The History of Human Population. *Science* 231:40–51.

Cohen, Joel. 1995. Population Growth and the Earth's Carrying Capacity. *Science* 269:341–346.

Cohen, Mark. 1977. *The Food Crisis in Prehistory: Overpopulation and the Origins of Agriculture.* New Haven: Yale University Press.

Cohen, Mark. 1989. *Health and the Rise of Civilization.* New Haven: Yale University Press.

Cohen, Mark. 1994. Demographic Expansion: Causes and Consequences. In *Companion Encyclopedia of Anthropology,* edited by Tim Ingold. New York: Routledge.

Cohen, Mark. 1998. *The Culture of Intolerance.* New Haven: Yale University Press.

Cohen, Roger. 1991. For Coke, World Is Its Oyster. *New York Times,* November 21, D1.

Cohen, Ronald, and Elman R. Service (editors). 1978. *Origins of the State: The Anthropology of Political Evolution.* Philadelphia: Institute for the Study of Human Issues.

Colley, Linda. 1992. *Britons: Forging the Nation 1707–1837.* New Haven: Yale University Press

Collier, George A., Jr. 1994. Roots of the Rebellion in Chiapas. *Cultural Survival Quarterly* 18:14–18.

Comaroff, Jean. 1985. *Body of Power, Spirit of Resistance: The Culture and History of a South African People.* Chicago: University of Chicago Press.

Connell, K. H. 1965. Land and Population in Ireland, 1780–1845. In *Population in History: Essays in Historical Demography,* edited by D. V. Glass and D. E. C. Eversley. Chicago: Aldine.

Conrad, Joseph. 1972 [1902]. *Heart of Darkness.* New York: W. W. Norton & Company.

Cook, Sherburne Friend, and Woodrow W. Borah. 1960. The Indian Population of Central Mexico, 1531–1610. *Ibero-Americana 44.* Berkeley: University of California Press.

Coon Come, Matthew. 1996. Remarks of Grand Chief Matthew Coon Come, Canada Seminar, Harvard Center for International Affairs and Kennedy School of Government, October 28, 1996.

Cordell, Dennis. 1994. Extracting People from Precapitalist Production: French Equatorial Africa from the 1890s to the 1930s. In *African Population and Capitalism: Historical Perspectives,* edited by Dennis Cordell and Joel W. Gregor. Madison: University of Wisconsin.

Crosby, Alfred W. 1986. *Ecological Imperialism: The Biological Expansion of Europe, 900–1900.* Cambridge: Cambridge University Press.

Dayal, Jaya and Jim Lobe. 1995. Poverty-Global: Poor People, Rich Banks and Good Intentions. Interpress Third World News Agency, Oct 21, 1995.

Deiron, Pablo A. 1991. Protestant Fundamentalism in Latin America. In *Fundamentalisms Observed,* edited by Martin E. Marty and R. Scott Appleby (Fundamentalism Project, volume 1). Chicago: University of Chicago Press.

Dettwyler, A. Katherine. 1994. *Dancing Skeletons: Life and Death in West Africa.* Prospect Heights: Waveland Press.

Diamond, Jared. 1997. *Guns, Germs, and Steel: The Fates of Human Societies.* New York: W. W. Norton.

Dobyns, Henry F. 1983. *Their Number Become Thinned: Native American Population Dynamics in Eastern North America.* Knoxville: University of Tennessee Press.

Drèze, Jean, and Amartya Sen. 1989. *Hunger and Public Action.* Oxford: Clarendon Press.

Driscoll, David D. 1992. *What is the International Monetary Fund?* Washington, DC: International Monetary Fund.

Dubos, Rene. 1968. *Man, Medicine, and Environment.* New York: Mentot.

Dubos, Rene. 1987 [1952]. *The White Plague; Tuberculosis, Man, & Society.* New Brunswick: Rutgers University Press.

Dunaway, Wilma A. 1996. *The First American Frontier: Transition to Capitalism in Southern Appalachia, 1700–1860.* Chapel Hill: University of North Carolina Press.

Duncan, Earle. 1994. Indigenous Identity at the Margin: Zapatismo and Nationalism. *Cultural Survival Quarterly* 18:26–30.

Durning, Allan. 1992. *How Much Is Enough: The Consumer Society and the Future of the Earth.* New York: W. W. Norton.

Edgerton, Robert B. 1989. *Mau Mau: An African Crucible.* New York: The Free Press.

Edwards, Michael, and David Hulme. 1995. *Non-Governmental Organizations—Performance and Accountability: Beyond the Magic Bullet.* London: Earthscan Publications.

Eisenstein, Zillah. 1997. Stop Stomping on the Rest of Us: Retrieving Publicness from the Privatization of the Globe. In *Feminism and Globalization: The Impact of the Global Economy on Women and Feminist Theory,* edited by Alfred C. Aman, Jr. *Indiana Journal of Global Legal Studies* Spring 1997 (special issue).

Ember, Carol R. 1983. The Relative Decline in Women's Contribution to Agriculture with Intensification. *American Anthropologist* 85:285–304.

Endelmann, Mark. 1987. From Costa Rican Pasture to North American Hamburger. In *Food and Evolution: Toward a Theory of Human Food Habits,* edited by Marvin Harris and Eric Ross. Philadelphia: Temple University Press.

Ensminger, M. E. 1991. *Animal Science.* Danville, IL: Interstate Publishers.

Erasmus, Charles J. 1972. *In Search of the Common Good: Utopian Experiments Past and Future.* New York: The Free Press.

Erlich, Paul R. 1968. *The Population Bomb.* New York: Ballantine Books.

Ehrlich, Paul R., and Anne H. Ehrlich. 1990. *The Population Explosion.* New York: Simon & Schuster.

Evans-Pritchard, E. E. 1940. *The Nuer.* Oxford: Oxford University Press.

Ewald, Paul. 1993. The Evolution of Virulence. *Scientific American* 269:86–93.

Farmer, Paul. 1992. *AIDS and Accusation: Haiti and the Geography of Blame.* Berkeley: University of California Press.

Fernández-Kelly, María Patricia. 1983. *For We Are Sold, I and My People: Women and Industry in Mexico's Frontier.* Albany: State University of New York Press.

Fey, Harold, and D'Arcy McNickle. 1970. *Indians and Other Americans: Two Ways of Life Meet.* New York: Harper & Row.

Firth, Raymond. 1959. *Social Change in Tikopia: A Re-Study of a Polynesian Community after a Generation.* London: Allen & Unwin.

Fjellman, Stephen M. 1992. *Vinyl Leaves: Walt Disney World and America.* Boulder: Westview Press.

Flannery, Kent V. 1972. The Cultural Evolution of Civilization. *Annual Review of Ecology and Systemics* 3:339–426.

Flannery, Kent V. 1973. The Origins of Agriculture. In Siegel, Beals, and Tyler, eds., *Annual Review of Anthropology* 2:271–310.

Foster, John Bellamy. 1993. "Let Them Eat Pollution": Capitalism and the World Environment. *Monthly Review* 44:10–11.

Freire, Paulo. 1970. *Pedagogy of the Oppressed.* New York: Continuum Publishing Company.

Freire, Paulo. 1988. *The Paulo Freire Reader.* New York: Continuum Publishing Company.

Fried, Morton H. 1967. *The Evolution of Political Society: An Essay in Political Anthropology.* New York: Random House.

Garrett, Laurie. 1994. *The Coming Plague.* New York: Farrar, Strauss & Giroux.

Geertz, Clifford. 1963. *Agricultural Involution: The Process of Ecological Change in Indonesia.* Berkeley: University of California Press.

Gellner, Ernest. 1983. *Nations and Nationalism.* Ithaca: Cornell University Press.

Ginsburg, Faye. 1993. Saving America's Souls: Operation Rescue's Crusade against Abortion. In *Fundamentalisms and the State: Remaking Polities, Economies, and Militance,* edited by Martin E. Marty and R. Scott Appleby (Fundamentalism Project, volume 3). Chicago: University of Chicago Press.

Gleissman, S. R. 1988. Local Resource Use Systems in the Tropics: Taking Pressure Off the Tropics. *Tropical Rainforests: Diversity and Conservation,* edited by F. Alemeda and C. M. Pringle. San Francisco: California Academy of Sciences.

Goodenough, Ward. 1963. *Cooperation in Change.* New York: Wiley.

Gossen, Gary H. 1994. Comments on the Zapatista Movement. *Cultural Survival Quarterly* 18: 19–21.

Gould, Peter. 1993. *The Slow Plague: A Geography of the AIDS Pandemic.* Cambridge: Blackwell.

Goulet, Denis. 1971. *The Cruel Choice: A New Concept in the Theory of Development.* New York: Atheneum.

Greider, William. 1997. *One World Ready or Not: The Manic Logic of Global Capitalism.* New York: Simon & Schuster.

Guha, Ramachandra. 1990. *The Unquiet Woods: Ecological Change and Peasant Resistance in the Himalaya.* Berkeley: University of California Press.

Guttmann, Myron. 1988. *Toward the Modern Economy: Early Industry in Europe, 1500–1800.* New York: Alfred A. Knopf.

Guttmann, Robert. 1994. *How Credit-Money Shapes the Economy: The United States in a Global System.* London: M. E. Sharpe.

Handwerker, W. Penn. 1989. *Women's Power and Social Revolution: Fertility Transition in the West Indies* (Frontiers of Anthropology, volume 2). Newbury Park: Sage.

Hanson, F. Allan. 1993. *Testing, Testing: Social Consequences of the Examined Life.* Berkeley: University of California Press.

Hardin, Garrett. 1968. Tragedy of the Commons. *Science* 162:1243–1248.

Hardin, Garrett, and John Baden. 1977. *Managing the Commons.* New York: W. H. Freeman.

Harding, Susan. 1991. Imagining the Last Days: The Politics of Apocalyptic Language. In *Accounting for Fundamentalisms,* edited by Martin E. Marty and R. Scott Appleby (Fundamentalism Project, volume 4). Chicago: University of Chicago Press.

Harris, Marvin. 1971. *Culture, Man, and Nature.* New York: Crowell.

Harris, Marvin. 1986. *Good to Eat: Riddles of Food and Culture.* New York: Simon & Schuster.

Harris, Marvin. 1987. *The Sacred Cow and the Abominable Pig.* New York: Touchstone.

Harris, Marvin, and Eric B. Ross. 1987a. *Death, Sex, and Fertility: Population Regulation in Preindustrial and Developing Societies.* New York: Columbia University Press.

Harris, Marvin, and Eric B. Ross. 1987b. *Food and Evolution: Toward a Theory of Human Food Habits.* Philadelphia: Temple University Press.

Hobsbawm, Eric J. 1959. *Primitive Rebels: Studies in Archaic Forms of Social Movement in the 19th and 20th Centuries.* New York: Frederick A. Praeger.

Hobsbawm, Eric J. 1964. Age of Revolution: Seventeen Eighty-Nine to Eighteen Forty-Eight. New York: NAL/Dutton.

Hobsbawm, Eric J. 1975. *The Age of Capital: 1848–1875.* New York: Charles Scribner's Sons.

Hobsbawm, Eric J. 1990. *Nations and Nationalism since 1780: Programme, Myth, Reality.* Cambridge: Cambridge University Press.

Hobsbawm, Eric J., and Terence Ranger. 1983. *Inventing Tradition.* Cambridge: Cambridge University Press.

Hudson, E. H. 1964. Treponematosis and Man's Social Evolution. *American Anthropologist* 76: 885–901.

Howell, Nancy. 1979. *Demography of the Dobe !Kung.* New York: Academic Press.

Iannaccone, Laurence R. 1993. The Economics of American Fundamentalists. In *Fundamentalisms and the State: Remaking Polities, Economies, and Militance,* edited by Martin E. Marty and R. Scott Appleby (Fundamentalism Project, volume 3). Chicago: University of Chicago Press.

Ignatiev, Noel. 1995. *How the Irish Became White.* New York: Routledge.

Jahan, Roushan. 1995. Men in Seclusion, Women in Public: Rokeya's Dream and Women's Struggles in Bangladesh. In *The Challenge of Local Feminisms: Women's Movements in Global Perspective,* edited by Amrita Basu. Boulder: Westview Press.

Jaimes, Annette M. 1992. Federal Indian Identification Policy: A Usurpation of Indigenous Sovereignty in North America. In *The State of Native America: Genocide, Colonization, and Resistance,* edited by M. Annette Jaimes. Boston: South End Press.

James, C. L. R. 1963. *The Black Jacobins: Toussaint l' Ouverture and the San Domingo Revolution,* 2nd ed. New York: Random House.

Jardine, Lisa. 1996. *Worldly Goods: A New History of the Renaissance.* New York: Doubleday.

Johnson, Paul E. 1978. *A Shopkeeper's Millennium: Society and Revivals in Rochester.* New York: Hill & Wang.

Juergensmeyer, Mark. 1993. *The New Cold War? Religious Nationalism Confronts the Secular State.* Berkeley: University of California Press.

Juergensmeyer, Mark. 1996. The Worldwide Rise of Religious Nationalism. *Journal of International Affair* 50:1–20.

Junas, Daniel. 1995. Rise of Citizen Militias: Angry White Guys with Guns. *Covert Action Quarterly* Spring:22–25.

Kanogo, Tabitha. 1987. *Squatters and the Roots of Mau Mau 1905–1963.* Athens: Ohio University Press.

Kanter, Rosabeth Moss. 1972. *Commitment and Community: Communes and Utopias in Sociological Perspective.* Cambridge: Harvard University Press.

Kearney, Michael. 1991. Borders and Boundaries of State and Self at the End of Empire. *Journal of Historical Sociology* 4:58–74.

Kemp, Amanda, Nozizwe Madlala, Asha Moodley, and Elaine Salo. 1995. The Dawn of a New Day: Redefining South African Feminism. In *The Challenge of Local Feminisms: Women's Movements in Global Perspective,* edited by Amrita Basu. Boulder: Westview Press.

Kennedy, Paul. 1993. *Preparing for the Twenty-First Century.* New York: Random House.

Kenyatta, Jomo. 1962. *Facing Mount Kenya.* New York: Random House.

Kincheloe, Joe L. 1997. McDonald's, Power, and Children: Ronald McDonald (aka Ray Kroc) Does It All for You. In *Kinderculture: The Corporate Construction of Childhood,* edited by Shirley R. Steinberg and Joe L. Kincheloe. Boulder: Westview Press.

Korten, David C. 1990. *Getting to the 21st Century: Voluntary Action and the Global Agenda.* Hartford: Kumarian Press.

Korten, David C. 1995. *When Corporations Rule the World.* Hartford: Kumarian Press.

Kowinski, William Severini. 1985. *The Malling of America: An Inside Look at the Great Consumer Paradise.* New York: William Morrow.

Kumar, Radha. 1995. From Chipko to Sati: The Contemporary Indian Women's Movement. In *The Challenge of Local Feminisms: Women's Movements in Global Perspective,* edited by Amrita Basu. Boulder: Westview Press.

Kuper, Leo. 1990. The Genocidal State: An Overview. In *State Violence and Ethnicity,* edited by Pierre L. van den Berghe. Boulder: University of Colorado Press.

Kuran, Timur. 1993. Fundamentalisms and the Economy. In *Fundamentalisms and the State: Remaking Polities, Economies, and Militance,* edited by Martin E. Marty and R. Scott Appleby (Fundamentalism Project, volume 1). Chicago: University of Chicago Press.

Landes, David S. 1969. *The Unbound Prometheus: Technological Change and Industrial Development in Western Europe from 1750 to the Present.* Cambridge: Cambridge University Press.

Lappé, Marc. 1994. *Evolutionary Medicine: Rethinking the Origins of Disease.* San Francisco: Sierra Club Books.

Lasch, Chistopher. 1977. *Haven in a Heartless World: The Family Besieged.* New York: Basic Books.

Leach, William. 1993. *Land of Desire: Merchants, Power, and the Rise of a New American Culture.* New York: Pantheon.

Leacock, Eleanor. 1983. Interpreting the Origins of Gender Inequality: Conceptual and Historical Problems. *Dialectical Anthropology* 7:263–283.

Leacock, Eleanor. 1986. Women, Power, and Authority. In *Visibility and Power: Essays on Women in Society and Development,* edited by Leela Dube, Eleanor Leacock, and Shirley Ardener. Delhi: Oxford University Press.

Leaf, Murray. 1984. *Song of Hope: The Green Revolution in a Punjab Village.* New Brunswick: Rutgers University Press.

Lears, T. J. Jackson. 1983. From Salvation to Self-Realization: Advertising and the Therapeutic Roots of the Consumer Culture, 1880–1930. In *The Culture of Consumption: Critical Essays in American History, 1880–1930,* edited by Richard Wrightman Fox and T. J. Jackson Lears. New York: Pantheon.

Lenin, Vladimir I. 1976. *Imperialism, the Highest Stage of Capitalism.* San Francisco: China Books & Periodicals.

Levine, Daniel H. 1986. *Religion and Political Conflict in Latin America.* Chapel Hill: University of North Carolina Press.

Lewellen, Ted C. 1983. *Political Anthropology: An Introduction.* South Hadley: Bergin & Garvey.

Lincoln, Bruce. 1989. *Discourse and the Construction of Society: Comparative Studies of Myth, Ritual, and Classification.* Oxford: Oxford University Press.

Livi-Bacci, Massimi. 1992. *A Concise History of World Population.* Cambridge: Blackwell.

Lloyd, Cynthia B. 1994. High Fertility at the Level of the Family. In *Population and Development: Old Debates, New Conclusions,* edited by Robert Cassen. New Brunswick: Transaction.

Low, Patrick. 1993. *Trading Free: The GATT and US Trade Policy.* New York: Twentieth Century Fund Press.

Lutjens, Sheryl L. 1994. Remaking the Public Sphere: Women and Revolution in Cuba. In *Women and Revolution in Africa, Asia, and the New World,* edited by Mary Ann Tétreault. Columbia: University of South Carolina Press

Malthus, Thomas Robert. 1826. *Essay on the Principle of Population.* London: John Murray.

Mamdani, Mahmood. 1972. *The Myth of Population Control: Family, Caste, and Class in an Indian Village.* New York: Monthly Review Press.

Manning, Patrick. 1990. *Slavery and African Life: Occidental, Oriental, and African Slave Trades.* Cambridge: Cambridge University Press.

Maren, Michael. 1997. *The Road to Hell: How International Charity & Food Aid Damage the Third World.* New York: The Free Press.

Marx, Karl. 1972. *Ireland and the Irish Question: A Collection of Writings.* New York: International Publishers.

Marx, Karl. [1844] 1970. *Critique of Hegel's "Philosophy of Right."* Translated by Annette Jolin and Joseph O'Malley. Cambridge: Cambridge University Press.

Marx, Karl, and Frederick Engels. [1848] 1941. *Manifesto of the Communist Party.* New York: International Publishers.

Maybury-Lewis, David. 1997. *Indigenous Peoples, Ethnic Groups, and the State.* Boston: Allyn & Bacon

McCay, Bonnie J., and Louise Fortmann. 1996. Voices from the Commons. *Cultural Survival Quarterly* 20:24–25.

McCracken, Grant. 1988. *Culture and Consumption: New Approaches to the Symbolic Character of Consumer Goods and Activities.* Bloomington: Indiana University Press.

Mead, Margaret. 1961. *New Lives for Old.* New York: New American Library.

Meade, J. E. 1967. Population Explosion, the Standard of Living, and Social Conflict. *The Economic Journal* 77:233–255.

Meggitt, Mervyn. 1962. *Desert People: A Study of the Aalbiri Aborigines of Central Australia.* London: Angus & Robertson.

Menchú, Rigoberta. 1984. *I, Rigoberta Menchú: An Indian Woman in Guatemala.* Edited and with an introduction by Elisabeth Burgos-Debray. New York: Verso.

Miller, Michael B. 1994. *Bon Marche: The Bourgeoise Culture and the Department Store 1869–1920.* Princeton: Princeton University Press.

Mintz, Sidney W. 1985. *Sweetness and Power: The Place of Sugar in World History.* New York: Viking.

Mooney, James. 1965. *The Ghost-Dance Religion and the Sioux Outbreak of 1890.* Chicago: University of Chicago Press.

Munson, Henry, Jr. 1988. *Islam and Revolution in the Middle East.* New Haven: Yale University Press.

Nag, Moni (editor). 1975. *Population and Social Organization.* The Hague: Mouton.

Nagengast, Carole. 1994. Violence, Terror, and the Crisis of the State. *Annual Review of Anthropology* 23:109–136.

Nash, George. 1988. *The Life of Herbert Hoover: The Humanitarian (1914–1917)*. New York: W. W. Norton.

Nash, June. 1994. Global Integration and Subsistence Insecurity. *American Anthropologist* 96:7–30.

Nash, Manning. 1991. Islamic Resurgence in Malaysia and Indonesia. In *Fundamentalisms Observed*, edited by Martin E. Marty and R. Scott Appleby (Fundamentalism Project, volume 1). Chicago: University of Chicago Press.

National Abortion Federation. 1997. Incidents of Violence and Disruption Against Abortion Providers; http://www.prochoice.org/

Nations, James D. 1994. The Ecology of the Zapatista Revolt. *Cultural Survival Quarterly* 18:31–33.

Nerfin, Marc. 1986. Neither Prince nor Merchant: An Introduction to the Third System. *IFDA Dossier* 56:3–29.

Newman, Lucile F. (editor). 1990. *Hunger in History*. Oxford: Basil Blackwell.

Nigh, Ronald. 1994. Zapata Rose. *Cultural Survival Quarterly* 18:9–11.

Nigh, Ronald. 1995. Animal Agriculture for the Reforestation of Degraded Tropical Rainforests. *Culture and Agriculture*: 51–52:2–5.

Noriega, Jorge. 1992. American Indian Education in the United States. In *The State of Native America: Genocide, Colonization, and Resistance*, edited by M. Annette Jaimes. Boston: South End Press.

O'Brien, Jay. 1994. Differential High Fertility and Demographic Transitions: Peripheral Capitalism in Sudan. In *African Population and Capitalism: Historical Perspectives*, edited by Dennis Cordell and Joel W. Gregor. Madison: University of Wisconsin Press.

Oduol, Wilhelmina, and Wanjiku Mukabi Kabira. 1995. The Mother of Warriors and Her Daughters: The Women's Movement in Kenya. In *The Challenge of Local Feminisms: Women's Movements in Global Perspective*, edited by Amrita Basu. Boulder: Westview Press.

Omran, Abdel R. 1971. The Epidemiological Transition: A Theory of Epidemiology of Population Change. *Milbank Memorial Fund Quarterly* 49:509–538.

Ong, Aihwa. 1987. *Spirits of Resistance and Capitalistic Discipline: Factory Women in Malaysia*. Albany: State University of New York Press.

Ong, Aihwa. 1990. Japanese Factories, Malay Workers: Class and Sexual Metaphors in West Malaysia. In *Power and Difference: Gender in Island Southeast Asia*, edited by Jane Atkinson and S. Errington. Palo Alto: Stanford University Press.

Ong, Aihwa. 1997. Strategic Sisterhood or Sisters in Solidarity? Questions of Communitarianism and Citizenship in Asia. In *Feminism and Globalization: The Impact of the Global Economy on Women and Feminist Theory*, edited by Alfred C. Aman, Jr. *Indiana Journal of Global Legal Studies* Spring (special issue).

Oved, Yaacov. 1988. *Two Hundred Years of American Communes*. New Brunswick: Transaction.

Paddock, William, and Paul Paddock. 1967. *Famine—1975*. Boston: Little, Brown.

Pimental, David, and Marcia Pimental. 1979. *Food, Energy and Society*. New York: Wiley.

Platt, Anne E. 1996. *Infecting Ourselves: How Environmental and Social Disruption Trigger Disease*. Washington, DC: Worldwatch Institute.

Polgar, Steven. 1972. Population History and Population Policies from an Anthropological Perspective. *Current Anthropology* 13:203–211.

Polgar, Steven. 1975. Birth Planning: Between Neglect and Coersion. In *Population and Social Organization*, edited by Moni Nag. The Hague: Mouton.

Posey, Darrell A. 1996. Protecting Indigenous Peoples' Rights to Biodiversity. *Environment* 38:6–13.

Posey, Darrell A., John Frechione, and John Eddins. 1984. Ethnoecology as Applied Anthropology in Amazonian Development. *Human Organization* 43:95–107.

Presley, Cora Ann. 1992. *Kikuyu Women, the Mau Mau Rebellion, and Social Change in Kenya*. Boulder: Westview Press.

Preston, Julia. 1998. Feuding Villages Bring Mexican Region to Brink of War. *New York Times*, February 2, 1998; http://www.nytimes.com

Ramos, Alcida Rita. 1995. *Sanumá Memories: Yanomami Ethnography in Times of Crisis*. Madison: University of Wisconsin Press.

Reed, Richard. 1997. *Forest Dwellers, Forest Protectors: Indigenous Models for International Development*. Boston: Allyn & Bacon.

Reining, Conrad C. 1966. *The Zande Scheme: An Anthropological Case Study of Economic Development in Africa.* Evanston, IL: Northwestern University Press.

Restad, Penne L. 1995. *Christmas in America: A History.* Oxford: Oxford University Press.

Rich, Bruce. 1994. *Mortgaging the Earth,* Boston: Beacon.

Rifkin, Jeremy. 1992. *Beyond Beef: The Rise and Fall of the Cattle Culture.* New York: Dutton.

Robbins, Richard H. 1997. *Cultural Anthropology: A Problem-Based Approach,* 2nd ed. Itasca: F. E. Peacock.

Ross, Eric. 1980. *Beyond the Myths of Culture: Essays in Cultural Materialism.* New York: Academic Press.

Rugh, Andrea B. 1993. Reshaping Personal Relations in Egypt. In *Fundamentalisms and Society: Reclaiming the Sciences, the Family, and Education,* edited by Martin E. Marty and R. Scott Appleby (Fundamentalism Project, volume 2). Chicago: University of Chicago Press.

Rummel, R. J. 1994. *Death by Government.* New Brunswick: Transaction.

Sachedina, Abdulaziz A. 1991. Activist Shi'ism in Iran, Iraq, and Lebanon. In *Fundamentalisms Observed,* edited by Martin E. Marty and R. Scott Appleby (Fundamentalism Project, volume 1). Chicago: University of Chicago Press.

Sacks, Karen. 1979. *Sisters and Wives: The Past and Future of Sexual Equality.* Westport: Greenwood.

Salamon, Lester M., and Helmut K. Anheir. 1996. *The Emerging Nonprofit Sector: An Overview.* Manchester: Manchester University Press.

Sale, Kirkpatrick. 1991. *The Conquest of Paradise: Christopher Columbus and the Columbian Legacy.* New York: Alfred A. Knopf.

Sanderson, Stephen K. 1995. *Social Transformation: A General Theory of Historical Development.* Cambridge: Blackwell.

Sauvy, A. 1969. *General Theory of Population.* New York: Basic Books.

Scheper-Hughes, Nancy. 1992. *Death Without Weeping: The Violence of Everyday Life in Brazil.* Berkeley: University of California Press.

Scherer, Ron. 1996. Tourism Booms as World's Middle Class Goes Trekking. *Christian Science Monitor,* June 12; 1996:http://www.csmonitor.cm/archiveascii.html

Schmidt, Leigh Eric. 1995. *Consumer Rites: The Buying and Selling of American Holidays.* Princeton: Princeton University Press.

Schneider, Jane. 1993. Rumpelstilskin's Bargain: Folklore and the Merchant Capitalist Intensification of Linen Manufacture in Early Modern Europe. In *Cloth and Human Experience,* edited by Annette B. Weiner and Jane Schneider. Washington: Smithsonian Institution Press.

Schuler, Sidney, and Syed M. Hashemi. 1994. Credit Programs, Women's Empowerment, and Contraceptive Use in Rural Bangladesh. *Studies in Family Planning* 25:65–76.

Schumacher, E. F. 1975. *Small Is Beautiful: Economics as If People Mattered.* New York: HarperCollins.

Schusky, Ernest L. 1989. *Culture and Agriculture: An Ecological Introduction to Traditional and Modern Farming Systems.* New York: Bergin & Garvey.

Scott, James C. 1985. *Weapons of the Weak: Everyday Forms of Peasant Resistance.* New Haven: Yale University Press.

Sen, Amartya. 1990. Food Entitlements and Economic Chains. In *Hunger in History,* edited by Lucile F. Newman. Oxford: Basil Blackwell.

Service, Elman R. 1975. *Origins of the State and Civilization: The Process of Cultural Evolution.* New York: W. W. Norton.

Shalom, Stephen R. 1996. The Rwanda Genocide: The Nightmare that Happened. *Z Magazine,* April; http://www.lbbs.org/zmag/article/april96shalom.htm

Silverblatt, Irene. 1988. Women in States. *Annual Review of Anthropology* 17:427–460.

Silverstein, Ken, and Alexander Cockburn. 1995. Major U.S. Bank Urges Zapatista Wipe-Out: "A Litmus Test for Mexico's Stability." *Counterpunch* Vol. 2: No. 3, February 1.

Sinclair, Upton. 1971 [1906]. *The Jungle.* Cambridge, Mass.: R. Bentley.

Skaggs, Jimmy M. 1976. *Prime Cut.* College Station: Texas A & M University Press.

Smith, Anthony D. 1995. *Nations & Nationalism in a Global Era.* Cambridge: Blackwell.

Stack, Carole. 1974. *All Our Kin: Strategies for Survival in a Black Community.* New York: Harper & Row.

Stiffarm, Lenore A., and Phil Lane, Jr. 1992. The Demography of Native North America: A Question of American Indian Survival. In *The State of Native America: Genocide, Colonialism, and Resistence,* edited by Annette Jaimes. Boston: South End Press.

Stoll, David. 1994. "Jesus Is the Lord of Guatemala": Evangelical Reform in a Death Squad State. In *Accounting for Fundamentalisms,* edited by Martin E. Marty and R. Scott Appleby (Fundamentalism Project, volume 4). Chicago: University of Chicago Press.

Stone, Lawrence. 1976. *The Family, Sex, and Marriage in England 1500–1800.* New York: Harper & Row.

Sutherland, Daniel. 1989. *The Expansion of Everyday Life: 1860–1876.* New York: Harper & Row.

Taussig, Michael. 1977. The Genesis of Capitalism Amongst a South American Peasantry: Devil's Labor and the Baptism of Money. *Comparative Studies in Society and History* 19:130–155.

Taussig, Michael. 1987. *Shamanism, Colonialism, and the Wild Man: A Study in Terror and Healing.* Chicago: University of Chicago Press.

Taylor, Bron. 1995. Earth First! In *Ecological Resistence Movements: The Global Emergence of Radical and Popular Environmentalism,* edited by Bron Raymond Taylor. Albany: State University of New York Press.

Tétreault, Mary Ann. 1994. Women and Revolution: A Framework for Analysis. In *Women and Revolution in Africa, Asia, and the New World,* edited by Mary Ann Tétreault. University of South Carolina Press.

Thompson, E. P. 1967. Time, Work-Discipline and Industrial Capitalism. *Past and Present* 38: 56–97

Thoreau, Henry David. [1854] 1957. *Walden.* Boston: Houghton Mifflin.

Thornton, John. 1992. *Africa and Africans in the Making of the Atlantic World, 1400–1680.* Cambridge: Cambridge University Press

Thurow, Lester C. 1996. *The Future of Capitalism.* New York: Viking Penguin.

Tilly, Charles, Louise Tilly, and Richard Tilly. 1975. *The Rebellious Century, 1830–1930.* Cambridge: Harvard University Press.

Tsing, Anna Lowenhaupt. 1993. *In the Realm of the Diamond Queen: Marginality in an Out-of-the-Way Place.* Princeton: Princeton University Press.

UNAIDS/WHO. 1997. Global summary of the HIV/AIDS Epidemic, December 1997.

http://www.unaids.org/highband/document/epidemio/report97.html

United Nations. 1993. *Development Programme, Human Development Report.* New York: Oxford University Press.

U.S. Bureau of the Census. 1990. *Statistical Abstract of the United States: 1990* (110th ed.). Washington, D.C.

U.S. Bureau of the Census. 1992. *Statistical Abstract of the United States: 1992* (112th ed.). Washington, D.C.

U.S. Bureau of the Census. 1993. *Statistical Abstract of the United States: 1993* (113th ed.). Washington, D.C.

U.S. Bureau of the Census. 1994. *Statistical Abstract of the United States: 1994* (114th ed.). Washington, D.C.

van den Berghe, Pierre. 1992. The Modern State: Nation-Builder or Nation-Killer? *International Journal of Group Tensions* 22:191–208.

Vaughn, Megan. 1987. *The Story of an African Famine: Gender and Famine in Twentieth Century Malawi.* Cambridge: Cambridge University Press.

Wagar, W. Warren. 1991. *The Next Three Futures: Paradigms of Things to Come.* New York: Greenwood Press.

Wagar, W. Warren. 1992. *A Short History of the Future,* 2nd ed. Chicago: University of Chicago Press.

Wahid, Abu N. M. 1994. The Grameen Bank and Poverty Alleviation in Bangladesh: Theory, Evidence, and Limitations. *The American Journal of Economics and Sociology* 53:1–15.

Waits, William. 1992. *The Modern Christmas in America: A Cultural History of Gift-Giving.* New York: New York University Press.

Wallace, Anthony F. C. 1966. *Religion: An Anthropological View.* New York: Random House.

Wallace, Anthony F. C. 1987. *St. Clair: A Nineteenth-Century Coal Town's Experience with a Disaster Prone Industry.* New York: Alfred A. Knopf.

Wallace, Ernest, and E. Adamson Hoebel. 1952. *The Comanches: Lords of the South Plains.* Norman: University of Oklahoma Press.

Wallace, Mike. 1985. Mickey Mouse History: Portraying the Past at Disney World. *Radical History Review* 32:35–57.

Wallerstein, Immanuel. 1989. *The Modern World-System III: The Second Era of Great Expansion of the Capitalist World-Economy, 1730–1840s.* New York: Academic Press.

Wallerstein, Immanuel. 1990. Antisystemic Movements: History and Dilemmas. In *Transforming the Revolution: Social Movements and the World-System,* edited by Samir Amin, Girovanni Arrighi, Andre Gunder Frank, and Immanuel Wallerstein. New York: Monthly Press.

Wallis, Jim. 1984. *Agenda for Biblical People.* San Francisco: Harper San Francisco.

Ward, Martha C. 1996. *A World Full of Women.* Boston: Allyn & Bacon.

Weatherford, Jack. 1988. *Indian Givers: How the Indians of the Americas Transformed the World.* New York: Fawcett Columbine.

Weatherford, Jack. 1997. *The History of Money: From Sandstone to Cyberspace.* New York: Crown.

Weber, Eugen. 1976. *Peasants into Frenchmen: The Modernization of Rural France, 1870–1914.* Stanford: Stanford University Press.

Weber, Max. 1947. *The Theory of Social and Economic Organization.* Translated by A. M. Henderson and Talcott Parsons, edited by Talcott Parsons. Glencoe: The Free Press.

Weber, Max. 1958. *The Protestant Ethic and the Spirit of Capitalism.* Translated by Talcott Parsons. New York: Scribner.

Weiss, Thomas G., and Leon Gordenker (editors). 1996. *NGOs, the UN, and Global Governance.* London: Lynne Rienner.

Wells, H. G. [1895] 1942. *The Time Machine: An Invention.* New York: Henry Holt.

White, Benjamin. 1973. Demand for Labor and Population Growth in Colonial Java. *Human Ecology* 1:217–236.

White House Conference on Child Health and Protection. 1931. *The Home and the Child: Housing, Furnishing, Management, Income, and Clothing.* New York: Arno Press.

Wilson, Edmund. [1931] 1961. *The Shores of Light ("An Appeal to Progressives").* New York: Vintage Books.

Winters, Jeffery A. 1996. *Power in Motion: Capital Mobility and the Indonesian State.* Ithaca: Cornell University Press.

Wittfogel, Karl A. 1957. *Oriental Despotism.* New Haven: Yale University Press.

Wolf, Eric. 1967. *Peasants.* Engelwood Cliffs: Prentice-Hall.

Wolf, Eric. 1969. *Peasant Wars of the Twentieth Century.* New York: Harper & Row.

Wolf, Eric R. 1982. *People Without History.* Berkeley: University of California Press.

Woolf, Virginia. 1950. *The Captain's Death Bed and Other Essays.* New York: Harcourt.

World Bank. 1997. *World Development Report.* Oxford: Oxford University Press.

World Development Report. 1996. *From Plan to Market.* Oxford: Oxford University Press.

World Health Organization. 1995. *The Tobacco Epidemic: A Global Health Emergency;* http://www.who.ch/psa/toh/Alert/apr96/index.html

World Health Organization. 1995. *World Health Report;* http://www.who.ch/whr/1995//xsum95_e. htm

World Health Organization. 1997. 50 Facts of Health. *World Health Report 1997.*

Worsley, Peter. 1968. *The Trumpets Shall Sound: A Study of "Cargo" Cults in Melanesia,* 2nd ed. New York: Schocken Books.

Young, Crawford. 1993. The Dialectics of Cultural Pluralism: Concept and Reality. In *The Rising Tide of Cultural Pluralism: the Nation-State at Bay?* edited by Madison, Wis.: University of Wisconsin Press.

Yunus, Muhammad. 1994. Keynote Address delivered at the 85th Rotary International Convention, Taipei, Taiwan, June 12–15.

Name Index

Amin, Samir, 342
Amy, 39
Anderson, Benedict, 118
Anheier, Helmut K., 140, 141
Anthony, Susan B., 31
Aristide, Jean Bertrand, Father, 133
Armour, Philip and Simeon, 228
Atahualpa, 77
Ayatollah Khomeini, 381, 384

Bannan, Benjamin, 350
Basch, Linda, 132
Battuta, Ibn, 61
Baum, Frank L., 22, 27–29, 31
Beaud, Michel, 145
Boas, Franz, 18, 385
Bodley, John, 270, 275, 278, 280, 302
Borah, Woodrow, 79
Boserup, Ester, 155, 183, 357
Bouchard, Lucien, 299
Braudel, Fernand, 118
Broom, Haj, 313
Bryan, William Jennings, 386
Brzezinski, Zbigniew, 136

Caldwell, John, 171, 178
Carlin, George, 4
Carneiro, Robert, 117
Casement, Roger, 276
Castro, Fidel, 360
Chabner, Bruce, 267
Chase, Allan, 159
Chief Joseph, 31, 45, 354
Cody, William F., 225
Cohen, Mark, 182, 248
Colley, Linda, 122
Colon, Bartolome, 79
Columbus, Chistopher, 75, 76
Comaroff, Jean, 370, 375
Come, Matthew Coon, 299
Conrad's, Joseph, 276
Cook, Sherburn, 79
Cortés, Hérnan, 78
Crawford DíCamp, Morris, 18

Custer, George Armstrong, 373

da Gama, Vasco, 73
Da Vinci, Leonardo, 31
Darrow, Clarance, 386
Darwin, Charles, 157
de Las Casas, Bartolomíe, 79
de Lery, Jean, 73, 78, 80
Dettwyler, Katherine A., 194, 255
Diamond, Jared, 8
Díaz, Porfiro, 332
Dobyns, Henry F., 79
Dodge, Richard Henry, 225
Dougherty, Daniel, 353
Douglass, Frederick, 31, 45, 354
Dowie, Alexander, 376
Dubos, Reni, 251, 264
Durning, Alan, 208

Edgerton, Robert, 316–318, 322–325,
    327, 330
Edwards, Michael, 140, 141
Ember, Carol R., 170
Endelemann, Mark, 231
Engels, Friedrich, 36, 42, 44, 48, 49, 50,
    117, 157, 161, 306, 356, 368, 369
Evara, 374
Ewald, Paul, 245, 269

Fallwell, Jerry, 368, 389
Faludi, Susan, 391
Farmer, Paul, 238, 261, 263, 264, 267, 268
Firth, Raymond, 193
Fisk, Jim, 96
Fjellman, Stephen, 3, 29
Flannery, Kent, 118, 165, 222, 229
Ford, Henry, 19, 228, 229
Foster, John Bellamy, 234
Franklin, Benjamin, 41
Freire, Paulo, 395
Fried, Morton, 115

Gage, Matilda Joslyn, 27
Gage, Maud, 27

Garibaldi, Giuseppe, 119
Garrett, Laurie, 238, 252, 263, 265
Gellner, Ernest, 4, 110, 111, 113,
    115, 127
Giegfried, Andreí, 3
Ginsburg, Faye, 390
Gleissman, S. R., 232
Glick Schiller, Nina, 132
Goodenough, Ward, 280
Gottfried von Herder, Johann, 120
Gottlieb Fichte, Johann, 121
Gould, Peter, 260
Grey, Edward, 276
Grimm, Jacob and Wilhelm, 27
Guha, Ramachandra, 366

Habyarimana, Juvenal, 295
Hammond, George H., 228
Handwerker, Penn, 174
Harcourt, William, 317
Hardenburg, Walter, 276
Hardie, Keir, 123
Hardin, Garrett, 158, 365
Hargreaves, James, 91
Harris, Marvin, 117, 118, 165,
    222, 229
Henderson, Ian, 329
Hobbes, Thomas, 116
Hobsbawm, Eric, 113, 127, 128, 131
Hoover, Herbert, 18, 24
Howard, Oliver, 31
Howell, Nancy, 166
Hulme, David, 140, 141
Humbard, Rex, 387
Humboldt, Wilhelm Freiherr von, 121
Huxley, Elspeth, 324

Iannaccone, Laurence R., 389
Ignatiev, Noel, 31, 41, 42, 48

James, Henry, 21
John Paul II, 393, 395
Johnson, Paul E., 370
Juergensmeyer, Mark, 379

Subject Index

Text Credits

Page 1ff, from *Europe and the People without History,* by Eric Wolfe. Copyright © 1983 The Regents of the University of California.

Page 3ff, from *Vinyl Leaves: Walt Disney World and America,* by Stephen M. Fjellman. Copyright © 1992 by Westview-Press. Reprinted by permission of WestviewPress.

Page 21, from "Possession and the Extended Self," *Journal of Consumer Research* 15: 140–158, by R. W. Belk. Copyright © 1988. Reprinted by permission of The University of Chicago Press.

Page 30ff, from "Mickey Mouse History: Portraying the Past of Disney World," *Radical History Review* 32: 35, 53, by Mike Wallace. Copyright © 1985. Reprinted by permission of Cambridge University Press.

Page 113ff, from "Violence, Terror, and the Crisis of the State," by Carole Nagengast. Reprinted by permission of the author and the *Annual Review of Anthropology,* Volume 23, Copyright © 1994, by Annual Reviews, Inc.

Pages 234–236, from "'Let Them Eat Pollution': Capitalism and the World Environment." Copyright © 1993 by Monthly Review, Inc. Reprinted by permission of Monthly Review Foundation.

Page 270ff, from *Victims of Progress* (Third Edition), by John H. Bodley. Copyright © 1990. Reprinted by permission of Mayfield Publishing Company.

Page 317ff, from *Mau Mau: An African Crucible,* by Robert B. Edgerton. Copyright © 1989 by Robert B. Edgerton. Reprinted by permission of The Free Press, a division of Simon & Schuster.

Pages 390ff, from "Saving America's Souls: Operation Rescue's Crusade against Abortion," by Faye Ginsburg, in *Fundamentalisms and the State: Remaking Polities, Economies, and Militance,* Martin E. Marty and R. Scott Applesby (eds.). Copyright © 1993, Reprinted by permission of the University of Chicago Press.

Pages 397–398, from "'Jesus Is the Lord of Guatemala': Evangelical Reform in a Death Squad State," by David Stoll, in *Accounting for Fundamentalisms,* Martin E. Marty and R. Scott Applesby (eds.). Copyright © 1994. Reprinted by permission of The University of Chicago Press.

Photo Credits

Page 5, Eunice Harris/The Picture Cube; Page 13, Anthro-Photo File; Page 16, Johannes Kroemer/Sygma; Page 23, AP/Wide World Photos; Page 28, Corbis-Bettmann; Page 30, David Ball/The Picture Cube; Page 36, UPI/Corbis-Bettmann; Page 37, Craig Strong/Gamma Liaison; Page 43, The Granger Collection, New York; Page 47, Corbis-Bettmann; Page 54, Reuters/Keith B. Richburg/Archive Photos; Page 65, North Wind Picture Archives; Page 69, Corbis-Bettmann; Page 80, 83, North Wind Picture Archives; Page 85, Corbis-Bettmann; Page 91, 99, The Granger Collection, New York; Page 108, David McIntyre/Black Star; Page 114, Camerique/The Picture Cube; Page 122, North Wind Picture Archives; Page 126, Russell D. Curtis/Photo Researchers, Inc.; Page 129, Reuters/Darren Whiteside/Archive Photos; Page 134, Mike Greenlar/The Image Works; Page 152, Johan Berglund/Impact Visuals; Page 158 right, Ira Kirschenbaum/Stock, Boston; Page 158 left, AP/Wide World Photos; Page 168, North Wind Picture Archive; Page 172 left, Bruce Paton/Impact Visuals; Page 172 right, Kindra Clineff/The Picture Cube; Page 180 left, Scott J. Witte/The Picture Cube; Page 180 right, David Austen/Stock, Boston; Page 187, Earl Roberge/Photo Researchers, Inc.; Page 192, Bernard Bisson/Sygma; Page 197, Sean Sprague/ Impact Visuals; Page 205, Gilles Saussier/Gamma Liaison; Page 211, Ellen Dooley/Gamma Liaison; Page 215, Culver Pictures; Page 221, Corbis-Bettmann; Page 226, The Granger Collection, New York; Page 230, McLaughlin/The Image Works; Page 239, Sean Sprague/Impact Visuals; Page 243, Grace Davies/The Picture Cube; Page 251, The Granger Collection, New York; Page 262, Leah Melnick/Impact Visuals; Page 266, Sean Sprague/Stock, Boston; Page 271, AP/Wide World Photos; Page 277, UPI/Corbis-Bettmann; Page 282, The Granger Collection, New York; Page 290, J. R. Ripper/Impact Visuals; Page 293, Paul Dix/Impact Visuals; Page 297, Thierry Orban/Sygma; Page 308, The Granger Collection, New York; Page 318, North Wind Picture Archives; Page 328, UPI/ Corbis-Bettmann; Page 331 left, Corbis-Bettmann; Page 331 right, Jacques Torregano/Gamma Liaison; Page 341, Corbis-Bettmann; Page 344, Archive Photos; Page 348, 351, The Granger Collection, New York; Page 355, UPI/ Corbis-Bettmann; Page 357, The Granger Collection, New York; Page 364, Bob Daemmrich/The Image Works; Page 369, Jay Mallin/Impact Visuals; Page 372, The Granger Collection, New York; Page 378, Julio Etchart/Impact Visuals; Page 383, M. Shandiz/Sygma; Page 387, Culver Pictures; Page 391, Reuters/Jeff Mitchell/Archive Photos; Page 394, B. Bisson/Sygma.